Richard C. Shimeall

Christ's Second Coming, Is It Pre-Millennial or Postmillennial?

The great question of the day, scripturally, historically, and philosophically considered

Richard C. Shimeall

Christ's Second Coming, Is It Pre-Millennial or Postmillennial?
The great question of the day, scripturally, historically, and philosophically considered

ISBN/EAN: 9783337236984

Printed in Europe, USA, Canada, Australia, Japan

Cover: Foto ©Lupo / pixelio.de

More available books at **www.hansebooks.com**

TESTIMONIALS

FROM THE

RELIGIOUS AND SECULAR PRESS,

OF THE

REV. R. C. SHIMEALL'S TWO WORKS,

ON

CHRIST'S SECOND COMING:

THE GREAT QUESTION OF THE DAY.

Is it Pre- or Post-Millennial?

SCRIPTURALLY, HISTORICALLY, & PHILOSOPHICALLY CONSIDERED.

OUR BIBLE CHRONOLOGY,

HISTORIC AND PROPHETIC,

Harmonized with the Chronology of Profane Writers, etc.,

DEMONSTRATED.

NEW YORK:
PUBLISHED BY JOHN F. TROW & CO.

PHILADELPHIA: POST OFFICE BOX 1109.

[PUBLISHERS' CIRCULAR.]

JOHN F. TROW & CO., 50 GREENE ST.

SHIMEALL'S NEW WORK

ON

CHRIST'S SECOND COMING:

THE GREAT QUESTION OF THE DAY.

IS IT PRE- OR POST-MILLENNIAL?

WITH A REPLY TO PROF. SHEDD ON

"ESCHATOLOGY,"

ETC., ETC.

TESTIMONIALS FROM THE RELIGIOUS AND SECULAR PRESS.

In presenting this work before the public, the author does so on the simple ground that, despite the indifference, prejudice, or hostility arrayed against the subject of which it treats from its past perversion and abuse, it is nevertheless, from its intrinsic importance as a matter of Divine Revelation, *fairly entitled to inquiry and discussion* as "the Great Question of the day." All that he asks of any person into whose hands this volume may fall, is a careful perusal of it, and a candid decision as to the merits of the two main points involved: "IS THE SECOND COMING OF CHRIST PRE- OR POST-MILLENNIAL?" It is a subject that has employed the devout thoughts and earnest pens of the most profoundly learned and eminently pious and distinguished in the Christian Church of every age,—ancient, mediaeval, and modern. But still the Church continues to be divided on the great question involved, both as to the *manner* and *time* of that stupendous event. This volume presents a view of *both sides* of the question at issue, on the grounds both of the *scriptural* arguments and the *historical* developments of the doctrine; and hence will be found to furnish a *complete exhibit* of all that is essential to a thorough knowledge of the subject.

The publishers can also supply those who desire it with the author's other elaborate work, "*Our Bible Chronology, Sacred and Profane, Historic and Prophetic, Critically Examined and Demonstrated, and Harmonized with the Chronology of Profane Writers,*" etc. This work has been critically examined by a number of our ripest scholars at home and abroad, and has been decided as entitled to the rank of a *standard work* on the subject.

JOHN F. TROW & CO.

TESTIMONIALS.

"From the New York Observer."

"This is a laborious treatise upon a subject that has occupied much of the time and attention of the Church. It professes to be free from all extraneous matter, and to exhibit *all the theories* that have obtained in the Christian Church, from the early post-apostolic age to the present times. The abstract testimony of the Holy Scriptures respecting the second coming of Christ is first presented. This is followed by an examination of the question whether this coming is *past, present,* or *future.* Under this head the various theories of MILLER, GROTIUS, BUSH, and others, are discussed with much patience and learning. The fifth chapter is devoted to the consideration of *sacred philosophy,* to the Scriptural doctrine of the RESURRECTION of Christ, of the righteous, and of the wicked, *as these depend upon, and are connected with,* His second coming. A *complete synopsis* of the Millennarian Scheme is given in the closing chapter. *The whole work evinces great sincerity and devotion, and is an interesting and important presentation* of millennarian views."

"The Christian Times and Episcopal Register."

"This work is based upon the author's 'BIBLE CHRONOLOGY,' a work that has gained *high commendation* both in this country and in England, and which stands among the most valuable works relating to the subject. The preface contains a concise account of the *different theories* that have been entertained on this subject at different times, and is followed by an *appeal*, addressed to Bishop Potter and the other prominent clergymen of this city, who entertain what is called the post-millennial view. He invites them in the most pointed manner to give a reason for the hope that is in them, and challenges them to refute his own view, which is the pre-millennial. . . . *This work is the result of a lifetime of thought and study.* It is very full in all its details; it is written in an impartial Christian spirit, and is distinguished by much ability; and, when taken in connection with the previous volume, furnishes what will generally be desired for the study of this great question."

"**The Christian Advocate and Journal.**" (Meth. Episc.)

"The writer of this volume is a venerable minister of the Presbyterian Church, and a writer of good reputation for candor and research. In composing this volume, he has evidently written from the impulses of his heart, no less than at the dictates of his judgment, maintaining his own theory with an affectionate earnestness. He holds that Christ's second coming will be PRE-MILLENNIAL, or that the great period in the progress of the ages of Christ's kingdom designated by that term—which he does not slavishly limit to a thousand of our solar years—will *follow* the resurrection and the general judgment. *Of the conclusiveness of his arguments we confess our inability to decide confidently,* THOUGH WE INCLINE TO COINCIDE WITH HIS VIEWS ON THAT POINT. We are also quite willing to concede that the subject is one of *deep interest* to the believer in Christ; and we can, in all sincerity, recommend this volume to any who may desire to examine the subject, which is here discussed *exhaustively,* though not *tediously.* Though necessarily somewhat controversial, it is written in a kindly tone, and carries with it a devout and reverential faith."

"**The Christian Intelligencer.**" (Ref. Dutch Church.)

"The author of this elaborate treatise is a sincere and devout believer in the pre-millennial advent of our Lord. Our personal respect for Mr. Shimeall, and interest in the question he has discussed, have led us to examine this work with care. . . . Having read many books written in favor of this theory, we are free to say that we consider this *by far the ablest work* in support of the pre-millennial scheme of interpretation we have yet seen. It is unusually free from dogmatism, and is unencumbered with fanciful applications of events to suit the requirements of a theory. *The appeal is made to Scripture as the final authority,* and that, the author thinks, is plainly in favor of the system he advocates. . . . And as he has selected certain eminent divines to *sit in judgment* upon his performance, and decide whether he is *orthodox* or *heretical,* we await with patience *their verdict.*"

"The Presbyterian." (Philadelphia.)

"The author maintains the pre-millennial views of Christ's coming, and reviews *the whole question* with a clear understanding of all that can be alleged for its correctness. He has given to the study of this question much time and attention, *and is well furnished for its defence against those of opposite views.* His book, therefore, will be found to contain all that is material for the *full exposition* of the subject, and with little of the asperity of controversy."

"The Evangelist."

"This volume is an elaborate discussion of what the author deems 'the great question of the day—Is Christ's second coming pre-millennial or post-millennial?' After a quite extended discussion, preparing the way for his conclusions, he sets forth his position, 'that there is to be no intervening millennium between the second coming of Christ and the day of judgment: in other words, that that event, when it does take place, will be pre- and not post-millennial. The second portion of the work is devoted to a reply to Professor Shedd's Eschatology in his 'History of Christian Doctrine.' Dr. Hatfield's views in his recent articles (published in the American Presbyterian and Theological Review) are also noticed. The author's views " are presented with care and candor, and evince much careful examination and an extended acquaintance with the subject."

"The Prophetic Times: A New Serial." (Philadelphia.)

"We hail this book by Mr. Shimeall with great satisfaction, as an able and seasonable contribution to the literature of this great theme. . . . It is the product of a learned and faithful explorer, and treats the various theories and aspects of the subject with comprehensiveness, judiciousness, and power. Taking the Bible as an intelligible book, which we are to interpret as we do any other serious writings meant for the enlightenment of mankind, he has reached the same conclusions to which every intelligent and honest investigator has come, or must come, who accepts the Scriptures in their plain literal import, which we claim to be the only true way of receiving them. In other words, he is a thorough *millenarian.*

"His method of treating the subject includes, First, an appeal, respectfully addressed to leading anti-millenarians, in which certain important points touching the merits of the subject, and the objectionableness of their manner of meeting them are well put; second, An abstract of the testimony of the Scriptures respecting the second coming, both as to the *substance* of the doctrine and its *practical* uses; third, An examination of the several false theories that have been put forth on the subject, show ing their unscriptural and unsatisfactory character, and utterly refuting them. This constitutes the largest part of the book, and what the author considers the *principal want* of a numerous class of clergy and laity, which he has mainly labored to supply. Various leading questions involved are then discussed separately, as also the nature of the RESURRECTION AND THE FUTURE ATTRIBUTES AND OFFICIAL DIGNITIES OF THE SAINTS; concluding with "A complete Synopsis of the Millenarian Scheme of the Second Coming." All this comprises 320 large octavo pages. Then follows a reply to Prof. Shedd's 'Eschatology,' embracing 117 pages, and setting forth the millenarianism of the ancient, mediaeval, and modern Church. This is a valuable part of the book, in which Prof. Shedd's 'History' is completely put to shame, as it deserves to be as respects *this* subject. To all this is added some 20 pages of valuable notes, with an index to the whole.

"We thank Mr. Shimeall for this timely and able production, and heartily recommend it for its fairness, its comprehensiveness, its general soundness of exegesis, and its manly honesty, respectfulness, and just conclusions. He who values the truth on this great theme cannot fail to value this book. We shall rejoice in finding it extensively circulated and attentively studied. *The means of a large acquaintance with the whole subject may be found in it.*"

"The Evening Post."

"We have already noticed one or two works of this nature, and that before us is one of the most remarkable for its research and the care with which it is written. Mr. Shimeall has given to the subject of his work the study of many years. His treatise bears evidence, not only of the zeal with which he maintains his own view of the subject, but of the diligence with which he has explored the writings of others. In regard to the Second Advent of the Messiah, he has collected *all the different theories* which have been proposed, stated the arguments in their favor and replied to them in all instances in which he does not accept them. . . . This second coming of Christ, according to Mr. Shimeall's view, is to precede and usher in the Millennium. It will *prepare the way* for that age of innocence, peace, and love which is to succeed the present age of dissension, bloodshed, and crime, and to which millenarians look with earnest longings for its immediate arrival. Although Mr. Shimeall acknowledges himself in the *minority*, he gives the names of various eminent persons, both of *ancient* and *modern* times, who have adopted views similar to those set forth in his book.

"A part of the volume is taken up with a Reply to PROF. SHEDD, of the Union Theological Seminary in this city, who, in his "History of Christian Doctrine," affirms that Millenarianism, by which he means similar views to those held by Mr. Shimeall.

has never been the recognized doctrine of the Christian Church. Mr. Shimeall takes issue with him on this point, and brings forward many examples of persons in the *early ages* of the Church, and the *middle ages*, and in *modern times*, who were MILLENARIANS. Lest the view taken by Mr. Shimeall should be confounded with what is called *Millerism*, he takes care to show wherein he differs from the Millerites. In the first place, *he denies the possibility of fixing the day and hour of Christ's Second Coming*, though he holds that there are certain symptoms from which its *near approach* is to be inferred. In the second place he maintains that *the conflagration of the world is not, as the Millerites hold, contemporaneously with this second* [pre-millennial] *advent of the Messiah*, since the promised reign of Christ on earth could not in that event take place.

"The reader may not accept Mr. Shimeall's conclusions, but he cannot look over the book without being interested in the discussion of a question which has engaged the thoughts of many eminent men in every age of the Christian Era, and which could occupy such a mind as that of (Sir Isaac) Newton."

"The Journal of Commerce."

"CHRIST'S SECOND COMING," is the title of an octavo volume by Rev. R. C. Shimeall, a member of the Presbytery of New York, who has devoted his energies and studies to the subject, and produced various works heretofore more or less related to it. In the present volume he has gathered a large amount of controversial matter on the Millenarian question, and presents with great energy his peculiar views. The author endeavors to give the reader a view of *all the theories* which have prevailed in various ages and countries on the Second Coming, and to furnish *in a clear and condensed form a great mass of information suited to answer inquiries often made*. He states that the reader will find the subject discussed 'free from all intricacy, even to the plainest mind.'"

"The New York Times."

The writer of this volume is well known for the extent and wide range of his studies, connected with the interpretation of the Prophetical Scriptures. All he asks for it *is a fair and candid examination* of his theory, in the interests, not of victory, but of truth, and he brings forward the names of some of the most venerated teachers and theologians of the day—under whose auspices the work appears—*to show that he is at least entitled to this consideration*. It will at once be seen that the subject of the book places it beyond the pale of ordinary newspaper discussion. . . . Still it is undeniable that many devout minds have found support and nourishment in the investigation of the prophetical records, and to all who indulge in this study, MR. SHIMEALL'S book will be welcome."

"The World,"

"It is impossible to over-estimate the importance of the subject which Mr. Shimeall discusses and exhausts in this volume of some five hundred pages. The first part of the work is devoted to the somewhat unreasonably vexed question of the SECOND COMING OF CHRIST. The author addresses an argumentative appeal to *ten clergymen of eminence*, including Bishop Potter and Mr. Henry Ward Beecher,—who will not probably answer him,—to reconsider their habitual '*post-millenarianism*,' and ascertain, while there is yet time, whether he may not be wholly in the wrong; and it is very certain that if these clergymen, failing to respond to his appeal, should eventually prove to have been in the wrong, the consequences both to themselves and to their congregations must be such as it is by no means agreeable to contemplate.

"We are standing now, according to Mr. Shimeall, within some *three years* of the most eventful period of human history. Historical chronology will close, as this devoted student of the 'Second Coming' assures us, with the year 1868. . . . It should be said that Mr. Shimeall, however, while he asserts the *pre-millennial* coming of Christ, argues earnestly against the *pre-millennial conflagration of all things*. . . . Perhaps the most interesting part of Mr. Shimeall's work, and that with which *post-millenarian* divines will find it hardest to deal, is the fourth section of the third chapter on 'ESCHATOLOGY,' in which he recites the '*authentic history of Chiliasm*' since the Reformation. In this section he confronts Professor Shedd with the illustrious and almost inspired Joseph Mede, and with Millenarian authorities of no less weight than John and Charles Wesley, Augustus Toplady, and Bishop Heber.

"Such men as these may have been utterly in the dark, mad, crude, and incompetent; but if this was the case, *why does their spirit rule in the churches*, and *why are their psalms, and hymns, and spiritual songs*, in all lands where the English tongue is known, *the delight and consolation of believers?*"

"The Commercial Advertiser."

"REV. RICHARD C. SHIMEALL has published a work entitled 'Christ's Second Coming,—Is it *Pre*-Millennial or *Post*-Millennial?' To the Scriptural, historical, and philosophical examination of this subject, Mr. Shimeall has devoted himself for many years. The subject of the Millennium, or the Second Coming of Christ, has been for ages held and exhibited in various and conflicting forms by numerous writers. We have, in the first place, the *Anti-Millenarians*, who allege that the Millennium is *past*. Then we have *Post-Millenarians*, who hold that the Second Coming of Christ will not occur till its *conclusion*.

A third School holds to a *future* Millennium *preceded* and *introduced* by, the Second Coming of the Saviour, etc. To this School the author of the present volume belongs.

"Mr. Shimeall enters into a very elaborate and extended review of the *various theories* heretofore held in regard to the Millennium, and *with much force of reasoning* endeavors to show how all systems except the last-named, fail to meet the claims of prophecy and Scripture."

"Zion's Herald." (Boston.)

"The author of the above-named work is a Presbyterian minister, who has evidently studied and thought upon his theme with a great deal of care, as 'the great question of the day.' *He writes with candor, fairly presenting both sides of the question.* His plan is, *first*, to present a view of all the principal 'theories' that have obtained in the Christian Church from the close of the Apostolic age to the present time; *secondly*, to show the scriptural and historical ground on which the different parties claim to rest their views; and, *thirdly*, to examine carefully each theory on its respective merits so as to enable the reader to decide for himself on which side the truth lies. He gives a complete view of the scriptural argument and of the history of the doctrine of Christ's Second Coming as found among the Ancients, Medievals, and Moderns.

"The three principal theories discussed are, 1. That the Millennium is already past; those who embrace it are called *Anti-Millenarians*; 2. That it is still future, and that the second coming of Christ will not take place until after the Millennium; its advocates are called *Post-Millenarians*; 3. That the Millennium is still future, but that the second coming of Christ will take place before the Millennium—its adherents are called *Pre-Millennialists*. The author takes sides with the last. The book may be read with profit by all parties, as it contains much reliable information on the subject."

"The Israelite Indeed."

"This is a work which should be read by all who love our Lord and Saviour Jesus Christ. It enters into all the views which have been held in any portion of the Church concerning our Lord's coming again. *It is one of the ablest works we have met with* on this important and interesting subject, and will well repay for the reading. Let all who love the Lord's appearing read this work and get their souls warmed up on this delightful theme."

This work has been published by the patronage of a large number both of the *Clergy* and the *Laity*, of different denominations, among whom are the following:

Rev. THOMAS DEWITT, D. D.
" J. T. DURYEA.
" E. P. ROGERS, D. D.
" W. R. GORDON, D. D.
" A. R. THOMPSON, D. D.
" J. T. DEMAREST, D. D.
" S. R. JOHNSON, D. D.
" J. H. WESTON, D. D.
" J. COTTON SMITH, D. D.
" A. H. VINTON, D. D.
" W. R. WILLIAMS, D. D.

Rev. R. U. HOWLAND, D. D.
" J. H. HOUGHTON, D. D.
" W. A. SCOTT, D. D.
" J. M. STEPHENSON, D. D.
" A. E. CAMPBELL, D. D.
" JOSEPH SCUDDER.
" JOHN M. KREBS, D. D.
" THOMAS HASTINGS, D. D.
" S. D. ALEXANDER, D. D.
" JOHN MANNING, D. D.
" JOHN QUINCY ADAMS.

Brooklyn, REV. JAMES EELLS, D. D., REV. J. H. VAN DYKE, REV. J. E. ROCKWELL, D. D.

Jersey City, REV. C. K. IMBRIE, D. D., REV. P. D. VAN CLEEF, D. D.

Williamsburg, REV. J. D. WELLS, D. D.

PETER LORILLARD, ESQ.
S. W. BENEDICT, ESQ.
S. A. SCHIEFFELIN, ESQ.
E. S. JAFFREY, ESQ.
A. W. BRADFORD, ESQ.
PETER NAYLOR, ESQ.
DAVID OLIPHANT, ESQ.
WM. VERNON, ESQ.
CHARLES SCRIBNER, ESQ.
F. T. BETTS, ESQ.
S. A. CHURCH, ESQ.
THEODORE BOURNE, ESQ.

CHARLES G. HARMER, ESQ.
J. W. P. MORRISON, ESQ.
A. B. CONGER, ESQ.
WM. B. CROSBY, ESQ.
HOMER MORGAN, ESQ.
JON. THOMPSON, ESQ.
JOHN T. CRANE, ESQ.
W. H. H. MOORE, ESQ.
BENJ. R. WINTHROP, ESQ.
BENJ. DOUGLASS, ESQ.
JAMES SUYDAM, ESQ.
C. F. HUNTER, ESQ.

New Standard Work.

OUR BIBLE CHRONOLOGY,

HISTORIC AND PROPHETIC,

CRITICALLY EXAMINED AND DEMONSTRATED,

AND

Harmonized with the Chronology of Profane Writers, &c.

WITH A MAP OF THE ANCIENT WORLD, A CHART OF THE COURSE OF EMPIRES, AND OTHER ILLUSTRATIONS. FIFTY-FOUR PAGES OF TABULAR MATTER, CHRONOLOGICAL AND GENEALOGICAL, SACRED AND PROFANE,

BY REV. R. C. SHIMEALL.

We call your special attention to the work referred to above, which, from the importance of the subjects of which it treats, and the interest which is being daily awakened in its behalf, both in England and in this country, shows its peculiar adaptation to the present times. Several editions of the work have been disposed of, including among its patrons the clergy of all the different denominations—Presbyterian, Episcopalian, Dutch Reformed, Methodist, Baptist, etc. It is also peculiarly adapted to the use of Bible Classes, Sabbath Schools, and other institutions of learning, and forms a much-needed appendage to the Family Bible. It forms a handsome *royal octavo* volume of about 250 pages, bound in substantial cloth, and contains all the matter embraced in the author's Biblical and Ecclesiastical Charts, (originally published at $10 *each* per copy,) and in a much more convenient form for ordinary use.

The author's aim in this volume has been to reach a *reliable* result in regard to the exact chronology of the world from the commencement of human history. The work was commenced at the request and by the encouragement of several of the most distinguished clergy of New York city, who were cognizant of the fact that Mr. S. had devoted many years of indefatigable research and labor in this department of Biblical literature. His *mode* of treating the subject will be found entirely original. It embraces a thorough examination of every system and theory, historic and prophetic, sacred and profane, ancient and modern, of those who have heretofore occupied this field. It takes into account all the objections, difficulties, and discrepancies that are alleged as insuperable to a satisfactory adjustment of the world's chronology, and claims to have produced what amounts to "A SELF-DETERMINING TEST" of this long litigated and intricate subject.

The *plan* of the author—taking as his STAND-POINT the present state of the question of *sacred* chronology as involved in that of the *profane*—is, first, to vindicate the authenticity and inspiration of the Mosaic Records, against the alleged vastly greater antiquity of ancient nations, particularly that of Egypt, as advocated by the school of modern Egyptologists; second, to settle the question as to which of the two versions of Scripture, the Hebrew or the Septuagint, (between which there is a *chronological* difference of about 2,000 years,) is *authoritative* in determining the chronology of human history; and third, to produce an *exact harmony* of the profane with the sacred records, from the Creation and fall of man to the Nativity. And while the author places his work in the hands of all upon its merits, the Press, both Religious and Secular, has reviewed it with favor. It has also been critically examined and pronounced *a Standard Work*, by many eminent Scholars and Divines, among whom are

REV. THOMAS DEWITT, D. D., *Collegiate Ref. Dutch Church.*
REV. SAMUEL R. JOHNSON, D. D., *Dean of the Gen. Theol. Seminary of the P. E. C.*
REV. FRANCIS L. HAWKS, D. D., LL. D., *Late Rector of Calvary Church.*

Rev. John M. Krebs, D. D., *Presb. Church, Madison Av.*
Rev. Charles K. Imbrie, D. D., *Presb. Church, Jersey City.*
Rev. John Cumming, D. D., F. R. S. E. *Scotch National Church, London.*

Price of Single Copy - - - - - - $2 50

N. B.—The work will be forwarded to any part of the United States (postage free) on the receipt of the price ($2 50) on application to John F. Trow, 50 Greene St., or to the author, No. 371 West 35th Street.

Just Published by the same Author.

THE POLITICAL ECONOMY
OF
PROPHECY,

WITH

SPECIAL REFERENCE TO THE CIVIL, MILITARY, AND ECCLESIASTICAL

RISE AND CAREER

OF

THE ROMAN EMPIRE,

AND OF ITS LAST EMPERORS,

THE THREE NAPOLEONS.

WITH AN APPENDIX ON

THE POPE'S LATE ENCYCLICAL,

AND

THE FIRMAN OF THE SULTAN OF TURKEY.

PROPHETICALLY AND HISTORICALLY DEMONSTRATED.

ILLUSTRATED BY PORTRAITS OF THE NAPOLEONIC FAMILY; A CHART OF THE COURSE OF EMPIRE; MAPS OF THE HOLY LAND, ETC.

ONE VOLUME DUODECIMO. PRICE $1 75.

JOHN F. TROW & CO., 50 Greene Street.

PHILADELPHIA: POST OFFICE BOX 1199.

CHRIST'S SECOND COMING:

IS IT PRE-MILLENNIAL OR POST-MILLENNIAL?

(THE GREAT QUESTION OF THE DAY),

Scripturally, Historically, and Philosophically Considered.

WITH A REPLY TO PROF. SHEDD ON

"ESCHATOLOGY,"

OR THE MILLENARIANISM OR CHILIASM OF THE ANCIENT, MEDIÆVAL, AND MODERN CHURCH.

ALSO, REMARKS ON AN ARTICLE WRITTEN UPON THE SAME SUBJECT, BY THE REV. E. F. HATFIELD, D. D.

BY

THE REV. RICHARD CUNNINGHAM SHIMEALL,

MEMBER OF THE PRESBYTERY OF NEW YORK,

AUTHOR OF OUR BIBLE CHRONOLOGY, HISTORIC AND PROPHETIC, DEMONSTRATED; AN ILLUMINATED SCRIPTURAL CHART OF HIST., CHRON., GEOG., AND GENEALOGY; A CHART OF UNIVERSAL ECCLESIASTICAL HISTORY; WATTS' SCRIPTURE HISTORY ENLARGED; END OF PRELACY; A TREATISE ON PRAYER, ETC., ETC.

NEW YORK:
PUBLISHED FOR THE AUTHOR,
BY JOHN F. TROW, 50 GREENE STREET,
AND RICHARD BRINKERHOFF, 48 FULTON ST
FOR SALE AT ALL THE BOOKSTORES.
1866.

Entered according to Act of Congress, in the year 1864, by

REV. R. C. SHIMEALL,

In the Clerk's Office of the District Court of the United States for the Southern District of New York.

JOHN F. TROW,
PRINTER AND STEREOTYPER,
50 Greene Street.

TO THE READER.

The subject involved in the Great Theological Question of the day in reference to the SECOND COMING OF CHRIST, from its adaptation to the times we live in, *more than any other*, appeals to and demands the serious consideration of every reflecting and unbiassed mind.

This Treatise owes its origin to the *absence* of any work extant adapted to the wants of a numerous class of persons, both of the clergy and the laity, who have solicited of the writer a reference to such helps as were best calculated to aid their inquiries in these premises.

Two requisites are indispensable to such a work. First. Freedom from all *extraneous* matter appertaining to this subject. Second. An exhibit of *all the theories* that have obtained in the Christian Church from the early post-apostolic age to the present time. These must be carefully examined in the light of Scripture and of history, the reader being left to decide for himself as to which is entitled—under the guidance of the Holy Spirit—to his adoption and belief.

It will be well here to state, for the information of those not generally conversant with this subject, that the expositors who have already occupied this field, may be divided into the *three following classes,* viz.:

I. Those technically called ANTI-*millenarians,* who allege that the Millennium of Rev. xx. 1-6 *is already Past.* From this class of writers have originated *three distinct Theories,* which will be found explained in the Preface.

II. The next class are called POST-*millenarians,* who, though they maintain that the Millennium is *still future,* yet allege that the Second Personal Coming of Christ is POST-*millennial.*

III. The third class are denominated PRE-*millennialists.* This class of writers, while they also hold that the Millennium is *still future,* yet affirm that the Second Personal Coming of Christ takes place BEFORE, and in order to the ESTABLISHMENT of, the Kingdom of the Son of Man.

The subjects discussed will be found *free from all intricacy*, even to the plainest mind.

While in the "SEQUEL to Our Bible Chronology," the *various Theories* which have obtained in the Christian Church are fully and candidly examined in the light of Scripture and of fact *on their merits;* the "REPLY to Rev. Prof. Shedd's article on Eschatology," will be found to furnish a complete history of Millenarianism, Ancient, Mediæval, and Modern.

All we ask of the reader is, that he will "*stand in the way, and see, and ask for the old paths, where is the good way, and walk therein,*" that he may "*find rest for his soul*" from the confusion and perplexity so prevalent on this momentous subject.

R. C. S.

EXTRACTS—TESTIMONIES TO CHRIST'S SECOND COMING.

"*We affirm that* THE REDEEMER'S SECOND APPEARING IS THE VERY POLAR-STAR OF THE CHURCH. *That it is so held forth in the New Testament, is beyond dispute.*"—(*Christ's Second Coming:* by the REV. DAVID BROWN, *of St. James's Free Church, Glasgow.*) This writer is a POST-millenarian.

"*As an incentive to repentance and holiness to sinners—as a motive to watchfulness, prayer, zeal, and diligence on the part of Christian ministers and people—more prominence is given to it* [THE SAVIOUR'S SECOND COMING] *in the pages of the New Testament than to any other. The apostles never failed to give point and pungency to their warnings and exhortations, by solemn reference to the certainty and suddenness of the Lord's coming.*"—(BISHOP HENSHAW *on the Second Advent.*) This writer was a PRE-millenarian.

"*This was the great theme on which St. Paul dwelt, to animate the first Christians in their trials, and to console them in their afflictions.* . . . *It* [THE SECOND COMING OF CHRIST] *is the principal topic of the Apocalypse of St. John; and to this he especially directs the attention of the first Christians.*"—(*Very Rev.* J. BAPTIST PAGANI'S *End of the World.*) A Roman Catholic writer.

"*Our looking at Christ's Second Coming* as at a distance,"—*the very attitude and sin of the Church generally of this day*—"*is the cause of all those irregularities* which render the thought of it terrible *to us.*" (MATTHEW HENRY, *Com. on Luke xii.* 45, 46.).

CONTENTS.

	PAGES
SUMMARY OF SUBJECTS	iii–xii
PREFACE	xiii–xx

AN APPEAL, respectfully addressed to the following clergy, selected as the *Representatives* of the Leading Evangelical Protestant Churches, on the Great Theological Question of the Day, viz.: Is the Second Personal Coming of Christ *Pre* or *Post*-Millennial? The RIGHT REV. HORATIO POTTER, D. D., Bishop of the Diocese of New York; the REV. N. L. RICE, D. D.; the REV. WILLIAM ADAMS, D. D.; the REV. T. E. VERMILYE, D. D.; the REV. EDWARD LATHROP, D. D.; the REV. JOHN MCCLINTOCK, D. D.; the REV. HENRY WARD BEECHER; the Rev. CHARLES HODGE, D. D., of the Princeton Theological Seminary; the REV. W. G. T. SHEDD, D. D., of the Union Theological Seminary, N. Y.; the REV. J. T. BERG, D. D., of the New Brunswick Theological Seminary, N. J. . . . xxi–xxxi

PART I.

INTRODUCTION.

ABSTRACT TESTIMONY OF THE HOLY SCRIPTURES, REGARDING THE SECOND PERSONAL COMING OF CHRIST.

SECTION I. Doctrinal.—Old Testament	33–39
New Testament	39–48
SECTION II. Practical Uses of said Doctrine	48–53

PART II.

AN EXAMINATION OF THE QUESTION—IS THE SECOND COMING OF CHRIST, AND THE SETTING UP OF HIS KINGDOM, PAST, PRESENT, OR FUTURE?

Preliminary Remarks—The most Prominent Theories that have obtained in the Church from Early Apostolic Times on this Subject 54–56

CHAPTER I.

FIRST THEORY: MILLERISM.

THIS THEORY ALLEGES, THAT ALL THE PROPHECIES WHICH SET FORTH THE RESTORATION, CONVERSION, AND POLITICAL PRE-EMINENCE OF THE TWO KINGDOMS OF JUDAH AND ISRAEL, OR THE TEN TRIBES, WERE VERIFIED BY THE RETURN OF THE JEWS FROM THE BABYLONISH CAPTIVITY.

Introduction—Derivation of the Theory 57–67

SECTION I. Alleged Independence of the Jews, after their Return from Babylon 67–68

SECTION II. Alleged Reconciliation of do. . . . 68–71

SECTION III. Alleged Spiritual Revivals which followed do.—Rebuilding of Temple—Restoration of Sacrifices, etc.—Objections—Answered 71–77

SECTION IV. Further Objections—Silence of N. T. on the Future Return of the Jews 77

SECTION V. Argument drawn from the Alleged Differences of the Two Covenants, Gal. iv. 22–31—Examined and Refuted . 77–98

CHAPTER II.

SECOND THEORY: AS ADVOCATED BY GROTIUS, PRIDEAUX, VINT, PROF. GEO. BUSH, ETC.

THIS THEORY ALLEGES, THAT THE PROPHECIES RELATING TO THE SECOND COMING OF CHRIST, AND THE ERECTION OF THE MILLENNIAL KINGDOM, WERE FULLY VERIFIED BY THE OVERTHROW OF PAGANISM AND THE ESTABLISHMENT OF CHRISTIANITY IN

THE ROMAN EMPIRE, UNDER CONSTANTINE THE GREAT, IN
A. D. 323, AS FOUNDED UPON REV., CHAP. XX. 1–7.

Their Arguments in Defence of, Stated	99–107
Examined and Refuted	107–117

CHAPTER III.

THIRD THEORY: AS ADVOCATED BY THE POPULAR WRITERS OF THE DAY.

THIS THEORY ALLEGES ALL THE PROPHECIES RELATING TO THE SECOND COMING OF CHRIST AND THE ESTABLISHMENT OF HIS KINGDOM IN THE WORLD, TO HAVE BEEN VERIFIED BY THE JUDGMENTS INFLICTED UPON THE JEWISH NATION AND POLITY, AT THE DESTRUCTION OF JERUSALEM, ETC., BY THE ROMAN ARMY UNDER TITUS, IN A. D. 70, AS FOUNDED UPON THAT PORTION OF OUR LORD'S PROPHECY CONTAINED IN MATTHEW, CHAP. XXIV. 27–30.

Quotations from	118–123
Their Arguments, etc., in Support of, Stated	123–126
Examined and Refuted, in Three Particulars	126–127
I. The Figurative and Literal Theories of Interpretation	127–130
II. Reply to their Expositions, etc.	131–160
III. Direct Literal Interpretation of this Prophecy, taken in Connection with its Chronological Stand-points, etc.	160–182

CHAPTER IV.

FOURTH THEORY.

THIS THEORY ALLEGES, THAT THE PROPHECIES RELATING TO THE KINGDOM OF HEAVEN, AND THE REIGN OF CHRIST ON EARTH, REFER TO THE FIRST INTRODUCTION AND ESTABLISHMENT OF THE CHRISTIAN CHURCH; THE DISPENSATION OF WHICH MERGES INTO, FORMS A PART OF, AND ENDS WITH, THE CLOSE OF THE MILLENNIAL STATE; WHEN, IT IS AFFIRMED, CHRIST WILL PERSONALLY APPEAR AT THE JUDGMENT DAY, AND SIMULTANEOUSLY RAISE FROM THE DEAD BOTH THE

RIGHTEOUS AND THE WICKED, WHEN THE ONE SHALL BE
REWARDED AND THE OTHER PUNISHED, ETC.

Introductory Remarks—Difficulties—The Question Stated . . 182–185

FIRST THESIS. Of the Alleged Identity of "the Times of the Gentiles," with the Christian Dispensation and the Millennial Era.

Proof that these Two Eras are not Identical 185–188

SECOND THESIS. This Thesis Alleges, that the Christian Church, during "the Times of the Gentiles," is Identical with "the Kingdom of Heaven"—"of God"—of "the Son of Man," etc.; also that, Forming a Part, it is to Run Onward to the Close of the Millennial Era.

Proof that the Christian Dispensation and the Millennial Era are Separate and Distinct 178–200

The Argument Continued, as Derived from the Chronology of Scripture, Historic and Prophetic 200–204

QUERY. IS THE UNIVERSAL CONFLAGRATION OF THE EARTH PRE OR POST-MILLENNIAL?

Answer to 204–216

PART III.

AN EXAMINATION OF THE QUESTION—WILL THE SECOND COMING OF CHRIST, AS AN EVENT STILL FUTURE, CONSIST OF AN ALLEGORICAL OR SPIRITUAL COMING; OR WILL IT BE LITERALLY A CORPOREAL OR PERSONAL COMING; AND WILL IT BE PRE OR POST-MILLENNIAL? SCRIPTURALLY AND PHILOSOPHICALLY CONSIDERED.

The Discussion of the Fourth Theory resumed, in Connection with the

THIRD THESIS. This Thesis Alleges, that as the Idea of a Kingdom involves the Presence and Reign of a King; so, throughout the prolonged period of "the Times of the Gentiles" onward to the End of the Millennium, its Advocates insist that Christ has reigned, and will continue to reign after an Invisible or Spiritual Manner.

	PAGES
Introductory Remarks	217–219

SECTION I. An Examination of the Alleged Identity of the Christian Church with "the Kingdom of Heaven," etc.; and of Christ's Spiritual Reign over it as King 219–232

SECTION II. A Demonstration that there is to be no intervening Millennium between the Second Personal Coming of Christ and the Day of Judgment; in other words, that that Event, when it does take place, will be Pre and not Post-Millennial. This Section is divided into two parts:

PART I. Direct Scriptural Proof that there is to be no intervening Millennium between the Personal Second Coming of Christ and the Day of Judgment 232–243

PART II. A Demonstration that the Ideas and Language of the New Testament Writers in reference to the Personal Second Coming of Christ and the Judgment of the Great Day, were Derived from and Founded upon the Prophetic Statements of the inspired Pre-Christian Jewish Writers regarding them. 243–254

Conclusion 254–256

CHAPTER V.

SACRED PHILOSOPHY, CONSIDERED IN ITS APPLICATION TO THE SCRIPTURAL DOCTRINE OF THE RESURRECTION OF CHRIST, AND OF THE RIGHTEOUS AND THE WICKED DEAD, AS DEPENDENT UPON, AND CONNECTED WITH, HIS SECOND COMING.

Preliminary Remarks 257–258

SECTION I. An Inquiry into the import of the terms, Spiritual, Corporeal, and Personal, etc. 258–263

SECTION II. A Demonstration of the Scriptural Doctrine of a *Literal Resurrection* of the Dead. Arguments: 1st, As derived from *Analogy;* 2d, As an *Elementary* Doctrine of the New Testament 263–268

SECTION III. A Special Inquiry into the *Mode* or *Form* of CHRIST'S Resurrected State—Preliminary Remarks . . . 268–271

Not a *Spiritual* Resurrection—Proofs 271–278

SECTION IV. A Scriptural Exhibit of the Nature, Attributes, and Official Dignity of the Literal or Personal Resurrected and Glorified Humanity of Christ 278

PART I.

Of the Nature of Christ's Resurrected Humanity.

1st. Negatively. Could not have been *purely Spiritual* . . 278–279
2d. Positively. Difference between a *Spiritual* and a *Spiritualized* body—Did not become *Angelic*—Objection, drawn from a number of *Extraordinary Circumstances and Actions* of Christ after his Resurrection—Explained 279–285

PART II.

What is revealed of the Attributes *and* Official Dignity *of the Resurrected Human Nature of Christ.*

I. An Exemplification of, in the *Transfiguration* on the Mount . 285–287
II. A Further View, as connected with Christ's *Divine Attributes*, 287–288
III. Also, as derived from Christ's Resurrected OFFICIAL DIGNITY—1st, As *Intercessor*—2d, As *Judge*—3d, As *King* . . 288–290

SECTION V. Concluding Scriptural Proof, that the Second Coming of Christ will be pre-Millennial and Personal.

I. It will be *pre-Millennial* 290–294
II. It will be *Personal* 294–297

CHAPTER VI.

A COMPLETE SYNOPSIS OF THE MILLENARIAN SCHEME OF THE SECOND PERSONAL COMING OF CHRIST AND OF THE MILLENNIAL ERA, AS TAUGHT IN HOLY SCRIPTURE . . . 298–320

PREFACE.

THE Creeds, Confessions of Faith, Articles of Religion, and covenants of every branch of the Church throughout Christendom, Roman, Greek, and Protestant, recognize the doctrine of the second coming of the Lord Jesus Christ, in resurrection power, as an undoubted scriptural truth.

Nevertheless, from an early period of her history, the Christian Church has been *at issue* with herself on the great question regarding the nature and purposes of that event, and of the period when it shall take place.

The *theories* which have obtained the greatest notoriety on this subject since the time of the famous Origen, between A. D. 204 and 254, are the following:

I. The first theory is that of *Augustine*, bishop of Hippo, who flourished between A. M. 390 and 430 (advocated also by Primasius, Andreas, Bede, etc.), of a *spiritual resurrection*, which—as this ancient writer followed the computation of the LXX for the epoch of the nativity, viz., in the middle of the sixth chiliad of the world's history—he affirms is dated from the *first* coming of Christ, by whom Satan was wounded, and the strong man disarmed and ejected from the hearts of men, etc.,—the *term* of its continuance to be the remainder of the said sixth chiliad.

II. The second theory is that put forth by *Hammond* and *Grotius*, between A. D. 1641 and 1660. These writers allege, that the second coming of Christ consists of an *ecclesiastical resurrection*, etc., and that it commenced with the opening of the IVth century continued one thousand literal years, and ended in the XIVth century.

III. The third theory is that of *Dr. Whitby*, whose death occurred in A. D. 1726. He taught that the resurrection of the martyrs, etc. (Rev. xx. 4), is to consist of *a signal revival of pure Christian principles*, the time of which is still future, and is to follow the destruction of Anti-Christ, etc.; after which, the whole earth being permeated with these Christian principles, Christ is to commence a *spiritual* reign over the nations for a thousand years. It is this theory which has formed the basis of the current theology of the Christian Church since his time.

I add here, that the *three* following principles of interpretation of the prophetic Scriptures have been resorted to, in the advocacy of the leading features involved in the three above-named theories, to wit:—of the first three, which affirm that the second coming of Christ is *already past*,

1. The first class of writers allege *all* the prophecies relating to that event to have been verified in the Restoration, etc., of the two kingdoms of Judah and Israel or the Ten Tribes, *at the time of the return* of the Jews from the Babylonian captivity.

2. The second class of writers differ from the first, in that they contend for the fulfilment of *all* the prophecies referring to the second coming of Christ, and the establishment of His kingdom in the world, by the judgments inflicted upon the Jewish nation, and the overthrow of their polity, *at the destruction of Jerusalem* by the Roman legions under Titus, in A. D. 70.

3. The third class of these writers, in opposition to the first two, hold that all the prophecies relating to Christ's second coming, and the setting up of His millennial kingdom on earth, were fully verified *by the overthrow of paganism, and the establishment of Christianity* in the Roman empire, under Constantine, in A. D. 325. Another theory:

IV. This theory, combining those both of *Augustine* and *Whitby* as the basis on which it stands, alleges that those prophecies which speak of "the kingdom of heaven," "the kingdom of God," "the kingdom of the Son of Man," etc., as associated with the reign of Christ on earth, refers to the *first introduction and establishment* of the Christian Church; the dispensation of which, being identical with "the kingdom of heaven" over which Christ reigns by His spirit, merges into, forms a part of, and ends with, the *close* of the millennial age, etc.; at which time Christ is to personally appear, simultaneously raise the dead, both just and unjust, and dispense to them rewards and punishments according to their works. This makes the Millennium to be *future*.

But, in addition to these four theories, and the principles applied in remoulding and amplifying them, there is—

V. A fifth system, which maintains that the Christian Church and "the kingdom of the Son of Man" are entirely separate and distinct; that there is to be a *literal resurrection* of departed saints and martyrs, to take place *at* the second personal coming of Christ, before, and in order to, the *setting up* of the kingdom of Christ, and over which they are to conjointly reign for a thousand years; also that, during that period, Satan is to be restrained from tempting, harassing, and injuring mankind; and that, *at the close* of that period, the wicked dead are to be raised, judged, etc. (Rev. xx. 4, 5).

Now, it is obvious to the plainest mind, that these *variant* Theories, and the principles applied to their elucidation, cannot be made to harmonize with the "*one faith*" in these premises, as revealed in the inspired word. Indeed, *one only* of the number can claim to be in accordance with that immutable "faith" at first "delivered to the saints." On this ground, many are wont to plead that the truth in this matter lay beyond our reach. In other words, that the *prophecies* are among those "deep things" of "the mysteries of God's will," which it was never intended should be understood,—at least, until they are *fulfilled*. Especially is this objection urged against the *prophetical dates*. Mr. Miller and others, it is said, have been mistaken. Therefore, no man living can reach anything definite or reliable regarding them. Aye, and that in the face of that positive declaration of the inspired Apostle Peter, that "we have a *more sure word* of prophecy," respecting which we are admonished that "we all do well to *take heed*, as unto a light which shineth in a dark place, until the day dawn, and the day-star arise in our hearts" (2 Peter i. 13); and who also tells us, that the old prophets "have inquired and searched *diligently*, who prophesied of the grace that should come unto us; searching *what*, or *what manner of time*, the spirit of Christ which was in them did signify, when it testified beforehand the sufferings of Christ, and the GLORY that should follow." (1 Peter i. 10, 11.) And also of the apocalyptic benediction, "*Blessed* is he that readeth, and they that hear the words of this prophecy, and keep those things which are written therein; for the time is at hand." (Rev. i. 3.) But,

We deferentially ask: Do we not reason otherwise in regard to other portions of the equally "deep things" of God's revealed mysteries? All that we now plead for in reference to "the great theological question of the day," as indicated in the title page of this volume, is, *that it is a fair subject for candid and open discussion.* Why, then, should it be made an exception, as an acknowledged part of the "*all Scripture* given by inspiration of God?" Surely, because men differ in their views respecting it forms no just grounds why it should be ignored. If, for example, the rule for the *rejection* of a matter of divine revelation be the measure of its misrepresentation, perversion, or abuse, then what becomes of our common Christianity? Try it in its application to the doctrine of the proper deity of Christ, as "God manifest in the flesh"—of the personality and deity of the Holy Spirit, of justification by faith, of perseverance in grace, of future retributions, etc. These, *one and all*, on the above principle, having each in their turn been *alike* perverted, opposed, and denied, had been alike erased from the escutcheon of our common Christianity, like a name inscribed upon the sand!

There are few, we opine, among those who professedly receive the "Scriptures as given by inspiration of God," who are willing to risk their eternal salvation on such an alternative. What? Close our Bibles, obliterate the Sabbath, shut up our churches, annihilate the ministry, and trample the ordinances of our holy religion under foot, in a word, reject Christianity, because, forsooth, the *variant theories* which have obtained among men have availed to pervert and abuse them? "The children of this world," in their treatment of the occult sciences, "are wiser in their generation." With them, these have advanced, and continue to advance in the scale of exactitude, just in proportion as they have *suffered* from the errors and abuses of men. Would we not do well to take an analogous lesson from them?

Let the reader, then, bear in mind, that all misconceptions, perversions, and abuses of scriptural truth, whether of doctrines or of the prophecies, being the result either of ignorance, mere party zeal, or open hostility, are to be subjected to the ordeal of God's holy word, which is to "*try* every man's work, of what sort it is."

(1 Cor. iii. 13.) Whatever respect we may have for the persons or of confidence in the opinions of the learned, either of the past or the present age, in matters of revealed truth, we can " call no man master." In the words of Chillingworth, "THE BIBLE, AND THE BIBLE ALONE, IS THE RELIGION OF PROTESTANTS." In the exposition, therefore, of the great and sublime doctrine of the second personal coming of the Lord Jesus Christ, as set forth in this volume, our motto is, " *To the law and to the testimony:* if we speak not according to this word, it is because there is no light in us." (Isa. viii. 20.)

And, although " many have taken in hand to set forth in order a declaration of those things" which have been so fully revealed in Holy Scripture on this subject, it is nevertheless undeniable, that in the *popular* theological nomenclature of the day, through both the pulpit and the press, it has either been so sublimated, mystified, etherealized—so mutilated—so confounded with other of the great acts and purposes of "God in Christ," on the one hand; or so neglected, ignored, or held up to contempt, on the other; that there is *a need-be*, to put forth the endeavor to rescue it from those prejudices which *false* glosses and theories have created in regard to it. Why: if Bishop Colenso's semi-infidel attack upon the inspired Pentateuch of Moses has called forth some four hundred replies in its defence, on both sides of the Atlantic; is it unreasonable that this *first* attempt to thoroughly canvass the variant and conflicting theories, ancient and modern, on the subject in hand, should be put forth to *redeem* it from the errors and delusions which have obtained in the church? We concede that treatises, not a few, have appeared, from time to time, especially within the last half century, on both sides of this great theological question of the present day. But, in the judgment of the writer, not one of them has fairly grappled with the difficulties, and met and removed the objections of antagonist writers. Nor can this be accomplished, except by a careful, patient, candid, and thorough examination of said question *on its merits*, separately from, and independently of, all superfluous and extraneous matters.

In our endeavor, therefore, to *restore* this glorious doctrine of the Lord's second coming to its proper place in the great firmament of revealed truth—that doctrine which has inspired the faith, nourished the hope, kindled the love, and supported the constancy of the chosen people of God, from the first hour of promised redemption through Christ to the present—we have conducted our examinations of it (in connection with all the theories and principles of interpretation that have obtained, so far as entitled to notice), on the only true basis, to wit, that of *analyzing* each theory separately and subjecting it to the threefold test of truth, " scripturally, historically, and philosophically considered." How far we may have succeeded in this endeavor, we leave for the future to determine. Duty is ours; results belong to God.

In conclusion, we have only to add that, adopting as our standpoint that the second personal coming of our Lord is *Pre*-millennial, we enter our *protest* against its being confounded with that of modern *Millerism*. To explain.

1. Millenarians, together with the advocates of the current theology of the Church, and the Millerites, *all* maintain that the second personal coming of Christ is to take place *at the close* of that period called in the New Testament (Luke xxi. 24, and Romans xi. 25) " the times of the Gentiles."

2. The circumstance which has led to a *confounding* of Millenarianism with Millerism, is the *proximate nearness* of that event, as alleged by both; whereas the advocates of the popular theory, on the hypothesis that " the times of the Gentiles " merge into, form a part, and end at the close of the millennial era, affirm that it takes place *after* that period. But,

3. Both Millenarians, and the advocates of the popular view, at least for the most part, maintain the existence on earth of *a millennium of blessedness* of the saved nations in the flesh for a thousand years.

4. On the contrary, Millerism *denies* this. The only difference, however, between the theory of Mr. Miller and that of the popularly received view of the Church of the present day is, that, as both place the second personal coming of the Lord *at the close* of " the times of the Gentiles," Mr. Miller *antedated* that event, by alleging that it was to occur in A. D. 1843, instead of at the end of the thousand years. On all other points, there is *an exact* correspondence between Millerism and the current view of the Church, in regard to all the events which are to *follow* the second personal coming of Christ, *e. g.*, the universal conflagration of the earth, etc., and the immediate introduction of the human race into their eternal state of bliss or of woe. Again,

5. While, according to the theory of Millerism, time was to

close and eternity to begin *immediately after* A. D. 1843; Millenarians, in unison with the advocates of the popular view, maintain that time does not end, *until the close* of the millennial era. Nevertheless,

6. While Millenarians affirm that the second personal coming of Christ is *pre*-millennial, the prevailing theology of the Church alleges it to be *post*-millennial. Hence the difference between the two classes of writers as to the *nature* of Christ's reign over the saved nations in the flesh during the millennium; the former insisting that it is a *literal, personal* reign; the latter, that it is to consist of a *spiritual* reign only. It is in place here, therefore, to *account* for this difference of views on this momentous subject.

We observe, then, that while the remote occasion of it arises from the different rules of interpretation of the prophetic Scriptures, Millenarians adopting the *literal,* and their opponents the allegorical or *spiritual* rule (which matter will be treated of in its proper place in the sequel); the immediate or direct occasion is that *some* millenarian writers—prominent among whom is the Rev. Dr. Cumming of London—allege that the second personal coming of Christ not only, but also the universal conflagration of the earth, is *pre*-millennial.

Now, *we* maintain that this is one among a number of millenarian crotchets, which tend to bewilder and confound many sincerely honest and inquiring minds. Indeed, it forms *the great stumbling block* in the way of an acceptance of the truth in these premises. *Post-*Millenarians, for example, cannot reconcile the above alleged universal conflagration of the earth as being *pre*-millennial, with the fact of the *perpetuity* of those races of men who are to people the earth during the millennium. The question, what is to become of them while that process is going on, no Millenarian, on the above hypothesis, ever has, or ever can answer. It is *a stupendous theological misnomer!* The Scriptures clearly teach—as will be shown in the proper place—that the universal conflagration is *post*-millennial. "Convince me of this," says a distinguished *post*-millenarian clergyman, recently, "and I will adopt the millenarian view, that the second personal coming of Christ is *pre*-millennial." It results, therefore,

First. That the only difference between the theory of Millerism and the current theology of the Church, on the subject of Christ's second personal coming is, that the latter insists there is to be a millennium *before* that event takes place. While,

Second. True millenarianism maintains, against the Millerites, a *future* millennium of blessedness to the saved nations in the flesh; and against the popular view, that the second personal coming of Christ *is not post*, but *pre*-millennial.

The writer has no ambition to be thought "original" in the production of this treatise, beyond what may be conceded of the *method* adopted in these discussions. While he acknowledges his obligations to both classes of expositors occupying the extensive field over which he has passed, to avoid encumbering his pages with lengthy quotations, he has preferred to adopt his own phraseology, for the most part, in availing himself of any suggestions or facts necessary to his purpose.

May the Holy Spirit guide the inquiring mind into all truth, for Christ's sake.

NEW YORK, *Jan.*, 1865.

AN APPEAL,

RESPECTFULLY ADDRESSED TO THE FOLLOWING CLERGY,

> The Right Rev. Horatio Potter, D. D., Bishop of the Diocese of New York.
> The Rev. N. L. Rice, D. D., Pastor of the Fifth Avenue Presbyterian Church, cor. of 19th Street (Old School).
> The Rev. T. E. Vermilye, D. D., Associate Pastor of the Collegiate Reformed Dutch Church.
> The Rev. William Adams, D. D., Pastor of the Presbyterian Church, Madison Square (New School).
> The Rev. John McClintock, D. D., Pastor of the St. Paul's Methodist Episcopal Church, Fourth Avenue.
> The Rev. Edward Lathrop, D. D., Pastor of the Tabernacle Baptist Church, Second Avenue.
> The Rev. Henry Ward Beecher, Pastor of the Plymouth Congregational Church, Brooklyn.
> The Rev. Charles Hodge, D. D., Professor in the Princeton Theological Seminary, New Jersey.
> The Rev. W. G. T. Shedd, D. D., Professor in the Union Theological Seminary, University Place, New York.
> The Rev. J. T. Berg, D. D., Professor in the Theological Seminary of the Reformed Dutch Church, Brunswick, New Jersey.

Dear Brethren:

The appeal here offered for your consideration, is prompted by no other motive than that of eliciting the truth, as connected with the subject discussed in this treatise. Nor do we feel that any apology is called for, other than what may be found in the nature and importance of the subject itself. As the professed "ambassadors" of the Lord Jesus Christ, appointed to "watch for souls as they that must give account,"[1] however diversified our ecclesiastical relations, positions, or circumstances, yet, in the matter of this appeal to you, we must be pardoned, if, for the nonce, we consider you as placed, one and all, on the common platform of that ministerial equality and responsibility, primitively applied to the college of the apostles, when reminded by their divine Lord and Master, "*All ye are brethren.*"[2] Especially can no legitimate exception be taken to this at a time like the present, when we are in the midst of a signal movement, in high and responsible quarters, having for its object the expurgation of *schism* from the Church, under the motto (to use the language of the Rev. Dr. Dix, rector of Trinity Church, in his recent discourse on *Church Union*, delivered in the Congregational Broadway Tabernacle), " we must have a union in the Church," in conformity with " a union of the States."

It is quite superfluous to add, reverend sirs, that the purport of this appeal implies that, on " the great theological question of the day," in reference to the second coming of Christ, to wit, " Is it *pre* or is it *post*-millennial?" you are the advocates of the *latter* hypothesis. That is, you all allege that that event is *post*-millennial. And hence, your unremitting efforts to head off the influence of the teachings of your *pre*-millennial opponents, in a form and manner somewhat as follows :—Either by your silence on the subject, or through the medium of the pulpit and the press, you labor to inculcate in the minds of your people, first, that to agitate this question of the second coming of Christ, etc., *tends to promote* sadness and melancholy, and to instigate the worst forms of fanaticism and delusion. Second. By telling them that it is a subject *too remote* to interest our inquiries. Third. By reminding them that the most learned and pious in the Church *disagree* among themselves, both as to the events of prophecy, and the time of their fulfilment ; and that, therefore, it does not come within the range of legitimate inquiry. And finally, fourth, you are unremitting in your endeavors, through both your public and private intercourse with your people, to infuse into their minds the idea, that it is *a matter of indifference* whether the second personal coming of Christ is to be *pre* or *post*-millennial ; and hence your inculcation of the sentiment, that preparation for death, which you allege

---

[1] Heb. xiii. 17. [2] Matt. xxiii. 8.

is identical with the second coming of Christ, is *the great motive to be employed* in urging men to faith, repentance, and a holy life. Hence my appeal to you.

And in the first place, while we concede, reverend sirs, that there have sprung up in different ages of the Church, both ancient and modern, some of the worst forms of fanaticism and delusion on this subject, yet I appeal, whether they have not originated from the *abuses* of God's prophetic word by ignorant, ambitious, and misguided men, rather than from the *study* of that word? Why, sirs, you may find a sprinkling of Millenarians in most of the Churches of which you are the distinguished representatives. There are the Right Rev. Bishop Southgate, Bishop Hopkins, of Vermont, Bishop McIlvaine, of Ohio, the Rev. S. H. Tyng, D.D., and the Rev. Francis Vinton, D.D., of the Episcopal Church; the Rev. C. K. Imbrie, D.D., the Rev. Dr. McCartee, and others, of the Presbyterian Church; and the Rev. Drs. Gordon and Demarest, with others, in the Reformed Dutch Church, etc., etc.; all of them in high repute for their learning, position, piety, and zeal. Do you account these as the subjects of fanaticism and delusion?

Then, second. In regard to the alleged *remoteness* of that event, we appeal. Now, what if it should turn out that, instead, it is "nigh at hand, even at the doors?" On this point, we admit that it savors of the most rampant fanaticism for any to pretend, as did Mr. Wm. Miller, that we can determine the "*day and hour*" of that event, concerning which Jesus declared, that "no man knoweth, no, not the angels in heaven, neither the Son, but the Father only."[1] Yet, we appeal. Has not God, in infinite condescension and mercy, been pleased to make known to the Church, through the combined medium of the chronology of prophecy and the concurrent "signs of the times," *the period about when* it may be expected? Why, reverend sirs, your *own* theory claims to do this. As *post*-millenarians, you tell us that it is to take place at the end of "the times of the Gentiles," which, you say, transpires at the "delivering up" of the millennial kingdom by the Son to the Father, upon *the close* of that era. But, we repeat, should it turn out that "the times of the Gentiles" close *before*, instead of at the end of that period: in other words, that these are *two* separate and distinct dispensations; then it will follow that, as the second personal coming of Christ is to take place at the end of

[1] Matt. xxiv. 36.

"*the times of the Gentiles,*" your alleged theory of the remoteness of that event will prove to be fallacious. We request your special attention to this point, as discussed in this sequel.

On one cardinal point, then, reverend sirs, we are agreed, to wit, that at "the time of the end,"[1] (*i. e.*, the end of "the times of the Gentiles,") the *previously veiled* vision,[2] though it was to extend over a long and dreary season of moral darkness and desolation, yet at last was destined to "*speak*, and not lie."[3] And for what, pray? Why, that the faithful in Christ Jesus who believe in, and are watching and praying for "the coming of the Lord," when they shall *see* "the things" spoken of as "SIGNS" of the *proximate* realization of their faith and hope, *begin* to come to pass in concurrence with the CHRONOLOGY which pointed them out, they might "look up and lift up their heads" at their approaching "redemption." (Compare Daniel xii. 12, 13 with Luke xxi. 25–36.) While on the other hand, of the "scoffers of the last times," who, "walking after their own lusts," shall exclaim, "*Where is the promise of His coming?* for since the fathers have fallen asleep all things continue as they were from the beginning of the creation," shall cry, "peace and safety," *then* shall sudden destruction come upon them as a woman in travail, and they shall not escape."[4] Besides, reverend sirs, does not the Apostle say, in addition, "But ye, brethren, *are not* in darkness, that that day should overtake *you* as a thief. Ye are all the children of *light*, and of *the day:* we *are not* of the night, *nor* of darkness?"[5]

But this *knowledge* of the proximate coming of the Lord, I need not inform you, reverend sirs, involves much of careful, prayerful, diligent, laborious, and persevering "inquiry and searching of what," as to the *events* of prophecy, "and *what manner of time* the spirit of Christ which was in the old prophets did signify, when it testified beforehand the sufferings of Christ, and THE GLORY that should follow."[6] Here, reverend sirs, is a door open for *self*-appeal. Have *we* done this? If not, why? As those who are appointed to "watch for souls as they that must give account," what excuse have we to offer? And now,

Third. As to the alleged *disagreement* among the most learned and pious expositors of prophecy. On this subject, reverend sirs, we appeal, that, even admitting this to be so, does it justify us in

---

[1] Dan. xii. 9. [2] Ib. verses 8, 9. [3] Habak. ii. 1–3. [4] 2 Pet. iii. 4; 1 Thess. v. 3. [5] 1 Thess. v. 4, 5. [6] 1 Pet. i. 11.

the neglect to *study* God's prophetic word—that "more sure word of prophecy" concerning which St. Peter tells us that "we all do well to take heed, as unto a light which shineth in a dark place;" aye, and to *continue* to do so, "until the day dawn, and the day-star arise in our hearts?"[1] How otherwise can we hope to reap the fruits of that apocalyptic benediction—"*Blessed* is he that readeth, and they that hear the words of this prophecy, and keep those things which are written therein?"[2] How, to "*fully* preach the Gospel of Christ,"[3] bringing out of the exhaustless "treasury of God's word things both *new* and *old*" for the instruction and edification of the Lord's people, "that we may present every man *perfect* in Christ Jesus?"[4]

But, reverend sirs, we must beg to demur to this averment. True, expositors on both sides of this "great theological question of the day," *do differ* in their interpretations of it. We affirm, however, that, so far as Millenarians are concerned, these differences relate not so much to the detailed events of prophecy, as to the *chronology* of those events. In regard to the first—the *events* predicted, we venture to affirm that, within the last half century, and particularly within the last twenty-five years, there has existed *greater harmony* of views among the learned and pious who have written on this subject, than on any other mooted question in the entire range of the cardinal doctrines of Christianity. And as to the second—the *chronology* of prophecy, their variations on the whole predestined period of six thousand years from the creation and fall to the close of " the times of the Gentiles," do not exceed more than about ten years; while the more *exact* of them—and they are by far the larger number—agree to within from one to four years. The fact is, Millenarians do not pretend to infallibility as interpreters of God's word. And so, some few of them, at least, either from a *partial* acquaintance with the subject, or a neglect to properly *discriminate* between things which differ, have contributed not a little, as we have remarked in the preface, to perplex the minds of inquirers. But, after all, what is the *chaff* to the *wheat?* saith the Lord.[5] And is it not, we submit, a fearful thought, IF, perchance, the very errors which originate in the infirmities of the Lord's servants, should be designed, in His all-wise providence, as *a test* of our fidelity in "searching the Scriptures daily, whether these things be so,"[6] and, in case of our neg-

[1] 2 Pet. i. 19.   [2] Rev. i. 3.   [3] Rom. xv. 19.   [4] Compare Matt. xiii. 52 with Col. i. 28.
[5] Jer. xxiii. 28.   [6] Acts xvii. 11.

lect to do this, to "*blind the minds*"¹ of those who, on the ground of the above pretext, reject the truth? We pass to the next article.

Fourth. In regard to the plea, that *it is a matter of indifference* whether the second coming of the Lord is *pre* or *post*-millennial. On this subject we appeal. Are not the best, the dearest interests of the Church and people of God, dead and living, and the solemn destinies of an impenitent and ungodly world for time and for eternity, *involved in,* yea, *bound up with* that momentous event, the judgment-coming of the Lord? Why, reverend sirs, what saith the Apostle John? "Beloved, now are we the sons of God, and it doth not yet appear what we shall be; but we know, that *when* He shall appear, we shall be like Him, for we shall see Him as He is."² That is, as St. Paul declares, that *then*, "THE LORD HIMSELF shall descend from heaven with a shout, with the voice of the archangel, and with the trump of God." For what? Why, to "*change* the vile bodies" of those who "sleep in Him," that they "may be made like unto *His own* glorious body," and that "the dead in Christ may rise *first*." Nor this only. For the Apostle adds: "*Then*, we which are alive, and remain unto the coming of the Lord, shall be caught up together with them in the clouds, to meet the Lord in the air; and so shall we *ever be with the Lord.*"³ And, on the other hand, Christ will *then* "be revealed from heaven in flaming fire with His mighty angels,"—for what? Why, to "*take vengeance* on them that know not God, and that obey not the Gospel of our Lord Jesus Christ; who shall be punished with everlasting destruction from the presence of the Lord, and from the glory of His power."⁴ Now if, reverend sirs, these and the like events *are to accompany* the second coming of Christ, how can it be said to be a matter of *indifference* whether that event is to be *pre* or *post*-millennial? For it is certain that, IF, as we have said, that event turns out to be *pre*-millennial—and this, mark, depends entirely upon the question whether or not "the times of the Gentiles" be a dispensation *totally separate and distinct from* the millennial era, and to which we have asked your special attention—then it follows, that all those splendidly glorious and awfully terrific events, instead of being remote from the present generation, are "*nigh at hand,*" yea, "*even at our doors.*"

¹ 2 Cor. iii. 14; iv. 4; 2 Thess. ii. 11.
² 1 John iii. 2.
³ Compare 1 Thess. iv. 13-17 with Philipp. iii. 21.
⁴ 2 Thess. i. 7-10.

You must, therefore, pardon me, reverend sirs, if I affirm on this point, that with me it is an article of faith that your individual salvation and mine, with all others of this day, depends upon our being *right* in this matter. It is only to those " who," in faith and hope, " look for Him," that " He will appear the second time without sin unto salvation." [1]

And finally, in regard to the other plea—the urging of death, as *the great motive* to faith, repentance, and a holy life, etc. Now, reverend sirs, we appeal, can there be, in the light of Holy Scripture, a fallacy, yea, a delusion, more at variance with the plainest teachings of Christ and His apostles? This is not the place to argue the point in hand. We therefore respectfully refer you to Part I. of this treatise, under the head of the second thesis—*the practical tendencies* of the scriptural doctrine of the second coming of Christ, in proof that *the great motive* to repentance, to the love of Christ and of one another, to mortifying of sinful lusts, to general obedience and holiness of heart and of life, to works of mercy, to watchfulness, to moderation and sobriety, to patience and long-suffering under trial, and, though last, not least, to *ministerial* fidelity and diligence in their vocation—in a word, to the exercise of every Christian virtue, is not death, but *a preparation* " to stand before the Son of Man" at his coming.[2] And, reverend sirs, we appeal, is not the reason of this most obvious? The second coming of Christ, in all ages, has constituted the *faith* and *hope* of the Church, both on earth and in heaven. Why, reverend sirs, are you not aware—and if not, should you not be aware— that out of the *forty-one* prophets who have spoken to us in the Old and New Testaments, only *six* of them foretold of the FIRST coming of Christ, and that these six impliedly, that is, with greater or less distinctness, refer also to that event; while *all* the others, in almost numberless places, and in every variety of form, predict in the most positive terms the SECOND coming of Christ? Again. Are you not also aware—and if not, ought you not to be aware—that the *scope* of prophecy, spanning, as it does, the entire period of the predestined six thousand years from the creation and fall to the close of " the times of the Gentiles," points the eye of faith to the SECOND PERSONAL coming of Christ? And that hence, while all the Old Testament saints " *died in the faith* " of that event as " seeing it afar off," [3] those of the New Testament, im-

---

[1] Heb. ix. 27, 28.   [2] Luke xxi. 36.   [4] Heb. xi. 13.

mediately upon their conversion, being pointed to it as *imminent*, "*Looked* for that blessed hope, the glorious appearing of the great God, even our Saviour, Jesus Christ?"[1] and that, "*loving* His appearing,"[2] they *hastened unto* the coming and kingdom of God,"[3] prompted by the "desire to depart and to be *with* Christ, which is far better."

But, reverend sirs, having said thus much, we must here further add, by the way, that *the times we live in* are portentous of the most stupendous events, alike in the national, political, civil, social, and ecclesiastical departments of *the State* and of *the Church*. "There *are now* signs in the sun, and in the moon, and in the stars; and upon the earth, distress of nations with perplexity; the sea and the waves *are now* roaring," while "men's hearts are failing them for fear, and for looking after those things that are coming upon the earth; for the powers of heaven *are now* being shaken,"[4] and that in a manner and to an extent never before known in the history of the world. And what can these earthquake upheavings and revolutions in the Church, and among the nations, kingdoms, empires, and states of "the wide, wide world" indicate, if they be not a *verification* of that prophecy in Ezekiel, chap. xxi. 27—"I will overturn, overturn, overturn *it*,"—that is, the state or condition of the world as at present constituted—"and *it* shall be no more, until He come whose right it is: *and I will give it* Him." (See Dan. ii. 35, 44; and vii. 11–14.) Does it not then become those who claim to be the "ambassadors" of the Lord Jesus Christ—the "watchmen" placed upon the ramparts of the Church of this day, to "see" to it "that we refuse not Him that speaketh: for if they escaped not who refused Him that spake on earth, much more shall not we escape, if we turn away from Him that speaketh from heaven; whose voice then shook the earth: but *now*, He hath promised, saying, Yet once more I shake not the earth only, but also heaven. And this word, Yet once more, signifieth *the removing* of those things that are shaken, as of things that are made; that those things which *cannot be shaken* may remain. Wherefore we, receiving a kingdom which cannot be moved, let us have grace, whereby we may serve God acceptably, with reverence and godly fear. For our God is a consuming fire."[5]

[1] Titus ii. 13.   [2] 2 Tim. iv. 8.   [3] 2 Pet. iii. 12.   [4] Philipp. i. 23.
[5] Heb. xii. 25-29.

Ah yes, reverend sirs. "*Our God . . . a consuming fire.*" We should not forget this. Surely, if that self-denying, faithful, suffering, inspired, and miracle-working Paul said, "I keep under my body, and bring it into subjection; lest, by any means, when I have preached to others, I myself should be *a castaway*,"[1] it becomes *us* to keep this his example before us, if we would escape the "consuming fire" of God's wrath against *the act* of ministerial unfaithfulness above indicated. Nor can we suggest a more timeous and effective *motive* to this than that we turn to, and ponder over, that tremendously awful picture of ministerial responsibility for the proper *use* or *abuse* of the talents committed to our trust, so graphically depicted in the prophecy of Ezekiel, chap. xxxiii. verses 1-9. "The word of the Lord came unto me, saying, Son of Man, speak to the children of my people, and say unto them, When I bring the sword upon the land, if the people of the land take a man of their coasts, and set him for their watchman; if, when he seeth the sword come upon the land, he blow the trumpet, and warn the people; then, whosoever *heareth* the trumpet, and *taketh not* warning, if the sword come and take him away, his blood shall be upon *his own* head. He heard the sound of the trumpet, and took not warning: his blood shall be upon him. But he that *taketh warning* shall deliver his soul. But if the WATCHMAN see the sword come, and *blow not* the trumpet, and the people *be not* warned; if the sword come, and take any person from among them, he is taken away *in his iniquity;* but *his blood* will I require at the WATCHMAN's hand."

"So thou, O Son of Man, I have set thee a watchman unto the house of Israel: therefore thou shalt hear the word *at my mouth*, and warn them *from me*. When I say unto the wicked, O wicked man, thou shalt surely die; if thou *dost not* speak to warn the wicked from his way, that wicked man shall die in his iniquity; but his blood will I require *at thine hand*. Nevertheless, *if* thou warn the wicked from his way, to turn from it; if he do not turn from his way, he *shall die* in his iniquity; but thou hast *delivered* thy soul."

Now, reverend sirs, here is a plain parallel drawn, first, between the exposure of the children of Israel to the danger of the *literal* "sword," in the destruction of their bodies; and the *spiritual*, in destroying their souls. Second. Between the duties and

[1] 1 Cor. ix. 27.

responsibilities of the *two classes* of "watchmen," when they see the swords coming upon them. And third. The *equity* of the divine procedure, as hypothecated of the faithfulness or unfaithfulness of the "watchmen," in their *giving* or *withholding* the needful warning. And what a fearful alternative! If warned, and the "people take the warning, they *live:* and "the souls of the watchmen are delivered. If not warned, the people *shall die* in their iniquity, but their blood will be required *at the watchman's hand!*"

Now, reverend sirs, you will doubtless agree with us, that there is an exact analogy between the above parallel of the children of Israel and *their* watchmen, and the relations, duties, and responsibilities of the *Christian* ministry to the people of this day. In regard to the coming of the *literal* sword, did not Jesus warn the Jews, "And when ye shall see Jerusalem compassed with armies, then know that the desolation thereof is nigh. Then let them which are in Judea flee to the mountains,"[1] etc. But, on the principle that to be forewarned is to be forearmed, we are not only to do this in times of *national* calamities, but especially in seasons of *spiritual* decay, abounding iniquity, waxing coldness, and the exposure of the professing people of God to the errors, heresies, schisms, and superstitious delusions thence arising, are we called upon to be "armed with the *whole armor of God,*"[2] and to "warn every man, and teach every man in all wisdom,"[3] by "earnestly contending for that faith once delivered to the saints,"[4] and especially that article of faith which respects the *second personal* coming of the Lord Jesus, "that we may present every man perfect in Him."[5]

But, reverend sirs, on the subject of this fundamental article of the Christian faith—"the great theological question of the present day"—we are unhappily at issue. We repeat, *you* maintain that that event is *post*-millennial; *we*, on the other hand, maintain that it is *pre*-millennial. The difference between us, therefore—inasmuch as we must both admit, as I have said, that the best and dearest interests of all men for time and for eternity are involved in the question of *the time* of the second coming of Christ, whether it be *pre* or *post*-millennial:—the difference between us involves HERESY on this subject, either on *your* part, or on *mine*. There is, reverend sirs, no evading this alternative.

[1] Luke xx. 20, 21. [2] Eph. vi. 11. [3] Col. i. 28. [4] Jude v. 3. [5] Col. i. 28.

Finally, reverend sirs, we can only repeat, that, in tendering to you this appeal, we do it with no feelings of personal disrespect to any of you. So far from it, from your acknowledged eminence in scholarship, in the prominence of your respective positions in the Church of Christ as learned divines, and in view of that unbounded influence which you have long wielded and still continue to wield over the minds of all brought within your reach, personally and throughout the whole Church, we yield to you, as we are in duty bound, all due honor. But our deep conviction is, *that the time has fully come* when there can be no further evading of this " great theological question of the present day," as to whether the second personal coming of the Lord is to be *pre* or *post*-millennial. It must be met, and discussed *on its own merits*. We have fairly opened the way for you to do so in this " Sequel to Our Bible Chronology, historic and prophetic," etc. We suppose that all of you, or the most of you, have that work in your libraries. Take the two together. Carefully canvass the several theories, which we have scripturally, historically, and philosophically examined on this subject. If we are *wrong*, point it out, and we pledge ourself to *recant*. If we are *right*, though we know how hard it is to confess that one is in error, yet, for the sake of truth, have the magnanimity to confess it. *The whole Church* will applaud you for it: while each and all of you will have the pleasure to reflect that you will have thrown the weight of your combined influence in the scale of truth, in preparing the people of this generation " *to stand before the Son of Man at His appearing and kingdom.*"

       I remain, reverend sirs,
         Yours, in Christ,
           R. C. SHIMEALL,
         Member of the Presbytery of New York.

NEW YORK, *July*, 1864.
  No. 371 West 35th street.

PART I.

INTRODUCTION.

Abstract Testimony of the Holy Scriptures, regarding the Second Personal Coming of Christ.

THE great central truth, around which, like the planets around the sun, all the others revolve, is, "God manifest in the flesh,"[1] in both His Humiliation and Exaltation.[2] It "became Him *first* to suffer, *before* He could enter into His glory."[3] It is the *latter* subject, with which we are more immediately concerned in the following treatise. We shall, in dependence upon the grace of God, seek to know what is "the mind of the Spirit," in relation to the second personal coming of the Lord Jesus Christ, as an *abstract* scriptural truth, by presenting it to view in its twofold aspect, doctrinal and practical.

SECTION I.

DOCTRINAL.

I. On this part of the subject, our quotations must be limited, for want of space, to the most prominent and pertinent proof-texts, only observing, by the way, that the doctrine of Christ's

---

[1] 1 Tim. iii. 16.   [2] 1 Pet. i. 11.   [3] Luke xvii. 25; xxiv. 26.

second coming is not confined to any one part of Scripture. We begin with

The Old Testament.

Sir Isaac Newton, who wrote an elaborate work on the prophecies, has well said, that "there is scarcely a prophecy of the Old Testament which does not in something or other relate to *the second coming of Christ.*" Let us apply this remark to the first promise of grace to man—" And I will put enmity between thee (the serpent-tempter) and the woman, and between thy seed and her seed: it (the woman's seed, Christ) shall bruise thy head, and thou shalt bruise his heel." [1] Now, on this passage I observe, that Christ's incarnation of the Virgin Mary by the power of the Holy Ghost, teaches us that He is the woman's promised " seed ; " while His *crucifixion* on the cross was explanatory of the bruising of His heel by satanic power and malice. At the same time the wondrous prodigies attendant upon the tragical scene of Calvary,

"When God the mighty Maker died
For man the creature's sin,"

furnished evidence that He *triumphed* over the serpent-tempter, by "leading captivity captive, and purchasing gifts for men." [2] This, however, was but the first blow inflicted upon the "head" of the "strong man armed," by the hand of "the stronger than he." His final bruising is reserved for the *future.* Satan, as "the god of this world," "the prince of the power of the air," still "works in the children of disobedience, leading men," not only individually but also nationally, "captive at his will." The ultimate triumph awaits the incarceration, and the final casting of the serpent in the lake of fire,[3] both of which acts are *future,* and are to be consummated at the period of the second coming of Christ.

The next prophecy of this event is that of Enoch, as recorded by the apostle Jude. "And Enoch, the seventh from Adam, prophesied of these, saying, Behold, the Lord cometh with ten thousand of his saints, to execute judgment upon all," etc. Christ's *first* coming was on an errand of *mercy.* It announced the proffer of "peace on earth, and of good will to man." But, at His *second* coming, though, "to them who look for him, he will appear the second time without sin unto salvation ; " [4] yet, man's probationary

[1] Gen. iii. 14, 15.   [2] Ps. lxviii. 18 ; Eph. iv. 8.   [3] Rev. xx. 10.   [4] Heb. ix. 28.

economy under the gospel dispensation having then closed, He will pour out the libations of His wrath upon the impenitent and incorrigible contemners of His word.¹ The fact that His first coming was not attended with "ten thousand of his saints," is proof decisive that Enoch's prophecy refers to His *second* coming.

The same holds true of the "*Prophet*" predicted by Moses, to whom the people should "hearken."² Also of the "*Shiloh*" of Jacob, unto whom "the gathering of the people should be."³ The same of the "*Star*" of Balaam, who was to "rise out of Jacob and have dominion."⁴ Now, though these several prophecies related primarily to the *first coming* of Christ, yet neither of them was fully verified by that event. For, of the *first*, our blessed Lord, as the great prophetic "Teacher sent from God,"⁵ complained of the people, "Ye will not come unto me, that ye might have life."⁶ But, a predicted period never yet realized will come, when "neighbor will no more say to neighbor, know ye the Lord; but when *all* shall know him from the least to the greatest."⁷ So of the *second*. After all the gatherings to Christ that have taken place out of all the nations of the earth for more than eighteen hundred years, it has been, and still is, true of the church that she remains emphatically a "*little flock*."⁸ But it is predicted of her that "in the last days, the mountain of the Lord's house shall be established in the top of the mountains, and shall be exalted above the hills," and that then "*all nations* shall flow unto it."⁹ No one will pretend that this universal ingathering unto Christ has ever yet been fulfilled. And so of the *third*. The "Star" CHRIST, that arose out of Jacob at the first coming, so far from then having the "*dominion*" predicted of him, was "cast out and killed," as the rightful "heir," and his inheritance seized by his murderers.¹⁰ But it is predicted of him that he *shall* reign, and his dominion shall extend from sea to sea, and from the rivers to the ends of the earth. These latter predictions, therefore, not having been *fully* verified by the events of the *first*, must depend upon and await the SECOND, coming of Christ.

I pass on to the remarkable prophecy of Job, respecting this event, in the following words:—"I know that my Redeemer liveth, and that he shall stand at the latter day upon the earth: and

---

¹ Rev. xvi. etc.   ² Deut. xviii. 15; Acts iii. 22.   ³ Gen. xlix. 10.
⁴ Numb. xxiv. 17-19.   ⁵ John iii. 2.   ⁶ John v. 40.   ⁷ Jer. xxxi. 34.   ⁸ Luke xii. 32.
⁹ Isa. ii. 2; Micah iv. 1.   ¹⁰ Matt. xxi. 28.

though, after my skin worms destroy this body, yet in my flesh shall I see God; whom I shall see for myself, and mine eyes shall behold, and not another; though my reins be consumed within me."[1] There are not a few in the school of modern biblical critics, who affirm that this passage of Job is to be understood simply of that *change in his experience,* from a state of adversity and bodily suffering,[2] to that of his restoration to redoubled prosperity and blessing,[3] *in this life;* an hypothesis founded upon the words, "as the cloud is consumed and vanisheth away; so he that goeth down to the grave shall come up no more." Also, "If a man die, shall he live again?" And again, "When a few years are come, then shall I go the way whence I shall not return."[4] It is hence alleged by these writers, that Job was totally ignorant both of the doctrine of man's *immortality* and of a future *resurrection;* and therefore that this passage can have no reference to the *future* second coming of Christ, etc. The fallacy of this hypothesis, however, is sufficiently obvious from Job's words when speaking of the *dead,* "He shall return no more *to his house,* neither shall *his place* know him any more."[5] That is, all his relations *with this life* are ended forever, equivalent to the passage, "if the tree fall towards the south, or towards the north, in the place where the tree falleth, there it shall be."[6]

Again. That Job was at least no less acquainted with the doctrine of man's immortality and of the resurrection of the dead at the last day, as connected with, and dependent upon, the *second coming* of Christ, than those of Enoch, and Moses, and Jacob, etc., is clear from the sense in which this passage is understood by the Jewish rabbies. Mr. C. W. H. Pauli, in his "Analecta Hebraiaca," having rendered the clause in the 25th verse, "And he that is the Last (the Christ) shall stand upon the dust," i. e., the earth; in opposition to the above perversion of its true meaning, says: "I rendered אחרון, *He that is the Last,* not only because I am fully convinced from the whole context that Job meant to say to his friends, 'I do not look for any deliverance at *your* hands, but my hopes are fixed upon HIM, who is the resurrection and the life;' but also the ancient rabbies have taken this word אחרון in the sense of God." He then gives "the words of Nachman, whose

---

[1] Job xix. 25-27. [2] Job i. *passim.* [3] Job xix. 10-15. [4] See Job vii. 9; xiv. 14; xvi. 22
[5] Job vii. 10. " Eccles. xi. .

valuable commentary is found in the Bibl. Magn. Hebraiaca, viz.: [We omit the Hebrew.]—

"He (Job) saith, he wishes that his companions would show him compassion and not persecute him, desiring that his words might be written down (verses 23, 24); perhaps others who would hear his arguments would show him pity, although he knew that he could not be redeemed by them; but by *that Redeemer* who was able to redeem him; He, who is the Living-One from eternity, even He, who is remaining after all created beings, because He endures forever, and that is, the blessed God." He also quotes R. Peritzol, and Ralbag, as speaking to the same effect.[1]

We now pass to the Psalms of David, in which this great event is frequently set forth in the most emphatic and glowing terms. The following, as an example, must suffice: "Our God shall come, and shall not keep silence: a fire shall devour before him, and it shall be very tempestuous round about him. He shall call to the heavens from above, and to the earth, that he may judge his people."[2]

The next inspired witnesses to this same truth, are the old prophets, whose predictions regarding it are so numerous, and announced on such a variety of occasions, that I must content myself to group together a small portion of them only, with little or no comment. I commence with the following from

Isaiah. "And there shall come forth a *Rod* out of the stem of Jesse, and a *Branch* shall grow out of his roots.... which shall stand as an ensign of the people: to it shall the Gentiles seek; and *His* rest shall be glorious."[3] It will require but a cursory glance at the context, to perceive that this prophecy relates exclusively to the *second coming* of Christ, to "smite the earth with the rod of his mouth, and with the breath of his lips to slay the wicked;"[4] "and to fill the earth with the knowledge of the Lord, as the waters cover the sea."[5]

Jeremiah repeats the same prophecy thus:—"Behold, the days come, saith the Lord, that I will raise unto David *a righteous Branch*, and *a king* shall reign and prosper, and shall execute judgment and justice in the earth. In his days Judah shall be saved, and Israel shall dwell safely: and this is his name whereby

---

[1] Paulis, *Analecta Hebraiaca*. Oxford, 1839, p. 199.   [2] Ps. l. 3, 4. See, also, Ps. lxxii. and xcvi. to cii. inclusive.   [3] Isa. xi. 1–10.   [4] Ib. verse 4. See also 2 Thess. ii. 8.
[5] Ib. verse 9. Compare also verses 2–9 with chap. liii. 1–12; li.–xxiv. to xxviii. and xl. to the end.

he shall be called, THE LORD OUR RIGHTEOUSNESS."[1] At the *first* appearing, our blessed Lord, so far from realizing the things here predicted of Him, was *rejected* as a king, and was crucified by the Jews, which resulted in the overthrow of their civil and ecclesiastical polity, the destruction of their city and temple, and their dispersion among all nations, where, with the Ten Tribes who are still in exile, they remain captives to this day. This prophecy, therefore, must be *prospective* of Christ's return from heaven.

Ezekiel refers to the same event in that beautiful passage, "Behold, the glory of the God of Israel came from the way of the east; and his voice was like the voice of many waters: and the earth shined with his glory."[2] Totally unlike this, His *first* coming: such was then the humiliation of the Incarnate Word, that, "as a tender plant, and a root out of a dry ground," when seen, he was adjudged to have neither "comeliness nor beauty," to attract the eye. "He was oppressed and afflicted, yet he opened not his mouth. He was brought as a lamb to the slaughter."[3] The sun refused to look upon the deed! "From the sixth hour there was darkness over all the earth unto the ninth hour."[4] The next testimony is given in the words of

Daniel, which, for sublimity of conception and boldness of imagery, well befits the theme. "I saw in the night visions, and behold, *one like the Son of Man came with the clouds of heaven*, and came to the ancient of days, and they brought him near before him. And there was given him dominion, and glory, and a kingdom, that all people, nations, and languages should serve him,"[5] etc.

Joel prolongs the same theme, as follows: "The sun and the moon shall be darkened, and the stars shall withdraw their shining. *The Lord* also shall roar out of Zion, and utter his voice from Jerusalem, and the heavens and the earth shall shake; but *the Lord* will be the hope of his people, and the strength of the children of Israel."[6] Corresponding with this prophecy of the Lord's *second* coming is the following from

Haggai, thus:—"Yet once, saith the Lord of hosts, it is a little while, and I will shake the heavens and the earth, and the dry land. And I will shake all nations, and *the Desire of all nations* (the Christ) shall come."[7] And to this the prophet

---

[1] Jer. xxiii. 5, 6. [2] Ezek. xliii. 2; ch. xxxvi. Compare also Dan. x. 5 and Rev. i. 7. [3] Isa. liii. [4] Matt. xxvii. 45. [5] Dan. vii. 13, 14. See also verses 9–12; compared with Isa. ix. 6, 7 and Ezek. i. 26–28. [6] Joel iii. 15, 16. Compare ii. 10, 31; Isa. xiii. 10 Matt xxiv. 29; Luke xxi. 25, 26; Rev. vi. 12, 13. [7] Hag. ii. 6, 7.

Zechariah thus responds:—"And *the Lord my God* shall come, and all his saints with him.".... "And his feet shall stand in that day *upon the mount of Olives* which is before Jerusalem,"[1] etc. Finally, to the above,

Malachi adds the last link to this golden chain of prophetic testimony in the Old Testament to this great truth. He says: "For, behold, the day cometh that shall burn as an oven; and all the proud, yea, and all the wicked shall be as stubble, etc..... But unto you that fear my name shall *the sun of righteousness* arise with healing in his wings," etc. "For the Lord whom ye seek, shall suddenly come to His temple, even the messenger of the covenant whom ye delight in: Behold *He shall come*, saith the Lord of hosts."[2] Now, in whatever sense this prophecy may be applied to the circumstances of the *first* coming of Christ, it cannot be maintained that it was verified in *all its parts*. Christ came not then to "*destroy* men's lives,"[3] but "to seek and to save them that were lost."[4] Neither did men then "*delight*" in him. For, being "not sent but unto the lost sheep of the house of Israel,"[5] we read that "He came unto his own, but His own received Him not."[6] Nor did his own followers then "go forth, and grow up, and become as calves of the stall."[7] For they were all "scattered, as sheep having no shepherd."[8] It must, therefore, have an *ulterior* reference to that day of which the prophet speaks when he says, "But who may abide *the day* of His coming? and who shall stand when He *appeareth?* For he is like a refiner's fire, and like fuller's soap:"[9] even that day when, with the winnowing "fan in his hand, He will thoroughly purge his floor, and gather the wheat into his garner."[10] Pass we now to

The New Testament.

Here, the light of prophecy on this momentous subject is reflected with a greatly augmented brightness. We open this testimony with the angelic announcement respecting the Son of God, as the Son of Mary, in these memorable words: "He shall be great, and shall be called the Son of the Highest: and the Lord God shall give unto Him *the throne* of His father

---

[1] Zech. xiv. 5, and verse 4. See also chap. xii to xiv. inclusive. [2] Mal. iv. 1, 2
[3] Luke ix. 56. [4] Ib. xix. 10. [5] Matt. xv. 24. [6] John i. 12. [7] Mal. iv. 2
[8] Matt. ix. 36. [9] Mal. iii. 1, 2 [10] Matt. iii. 12.

David: and He shall reign over the house of Israel forever; and of His kingdom there shall be no end!"[1] It is here to be observed, that, inasmuch as there was nothing connected with our Lord's humiliation in the flesh, which could possibly meet the terms of this prophecy respecting him, we are compelled to apply it to that of his predicted "*glory*" which was to *follow* " his "sufferings,"[2] when He should be "revealed from heaven in flaming fire with His mighty angels, to take vengeance on them that know not God, and that obey not the gospel;"[3] and when, "wearing His many crowns,"[4] and *seated* on His father David's throne, "the kingdom, and dominion, and greatness of the kingdom under the whole heaven should be given to him" and to his "saints."[5]

We quote a second angelic prediction of this event. "And while they (i. e., the disciples of Galilee) looked steadfastly toward heaven as He went up, behold, two men stood by them in white apparel; who also said, Ye men of Galilee, why stand ye gazing up into heaven? This same Jesus which is taken up from you into heaven, *shall so come in like manner* as ye see Him go into heaven."[6] But, let us see what Christ Himself said, concerning this doctrine. A little prior to His crucifixion, with a view to console His desponding disciples in the prospect of His separation from them, He said: "Let not your hearts be troubled: ye believe in God, believe also in me. In my Father's house are many mansions:" ... "and I go to prepare a place for you, and if I go and prepare a place for you, I WILL COME AGAIN, and receive you unto myself: that where I am, there ye may be also."[7]

On another occasion Jesus said to the Jews, seeing that they still persevered in rejecting Him as their Messiah, "Behold, your house is left unto you desolate"—a prediction this, of the overthrow of their polity and the destruction of their city and temple by the Roman legions—to which He adds, "For I say unto you, ye shall not see me henceforth, till ye shall say, *Blessed is He that cometh in the name of the Lord.*" Here our blessed Lord refers, though indefinitely, to *the time* of His "return" from heaven, whither He was going to prepare those "many mansions" for His faithful followers, spoken of in the last preceding passage.

Again. By way of correcting an *error* into which His disciples had fallen, as though the Messianic kingdom was *then* to be

---

[1] Luke i. 31-33.   [2] 1 Pet. i. 11.   [3] 2 Thess. i. 8, 9.   [4] Rev. xix. 12.
[5] Dan. vii. Compare verses 13, 14 with 21, 22 and verse 27.   [6] Acts i. 10, 11.   [7] John xiv 1-3

restored to them; Jesus predicts that *a long interval* would ensue, between His ascension and His coming again. "He said unto His disciples, The days will come, when ye shall desire to see one of the days of the Son of Man, and ye *shall not* see it." That is, they should not see it according to *their* expectation of it: not that they should *never* witness it. For, He proceeds to notify them of a "*sign*," which should indicate *when* it was about to take place. He says: "As the lightning that lighteneth out of one part under heaven, shineth unto another part under heaven, so shall also the Son of Man be in His day."[1] It was on this ground also that, *after* His resurrection, being asked by His disciples, "Lord, wilt thou *at this time* restore the kingdom to Israel?" He said, "it is not for *you*," that is, those of *this* generation, "to know the times or the seasons, which the Father hath put in his own power."[2] Not that these "times and seasons" should *never* be revealed. The veil of obscurity then thrown over them, should be withdrawn at the proper time—"*the time of the end.*"[3] That "time" having come, the celestial "sign"—the "*lightning*" in the heavens—should indicate to all the tribes of the earth, the *approaching* fulfilment of what He had said,—"They shall see the Son of Man coming in the clouds of heaven, with power and great glory."[4]

But, in addition to the above prophecies of Christ respecting His second coming, and especially as we find that event elaborated in the xxivth of Matthew, the xiiith of Mark, and the xxist of Luke, the same great truth is set forth in those parables, which form a *continuation* of that sublime discourse; for example, the parable of the Chief Servant, Matt. xxiv. 45–51. In the case of his unwatchfulness and improper behavior, if found saying "in his heart, my lord *delayeth* his coming," etc., we are told that "the lord of that servant shall come in *a day* when he looketh not for him, and in *an hour* that he is not aware of; and shall cut him asunder, and appoint his portion with the hypocrites: there shall be weeping and gnashing of teeth." (Verses 50, 51.)

So also the illustrative parable of the ten virgins, Matt. xxv. 1–13. In it is taught the necessity of being in readiness for *the coming* of the Lord to receive His people into his presence and glory. Hence the enforcement of the admonition, "Watch, therefore, for ye know neither the day nor the hour wherein the Son of

---

[1] Luke xviii. 22-24. [2] Acts i. 6, 7. [3] Dan. xii. 4. [4] Matt. xxiv. 30.

Man cometh." Moreover, in this parable, the midnight cry is heard, "Behold, the Bridegroom cometh!" It is in this character that our Lord is represented as coming at the last day, in the Apocalypse, chap. xix. 7–9. The termination of the day of proffered grace, and the final separation, at the judgment of *the living* nations, between the just and the unjust, are graphically delineated in the sequel of the parable.

To these may be added the parable of the talents delivered to the servants, Matt. xxv. 14–30. In it we have an illustration of the Lord's *personal withdrawal* from his servants, after giving them their charge (v. 15); then, "after a long time," of His *return to reckon* with them: i. e., to bring them to judgment; when, to the faithful, there is the *reward*, by exalting them to dominion (v. 23), and their admission to the joy of their Lord: to the unfaithful, *punishment*, denoted by the casting of the unprofitable servant into outer darkness (v. 30). The parable of the nobleman who distributes among his servants ten pounds, and takes his "journey into a far country *to receive a kingdom and to return*,"[1] is of similar import, only that it brings more fully into view than in the other, the *design* of Christ's personal absence from the Church during the interval from His ascension to His second coming, namely, to await His *full investiture* of His kingly prerogatives, as the pre-ordained PRINCE OF THE KINGS OF THE EARTH."[2]

We shall now conclude this golden chain of testimony to the doctrine of Christ's second coming by passing on to the *epistolary* writings, that we may ascertain what the inspired Apostles taught on this subject. It is of the first importance here to observe, that what our blessed Lord, as above, had predicted of this event, "formed the great *text-book* from which the Apostles and primitive Christians mainly derived, not only their doctrines, but their illustrations, of the second coming of Christ, and the destinies of men that shall result!" And thus was fulfilled our Lord's avowed intention of *keeping his words* before the Church in all ages: "And what I say unto *you*, I say unto *all*, WATCH!"

The Apostles Paul and Peter, and James and Jude, and John, as the amanuenses of the Holy Spirit in perpetuating the doctrine of the Lord's second coming, speak of it *in every variety of form* that is calculated to arrest the attention, and to keep

---

[1] Luke xix. 11–27. [2] Rev. i. 5.

alive in the Church a spirit of prayer, and watchfulness, and patient waiting for that event. And, mark: they all treated of it as the foundation of the hope of "eternal life," *from the beginning.* In expectation of their admission to an "inheritance incorruptible, and undefiled, and that fadeth not away" at the Lord's second appearing, believers are spoken of as "*waiting* for the Son of God from heaven," [1] and as "*loving* that appearing." [2] Yea, with the eye of faith fixed on Christ the Coming One, not only in His suffering, but in His glorified humanity, they were strengthened to endure "trial of cruel mockings and scourgings, yea, moreover, of bonds and imprisonments; and also to be stoned, and sawn asunder, and tempted: to be slain with the sword, to wander about in sheep skins and goat skins, being destitute, afflicted, tormented: also to wander about in deserts, and in mountains, and in dens and caves of the earth." [3] "Walking by faith and not by sight as seeing Him who is invisible," [4] they had their "conversation [πολίτευμα, *citizenship*] in heaven, whence also they *looked* for the Saviour, the Lord Jesus Christ, who," when He comes, "shall change our vile body, and fashion it like unto His own glorious body, according to the working whereby He is able to subdue all things to Himself." [5]

Hence St. Paul, having said, 1 Thess. iv. 16, "For *the Lord* HIMSELF shall descend from heaven with a shout, with the voice of archangel, and with the trump of God," continues his discourse on the subject of Christ's judgment-coming as to its results, first, in the *punishment* of the wicked, thus: "And to you who are troubled, rest with us, when the Lord Jesus shall be revealed from heaven with his mighty angels, in flaming fire, taking vengeance on them that know not God, and that obey not the Gospel of our Lord Jesus Christ: who shall be punished with everlasting destruction from the presence of the Lord, and from the glory of His power" (2 Thess. i. 7-9): and second, in the *reward* of his suffering and faithful followers, by the resurrection of those who sleep in Him, and the rapture of the living saints. His words are: "And the dead in Christ *shall rise first:*" to which he adds, "*Then we which are alive and remain,* shall be caught up together with them in the clouds, to meet the Lord in the air; and so shall we ever be with the Lord." (1 Thess. iv.

---

[1] 1 Cor. i. 7; 2 Thess. iii. 5.   [2] 2 Tim. iv. 8.   [3] Heb. xi. 36-38.
[4] Heb. xi. 27.   [5] Philipp. iii. 20.

16, 17.) And finally, third, in regard to this doctrine of the Lord's second coming, he tells his Thessalonian brethren, 1 Thess. v. 1–5, "But, of the times and seasons, brethren, ye have no need that I write unto you. *For yourselves know perfectly*, that the day of the Lord so cometh as a thief in the night. For when they"—i. e., the scoffers of the last days, who, as Peter predicted of them, shall exclaim, " Where is the promise of His coming?"[1] etc.—" when they shall say, Peace and safety: then sudden destruction shall come upon them, as travail upon a woman with child, and they shall not escape." And he again adds: " But *ye*, brethren, *are not* in darkness, that that day should overtake you as a thief. Ye are the children of *light*, and of *the day:* we *are not* of the night, nor of darkness."

We ask, therefore, Whence was it that these Thessalonian brethren " *knew perfectly*, that the day of the Lord's " coming to raise the dead and change the living saints, " would so come as a thief in the night?" There is no intimation whatever, that they learned it from Paul, or from any of the other apostles. All the epistolary writings, from 1st Corinthians to the Apocalypse inclusive, were written *subsequently* to our Lord's repeated and varied declarations and illustrations of this sublime subject. They, therefore, only take up and prolong the theme so largely discoursed of by the old prophets, and also by HIM who " spake as never man spake."

On the general subject of the testimony of the New Testament to this doctrine, it may not be out of place here to observe that, paradoxical as it may appear, it is no less a cause of lamentation than of surprise, that the circumstance of the *frequency* of its occurrence seems but to *weaken* the impression that it was designed to produce. Such a result, surely, can only be accounted for, on the ground of the ascendency of the *sensual* or worldly, over the *spiritual* life, of the Church. Long exemption from being called to *suffer* for Christ's sake, has almost totally crushed out that spirit of aspiration after things heavenly,—in other words, of a readiness to be " crucified to the world with its affections and lusts,"—which characterized the Church of primitive and of later times. Hence the loss, to *the Church of this day*, for the most part, of a Scriptural view and appreciation of this doctrine, *as the foundation of her faith and hope*. In the endeavor, there-

[1] 2 Pet. iii. 4.

fore, to recover the Church to an acceptance of this fundamental article of "the faith once delivered to the saints," we propose to reproduce, in a condensed form, a few of the many expressions under which this doctrine is represented in the Gospels and Epistles. To this end, we shall group them together under the following heads. It is, perhaps, most usually styled,

I. "*The presence of Christ*,"— Ἡ παρουσία τοῦ Χριστοῦ. 2 Pet. i. 16: "For we have not followed cunningly devised fables when we made known unto you the power *and coming* of our Lord Jesus Christ, but were eye-witnesses of his majesty." This passage relates to Christ's transfiguration on the mount, as recorded in Matt. xvii. 2-5; Mark ix. 1-7. But, though it transpired during the period of the *first* coming of Christ, it was but the type and earnest of the glory of the *second*. Again. To the question of the disciples, "What shall be *the sign* of thy coming?" Matt. xxiv. 3, Christ replied, "As the days of Noah were, so shall also *the coming* of the Son of Man be" (verses 37, 39). The Apostle James said, "Be ye also patient, brethren, stablish your hearts: for *the coming* of the Lord draweth nigh" (chap. v. 7-9). So St. Paul: "Now we beseech you, brethren, by *the coming* of our Lord Jesus Christ, and by our gathering together unto Him, that ye be not soon shaken in mind," etc. For, "that wicked . . . the man of sin and son of perdition . . . shall be revealed, whom the Lord shall consume with the spirit of His mouth, and shall destroy" (i. e., after the example of His transfiguration) "with the brightness of *His coming*." (2 Thess. ii. 1-8.) See also 1st Thess. i. and ii. passim. St. Peter also speaks of "looking for and hasting unto *the coming* of the day of God, wherein the heavens being on fire, shall be dissolved," etc. (2 Peter iii. 12.) And again St. Paul: "But every man in his own order; Christ the first fruits: afterward they that are Christ's *at His coming*." (1 Cor. xv. 23.)

II. His "*appearance*," or "*Epiphany*,"—Ἡ ἐπιφανεῖα. 1 Tim. vi. 14: "That thou keep this commandment without spot, unrebukable, until the *appearing* of our Lord Jesus Christ." 2 Tim. iv. 8: "Henceforth there is laid up for me a crown of righteousness, which the Lord, the righteous Judge, shall give me at that day; and not to me only, but unto all them also that love His *appearing*."

III. "*Christ's coming*,"—Χριστὸς ἐρχόμενος. Matt. xvi. 28: "Verily, I say unto you, There be some standing here, which shall not taste of death, till they shall see the Son of Man *coming* in His kingdom." This "kingdom," however, in its *full* manifestation, was not in their day restored to them. But they were to be the eye-witnesses of it in its *type* and *earnest*, which occurred about six days after on the mount of transfiguration. (Matt. xvii. 1, 2; Luke xvi. 26.) "For whosoever shall be ashamed of me and of my words, of him shall the Son of Man be ashamed, when He *shall come* in His own glory," etc. Luke xxi. 27: "And then shall they see the Son of Man *coming* in the clouds of heaven with power and great glory." Acts i. 2: "This same Jesus, which is taken up from you into heaven, *shall so come* in like manner, as ye have seen Him go into heaven." Zech. xiv. 5: "And the Lord my God *shall come*, and all the saints with thee." Mal. iii. 1: "And the Lord, whom ye seek, *shall suddenly come* to His temple," etc. St. Paul, 1 Cor. xi. 26, connects this doctrine with the solemn commemoration of the sufferings and death of Christ in the Lord's Supper: "For as oft as ye eat this bread, and drink this cup, ye do show the Lord's death *till He come.*"

IV. "*The day of Christ,*"—Ἡ ἡμέρα τοῦ Χριστοῦ. 1 Cor. i. 8: "Who shall also confirm you unto the end, that ye may be blameless *in the day* of our Lord Jesus Christ." 2 Cor. i. 14: "As also ye have acknowledged us in part, that we are your rejoicing, even as ye also are ours *in the day* of the Lord Jesus." 2 Pet. iii. 10: "But *the day* of the Lord will so come as a thief in the night," etc. Philipp. ii. 16: "Holding forth the word of life; that I may rejoice in *the day* of Christ, that I have not run in vain, neither labored in vain." Joel ii. 31: "The sun shall be turned into darkness, and the moon into blood, *before the great and terrible day* of the Lord come."

V. "*The end,*"—Τὸ τέλος. "And this gospel of the kingdom shall be preached in all the world for a witness unto all nations, and then shall *the end* come."

VI. "The close of the age," or "Dispensation,"—Ἡ συντελεία τοῦ αἰῶνος. "Lo, I am with you alway, even unto *the end* of the world." (Matt. xxviii. 20.) "The harvest is *the end* of the world: and the reapers are the angels. As therefore the tares are gathered and burned in the fire; so shall it be in *the end* of this world,"¹ etc. (Matt. xiii. 39, 40, 49.)

---

[1] In the passages the Greek is, not κοσμος, *habitable earth*, but αιωνος, *age* or *dispensation*.

VII. Ἡ φανέρωσις τοῦ Χριστοῦ. "When Christ, who is our life, *shall appear*, then shall ye also appear with him in glory." (Col. iii. 4.) "And when the Chief Shepherd *shall appear*, ye shall receive a crown of glory that fadeth not away." (1 Pet. v. 4.) "Beloved, now are we the sons of God, and it doth not yet appear what we shall be: but we know that, when He *shall appear*, we shall be like Him, for we shall see Him as He is." (1 John iii. 2.)

VIII. Ἡ ἀποκάλυψις τοῦ Χριστοῦ. 1 Pet. i. 5 : "Who are kept by the power of God through faith unto salvation, ready to be *revealed* in the last time." (See also verse 7.) 1 Pet. iv. 13: "But rejoice, inasmuch as ye are partakers of Christ's sufferings; that, when His glory shall be *revealed*, ye may be glad also with exceeding joy."

We conclude this presentation of the evidence in support of the *doctrine* of the Lord's second coming, with the remark, that an event, thus so extensively and variously exhibited to our view in the scriptures of the Old and New Testaments, could not but have been designed as a subject of frequent, prayerful, and solemn meditation by the church and people of God *in all ages.* And especially does this hold true of those who, in the dispensations of God's providence and grace, shall be found upon the earth at *"the time of the end,"* when the great "mystery of God," as involved therein, *is about to be "finished."*

How then, I ask, can any who *wilfully* close their minds to this truth, avoid incurring the guilt, and its attendant penalty, of those who *"take away* from the words of the prophecy of this book," either by overlooking, or perverting, or denying it? Surely, God, in retributive justice, "will take away *his part* out of the book of life, and out of the holy city, and from the things which are written in this book:" wherein, besides that in every chapter of St. Paul's two epistles to the Thessalonians, the theme of the Lord's second coming is at least *once* introduced, the attentive reader of the Revelation will find that, from its beginning to the end, it is constantly presented to view as *the one great hope and consolation of the church,* in all her appointed pilgrimage;—like an heavenly beacon, it cheers her on through the impending storm; like a glimpse to the laboring mariner of the peaceful haven in the distance, she is constantly encouraged through faith "to lift up the hands that hang down, and the feeble knees." (Heb. xii. 13.)

Thus, then, we see, that while *a Saviour to come in His glory* was held up to the faith and hope of the Old Testament saints, *before* He personally "appeared to put away sin by the sacrifice of Himself" on the cross; the same faith in and hope of His *return* from heaven in the clouds with power and great glory, both *before* and *after* His ascension, were set before the church by Christ and His inspired apostles, with additional lustre and distinctness of utterance. And, with this evidence before us in support of the *abstract* doctrine of the second coming of Christ, we pass to consider it in its practical aspect.

SECTION II

PRACTICAL.

This is connected with *the incentives* to faith, repentance, and a holy life. As we have already said, a belief in this doctrine of Christ's second coming, during the antediluvian, Mosaic, and early Christian age of the Church, operated in keeping in constant exercise a "*looking for* that blessed hope, the glorious appearing of the great God, even our Saviour, Jesus Christ."[1] In other words, the eye of faith centred in that event, as the *polar star* of the church's undying "hope" of her final triumph over sin, the world, and Satan; and hence operated as *the all-inspiring motive,* to keep herself "unspotted" from the moral contaminations of earth, that she might be presented as "a chaste virgin to Christ"[2] *at "His appearing."*[3]

But, I ask,—and I put the question with deep solemnity—Has this faith and hope in Christ's second coming *been retained* by the professing church, in the sense in which it was received, from Abel down to the time of John in the Isle of Patmos? Or, if we except an adherence to this doctrine by the early *post-*apostolic church down to the opening of the IVth century, has it been permitted since to hold a corresponding *practical influence* over the lives and conduct of those who have professed and called themselves Christians?

We judge no man. Nevertheless, on this subject, we appeal: —if we except a few "burning and shining lights," who, "like angel visitants, few and far between," have appeared upon the stage within the last sixteen centuries, the *current* theology of

---

[1] Titus ii. 13.   [2] 2 Cor. xi. 2.   [3] 1 Pet. i. 7.

the Church has unceasingly taught that meditation on death and judgment, and on the glories of heaven and the pains of hell, are *the great motives* to repentance, and the keeping the mind in a proper tone as it regards *the future:* while it is strenuously objected that, to insist on such a doctrine as the one here presented to view, is of *a purely theoretical* character, and tends only to fanaticism and delusion. On this subject, then, I beg indulgence to remark,

1. That, of the first of these motives—*preparation for death,* etc.,—it is not so much an exhibit of the brief and uncertain tenure of life, and the solemnities of the judgment and a future state, as motives to repentance, etc., to which we object; as that they are made *pre-eminent*, as such, over a much more important, and, as we contend, *the only* truly Scriptural motive to that end. Of the numerous passages that might be given in illustration, take, for example, the following: "Therefore, be ye also ready, *for*, in such an hour as ye think not, *the Son of Man cometh.*"[1] Here, evidently, the declared *unexpected return* of the Son from heaven, and *not* death, is presented as *the* motive of preparation to meet, *not* "the king of terrors,"[2] *but "the Son of Man;"* and not, further, to meet "the Son of Man," as though He came *to us* at death. Rather, the striking of that fatal blow is inflicted by the coming of "*the King of terrors,*"[3] whose work it is, by the judicial permission and command of the God of *providence*, to inflict upon us the *penalty* due to our sins; which penalty, as to the circumstances of the time, place, and manner of its infliction, forms *no part* of Christ's mediatorial work. As in the case of the rich worldling in the Gospel, we read that it was, *not* Christ, but "GOD that said unto him, Thou fool, this night shall thy soul be required of thee!" i. e., at the hand of the rider of the "pale horse," whose "name was *Death.*"[4] Nor is there any exemption from this penalty, during the "reign of Death" in and over our world.[5] Saint and sinner alike fall victims to his relentless power.[6] "It is appointed unto men once to die, and *after* that, the judgment."[7] At death, while the body is laid in the grave, the soul "*returns to* God who gave it."[8] So far from Christ's coming even to the saints, at death, their souls, disenthralled from their clay tenement, *go to Him!* Hence their "desire to depart, that

[1] Matt. xxiv. 44. [2] Job xviii. 14. [3] Ib. [4] Rev. vi. 8. [5] Eph. ii. 2.
[6] Eccles. ii. 14, 15; viii. 14; ix. 11. [7] Heb. ix. 27. [8] Eccles. xii. 7.

they may be *with* Him."[1] Besides, death, in any view we may take of it, is *unnatural* to us. Death has robbed us of our pristine state, and is therefore our *greatest enemy*. For this reason it is that we *dread* death. Accordingly, the blessed "Gospel," which "brings life and immortality to light,"[2] instead of preaching up *death* to us as a motive to repentance, etc., points our eye of faith to HIM, who, at His first appearing, "came to *deliver* them who, through *fear of death*, were all their life-time subject to bondage;"[3] and who, when He shall "appear the *second* time," comes as "*the judge* of the quick and the dead," seated on His "white horse," wearing His "many crowns," as He whose name is "Faithful and True,"[4] to "*destroy* him that has the power of Death, that is, the Devil."

Again:

2. As to the other article—that of urging *a meditation of death*, etc., as a motive to Christian constancy. In so far as this motive is made to rest upon the expectation of an immediate entrance, *at that juncture*, into a state of *perfect* blessedness; we can only now say, that we know not of a single passage of Scripture that warrants any such expectation. That the souls of the faithful departed do, *immediately after death*, enjoy a state of blessedness which "passeth all understanding,"[5] and that they do visibly behold the Lord, as He is seated upon the throne of "intercession" "at the right hand of the Majesty in the heavens," we fully believe. But this state, we are not to forget, is that of a *separation* of the soul from the body. Hence, that that conscious blessedness, that rest, whatever it be, is not and cannot be *then* consummated, is evident from the opening of the fifth Apocalyptic "Seal," respecting which St. John says, "I saw, *under the altar*, the souls of them that were slain for the word of God, and for the testimony which they held: and they cried with a loud voice, saying, *How long*, O Lord, Holy and True, dost thou not avenge our blood on them that dwell on the Earth!"[6] and of them it is said, that "white robes"—which is interpreted to be "the righteousness of the saints"[7]—"were given to every one of them; and it was said unto them, that they *should* "*rest yet for a little while*, until their fellow-servants also, and their brethren, that should be killed as they were, *should be fulfilled*."[8]

[1] Philipp. i. 23.   [2] 2 Tim. i. 10.   [3] Heb. ii. 15.   [4] Rev. xix. 11–16.
[5] Philipp. iv. 17.   [6] Rev. vi. 10.   [7] Ib. xix. 8.   [8] Ib. vi. 11.

ITS PRACTICAL ASPECT. 51

We cannot now enter into a full exposition of this momentous subject. It must suffice for the present, to refer the reader to the latter part of the prayer, as found in the burial service of the Church of England, as, in our view, presenting the Scriptural idea of the *existing beatitude* of those who "sleep in Jesus."[1] It is in these words:

"Almighty God . . . we give Thee hearty thanks for that it has pleased Thee to deliver this our brother out of the miseries of this sinful world; beseeching Thee, that it may please Thee *shortly to accomplish* the number of thine elect, and *to hasten* thy kingdom; that we, and all those that are departed in the true faith of Thy holy name, *may have our perfect consummation and bliss*, both in body and soul, in Thy Eternal Kingdom, through Jesus Christ our Lord."

We only add, that it is declared of the "souls" of these martyrs *now* "under the altar," that they are destined to "*sit on thrones*,"[2] and *wear* "*crowns*,"[3] and bear in their hands the "*palms*" of celestial triumph,[4] and that they "*shall reign on earth*."[5] But this cannot be, until their bodies and souls are *reunited*, at "the resurrection of the just."[6] This, however, is *dependent upon* the second coming of Christ. "Christ the first-fruits: afterward, they that are Christ's *at His coming*."[7]

It follows, therefore, that THE SECOND COMING OF CHRIST, and *not* death, is the great, practical, Scriptural *motive* to Christian constancy.

And so of every other motive to *practical godliness*. Indeed, the more we examine the Scriptures on this point, the more clearly shall we see this. Do you ask what is the Scriptural motive,

(1.) To *repentance?* I answer, it is the second coming of Christ. "*Repent* ye, therefore, and be converted . . . and He shall *send Jesus* . . . whom the heavens must receive, until the times of restitution of all things."[8]

(2.) What, to *love Christ?* I answer, the same. "If any man *love not* our Lord Jesus Christ, let him be anathema, maranatha:" which, being interpreted, is, "Let him be accursed. *The Lord cometh*."[9]

(3.) What, to *love one another?* I answer, the same. "And the Lord make you to increase and abound *in love* toward one

---
[1] 1 Thess. iv. 14.   [2] Rev. xx. 4.   [3] Ib. iv. 4.   [4] Ib. vii. 9.   [5] Ib. v. 10.
[6] Luke xiv. 14.   [7] 1 Cor. xv. 23.   [8] Acts iii. 19-21.   [9] 1 Cor. xvi. 22.

another, and toward all men, even as we do toward you: *to the end* He may stablish your hearts unblamable in holiness before God, even the Father, *at the coming* of our Lord Jesus Christ, with all His saints."[1]

(4.) What, *to mortification of earthly lusts?* I answer, the same. "When Christ who is our life *shall appear*, then shall *ye also appear* with Him in glory. *Mortify*, therefore, your members which are upon the earth," etc.[2]

(5.) What, *to general obedience and holiness?* I answer, the same. "We know that, *when He shall appear*, we shall be like Him, for we shall see Him as He is. And every man that hath this hope in him, *purifieth himself*, even as He is pure."[3]

(6.) What, *to spirituality of mind?* I answer, the same. "For our conversation [πολίτευμα, citizenship] is in heaven, *from whence we look for the Saviour*, the Lord Jesus Christ, who shall change our vile bodies," etc.[4]

(7.) What, *to works of mercy?* I answer, the same. "When the Son of Man shall come in His glory, . . . then shall He say to them on His right hand, Come, ye blessed of my Father, *inherit* the kingdom, etc.; for I was hungry, and ye gave me meat, etc.: for, as much as ye have *done it* unto one of these little ones, ye have done it unto me."[5]

(8.) What, *to watchfulness?* I answer, the same. "Let your loins be girded about, and your lights burning . . . Blessed are those servants whom the Lord, *when He cometh*, shall find *watching*."[6]

(9.) What, *to moderation and sobriety?* I answer, the same. "Let your *moderation* be known unto all men. The Lord is at hand."[7]

(10.) What, *to ministerial fidelity and diligence?* I answer, the same. "For what is our *hope*, or *joy*, or *crown of rejoicing?* Are not even ye in the presence of the Lord Jesus Christ at *His coming?*"[8] And finally,

(11.) What, *to patience and long-suffering?* I answer, the same. "Be ye also *patient:* stablish your hearts: for *the coming* of the Lord draweth nigh."[9]

---

[1] 1 Thess. iii. 13. [2] Col. iii. 4, 5,; Tit. ii. 11-13. [3] 1 John iii. 2, 3; ii. 28; Matt. xvi. 27 Rev. xxii. 12. [4] Philipp. iii. 20, 21. [5] Matt. xxv. 31-36. [6] Luke xii. 35-37; 1 Thess. v. 4, 5; Rev. xvi. 15. [7] Philipp. iv. 5; 1 Pet. i. 13. [8] 1 Thess. ii. 19 Matt. xxiv. 46; 1 Tim. vi. 13; 2 Tim. iv. 1, 2; 1 Pet. v. 1-4. [9] James v. 7, 8; 2 Thess. i. 4-7; Heb. x. 36, 37; 1 Pet. i. 6, 7.

Having thus set before the reader the Scriptural evidence of the *doctrine* of the Lord's second coming; and also pointed out its designed tendency in a *practical* aspect, we can only add the prayer, that we may all have grace to "look" forward to and "love his appearing," as our only hope of preparation to "*stand before the Son of Man*," when,

"In pomp and majesty ineffable,"

"He shall descend from heaven with a shout, with the voice of the Archangel, and with the trump of God."

PART II.

An Examination of the Question—Is the Second Coming of Christ, and the Setting up of His Kingdom, past, present, or future?

PRELIMINARY REMARKS.

In the discussion of the subject to which the reader's thoughts are now directed, viz., an examination of the question—Is the Second Coming of Christ, and the Setting up of His Kingdom, past, present, or future?—let us suppose that, *for the first time*, he is brought into contact with the Scriptural doctrine, etc., of that event, as set forth in Part I. of this treatise. With a mind entirely unbiassed by previous contact with speculating theories, the query is, What would be the impressions, convictions, and conclusions of his mind in reference to it? Undeniably, the prophecies of that event as presented by the writers of the Old Testament, and by Christ and His apostles in the New, point to *a period* in the Divine purpose when "the Church of God, which He purchased with His own blood,"[1] should assume the form and dimensions of a "kingdom" of unrivalled splendor and dominion under the reign of Christ, the Messiah, as "king;" by an extermination of all His and her enemies, and the establishment and perpetuity of a state of universal peace, prosperity, and righteousness in the earth.

I now, therefore, submit: Taking into view the prophecies of this event *as a whole*, would not such a reader, receiving them as

[1] Acts xx. 20.

a revelation from God, and interpreting the language in which they are given in its natural or grammatical sense, infer that it was *still future?* Look at the subjects embraced in them. Taken in connection with the coming of the Lord, they announce, *first*, that Jesus, in his *kingly* character, as "the Son of the Highest, has the promise that He shall sit on the throne of His father David, and reign over the house of Jacob forever," etc.;[1] *second*, that those who now "sleep in Christ" shall be raised from the dead, while those who are alive at His coming shall be changed, and caught up to meet Him in the air;[2] and *third*, that Christ is then to commence, jointly with His risen and glorified saints who are to reign with Him on the earth, to "judge the world in righteousness, and to rule the nations upon earth." Now, who will venture to affirm that all these prophecies have *already* been verified?

Strange to tell, there are eminent writers not a few, who, in one form or another, *have taught* that the coming of Christ the second time to establish His kingdom among men, either transpired *centuries ago*, and that it has *already* run its course; or that it *now* exists, and is to continue for an indefinite time. It will be indispensable, therefore, to an intelligent understanding of *the various theories* which have been brought to bear upon this great subject, candidly to examine their respective merits; compare each with the other; and the whole with what the writer deems to have been revealed to both prophets and apostles, by "the Spirit of Christ which was in them."

The most prominent of these theories are the following. The prophecies referring to this event, it is contended by some, were verified,

1. By the Restoration of the Jews from the Babylonish captivity.

2. Another class allege that they received their accomplishment in the overthrow of Paganism and the establishment of Christianity in the Roman empire, under Constantine the Great, in A. D. 323.

3. A third class affirms their fulfilment in the judgments inflicted upon the Jewish nation and polity, at the destruction of Jerusalem by the Roman legions in A. D. 70.

4. And a fourth class, that the kingdom and reign of Christ on

---

[1] See page 39 of this Work.   [2] Ib. 43.

earth are *identical* with the establishment of the Christian Church, the dispensation of which is to continue until the close of the millennial age, when He will raise the dead, judge the world, and deliver up the kingdom to God, etc.

I here remark, that the *theology* of these various theories is so interwoven with much that is written on this subject of the second coming and reign of Christ by modern interpreters of prophecy, that nothing further need be added by way of apology, for the space appropriated to them in these pages. They will be discussed *seriatim*, each under a separate chapter. As preliminary thereto, it will be well to premise:

First. That the phraseology, the kingdom and reign of Christ, and the millennial era of the Church, is used by all writers interchangeably as denoting *the same thing*.

Second. This being so, I remark that it is reasonable to suppose—indeed it is indispensable—that any theory which advocates the second coming of Christ and the establishment of His kingdom on earth, either as already past or as now existing, should partake of *all* the characteristics of both, as specified in prophecy respecting them.

Third. It is here also specially to be borne in mind that all these theories, except the first, interpret the second coming of Christ in the sense of either a *providential*, or of a *figurative* or *spiritual* coming. This is done to avoid a dilemma otherwise fatal to them, to wit, that in no sense can it be maintained that a *literal* or *personal* coming of Christ has transpired, within the limits assigned by them to that event. It is clear, however, that *if* such a literal or personal coming of Christ is an event yet *future,*—which all these writers admit—it will follow, according to their own showing, that there are to be *three*, instead of two, comings of Christ.

Fourth. But if, on examination, the theories to pass under review *fail* to furnish evidence from Scripture and from fact, of the second coming of Christ, and of the setting up of His kingdom in the world, *under either of the forms for which they contend*, it will leave the way fairly open for the separate consideration of that subject in a subsequent part of this Treatise.

With the way thus prepared before us, we proceed to an examination of those theories which maintain that the second coming of Christ *is already past*, of which there are three theories.

CHAPTER I.

FIRST THEORY: MILLERISM.[1]

THIS THEORY ALLEGES THAT ALL THE PROPHECIES WHICH SET FORTH THE RESTORATION, CONVERSION, AND POLITICAL PREEMINENCE OF THE TWO KINGDOMS OF JUDAH AND ISRAEL OR THE TEN TRIBES, WERE VERIFIED BY THE RETURN OF THE JEWS FROM THE BABYLONISH CAPTIVITY.

If this be so, it follows that the *recovery*, by Judah and Israel, of "the first dominion"[2] promised to them under their Messiah, in other words, the Millennium of the Scriptures—for there can be no millennium on earth without the Jews—has become a matter of *history*, in the place of prophecy yet to be fulfilled.

The important bearing which this theory has upon the *general subject* of our present inquiries, calls for a special examination of its merits. We will lay before the reader in the outset as plain a statement as we can of the facts in the case.

First, then, I observe: There are many of the prophecies of the Old and New Testaments, which speak of the *return* of the Jews to their own land, in immediate connection with the contemporaneous *personal presence* of the Messiah as their King.

But those mighty men of renown of former days, Beza, Prideaux, Pareus, Willet, and Owen, together with those worthies of modern times, Simeon, and Scott, and Faber, of England; and the Rev. Dr. Berg, of our own country, stoutly maintain a *future* literal restoration of the Jews to Palestine; whilst at the same time they *deny*, that the second personal coming of Christ is in any way connected with that event; or, in other words, that it is *pre-millennial*.

On the other hand, that class of writers with whom we are *now* more specially concerned, whilst they *admit* a second personal coming of Christ as future, do at the same time *deny* the future restoration of the Jews, affirming that *all the prophecies relating to that event were fulfilled by their return from the Babylonish captivity*. In this theory, therefore, there is a double purpose, viz., first, to *evade* the doctrine of the second personal coming

---

[1] The writers on this subject are Rev. Wm. Miller, Rev. George Storrs, Rev. F. G. Fox, Rev. Josiah Litch, Rev. J. Oswold, A. M., and others.
[2] Micah iv. 8.

of Christ as being *pre*-millennial; and second, to *escape* the dilemma attendant upon the theory of the other writers above mentioned, all of whom, while they contend for the future literal restoration of the Jews, etc., yet affirm that Christ will reign over them *spiritually:* at the same time alleging that the personal coming of Christ is *post*-millennial. This, we repeat, is to make out *three*, instead of two, comings of Christ.

Now it will, we think, be conceded that, of the two horns of this dilemma, the *latter* has the decided vantage ground over the former. It will be found, unless we greatly mistake, that writers on this subject must either admit that the second personal coming of Christ is *pre*-millennial, or adopt the theory which *denies* the restoration of the Jews as being still *future.*

Having thus defined the position of these writers in the premises, we return to the advocates of the theory under consideration.

The first thing to be noted in regard to them is, a consciousness of the difficulty which their theory must encounter, from the *very terms* in which the prophecies relating to the Jewish restoration are couched. We here refer to the obvious disproportion between the glowing language of the prophets in relation to that event, and the circumstances attendant upon the termination of the Babylonish captivity. All this, however, is attempted to be obviated by the objection, that the above argument "is more plausible than solid." It is said in the first place, that, "by forming our estimate of the character of these events, not by our feelings, but by a reference to those of the persons *actually* concerned in them, we shall not think that the disproportion" here spoken of "between the prophetic language and those events, is quite so great as might, at first, be supposed." And second, "that the prophecies in question have a reference to things, compared with which any events, connected with *mere* Jewish interests, have no importance," etc.

But to this it may be replied: Are we then to understand that the statements of the old prophets on this subject are *exaggerated?* that the *fulfilment* of God's promises and prophecies is not equal to what the language used might lead us to expect? and, that the substance of the things hoped for is *inferior* to the shadow of them? If so, does it not follow, that such an assumption savors of a neological leaven? Surely, if men may thus lower and evade the language of Scripture, there is nothing the force of which may not be got rid of in like manner; and the writings of the prophets—or rather the *voice* of the Holy Ghost in them—must be looked upon as no better than hyperbolical bombast!

And so, also, of the estimate of the *events* pointed at in the prophecies by our feelings, instead of the feelings of those actually concerned in them. Has it then come to this, that "the *character* of the events" which God predicted by His prophets, is to be affected either by our feelings, or theirs, or by those of any other class of persons? Is the *inspiration* of the Holy Ghost to be tested, after all, by the various and opposite expectations of men? —is it to be resolved into *our* natural or religious enthusiasm? And are the images of future events exhibited to the Church through the medium sometimes of an excited, sometimes of a depressed, and often of a distorted imagination?

And, in conclusion on this subject: If God so please, who, or what is man, that *he* should presume to decide as to what "events, connected with the Jewish interests," should or should not be of "importance?" Let us suppose an allusion here made to the personal manifestation of Messiah to the Jews on their restoration. We might ask, not only on the score of the *probability*, but the *possibility* of such an event, "Is anything too hard for the Lord?"[1] Is our unbelief to be the measure of His truth? If a Jew had objected, *before* the events, the improbability, approaching not only to moral, but to *physical* impossibility, that Messiah could ever be born of a virgin: suppose, further, he had objected the improbability of such a *religion* as that of Christ, with such apparently inadequate support, and so contrary to men's prejudices and passions, ever so prevailing in the world, as that one day *all nations* should bow to Him:—how would such an objector meet this antagonist, but by arguments that would equally refute his own? namely, *faith* in the truth and power of God!

But enough of this. Let us now, as briefly as may be, proceed to the proofs and arguments alleged in support of this theory. Assuming that no such an event is in the womb of the future, it is affirmed,

I. That the predicted reconciliation to take place between Judah and Israel has already been verified *in the restoration from the Babylonish captivity.* In proof, we are referred, as the *foundation* on which this theory rests, to the following passage, Jer. l.

---

[1] Jer. xxxii. 27.

4, 17, and 33, 34, as an express prophecy of the *return* of "the children of Israel and the children of Judah together from Babylon under Cyrus. It is hence argued that, to expect their return as yet future, is to expect a new schism in the nation, for which no plausible reason can be assigned; and a mutual reconciliation, for which no cause, without such a schism, could exist. In a word, it is insisted, 1st, that the nation was *then* restored, and assumed an *independent* character; 2d, that this restoration was attended by an *extinction* of the national schism; and 3d, that it was accompanied with a *spiritual revival:* all of which, if founded in truth, as they involve the cessation of the old feud which divided the two kingdoms, and they became merged into one under the common denomination of JEWS, demonstrate the *moral impossibility* of any return in the future.

From a desire to give the advocates of this theory the full benefit of all that can be adduced in its support, as claimed to be derived from the Scriptures of the Old and New Testaments, and from profane writers, we herewith lay before the reader the *materiel* out of which their alleged evidence to that end is derived.

1. In defence of the first of the three above-named postulates, to wit, that *at the time* of the nation's return from Babylon, it assumed an independent character, we are referred to the following from Josephus, lib. xi. chap. v. 7, where he says:—"So the Jews prepared for the work. This is the name they are called by, from the day that they came up from Babylon: which is taken from the tribe of Judah, which came first to these places: and thence both they and the country gained that appellation."

Now, inasmuch as the passage quoted from Jer. l., as the *foundation* on which the superstructure of this theory is built, includes the restoration of *all* the children of Judah and of Israel, or the ten tribes; so, in order to the *complete* establishment of their joint national independence at that time, the restoration here contended for must embrace the two kingdoms *as a whole*. Accordingly, these writers infer such to have been the case, 1st, on the ground that the *Jews* are spoken of by Josephus as having "first" returned, etc., which of course implies, that those of the children of *Israel* followed afterward; and 2d, from the alleged failure to find the lodging place of the ten tribes, on the part of those who are looking for their *future literal* restoration to the land of their fathers. And, in confirmation of this, we are referred to the writer of the Maccabees, (chap. iv. 59; and v. 3, etc.), who gives to the *united* population the name of Israel.

Let us, however, enter a little more into the *historic* evidence, adduced by the advocates of this theory, in support of the point under discussion. One of the ablest writers in its defence, having traced the history of Jewish affairs from the period of their restoration by Cyrus, and then through the fortunes which followed them by the overthrow of Medo-Persia at the hand of Alexander the Great, the division of his empire after his death into four kingdoms, and the important bearing with which the friendship or hostility of the Jews in Judea were regarded by their contending rivals, down to the time when their national independence was recognized under the sway of the Asmonæan princes, says:—"In the year B. C. 143, Simon, brother of Judas Maccabæus, was acknowledged by Demetrius, *king of Syria*, as high-priest and prince of the Jews; and so remarkable was this transition from a provincial to a national state, that it became an *epoch* in the history of the Jews, and an *era* from which subsequent events were dated;" and, that "the nation continued *absolutely* independent till the year B. C. 63, that is, during a period of eighty years, until Pompey took the city of Jerusalem."

Again: In meeting an objection "that the condition of the Jews" during this interval "was very contemptible compared with their condition under the former race of kings," this writer draws a comparison between their state when, in the reign of Jehoshaphat, Judea being invaded by the Moabites and Ammonites, they were unable to repel their foes;[1] and that "under the Maccabæan kings, when Moab and Ammon were completely extinguished as nations, and the Edomites were compelled by Hyrcanus, the son of Simon, to adopt the rite of circumcision, from which time *they ceased* to have a national existence."

Once more: In further proof of the national independence, unity of interest and purpose, and numerical power of the restored Jewish nation, we are transferred to the time of the Roman Emperor Caligula, who, being "intoxicated with power, resolved that he must be honored as a god." To this end, he "gave orders that his image should be set up in all the temples dedicated to religious worship throughout the empire." In this "he found no difficulty till the question came to be about the desecration of Jehovah's

[1] 2 Chron. xx. 3.

temple in Jerusalem. Here," however, " he found a resistance not to be overcome." " Petronius, the governor, upon receiving the imperial mandate," aware of "the power of the Jews who inhabited the countries beyond the Euphrates," according to the statement of Philo, became greatly alarmed. "For he knew," says Philo, "not by report, but by experience, that Babylon, and many other of the provinces, were in the possession (κατεχομενας) of the Jews." So Josephus, also, "speaking of the Jews living beyond the Euphrates," says,—" While the ten tribes are beyond the Euphrates until now, and are an immense multitude, and not to be estimated by numbers," etc. And finally, we are referred to " Agrippa's letter to Caligula, in which he endeavors to dissuade him from desecrating the temple in Jerusalem."—" But concerning the Holy City, I must speak what is fitting. This, as I said before, is my country, and the metropolis, not of one territory, but of very many, on account of the *colonies* that she has sent out to various places," etc. " Then follows an enumeration of the different parts of the world in which the Jews are to be found," exclusive of "those beyond the Euphrates" alluded to by Philo and Josephus, of whom, he adds, " I say nothing," etc.

2. Further, on this subject. In reference to the evidence of the *reconciliation* of Judah and Israel, or of the unity of interest and purpose of the nation, etc., during this period, Philo is quoted as saying,—" For every year deputations are sent, bringing much gold and silver to the temple, collected from the first-fruits; and they travel by ways hard to be passed over, but which seem to them, from their religious zeal, like the best roads," etc. Now, these " deputations," it is said, " were the *representatives of the ten tribes* living beyond the Euphrates, who, being descended of those who departed from Judah, bring their annual offerings to Jerusalem; by which act they acknowledge it as the centre, both of civil and religious unity of the whole nation. Also, that the persons whom Judas went to assist, as spoken of in the 1st Book of Maccabees, being residents in Galilee, must have belonged to the *ten tribes*. And it is hence demanded: " Is this no proof of the *healing* of the national breach? It was not to Dan, nor to Bethel, that they went. But to *Jerusalem*." Aye, and in bearing their precious offerings to the Holy City, their "joy was of so intense a kind as to make them overlook inconveniences and dangers of every kind attending their long and tedious journey."

3. And now, as to the last point—*the spiritual revivals.* It is contended by these writers "that such revivals might be fairly expected from the language of the prophets, when speaking of the *return* of the Jews to their land:" and that they "do not consider any events that did not involve them, a fulfilment of those prophecies." But they insist, "that such revivals *did take place,* appears from the testimony both of Ezra and Nehemiah. See Ezra, iii. and x.; and Nehemiah, viii. and xi.; also, 2 Maccab., x., etc.

So much, then, according to this theory, for the *historical* facts and evidences of the millennium of the Scriptures, as alleged to have been verified in the complete restoration, reconciliation, and conversion of the children of Judah and Israel, or the ten tribes, *to* and *in* their own land, *on their return from Babylon.*

II. We pass now to a series of arguments adduced by these writers, in addition to the above, *against a future literal* return of the Jews to Canaan: of which,

1. The *first* "is founded on the necessity," upon that hypothesis, "of connecting with the literal return, the literal rebuilding of the temple; and with it, of course, the literal restoration of sacrifice," etc. It is hence argued, that *if* the return of the Jews at some future period is to be followed by such consequences, "there is such an evident *reductio in absurdum* as involves *falsity* in the assumption;" there being *no* prophecy which points either to the rebuilding of the temple, or the restoration of sacrifice, *after* the destruction of the Holy City, etc.

2. A *second* argument to the same end, is founded upon the alleged fact "that the New Testament is *silent* about the restoration of the Jews to their land. The destruction of the temple, and the desolation of the Holy City," it is said, "are foretold, with their consequences: but, *not a word of comfort,* as was the case *previous* to the Babylonish captivity. The ejectment from the forfeited inheritance is *final.* The kingdom is taken away from the "wicked men, and given to a nation bringing forth the fruits thereof." "God," it is declared, "will remember His covenant with literal Judah *no more for ever,* neither shall it come into mind." "And when Paul, in the xi.th of Romans, denies that God has cast away His people, the benefit from which they are not excluded is *spiritual* and *personal,* having respect, at that time, to "the election of grace," and ultimately, to "turning away ungodliness from Jacob." And,

3. A *third*, and the last and principal argument against the future literal restoration of the Jews to their land, "is founded upon the respective characters of the *two covenants*. Many strange things," these writers tell us, "have been written in our strange times on the subject of the covenants. But the matter stands clearly unfolded by the apostle in Galatians, chap. iv., 22–31. The one covenant is entirely confined to *temporal* things, and the other to *spiritual* things. The former passed away on the death of Christ, with all its provisions and its promises. To talk *now* of the Jews as a peculiar people, and as having any temporal promises," it is affirmed, "is to *revive* the covenant that God has superseded."

Thus have we laid before the reader, so far as we are aware, *the entire strength* of the proof-texts, historical facts, and other arguments, adduced in support of the theory, that the return of the Jews from Babylon verified all that the prophecies point out, in reference to the destiny of Judah and the ten tribes. We have also purposely abstained from remarks in reply, with a view to avoid a break in the chain of evidence furnished in advocacy of it. But, as "he that is *first* in his own cause seemeth just"—and we readily concede the apparent force of the reasoning employed in its defence—" but his neighbor cometh and *searcheth* him:"[1] So, having sundry serious objections to advance against both the *foundation* on which it rests, and the *superstructure* built upon it, we submit the following to the consideration of all candid and impartial minds.

Let us, then, examine,

I. The *foundation*, on which this theory rests.

1. I remark in the first place, as I have already said, that this theory involves the necessity of demonstrating the *entire* restoration, not only of the children of *Judah*, but those also of the *Ten Tribes*, from the Babylonish captivity by the edict of Cyrus, in order to sustain the alleged prophecy of it in the l.th chap. of Jeremiah *in its integrity*. If it *fails* to do that, the whole is swept away. That it does not and cannot do that, will, we submit, appear evident from what follows:—

(1.) There is no proof in Scripture of a single family having returned from *each* of the ten tribes. It can only be shown that a *few* from several of them, did so. This, however, it is to be borne

[1] Prov. xviii. 17.

in mind, can only be accounted for from the fact, that there always was in Ephraim *a remnant*, who had their hearts toward Jerusalem, and who did not fall into the idolatrous practices of the nation in general. It was to prevent *their* example from drawing back the whole nation, that the calves were first set up in Dan and Bethel:[1] And, when Hezekiah kept a solemn passover in Jerusalem, and invited Ephraim and Manasseh to attend, though the great body of Israel "laughed [the messengers] to scorn and mocked them; nevertheless divers of *Asher* and *Manasseh* and *Zebulun* humbled themselves, *and came to Jerusalem*."[2] Of *these*, then, it was, who, *never having left* Judah, returned with them from the Babylonish captivity. Of those of the Ten Tribes carried captive into Assyria by Shalmanezer,[3] there is not the least evidence that *one* of them availed himself of the proclamation of Cyrus to return with Judah. Then further,

(2.) So far as the inhabitants of *Samaria* were concerned, between whom and the Jews there existed the greatest enmity *after* the return from Babylon; so we know that the Jews in the time of Christ regarded them with *great antipathy*,[4] which is anything but evidence that the ancient quarrel and ground of jealousy were *removed*. At the time of the return from the Babylonish captivity, therefore, these Israelites held to *Judah*, a relation analogous to that of the mixed multitude of Egyptians, who accompanied them at the former exodus.[5] But surely, no one would say on that account, that *Egypt* went up! Once more,

(3.) What is *decisive* of this point is the fact, that this very case is contemplated in prophecy, *distinct from and independent of*, the restoration from Babylon. In Ezek. xxxvii. 16, 17, the prophet is directed to "take one stick and write upon it, For JUDAH, and *for the children of Israel his companions*. Here we have Judah and his companions of the house of Israel, as they attached themselves to him *before* and *during* the captivity; and, as we admit, came up with him from Babylon. But is this all? "Then take another stick and write upon it, For JOSEPH, the stick of Ephraim, and *for all the house of Israel his companions:* and join them one to another in one stick."[6] The advocates of this theory, therefore, are bound to show us the complete fulfil-

---

[1] Compare 1 Kings xli. 32 with 2 Chron. xi. 14-17.
[2] 2 Chron. xxx. 10-12.
[3] 2 Kings xvii. 1-5 and verse 23.
[4] John iv. 9.
[5] Exod. xii. 38; Numb. xi. 4.
[6] Ezek. xxxvii. 16.

ment of *both features* of this prophecy, in the alleged return from Babylon: not only the *union* of Judah with *some* of the children of Israel his companions; but also with "Ephraim and the *tribes* of Israel, his fellows" (ver. 19), even " *all* the house of Israel, his companions." And this, we conceive, it is utterly out of their power to do, there being *no* recorded events at all to correspond with both the circumstances so precisely described and distinguished in this place. Finally,

(4.) It remains to be proved, that Jer. l. 3, 17, 33, selected as the *foundation* of this theory, refer to a restoration of Israel, or the Ten Tribes, at the time of the taking of Babylon by the Medes; nor do they in all the instances, obviously relate to *any* restoration of Israel at all. The error of these writers on this subject, arises from their overlooking an important principle of prophetic interpretation; viz., that the spirit which spake by the prophets frequently contemplates *two events;* the one being either a *type* or *earnest* of the other. The latter and greater is the one kept chiefly in view, and the description of it is consequently in many respects unsuitable to the *minor* event, and altogether overcharged, if it be limited to it. On the other hand, there are occasional allusions which *must* be limited to the minor event. Thus we admit in Jer. l. and li. a plain and obvious reference to the taking of *Babylon* by the Medes; but we equally insist upon a reference in it to the destruction of the *mystic Babylon*, or, at least, to some event of far greater extent and scope, and accompanied by circumstances which have as yet had *no* fulfilment. For example, we ask the abettors of this theory,—Is there not a reference in Jer. li. 19-24 to Israel as " the Lord's *battle-axe*," etc., which is made instrumental in the vengeance on Babylon?—was Israel made " a weapon of war in the Lord's hand" in the time of Cyrus, or in any way instrumental in inflicting that vengeance? We would further ask, Were the Lord's people *called out of Babylon* (verse 45), and afforded an opportunity of escape, *previous* to the taking of Babylon by the Medes? Is not this verse, therefore, plainly parallel with Rev. xviii. 4, and a mark that *mystical Babylon* is intended? And once more, was Babylon destroyed by Cyrus *in the manner* stated in verses 13 and 26? Was the conquest and change of dynasty which then took place *an end* of that city?

The foundation of this theory being thus disposed of, we might well spare ourself the labor and the reader the time of pursuing the subject further. There is, however, a need-be, to take a survey of the imposing proportions of,

II. The *superstructure*, which not a few of the wise and good of our day have erected upon it. Permit me here to say, that I think I am not very wide the mark when I affirm, *that there is no other point connected with a solution of the great theological question of the day now under discussion*, viz., the second coming of Christ, *that forms an equal obstacle to a right determination of it.* I hold, that the numerous prophecies which set forth the restoration, reconciliation, and national preëminence of Judah and Israel in their own land, *form the key* to a correct interpretation and application of all the other unfulfilled prophecies of God's Word, and especially that relating to the question, whether Christ's second coming is to be *pre*, or *post*-millennial. Keeping this in view, let me indulge the hope, that adherence to a long-cherished theory will give way to the force of evidence, if, in the end, it is found to vanish,

> "Like the baseless fabric of a vision,
> Which leaves not a wreck behind."

To save the labor of transcribing from the articles replied to, the reader will please refer to them as numbered 1, 2, 3, etc., with which ours *in brackets* will correspond.

With these remarks premised, we pass to a notice, first, of the alleged facts and arguments, with their inferences, as contained in the *historic* allusions adduced in support of this theory. We shall divide it into sections.

SECTION I.

OF THE ALLEGED INDEPENDENCE OF THE JEWS, AFTER THEIR RETURN FROM BABYLON.[1]

[1.] On this subject, we have to object,

First, that these writers do not fairly meet the argument from Scripture, their expositions being confined to *a part* only of the prophecy. Supposing that they make out something like a fulfilment of this portion, they take for granted that the *whole* was fulfilled.[2]

Second, as it respects the testimony cited from Josephus,[3] all

---

[1] See pages 60–62.   [2] See pages 59–62.   [3] See page 60.

that can be said of it is, that those families out of a *few* of the Ten Tribes, who adhered to Judah *after* the dismemberment of the kingdom, instead of accompanying, they *followed* those of Judah, who were the "*first*" to return to Babylon.

Third, we have already shown, that Jer. l. 3, 17, 33, and chap. li., can have *no* reference to the restoration from Babylon.[1] We now pass to the argument drawn from the statements of Philo, Agrippa, etc.[2] Now, even admitting that it were in other respects complete, it is faulty in this particular: that the promises to Judah and Israel intimate that the restoration of the two nations shall be *under a prince of the house of David:*[3] whereas the Asmonæan princes, besides that they were never independent, but *tributary*, the Maccabees ruled to the *exclusion* of the house of David. Nor can this theory ever be reconciled with those *promises* to Israel when restored and united under her Davidic head, that she shall be *mistress* over all other nations, and that they shall all be *tributary* to her,[4] an event which none can pretend has ever yet been realized. Again,

Fourth, the passage in Josephus which speaks of "the ten tribes" who, in his time, were "beyond the Euphrates," and which he represents as "an immense multitude," etc., only shows that he considered them as yet *unrestored*. Now, we do not deny that there were large numbers of Jews scattered over various parts of Europe *after* the Babylonish captivity. But this is no proof that they were *of* the ten tribes, or that the "colonies" sent forth by the Jews into territories under Jewish dominion, were *independent*.

SECTION II.

OF THE ALLEGED RECONCILIATION OF JUDAH AND ISRAEL, AFTER THEIR RETURN FROM BABYLON.[5]

[2.] As it regards the deputations sent to Jerusalem, we remark,

First, that we do not see, in this circumstance, any clear and satisfactory evidence, that the national breach between the two kingdoms was *healed*. If these persons had been deputed from

---

[1] See pages 59, 60, 66.   [2] See page 62 of this Work.
[3] See Jer. xxx. 1-9; Hosea iii. 4, 5; Zech. xii. 10; Ezek. xxxiv., xxxvii. etc.
[4] See Isa. lx. 1-7.   [5] See pages 62, 63.

the ten tribes in their collective capacity, it would imply that they had *nationally* renounced their idolatrous practices; which, as regards the bulk of the nation, is contrary to the *predictions* respecting them whilst in their scattered state,[1] and also to *historic* testimony. It is clear, therefore, that they could have been none other than representatives from those *Jewish* colonies scattered in various parts of Europe, among whom, doubtless, were those of the "*divers* from the tribes of Asher and Manasseh, and of Zebulun," who had united themselves to Judah *previous* to the captivity of Israel;[2] and this number must have been considerable, since even in the worst of times, during the tyranny and abominations of Ahab and Jezebel, there were 7,000 who did not bow the knee to Baal.[3] Nor was it so much the civil and political, as the *religious* character of Jerusalem, that attracted them thither. Jerusalem was "the city which the Lord had chosen, whither the tribes should go up."[4] Again,

Second, how, we ask, is it to be accounted for, if the two nations of Judah and Israel had become *one* at the return from Babylon, that there should be *no living traces of that union?* It is remarkable, that whilst there are thousands who can trace themselves to be of *Judah* and *Benjamin*, and also of *Levi* (who was common to both nations), we believe none can be found to trace themselves to the *ten tribes*. And as to the inhabitants of Galilee being of the ten tribes, the best test would be to prove it by an appeal to the *genealogy* of the families or persons mentioned as resident there. But on this subject silence reigns supreme. The fair inference therefore is, that the mixed Israelitish multitude who *followed* Judah at the return from Babylon, though *of* the ten tribes, yet (having separated from them *before* their captivity under Shalmanezer) could not have formed any part of them. The circumstance that all efforts to ascertain the present whereabouts of the ten tribes have proved unavailing, is no evidence that they *have not now* a separate and independent existence.

And, *third*, as to the alleged *revival* of the old quarrel in the event of their restoration being *future*, it is sufficient, according to our view of the matter, amply to fulfil the prophecy, that the ten tribes went into captivity in a state of *alienation from* Judah; and that when they, with Judah, shall be restored, the very

---

[1] See Deut. xxviii. 64.   [2] 2 Chron. xxx. 10–12.   [3] 1 Kings xix. 18.   [4] Ps. cxxii. 4.

agency employed in effecting their national *union*, will effectually eradicate their national *animosity*.

And so, *fourth*, in reference to the argument founded upon the alleged *improbabilities* of the future restoration of the ten tribes. We oppose to it the following positive "Thus saith the Lord." We find it written of Israel: "If any of thine be driven out unto the utmost parts of heaven, from *thence* will the Lord thy God *gather* thee, and from thence will he *fetch* thee: and the Lord thy God *will bring thee* into the land which thy fathers possessed, and thou shalt possess it."[1] Here please mark: the expression, "if *any* of thine," implies that the return will be, not of a part of Israel, but of all: not *one* will be left behind. For, "it shall come to pass in that day, that the Lord shall beat off from the channel of the river unto the stream of Egypt" (nothing like which occurred at the alleged return of the ten tribes from Babylon. Compare also Isa. xi. 15), "and ye shall be gathered *one by one*, O ye children of Israel."[2] Nor this only. As if to anticipate this very objection to such an event, the prophet describes Zion as thus exclaiming on the return of her children: "Then shalt thou say in thine heart, Who hath begotten me these, seeing I have *lost* my children, and am desolate, a captive, and removing to and fro? and who hath brought up these? Behold, I was left alone: *these, where had they been?*"[3] Ah, "is anything too hard for the Lord?" The advocates of this theory say that such a restoration is *abstractly* possible. We say, we *believe* that it will come to pass.

One word, in conclusion, as to the *ground* of this argument. It is made to rest upon the alleged *utter extinction* of the nations of Edom, Moab, and Ammon, at the hand of Israel, *at the time of their* return from Babylon. These writers demand, "Where are these nations now?" And they hence argue, "Unless they are supposed to *revive*, they cannot be overthrown. Their revival, they say, is not very *probable;* and, in the same proposition, they infer the *improbability* of the return of the Jews, seeing that return was to be *followed* by the destruction of these nations," etc. But it is particularly unfortunate for this argument, that a "thus saith the Lord" declares, "Yet will I bring again the captivity of Moab in the latter days, saith the Lord." (Jer. xlviii. 47.) And

---

[1] Deut. xxx. 4, 5. [2] Isa. xxvii. 12. [3] Ib. chap. xlix. 21.

again: "I will bring again the captivity of the children of Ammon, saith the Lord." (Jer. xlix. 6.)

SECTION III.

OF THE ALLEGED SPIRITUAL REVIVALS WHICH FOLLOWED THE SO-CALLED RETURN OF JUDAH AND ISRAEL FROM BABYLON.

3. [3.] We admit that there was a work of grace among the Jews in the time of Ezra and Nehemiah: but we cannot allow Acts ii. 16, 17, and xv. 14, to have anything to do with the revival which is foretold as accompanying the *restoration* of Israel, seeing that it was a work which was contemporaneous with the casting off of the Jews, instead of their return from captivity. Matt. xxiii. 38, 39; see also Rom. xi. 15. Moreover, we have a particular description of the *manner* in which the national conversion of the Jews will be brought about, in Zech. xiv. 4, 5, and chap. xii. 9–14, which see. Was there any such a *revival* at the return from Babylon?

We now proceed to the other arguments adduced by these writers against the future literal return of Judah and Israel to their own land.

First. *Those relating to the temple, and the restoration of sacrifices,* etc. Suppose we admit, for the sake of argument, that *no* satisfactory solution has been or can be given, of the rebuilding of the temple, etc., as described in the xliid and xliiid chapters of Ezekiel's prophecy. Of one thing we are certain: that at the return of the Jews from the Babylonish captivity, they did not set about the erection of their new temple *on the plan* revealed to that prophet *during* the captivity. And no one, we are persuaded, taking the prophecy as it stands, will affirm its literal fulfilment before Christ, or that it has been fulfilled, or is now fulfilling, under the Christian dispensation, in a *mystical* sense.

That remarkable prophecy of Haggai, chap. ii. 2, 9, respecting *the second temple*, has an important bearing on this subject. The prophet having asked, "Who is there left among you that saw this house in her first glory? And how do ye see it now? Is it not in your eyes in comparison of it as nothing?" adds—"the glory of this *latter house* shall be greater than of the former, saith the Lord of Hosts." Now, it is here to be noted, in the first place, that the "house," on which the Jews then looked, was little better than a heap of ruins (see verses 1–4). But even when *rebuilt*, its magnificence was "as nothing" compared with that erected by Solomon.[1] The question, therefore, is, In what was to consist the predicted *greater glory* of this latter house over the first? If we are to rely upon the current interpretation, it was verified by the appearance of Messiah in the temple, during His first coming. But, besides that Christ appeared, not in that second, but a *third* house—that called the temple of Herod, we may, I submit, without the fear of derogating aught from His claims to true and proper divinity as "God manifest in the flesh," call in question the consistency of such an application of the above prophecy to that event. Had the *transfiguration* of our blessed Lord occurred in the temple instead of on the mount,[2] there had been some color of a pretext for its support. The circumstance, however, of the *place* of manifestation of this glorified humanity of Jesus, taken in connection with His positive command to His disciples after they descended from the mount, viz., "tell the vision to no man until the Son of man be risen again from the dead,"[3] show clearly that, from the manger to the cross, the "*glory*" of the God-man Mediator—if we except the miraculous attestations of it during His ministry—was veiled beneath the mantle of His humiliation. During His first appearance in the flesh, Jesus was accounted as "a root out of a dry ground"—as one "having neither form nor comeliness whereby we might desire him"—as "a man of sorrows and acquainted with grief"—yea, as one who was "despised and rejected of men."[4] Nor did all the concentrated displays of the wisdom and power of Christ, whether *in* the temple or *out of it*, prevail with those to whom as a nation He was sent, to accept Him as their Messiah. "*The veil* still remained on their hearts."[5] He came to His own, but His own received Him not."[6] In a word, Christ came first to "suffer:" "the glory was to follow."[7]

---

[1] The amount of gold and silver said to have been expended in building the temple of Solomon was one hundred thousand talents of gold and a thousand thousand talents of silver (2 Chron. xxii. 14), amounting to upwards of £800,000,000 sterling; which, says Dr. Prideaux, was sufficient to have built the whole temple of solid silver, and greatly exceeds all the treasures of all the monarchs of Christendom.—Prid. *Connec.* vol. I., p. 5.

[2] Compare Matt. xviii. 1–5 with Mark ix. 1, 2 and 3–7.   [3] Matt. xvii. 9; Mark ix. 9.
[4] See Isa. liii.   [5] 2 Cor. iii. 14.   [6] John i. 11.   [7] 1 Pet. i. 11.

We think, then, we are safe in the inference, that the "greater glory" of which the prophet Haggai speaks, relates, not to Christ's appearance in the temple of Herod, but to that of a temple *future* to any which had preceded it. The comparison instituted by Haggai above, is that between the glory of one "house" and that of another "house"—of the temple of Ezekiel with those erected by Solomon, Zerubbabel, and Herod. This, we submit, will appear obvious to any one who will take the trouble to compare the ground-plan of Solomon's temple, as given by Calmet and Prideaux, with that of Ezekiel, as delineated by Poole. The difference is so great as scarcely to bear a resemblance. Solomon's temple was 60 cubits long, 30 broad and 30 high.[1] Zerubbabel's was ordered to be 60 cubits long, and 60 broad.[2] And Herod's was 100 cubits long.[3] Solomon's temple was in a square of 60 cubits. Ezekiel's is to be in a square of 500 cubits.[4] The proportion of Ezekiel's temple, therefore, to that of Solomon will be as 500 to 60, or as the *glory* of King *Messiah* will surpass the glory of king Solomon. In this sense, then, the "glory of this *latter house*" will exceed that of the former. Again:

Second. As to the Restoration of Sacrifices. The prophet was specially ordered to show to the house of Israel, provided they were ashamed of their iniquities, *the whole pattern, and forms, and ordinances, and laws*, of this house, with a charge to *keep* one and all of them. (Chap. xliii. 10, 11.) Now, that the Jews who returned with Zerubbabel [Nehemiah] were ashamed, appears from Neh. ix. 1–3; yet no reference or allusion seems to have been made to this revelation of Ezekiel, either in a literal or spiritual sense. So far from it, though Ezekiel himself was commanded to take of the seed of Zadok, and with them to officiate in the ordinances and sacrifices, yet we are nowhere informed that he did so. The conclusion, therefore, is, that the reason of their omission was that their observance was to be reserved *for the future*.

To this, however, it is objected that the offering of sacrifices appears *incongruous* with the deliverance of the animals from bondage during the millennial dispensation, etc. But to this it may be replied, that the law in regard to the brute creation, "the spirit of the beast goeth downward,"[5] is applicable alike to all

---

[1] 1 Kings vi. 3, 4; 2 Chron. iii. 3, 4.   [2] Ezra vi. 3.   [3] Josephus, book xv. chap. 14.
[4] Ezek. xlv. 2.   [5] Eccles. iii. 21.

time, as well *before*[1] as after the fall. We know of no scripture which teaches that they shall at any period, " the times of restitution of all things "[2] not excepted, be rendered, like man, absolutely *immortal*. And, if it were befitting that the brute creation, though "made subject to vanity unwillingly,"[3] was nevertheless offered in sacrifice from the time of Abel as typical of the sacrifice of the woman's seed to come, we see not why they may not be used in the Divine purpose as a *commemorative* ordinance of that event during the millennial age.

It is also objected, that the future offering of sacrifices is *incompatible* with St. Paul's reasoning in the Epistles to the Galatians and Hebrews, where, having argued the inefficacy of the legal sacrifices to atone for sin, and the sufficiency to that end of the one offering of "Christ," who as "our passover was slain for us;" such a revival of them would seem to be a return again to the "beggarly elements" from which the Church has been delivered. To this, however, we deem it sufficient to observe, that the facts of the case, in that the apostles *themselves* continued to offer sacrifices and to observe Jewish feasts for thirty-seven years subsequent to the death of Christ, furnish evidence that these things were not removed *on account of* the death of Christ. As institutions of the Church under the Christian dispensation, they, together with the polity of the Jewish commonwealth, were set aside after the fall of Jerusalem and the dispersion of the nation in A. D. 70, and were *suspended* "until the time come when they shall say, Blessed is He that cometh in the name of the Lord."[4]

And finally, on this subject, we think it sufficient to remove all doubt, in regard both to the future literal rebuilding of the temple and the revival of sacrifices as a *commemorative* ordinance during the millennial dispensation, to refer to the fact that no such events occurred, as preceding the visit of Christ to the temple, to which the prophet Haggai points in chap. ii. 6, 7, and verses 20–22; in addition to which, in verse 23, we have a clear and unequivocal prophecy of the *future* prosperity and glory of

---

[1] This idea may somewhat startle the reader. Let him, however, reflect, that the very penalty annexed to a partaking of the fruit of the interdicted tree,—" In the day thou eatest thereof thou shalt surely *die*," i. e., so far as it respected the matter of an organic death, implies that our first parents, even in *innocence*, must have had a knowledge of what *death was*. But, in regard to human beings, this knowledge could only have been derived from what they saw of *the ravages of death* among the lower orders of creation.

[2] Acts iii. 21.   [3] Rom. viii. 20.   [4] Matt. xxiii. 39.

Christ's kingdom (a prophecy which can in no sense be applied to the Church during the present dispensation), under the name of Zerubbabel, as His ancestor and type. But,

Third. Should this and the preceding facts and evidences be deemed undecisive of the question in hand, of the numerous passages that might be adduced to the same end, we select that of Deut. xxx. 3-6, the following analysis of which will be found to place the matter beyond the reach of further controversy.

1. On the return of the Jews from their captivity, it is here predicted that they shall be "gathered from all the nations whither the Lord their God hath scattered them," reaching even "unto the uttermost parts of heaven." (Verses 3, 4.) But their return under Cyrus was confined almost exclusively to those who came up from Babylon.

2. It was predicted of the Babylonish captivity, thus: Deut. xxviii. 36, "The Lord shall bring *thee, and thy king* which thou shalt set over thee, unto a nation which neither thou nor thy fathers have known." This was fulfilled, as recorded in Dan. i. 1, 2, when Nebuchadnezzar invaded Jerusalem, and carried Jehoiakim, king of Judah, a captive to Babylon. But in the prophecy, Deut. xxx. 3, 4, *no* mention is made of their having a king, the "sceptre," after Shiloh came, having "departed from Judah," since which they have been "without a king, and without a prince, and without a sacrifice, and without an image, and without an ephod, and without teraphim." But, after abiding thus for "many days," saith the Lord, "the children of Israel shall return, and seek the Lord their God, and *David their king:* and shall fear the Lord and His goodness *in the latter days.*"[1]

3. Compare the *number* of the captives who returned from Babylon with what is predicted of their increase at the time of their final restoration. At the exodus from Egypt there were about 600,000 on foot that were men, besides children, together with the mixed multitude.[2] But in the return from Babylon the whole number, including the congregation proper, together with men-servants, maid-servants, and singing-men, and singing-women, did not amount to the total of 50,000 persons. (See Neh. vii. 66.) Whereas, according to the prophecy of Hosea, chap. i. 10, 11, they are yet to be "multiplied above their fathers," for, saith he, "The number of the children of Israel shall be *as the sand of the*

[1] Hosea iii. 5.   [2] Exod. xii. 37, 38.

sea, which cannot be measured nor numbered. . . . . Then shall the children of Judah and the children of Israel be gathered, and appoint themselves *one head*, and they shall come up out of the land: for great shall be the day of Jezreel (or seed of God)." And,

4. The prophecy in verse 6, "and the Lord thy God shall circumcise thine heart, and the heart of thy seed, to *love* the Lord thy God," etc. Whatever may be said of the revivals of religion among the Jews under Ezra and Nehemiah, and the time of the Maccabees; yet, when Stephen addressed them, Acts vii. 51, his language was, "Ye stiff-necked and uncircumcised in heart and ears; ye do always resist the Holy Ghost: as your fathers did, so do ye." Now, here is the evidence of their having *fallen away from* their steadfastness in God, *after* their return from Babylon. Whereas, at their final ingathering "from all countries whither they have been driven," their covenant-God declares, "And I will make an everlasting covenant with them, that I will not turn away from them to do them good; but I will put my fear in their hearts, that they shall not depart from me. Yea, I will rejoice over them to do them good, and I will plant them in this land assuredly, with my whole heart, and with my whole soul, ... for I will cause their captivity to return, saith the Lord."[1]

As an aid to the student of prophecy, it will be well for him to consult, on this subject, the following passages, viz.: Lev. xxiv. 40-45. Deut. xxx. 3-6. Isa. i. 26, 27; x. 20-22; xi. 11-14; lx.; lxi. 4-7. Jer. iii. 18-23; xvi. 14-18; xxiii. 3-8; xxx. 18-22; xxxi.-xxxiii. 19-22; l. 4-20. Ezek. xi. 16-19; xx. 34-40; xxviii. 24-26; xxxvi., xxxvii., xxxviii., xxxix., xl. Hosea iii. 5. Joel ii. 21-32. Amos ix. 9-15. Micah ii. 21; iv. 6-8. Zech. i. 18-21; viii.-xii. 6-14, and xiii. 1.

But, not to prolong this discussion, whatever may be thought of our exposition of the prophecy of Haggai, chap. ii. 9, of this we are certain: *first*, that it could not have been verified in the return of the Jews from Babylon, and of the worship then instituted; *second*, that it is equally obvious that Christ's presence in the temple did not meet the terms of the prophecy; and hence, *third*, that the latter chapters in Ezekiel's prophecy are to be taken, not in a spiritual, but in a *literal* sense.

---

[1] Jer. xxxii. 36-44. See also chap. xxxi. 31-40.

SECTION IV.

We now pass to the argument against the future literal return of the Jews to their own land, as founded,

2. [2.] *On the alleged silence of the New Testament on that subject.*[1] "Silence," indeed! We cannot but express our astonishment that devotion to a preconceived theory should so blind the minds even of good men, as to lead them to overlook all those passages which militate against it. "Not a word of comfort," it is said, "accompanied our Lord's prophecy of the destruction of the Holy City, etc., with its consequences!" It may not here be superfluous to remind the reader that Matt. xxiii. 34-39 forms the *introductory* part of the great prophecy of Christ, as continued through chapters xxiv. and xxv. Now, in chap. xxiii. 38, Christ had predicted of the Jews, "Behold, your house shall be left unto you desolate." But He immediately adds, verse 39, "For I say unto you, ye shall not see Me henceforth, till ye shall say, Blessed is He that cometh in the name of the Lord." Was there no comfort in that? Again: As the dispersion of the Jews and the treading down of Jerusalem was to continue "until the times of the Gentiles should be fulfilled;" and they were told that when the things should "*begin* to come to pass," that were to foreshadow the close of that period, they were to "*lift up their heads*" at their approaching "redemption,"[2]—was there no comfort in that? Nor can we understand verse 31, respecting the "gathering together of the *elect* from the four winds with a great sound of a trumpet," (not, mark, that "last trump," which is to awake "the dead in Christ," but that of which the great trumpet of jubilee was the type,) other than of the recovery from their captivity of those who, "as touching the election, are beloved for the fathers' sake." (Rom. xi. 28.) At least we are persuaded that believing Jews, having their eye on Isaiah xxvii. 13, would find "comfort" in this part of our Lord's prophecy.

SECTION V.

Fourth. We have at length reached the most important of all the objections urged by this theory against the future literal restoration of the Jews to their own land.[3]

[1] See page 63.   [2] Luke xxi. 28.   [3] See page 64.

3. [3.] *It is predicated of the alleged differences of the two covenants*, Gal. iv. 22–31 ;—the covenant of works, which is affirmed tobe confined entirely to *temporal* things ; and the covenant of grace, as relating to those which are exclusively *spiritual*.

Now, we readily concede, that "many strange things" have been written and preached in our times on these two covenants. The result is the utmost confusion of views, in regard to *the spiritual relation* of the lineal descendants of Abraham, Isaac, and Jacob, to the Lord Jesus Christ as "the minister of the circumcision for the truth of God, to confirm the promises made unto the fathers" (Rom. xv. 8), and to the "good olive-tree" or Church of God, present and future, as set forth by the old prophets, and as illustrated by St. Paul in the xith chapter of his epistle to the Romans.

The solution of the difficulties involved, depends solely upon a right apprehension of the nature and design of THE ABRAHAMIC COVENANT.

The question is, Was it the old Adamic covenant of works, as re-promulgated at Sinai? Or, was it the original covenant of redemption, or of grace, in a newly-revised and enlarged form? If the former, then it was a mere *temporary* compact, having respect only to temporal things, and has long since ceased to exist. If the latter, then, whatever its temporal behests, it was essentially *a spiritual compact* or covenant of grace, and, from its very nature, must be perpetual. If the former, then the Church-state under the Jewish commonwealth was an isolated institution, having no relation whatever to that under the Christian dispensation. If the latter, then the Church *is one and the same* throughout all time, subject only to those external changes incident to her onward progress through successive dispensations.

Our first remark regarding this covenant is, that, primarily, it has for its foundation Abraham's seed, CHRIST, as the preordained pledge and surety for the fulfilment of all its stipulations. "He saith not, as to seeds as of many, but as of one, and to thy seed, which is Christ."[1] He is therefore called "the minister of the circumcision for the truth of God, to *confirm* the promises made unto the fathers."[2]

Then, second. Of these promises made unto the fathers, we observe, that they include, first, Abraham, Isaac, and Jacob, to-

---

[1] Gal. iii. 16.   [2] Rom. xv. 8.

gether with their multitudinous *lineal* seed; and second, the *Gentiles* of all nations, who were to be blessed through them.

We repeat, therefore, that the point to be determined is, *the relation*, past, present, and prospective, of the former to the latter, and of both to Christ, as set forth in the terms of this covenant.

It is almost superfluous to add, that whatever either the old prophets, or Christ and his apostles said of the past, present, and future destiny of the *literal* Israel, must accord with the original stipulations of that covenant, first, in regard to their connection with the inheritance of the land of Canaan, and the conditions upon which they were to obtain it; and second, with that part of the covenant which, reaching *beyond* them, was to render them the medium of blessing to all the Gentile nations of the earth.

Whatever theory, therefore, is found to *clash* with these covenanted stipulations, must be radically erroneous. Yea, more: it must be HERETICAL. The theories which have principally obtained currency in the Church of the present day on this subject are the two following:

I. Of the two covenants mentioned (Gal. iv. 22–31), it is affirmed that the one covenant, the Abrahamic—which is assumed to be *identical* with the Sinai covenant or law of works which "gendereth to bondage,"—is confined to *temporal* things; and the other, called the *New* covenant under the Christian dispensation, to *spiritual* things. The former, it is said, passed away at the death of the Messiah, with all its provisions and its promises; hence that, "to talk *now* of the Jews as a peculiar people, and as having any temporal promises, is to revive the covenant which God has superseded." Also, "that there is no evidence for supposing that there is in the nature of the new covenant anything that admits of its identification with material localities." In other words, this theory maintains, that the Abrahamic covenant is A MERE ECCLESIASTICO-POLITICAL CONSTITUTION, having for its outward badge the seal of circumcision, as a mark of national carnal descent; and that, as such, it had respect, *exclusively*, to the temporal promises of the land of Canaan, the possession of which was made to depend on the nation's obedience to the law of works; but that the nation, having failed to comply with its demands, have *forfeited* the promises, and that "their ejectment from the land is *final*."

It is hence argued, that, under these circumstances, the law of works having been *abrogated* by the obedience and death of Christ, the Jews are now placed, as individuals, on the platform of the new Christian covenant, in common with the nations of the Gentiles; and who, so far as they believe in Christ, etc., together constitute the *spiritual* Israel of God under the present dispensation. And so, when Paul tells us (Rom. xi. 26) that "*all* Israel shall be saved," he means an Israel which is not constituted of family descent from Abraham—that "all are not Israel who are of Israel"[1]—that "he is not a Jew who is one outwardly; neither is that circumcision which is outward in the flesh: but he is a Jew, which is one inwardly; and circumcision is that of the heart, in the spirit, and not in the letter,"[2] etc. And, finally, that to the Jewish nation who persevered in rejecting Him, Jesus said, "Ye *shut out* the kingdom of heaven against men, and neither go in yourselves, nor suffer them that are entering to go in:"[3] and that Paul and Barnabas therefore subsequently declared to them as those to whom "the word of God was first spoken, Seeing ye put these things from you, and judge yourselves unworthy of everlasting life, lo, we turn to the Gentiles."[4] And thus, it is affirmed, that "the kingdom of God *was taken from them*, and given to a people (the Gentiles) bringing forth the fruits thereof."[5]

II. On the other hand, it is contended that the Abrahamic covenant is *identical* with the original promise of redemption by the woman's seed Christ,[6] only in a revised and enlarged form. In other words, that it was *the covenant of grace*, entered into with that patriarch as the preordained "heir of the world,"[7] and of whom Christ, as "the heir of all things,"[8] was to come, as the surety and pledge of the fulfilment of all its stipulations, first, to His *lineal* descendants, the multitudinous seed to whom was given the promise of the land of Canaan; and second, to the *Gentile nations* who were to be blessed through them. Also that, while to them the rite of circumcision was an external badge of *national* distinction, it was at the same time, as with their great progenitor, "a seal of the righteousness of faith;" this latter, and *not* their obedience to the covenant of works, being the true and only divinely appointed condition on which depended their inheritance of the land promised to their fathers.

[1] Rom. ix. 6. [2] Rom. ii. 28, 29. [3] Matt. xxiii. 13. [4] Acts xiii. 46.
[5] Matt. xxi. 43. [6] Gen. iii. 14, 15. [7] Rom. iv. 13. [8] Heb. i. 2.

It will be perceived at a glance that these two theories are as divergent as the opposite poles. This latter, clearly distinguishing the Abrahamic, as the new covenant of grace, from the Sinaic covenant of works, asserts *its perpetuity*, and the *identity* of the Church of God, under successive dispensations. It shows that that covenant, as it respects the *subjects* embraced within its capacious grasp, whether Jews or Gentiles, has to do with both spiritual and temporal things, the latter, as it respects the *literal* Israel, being dependent upon, and held in subservience to, the former.

If it be asked, Wherefore, then, the *failure* of Israel to obtain the inheritance promised to them? we reply by a reference to the Pauline declaration, "because they sought it, *not by faith*, but as it were by the deeds of the law."[1] Yes, this was the "*stumblingstone*" on which they fell.[2] Instead of securing their title to the promised inheritance by faith in the mediatorial work of Abraham's "seed," which is *Christ*,[3] as the surety and pledge for the fulfilment to them of *all* its stipulations, like the young ruler in the Gospel,[4] they sought it by placing themselves under the "Hagar," or Sinai covenant of works.[5] And, as it forms no part of the moral government of God to interfere with the free, voluntary choice of his creatures, he left them under that covenant, as *a test* of their fidelity to him.

Their history is the record of their *failure* to comply with its rigorous but righteous demands. Hence their almost total, long-protracted alienation from the promised land, as depicted in the nation's lamentation as given in the words of Isaiah, chap. lxiii. 17, 18: "O Lord, why hast thou made us to err from thy ways, and hardened our hearts from thy fear? Return, for thy servants' sake, the tribes of thine inheritance. The people of thy holiness have possessed it"—i. e. the land—"*but a little while:* our adversaries have trodden down thy sanctuary,"[6] etc. Alas, how true this! If we except Israel's temporary possession of the land of Canaan after its division by Moses and Joshua, and subsequently under David, etc., down to the captivities, first, of the ten tribes, and then of Judah, they have verily been a people scattered and peeled, a hiss and a by-word to all nations.[7] Their national sins—their unbelief, idolatries, and incorrigible wickedness—show wherefore it was that "the Lord made them to err

---

[1] Rom. ix. 32. [2] Ib. [3] Gal. iii. 16. [4] Matt. ix. 18. [5] Gal. iv. 24.
[6] Isa. lxiii. 18. [7] Zeph. ii. 15; Joel ii. 17.

from his ways, and hardened their hearts from his fear, and delivered their land into the hands of their adversaries to be trodden under foot,"[1] while they have been dispersed as captives among all nations, *even to this day.*

There was, however, a "mystery of the Divine Will," which underlay all this, that is not discernible on the surface. It stands connected with the purposes of the author of the Abrahamic covenant, viewed as a whole. In the accomplishment of *all* the stipulations of that covenant, we are specially to bear in mind that it respected the *lineal* multitudinous seed of Abraham not only, but also the *Gentile* nations who were to be blessed through them. Now, it was from a view of the stupendously mysterious method of the Divine procedure in the accomplishment of this latter purpose which led the Apostle to exclaim, "O the depth of the riches, both of the knowledge and wisdom of God! How unsearchable are his judgments, and his ways past finding out!"[2] This deep "wisdom of God in a mystery," involved the "fall" of Israel by "unbelief," as the *medium* of securing "the riches of the world;" and the "diminishing of them," as the *medium* of "the riches of the Gentiles." (Rom. xi. 12.) "The casting away of them was the reconciling of the world" (v. 15). "*Because* of unbelief (v. 20) they, as the natural branches (v. 21), were broken off (v. 17) from the good olive-tree" (v. 24), that the believing Gentiles might be grafted in among them," and thus, "*with them*, be made to partake of the root and fatness of the olive-tree" (v. 17).

Thus it was, that in the purpose of Him that "worketh all things after the counsel of His own will," the apostasy of the literal Israel as a nation under the law of works, was made the *occasion* of the fulfilment of that part of the Abrahamic compact which stipulated, "In thee and in thy seed shall all the families, kindreds, and nations of the earth be blessed."[3] And thus it is that "SALVATION IS OF THE JEWS."[4]

We hence reach the momentous inquiry,—Was the exscinding of Israel as a nation from the good olive-tree on account of their unbelief, *final?* Did Israel thereby lose all further interest, as a nation, in the covenanted stipulations entered into with their fathers respecting them? Was their ejectment from the promised inheritance of Canaan to be *perpetual?* Let St. Paul an-

---

[1] Isa. lxiii. 18. [2] Rom. xi. 33. [3] Gen. xii. 3; Acts iii. 25.
[4] Compare Gen. xii. 3 and xxii. 18 with John iv. 32.

swer. Still treating of Israel as a nation, he says: "If the fall of them be the riches of the world," etc., "how much more their *fulness?*" (v. 12.) And again: "If the casting away of them be the reconciling of the world, what shall *the receiving* of them be but life from the dead?" (v. 15.) Hence the declaration, "And they, also," i. e., *the nation* of Israel, "if they abide not still in unbelief, shall be grafted in:" i. e., shall be restored to their place in the good olive-tree from which they were broken off; "for," says the Apostle, "God is able to graff them in again" (v. 23).

Now, nothing can be more distinctly marked and defined, than the positions of the parties here treated of, in respect to their *relations* to the "good olive-tree" or Church of God under the Christian dispensation. Undeniably, the apostle speaks of a *future* destiny of Israel as a nation, totally independent of whatever may be their individual relation to the Christian Church, during the present economy, in common with the Gentiles. The argument throughout this entire chapter is, to show that "God *hath not* cast away his people," i. e., Israel, "whom he foreknew" (ver. 2); that, "as concerning the gospel," they were *enemies* for the Gentiles' sakes: but that, "as touching the election, they were *beloved* for the fathers' sakes" (ver. 28). "For as the Gentiles in times past had not believed God, yet *now* have obtained mercy through their unbelief: even so have Israel now not believed, that through the mercy of the Gentiles, *they* also might [hereafter] obtain mercy" (vv. 30, 31). I repeat, might *hereafter* obtain mercy. This is evident from St. Paul's statement, that "blindness in part—mark, not total, but—"blindness *in part* has happened to Israel." . . . How long? Forever? Nay, verily, but "*until* the fulness of the Gentiles be come in" (v. 25). Hence his argument, that although "their minds were blinded," so that "even unto this day, when Moses is read, the *veil* is upon their hearts in the reading of the Old Testament; nevertheless," says the apostle, "when it shall turn to the Lord, the veil shall be taken away" (2 Cor. iii. 14–16). That notable prophecy of our Lord respecting Israel as a nation (Luke xxi. 24), points to *the same time* with that of St. Paul as above, for the removal of this "veil from their hearts." "And ye shall be led captive into all nations, and Jerusalem shall be trodden down of the Gentiles, *until* the times of the Gentiles be fulfilled." In both passages, reference is made to the *close* of "the times of the Gentiles." The fulness of the evidence, therefore, that Israel's inheritance of the promise regarding *the land* depended, not on their obedience to the law, but on "the righteousness of *faith*, must await the *completion* of that period. The security to them of the temporal behests of that covenant as Abraham's lineal multitudinous seed, by virtue of their interest in its spiritual engagements in their behalf, will *then* stand out in bold relief. The declaration of the Holy Ghost,—"For this is my covenant with them, when I shall take away their sins" (Rom. xi. 27), will then, and not "*until*" then, be fully verified unto them. We shall *then* understand why it was that "God hath concluded them all," i. e., the nation of Israel, "in unbelief," namely, "that he might have mercy upon *all*" (v. 32). In a word, *then* it shall be seen, that "the gifts and callings of God" in respect to the *national* Israelite "remnant according to the election of grace" (v. 5), "are without repentance" (v. 29); for *then* "there shall come out of Zion the Deliverer," that is Jesus, who, "as the minister of the circumcision for the truth of God to *confirm* the promises made unto their fathers," "*shall turn away* ungodliness from Jacob" (v. 26).

It results, therefore, that, to affirm that the Abrahamic covenant is *identical* with the old Sinai covenant of works—that it was a mere ecclesiastico-political constitution, with the outward badge of circumcision as a mark of national descent—that its promises in regard to literal Israel had respect only to temporal things—that it was abrogated by the obedience and death of Christ, and that therefore God will remember his covenant with them no more forever—and that, consequently, they are now entirely lost, only as they are merged, as individuals, into the *spiritual* Israel in common with the believing Gentiles,—we repeat, to affirm all this, is to involve the entire statements and reasonings of St. Paul, as set forth in reference to them as contradistinguished from the Gentiles, into a mass of the most unaccountable and unsurpassed absurdities and contradictions!

So far from this, the entire line of the apostle's argument demonstrates, *first*, that, consequent of the national apostasy of Israel under the law of works, they were *for a time set aside*, as a punishment for their sins, by a long-protracted captivity. "Their house was left unto them desolate."[1] And this to the end that, meanwhile, *second*, the door of grace and salvation, according to

[1] Matt. xxiii. 38.

the provisions of the Abrahamic compact, might be opened to the Gentiles of all nations. In other words, "that the blessing of Abraham," as the preordained "heir of the world," "might come on the Gentiles through Jesus Christ" as "the Heir of all things," "that we might receive the promise of the Spirit through faith" (Gal. iii. 14). The "fall" of literal Israel, and their consequent excision from the good olive-tree, as we have seen, was necessary, in order to *give scope* to the "taking out of (or from among) the Gentiles, a people *for Christ's name.*" (Acts xv. 14.) But that, so far from this resulting in the literal Israel's final ejectment from all interest in that covenant *as a nation*, the apostle shows, *third*, that when the above ingathering of the Gentiles during the period allotted to them shall have been accomplished, they (i. e., the nation of Israel) should be *re-engrafted* into their own olive-tree, by and through the direct agency of their Messianic Deliverer. We defy the utmost ingenuity of the most astute casuist, by any fair interpretation of the apostle's language, to escape these deductions.

In order, however, to place this matter in a succinct and definite form before the mind of the reader, we submit the following additional considerations, as decisive of the points at issue.

First. In regard to Gal. iv. 22-31, we observe, that it cannot be from the circumstance that the apostle sets forth the subject in an *allegory*, "that the one covenant is entirely confined to *temporal* things, and the other to *spiritual* things;" for this would apply to both covenants. And if it be from the mere circumstance that Jerusalem is spoken of as "Jerusalem which is above," let it be remembered, that this *same* Jerusalem is destined to "*come down* from God out of heaven" in the regenerated earth, where "the tabernacle of God is to be with men." (Rev. xxi. 2, 3.) Again,

Second. It is very plain from Gal. iii. 15-18, that what St. Paul means by the *new* covenant, or covenant of promise, is that which was first begun with Abraham, and reiterated and amplified with Isaac and Jacob, and is hence spoken of in Ephes. ii. 12 in the plural, "as covenants of promise." And here it is to be specially borne in mind that *the land of Canaan* is repeatedly promised to these three patriarchs personally and respectively, as well as to their seed. The promise to each of the three patriarchs is, —" to *thee* will I give it, *and* to thy seed." But, as we have already stated, while the *posterity* of Abraham have had a temporary possession of the land,[1] Abraham, Isaac, and Jacob have not, but were strangers in it. (See Gen. xiii. 15; xvii. 8; xxvi. 3; xxviii. 13; Exod. vi. 3, 4). There must, therefore, be a *special* fulfilment of the promise to *them*, as well as to their posterity. Nor, in regard to Abraham's seed, has the promise been fully accomplished, even in its literal sense. Their occupancy of it, after its conquest under Moses and Joshua, and its division amongst the twelve tribes, and subsequently under David, etc., was but an *earnest* of a more extensive and complete fulfilment to them of the original promise. This promise has *never* yet been verified to them. (See Acts vii. 4, 5; and Heb. xi. 13–16, 39). Nor will it be, *until* the time comes for the removal of the "veil from the heart" of "the remnant" seed "according to the election of grace." *Then*, in virtue of the faithfulness of Abraham's "seed," which is primarily CHRIST (Gal. iii. 16); when He as their "Deliverer" shall appear to "turn away ungodliness from Jacob," all "the children of promise," or the multitudinous seed, shall be *restored* to their long alienated inheritance, the land which, in Isaiah viii. 8, is especially called "IMMANUEL'S LAND;" and under such circumstances, if the context be regarded, as to show that a "material locality is designed." Finally,

Third. In reference to the *nature* and *design* of the Abrahamic covenant, the following Scriptural view of it will, we think, place both beyond the reach of further cavil. Let it be observed, then,

1. That the *Old* covenant, or law of works, which the apostle tells us was to be "done away in Christ," is totally separate and distinct from the Abrahamic, will appear from the following comparison of the two:

Abraham was called from *Ur of the Chaldees*.	Moses was born and reared in *Egypt*.
The covenant transaction with Abraham took place in *Canaan*.	That with Moses on the Mount Sinai, in *Arabia*.
The covenant with Abraham was imprinted *in the flesh*.	That with Moses was engraven on *two tables of stone*.
The covenant with Abraham was instituted, A. M. 2083.	That with Moses, 430 years *after*, A. M. 2513.
Finally, the covenant with Abraham was *founded on faith*.	That with Moses was *founded on works*.

This last-named fact leads to a second remark, viz.:

[1] See page 81.

2. That the Abrahamic covenant is *an absolutely spiritual compact.* The design of this covenant was, the preservation of the knowledge and worship of the One True God and of religion in the world. At the time of its institution, Polytheism, or the worship of false deities, had almost totally eradicated the last vestige of a knowledge of the true God and his worship in the earth. "Even Terah, the father of Abraham, and the father of Nachor, who dwelt on the other side of the flood in old time, *served other gods.*"[1] Hence the necessity for the calling out from the idolatrous mass, of *an elect nation* to serve God. This was effected by the institution of the covenant under consideration. And that this covenant, as we have said, was an absolutely spiritual compact, will appear,

(1.) From the *personal character* of the individual with whom that covenant was made. He was not a worldly and ambitious prince, but a pious patriarch. God had "redeemed"[2] him from the idolatry of his father's house, ere he left "Ur of the Chaldees." When, therefore, he received the divine mandate to repair to Canaan, we read of him that he "believed God" concerning all that He had said, and that that faith "was *counted* unto him for righteousness."[3] See now, in further evidence of this,

(2.) The solemnity which marked the *inauguration* of this covenant with Abraham, together with the Divine pledge therein given. The descended Deity appears to Abraham, and says: "I am thy shield, and thy exceeding great reward."[4] And again: "I am the Almighty God: walk before me, and be thou perfect: and I will make my covenant between me and thee, and will multiply thee exceedingly. Thy name shall be Abraham, for a father of many nations have I made thee. Kings shall come out of thee." And, "I will be a God unto thee."[5]

But, we remark in this connection, what is very important to bear in mind, that this covenant included both *Sarah* and the *lineal* descendants of Abraham as well as himself. "Thou shalt call thy wife *Sarah,*" saith God to Abraham, "and I will bless her and give thee *a son* of her: she shall be a mother of nations: kings of people shall be of her;"[6] and, "I will establish my covenant between me and thee, and thy seed after thee, in their generations, for an everlasting covenant—and I will be their God."[7]

---

[1] Josh. xxiv. 2. [2] Isa. xxix. 22. [3] Compare Gen. xli. 4 with Rom. iv. 4, 5.
[4] Gen. xv. 1. [5] See Gen. xvii. 1–6 and verse 7. [6] Gen. xvii. 15, 16. [7] Ib. ver. 7, 8.

Nor these only. For Jehovah adds, "And in thee and in thy seed shall all the families and nations of the earth be blessed." (Compare Gen. xii. 3 with xxii. 18.) To this we add,

(3.) That *circumcision*, which was the outward badge or seal of this covenant, like *baptism*, the external seal of the gospel covenant, was a spiritual ordinance. That is, it denoted the necessity of the same internal *spiritual* change on the part of its recipient, as a security to him of the benefits of the covenant, as that denoted by the rite of Christian baptism. Is it declared of the latter, "He that believeth and is baptized shall be saved?"[1] Of the former it is said, "Abraham received the sign of circumcision, a *seal* of the righteousness of faith."[2] Hence,

(4.) The *condition* of the blessings conferred by the Abrahamic covenant was *true religion*, as well as external obedience. The apostle, speaking of "the promise that Abraham should be the heir of the world," says that "it was not to him or to his seed, through the law, but through the righteousness of *faith*."[3] But this constitutes the distinguishing feature of Christianity, as contradistinguished from the law of works. Accordingly, to show the exact correspondence of the nature of both, the apostle says: "And the scripture, foreseeing that God would justify the heathen through faith, preached before *the gospel* to Abraham."[4] Therefore it is that, while "Jesus Christ" (the author of the gospel, and the surety and pledge for the execution of the stipulations in the covenant in behalf of all the parties interested) "is the minister of the circumcision for the truth of God"—not, mark, to destroy, annul, and abrogate, but—"to *confirm* the promises made unto the fathers,"[5] in reference to their *lineal* multitudinous "seed," He secures salvation, also, to all the *Gentile* nations of the earth. The apostle, therefore, arguing from the spiritual nature of the Abrahamic compact, and the spiritual condition on which is suspended an interest in its behests, says: "Now this I say, that the covenant (Abrahamic) which was confirmed before of God in Christ, the law (or covenant Mosaic), which was four hundred and thirty years after, *cannot disannul*, that it should make the promise (i. e., the covenant Abrahamic) of none effect."[6]

It hence follows, that the Abrahamic covenant was not superseded, but *confirmed*, by the introduction of Christianity. Noth-

---

[1] Mark xvi. 16. [2] Rom. iv. 11. [3] Ib. iv. 13. [4] Gal. iii. 8.
[5] Rom. xv. 8. [6] Gal. iii. 17.

ing can be more evident than the fact of its perpetuation under the two dispensations, Jewish and Christian.

This involves another fact—that of the *twofold relation of the parties* embraced in the covenant compact, to St. Paul's "good olive-tree." This symbol, denotive of the Church-state, as more formally organized at the institution of the covenant with Abraham, first encircled within its spiritual pale the believing patriarch and his lineal seed. But, as a visible body on earth, in order to carry out its graciously benevolent designs, it became necessary not only to form this covenant relation with one who had retained the knowledge and worship of the true God, but also to select *a new territory* as the theatre of its development. Hence the connection of that covenant

3. With *temporal things*. No sooner, therefore, than the believing patriarch, obedient to God's command while yet in "Ur of the Chaldees," had set his foot on the land which "God had showed him,"[1] having given him reiterated assurances of the Divine favor and protection, He appeared to him on the plain of Mamre, and said:

"*Unto thy seed will I give this land,*"[2] even "all which thou seest, from the river of Egypt, unto the great river, the river Euphrates.[3] To thee will I give it, and to thy seed forever, for an everlasting possession."[4]

Canaan, at this time, was occupied by those *idolatrous* nations, the Kenites, and the Kenizzites, and the Kadmonites, and the Hittites, and the Perizzites, and the Rephaims, and the Amorites, and the Canaanites,[5] etc., all of whose religious systems were so many *rivals* to that of Him who has declared, "I will not give mine honor to another, nor my praise to graven images."[6] As these nations occupied this "goodly land"[7] only as invaders, as a matter of right they could not retain it. Consequently, the bequeathment of it to others, by its only lawful Proprietary—for it is described as "a land which the Lord God *careth for:* that the eyes of the Lord God are always upon it, from the beginning of the year even unto the end of the year"[8]—violated no principle either of equity or of justice toward them.

But Israel, as we have seen, seeking to retain possession of it under the Sinai covenant of works, and *failing* to comply with its

---

[1] Gen. xii. 1.   [2] Ib. xii. 5–7.   [3] Ib. xiii. 15.   [4] Gen. xvii. 8.   [5] Ib. xv. 19–21.
[6] Isa. xlii. 8; xlviii. 11.   [7] Deut. viii. 7–9; 2 Kings xviii. 32.   [8] Ib. xi. 12.

demands of perfect obedience, were driven into captivity; while, on the one hand, the land has remained in the hands of those who have "spoiled them;"[1] and, on the other, the door of the covenant, during the period of their excision from the "good olive-tree" under the Christian dispensation, is thrown open for the engrafting, in their place, of the Gentile scions, as those who are to constitute, in a peculiar sense, "*a people for his name.*" We repeat: on account of the spiritual whoredom of "Israel," and of her more "treacherous sister, Judah," God had issued against both "*a bill of divorce.*"[2] And, persisting in their united refusal to "return from their back-slidings"—to "circumcise themselves before the Lord," by "taking away the foreskins of their *hearts*," and to "wash their *hearts* from wickedness, that they might be saved;"[3]—therefore saith their covenant God by the mouth of Isaiah, "ye shall leave your name for a curse among my chosen: for the Lord God shall slay thee, and call his servants by *another name.*"[4]

Now, this was fully verified when, Israel having been "cut off" from "the good olive-tree," on account of their continuance in "unbelief," and the Gentiles by faith in Christ were graffed into their place, "the disciples were first called *Christians* at Antioch."[5] Thus, in accordance with that part of the covenant pledge of God with Abraham, "In thee, and in thy seed, shall all the nations, families, and kindreds of the earth be blessed," under the Christian economy, "*in every nation*, he that feareth God and worketh righteousness, is accepted of Him."[6] Aye, "accepted of Him:" and that, in a way and manner essentially different from the relation to him of the literal Israel. For, while Jesus the Messiah, as "the minister of the circumcision for the truth of God," was the divinely appointed surety and pledge to "confirm the promises" made to them concerning the restoration of the land; God the Father, as the author and rectoral Head of that covenant, united *Himself* to Israel as her husband. "The word of the Lord came to Jeremiah, saying, Go and cry in the ears of Jerusalem, saying, Thus saith the Lord; I remember thee, the kindness of thy youth, the love of thine espousals, when thou wentest after me in the wilderness, in a land that was not sown."[7] For, saith he, "I am married unto you."[8]

---

[1] Isa. xlii. 22; Ezek. xxxix. 10. [2] Jer. iii. 6–11. [3] Jer. iii. 12; and iv. 4, 14.
[4] Isa. lxvi. 15. [5] Acts xi. 26. [6] Acts x. 35. [7] Jer. ii. 2. [8] Ib. iii. 14.

But, the "King's Son" must have his bride also. And, as the literal Israel, to whom the invitation to the marriage feast was first given, "all with one consent began to make excuse" and finally refused to come,[1] "lo," He "turned to the Gentiles," "*to take out of* (or from among) *them*" that "holy nation and royal priesthood, and peculiar people,"[2] who should constitute His bride—"THE BRIDE, the Lamb's wife."[3]

What, then, is "the bill of divorcement" against Israel never to be *revoked?* Is her ejectment from the promised inheritance of the land as its rightful heir, final? Will God remember His covenant engagements with Abraham and his lineal multitudinous seed no more forever? Let the old prophets answer. In regard, first, to the bill of divorcement against ISRAEL, it is written, "Turn, O backsliding children, saith the Lord, for I *am* married unto you; and I will take you, one of a city, and two of a family, and I will bring you to Zion." "And I will betroth thee unto me *forever:* yea, I will betroth thee in righteousness, and in judgment, and in loving kindness, and in mercies. I will even betroth thee unto me *in faithfulness:* and thou shalt know the Lord."[4]

Second. Israel is still in captivity. Judah is still dispersed among all nations. The whole land still remains desolate. "Yet, saith the Lord, *will I not* make a full end."[5] And so, when "the fulness of the Gentiles shall be come in," and their Messiah, "THE DELIVERER, shall come to Zion to turn away ungodliness from Jacob," by removing "the veil" of unbelief which yet remains over "their hearts," the prophet Isaiah assures us of the *universality* of their promised restoration. "He shall gather together the dispersed of Judah from the four corners of the earth: and He shall gather together the outcasts of Israel."[6] And, finally,

Third. The prophet Moses, having alluded to the circumstances of Israel's sin and guilt in "despising God's judgments and abhorring his statutes," adds these remarkable words: "*Yet for all that,* when they be in the land of their enemies, I will not cast them away, neither will I abhor them, to destroy them utterly, and to break my covenant with them: for I am the Lord their God. But I will for their sakes *remember* the covenant of their ancestors, whom I brought forth out of the land of Egypt, that I might be their God: I am the Lord. I will remember my covenant with

---

[1] Luke xiv. 18.   [2] Titus ii. 14.   [3] John iii. 29 ; Rev. xxi. 9.
[4] Jer. iii. 14 ; Hosea iii. 19, 20.   [5] Jer. iv. 27.   [6] Isa. xi. 12.

Jacob, and also my covenant with *Isaac*, and also my covenant with *Abraham* will I remember; and I will remember THE LAND."

Then, further, when the ingathering of that "consecrated host of God's elect" from among the Gentiles (during the period of Israel's continued dispersion and the treading down of the holy city), who are to constitute "*the bride* of the Lamb," shall have been consummated, the prophet Isaiah, having an eye to the predicted *conversion* of all nations which is to immediately follow the *close* of "the times of the Gentiles," and the accomplishment of which is made to depend upon Judah's and Israel's restoration to and national conversion in their own land, says: "The Lord God, which gathereth the outcasts of Israel, saith, Yet will I gather *others unto Him* besides those—i. e., the Jews—that are gathered unto him."[2] Now, that these can be none other than the Gentile nations which, having escaped those terrific "judgments" that shall fall upon the last great anti-christian confederacy in their invasion of Jerusalem as described by Zechariah, chap. xiv. 1–3, "shall learn righteousness," may be seen from the following: "Behold, I will lift up my hand to the *Gentiles*, and set my standard to the people."[3] "Behold, these shall come from far; and lo, these from the north and from the west; and these from the land of Sinim."[4] "And the *Gentiles* shall come to *thy* light, and kings to the brightness of *thy* rising."[5] "Then *thou* shalt see, and flow together, and *thy* heart shall fear, and be enlarged: because the abundance of the sea shall be converted unto *thee;* the forces of the Gentiles shall come unto *thee*."[6]

But it is of special importance to understand the *order* of the Divine procedure in the accomplishment of these events, and also the *agencies* through whom, and the *means* by which they are to be brought about. On these subjects, the prophets are very explicit.

I. *Of the Jewish nation.* The priority of the restoration of the house of *Judah* to that of Israel, may be gathered from the circumstances and instrumentalities connected with each. For instance: the exhaustion of the Turkish power, the only political impediment to the restoration of the house of Judah to Palestine, is set forth under the symbol of the "drying up of the mystical Euphrates."[1] This effected, and their conversion follows, as describ-

---

[1] Lev. xxvi. 44, 45 and v. 42. [2] See Gen. xlix. 10; Isa. lvi. 8; John x. 16; xi. 52; Eph. i. 10; ii. 14-16. [3] Isa. xlix. 22. [4] Ib. ver. 12. [5] Ib. lx. 3. [6] Ib. ver. 5. [7] Rev. xvi. 12-14. That "*the great river Euphrates*," mentioned Rev. ix. 14, as interpreted to signify the

ed by Zechariah,—"AND HIS (CHRIST'S) *feet* shall stand in that day upon the mount of Olives which is before Jerusalem."[1] The "day" here spoken of, is the same with the time when the *personally manifested Christ* "shall fight against" the anti-Christian invaders of the holy city, as described in this chapter. For, says the prophet, "The Lord my God shall come, *and all His* [resurrected and glorified] *saints with Him.*"[2] It is *then* shall be verified the promise, "And I will pour upon the house of Judah and the inhabitants of Jerusalem, the spirit of grace and of supplications; and they shall *look upon me whom they have pierced*, and they shall mourn for him, as one mourneth for his only son, and shall be in bitterness for him, as one who is in bitterness for his firstborn."[3] And thus, after the example and pattern of the conversion of St. Paul, as "one born out of due time," his brethren are *as* "*a nation* born at once."[4]

Then further. "The house of Judah and inhabitants of Jerusalem" having thus repented of their sins and received their Messiah, this work of the conversion of the nations *miraculously* commenced by Christ PERSONALLY, will be continued in exact analogy to the first propagation of the gospel among the Gentile

---

Mahometan or Turkish power, (the same with the "little horn" of Daniel's second vision, chap. viii.,) is not founded in fancy, we here quote the opinions of several of the most distinguished expositors of prophecy for the last two centuries. Brightman, a Fellow in Queen's College in Cambridge, in Elizabeth's time, speaking of this subject in 1636, says, "It is not to be doubted but that these angels (referring to the four angels bound on the banks of this great river, or the four *Sultanies* of Bagdad, Damascus, Aleppo, and Iconium) be the Turks; and to this opinion do most interpreters consent." So also the profoundly learned Joseph Mede, who, A. D. 1650, "interprets the four angels to signify so many Sultanies or *kingdoms*, into which the Turks were divided;" and he quotes them from Richerius to be, "the first Asia Minor, the second Aleppo, the third Damascus, and the fourth Antioch." And Sir Isaac Newton, in his observations on the Apocalypse, adopts and applies this view. Tillinghast also says,—"By the general consent of expositors, it hath reference to the Turkish power." Mr. Durham, in 1660, gives an explanation harmonizing, on the whole, with the preceding extracts: so does Mr. Petto in 1693; and Fleming, in his work on the Apocalypse in 1700.

So, the *fate* of this power, and the *time* of its destruction, as described Rev. xvi. 12-14. Daniel says it "*shall be broken without hand.*" (Chap. viii. 25.) St. John, that it shall be "*dried up.*" And this, to the end "THAT THE WAY OF THE KINGS OF THE EAST MIGHT BE PREPARED." On this passage, says Brightman, "that people is here signified by these kings, for whose sake alone the Scriptures declare that the waters were dried up of old; viz.: THE JEWS." So of the distinguished Joseph Mede. "The kings of the East," says he, "are the Jews." The same of Tillinghast. He says, "By the kings of the East we are to understand THE JEWS, who, upon the pouring out of this vial, (the sixth,) shall return to their own land, and be converted unto Christ; and I take it," he adds, "that the pouring out of this vial prepareth the way for both;" i. e., the destruction of the Turkish power or Mahometan little horn of Daniel's he-goat, and the restoration to Palestine, and conversion of God's covenant people, THE JEWS. At the same time, of course, falls the Mahometan power as the scourge of the apostate Eastern or Greek Church.

[1] Zech. xiv. 4.   [2] Ib. ver. 5.   [3] Ib. xii. 10.   [4] Isa. lxvi. 8.

nations, until the whole earth is subdued to His authority. The next in order, therefore, comes,

II. Those of *the Gentile nations of Christendom*. Of these the prophet thus speaks, chap. lvi. 8: "The Lord God, which gathereth the outcasts of Israel," (used in this place to denote the *house of Judah*,) "saith, Yet will I gather *others* to him, besides those that are gathered to him." That is, those "Gentiles that shall come to *his* light, and kings to the brightness of *his* rising." (Isa. lx. 3.) Who these Gentiles are, may be gathered from what the prophet Zechariah says of those that are "*left of the nations* which came against Jerusalem" at the time of its last invasion, as described, chap. xiv. verses 1, 2, and 16, namely, the last anti-Christian confederacy, against whom the Lord Jesus "fights as in the day of battle," verse 3. For, it is in the midst of "the judgments" that will be inflicted upon them, that prophecy declares "the people will learn righteousness."[1] Now, that these unconverted Gentile nations lay within the bounds of Christendom, appears from the following, Isa. lxvi. 18: "It shall come, that I will gather *all nations*, and they shall come, and see my glory." That is, when the Lord shall "arise and shine upon Judah, and when His glory shall be risen upon him." (Verse 1.) And this "glory" shall consist of a *miraculous* display of the Divine Power in their behalf; for, says the prophet, "And I will set my sign among them."[2] And again: "Behold, I will lift up my hand to the Gentiles, and set my standard to the people."[3] Thus their conversion. This done, and these newly-converted Gentiles of Christendom shall be sent,

III. *To the idolatrous Heathen.* For of those it is also predicted that the time will come when *they* "shall cast their idols of silver, and their idols of gold, which they made each one for himself to worship, to the moles and to the bats."[4] And this will be, "when God arises to shake terribly the earth,"[5] the very time this, of which we now speak. For, says the prophet, they shall be sent "unto the nations, to Tarshish, Pul, and Lud, that draw the bow; to Tubal and Javan, and to the isles afar off, that *have not heard* my fame, *neither have seen* my glory: and they," i. e., the converted Gentiles of Christendom, "shall declare my glory among the Gentiles" of *Heathendom*. Aye, like the Apocalyptic "angel

---

[1] Isa. xxvi. 9. [2] Ib. lxvi. 19, 21. [3] Ib. xlix. 22, and verse 12.
[4] Ib. ii. 18-22. [5] Ib. lxvi. 19, 21.

flying through mid-heaven, having the everlasting gospel to preach to all nations, and kindreds, and tongues, and people,"[1] they shall neither tire nor faint, until the universal world of mankind shall be converted to the Lord Jesus Christ. Then shall be verified the promise, "the heathen shall be given to Him for His inheritance, and the uttermost parts of the earth for His possession."[2] And now, in reference to,

IV. *The House of Israel*, or *the Ten Lost Tribes*. It would be irrelevant to the subject in hand to enter into the question of the whereabouts of the lost Ten Tribes of Israel. Speculation here is of little worth. Suffice it to say, that however lost to the eye of man, they are known to God. Of this we may be assured, that they are still inhabiting those remote regions in *Assyria*, whither *all* the Ten Tribes were carried captive by Ezarhaddan, or Shalmanezer, in A. M. 3307.[3] What principally concerns us now, is the fact that prophecy makes their conversion, unlike that of the house of Judah, to *precede* their restoration to Palestine. He that hath said, "Fear not thou, O Jacob my servant, and be not dismayed, O Israel: for, behold, I will save thee from afar off, and thy seed from the land of their captivity, and Jacob shall return and be at rest,"[4] etc., also declares, "Therefore they shall come *and sing* in the heights of Zion,"[5] etc., " when God *has* executed judgments upon all those that despised them round about."[6] Yes: it is "when they are *at hand to come*,"[7] that is, are ready to return to their own land, that "the Lord *Himself* shall go before them." Accordingly, their covenant-God having declared of Israel, "I have loved thee with an everlasting love; therefore with loving kindness have I drawn thee:"[8] by the secret workings of the Holy Spirit's influences, as in the case of "the house of Judah," etc., their souls are stirred up within them to receive and to believe in their MESSIAH, and to repent of their sins, as preparatory to their return "with weeping and with supplications,"[9] etc. Hence, when this event transpires, the words, "*I have* blotted out as a thick cloud thy transgressions, and as a cloud thy sins,"[10] etc., show that their conversion has taken place *prior to* their return.

In further confirmation of the above, I now add, that what is said of them when they shall have been restored to their own

[1] Rev. xiv. 6. [2] Ps. i. 8. [3] Compare 2 Kings xv. 29 and xvi. 9 with 2 Kings xvii. 20.
[4] Jer. xlvi. 27, 28. [5] Jer. xxxi. 1-14. [6] Ezek. xxviii. 24-26.
[7] Is. xxxvi. 1-6, and 7-15. [8] Jer. xxxi. 3. [9] Ib. ver. 9. [10] Isa. xliv. 1, 2.

land, is decisive of this point. Read the following prophecy, "*And in that day*"—that is, the day of their national conversion as above—"the Lord shall set His hand again *the second time*"—that of Judah having been the first—"to recover the remnant of His people which shall be left from Assyria, and from Egypt, and from Pathros, and from Cush, and from Elam, and from Shinar, and from the islands of the sea," etc. "And there shall be an highway for the remnant of His people which shall be left of Assyria, like as it was to Israel in the day that he came up out of the land of Egypt." And so, as they advance along the track of their "highway," the prophet tells us that "the Lord with His mighty wind shall shake His hand over the river," (i. e. the Nile,) "and shall smite it in the seven streams thereof, and make men go over *dry shod*." The meaning here is, that as their course will lay across "the tongue" (or bay, margin) " of the Egyptian sea," it will, like that of the Red sea some 3,500 years before, be divided at the approaching footsteps of the returning Ten Tribes; and thus, as in the instance of their former deliverance out of Egypt, furnish them with a *miraculous* passage to the opposite shore. And, this point attained, the prophet informs us that the newly-converted Gentiles described above, "shall bring" all these Israelitish "brethren" of the Jews "*for an offering unto the Lord* out of all nations, upon horses, and in chariots, and in litters, and upon mules, and upon swift beasts, to my holy mountain, Jerusalem, saith the Lord, as the children of Israel bring a clean vessel in the house of the Lord. And I will also take them for *priests* and for *Levites*, saith the Lord."[1] But,

V. On this subject of the universal conversion of the world of mankind to Christ, there is in Isaiah, chap. xix., a prophecy which relates especially to ancient *Egypt* and *Assyria*, which must not be passed over. In the first seventeen verses, the prophet, having denounced a series of the most terrible judgments against Egypt, follows them up by a prediction of *final* mercy to her, and also to Assyria, and of their connection with restored Judah and Israel in Palestine. Though the Lord declares that He would "*smite Egypt*" for her past persecution of His chosen people Israel, by giving her up for a time into the hands of the last Antichrist, etc., yet it would be only that He might *heal it ;* for, "in that day, they shall even turn to the Lord, and He shall be entreated of

---

[1] Isa. xi. 11-16, and Zech. x. 10, 11.   [2] Isa. xi. 11-16

them, and *heal them.* In that day, there shall be an altar to the Lord in the midst of the land of Egypt, and a pillar at the border thereof to the Lord. And it shall be for a sign, and for a witness unto the Lord of Hosts in the land of Egypt: for they shall cry unto the Lord, because of their oppressors;" that is, Antichrist and his confederate hosts who have invaded their land. And then the prophet adds, " And He shall send them a SAVIOUR and a GREAT ONE, *and He shall deliver them.* And the Lord shall be known in Egypt, and the Egyptians *shall know the Lord* in that day, and shall do sacrifice and oblation: yea, they shall vow a vow unto the Lord, and shall perform it. . . . In that day shall five cities in the land of Egypt speak the language of Canaan, and swear by the Lord of Hosts," etc. And, finally: " In that day shall there be a highway out of Egypt to *Assyria,* and the Assyrian shall come into Egypt, and the Egyptian into Assyria, and the Egyptians shall serve *with* the Assyrians. In that day shall ISRAEL be third with *Egypt* and with *Assyria,* even A BLESSING in the midst of the land: whom the Lord shall bless, saying, Blessed be Egypt my people, and Assyria the work of my hands, and Israel mine inheritance." (Verses 18–25.) [1]

And moreover, we are assured that, when the time for the accomplishment of this mighty moral revolution in the world shall have come, contrary to the popular expectation, "THE LORD," by those combined human and supernatural or miraculous agencies which He will employ to that end, " will *cut short* His work in righteousness; for a *short work* will the Lord make in the earth." [2]

And now, see the *result* of this work. First. The "two sticks," that is, Judah and Ephraim, or the Ten Tribes of Israel, having been restored to that land from which they had been separated during the prolonged period (as will be shown in the sequel) of the mystical "seven times," or 2,520 years of chastisement for their sins, as predicted by Moses, (Numb. xxvi. 18, 21, 24, 28,)—"the times of the Gentiles" mentioned Luke xxi. 24, and Rom. xi. 25—and again *united* in that land, and in their converted state, shall become " *one stick* in the hand of the Lord upon the mountains of Israel." [3] Nor this only. For, the nations of the Gentiles, both nominally Christian and Heathen, together with Egypt and Assyria, shall be converted, and thus " *flow unto*

---

[1] Consult also Isa. xi. 10; xlii. 1–17; liv. 1–17; lv., lxi., lxvi.; Jer. xvi. 16–21; Mic. iv. 1–5; Zech. viii. 20–23, and chap. x.   [2] Rom. ix. 28; Matt. xxiv. 22.   [3] Ezek. xxxvii. 15–17.

them."[1] And thus will be verified God's covenant faithfulness, first, to the *lineal* multitudinous seed of Abraham, and second, the promised blessing, through them, to the nations, kindreds, and tongues of *the Gentiles.*

In conclusion, then, we submit that we have demonstrated the utter fallacy of the theory of *Millerism* at the head of this chapter, which alleges the fulfilment of *all* the prophecies that set forth the restoration, union, and conversion of Judah and Israel, or the Ten Tribes, to and in the Holy Land, *by the return of the Jews from the Babylonish captivity.* Not to go into a recapitulation of the ground over which we have passed, suffice it to say, that we have carefully and candidly weighed, and, we hold, successfully *refuted* every argument and fact, as based either on Scripture or history, brought against the predicted *future* restoration, union, and conversion of the literal seed of Abraham to Palestine; and have shown that, when that event does take place, their national conversion is dependent upon, and can only be effected by, THE PERSONAL MANIFESTATION to them of the Lord Jesus Christ; the ingathering of the Gentiles to them; and the establishment of Christ's kingdom and reign over them as their Messiah.

I will only add, by the way, that as all expositors, except the Millerites, admit that the Jewish nation is to remain in captivity, and Jerusalem is to be trodden down of the Gentiles, "*until* the times of the Gentiles be fulfilled" (Luke xxi. 24; Rom. xi. 25); it will follow, unless that period can be shown to be *identical* with the millennial era and to *end* with it, that "THE DELIVERER'S coming to Zion to turn away ungodliness from Jacob," *must be* PRE *not* POST-millennial.

[1] Isa. lx. 5.

CHAPTER II.

SECOND THEORY: AS ADVOCATED BY GROTIUS, PRIDEAUX, VINT, PROF. GEO. BUSH, ETC.

THIS THEORY ALLEGES, THAT THE PROPHECIES RELATING TO THE SECOND COMING OF CHRIST AND THE ERECTION OF HIS MILLENNIAL KINGDOM, WERE FULLY VERIFIED BY THE OVERTHROW OF PAGANISM AND THE ESTABLISHMENT OF CHRISTIANITY IN THE ROMAN EMPIRE, UNDER CONSTANTINE THE GREAT, IN A. D. 323.

THE most modern and popular advocate of this theory is the late Professor George Bush. He borrowed it from the writings of Grotius, Prideaux, Vint, etc. It is founded upon their exegesis of Rev. xx. 1-7.

The nature and character of the Millennial state of the Church, according to these writers, is made to consist "in the cessation of the pagan persecutions, and the extirpation of idolatry and polytheism" in the Roman empire *under Constantine the Great;* is to continue until "the appearance of the Antichrist" predicted by St. Paul, 2 Thess. ii. 3-12, whose "reign is to last three and a half *literal* years; and is *shortly to precede* the second coming of our blessed Lord to judgment," etc.

The interval between these two extreme points, i. e., "the Millennium, or the *thousand years* mentioned by St. John," is regarded by them as the period "during which Satan was bound and the saints reigned with Christ" in a state of "general peace and prosperity to the Christian Church," etc.; but whether this interval of blessedness has *already* expired, or is *still* running on, they are not agreed.

In what we have to offer on the subject of this theory, we shall confine ourself, for the most part, to a review of Prof. Bush's "Treatise on the Millennium;" which will involve an examination of the *symbolical imagery* employed by the Holy Spirit in the passage under consideration, as interpreted and applied by him in its defence.

Speaking of "the doctrine of the Millennium," as founded on Rev. xx. 1-7, this writer affirms,

First. That it "is the *only express passage* in the Scriptures, in which mention is made of a period of a *thousand years*, in connection with the prospective lot of the Church,"[1] and,

Second. That its *only key* of interpretation is made to consist of "what is to be understood by the dragon, or the Satan (the adversary) who is to be bound; what by his binding; and what by the bottomless pit in which he is represented as being shut up."[2]

1. In reference to the "DRAGON" (verse 2), he enters upon a long, labored, and learned disquisition, to prove, *first*, that, according to the symbolic language of the Apocalypse, he denotes "a standing symbol of Paganism, including in that term the twofold idea of despotic government and false religion"[3]—or in other words, that he is "*Paganism personified;*"[4] and *second*, "the *identity* of the dragon which is bound [verses 1, 2], with the dragon which was cast out of heaven."[5] [Chap. xii. 3–8.]

The Professor then argues, that "*if* this be the true meaning of the dragon, his being seized, bound, and incarcerated for a thousand years, must necessarily signify some *powerful restraint* laid upon this baleful system of error,"—i. e., Paganism—"by which its prevalence, through the above-mentioned period, is vastly weakened, though not utterly destroyed."[6]

And he continues, "*if* this be the true meaning of the binding of the dragon, then, his being 'cast into the bottomless pit,' etc., if we mistake not, is intended by the spirit of prophecy to signify *the unknown world*, comprising the immense, unexplored, undefined, boundless regions which stretched beyond the limits of the Roman empire, particularly to the north and east;"—i. e., the territory which embraced the more obdurate Pagan subjects of Constantine's bitter and implacable rival, Licinius, etc., in the *eastern* branch of the empire—"where," says he, "Satan had long established his throne, where he ruled with undivided sway, and where idolatry, in its most frightful and horrid forms, has ever held a disastrous dominion."[7]

But this is not all. During this alleged *absence* of the "dragon," thus "cast down," "bound," "shut up," and "sealed" in "the bottomless pit" or abyss; that is, during this season "of general peace and prosperity of the Christian Church" for a thousand years; and "commencing about the time of the suppression of Paganism," or binding of Satan, or the dragon; he affirms was "the *rise of the beast*" of Rev. xiii. 1, "having seven heads and ten horns, and upon his horns ten crowns," etc. But for what

---

[1] Treatise on the Millennium, pref. p. x.   [2] Ib. pref. p. x.   [3] Ib. p. 93.
[4] See p. 146.   [5] Ib. p. 142.   [6] Ib. p. 146.   [7] Ib. p. 159.

purpose? Let the learned author answer. The dragon, he says, "conscious of his being forced to withdraw in his own proper person, ... resolves on thrusting upon the vacated stage another agent, who should act as his *Vicegerent*, and into whom he determines to *transfuse* the full measure of his own Satanic spirit and genius. This was no other," adds he, "than the seven-headed and ten-horned beast that arose out of the *sea!*" etc.

The Millennial Church, then, we conclude, must have been vastly benefited by this important *exchange* of the "dragon" for the "beast." Indeed, the Professor himself seems to have been considerably startled at this idea, and therefore says, "This may strike the reader as a very revolting conclusion; but this conclusion," he adds, "we know not how to avoid, nor can we see how any one can avoid it, who *admits* the premises on which it rests."[1]

Now to all this we readily reply, neither do we. Indeed, who does not know that the right interpretation of any subject depends upon a correct understanding of the *premises* on which it rests? But in this, we must insist, lay all the difficulty in the Professor's ingeniously wrought theory. For, to say nothing of his violation of the laws of interpretation of the symbolic imagery of prophecy, by an indiscriminate jumbling together of the dragon with the beast, whether with *one* head or *seven*, or whether with horns and crowns, or *no* horns or crowns at all, the Professor, as the expositor of the Apocalypse, furnished himself with the amazing facility which marks his application of them *en masse*, as denotive of "the *extirpation* of idolatry and Paganism" from the Roman empire; and to confine the golden period of peace and prosperity of the Millennial Church *under the reign* of Constantine, and that of his successors, to the space of what he calls one thousand years!

Now, the readiest mode of exposing the *fallacy* of all this, will be to place before the eye the several descriptions given of these objects, thus:

The first, Rev. xii. 3, etc.	The second, Rev. xiii. 1.
"And there appeared another wonder in *heaven:* and behold, *a great red dragon*, having seven heads and ten horns, and seven crowns upon his *heads*."	"And I stood upon the sand of the *sea*, and saw a *beast* rise up out of the sea, having seven heads and ten horns, and upon his horns ten crowns, and upon his heads *the name of blasphemy*."

[1] Treatise on the Millennium, p. 147.

The third, Rev. xx. 1–3.

"And I saw an angel come down from heaven, having the key of the bottomless pit, and a great chain in his hand. And he laid hold on the dragon, that old serpent, which is *the devil and Satan*, and bound him a thousand years, and cast him into the bottomless pit, and shut him up, and set a seal upon him, *that he should deceive the nations no more*, till the thousand years should be fulfilled: and *after* that he must be loosed for a little season," etc.

Now, the plainest-minded Christian cannot but perceive at a glance *the marked distinction* between these various objects revealed to the Apostle John. Take, for example, the *first* and *second*. While the points of *resemblance* consist only in this, that both have seven heads and ten horns, yet they differ in the following particulars:

1. In *name*. The one is called a "*dragon;*" the other a "*beast.*"

2. In *origin*. The "dragon" is "cast out of *heaven;*" the "beast" rises "up out of the *sea*," and receives his power *from* the dragon; for, although the dragon is represented as "*having seven heads and ten horns,*" yet, as we shall see, the latter is only his *subordinate agent* in the execution of his purposes. Hence,

3. The *mutation* to which the "beast from the sea" is subjected. First, he appears with "seven crowns upon his *heads;*" which crowns are subsequently transferred to his *ten horns*, and upon his heads is written "*the name of blasphemy.*"

4. That the dragon and the beast *are not* identical, will appear from the following: In the first place it is to be observed, that so far from the dragon being a *symbol* of "paganism personified," the Holy Spirit says that he is "that old serpent called the *Devil* and *Satan*." On the other hand we read that "the dragon gave his power, and seat, and great authority *to the beast.*" (Rev. xiii. 2.) Again: the "beast," with his seven crowned heads, as the *agent* of the "dragon," *is* symbolical of the Pagan "despotic government," under which form, having accomplished his mission and received his fate, the draconic Devil, or Satan, *changes his tactics*, by transferring the crowns from the seven heads to the *ten horns* of the beast, while on his seven heads are inscribed the name of blasphemy, under which *new form* he becomes the symbol of "*false religion*," or Papal anti-Christianism, to which power it was given to "make war with the saints, and to overcome

them;"[1] and that power was given him also over all kindreds, and tongues, and nations, and people."[2]

Then again. Take the *first* and *third* of the above representations. Here, we admit, that the dragon of Rev. xii. 3, *is identical* with that of chap. xx. 2; for, of this last, as of the first, the Holy Spirit says that he is "that old serpent, which *is* the devil and Satan." But, mark the difference in the account given of the dragon in these two places. In chapter xii. 9, it is said of him that "he was cast out *into the earth*, and his angels were cast out with him." Where? Into the "bottomless pit" or abyss? Nay. For though "the heavens rejoice, and they that dwell in them" (v. 12), "because the accuser of the brethren is cast down," etc. (v. 10); yet the prophetic voice proclaims, "Woe to the inhabitants of the *earth*, and of *the sea!* for THE DEVIL is come down unto you, having great wrath, because he knoweth that he hath but a short time" (v. 12). On the other hand, the account given of this same dragon in chap. xx. is, that he is "*cast into the bottomless pit*, and is shut up, and a seal set upon him, that he should deceive the nations no more, *till* the thousand years should be fulfilled," etc.

Now then, to show the *fallacy*, first, of confounding the dragon and the beast with the symbolic agents employed by him; and second, of insisting on the identity of the dragon and the beast; and third, of representing that the circumstances of the agencies, time, place, etc., connected with the dragon of chap. xii. and xx. *are the same;* it is only necessary to remark,

(1.) If the dragon of chap. xii. and xx., and the beast of chap. xiii. are identical, and denote "a standing symbol of Paganism;" and the seizing, binding, and incarceration for a thousand years, etc., of the dragon in the bottomless pit or abyss, signify the "extirpation of paganism from the Roman empire" under Constantine; how are we to reconcile the *presence* of the dragon with the beast, *at the time* of the transference of the power of the former to the latter? And, mark, this fact is admitted by Prof. Bush; for, how otherwise could the dragon, as he says, "*transfuse* the full measure of his own satanic spirit and genius" into the beast? But again.

(2.) The "beast" of chap. xiii. was *worshipped*—"all the world wondered after him" (verses 3, 4, 8). But, the "dragon"

[1] Dan. vii. 21, 22. [2] Rev. xiii. 7.

also was worshipped (v. 4). The question therefore is, if the dragon and beast are *identical,* where was the dragon *at this time?* Was he "bound with a great chain," and "cast into the bottomless pit and sealed?" If so, how are we to reconcile this with the declaration of Holy Writ, that, *during* his incarceration for "a thousand years," he was *to deceive the nations no more?* while here is an existing deception of "*all* who dwell upon the earth," of which *he* is the author, and so great as to secure to himself the homage of "*all the world!*" Nor is this all. For,

(3.) If we admit the above interpretation of these symbols, then the "great red dragon," being "*Paganism personified,*" when "cast into the bottomless pit," which, according to his interpretation is Paganism in "the unexplored regions of the north and east,"—and which, by the way, must have included the *eastern* branch of the Roman empire under Licinius—it follows, that Paganism must have been *cast into* Paganism! In other words, that the "great red dragon" must have been *cast into* HIMSELF!

It is almost superfluous to add further on this subject, that the very circumstance of finding the "dragon," when we come to chap. xx., introduced to our notice *without* any mention of his having "seven crowned heads and ten horns," is demonstrative that they were intended to denote his subordinate agents, as *distinct from* himself. He, symbolic of "that old serpent, which is the *devil* and *Satan;*" they, "his *angels.*" The same holds true of all the symbols of Daniel, e. g., like the ten-horned fourth beast of chap. vii. 7, 8, from among which there came up another "little horn;" and like the "he-goat" of chap. viii. 1-12, out of the "notable horn" of which, being broken, *four horns* came up in its stead, and from *one* of which there sprung up another "little horn;" and all of which occupy their respective spheres according to their relative symbolic import, so with this great red dragon of the Apocalypse: his being represented as invested with the appendages of "seven crowned heads and ten horns," all have their appropriate symbolic meaning as his *agents*. And, like as with the *body* of the "little horn" or beast, which arose up from among the ten horns of Daniel's fourth beast, which, though "slain, destroyed, and given to the burning flame," left the *life* of the beast himself to be "prolonged for a season and a time:" so with the "great red dragon" under review. Whatever was the fate of the seven crowned heads and ten horns of *the beast*, or the same, when transferred to his *ten horns* as his agents, acting under his authority, and inspired with "the full measure of his satanic spirit and genius" in upholding paganism or in persecuting the saints of God; yet he still lives, to transfuse *the same* "spirit and genius" into the same or future agents, and *with them* to receive the homage of the world!¹

Having thus, we submit, sufficiently exposed the misconstruction and consequent misapplication of the symbolic imagery of the Apocalypse adduced by Prof. Bush in support of the theory before us, we now propose to vindicate the nature, character, and duration of the MILLENNIAL STATE of the Church as *still future*, against other arguments alleged in proof that it is either *already past*, or that it is *still* running its course.

First. In regard to this writer's assertion, that Rev. xx. 1-7 "is the *only express passage* in the whole compass of the Scriptures, in which mention is made of a period of a thousand years in connection with the prospective lot of the Church," etc., we observe, that even admitting this to be so, yet of one thing we are certain,—it by no means diminishes the *sufficiency* of the proof respecting it; and especially so, when we consider, that ninety-nine hundredths of the Christian world receive as scriptural doctrines, *the change* in the observance of the Christian Sabbath from the seventh to the first day of the week, and the right of both sexes of admission to the holy communion, *without any express* passage whatever for either!

But this is not all. We *deny the truth* of the above statement respecting this passage, except in the single article of its mention of one thousand years, which, by the way, is reiterated in one form or other no less than *six times* in the *seven* verses! Of the other parts of the passage relating to the *Millennium*, there are *scores* of passages both in the Old and New Testaments, which teach the same great truth in the most "express" terms. Indeed, Prof. Bush himself, when speaking of the "latter-day glory" of the Church, says, that it "is abundantly testified by the predictions of the former and the latter prophets." But then he *denies* that the announcements of Isaiah and other ancient prophets regarding the "sublime visions of ultimate glory to the Church,"

---

¹ Compare Rev. xii. 11-18 and xvii. 12-18 with 2 Thess. ii. 3-5; 6-12.

are "parallel" with, or point to, "precisely the *same epoch* with the Millennium of the Apocalypse, chap. xx. 1–7."

One thing, however, is certain. There can be but *one* millennial state of the Church on earth. That ended, and the Son of God "shall have *delivered up* the kingdom to God, even the Father," when "the Son also himself shall be subject unto him that put all things under him, that God may be all in all;"[1] when "the general assembly and church of the first-born" shall enter upon the *eternal* blessedness of "the new heavens and earth," or supernal state.

It follows, therefore, either that the millennium, or the thousand years mentioned by St. John during which Satan was bound and the saints reigned with Christ, *commenced* with the cessation of the Pagan persecutions and the extirpation of idolatry and polytheism, *at the accession* of Constantine to the supreme sovereignty of the Roman empire, A. D. 323, and that it has either expired or is still running on; or, that that event is *still future*.

Now, the former is the theory of the Millennium advocated by the learned Grotius, Prideaux, and Prof. Bush. This latter writer, speaking of "the prevailing impressions"—"for," says he, "opinions they can scarcely be called—respecting the millennium; a term," he adds, "denoting, in its popular sense, *a future* felicitous state of the Church and the world of a thousand years' duration," etc.; and that this popular impression is indicated by the frequent use of the "phraseology,—millennial state, millennial reign, millennial purity, millennial glory," etc.—these "prevailing impressions," he says, "are to be traced to the influence of *a mere traditionary tenet*, which, having been received from our forefathers in childhood, have become with us a matter of mechanical repetition in after life, when

> "'The priest hath finished what the nurse began.'"[2]

And yet, superadded to his theory of a past or continued millennium as represented above, he insists that, in comparison with it, "a brighter and benigner period *is yet* to dawn upon our world —an era of preeminent peace, purity, and prosperity, constituting what is frequently called 'the latter day glory,' *is yet* destined to bless our globe, *succeeding* and compensating 'the years wherein we have seen trouble;' for this is abundantly testified by

---

[1] 1 Cor. xv. 24, 28.   [2] Treatise on the Millennium; pref. p. vii.

the predictions of the former and the latter prophets, and shadowed forth under many a significant parable, type, and allegory."[1]

We now ask, In what consists the *difference* between the Professor's views of the millennial or "latter day glory" of the Church, and the "prevailing impressions" respecting it, according to his own showing? Both are to take place *in* "our world," *on* "our globe." Both assert of it, that it is to be "a brighter and benigner period," infinitely transcending, in peace, purity, and blessedness, "the most favored epochs which have yet marked its annals." Both affirm that it is "a *coming* condition in the affairs of the Church," etc.; i. e., that it is still *future ;* and, both declare that all this "is *abundantly testified* by the predictions of the former and the latter prophets."

It becomes, therefore, an inquiry of grave and serious import, as to the *grounds* upon which this writer speaks of "the vast multitude" who are guided by the "prevailing impressions" respecting the millennium, as unable "to give a *reason* of the hope that is in them;" and to speak of them as "'knowing not what they say, nor wherefore they affirm;'" and to demand of them "upon what this, their expectation, is founded," and whether it has "unequivocally the warrant of any express declaration of Holy Writ."[2]

To test this matter, we yield to the demand here made, and join issue with the advocate of the theory here laid down.

Let it be assumed, then, that the millennial state of the Church *commenced* with "the cessation of the pagan persecutions and the extirpation of idolatry and paganism *under Constantine the Great:* it will follow, that, as the Scriptures make provision for but *one* such a state of the Church on earth, the learned Professor's idea, in comparison with, and addition to it, of "a brighter and benigner period as yet to dawn upon our world," *is a pure fiction !*

Then, in the next place, should it result, that the millennial state of the Church, as alleged to have commenced from the time of Constantine the Great, is a *falsification* both of Scripture and of historic fact, it will of course follow, that what the Professor represents in such glowing terms of the state of the Church "*yet* to dawn upon our world," *is precisely that future* millennium which, as he says, we have received "*by tradition* from our forefathers in childhood," and "mechanically repeat in after life."

[1] Treatise on the Millennium, preface, p. viii.   [2] Ib. ib.

Our first business will be to give a brief Scriptural view of the millennial state of the Church as described in Rev. xx. 1–7, taken in connection with "the abundant testimony of the former and the latter prophets" in relation to it.

And second, examine, historically, the millennium as alleged by the theory under review to have commenced under Constantine the Great, in proof that it is destitute of every characteristic of that state.

I. First then. *The Scriptural view of the Millennial state of the Church.* We shall here,

1. Give an *analysis* of the first seven verses of Rev. xx., with a view to determine what it teaches respecting the millennium, during the six times repeated one thousand years mentioned therein.

(1.) The first fact is, *the one thousand years' binding of the dragon,* which, as a symbol, the Holy Spirit interprets to signify "that old Serpent, which *is* the devil and Satan." (Verse 2.)

(2.) The second fact is, the consequent *one thousand years' exemption* of the nations from his deceptive devices. (Verse 3.)

(3.) The third fact is, that during this one thousand years, *some of the dead lived, sat on thrones, and reigned with Christ on the earth.* (Compare verse 4, with chap. v. 10; see, also, chap. xx. 6, and xxii. 5.) This is interpreted by the Holy Spirit to mean "THE FIRST RESURRECTION." (Verses 5, 6.)

(4.) The fourth fact is, that "*the rest of the dead,*" i. e., those who are to suffer the penalty of "the perdition of ungodly men," (2 Pet. iii. 7,) "*lived not again,* until this thousand years were *finished*" (verse 5. See, also, verses 11–15); and,

(5.) The fifth fact is, that, at the *expiration* of this one thousand years, "Satan shall be *loosed out of his prison* for a little season," etc. (verses 3, 7, and 8, etc.)

Here, then, we have described to us "*Satan,*" as the great adversary of God and man, and the disturber of the peace and prosperity of the Church, and the deceiver of the nations, bound with a great chain, cast into the bottomless pit, shut up, and a seal put upon him, etc., and all for what purpose? Why, "that he should *deceive the nations no more,*" at least "for a thousand years." Accordingly, in exact harmony with these representations, that same "Spirit of Christ" who revealed these things to the revelator, John, in the Isle of Patmos, inspired the old prophets, also, to speak of this glorious period of the Church, as, in the purpose of God, ultimately *set free* alike from the distractions of "error, heresy, and schism," and the cruel hand of the persecutor. Yes. Wrapped in prophetic vision, they were "moved by the Holy Ghost" to predict that *the time would come*, when, in the sense of "the unity of the faith once delivered to the saints,"[1] "*All shall know the Lord*, from the least to the greatest."[2] Also, that *then*, in the sense of the peaceable kingdom of the "BRANCH,"[3] it is said of Messiah, so glowingly set forth by Isaiah, that "Righteousness shall be the girdle of the loins, and faithfulness the girdle of the reins,"[4] of the King of Zion. Then, men "shall beat their swords into ploughshares, and the spears into pruning-hooks;"[5] for they "shall learn war no more." *Then* the ferocity of the *animal* creation shall be subdued. "The wolf shall dwell with the lamb, and the leopard shall lie down with the kid; and the calf, and the young lion, and the fatling together, and a little child shall lead them. And the cow and the bear shall feed; their young ones shall lie down together: and the lion shall eat straw like the ox. And the sucking child shall play on the hole of the asp, and the weaned child shall put his hand on the cockatrice's den. They shall not hurt nor destroy in all my holy mountain: *for the earth* shall be full of the knowledge of the Lord, as the waters cover the sea."[6]

And we now repeat, that it was in *this state* of the millennial Church, that St. John, the divine, "saw the souls of them that were beheaded for the witness of Jesus and for the Word of God, and which had not worshipped the beast, neither his image, neither had received his mark upon their foreheads, or in their hands;" not now, mark, as "*under the altar*, crying, How long, O Lord God, holy and true, dost thou not avenge our blood on them that dwell on the earth;" but, as "*living and reigning with Christ a thousand years*." (Rev. xx. 4.)

This very limited glance of the Scriptural representations of the millennial period of the Church, must suffice. We now pass,

II. *To an historical examination of the alleged theory of the Millennium*, as advocated by Grotius, Prideaux, Vint, and also Prof. Bush. We have seen in what consists the alleged

---

[1] Eph. iv. 3.   [2] Isa. xxxi. 34.   [3] Zech. vi 12.   [4] Isa. xi. 5.
[5] Isa. ii. 4.   [6] Isa. xi. 5–9.

nature and character of the millennial state of the Church, according to the theory of the writer under review, viz.: "in the cessation of the Pagan persecutions, and the extirpation of idolatry and polytheism," as the results of what is claimed to be the *conversion* of Constantine the Great to Christianity.

Now, that this event, together with its accompanying circumstances, should have been regarded as *a most brilliant triumph* of the cross of the Nazarene over the molten image, awakens no surprise. It was the disenthralment of a long-suffering and bleeding Church from an ordeal of persecution, which had well-nigh exterminated her from the earth. But, that this event should have been construed into the *commencement* of St. John's predicted one thousand years' millennial peace, purity, and prosperity of the Christian Church, we must confess, both astonishes and confounds us. To show its utter fallacy, we ask the reader to accompany us,

1. To a view of the *circumstances* connected with the so-called conversion, life, and acts of Constantine the Great, under whose imperial sway this alleged *millennium* is declared to have commenced. Constantine ascended the throne of the Cæsars in A. D. 306, soon after which he professed himself a convert to the Christian faith. The fact that his father Constantius had been favorably inclined toward Christianity, and that his mother Helena had adopted it, added to the declared *miraculous appearance of the cross* to him in the heavens when about to engage in conflict with his rival, Maxentius, all contributed to his renunciation of the pagan religion. His conversion, however, was gradual, and was only partially avowed in the *eighth* year of his reign; nor, according to the best authorities, did he receive Christian baptism, until a little before his death, A. D. 337, making in all, between his public avowal of Christianity and his baptism, an interval of about *twenty-four* years!

Then consider, that among the *acts* of his life, is registered that of *homicide!* His son Crispus, and afterward his wife Fausta, both suffered death at his hand. In law there are three species of homicide—justifiable, excusable, and felonious. Which of these will apply to *his* case, we submit to the decision of others.

Again. It is to be specially noted, that, under Constantine, *Church and State were united*, than which no other circumstance so effectually contributed to the erection and establishment, as we shall presently show, of the great anti-Christian *Papal power* This leads us,

2. To another consideration, to wit, that the peace and prosperity of the Church which followed Constantine's reign, by no means comports either with the *Scriptural* character of the millennium, nor with what is affirmed of its great but *indefinite* length, as described by the thousand years of St. John. Indeed, it is to *avoid* the dilemma here indicated, that the advocates of the theory that the millennium is either already past, or that it is now running its course, unite in their eulogiums of this golden Constantinian age, as *the era* of its commencement. On this subject our author in his "Treatise" says, "No facts in the chronicles of the past are more notorious, than that paganism under Constantine and his successors did, after a desperate struggle, succumb to Christianity in its triumphant progress."[1] And he quotes the following from Gibbon, who, speaking of the reign of Constantine, remarks, "Every motive of authority and fashion, of interest and reason, now militated on the side of Christianity."[2] But, he adds, "two or three generations elapsed before their victorious influence was universally felt. . . . ." "The pious labor which had been suspended near *twenty years* since the death of Constantine, was vigorously resumed and finally accomplished, by the zeal of Theodosius."[3] "The gods of antiquity," says he, "were dragged in triumph at his chariot wheels. In a full meeting of the Senate, the Emperor proposed, according to the forms of the republic, the important question, Whether the worship of *Jupiter* or that of *Christ* should be the religion of the Romans. On a regular division of the Senate, Jupiter was condemned and degraded by a very large majority."[4] And, finally, this historian is quoted as saying, that "so rapid, yet so gentle, was the fall of paganism, that only twenty-eight years after the death of Theodosius, the faint and minute vestiges were no longer visible to the eye of the legislator."[5]

Now this, especially when viewed as emanating from the pen of an *infidel* historian, is all very fine; and, in order to inspire us with the same confidence in his *authority* as our author himself felt, he speaks of his "pen" in a certain instance of accom-

---

[1] Treatise on the Millennium, p. 146. [2] Ib. p. 148; GIBBON's *Decline and Fall*, etc., p. 332.
[3] Ib. p. 151; *Decline and Fall*, p. 464.   [4] Ib. p. 151; *Decline and Fall*, p. 464.
[5] Ib. p. 149; *Decline and Fall*, p. 469.

plished prophecy, as seeming "to have been guided by *the spirit of inspiration;*"¹ and that the reader of his works "will find in the concluding part of the twentieth chapter of the Decline and Fall, a more valuable commentary on *this* part of the xxth chapter of the Apocalypse, than is furnished by *all* the professed expositors who 'have taken in hand to set forth in order a declaration of the things contained in it.'"²

But, let us examine the *phraseology* of Gibbon on this subject. He makes the "every motive" of Constantine in "the extirpation of idolatry and polytheism" to consist of the following elements— "authority," "fashion," "interest," "reason:" than which, there can be none other more directly *opposed to* the unearthly nature of the gospel of Christ. And when he comes to the time of Theodosius, the triumphs of Christianity are suspended upon the *capricious* vote of a majority in "a full meeting of the Senate," to be decided "according to the forms of the *Republic!*" A splendid specimen, this, of the primitively ordained mode of propagating Christianity! And, withal: what a glorious, brilliant *commencement* of the millennial peace, purity, and prosperity of the Church! Rather may it be said that "*the Church,*" being thus placed by Constantine under the protective wing of "*the State,*" was seduced into that somewhat protracted courtship, so to speak, "with the kings of the earth," as finally ultimated in the *birth* of that stupendous power, THE PAPAL APOSTASY;"³ a power symbolized by the "*little horn*" of Dan. vii. 8, 11, 20, 21, 24, 25, and with which synchronizes that "beast that rose up out of the *sea,*" to whom the "dragon" delegated his power. (Compare Rev. xii. 3 with xiii. 2, 4, and verses 5–8.) This same power is also symbolized by "*the great whore of Babylon* that sitteth upon many waters," "with whom the kings of the earth have committed fornication," while the "inhabitants of the earth have been made drunk with the wine of her fornication." (Rev. xvii. 1, 2.) Eusebius, Socrates, and Theodosius, all unite in the affirmation that with Constantine the Great *commenced* the exercise of a vast power in the Church, which was retained and wielded by many of his successors. "They convoked councils, and presided over them. They elevated bishops, composed contentions, reformed abuses, admitted appeals, constituted judges in ecclesiastical cases, deposed the clergy, and made laws in religious rites," etc.

¹ Treatise on the Millennium, p. 139. ² Ib. p. 150. ³ See 2 Thess. ii. ver. 3 and 7 compared.

It is scarcely necessary to repeat that we are now speaking of the *acts*, not of Roman bishops, but of Romon *emperors*. Was it, then, with these latter that the Lord Jesus Christ, as the great Head of the Church, said, "Lo, I am with *you* alway, even unto the end of the world?" No! The Church of Christ, the *faithful* of whom had almost totally perished by persecution, as *a test* of her fidelity to Him under a change of circumstances, was now translated from the fiery ordeal of the stake to courtly favor. The *same national* arm that for the three preceding centuries had been raised to crush, was now turned to the *protection of* the Church. Constantine the Great, both in character and design, became in some sort to the *Christian* what Cyrus was to the *Jewish* Church. But we are compelled to say, *unlike* the liberated captives of Babylon at the hand of the Persian monarch, the Christian, while engaged with one hand in repairing the ravages of ten severe storms of persecution, *overlooked* the necessity of retaining in the other those weapons of defence indispensable in warding off the insidious and seductive influences of worldly princes, whose "every motive" was prompted by "authority," "fashion," "interest," and "reason." In other words, *the Church succumbs to the world!* "Reason," or the *expediency* of things, takes the place of Scripture; "interest," or *worldliness*, that of spirituality of heart and of life; "*fashion*," or the pomps and vanities of the present state, that of self-denial for Christ's sake; and "authority," *political*, that of the primitively legitimate exercise of authority *ecclesiastical*. In conclusion, on this subject, the Church was now enabled—comparatively, we mean—to bask for a time in the sunshine of prosperity. She walked, so to speak, in a garden of roses. She reclined upon a bed of down. Arrayed in gorgeous attire, "she fared sumptuously every day." She was wafted along by the chariot of *the State!*

But, we now ask: Was the Church, in her internal and external condition during the IVth century and onward, possessed of *any one* feature of her predicted millennial peace, purity, and blessedness? We unhesitatingly affirm *that she was not*. To say nothing of the prevalent *opposition* to Christianity down to the time of Constantine, despite all the eulogized peace and glory of the confederated Church and State; as early as in A. D. 325, being the twentieth year of that emperor's reign, he was compelled to convoke a council, over which he himself presided, composed of

8

318 bishops, for the express purpose of suppressing one of the most extensive and fatal *heresies* that ever infested the Church: we mean that of *Arianism*. But, was that heresy suppressed? So far from it, between the constant vacillations of the emperor himself in regard to the orthodox and heterodox parties; and the perfidy, inconstancy, and rage of the Arian sectarists against the Trinitarian; the heresiarch Arius procured from Constantine the *expulsion* from his see of Eustathius of Antioch, and also the *deposition* from his bishopric of Alexandria, and his repeated exile of the good Athanasius. Nor was this all. By the connivance of this Christian, this orthodox emperor, several Arian or heretical councils were held,—as those at Tyre, at Antioch, at Sardica, at Nice, in Thrace, etc.; and, as every scholar of ecclesiastical history knows, this very Arian heresy, *during* this same IVth century of alleged millennial happiness of the Church, had nearly overspread *the entire Christian world!*

Then again. To the Arian heresy of this century may be added that of Photinus, Apollinaris, Macedonius, Donatus, etc.; all of whom, in one form or other, denied the *Divinity* of Christ, and of the Holy Spirit, or distracted the Church by *schism*. And so far from the Church being exempt from *persecution* during this century, though the last and most cruel of the *ten* inflicted by the Pagans under Diocletian and Maximian,— and which commenced A. D. 303,—was finally suppressed as far as the influence of Constantine extended in the west; yet in the east Licinius continued it with unabated fury; and, after the death of Constantine, by Constantius and Valens against the *orthodox*, with the intermediate and bloody reign of the apostate Julian.

Again. In the IVth century the Roman empire was *divided*. In the Vth it was rent into *ten kingdoms*. And under Justinian, A. D. 533, the construction of a model for THE SPIRITUAL HIERARCHY of the Papal dominion was laid, by an edict of Justinian, in constituting John II., the Patriarch of Rome, *the head* of the universal Church,—*alias*, the vicegerent of Jesus Christ upon earth! Hence another consideration, proving the misapplication of the prophecy in Rev. xx. 1–7, to the interval from Constantine onward; it is this:

3. That the *subsequent* state of the Church from the close of the so-called golden period down to the present time, shows it to have been any other than one of general peace, purity, and prosperity.

It may be as well to premise in this place, in regard to what these writers affirm of the "thousand years" in this passage as denoting an *indefinite* length of time, that a comparison of St. Peter's 2d Epistle, chap. iii. 7, will show its fallacy. In proof that the "thousand years" in both passages refer to the *same* period, viz., the *judgment-coming* of the Lord, St. Peter says, "But the heavens and the earth which are *now*, by the same word are *kept in store*, reserved unto fire against the day of judgment and perdition of ungodly men;" which "day of judgment," etc., he explains in the 8th verse, thus: "But, beloved, be not ignorant of this one thing, that *one day* is with the Lord [as] *a thousand years*, and *a thousand years* [as] *one day*," i. e., "the day (ἡμέρα) of judgment" is as a thousand years—*one judgment-day*. St. Peter's reservation of "the heavens and the earth that now are," therefore, extends from the *commencement* of the thousand years' judgment-day to the period of the "perdition" awarded to "ungodly men" *at its close*, which exactly harmonizes with "the rest of the dead," who, according to St. John, lived not again, "*until* the thousand years were finished." (Rev. xx. 5.)

But, as we have said, the greatest confusion prevails among the advocates of this theory as to *the period* in question. Prof. Bush applies it, as we have seen, to "the extirpation of idolatry and paganism from the Roman empire under Constantine, which, if we are to understand it to reach down to the appearance of THE ANTICHRIST, as that personage *has not yet* shown himself upon the stage, according to this hypothesis, it has already been running on no less than 1537 years! On the other hand, if we take the Professor's theory, viz., that the millennium is already *past*, when we come to his golden period of peace and prosperity to the Church under Constantine and his successors, and which he confines to the space of what he calls a thousand years, we are straightway informed that it means "*one or two centuries;*" (!) for, on page 128 of his "Treatise," he makes the suppression of paganism in the Roman empire to extend only "one or two centuries beyond its public and incipient suppression by Constantine in A. D. 323!

To return now to the subject in hand. From the edict of Justinian in A. D. 533, commenced the reign of that period which enveloped the Church throughout Christendom in the deepest spiritual darkness *for more than nine succeeding centuries.* And, during this period, what a tissue of outrages were perpetrated against all law, Divine and human? of acts of inhumanity the most barbarous? of superstitions the most debasing? of heresies the most alarming and dangerous? Indeed, the minds of men throughout this entire period were brought under *the most servile bondage* to those master-spirits who had dethroned reason, and usurped universal dictation over the consciences of men. Ignorance, ambition, avarice, superstition, a Christianized idolatry, cruelty, and bloodshed, followed everywhere in their train, and spread around them a moral desolation, to which history was before a stranger. "Mercy and truth," and "righteousness and peace," seemed to have bid the Church an eternal adieu. The darkness into which she had been so long enveloped; the pelting storms of adversity which had so long directed their fury against her; and the gross ignorance, superstition, and corruption in doctrine and morals, both among priests and people, which abounded within her; all seemed to indicate that God, though He had purchased the redemption of the Church with His own blood, had nevertheless surrendered her up as a prey, to be torn piecemeal by the pitiless hands of a race of ecclesiastical demagogues and secular tyrants.

In conclusion, let me now ask the reader to compare the *scriptural* description given of the nature and character of the millennial state of the Church in a previous page,[1] with the *historic* character of the period assigned to it by this theory; and I ask: Would it have ever entered his mind that the state of the Church from the time of Constantine the Great down to the present, or *any portion* of that interval, had constituted the predicted exemption of the Church from all physical and moral evil? Above all, would he, from the *present* aspect of the times, as viewed in its relation to the existing character and influence of religious truth and morals, infer that she is *now* enjoying that state? This would be to suppose the existence and prevalence in the world of the predicted millennium of the Bible, *in the very absence* of that peace, purity, prosperity, and glory, which is indispensable to that state, than which, we can conceive of no greater absurdity.

We leave this theory, therefore, with the remark, first, that in the application of the symbolic imagery of Rev. xx. 1–7 to the state and condition of the Church between the time of Constantine and the present day, as denotive of the *Millennium* promised

[1] See pages 108, 109.

as the object of her faith, and hope, and prayers, may be looked upon as a specimen of *figurative* interpretation run mad. We add,

Second. That the various heresiarchs of the present day—e. g., Unitarians, Universalists, etc.,—have made and still make vast capital out of the theology of those of the *orthodox*, who interpret the "DRAGON" referred to in Rev. xii. 3, and xx. 2, as signifying "*Paganism personified.*" This is to ignore the scriptural doctrine of the *actual personality* of that being whom the Holy Spirit declares to be represented by that symbol, viz.: "that old serpent, which is the devil and Satan." And finally,

Third. The Papal Church is brought under vast obligations to the *Protestant* advocates of this theory, for their zealous defence of *her* claims, as *free* from the imputation of constituting *one of the Antichrists* of the New Testament scriptures. For, if their interpretation of Rev. xx. 1-7, etc., be in accordance with "the mind of the spirit," the Church of all nations, under her enlightened, benign, and gentle reign, has been basking for centuries in the full sunshine of her *Millennial* or latter day glory!"

With the prayer, therefore, that the reader may reap the benefit of this much-needed exposure of the fallacy of the above theory, we call upon him to reject, at every sacrifice, the mere "doctrines and commandments of men,"[1] who "concerning the truth have erred,"[2] and that henceforth, "speaking the truth in love,"[3] he "may grow up into Him in all things, which is the head, even Christ,"[4]—we pass to an examination of the next theory connected with the subject in hand.

[1] Col. ii. 22. [2] 2 Tim. ii. 18. [3] Eph. iv. 15. [4] Ib.

CHAPTER III.

THIRD THEORY: AS ADVOCATED BY THE POPULAR WRITERS OF THE DAY.

THIS THEORY ALLEGES, ALL THE PROPHECIES RELATING TO THE SECOND COMING OF CHRIST AND THE ESTABLISHMENT OF HIS KINGDOM IN THE WORLD, TO HAVE BEEN VERIFIED BY THE JUDGMENTS INFLICTED UPON THE JEWISH NATION AND POLITY, AT THE DESTRUCTION OF JERUSALEM, ETC., BY THE ROMAN ARMY UNDER TITUS, IN A. D. 70.

This theory, like the two preceding, though on different grounds, *repudiates* the coming and reign of Christ on earth in His glorified humanity, *as future*. It is founded on that portion of our Lord's prophecy, contained in the xxivth chapter of St. Matthew's Gospel, from the 27th to the 30th verses inclusive:

27. "For as the lightning cometh out of the east, and shineth even unto the west; so shall also the coming of the Son of Man be.

28. "For wheresoever the carcass is, there will the eagles be gathered together.

29. "Immediately after the tribulation of those days shall the sun be darkened, and the moon shall not give her light, and the stars shall fall from heaven, and the powers of the heavens shall be shaken:

30. "And then shall appear the sign of the Son of Man in heaven: and then shall all the tribes of the earth mourn, and they shall see the Son of Man coming in the clouds of heaven with power and great glory."

The advocates of this theory, in their interpretations of the above prophecy, affirm,

1. That the "*lightning* shining from east to west," figuratively denotes the coming of the Son of Man *by the Roman army*, to invade and conquer Judea; its sudden flashes indicating the unexpected, rapid, and universal desolation that would follow.

2. That the "*eagles*" gathered around the "carcass" signify, that wheresoever the *Jews* are, thither shall the *Roman army* be gathered.

3. That the words, "*immediately after* the tribulation of those days," show that our Lord was not speaking of any distant event, but of something immediately consequent on the calamities predicted; and that must be, *the destruction of Jerusalem*. This was to consist of an utter desolation, and terrible destruction brought upon the nation, and upon the capital cities, analogous to the obscuration of the heavenly luminaries; or, that there should be

a destruction of their *ecclesiastical* and *civil* state, and of the *rulers* of both; these latter, for or on account of their state and dignity, being represented by the *sun*, *moon*, and *stars*, shorn of their brilliancy, fallen from their spheres, and involved in ruin. And finally,

4. That our Saviour proceeded to speak in the same figurative style, and in connection with the 27th verse, of the "appearance of the sign of the Son of Man in heaven," etc. (verse 30); the plain meaning of which, it is affirmed, is, that the destruction of Jerusalem should be such a remarkable instance of divine vengeance—*such a signal* manifestation of Christ "coming in the clouds of heaven with power and great glory," that all the Jewish tribes shall "*mourn*," and many would be led from thence to *acknowledge* Christ and the Christian religion, etc.

In a word, this theory, based throughout upon what is technically called the FIGURATIVE interpretation of the words of the prophecy, alleges that it teaches, not a personal, but a *providential* coming of Christ "by the Roman army," judicially to punish the Jews for their sins; which, however, is to result in their acknowledgment of and conversion to Him, as their Messiah.

But, unlike the first theory, though it affirms *the restoration of the Jews*, yet it denies all connection between it and *the second personal* coming of Christ, which that theory admits.

That the above is a fair and candid synopsis of their views, will appear, first, from the following interpretations given by them of its several parts; and second, from the arguments adduced in their support.

I. The *figurative interpretations* of this theory:

Verse 27. BISHOP PEARCE. "The *Roman army* entered into Judea on the east side of it, and carried on their conquests westward, as if not only the extensiveness of the ruin, but the very route which the army would take, *was intended* in the comparison of the lightning coming out of the east and shining even unto the west."

Other writers on this subject are the *mere echoes* of this learned prelate. As, for example,

BISHOP NEWTON. "The *Roman army* entered Judea on the east side of it, and carried on their conquests westward, as if not only the extensiveness of the ruin, but the very route which the army would take, *was intended* in the comparison of the lightning coming out of the east, and shining even unto the west."[1]

DR. ADAM CLARKE. "It is worthy of remark that our Lord, in the most particular manner, points out the very march of the *Roman army;* they entered into

---

[1] NEWTON *on the Prophecies*, London edition, p. 354.

Judea on the east, and carried on their conquests westward, as if not only the extensiveness of the ruin, but the very route which the army would take, *were intended* in the comparison of the lightning issuing from the east, and shining to the west."

DR. COKE. "His coming will not be in this or that particular place, but like the lightning, sudden and universal. The appearance of the *true* Christ will be as distinguishable from that of the *false* Christs, as lightning, which shineth all round the hemisphere, is from a blaze of straw; it is very remarkable, 'that the *Roman army* entered into Judea on the east side of it, and carried on their conquests westward.'"

DR. SCOTT. "The *Christians*, if they had not been forewarned, might have been deceived on another ground; for they expected their Lord to come, not to deliver, but to *destroy* Jerusalem; they were therefore reminded that his coming for this purpose would not be secret, or local; but like the 'lightning, which shineth' at once from east to west; for *in his righteous providence*, he would, with conspicuous and irresistible energy, desolate the whole land. The Roman armies entered Judea from the east, and carried their victorious ravages to the west, in a very rapid and tremendous manner."

COTTAGE BIBLE. "The meaning appears to be, that, as this surprising meteor shoots in the same instant from east to west, and pervades the whole horizon; so should *the Roman armies*, which attend the coming of the Son of Man, like a mighty tempest, at once cover the whole land of Israel."

DR. BENSON. "The coming of the Son of Man shall be in a very different manner, and for very different ends, from what you are imagining. It shall be like lightning, swift, unexpected, and destructive. His appearance will be as distinguishable from that of every false Christ, as lightning, which shines all around the hemisphere, is from a blaze of straw."

REV. ALBERT BARNES. "This is not designed to denote the *quarter* from which he would come, but the *manner*. He does not mean to affirm that the Son of Man will come from the east, but that he will come in a rapid and unexpected manner, like lightning. Many would be looking for him in the desert; many in secret places. But he said, it would be useless to be looking in that manner, . . . to any particular part of the heavens, to know where the lightning would next flash. In a moment it would blaze in an unexpected part of the heavens, and shine at once to the other part. So rapidly, so unexpectedly, in so unlooked-for a quarter, would be his coming." To this he adds—"The meaning is, *he would come by means of the Roman armies*." "The words, therefore, had doubtless a primary reference to the destruction of Jerusalem, but such an amplitude of meaning as also to express his coming to judgment." . . .

DR. WHITBY. "You will then need none to instruct you where Christ is, or to say to you, He is here, or there; for, *by the Roman army*, which shall pass through the territories of the Jews like lightning, his coming to take vengeance on that nation shall be manifest," etc.

In harmony with the interpretation of the "lightning" in the 27th verse, as denoting "the coming of the Son of Man" to destroy

Jerusalem by the Romans, the following will represent the view given by these writers of—

Verse 28. REV. ALBERT BARNES. "This verse is connected with the preceding by the word 'for,' implying that this is a reason for what is said there, that the Son of Man would certainly come to destroy the city, and that he would come suddenly. The meaning is, *he would come by means of the Roman armies;* " i. e., as eagles to devour their prey.

DR. WHITBY. His interpretation is more direct and explicit. He says, "Wherever the Jews, who, like dead carcasses, should be devoured by the Roman eagles, are, thither shall *he* [the Son of Man] fly with them, to tear and to devour them."

We pass to,

Verse 29. DR. WHITBY. This writer's comment may be selected as embodying the substance of this theory, though, in relation to *the time* intended by "the tribulation of those days," he differs, not only with *himself*, but from most others. He says: "It being foretold that this should happen *immediately after* the wasting of the Jews, by Vespasian's army flying quickly through Galilee, Idumea, and Judea; this cannot be taken *literally*, because no such thing then happened to the sun, moon, or stars. It must be, therefore, a *metaphorical* expression, to signify, as it doth frequently in the Old Testament, and other writers, an utter desolation, and terrible destruction, brought upon a nation, and upon the capital cities, compared to the sun and moon; for in this language the prophet Isaiah speaks of the destruction of Babylon, chap. xiii. 9-10 (which see). The indignation of God against the Idumeans is represented in like dreadful words, Isa. xxxiv. 3, 4; so is the destruction of Sennacherib and his people, Isa. li. 6; so the destruction of Egypt, Ezek. xxxii. 7. And in these words this very remarkable destruction is foretold by Joel, ' The sun and the moon shall be darkened, and the stars shall not give their light ' " (Joel ii. 31; iii. 15).

"This, therefore, saith Maimonides, 'is a proverbial expression, importing the destruction and utter ruin of a nation.' Artemidorus also saith, that, 'the sun darkened or turned into blood, and the stars falling, or disappearing, import the destruction of many people.' And in this sense it is almost incredible, which Josephus saith, viz.: that eleven hundred thousand perished in that siege." Whitby continues: "Another exposition of these words is this, that then there shall be a destruction of their *ecclesiastical* and *civil* state, and of the *rulers* of them both; according to these words of Maimonides, 'this metaphor imports, that men who for their state and dignity might be compared to the *sun, moon*, and *stars*, shall suddenly fall down as a leaf from the vine and from the fig-tree.'"

Then, as to *the time*, etc.

"And this happened," says Whitby, "a considerable time *before* the destruction of Jerusalem, when the thieves and zealots, saith Josephus, 'kept all the nobles and rulers of the country in close custody;' when the zealots 'slew and consumed the nobility, and made it their business to leave none of the men of power alive,' etc. This was to happen," he adds, "*before* 'the great and terrible day of the Lord,' or *at that time :*" for, "we learn this from the prophet Joel, that 'then shall the sun be darkened,' etc. This, therefore, cannot be referred to any time *after* the destruction of Jerusalem."

Here it may be observed, by the way, that, according to Dr. Whitby's own showing, the *first* theory here spoken of supposes that "the great and terrible day of the Lord" was that identical time when the Jewish nation met with its utter desolation *at* the siege and destruction of their capital during the war under Vespasian. And the prophecy of Joel was brought forward to sustain *that* position. Whereas the *second* theory, the destruction of their ecclesiastical and civil state, supposes that the day alluded to by Joel, when the sun, moon, and stars should be darkened, was "a considerable time *before* the destruction of Jerusalem!" And the prophecy of Joel is made to sustain *that* position also. The question therefore is, since these two theories depend upon a *different* application of the prophecy of Joel, differing essentially in regard to not only *the time*, but the *nature* of the darkening of the luminaries, inasmuch as the one must be erroneous if the other is true, how are we to *decide* between them?

Thus much for the learned Whitby.

DR. LIGHTFOOT, and DR. CLARKE after him, adopt the same general principles of exegesis. But Dr. Clarke, it will be seen, places the darkening of the sun, moon, and stars *after* the fall of Jerusalem. He says: "The word 'immediately,' shows that our Lord was not speaking of any *distant* event, but of something *immediately consequent* on calamities already predicted; and that must be, the destruction of Jerusalem." Quoting Lightfoot, he continues: "The Jewish heaven shall perish, and the sun and moon of its glory and happiness shall be darkened—brought to nothing. The *sun* is the religion of the *Church;* the *moon* is the government of the *state;* and the *stars* the *judges* and *doctors* of both."

To the above we add the following from

DR. ROBINSON. His explanation of this passage differs materially from the preceding writers, as to *the time* of the obscuration of the celestial luminaries. He says: "The subsequent desolation and calamity spoken of in Matt. xxiv. 29, 30, and the parallel passages, I refer to the overthrow and complete extirpation of the Jewish people *fifty years later* under Adrian; when they were sold as slaves, and utterly driven out from the land of their fathers." (*Harmony of the Gospels.*)

We now come to the expositions given of

Verse 30. These commentators understand this verse, taken in connection with the 29th, to refer either to the coming *of* the Romans, or to the coming (metaphorically) of Christ *with* the

Romans, and effecting the destruction and desolation described in verse 27, under the *similitude* of the darkening and falling of the luminaries of heaven. But whichever way it is modified, they do not understand Christ to have come in any other way than *judicially*, by the Romans, to inflict these terrible judgments on the Jewish nation.

DR. WHITBY remarks on verse 30, "Our Saviour's coming here, seems to import his coming *by the Roman army*, to besiege and to destroy Jerusalem and the unbelieving Jews, for so Christ seemeth plainly to interpret this '*coming of the Son of Man*,' verse 27," etc.

DR. CLARKE. "Then shall appear the *sign* of the Son of Man. The plain meaning of this is, that the destruction of Jerusalem will be such a remarkable instance of divine vengeance, such a *signal manifestation* of Christ's power and glory, that all the Jewish tribes shall mourn, and many will, in consequence of this manifestation of God, be led to acknowledge the Christian religion."

MR. BURKITT. "Then shall all the tribes of the earth *mourn ;* that is, then shall the Jews be convinced that their destruction was the punishment of their sins, in rejecting and crucifying Christ; and accordingly they that had pierced him shall *behold* him, and *mourn over* him," etc.

MR. WATSON. "The *sign* of the Son of Man is that demonstration of the supernatural character of the *judicial* visitation of the Jews, that to the Christians it should be as a sure sign that it was *Christ* who was then inflicting his vengeance upon his enemies, as though there should be *a visible personal* appearance of him. Even Josephus, a Jew, acknowledged in these events the special displays of the more immediate agency of an angry God; and much more, to Christians, would they be *the sign* of his majesty to whom 'all power in heaven and earth' had been committed, and thus prove a mighty confirmation of their faith."

MR. BURKITT. "There is *a threefold* coming of Christ spoken of in the New Testament. 1. His coming in his *Spiritual* kingdom by the preaching of the gospel among the Gentiles. 2. His coming to *destroy Jerusalem* forty years after his ascension. 3. His *final coming to judgment* at the great day. *All* these comings of the Son of Man, for their suddenness and unexpectedness, are compared unto lightning," etc.

We might easily extend these quotations, in illustration of the *figurative* expositions of the prophecy under consideration. The above, however, all of which are culled from the writings of those whom the church delights to honor as "Masters in Israel," are deemed sufficient for our present purpose. Our next business is to lay before the reader,

II. The *arguments* adduced by these writers in their support.

1. Assuming that "*the days of tribulation*," verse 29, refers to the calamities which befel the Jewish nation during the Roman

war; as the darkening of the sun, moon, and stars was to transpire "immediately after" that time, and as no such event occurred *literally*, therefore, it is contended, the passage is *metaphorical*, and must be understood in the sense above given of it. This is also alleged to be sustained by the use of similar prophetic imagery in reference to the destruction of Babylon, Idumea, Sennacherib and his army, Egypt, etc.; but especially of Jerusalem, by the prophet Joel, chap. ii. 30, 31, and iii. 15, and which, it is affirmed, is applied by the apostle Peter (Acts ii. 16–20) to the Jews of that age. Hence the plea both of necessity and of precedent for expounding the passage figuratively. Again,

2. The coming of the Son of Man was to *follow* the darkening of the celestial luminaries. And yet our Lord, in Matt. xvi. 27, 28, speaking of the "coming of the Son of Man in the glory of his Father," etc., adds, "There be some standing here, which shall not taste of death, *till they see* him coming in his kingdom." And again, Matt. xxiv. 34, he declares that—"ἡ γενεὰ αὕτη—*this generation* shall not pass away till all these things be fulfilled." Therefore, it is argued, as Christ's coming was to *follow* the above signs in the heavens, and yet was to transpire *before* all these men died, it is certain that that coming of Christ *cannot be* future. Dr. Clarke, in his comment on Matt. xvi. 27, says: "This seems to refer to Dan. vii. 13, 14, 'Behold, one like the Son of Man came to the ancient of days, and there was given to him dominion, and glory, and a kingdom, that all people, and nations, and languages, should serve him.' This was the *glorious mediatorial kingdom* which Jesus Christ was *now* about to set up, by the destruction of the Jewish nation and polity, and the diffusion of the gospel through the whole world..... It is *very likely* that the words do not apply to the final judgment, to which they are generally referred, but to the wonderful display of God's grace and power *after the day of Pentecost*." And on verse 28, he adds: "This seems to confirm the above explanation, as our Lord evidently speaks of the establishment of the Christian Church *after* the day of Pentecost; as if he had said, 'Some of *you*, my disciples, shall continue to live *until* these things take place.' The destruction of Jerusalem and the Jewish economy, which our Lord here predicts, took place about *forty-three years* after this; and some of the persons now with him, doubtless survived that period, and witnessed the extension of the Messiah's kingdom."

Another passage, viz., John xxi. 22, is quoted to the same end. By an eminent divine it is thus stated: "'And Jesus said, If I will that he [John] *tarry till I come*, what is that to thee?' John's fellow-disciples spread abroad a report from this, that the Saviour had said to him that he should not die. But John himself remarks, that 'Jesus did not say, he shall not *die*,' but, 'if I will that he *tarry* till I come, what is that to thee?' In other words," continues this writer, "John understood Jesus, not as promising exemption from death, but only that he should live *until his coming*. And when, now, was that to be? If his coming meant the general judgment, then John would not have to die *at all;* for saints then alive are not to die, but to be immediately 'caught up to meet the Lord in the air,' doubtless with an appropriate metamorphosis. The *coming* in question, then, *after* which John was to die, and not before, must have been some coming *during* that generation. And what else could it be referred to, except to *his coming* to punish the unbelieving Jews?"

We add one more passage, adduced in support of the above *figurative* interpretation of Christ's coming. It is our Lord's declaration to the high priest, Caiaphas, Matt. xxvi. 64, "Hereafter shall *ye see* the Son of Man, sitting on the right hand of power, and coming in the clouds of heaven." The argument here is, as it is certain that the high priest could not live until the day of judgment, and as the second coming of Christ will be prior to the resurrection of the dead, and as it is not possible that the high priest could have lived to witness that event, therefore, it is concluded that the coming spoken of must be a figurative coming to destroy Jerusalem.

Finally. On this subject it is argued,

3. That there are many passages in the *poetical imagery* of the Old Testament which justify the *figurative* interpretation of the one before us. For example, Isa. lxiv. 1: "Oh that thou wouldst rend the heavens, that thou wouldst *come down!*" Hab. iii. 3: "God *came* from Teman." Gen. xi. 5: "The Lord *came down* to see the city and the tower." Exod. iii. 8: "I am *come down* to deliver thee out of the hand of the Egyptians," etc. The same is true of those passages which speak of God as *coming in a cloud, riding* on a cloud, etc.

Thus much, then, of this theory, which, by a *figurative* interpretation of our Lord's prophecy, Matt. xxiv. 27-30, alleges the fulfilment of all the prophecies which relate to His second coming, and the establishment of His kingdom in the world, by the judgments inflicted upon the Jewish nation and polity, *at the destruction of Jerusalem by the hand of the Roman legions, in* A. D. 70.

It is almost superfluous to remark, that the learning, talents, and acknowledged piety and exalted position of those from whose writings we have quoted in illustration of their theory, and in the arguments adduced in its support, have secured to them an unbounded influence *in moulding the theology of the modern church*. Their theory of interpretation of the subject in hand, has become almost universally and permanently incorporated with the standard biblical literature of the day. Their commentaries and other writings have formed, and still form, the *text-books* of all our theological schools, and their *opinions* are endorsed and promulgated by the ministry, and received by the membership of nearly the entire church. And, so deeply rooted is this theory in the minds of nearly all who in this day " profess and call themselves Christians," that an attempt to change the current of thought on this momentous subject, is about as hopeless a task as would be that of altering the deep-worn courses of our rivers.

And yet, it will be admitted by all, that these men, however renowned, were but mortal. Why then, it may be asked, account them infallible? which men do, by yielding *implicitly* to their dogmas. In regard to all other matters of investigation, men choose to think for themselves. Why not in matters of *theology* as well?

We choose to do so. While we yield to none in paying that deference to the authority of great names which is their due, yet we can, in the matter of the *inspired* verities, " call no man master;" for "*one* is our Master, even Christ."[1] And our conviction is, that it is now too late in the day of our probation to pin our faith either upon the teachings of uninspired men, or of like stereotyped creeds. " *To the law and to the testimony:* if we speak not according to this word, it is because there is no light in us."[2] They have written on this subject. Their ponderous tomes, or octavos, or duodecimos, find a place, in larger or smaller numbers, in almost every Christian hamlet throughout the land. And now, while we would " magnify our office,"[3] yet with no pretensions

---

[1] Matt. xxiii. 8.   [2] Isa. viii. 16.   [3] Rom. xi. 13.

beyond that of being "less than the least of God's servants,"[1] we also come forward with our *Reply*. In doing this, we propose, without further delay,

I. To examine the theory of figurative interpretation, applied by these writers to the prophecy under review.

II. To reply to the expositions given in support of their interpretations of this prophecy, and

III. Give a direct literal interpretation of this prophecy, taken in connection with its chronological stand-points.

The importance of this subject to the cause of truth, as we view it, is our only apology for the space given to it in these pages.

THE FIGURATIVE THEORY, ETC.

I. First, then. *We are to examine the theory of figurative interpretation applied by these writers to the prophecy under review.*

We remark then,

1. That it is a violation of all the laws of prophetic interpretation, to confound a figure of speech with a symbol. *Figures* are used for the simple purpose of *illustration* or *ornament*. Hence, the agents or objects to which they are applied, relate to the subjects of the acts or qualities which they ascribe to them. On the other hand, *symbols* are the *representatives* of the agents, objects, qualities, acts, conditions, or effects of others of a different and resembling class. In the next place, we observe,

2. That the use of metaphorical or figurative language, implies a knowledge or *idea* of what would be understood, if such language were used *literally*. In other words, figures are to the literal agents or objects illustrated, what *shadows* are to the *substance*. We cannot use a figure without having in view the *literal* thing from which the figure is derived. For example: If we speak of a man as the *pillar* of the state, we have in view the nature of a *literal column* at the same time. If we say Christianity is the *sun* of the world, it implies that we have a previous understanding of the nature of the sun as the *source of light*, etc. Thus the one illustrates the other.

The use of *symbolical* language, on the other hand, is employed as *prophetical representatives* of the objects, acts, etc., of men bearing a resemblance to them. Thus, in Daniel's vision (chap.

---

[1] 1 Cor. xv. 9; Eph. iii. 8.

vii.), wild beasts are employed by the Holy Spirit to *represent* cruel, bloody, and destroying men: powerful creatures in the animal world that prey on inferior beasts, being *put in the place of men* in the political and religious world, of a *corresponding* character toward mankind; and the destructive *acts* of the one, are employed to represent the resembling destructive *acts* of the other. In like manner, in the Apocalypse, candlesticks are used to *represent* churches, and stars, the teachers of religion, etc., the former to *support* the latter, whose work it is to spread the light of the gospel in the world. But, we now add,

3. That the advocates of the figurative theory of interpretation, overlooking entirely the above distinction, convert *figures* into *symbols*, and thus employ the agents, acts, and events of which they treat, as though they were the *representatives* of those of another class: in other words, that their literal meaning is but the *shell*, under which a spiritual or mystical sense, which it is alleged is their *only true* sense, is *veiled*. For instance, take the prophecy of Isa. ii. 1–5: the *subjects* of which the affirmation is made, viz., "the mountain of the Lord's house"—"all nations shall flow into it"—"many peoples"—"Jehovah's house," etc., are all interpreted and applied in a spiritual or mystical sense, to denote the *conversion* of the Gentiles to the Christian faith, and their *ingathering* into the Christian Church, etc.

To show the error, however, of thus changing the above and similar figures of speech into symbols, it only need to be asked: How can *all* nations be supposed to stand for *other* nations, when there are *no other nations* in the world? And again: to transform these figures into symbolical representatives of other things, would necessarily involve, in the application of the symbol, a reference to nations of *some other orb*, which is impossible.

4. This, then, is the *origin* of the figurative interpretation of the prophetical scriptures. Suffice it to say, that it was totally unknown to the fathers of the first two centuries of the Christian age. ORIGEN, who flourished in the early part of the third century (from A. D. 204), is the father of it. It has been adopted, for the most part, by the Church from his time to the present. This system of interpretation, as applied to the prophecy of Christ, Matt. xxiv. 7–30, however, seems to be traceable to BP. PEARCE, from whom Bp. Newton, Whitby, and the others have copied it.

5. We now proceed to adduce the following *admitted use* of

the figurative language of prophecy, in proof that these figures of speech are, as we have said, *literal illustrations*, and *not* symbolical representatives of the objects and acts to which they refer. Such passages are always found in the evidently and confessedly poetic portions of the prophecies. Take the following, as a few of the many examples which might be given:[1]

(1.) Isa. xiii. 1. This is a clear example of *figurative* prophecy, illustrating the *literal* overthrow of Babylon.

(2.) Isa. xiii. 9. After this *figurative* description, follows the *literal* explanation, which, in so many words, tells us that it refers to the *overthrow* of Babylon by the Medes.

(3.) Ezek. xxxii. The same, and is applied to the *literal* destruction of Egypt.

(4.) Jer. xv. 9. The context gives a clearly *literal* application of the language to the judgments of God upon Jerusalem and the Jews, on account of the sin of Manasseh, the king.

(5.) Ezek. xxxii. 7, 8. The inspired writer goes right on to say, expressly, that it refers to the *literal* desolation of Egypt by the king of Babylon.

(6.) Amos viii. 9. This is both preceded and followed by clear and *literal* applications to the judgments of God upon the Jews, for their oppressions and idolatry.

(7.) Joel ii. 10, 11. This is preceded by a description of a visitation of the locusts, under the idea of an *army;* and it is followed by a plain statement (verses 20, 25) of the fact that it means a *literal* visitation of locusts and other destroying insects; and,

(8.) Of those passages which speak of God as *coming* in a cloud, *riding* upon a cloud, etc., they either state, or refer to the *fact,* so prominent in the early history of the Jews, that God did *literally* come down in a cloud, that he *dwelt* in a thick cloud, that he *literally* made clouds and darkness his pavilion, and that he *literally* marched forth "in the pillar of a cloud," etc.

Another point which it is of importance to observe in this connection, is,

6. The evidence, that our leading divines have been led, unconsciously, and therefore without doubt honestly, to adopt an *erroneous theory* of prophetic interpretation, and that their *expositions* of prophecy, as a consequence, abound with instances of embarrassment, indefiniteness, self-contradiction, and palpable mis-

[1] The reader is requested to turn to the passages referred to.

conceptions of the subjects treated of. We cannot better express ourself on this point, than by quoting the observations of Dr. Tower, in his "Illustrations of Prophecy," vol. ii. p. 160. This writer, though an advocate of the *figurative* theory, yet was of too penetrating and logical an order of mind, not to perceive, and too honest not to expose, the glaring inconsistencies of his colleagues, when satisfied that they *misapprehended* any portion of God's prophetic word. Referring to the prophecy of our Lord, Matt. xxiv. 27–30, he says:

"That this prophecy of Jesus is of very difficult interpretation, is very generally admitted. Grotius and Lowth, Sykes, Benson, and Macknight, Bp. Watson, and the Taylors, have, Mr. Nesbitt acknowledges, (he is here speaking of the *second* coming of Christ,) 'all of them, without exception, manifestly discovered their *embarrassment*, and the difficulties which they labored under, in considering this subject.'" "Surely," resumes the Doctor, "this affords a strong presumption, that they have *all failed* of discovering the true import of Christ's celebrated prediction." And again, says Dr. Tower, quoting verse 30, "The expression translated, 'all the tribes of the earth,' Bp. Newton asserts, signifies merely the *Jewish tribes* inhabiting the province of Judea; and he maintains that this passage plainly signifies, 'that the destruction of Jerusalem will be such a remarkable instance of Divine vengeance, such a signal instance of *Christ's* power and glory, that all the Jewish tribes shall mourn.' But, unfortunately for this interpretation," he adds, "it is completely at *variance* with the testimony of civil and ecclesiastical history. So far from authorizing us to conclude that the Jews discerned or acknowledged, in the destruction of their city, any display of Christ's power; or that they attributed to their rejection of him, and the cruel death which he received at their hands, the overthrow of their armies, their capital, or their polity; it informs us that *they still* insulted the memory of their crucified Messiah, and *still* remained hardened in infidelity."

Our design in the preceding remarks on the subject of the *figurative* and *literal* interpretations of the prophetic scriptures in general, is simply to furnish a guide to the mind of the reader, in determining its merits, when applied by its advocates to the several parts of the prophecy of our Lord now under special consideration. This brings us,

II. *To our proposed reply to the expositions given in support of their interpretations of it.*

We will take up each part of the above prophecy, with its comments, in their consecutive order.

The reader will perceive, by referring to the synopsis of the theory in hand (pages 118-123), and to the arguments adduced in its support (pages 123-126),

1. That Matt. xxiv. 27 is interpreted to mean — That the lightning shining from east to west, figuratively denotes the coming of the Son of Man by the Roman army, to invade and conquer Judea; its sudden flashes indicating the unexpected, rapid, and universal desolation that would follow.

Before entering upon the subject, however, we would observe, once for all, that we shall maintain that the prophecy before us, like those portions which precede it from verse 1 to 26 inclusive, and those which follow it from verse 31 to the end of the chapter (with the exception of verse 28), *is not* to be interpreted by the laws which are applicable either to the figurative or the symbolical interpretations of other prophecies, but that it is *literal* throughout. And here I beg to remark, that it will, perhaps, be a matter of surprise to the reader to be informed that these very advocates of the figurative interpretations given by them of the 27th and 30th verses, inclusive, of this prophecy, themselves admit that *all* the other parts of it are to be taken *literally!* Surely, then, the onus remains with them to *prove* the sudden and extraordinary transition alleged to have been made by our Lord in this part of His great prophecy, from the literal to the figurative. This fact *of itself*, we submit, is sufficient to awaken in the mind of the most ardent and zealous advocate or admirer of this theory, at least a strong suspicion of its unsoundness.

Besides. Let it here be borne in mind, that the points at issue are not to be decided by mere assertion, or as a mere matter of opinion, however supported by great names. We shall show that the question of interpretation involved, *is purely one of fact.* On this hypothesis alone, we shall rest the whole issue of our reply.

With these preliminaries in view, we proceed to observe, that the passage before us, taken as a whole, is explained by these writers *figuratively*, to denote, as we have said: 1st, the invasion and destruction of Judea and Jerusalem, together with the ruin of the Jewish nation and polity, by the Roman legions, which should be like the sudden and irresistible flash of the "lightning," from east to west (v. 27); while, 2d, this destruction is compared to the darkening of the heavenly luminaries, which was to take place "immediately after," and to be effected by, the agency of said invading armies (v. 29); which invasion and its consequences, 3d, is described under the similitude of ravenous "eagles," the Romans, gathered around the fallen carcasses of the Jews (v. 28); and, 4th, that all this was intended to portray the grand, sublime, and momentous event, the *second* coming of Christ; which is described to be a metaphorical coming, by or with the Romans, as *representatives* of Christ, to inflict said punishments upon the Jews, etc.; and that this their destruction would be as ample a manifestation of Christ's power and glory as if He was *Himself* to come visibly in the "clouds of heaven," etc.; so that "all the tribes of the earth," i. e. the Jews, "seeing the *sign* of the Son of Man in heaven," and that it was He whom "they had pierced," would "behold Him and mourn over Him," and that "many, believing in Him, would become Christians," etc.

It is here important to observe, by the way, that Mr. Watson takes the liberty of substituting, against the plain words of the the passage, "all the tribes of the earth shall mourn," the word, "*Christian*," thus:—"The sign of the Son of Man," he says, "is that demonstration of the supernatural character of the *judicial* visitation of the Jews, that to the *Christians* it shall be as sure a sign that it was Christ who was then inflicting His vengeance upon His enemies, as though there should be a *visible personal* appearance of Him," etc.

Now, let it here be distinctly noted, that these writers deny that the above passage has any reference to a *personal* coming of Christ, except, at most, in a secondary and remote sense. In other words, they contend that its primary meaning is, Christ's *providential* coming, judicially to punish the Jews for their sins.

Our method of reply will be, to take up each verse consecutively, making reference at the same time to the others, in order to show their mutual relations to one another. The first in course is,

Verse 27.[1] On this passage we observe,

---

[1] See comments of Bp. Pearce, Bp. Newton, Dr. Clarke, Dr. Coke, Dr. Scott, The Cottage Bible, Dr. Benson, Rev. Mr. Barnes, and Dr. Whitby, on this verse, p. 119-120.

(1.) That there is a *contrast* here of one subject with another but *no* figure to illustrate one subject by another. We must bear in mind, that our blessed Lord was now addressing Himself, not to the literati of His day, or to minds inured to the subtleties of abstruse metaphysical speculations, such as abound in our age; but, to the common people, who would construe every word He uttered in accordance with the meaning of language *then* in use. Again,

(2.) The disciples, at this very time, believed in and were looking for *the speedy second personal appearing* of their Divine Master, who had said to them only a little before, that though "their house was to be left to them desolate," yet the time would come when "they should say, Blessed is he that cometh in the name of the Lord."[1] Hence their question to Him, Matt. xxiv. 3, "What shall be *the sign* of Thy coming?" In the next place,

(3.) In verses 23-26 of this chapter (xxiv.), Christ had predicted the appearance among them of "false Christs," etc. We therefore affirm, without the fear of successful refutation, that the contrast of which we now speak, lay between the coming of these *false* Christs and His own coming as the *true* Christ, verse 27 furnishing as much of an answer to the above question in reference to "*the sign*" of His coming as was deemed necessary, by way of warning them against being deceived by these impostors; so that when men should say, "Behold, He is in the desert, or in secret places," they might certainly know that it was not His coming, as that should be signalized only by the lightning's flash athwart the heavens from east to west. Hence the connection between the 23d–26th verses and the 27th. We repeat, the contrast is between the *manner* of the coming of the false and of the true Christ, both being as *personal* as language can make them. Accordingly,

(4.) When, in the 30th verse, our Lord describes to them *His actual* coming itself, He affirmed that He would come "in the clouds of heaven," and that "all the tribes of the earth" would see Him come in that manner. Finally,

(5.) Whence, then, we ask, the authority for converting Christ's language, in verses 27 and 30, into *figures*, as denotive of the sudden manner in which the Roman armies were to come against Judea, Jerusalem, and the Jews? Are we to suppose

[1] Matt. xxiii. 38, 39.

that our Lord did not know what were the ideas of the disciples as to the *nature* of His coming? If, then, He spake of a figurative coming, while they were expecting Him to come personally, is it not natural to conclude that He would at once have *corrected* their error by telling them—"You are mistaken in your impression that I am to come personally: it is not a personal coming, as the 'false Christs' will pretend; but only a *figurative* or *judicial* coming: I mean simply that I am to come in judgment by means of the Roman armies." This would not only have guarded them from all danger of deception on this point, but also would have prevented succeeding generations from misapprehending Him. But our Lord did no such thing.

The conclusion, therefore, we submit, is, that the theory under review, so far as this verse is concerned, fails rightly to interpret our Lord's words. We pass to

Verse 28.[1] The 27th verse, as we have seen, is limited to the contrast between the coming of the *true* Christ and those of the *false*. There the comparison ends, and they disappear from the stage of the prophecy. The reference to Christ's coming in this verse, therefore, is *parenthetical*, and relates, by way of anticipation, to the subject of His *actual* coming, as set forth more at large in verse 29, which speaks of the *signs* which are to appear "immediately after" the "tribulation of those days" spoken of in verses 21 and 22; while verse 30 describes the *manner* of that actual coming; thus marking the chronological order of the events that are to precede and accompany that coming.

It is admitted that the terms, "eagles" and "carcass," in verse 28, are figures. But, in view of the relation which verses 27, 29, and 30, bear to each other, it is evident,

(1.) That verse 28 can have *no* reference to the coming of the "false Christs," spoken of in verses 23-26, as "eagles" to prey upon the "carcasses" of the Jews. The reference made to them is confined to the description given of the difference between the manner of their coming and that of Christ, as delineated by the flashing of the lightning. The question then is, what is intended by these figures? We reply,

(2.) That they can have no reference to the coming of the Roman armies as "eagles," to prey upon the "carcasses" of the Jews. True, among the images and other devices of the Roman

---

[1] See the comments of Barnes and Whitby on this verse, p. 121.

ensigns, that of the eagle was very conspicuous. True also, there are in the Old Testament several references to the habits of this bird, to denote ravaging armies. Still, as we have proved that verse 27 has *no* reference whatever to the Roman armies, so verse 28, if applied to them, would derange the entire chronological order of the events predicted in verses 27, 29, and 30. This fact of *itself* furnishes sufficient evidence, that neither the image of the eagle on the Roman ensign, nor the reference to its ravaging habits in the Old Testament, can justify the application of the figures in this verse to the Roman armies gathering against the Jews. Besides, there is *no analogy* between the habits of that bird in coming upon its prey, and that of the Roman armies in ravaging the Jews. The eagle is not gregarious, and does not make its attacks in great numbers, like armies. It is an unsocial bird;[1] and, to quote Watson's Dictionary, "Providence has constituted it a *solitary* animal; two pairs of eagles are never found in the same neighborhood, though the genus is dispersed in every quarter of the world."

But, all is made clear, and in unison with the prophecy, by connecting the 28th verse with verses 27, 29, and 30. These last-named verses relate, as we have said, 1st, to the *sign* of Christ's coming; and 2d, to the *manner* of His actual coming; and which, when taken in connection with verse 28, show that the figures of the eagles and the carcasses therein employed, were designed to illustrate,

(3.) *The destruction of the ungodly at the second coming of Christ.* This hypothesis, we concede, may at first view strike the reader as far-fetched, novel, and, perhaps, chimerical. He, however, will admit equally with us, that the Scriptures plainly teach, that when "the Lord Jesus is revealed from heaven," it will be "in flaming fire," to "*take vengeance* on them that know not God," etc., and to "*reward* God's servants." (See 2 Thess. i. 7; and Rom. ii. 5-11).

As it regards the application of the figures in this 28th verse, however, the *agents* illustrated thereby cannot be Christ on the one hand, and the just and unjust on the other. Rather, the "eagles" are intended to denote the *angels*, as the agents employed in the destruction of the ungodly, and the separation from them of the righteous. Thus, in Matt. xiii. 30, we learn that, *at*

[1] Job xxxix. 27-30.

the second coming of Christ, it will be a time of separation between the righteous and the wicked, when the *angels* will be directed by our Lord to "gather together first the tares, and bind them in bundles to burn them, and to gather the wheat into barns."

And this, the great parabolic Teacher says, shall be at "*the end of the world*,"—αιων, i. e., age, or dispensation, called "the times of the Gentiles." (Luke xxi. 24; Rom. xi. 25.)

Now, we submit that Luke xvii. 34-37 is exactly parallel to Matt. xxiv. 28. Our Lord there refers us to the time when there shall be "two in one bed; the one shall be taken and the other left. Two women shall be grinding at the mill; the one shall be taken and the other left." Upon the announcement of this prophecy, the disciples said to Jesus, "Where, Lord? And he said unto them, Wheresoever the *body* (or carcass) is, thither will the *eagles* be gathered together."

Here, then, we are directed to *a time of separation*, between those most intimately associated in life. That time is stated to be, "When the Son of Man shall be revealed," which is to be at a period of the Church and the world analogous to "the days of Noah" and of "Lot" (verses 26-30), which is exactly coincident with "the end of the world" in Matt. xiii. 40-43.

It is scarcely necessary to add, in this connection, that in Luke xvii. there is not the remotest reference, from beginning to end, to the *Romans*. Indeed, the chronological note there given as to *the time* of said separation, viz., "in that night;" (and the second coming of Christ is represented as being in the night, Matt. xxv. 6;) and also the *nature* of the occurrence then to take place—not, mark, the escape of the one and the taking of the other, but a taking of one *from the side* of another that is *left*—is decisive against it.

As, therefore, 1st, Luke xvii. 34-37 is parallel with Matt. xxiv. 28; and as, 2d, the time of said separation refers, not to the coming of the Romans against Judea, Jerusalem, and the Jews in A. D. 70, but to the time "when the Son of Man is *revealed*," it follows, first, that the figures in this 28th verse refer to the destruction of the wicked by the angels at the second coming of Christ; and, second, that the theory under review which applies them to the Romans and the Jews, etc., is *fallacious*.

We come now to consider

Verse 29. The expositions given of this verse by the advocates of the figurative theory of interpretation, will render it necessary to notice, first, what they say of the *darkening* of the sun, moon, and stars; and, second, what, of *the time* of their occurrence.

I. The *darkening* of the sun, moon, and stars.[1] This is made to signify, 1st, "a *proverbial* expression, importing the destruction and utter ruin of a nation," etc.; and, 2d, "the *destruction* of their (i. e., the Jews') ecclesiastical and civil state, and of the rulers of both," etc., "who shall suddenly fall down as a leaf from the vine and from the fig-tree."

As what we have to say in reply to these explanations of the heavenly luminaries, will be brought out more fully in connection with our criticisms on the alleged *time* of their appearance, it will be necessary to say but little regarding them in this place. In unison with what has been said on the subject of the *laws* of prophetic interpretation, etc.,[2] though at the hazard of a seeming repetition, we in the very outset enter our protest against the fanciful, incongruous, and often contradictory expositions, attendant upon the popular system of metaphorizing the plainest *literal* declarations of God's word. We are, from conviction, unchangeably determined to expose to our utmost the fallacy of this theory, in our exegesis of the *un*figurative portions of the Bible; and in the *figurative* portions to be guided by what is, in immediate connection or otherwise, taught in *literal* prose.

We observe then, that we hold the passage before us to be strictly *literal;* that is, when Jesus said that "the sun should be darkened, and the moon should not give her light, and the stars should fall from heaven," he meant to be understood to speak of them as literally as when he said, "and all the tribes of the earth *shall mourn*," when they behold them. And wherefore, pray, should these celestial phenomena be thought a thing "incredible," any more than in the instance of the recorded arresting of the sun by the command of Joshua;[3] or the darkening of the sun, and of the other natural prodigies attendant upon the crucifixion of the Son of God?[4] See the argument of the figurativists as founded on Joel ii., iii. etc., and reply, pp. 142-146.

But, as before observed, this exposition, if we mistake not, will be abundantly confirmed by what we have to offer on the subject of,

[1] See comments by Barnes and Whitby, page 122, etc.   [2] See pages 127-129.
[3] Josh. x. 12.   [4] Matt. xxii. 50-53.

II. *The time* assigned to this darkening of the sun, and moon, and falling of the stars, etc. Our Lord's words are explicit. He says it shall be "*immediately* after the tribulation of those days," etc. Now, in order to determine the time for the commencement and close of this momentous period as indicated by the phrase "those days," we must ascertain in what consisted *the "tribulation"* here spoken of. All depends upon this. The allegorists, as we shall see, in applying the darkening of the heavenly luminaries as denotive of it, introduce into their interpretations the greatest possible uncertainty and confusion.

It is here to be particularly noted, that however these writers differ either with themselves or with each other on this point, all agree that the "days" here spoken of, are embraced in the *unparalleled calamities* described in verses 21, 22, and Mark xiii. 19: "For then shall be great tribulation, such as was not since the beginning of the world to this time, no, nor ever shall be;" which "days" were to be so intensified in their character compared with all preceding calamities, that, "except they should be *shortened*, no flesh should be saved." Mark's words are, "In those days shall be affliction, such as was not from the beginning of the creation which God created unto this time, *neither shall be.*"

Now, viewed from any stand-point adopted by these writers, this hypothesis is fundamental to their theory. For, the darkening of the sun, moon, and stars, etc., whether interpreted to signify "the wasting of the Jews by Vespasian's army flying quickly [like the lightning's flash, v. 27] through Galilee, Idumea, and Judea," and which it is alleged brought "an utter desolation and terrible destruction upon their nation and their capital cities;" or as denoting the "destruction of their ecclesiastical and civil state, and the rulers of both;" if these calamities were those referred to by our Lord in the above passages, it follows that they must have exhausted *all* that was intended to be embraced therein.

But, in direct opposition to this view, we affirm, first, that our Lord's description of the unparalleled calamities which were to fall upon the Jews in verses 21, 22, and Mark xiii. 19, refer to *a period entirely future to* the destruction of their country, nation, and polity, by the Romans; and,

Second. That the time assigned to the darkening of the sun, moon, and stars, etc., is *subsequent* to the close of these calamities.

But of this in its proper place.

Let us now see what these writers say of *the time* for the commencement, etc., of the "tribulation" referred to. We turn,

1. To DR. WHITBY. When treating of the first theory above, which applies the celestial phenomena to denote the coming of the Roman armies to besiege and destroy the nation and capital cities of the Jews, Dr. Whitby tells us that the "tribulation of those days" "were accomplished *during* the war under Vespasian!" But, when we come to the second theory, which makes the same celestial phenomena to denote the destruction—and that by the same Roman army—of the ecclesiastical and civil state, and of the rulers of both (and which he also adopts); this is made by him to refer to "a considerable period *before* the destruction of Jerusalem, when the thieves and zealots, says Josephus, 'kept all the nobles and rulers of the country in close custody; and when the zealots slew and consumed the nobility, and made it their business to leave none of the men of power alive."

But this is not all. According to these writers, in verse 30 we have not a personal, but a *judicial*, coming of the Lord, "by the Roman army," to punish the wicked Jews. Well, and what time does Dr. Whitby fix upon for this judicial coming of the Lord? Does he *now* speak of the invasion of the country? Does he *now* speak of that time of tribulation in "the wasting of the Jews by Vespasian's army quickly flying through Galilee, Idumea, and Judea? No. Does he *now* speak of that period "a considerable time *before* the destruction of Jerusalem," when, according to his own showing, their "ecclesiastical and civil state, and the rulers of them both" were destroyed? No. When, then, was it? Let the learned Doctor himself answer. His own words are, "Our Saviour's coming here, seems to import his coming by the Roman army to *besiege* and *destroy* Jerusalem, and the unbelieving Jews; for so Christ seemeth plainly to interpret this 'coming of the Son of Man,' verse 27. 'The coming of the Son of Man shall be as the lightning shining from east to west; for, wheresoever the Jews are, thither shall the Roman army be gathered,'" i. e., like the eagles devouring their prey! Indeed! Then this judicial coming of the Lord spoken of in verse 30, *was not* the coming of the Roman army when they made the invasion; it *was not* that visitation that brought about the tribulation of those days under Vespasian; neither was it the destruction of their ecclesiastical and civil state, etc., which took place a considerable time *before* the destruction of Jerusalem," when their sun and moon were blotted out, and their rulers fell to the earth like untimely fruit from the vine and fig-tree. None of these. But it was the *judicial coming* of the Lord, to besiege and destroy Jerusalem and the unbelieving Jews, AFTER the nation and their capital cities were destroyed, and their ecclesiastical and civil polity had been blotted out. Yes, then it was that the Lord came, by the Romans, to punish them!

Again. Other advocates of this theory maintain, that "the tribulation of those days" refers especially to the horrors of the *final* and fatal siege of the holy city. This is the theory of Br. NEWTON, in his dissertations on the prophecies, and has been adopted, with little or no variation, by Drs. Clarke, Scott, Coke, etc., and by Watson and Barnes. And,

Finally. DR. ROBINSON, in his Harmony, making a similar figurative application with the others, as to the things signified by "the sun, moon, and stars," etc., says that "The *subsequent* desolation and calamity spoken of in Matt. xxiv. 29, 30, and the parallel passages"—(by which we suppose the Doctor means verses 21, 22, and Mark xiii. 19: while in the other instance, he must allude to the *antecedent* calamities mentioned Matt. xxiv. 4-13)— "I refer to the overthrow and complete extirpation of the Jewish people *fifty years later*, under Adrian," etc.

Here, then, while Dr. Robinson differs from all his co-laborers as to *the time* for the commencement and close of the unparalleled tribulation; so they leave Dr. Whitby to stand alone in his paradoxical theory.

As it respects the theory of this latter writer, we remark, that to conclude that "the tribulation of those days" refers to a period *anterior to* the final siege," unavoidably involves the following difficulties, viz., first, that our Lord, in the exceedingly minute details of this prophecy, entirely omitted any reference to this last notable siege, though it consummated the ruin both of the Church and nation! Second. That if this *final* siege be the one intended by the darkening of the sun and moon, etc., then we must suppose that our Lord passed, by a sudden and unexplained transition, from one of the most *literal* prophecies of that event,[1] to the most highly *figurative* language that can be found in all the confessedly poetic departments of the Bible! and, third,

---

[1] See Luke xxi. 5-24, first clause: with which compare Matthew and Mark.

another result is, that there was *far less* of " tribulation" in the first than in the last siege. Whereas the first siege resulted in the death of only 300,000 Jews during *three or four years*, the last was marked by the destruction at "the edge of the sword" (Luke xxi. 24) of not less than 1,100,000 people *in six months!*

The truth is, Dr. Whitby was logician enough to perceive, that previously to, or during that siege, the so-called sun, moon, and stars of the nation perished; and he could not bring himself to the task of showing that it was afterward. It was this circumstance that forced him into the above unsuccessful, and what we conceive to be self-contradictory, efforts, to fix "the tribulation of those days" at an *earlier* period of the war.

But, enough of this. The theory, as presented by the other writers on this subject, contains just two points:—1st, That " the tribulation of those days" refers to the siege and destruction of Jerusalem; and 2d, that immediately after this siege, would occur the obscuration, etc., of the heavenly luminaries; which they apply to the Jewish Church and State, as thus expressed by Dr. Lightfoot:—" The Jewish heaven shall perish, and the sun and moon of its glory and happiness shall be darkened—brought to nothing. The sun is the religion of the Church; the moon is the government of the State; and the stars are the doctors of both." This states specifically the usual interpretations given of the passage.

Without further preliminaries, we now proceed to adduce the facts and arguments in support of the *opposite* view to that advocated by these writers, and observe,

First. That our Lord's description of those unparalleled calamities in verses 21, 22, and Mark xiii. 19, which were to fall upon the Jews, refers to a period *entirely future to* the destruction of their country, nation, and polity, by the Romans. And,

Second. That the time assigned to the darkening of the sun, moon, and stars, etc., is *subsequent to the close of* these calamities.

We here again repeat, that the issue in this important matter depends, not upon mere assertion or opinion, but upon facts.

The pivot upon which turns the issue in the premises, is the question of the *literal* or *figurative* character of the prophecy of Christ in Matt. xxiv. 27–30.

That there may be no ground for a continued misapprehension

regarding it, we here give what constitutes the *foundation* on which rests the theory we repudiate. It is simply this:

Its advocates assume, that as there was *no* literal fulfilment of the darkening of the sun, moon, and stars during the period of the Jewish troubles under the Romans, *ergo*, the language of the prophecy must be understood *figuratively*, to represent the providential or judicial coming of Christ, to destroy the country, nation, and ecclesiastical and civil polity of the Jews.

Let the reader not forget, in this connection, the fact that these same writers admit that all the other portions of this great prophecy of Christ are *strictly literal!*

That the part of it under review is *equally literal*, we shall now proceed to prove.

The subject in hand relates to matters both of interpretation, and of historic facts. Our arguments, of course, must hold a relation to both.

I. First, then. *Of the principle of interpretation* applied to the exposition of this 29th verse. Two classes of passages are adduced to sustain the figurative theory—the first, those that are alleged in proof that this passage will admit of *no other* interpretation: the second, that the event predicted, to wit, the darkening of the heavenly luminaries, received their *accomplishment* in those judgments inflicted upon the Jews, between the commencement and termination of their calamities under the Romans.

1. In regard to the first point, the advocates of this theory refer to numerous passages in the Old Testament, which, being *figurative*, are adduced in justification of so interpreting the words of Christ in that now before us. The reader will find several examples of these in pages 121 and 125 of this work. Still, the question to be determined is, not whether such figures of speech were ever used by the old prophets for purposes of illustration or ornament—which we admit—but whether *our Lord* employed the words, "darkening of the sun and moon, falling of the stars from heaven," etc., in verse 29, to signify the judgments that were to overtake the Jews?

On the *affirmative* of this question, great reliance is placed upon the two following passages, Joel ii. 30, 31, and iii. 15: "And I will show wonders in the heavens and in the earth—blood, and fire, and pillars of smoke. The sun shall be turned into darkness, and the moon into blood, before the great and terrible day of the

Lord come." (Joel ii. 30, 31). "The sun and the moon shall be darkened, and the stars shall withdraw their shining." (Chap. iii. 15). The passages are parallel. Now such writers as Patrick and Lowth, Dr. Clarke and others, say, "this very destruction of Jerusalem is represented" thus in these passages. The following quotations from their works must suffice. On Joel ii. 30, PATRICK and LOWTH say:

"This and the following verse principally point out the destruction of the city and temple of Jerusalem by the Romans, a judgment justly inflicted upon the Jewish nation for their resisting the Holy Spirit, and contempt of the means of grace." And Mal. iii. 1, 2, 5, and iv. 1, are referred to as pointing out the signs which were to immediately precede that destruction; while Josephus is quoted (De Bell. Jud., Lib. 6, cap. 31) in verification of their fulfilment, as predicted by Christ, Luke xxi. 11.—On verse 31, they write thus: "Comp. Mal. iv. 5. . . . The expressions here used, in the *literal* sense, import the failing of light in the sun and moon, whether by eclipses (when the moon looks of a bloody color) or any other cause; and here they denote the dark and melancholy state of public affairs at the destruction of the Jewish nation by the Romans, and the utter overthrow of that state and government." (See the Note upon Isa. xiii. 10.)

And so DR. CLARKE, on Joel ii. 30, ["wonders in the heavens and in the earth."] "This refers to the fearful sights, dreadful portents, and destructive commotions by which the Jewish polity was finally overthrown, and the Christian religion finally established in the Roman empire. See how our Lord applies this prophecy, Matt. xxiv. 29, and the parallel texts." And on verse 31, ["the sun shall be turned into darkness,"] he says: "The Jewish polity, civil and ecclesiastical, shall be entirely destroyed."

Such, then, is the mode of applying these passages from Joel, by all the commentators that give a *figurative* interpretation to the language in Matt. xxiv. 29. The issue, then, is distinct. We take the *negative*. Now for the proof: the prophet—or rather the Lord by the prophet—shall give his own explanation.

Let the reader now turn back to Joel ii. 30, 31. This, it is affirmed by these learned divines, relates to the *destruction* of the nation, and the civil and ecclesiastical polity of the Jews. But what does God say on the subject?

Verse 32: "And it shall come to pass, that whoever shall call on the name of the Lord shall be delivered: for in Mount Zion and in Jerusalem shall be *deliverance,* as the Lord hath said, and in the remnant whom the Lord shall call." Chap. iii. 1, 2: "For, behold, in those days, and in that time, when I shall *bring again* the captivity of Judah and Jerusalem, I will also gather all nations, and will bring them down to the valley of Jehoshaphat, and will plead with them there *for my people and for my heritage, Israel,* whom they have scattered among the nations, and parted my land." Then, in chap. iii., verses 3–6, follows a narrative of what Israel, Judah, and Jerusalem had suffered at the hands of their enemies. Verses 7, 8, of God's threatened judgments upon them therefor; and verses 9–14, of the manner in which those judgments should be visited upon them, etc. And then comes verse 15: "The sun and the moon shall be darkened, and the stars shall withdraw their shining." Verse 16: "The Lord also shall roar out of Zion, and utter his voice from Jerusalem; and the heavens and the earth shall shake." For what purpose? as precursors of the destruction of Jerusalem and the Jews by the Romans? Nay, verily. For, saith the prophet, "The Lord will be the *hope* of his people, and the *strength* of the children of Israel." Then, from the 17th to the 21st verses, inclusive, we have a most glowing description of God dwelling in Zion, *in the midst* of his ransomed people; and of the peace, prosperity, and abundance to be enjoyed by them, while they shall behold Egypt and Edom converted into a desolate wilderness, for their violence against the children of Judah. Yea, "Judah shall dwell forever, and Jerusalem from generation to generation." For, saith the Lord, "I will cleanse their blood that I have not cleansed: *for the Lord dwelleth in Zion.*"

Now let the reader particularly note that these two quotations from Joel are *inseparably connected.* The last verse of the iid chapter refers to the same time that the sun and moon are to be darkened. This is conceded by Dr. Lowth, who, on Joel iii. 1, "In those days, *at that time,*" says: "The time called 'the last days,' chap. ii. 28,"[1] etc. Also by Dr. Clarke. "Joel iii. 1: 'For, behold, in those days,—according to the preceding prophecy" [i.e. chap. ii. 28, etc.], "these days should refer to gospel times, or to such as should immediately precede them." On the other hand, it has been proved by the authority of God himself, that the first

---

[1] See Commentary of Patrick and Lowth.

verse of the iiid chapter refers to the *same days* spoken of in chap. ii. 28, etc. And, from the declaration of the Almighty, we learn that "those days" and "that time,"—i. e., the time during which the darkening of the heavenly luminaries takes place—*do not* refer to the utter desolation, destruction and ruin of Judea, Jerusalem, and the nation of the Jews by the Roman armies, but—and God is witness—to events *directly the reverse* of all this. It refers to the time when Jehovah " shall bring again the captivity of Judah and Jerusalem;" i. e., when, as the Lord says, "Jerusalem shall be holy, and when there shall no stranger pass through her any more." (Joel iii. 1, 17).

Here, then, these commentators, who, with one stroke of the pen, refer the darkening of the celestial planets to the destruction of the Jews by the Romans, acknowledge the unbroken' and inseparable connection between the iid and iiid chapters of Joel, when they come to comment on this very darkening of the sun, etc., *in connection with* the events with which it is so undeniably associated; and that, too, according to God's own explanation of it, in the iiid chapter; with another stroke of the pen, they totally abandon the ground of their former exposition, and refer it to other events, or confess their inability to understand it at all. Doctors Lowth and Clarke both adopt this course. The latter writer, commenting on Joel iii. 1, says: "But this is a part of the prophecy which is *difficult* to be understood. All interpreters are *at variance* upon it," etc. Then, after giving several examples of them, he concludes thus: "In this *painful uncertainty*, rendered still more so by the discordant opinions of many wise and learned men, it appears to be my province to confine myself to an explanation of the phraseology of the chapter, and leave the reader to apply it as may seem best to his own judgment." [!!!]

The reader will pardon our display of the dagger-points. They are merely designed as suggestive of the deep mortification that must have accompanied the penning of the above concession by such a writer as Dr. Clarke—the *cause*, we submit, the spiritualizing a passage where all was literal; the *effect*, the indefinite, confused, and contradictory conclusions, in its application to the events referred to. This will appear the more conspicuous, when we come presently to explain the nature and duration of the unparalleled calamities spoken of in Matt. xxiv.

21, 22, and Mark xiii. 19; and also the true chronology of the darkening of the sun, moon, and stars.

There is, however, one other point that we must not overlook, in reference to the quotations from Joel. The advocates of this theory refer us to St. Peter, and affirm that, having quoted this very passage in Joel, Acts ii. 16–21, he applies the darkening of the sun, moon, and stars *to the destruction of the Jews by the Romans;* proof demonstrative, they insist, that Matt. xxiv. 29 is to be interpreted *figuratively*, to denote that event.[1] So far from it, we defy the closest scrutiny of the passage to detect the least reference in it to the Romans, from beginning to end. As we have shown that the prophecy of Joel relates, *not* to the destruction *but* to the deliverance, etc., of the Jews; so we shall now prove, of the passage referred to in the Acts.

In the prophecy of Joel, the period designated as "those days," and "that time," in chap. iii. 1, which were to *commence* as described in chap. ii. 28, 29, were to continue, *until* the period for the darkening of the heavenly planets, as the precursors of the restoration of the Jews, and the final overthrow of their oppressors. Now, are we to suppose that the inspired apostle was ignorant of the fact, that the prophet Joel, when he spake of this darkening of the sun, moon, and stars in its relation to associated events, referred it to the *closing up* of the tribulation of the Jews at the great battle that should destroy their enemies? Who will pretend this? Accordingly, in his allusion to this prophecy, the apostle affirms, in the first place, that the dispensation of the spirit on the day of Pentecost of which Joel spake, had *begun* to run its course; and second, that his associating with this event the darkening of the heavenly luminaries, was simply to show, in harmony with the design of the prophet, that these "last days" were to continue, until, as he said to the Jews a little after, (see Acts iv. 21,) *until* " the times of restitution of all things, which God had spoken by the mouth of all his holy prophets, since the world began." In a word, the language of Peter in the Acts is to be taken as *God's commentary* on the text in Joel.

Thus much, then, in regard to this passage from Joel, which, by the way, constitutes the *chief reliance* of these commentators, in support of their figurative interpretation of Matt. xxiv. 29.

[1] See page 124.

2. But, there are several other passages pressed into service by these writers, to sustain the alleged interpretation given by them of the *metaphorical* import of the darkening of the sun and moon and stars, as denoting the second coming of Christ by the Romans, within the period of the then existing generation. Our Lord, say they, declared to his disciples that " *This generation* shall not pass, till all these things be fulfilled " (Matt. xxiv. 34); and also, that with this prophecy accord several other statements, which go to prove that the second coming of Christ spoken of in Matthew cannot be *future*. The first passage is,

Matt. xvi. 27, 28. Our Lord, having in v. 27 spoken of "the coming of the Son of Man in the glory of the Father," etc., adds, " There be some standing here which shall not taste of death, *till they see* the Son of Man coming in his kingdom " (v. 28). To this we answer, that v. 27 undeniably refers to Christ's coming to judgment. If, therefore, v. 28 refers to *the same thing*, it follows that that event transpired while some of the disciples were *still living!* and such, substantially, is the view taken of it by Dr. Clarke. In his note on v. 27—with which he considers Dan. vii. 13, 14, as collateral, he says: " This is the glorious *mediatorial kingdom* which Jesus Christ was now about to set up, by the destruction of the Jewish nation and polity, and the diffusion of the gospel through the whole world. . . . It is very likely that the words do not apply to the general judgment," etc. And on v. 28 he adds, " This verse seems to confirm the above explanation," etc. . . . It is " as if he had said, 'Some of you, my disciples, shall continue *until* these things take place.' The destruction of Jerusalem and the Jewish economy, which our Lord here predicts, took place about forty-three years after this; and some of the persons now with him, doubtless *survived* that period, and witnessed the extension of the Messiah's kingdom." etc. Now, to this we reply,

First. That in no sense can v. 28 be construed to denote the setting up, *at the time* referred to, of the so-called mediatorial kingdom of Christ, as here alleged. This writer makes the surviving disciples to have "witnessed the extension of the Messiah's kingdom" "*after* the day of Pentecost," and "the destruction of Jerusalem," by "the diffusion of the gospel through the whole world." Two facts demonstrate the utter fallacy of this statement: the first, that the gospel accomplished its entire circuit through the world *before* "the destruction of the Jewish nation and polity," and that, by these very disciples themselves. (Compare Matt. xxiv. 14 with Rom. x. 19.) The second, that the " Christian Church " *has not yet attained* " its final triumph" since "the destruction of the Jewish polity." The truth is, the reference in this verse to the " coming of the Son of Man in His kingdom," relates exclusively to the kingdom of Christ in *manifestation*, as contradistinguished from the "kingdom of God," or "of heaven," in "*mystery*," under and during "the times of the Gentiles." This latter "kingdom" is constituted of those who, down to the *end* of that period, are "taken out of (or from among) the Gentiles, to the praise of Christ's name,"[1] and *in* which they are prepared, " when the Son of Man shall come in His kingdom," to receive the welcome, " Come, ye blessed," etc. This 28th verse, therefore, relates to the coming of the Son of Man to *set up* His kingdom in its fulness and perfection, when His present office as our priestly Intercessor at the right hand of God shall have *ended;* and when, having "*received*" that kingdom" for which He has "taken a journey into a far country,"[2] He will "*return*," to take His seat, as David's "Son," on David's "throne," and thus commence and continue His *kingly* reign " over the house of Jacob forever."[3] For it should be borne in mind, that David was in no sense a *type* or forerunner of Christ in His mediatorial, but only His *kingly* office. Christ now fills the office of "*high-priest* over the house of God,"[4] which is " His body, the Church,"[5] "the kingdom of heaven" in "*mystery*," and over which, in His present character as "Intercessor at the right hand of God," He is " the Head."[6] But this is in no way inconsistent with the *literal* fulfilment of those many predictions of a *future* kingdom, when the existing dispensation shall have passed away. By not distinguishing between these two widely different dispensations, and confounding those passages which relate to them respectively, the greatest confusion has obtained among expositors of the Scriptures respecting them, to the great trouble and perplexity of candid inquirers.

Then again. These two verses in Matt. xvi. 27, 28, taken in connection with other collateral passages, it may be asked—Did Christ, *during* His alleged coming at "the destruction of

---

[1] Acts xv. 14. [2] Luke xix. 12. [3] Luke i. 32, 33.
[4] Heb. x. 21. [5] Col. i. 18.

Jerusalem," etc., come "with His angels?" Was there *then* any "appearance of the sign of the Son of Man in heaven?" Did Christ *then* "come in the clouds of heaven?" Was there *then* the sound of a trumpet, and a gathering together of the elect from the four winds of heaven?" And did Christ *then* "reward every man according to his works?" Surely, as it respects this last article, it cannot mean an act of gracious mediation, but of *strict judgment;* nor can it mean a national judgment, which in no sense is the rewarding of each and every man according to his works; for, sinners of a widely different degree of delinquency, in a time of national judgment, are involved in the same public calamities, the comparatively innocent sharing the penalty equally with the most guilty. It is certain, therefore, that the coming of Christ in the fulness of His glory to set up His *kingly reign*, could not have been verified by the judgments inflicted on the Jews at the period of the Roman invasion.

And yet, agreeably to the intent of Christ's words, in verse 28, those to whom He addressed Himself *did* "see" "the Son of Man coming in His kingdom." It was verified in the TRANSFIGURATION, a few days after, when Jesus took Peter, and James, and John, up into the mountain to meet Moses and Elias.[1] Of this spake Peter (1 Pet. i. 16-18): "For we have not followed cunningly devised fables, when we made known unto you the power and coming of our Lord Jesus Christ, but were *eye-witnesses* of His majesty. For He received from God honor and glory, when there came such a voice to Him from the excellent glory, This is my beloved Son, in whom I am well pleased. And this voice from heaven we heard, when we were with Him in the holy mount."

We pass to another passage, in which it is claimed that our Lord spake of His coming in reference to Jewish affairs.

John xxi. 22: "And Jesus said, if I will that he [John] *tarry till I come*, what is that to thee?" The argument of the figurativists here is, that Christ, by His coming, could not have meant "the general judgment; for, as the saints that are then alive are not to *die*, it would follow that *John* would not die at all. Therefore, the coming *after* which John was to die could not have refered to any other than Christ's coming to punish the unbelieving Jews during the generation *then* living.[2]

---
[1] Three of the Evangelists speak of this event in immediate connection with Christ's transfiguration on the mount: Matt. xvii. 2; Mark ix. 2; Luke ix. 29.
[2] See page 125.

To this it may be replied, if the disciples understood Christ in the sense here given, how came they to circulate the report that "that disciple *should not die?*" According to this theory, they had been frequently informed that Christ would come judicially to punish the Jews within the life-time of the men of *that* generation; and yet, because John should live to witness them, therefore John should *never die!* Marvellous logic, this!

The truth of the matter is simply as laid down in the following *facts:* 1st. Christ's remark concerning John was not made till *after* His resurrection, and also the instructions given to the disciples "of the things pertaining to the kingdom of God." (Acts i. 3.) 2d. These instructions, doubtless, included the important matter of Christ's coming to raise the dead and change the living. 3d. The whole Church at this time, and so on to St. Paul's penning of 2d Thess. ii. 1–4, believed that *a very short interval* was to elapse between the first and the second comings of Christ. 4th. They also understood the doctrine, as afterwards stated by St. Paul, 1 Cor. xv. 51, 52, that those who "*remain* unto the coming of the Lord," *would not die,* but be instantaneously "changed," and be "caught up to meet the Lord in the air." (1 Thess. iv. 13–18.)

Now, it was under these circumstances that our Lord had signified to Peter "by what death *he* should glorify God." This awakened his inquisitiveness to know somewhat of the destiny of the beloved *John.* Hence the question, "Lord, and what shall this man do?" To this Jesus replied, in the words before us, "If I will that he tarry *till I come,* what is that to thee? Follow thou me." When, therefore, we take into view the above instructions of Christ regarding His *second* coming, how natural was it for the disciples to infer that John was to be kept "alive *unto* the coming of the Lord, and also that, as a consequence, he would not die?" And yet Jesus said not unto him, "my will is that John shall tarry till I come;" but, "*if I will* that he tarry," etc., "what is that to thee," Peter? "Follow thou me." Whether that interval were of shorter or longer duration, an act of Christ's will was fully adequate to the preservation of John's life till He come again. But our Lord, looking to the *coming itself,* and *not* to the time when it should take place, proceeded to *suppress* the curiosity of Peter as to the destiny of his brother disciple by a mild rebuke: It is no concern of thine, Peter, whether John die *before* I come, or live *until* I come. "Follow thou me."

But finally, on this subject. Is it not surpassingly strange, that while these writers explain our Lord's remarks concerning John's tarrying *literally*, so soon as they touch the matter of *Christ's coming*, to which it relates, all suddenly becomes *figurative!* This, we must insist, is to substitute the most wild and fanciful speculations in divine things, in the place of that simple law of scriptural interpretation which enjoins—"Interpret every passage of God's word *literally*, unless there be a necessity to the contrary." Now, nothing is more evident than that the disciples, even *before* the crucifixion, were taught the doctrine of the second literal or personal coming of Christ.[1] And, as Christ's remark concerning the tarrying of John till He come, was *subsequent* to His prophecy of the destruction of Jerusalem, they must have understood both the coming of Christ and what was said of John's tarrying for it *literally*. Then, as they looked for the second personal coming of Christ as an event *nigh at hand*, it was perfectly natural for them to understand our Lord to have said that John should not die, but that he should live to see Him come in the clouds of heaven, and then be changed, and caught up to Him, like Enoch and Elijah, "in the air."

We leave the reader to decide between the obvious truth of the *literal*, or the equally obvious fiction of the *figurative* interpretation of this passage.

A third passage adduced in support of a figurative interpretation of Christ's coming, is founded on his address to the highpriest, Caiaphas.

Matt. xxvi. 64: "Hereafter *shall ye see* the Son of Man, sitting on the right hand of power, and coming in the clouds of heaven." The argument derived from this passage is this: As Caiaphas could not live until the day of judgment; and as the second coming will *precede* the resurrection, therefore, he could not *see* Christ come, etc. It is hence concluded that our Lord meant His *figurative* coming to destroy Jerusalem.[2]

This reasoning is claimed to be decisive against the literalist. We will examine it,

First, in reference to the words, "hereafter shall *ye* see," etc. These expositors restrict the seeing of the Son of Man, here, to the *person* of the high-priest himself. Then, of course, they will, in all consistency, apply the same restriction to the apostolic com-

---

[1] See John xiv. 1-3; xv. 16, 22, and intervening verses. [2] See page 125.

mand, "Go *ye*, therefore, and teach all nations.... and lo, I am with *you* alway, even unto the *end of the world*." And so, the entire college of the apostles must still be *alive!* The same holds true of St. Paul and his brethren, in regard to what he said of the second coming of Christ to raise the dead: "*We* shall not all sleep,"—i. e., die—"but *we* shall all be changed," etc. And "then, *we* which are alive and remain unto the coming of the Lord," etc. But this resurrection *has not yet* taken place. And so, Paul and his brethren must *still be alive!*

The fallacy of this theory in its application to Caiaphas, however, will be still more apparent from the circumstance, that there is no evidence that even *he* witnessed Christ's coming, in the sense here explained of it. We submit the following facts: Jerusalem was destroyed in A. D. 70. It was in the fifth or sixth year of Caiaphas' priesthood when Christ was arraigned before him, which was probably in the fortieth year of his age at least; and, about four years after, having incurred the displeasure of the emperor, he was deposed. If, therefore, he lived to witness the above catastrophe, it must have been about in his *eightieth* year. This is not impossible. But, we submit, the strong probability, amounting almost to moral certainty, is that, if he did not die long before, yet, being so eminent a man as the son-in-law of Annas, he fell *a victim* to the fury of the zealots, who, as Josephus informs us (De Bell. Jud. lib. 5, cap. 20), "slew and consumed the nobility, and made it their business to leave *none of the men of power alive*." Nor this only; for he adds (Lib. 4, cap. 11, 12), that they "abolished *the families* of the high-priests by succession, and placed in their room men ignoble and unknown, who neither belonged to the priesthood, nor knew what the office of high-priest meant;" all of which, the reader will bear in mind, took place *even before* the first invasion of the holy city by the Roman legions.

It is clear, therefore, that the passage did not refer the *seeing* of Christ at his second coming to Caiaphas personally; but that the *living nations*, of which himself and those whom our Lord was then addressing were the types, should "*hereafter see* the Son of man sitting on the right hand of power, and coming in the clouds of heaven," at that day when "*every eye should see him;* and they also which pierced him; and when all the kindreds of the earth should wail because of him." The statement, therefore, that, as the second coming of Christ *precedes* the resurrection;

and hence, that as Caiaphas was not to be raised until *after* that event, the coming spoken of above must mean a *figurative* coming of Christ to destroy Jerusalem, is a most unwarrantable assumption. It is founded either upon an entire ignorance, or a perversion, of the *order* of the events which accompany and follow that momentous crisis. For, in the first place, on the hypothesis of the second coming of Christ as preceding the resurrection as laid down by St. Paul, 1 Cor. xv. 51, 52, and 1 Thess. iv. 13–18, compared with Rev. xx. 1–6, and verses 11–15, the order of events is as follows: first, The dead in Christ, *at* the sounding of the last trump, shall be raised, and the believing saints then alive shall be changed, and together be caught up to meet the Lord in the air, etc. How long our blessed Lord and his saints will *remain* in that position, we are not informed. But, the *union* between himself and the saints of this first resurrection being consummated, *then*, in the next place, as Zechariah states (chap. xiv. 5, and v. 4), "The Lord God will come, and all his saints with Him," etc. But for what purpose? To raise the wicked dead? Nay, verily. But it is *to judge the living antichristian nations*, which, as I have said, answer to the *living* Caiaphas and others to whom Christ spake the words of this passage. Christ then comes, I repeat, *not* to raise the wicked dead—for not a word is said in our Lord's address to Caiaphas about a resurrection—but to "*take vengeance* on them that know not God, and that obey not the gospel of our Lord Jesus Christ" (2 Thess. i. 7–10); and who, being those who shall then "*see* Him, and *wail* because of Him;" third, shall be numbered among those wicked "dead" who shall not be raised, "*until* the thousand years" of millennial blessedness "are *ended*." (Rev. xx. 5.)

Viewed, therefore, in all its aspects, we appeal to the decision of every unbiased mind, as to the merits of the issue on this passage. We claim to have demonstrated, 1st, that the advocates of this theory assume, that the seeing the Son of Man, etc., was necessarily limited to Caiaphas. 2d. That they assume that the raised dead cannot see Christ. 3d. That their assumptions conflict with the plainest scriptural declarations in regard to the *two resurrections*, etc. And we now add, that, having shown that the other two passages claimed by these writers, so far from yielding support to their theory, prove it to be utterly fallacious, it follows that the other passage, viz., Matt. xxiv. 34: "This generation shall not pass away, till all these things be fulfilled," cannot, by any possibility, be made to apply to the generation of men *then living*. For, if this prophecy of Christ, in verse 29, is to be interpreted *literally*, His coming spoken of, instead of being figuratively used to denote the destruction of the Jewish nation in A. D. 70, refers to his judgment-coming in the clouds of heaven, *at the last day*. Consequently, *the* "generation" that was "not to pass away till all be fulfilled," must hold a relation to *that event*.

Having now animadverted upon the two classes of passages adduced in support of the figurative interpretation of this 29th verse of Matt. xxiv., viz., 1st, Joel ii. 30, 31, and iii. 15 (see pages 142–146); and 2d, Matt. xvi. 27, 28; John xxi. 22; Matt. xxvi. 64, and xxiv. 34 (pages 147–153), we now proceed to demonstrate, by the most indubitable scriptural testimony and historic facts,

I. That our Lord's description of the *unparalleled calamities* in Matt. xxiv. 21, 22, and Mark xiii. 19, which were to fall upon the Jewish nation, etc., refer to a period *entirely future to* the destruction of Jerusalem by the Romans in A. D. 70.[1]

This subject brings us into direct contact with "*the tribulation of those days*" spoken of by our Lord in Matt. xxiv. 29. The advocates of the figurative theory under review, affirm that this verse is collateral with verses 21 and 22 of this chapter; and that they one and all refer to the calamities that overtook the Jews *at* the destruction of Jerusalem. But, that this view is totally at variance with the true sense and proper application of the passages referred to, will, we submit, appear,

1. From the *connection* of this part of the prophecy with the following member of it as given by St. Luke, chap. xxi. 24:

"And ye shall fall by the edge of the sword, and shall be carried captive into all nations; and Jerusalem shall be trodden down of the Gentiles, *until* the times of the Gentiles be fulfilled."

Now, these words are *supplementary* to the record of Christ's prophecy as furnished by Matthew and Mark. By this we mean, that St. Luke supplies a portion of the prophecy as given by our Lord, which was *omitted* by the other two Evangelists. We think these variations may be accounted for from the fact, that Matthew and Mark wrote their respective Gospels for the benefit of the Jews; while Luke penned his for the use of the Gentiles. *They* were careful to insert a particular narrative of the predicted ap-

[1] See pages 139–141.

pearance among the Jews of the "false Christs," etc., down to the war and siege of the holy city; *he*, of the captivity and dispersion among the Gentiles, of those of them that should escape the edge of the sword during said siege. But, unless, indeed, we suppose one of the inspired writers to have *added* a passage that the Lord did not deliver—which would have been to falsify the record —this supplement forms as *essential a part* of the prophecy, as though it had been found in each of the Gospels.

We now observe, that the misapprehension and consequent confusion occasioned by these writers in their interpretations of the prophecy in hand, has arisen either from their having entirely overlooked this supplementary passage from Luke, or in assigning to it a wrong place in the chapter. And, inasmuch as both the nature and duration of "the tribulation of those days" referred to, can only be determined by *restoring* it to its legitimate position in the prophecy, it is to that point that we shall now direct the reader's mind.

Now, as already stated, those who claim verses 21 and 22 of this chapter, together with Mark xiii. 19, as collateral with verse 29, now under consideration, place the supplementary passage from Luke *opposite* to Matt. xxiv. 21, 22, and Mark xiii. 19, 20. Against this arrangement we are compelled to urge the following objections, viz.:

First. It makes the verse from Luke xxi. 24 to come in *before* verses 23 and 24, which refer to the false Christs, etc., whose appearance was to *precede* the Jewish calamities; whereas the supplementary passage undeniably speaks of calamities that were to *follow* the Jewish war. Again,

Second. The *chronology* of the "tribulation" predicted in the verse from Luke, makes it certain that the above Harmonists have misplaced it. That "tribulation" is there made to reach from the *end* of the Roman siege to the *close* of "the times of the Gentiles;" which period has not yet expired: whereas the calamities predicted by Christ, according to these writers, terminated more than *seventeen* centuries ago! Once more,

Third. By placing it opposite to Matt. xxiv. 22, and Mark xiii. 20, it makes our Lord predict a *shortening* of those very days of tribulation, lest all flesh should perish (of which He had spoken in the preceding verses), when He knew that they were to extend over a period of *eighteen hundred years!* It is simply absurd to speak of shortening the *longest* period of national dispersion that history records. How, then, is this supplementary prophecy of St. Luke to be made to harmonize with the application, by these writers, of the predicted unparalleled tribulation *to the time of* the Roman war?

This may suffice, by way of exhibiting the negative argument in these premises. We offer the following, in proof that the true position of St. Luke's supplement is, to place it *before* verse 29, which relates to the signs in the heavens. It is hence made to *follow* the description of the final siege (see Luke xxi. 5–22), and to *precede* the darkening of the heavenly luminaries, thus—Luke xxi. 20–23: "And when ye shall see Jerusalem compassed with armies, then know that the tribulation is nigh," etc. Then verse 24: "And they shall fall by the edge of the sword, and shall be led captive into all nations: and Jerusalem shall be trodden down of the Gentiles, *until* the times of the Gentiles be fulfilled." And then comes in Matt. xxiv. 29, which is collateral with Luke xxi. 25: "Immediately after the tribulation of those days," i. e., "the desolation" of the Jews by the Roman siege *previously* spoken of, "shall the sun be darkened," etc. Or, as St. Mark gives it: "But *in* those days, *after* that tribulation, shall the sun be darkened," etc. (Mark xiii. 24.) The 23d verse of Luke evidently takes in, first, "the desolation" of Jerusalem, etc., by the Roman invasion—"there shall be great distress in the land;" and, second, the unprecedented calamities which were to follow the close of the siege, down to the time of the darkening of the sun, moon, and stars, etc.,—"and wrath upon this people," as described by our Lord, Matt. xxiv. 21, 22, and Mark xiii. 19, 20.

Having thus assigned to St. Luke's supplement to Matthew and Mark its *true* chronological position in this great prophecy of Christ, we proceed to the proof that the predicted calamities described in Matt. xxiv. 21, 22, etc., as alleged to have been verified during the Roman siege,

2. Is contradicted by historic fact. We have the testimony of Josephus, that even *before* the siege, the direst anarchy prevailed both in Church and State; and that both the ecclesiastical and civil orders were deposed and destroyed, to the absolute subversion of all law and authority among the people. Speaking of the thieves and zealots who infested the city, the Jewish historian

tells us,[1] that they "kept all the nobles and rulers of the country in close custody," and that they "abolished the families of the high-priests by succession, and placed in their room men ignoble and unknown, who neither belonged to the priesthood, nor knew what the office of high-priest meant." Again; he says that "twelve thousand of the nobility perished after this manner; when the high-priests, and among them Ananus, were destroyed by the Idumeans," which Josephus reckons as "the *beginning* of their captivity,"[2] their national glory departed from them. Josephus adds, that the zealots "slew and consumed the nobility, and made it their business to leave none of the men of power alive."[3]

Nor this only. As though bent upon their own ruin, the factious Jews became divided into two parties, the leaders of whom, striving for the supreme dominion, fought not only against one another, but against the common people. "And because the city had to struggle with three of the greatest misfortunes, war, and tyranny, and sedition, it appeared upon the comparison that the war was the least troublesome to the populace of them all." Nor were these terrible calamities confined to the capital; there was in addition a regular combination of ruffians, called *Sicarii*, outside of the city, who carried on an indiscriminate crusade of murder, plunder, and desolation, together with a desecration of the holy places, i. e., *proseuche,* or houses of prayer, through every part of Judea.

And now, reader, bear in mind that *at this time,* some who succeeded in escaping from the metropolis, fled to Vespasian, to persuade the Roman general " to come to the city's assistance, and *save* the remainder of the people!" and especially remember that all this took place not far from *two years* before the destruction of Jerusalem!

Historically, therefore, the state of the case amounts to this:

(1.) The high-priest of the Jewish nation and many of his associates had been murdered, and the whole body of the priesthood overthrown; and, if there were any religious services, they were conducted by such wretches as the robbers saw fit to appoint.

(2.) Their temple was changed into a citadel and stronghold for an army of the vilest and most abominable robbers and murderers that ever disgraced the human race.

---

[1] *De Bell. Jud.,* lib 4, cap. 11, 12.   [2] Ib. lib. 4, cap. 19.   [3] Ib. lib. 5, cap. 20.

(3.) Their "holy houses" (synagogues) throughout the land had been pillaged and destroyed by the ruthless and bloody Sicarii.

(4.) Their judiciary and temple officers had either fled for their lives to the Romans, or had been murdered by the robber-gangs of the city, while their nobles and men of wealth perished by myriads. And finally,

(5.) Whether within the capital or throughout the borders of Judea, east, west, north, and south, the *ecclesiastical* and *civil* institutions of the nation were exterminated, and the country conquered and laid waste by the Romans, or ravaged by organized banditti.

And thus, reader, it continued to the end. These, we repeat, are the *historical facts* of the case. And yet, our commentators have trusted the interpretation of some of the most important parts of the Bible to the theory, the principal argument to sustain which lies in the assumption that the Jewish ecclesiastical and civil governments were destroyed "*after*" the destruction of Jerusalem!

What shall the writer say more? He claims to have settled the question by *undeniable* historic facts. If anything, let it be in the form of the following appeal to logic:

1. If by the heavenly luminaries be meant the ecclesiastical and civil States and rulers of the Jews, and the darkening of them refers to their destruction; and if this was effected by the Roman legions, it follows that it must have occurred either *before* or *during* the tribulation that resulted in their ruin.

2. But, inasmuch as the *object* of the war was to reduce the nation to obedience, or to bring it to ruin, it could not have *preceded* it.

3. It must therefore have occurred *during* the war. Recollect we are now speaking of the darkening of the sun, moon, and stars, as denoting the so-called *Jewish tribulation* at the hands of the Romans. We repeat, then, it must have occurred during the war. Now, it is undeniable, that that war did not cease until its object was effected. It is also undeniable, that the nation was in ruins *before* the war was ended. And it is a fact, also, that the predicted tribulation continued undiminished, if indeed it did not increase in severity, *to the last.*

It is, therefore, we submit, settled—historically and logically settled—that it was during, and *not* after, that time of trouble, that the so-called Jewish luminaries were darkened. And, what is decisive of this point, are those notable words of Christ, "*Immediately after* tribulation of those days, the sun shall be darkened," etc.; which shows conclusively that our Lord was not speaking of *that event* in the 29th verse of this chapter.

Having, then, as we claim, proved the fallacy of the metaphorical interpretations of the 27th, 28th, and 29th verses of this prophecy of our Lord, as urged by the advocates of the theory under review; and also historically demonstrated the *error* of applying it as denotive of the coming of the Romans, etc., it will be unnecessary to dwell at length upon

Verse 30. In regard to the comments given of this verse, it matters not whether, as stated by Dr. Whitby, we are to understand the coming of Christ in the sense of a *literal* coming of the Romans to execute his judgments upon the Jews; or to the subsequent manifestations of Christ by the *judgments* which he, by means of the Romans, inflicted. The popular view, by which we mean the view adopted by most of our modern divines, is thus expressed by Br. NEWTON: "Our Saviour proceeded in the same *figurative* style" (v. 30): 'and then shall appear the sign of the Son of Man in heaven,' etc. The plain meaning of it is, that the destruction of Jerusalem will be such a remarkable instance of divine vengeance, such a *signal* manifestation of the divine power and glory, that all the Jewish tribes shall *mourn*, and many will be led from thence to *acknowledge* Christ and the Christian religion." . . . "The destruction of Jerusalem will be as ample a manifestation of Christ's power and glory, as if He were Himself to come visibly in the clouds of heaven." [!!!]

Yes, reader. This is the theory of our Lord's *second* coming, adopted and advocated, in whole or in part, by such divines as Bps. Pierce and Newton, Drs. Whitby, Clarke, Lightfoot, Scott, Coke, Benson, Warburton, Robinson, etc., and the Rev. Messrs. Watson, Burkitt, Barnes, etc. Briefly, then, as it respects the *first* branch of this theory, its inconsistency, we submit, will become apparent, from the following arguments and facts:

(1.) *If* the coming of the Lord at the time here specified was merely "the coming of the Roman army to destroy Jerusalem and the unbelieving Jews," then it will follow, of necessity, that it occurred at the *same time*, since, in fact, it is affirmed to be the *same event.*

(2.) Again. The destruction of the Jewish Church and State, and city, and people, resulted from the coming of the Romans, and must, of course, have been *after* that coming, because results must be subsequent to the causes which produce them. Accordingly, as our blessed Lord delivered the whole of this remarkable prophecy with special regard to the *chronological* order of the events,

(3.) He describes the appearance of the "sign" of His coming, of the mourning of all the tribes of the earth, and of His actual coming in the clouds of heaven, as being "*after* the tribulation of those days," and subsequent, in the order of time, to the darkening of the sun, moon, and stars.

Reader, which shall we believe—the comments and opinions of men, or the teachings of Christ?

We have now, agreeably to our proposal in the outset, I., examined the theory of *figurative* interpretation, as applied by its advocates in their expositions of the prophecy under review; and II., we have replied somewhat at length to the *expositions* given of each verse of the prophecy. The reader may suppose that sufficient has been said on the subject. But, such is the writer's view of the importance to the Church, at this time, of a thorough understanding of the *scriptural import* of this prophecy, that, even at the risk of being thought to tax his indulgence beyond reasonable limits, he will venture to solicit his further consideration of what may be offered, as was proposed,

III. *In the form of a direct literal interpretation of this prophecy, taken in connection with its chronological stand-points.*

Agreeably to our proposed plan as connected with the expositions of this prophecy, everything will depend upon a proper classification of the *signs*, moral and physical, celestial and terrestrial, with which it is interspersed, in order to determine which of them form the precursors of the judgments of God that were to result in the destruction of the *Jewish* nation and polity and of the Holy City; and those that were to precede and accompany the *second future epiphany* of the Lord Jesus Christ. As preliminary to their application to the purposes intended in their announcement, it will be well to premise,

First. That, present to the mind of our blessed Lord in the prophecy before us, was *the period* of the "seven times" chastisement of the Jewish commonwealth on account of their sins, as predicted by Moses in the xxvith chapter of Leviticus and the ivth chapter of Daniel. Our next remark is,

Second. That much of the difficulty and embarrassment attendant upon a correct interpretation and application of these "signs" to the *times* and *circumstances* to which they refer, will be avoided by taking into view the prophecy of Christ *as a whole.* There are two causes which have operated greatly to obscure the subjects of this prophecy,—the habit, with many, of *limiting* the things spoken of to the xxivth of Matthew, the xiiith of Mark, and the xxist of Luke, on the one hand; and that of dividing it into two parts, on the other. An attentive examination of the context will show, that while the xxiiid chapter of Matthew, from the 34th verse, forms an *exordium* to the prophecy; and the xxist of Luke, as shown in a previous page,[1] comprises a *supplementary* commentary or paraphrase on the prophecy as given by Matthew and Mark, our Lord continues it unbroken to the end of Matthew xxvth.

Thus, as we shall see, the importance and impressiveness of this *crowning prediction* of all others contained in Holy Scripture, is vastly augmented beyond the comparatively narrow limits assigned to it by most writers. It will, in this view, be found to extend—as it respects the events foreshadowed by the "signs" designated—from the time of its first announcement to the close of this dispensation; which is immediately *proximate* to the period of the "coming of the Son of Man in the clouds of heaven, with power and great glory." As it respects,

1. The *exordium* to this prophecy, commencing, as we have said, with Matt. xxiii. 34. Our blessed Lord, in the preceding verses, proves the Jews to have been "the children of them that killed the prophets," and declares that they would "fill up the measure of their fathers" (verses 29–32). He then proceeds to predict that they would persecute and put to death those "prophets, and scribes, and wise men," whom He would send unto them: that so all the blood of the martyrs, from Abel to Zacharias,[2]

---

[1] See pages 154-156 of this work.

[2] Our Saviour here, I submit, spake of things that are not as though they had been, and hence *anticipates* what was to form the crowning act of the murder of His prophets by the Jews. This is evident from the following historic fact:

The Zacharias whom they were charged with having slain between the porch and the altar of the temple, could not have been the prophet Zechariah, whose writings are extant in our Bibles; nor Zechariah the son of Jehoiada the high-priest, who is mentioned, 2 Chron. xxiv. 20, 21, to have been slain in the court of the temple; but Zacharias, the son of Baruch (or Bara-

who was slain between the porch and the altar of the temple, should be visited upon that "generation" (verses 33–36). Then follows the Redeemer's pathetic lamentation over the obstinacy of the Jewish nation in rejecting Him, and His prediction that their "house should be *left unto them desolate;*" and that they "should not see Him henceforth," i. e., in His character as their "DELIVERER," till the arrival of the period when they "shall say, Blessed is he that cometh in the name of the Lord" (verses 37–39).

In the light, therefore, of these startling disclosures,—the desolation of their temple; His own departure *from* and return *to* them; and the *indefiniteness* of the period assigned to this last-named event,—how natural the exhibit, on the part of His disciples, of the deepest interest and concern in regard to them.

But failing to comprehend their full import, and in the hope of averting, so to speak, the impending ruin just denounced against their beautiful temple, as they follow the retreating footsteps of Christ in His withdrawal from the holy precincts, they "come to Him, for to show Him the buildings of the temple;"[1] and, as though to move His sympathies in its behalf by their deprecations of its threatened loss, while "one of them said, Master, see what manner of stones, and what buildings are here;"[2] others, expatiating on its magnificence, "spake of the temple, how it was adorned with goodly stones and gifts."[3] But all to no purpose. The Jews, in fulfilment of Daniel's prophecy, were about to "finish their transgression," *as a nation,* by the rejection and crucifixion of their Messiah, and thus to bring down upon themselves those *further* chastisements which form an important part of the burden of this prophecy. Our Lord, therefore, proceeds at once to say to them in reply: "See ye not all these things? Verily I say unto you, there shall not be left one stone upon another that shall not be thrown down."[4] Hence the desire of the disciples for further instruction on this momentous subject. To this end, as Jesus sat upon the mount of Olives, they come to Him privately, and propound to him three questions, in the precise order of the things announced, as already stated.

chias, as given by our Lord), who, as Josephus relates, was slain by the zealots *in the middle* of the temple, just before its destruction by the Romans under Titus, A. D. 70. In confirmation of this view, it may be remarked, by the way, that the Scripture nowhere expresses that the prophet Zechariah came to his death by *violence.* Hence the responsibility of *that* "generation" for the act.

[1] Matt. xxiv. 1. [2] Mark xiii. 1. [3] Luke xxi. 5.
[4] Matt. xxiv. 2· Mark xiii. 2; Luke xxi. 5, 6.

First. In reference to the predicted desolation of the temple, they ask, "*When* shall these things be?"

Second. Of His predicted return to them, they ask, "What shall be the *sign* of Thy coming?" And,

Third. Of the indefinite allusion made to the period assigned for His reappearing, they ask, When shall be "*the end* of the world?"

It will be well to observe here, in passing, the *variations* in these questions, as recorded by the three Evangelists. In Mark and Luke they embrace two particulars only. Mark has it, "Tell us, when shall these things be, and what shall be the sign when all these things shall be fulfilled?"[1] and Luke, thus: "But when shall these things be? and what sign will there be, when these things shall come to pass?"[2] while in Matthew, as above, there are three.

To explain this apparent discrepancy, it is only necessary to bear in mind, that there is nothing in the records of Mark and Luke that has any obvious connection with *the second coming of Christ;* hence, while in all the three Evangelists the first question is the same, "When shall these things be?" Mark and Luke only ask for *a "sign,"* by which they might know when these things were to be accomplished. But in Matthew, as we have seen, the context concerns not only the desolation of the commonwealth, polity, and temple of the Jews, but also the coming of Christ. "Behold, your house is left unto you desolate: for I say unto you, ye shall not see me henceforth, until ye shall say, Blessed is he that cometh in the name of the Lord."[3] The prophecy, as recorded by the three Evangelists, however, *taken as a whole*, furnishes internal evidence that the two of Mark and Luke embrace the same subjects as those included in the reply of Christ, as given by Matthew.

Before proceeding to the general subject of this remarkable prophecy of our Lord, we must be permitted to observe, how at war with all consistency is the opinion so prevalent among professing Christians of this day, that the great question: "*When* shall these things be?" is presumptuous and unlawful. The indulgence shown by our Lord in His reply to these inquiries of His disciples, together with those things spontaneously revealed to other servants of God;[4] above all, the *reproof* cast by Christ upon

[1] Mark xiii. 4.   [2] Luke xxi. 7.   [3] Matt. xxiii. 37-39.   [4] See Ps. xxv. 14.

the great bulk of the professing Israelites of His time, "*because* they knew not the times of their visitation;"[1] all of which arose from their neglect to "observe the signs of the times:"[2] all these things, we repeat, clearly lead to the conclusion that, to investigate "the times and seasons" noted in the Holy Scripture, is not only legitimate, but that believers are presumed to *know* them,[3] and are obnoxious to the imputation of the deepest hypocrisy, if they do not.

Having thus adverted to the circumstances which occasioned the announcement of this prophecy, we now pass,

2. To consider *its general scope and design.* The prophecy, as we have said, viewed as a whole, will be found to extend, in regard to the events foreshadowed by the "signs" designated therein, from the time of its *first* enunciation by our Lord to the *close* of "the times of the Gentiles," or "the end of the world," i. e., αιων, age, or dispensation under which we live, and thence, to the period of the *judgment-coming* of the Lord.

Now, if this can be made to appear, then, we submit, the *literal* takes the place of the figurative interpretation of *all* the parts of this prophecy, except Matt. xxiv. 28. But then, as we have shown, the things intended by the figures there used must be a reality: in other words, they must be *literally* verified.[4] It will hence follow, that the fallacy of limiting the entire class of "signs," etc., therein set forth, to the coming of Christ to destroy the Jews and Jerusalem, will be placed beyond the reach of further controversy.

After what has been said on this last-named subject, it would be a waste of time and paper to dwell at length upon the theories of an alleged *spiritual* and *providential* coming of Christ to destroy the Jews, etc. Still, that there may be left no room for further cavilling on these points, it may be well in this place to refer, in a form not previously given, to the *source* of the misapplication of the above signs in these premises. It is simply this: The advocates of these theories, having looked for a fulfilment of the events denoted by them within the lifetime of the men of *that generation,* have been led to confound the ordinary "signs" by which the Jewish nation was warned of its approaching doom, through the providential but invisible agency of the *Father,* with those miraculously portentous celestial and terrestrial phenomena which were to precede and accompany "*the coming of the Son of*

---

[1] Luke xix. 44. [2] Matt. xvi. 3. [3] 1 Thess. v. 1–4.
[4] See page 131 of this Work.

Man." The following comparison of the respective precursors of these events, will make this plain:

Of the first; those which were to precede the destruction of Jerusalem.	*Of the second;* those which were to precede Christ's second coming, during the season of unparalleled tribulation.
Matt. xxiv. 5–16.	Matt. xxiv. 21–29.
1. The appearance of false Christs and false prophets.	1. The appearance of false Christs and false prophets, who shall perform *miraculous* signs and wonders.
2. Wars and rumors of wars.	2. The coming of the Son of Man compared to the lightning's flash.
3. Famines, pestilences, and earthquakes in divers places.	3. The darkening of the heavenly luminaries, and the shaking of the powers of heaven.
4. Affliction, persecution, and death of Christ's followers, at the hand of their enemies.	4. "And *then* shall appear the sign of the Son of Man in heaven: and *then* shall all the tribes of the earth mourn; and they shall see the Son of Man coming in the clouds of heaven with power and great glory."
5. Abounding wickedness and religious formalism.	
6. The universal preaching of the gospel to all nations.	
Then comes the *immediate* sign—	
7. "When ye, therefore, shall see the abomination of desolation spoken of by Daniel the prophet, stand in the holy place ... Then let them which be in Judea flee," etc.	
Mark xiii. 5–15.	Mark xiii. 17–26.
The same.	The same.
Luke xxi. 8–19.	Luke xxi. 24–26.
8. The same. But He adds, "And when ye shall see Jerusalem compassed with armies, *then* know that the desolation thereof is nigh. *Then* let them which be in Judea flee," etc.	5. The prolonged period of the unparalleled tribulation, etc., St. Luke's supplement to Matt. xxiv. 29, "And ye shall be led captive into all nations; and Jerusalem shall be trodden down of the Gentiles, *until the times of the Gentiles shall be fulfilled.*"
9. Connected with these "signs," are also a series of directions given for the safety of the people of God. Matt. xxiv. 17, 18. Mark xiii. 15, 16. Luke xxi. 21.	6. This period ended, then comes the darkening of the heavenly luminaries, etc. To this He adds,
10. Also, of the *result* of this siege of Jerusalem by the Roman army, Luke adds, "And they shall fall by the edge of the sword," etc. See Luke xxi. 24, first clause.	7. "And upon the earth distress of nations with perplexity; the sea and the waves roaring; men's hearts failing them for fear, and for looking after those things that are coming upon the earth: for the powers of heaven shall be shaken."
	8. "And *then* shall they see the Son of Man coming in a cloud, with power and great glory."

Now who does not see, in the light of this comparison, a *marked difference* between those "signs" which were to presage the destruction of Jerusalem, etc., by the Roman army, and those which were designed to indicate the coming of the Son of Man? This confounding of the two classes of "signs," is the more extraordinary, when we reflect, that in the parallel passage of Luke (chap. xxi. 24–28) the most demonstrable evidence is furnished, that a *long interval* was to elapse, between the providential or judicial coming of the Father at the destruction of Jerusalem, and the coming of the Son of Man in clouds.

We now come to treat of the *period* appropriated in the prophecy, to the UNPARALLELED TRIBULATION spoken of by Matthew and Mark. Suffice it for the present to say (as we shall show in its proper place), that so far from this "tribulation" having been verified in the calamities, great as they were, that were attendant upon the destruction of the Holy City, it was not only *not* confined to, but it formed *no part of*, that event. Indeed, whatever may be alleged of the obscurity in which this remarkable prophecy is involved, yet the attentive reader of the Gospels in which they are recorded, cannot fail to observe the *chronological* consecutiveness of the events therein portrayed. For, in the first place, St. Luke, speaking of the "signs" that were to *precede* the coming of the Roman army, says, chap. xxi. 12, "but *before* all these things, they" (i. e. parents, and brethren, and kinsfolk, and friends) "shall lay their hands on you, and persecute you . . . and cause you to be put to death," etc.; while, second, of the "signs" which were to forewarn them more directly of that event, St. Matthew says, chap. xxiv. 8, "all these are the *beginnings* of sorrows:" to which St. Mark, chap. xiii. 7, and St. Luke, xxi. 7, add, "but the *end* shall not be yet." Then further, third. St. Luke, having spoken of the whole interval of the treading down of Jerusalem by the Gentiles, "until the times of the Gentiles be fulfilled," embraces it in that period called "*the days of vengeance*," in which "all things that are written may be *fulfilled*." Nor is this all. The three Evangelists, Matt. xxiv. 34; Mark xiii. 30; and Luke xxi. 32, testify that "this generation shall not pass away, till all these things be *fulfilled*." And finally, fifth. St. Matt. xxiv. 36, and Mark xiii. 32, speaking of the time of the coming of the Son of Man, says, "but of that day and that hour *knoweth no man,* no, not the angels in heaven, neither the Son, but the Father."

The way is now prepared to lay open the real scope and design of this prophecy.

This will be found, as we have said, to relate to "*the coming of the Son of Man in the clouds of heaven with power and great glory,*" which event was to be preceded by a long, protracted course of "tribulation," increasing in unprecedented severity toward its close; which latter circumstance, *as a "sign,"* was to indicate its near approach. To this subject we now address ourself. As introductory thereto, our business will be,

1. To determine the scriptural import of the phrase, "TIMES OF THE GENTILES," Luke xxi. 24. Now, "in searching what, or what manner of time, the Spirit of Christ" which inspired the old prophets "did signify, when it spake beforehand of the sufferings of Christ and the glory that should follow," we must go back to the period of the "*seven times*'" chastisement of Israel and of Judah on account of their sins, as predicted by Moses, Lev. xxvi., and by Daniel, chap. iv.

This period, as it is given, not in common time, but as a prophetical or mystical date, must be deciphered agreeably to the laws for the interpretation of the *symbols* of prophecy, thus:—as the term "time," etc., when used as a prophetical number,[1] denotes a year of 360 days, and each day is to be taken for a year,[2] the "seven times" or years give us a total of 2520 years. Taken in this sense, it marks out the *whole period* of Gentile domination over God's church and people, called "the times of the Gentiles."

But, in order to determine the date for the *commencement* of this period, as it was to reach down to the *close* of "the times of the Gentiles," it is indispensable that we ascertain whether the Scriptures, without going into the details of its chronology, has revealed to the Church a definitely fixed period from the creation and fall, to the close of these "times of the Gentiles," within which all the prophetical numbers were to run out.

In addition, then, to the *tradition* of the pre-Christian Jewish writers, that the six days of creation were designed to typically adumbrate 6000 years—2000 void, 2000 under the law, and 2000 under Messiah—to be followed by a seventh millennary of rest and

---

[1] See Dan. vii. 25.   [2] Ezek. iv. 1–6.   See Note D, IId Part.

triumph over their enemies: I say, in addition to this tradition of the Jews, the *Scriptures* directly recognize the same principle of analogy on this subject. For example: I ask, was not the first Adam[1] created as the *figure* of Him (Christ) that was to come?"[2] If then, we can go back to the fountain-head of time, and find in Adam a *type* of "the second man, the Lord from heaven,"[3] as He who, by a second creation was to "restore all things" from the ruins of the fall; why should it be thought a thing incredible, that the *six days* of formation of the material heavens and earth, and a *seventh* of rest, should also bear a like character? Wherefore did God create the world in six days, and rest the seventh? Why did He not employ five, eight, ten, or twelve days instead? And so, accordingly, St. Paul (Col. ii. 16, 17), alluding to the *typical* character of the preceding dispensations, speaks especially "in respect of the Sabbath days"—of which, the *seventh* day of the Creator's repose from his six days' work was the first—and denominates them "*a shadow* of good things to come." Or, if this be deemed an unwarrantable stretching of types in regard to the first Sabbath, I would direct the reader to Paul's use of the word Σαββατισμος—*Sabbatism*—in Heb. iv. 9; where, especially considering that it was Hebrew Christians whom he was addressing, and that, from long-continued usage, they could not do otherwise than associate it with a *chronological septenary*, he employed it to designate the saints' long-expected and ardently-prayed-for glorious time of rest with Christ.

If, therefore, as is undeniable, the inspired apostle applied the seventh day or first Sabbath of creation as a *type* of the heavenly rest, how can we consistently withhold from the previous *six days* of creative labor, a similar typical character, as denotive of the 6000 years that were to *precede* the seventh of rest? It is recorded of the anti-typal second Adam, that with Him "one day is as a thousand years, and a thousand years as one day."[4]

To the above we may also add the fact, that the early *post-Christian* fathers, with the additional light of the teachings of Christ and the writings of the apostles before them, continued to put forth the same sentiments; and that, mark, not as mere opinions based on Jewish tradition, but as an article of their Christian faith. (See Appendix, pp. 59–65).

This, then, we submit, is decisive of the question, that God

---

[1] 1 Cor. xv. 47. [2] Rom. v. 14. [3] 1 Cor. xv. 47. [4] 2 Pet. iii. 8.

has revealed to the Church the unalterable period of 6000 years, as the interval *within* which, under the three dispensations, Patriarchal, Jewish, and Christian, all his *ordinary* purposes of providence and grace were to be accomplished.

To determine, therefore, the time for the *commencement* of this mystical number, we have only to refer to the joint prophecies of the captivities of Israel and Judah, as announced by Hosea and Isaiah. Hosea, thus: "And the pride of Israel (the ten tribes) doth testify to his face: therefore shall Israel and Ephraim (the principal tribe of the ten) fall into captivity: Judah (the other division) shall also fall with them."[1] On the other hand, Isaiah pointed out *the very time* when these captivities should take place: "and within threescore and five years, Ephraim shall be broken, that it shall not be a people."[2]

Now, this last prophecy was made in the 2d of the 16 years of Ahaz's reign over Israel, A. M. 3377. The above 65 years is made up of the 14 from the 2d of Ahaz, and the 29 years' intervening reign of Hezekiah, down to the 22d of Manasseh, A. M. 3441, when the captivity of *Ephraim* took place under Esarhaddon[3] king of Assyria; and the same year, having caught *Manasseh* king of Judah hid in a thicket, he bound him in chains and carried him a captive to Babylon.[4] Then, by deducting the "seven times" or 2520 years of Lev. xxvi. from the 6000 years above, it throws us back to A. M. 3480, which date, though it falls 39 years after the personal captivity of Manasseh; yet, as by his repentance he was *restored* to his kingdom, it was not reckoned as having its *national* commencement until after that interval. Take the following in proof: "Manasseh *hath made* Judah to sin with his idols: therefore, thus saith the Lord God of Israel, behold, I am *bringing* (*i. e.*, by the personal captivity of their king) such evil upon Jerusalem and Judah, that whosoever heareth of it, both their ears shall tingle." The meaning here is, that the *nation*, not having repented of their idolatry, etc., during the above interval, was punished for the sins which Manasseh instigated,—and which consisted in the loss to them of their national independence,—and of which *his* captivity was but the prelude.

We have only to add, that while Israel or the ten tribes, from

---

[1] Hosea v. 5.   [2] Isa. vii. 8.   [3] The same with Asnappar, Ezra iv. 2, 10.
[4] Compare 2 Kings xvii. 24 with Ezra iv. 2, 10; and 2 Chron. xxxiii. 11.

the time of their captivity under Esarhaddan, have never effectually regained their national independence; so Judah, since A. M. 3480, have remained subjected to the dominancy over them of Gentilism. This, therefore, constitutes *the whole period* called "the times of the Gentiles," which, commencing B. C. 652, end in A. D. 1868: 652+1828=2520—and which, added to A. M. 3480, complete the 6000th year from the creation and fall.

Again. In confirmation of the exposition here given of the import of the mystical "*seven times*" of Moses, is the interpretation by Daniel of the vision of the colossal image as revealed to Nebuchadnezzar, showing that this domination of Gentilism over the Jewish commonwealth, was to extend from the period indicated by the "*head of gold*," through the intervening eras denoted by the other symbolic compartments of the Image,[1] down to the time when the *Messianic* "*stone* cut out without hands," *smites the image* on the ten toes of the feet, and the setting up of that "kingdom of the God of heaven, which shall stand forever."[2] But more especially, in the things "noted" in that monarch's second vision, that of the Great Tree, as *expository* of the first. This tree, it will be recollected, flourished, and was glorious in the eyes of men; but it was a thing against which Heaven watched, until at length the command was given, "Hew the tree down, and destroy it; yet leave the stump of the roots thereof in the earth, even with a band of iron and brass, in the tender grass of the field; and let it be wet with the dew of heaven, and let his portion be with the beasts of the earth, *till seven times* pass over him."[3]

Now, though this prophetic vision primarily referred to the *personal* history of the Babylonish monarch, and was verified in his being driven out from men to herd with the beasts of the field in a state of maniacy for seven literal years, at the end of which he was to be restored to his kingdom, etc.; yet, from the fact that, when the Messianic "stone" comes and smites the colossal image on his feet, it is still found standing complete *in all its parts*;[4] it is demonstrative that the Babylonish monarch, as the head of that image, is the *representative* of the Gentile

---

[1] The four metallic compartments of this image, composed of gold, silver, brass, and iron mingled with clay, represented the rise and fall successively of the four great monarchies that were to bear rule in the world successively, viz., the Babylonian, Medo-Persian, Grecian, and Roman.

[2] See Dan. ii. 44. [3] Dan. iv. 10-23. [4] Dan. ii. 34, 35. See also pages 239-241 of this work.

powers throughout. It hence follows, that the mystical number of "seven times" which was to pass over him during his maniacal exile in the expository vision of the great tree, must also regard him in his *representative* character, in the relation he holds to these Gentile powers. Consistency therefore requires, that while his state of maniacy symbolizes the wild and ferocious nature of those powers; the "seven times" which were to pass over them must run commensurate with *their whole existence.* This corresponds exactly with Daniel's representation of the period assigned to the mad career of these powers.[1] For, while of the four beasts he says that they "devoured, break in pieces, and stamped the residue with their feet,[2] of the first "little horn" (the Roman) he adds, that he "made war with the saints and prevailed against them, *until* the ancient of days came, and judgment was given to the saints of the Most High, and *the time* came that the saints possessed the kingdom."[3] So also, of the second "little horn" (the Mohammedan), he says that "his power shall be mighty, . . . that he shall destroy wonderfully, and shall prosper, and practise, and shall destroy the mighty and the holy people . . . *for many days*,"[4] i. e., for 2300 days, or years.[5]

Finally, on this subject. As out of the last of the four monarchies, the Roman, in conjunction with the Mohammedan superstition and infidelity, is to arise another power—*preëminent* in comparison of all that have preceded it,—and which the prophet denominates *a* "*king* that shall do according to his will, and that shall exalt himself, and magnify himself above every god, and shall speak marvellous things against the God of gods, and prosper till the indignation be *accomplished*,"[6] etc. ;—this, he adds, shall be "at the time when Michael, the great prince"—the MESSIAH, "who standeth for the children of his people," the Jews, "*shall stand up.*" Now this period, while it commences (as will be shown in the proper place) at the expiration of "the times of the Gentiles," introduces us to that *short unchronological* season of unparalleled affliction,[7] in the midst of which the Messianic "stone" comes in clouds to "deliver his people, every one

---

[1] This is exhibited in detail in Daniel's synchronic vision of the four rampant beasts—the two-winged Lion; the Bear with three ribs in his mouth; the four-headed and four-winged Leopard, and the nondescript Monster with ten horns, and another little horn; together with the little horn which sprang from one of the four horns of the rough goat in his second vision, etc. (See Dan. vii. 1–8; viii. 8–12.)

[2] Dan. vii. 19. [3] Ib. vii. 21, 22. [4] Ib. viii. 24–26. [5] Ib. verses 13, 14.
[6] Ib. xi. 31–39. [7] Matt. xxiv. 21, 22; Mark xiii. 19, 20.

that shall be found written in the book;" "awakes his saints that sleep in the dust of the earth;"[1] and changes those who shall be alive at his coming,[2] etc.

The incontrovertible inference from these statements, we submit, is, that the period designated by our Lord in this prophecy as "the times of the Gentiles," is no other than that revealed by His Spirit, first, to Moses, and subsequently to Daniel, under the mystical or prophetic form of "*seven times.*" Commencing, as we have seen, with the national captivity of Judah under Manasseh A. M. 3480, it is still running its course. But it is destined, we confidently affirm, to reach its utmost limit in A. D. 1868, at which time "*the fulness* of the Gentiles shall be come in."[3]

Yes, we repeat. Present to the mind of our Lord was this *identical* "seven times" of the old prophets, Moses and Daniel, when he predicted that unparalleled "tribulation" which was to *precede* his second coming, as we find it recorded by St. Luke: "and ye shall be carried captive into all nations; and Jerusalem shall be trodden down of the Gentiles, *until* the times of the Gentiles be fulfilled." (Chap. xxi. 24.) Yea, more: when He uttered those fearfully portentous words to the still obdurate Jews, Matt. xxiii. 38, "Behold, your house (temple) is *left* unto you desolate," it was as though he had said to them:

'That tribulation which, as predicted by Moses and Daniel, commenced with the captivity of Judah under Manasseh A. M. 3480, inflicted upon you by your long-offended covenant God on account of your sins at the hand of *the great Gentile* "*Desolator*" (perpetuated by transmission from the Babylonian, through the Medo-Persian and Grecian to the now Roman power), and which 685 years' endurance of it by you as a nation, *has failed* to humble and reform: that "tribulation," I repeat, is henceforth "*left*" to you, to run on in continued and increasing severity at the hand of *that same* Desolator, whose "overspreading of abominations shall make desolate" your once "pleasant land,"[4] together with your "Holy City" and "Temple," "not one stone of which shall be left, that shall not be thrown down." Yea, this great Desolator "shall so plant the tabernacle of his palaces between the sea in the glorious holy mountain,"[5] that

[1] Dan. xii. 1, 2. See also Zech. xiv. 1-6, etc.   [2] 1 Cor. xv. 51, 52; 1 Thess. iv. 13-18.
[3] Rom. xi. 25.   [4] Compare Dan. viii. 9 with ix. 27.   [5] Ib. xi. 45.

"you shall fall" at his hand "by the edge of the sword;" you shall *again* "be led captive into all nations, and Jerusalem shall be trodden down of the Gentiles, until the times of the Gentiles be fulfilled," or "until the consummation,"[1] which, while it will be to you "the time of Jacob's trouble,"[2] of "great tribulation," of "affliction, such as was not from the beginning of the creation which God created to that time, neither shall be,"[3] it will be to your relentless foe total and irremediable ruin.[4] For, "*you shall be saved out of it.*"[5]

We now unhesitatingly reiterate the statement, that this unparalleled tribulation, so far from being identical, has *no* connection whatever with the calamity of the Jewish nation prior to and during the Roman invasion, except as it was the result of, and hence followed, that event. This prophecy of our Lord, as already intimated, chiefly relates to the GREAT CRISIS, connected with the *closing* events of the present age. It alone, therefore, will be found to exhaust the fulness of the description.

Nevertheless, the providence of God has so arranged, that events similar in character, though less in importance, should previously occur, either as warnings, exemplifications, and sometimes as types of, the *consummation* that is to follow: so that the description of the great event becomes in part applicable to the forerunner. It is upon this principle that many of the prophecies of the Old Testament are applied to the New. For example: the context of Jer. xxxi. 15 makes it evident that it applies to the *great future* tribulation of the Jews; yet in the New Testament it is applied to a *minor* event which has already occurred, similar in kind, though less in degree.[6] So the 2d Psalm, which primarily refers to the *last* great antichristian apostasy, is quoted in a similar manner in Acts iv. 25-28. Compare also Zech. xii. 10 with John xix. 37; and Joel ii. 28 with Acts ii. 17.

It is hence evident, that on no other principle can we reconcile that part of Matt. xxiv. 5-16, together with the collateral passages in Mark and Luke, which relate to the "signs" that were to indicate the approaching destruction of Jerusalem by the Romans, with verses 21-27, etc., that refer to those which were to harbinger the "coming of the Son of Man" *at the close of* "the times of the Gentiles."

In this, however, we can see the most marked evidence of the

---
[1] Dan. ix. 27.   [2] Comp. Jer. xxx. 7 with Dan. xii. 1.   [3] Matt. xxiv. 21; Mark xiii. 19.
[4] 2 Thess. i. 3-10; ii. 8.   [5] Jer. xxx. 7; Dan. xii. 1.   [6] See Matt. ii. 18.

infinite wisdom and love of God our Redeemer. Prophecy, though throwing its strongest light upon the *concluding* events of the Gentile dispensation, and increasing in importance as time advances, is nevertheless rendered useful throughout *the whole period*, by admitting of being *applied*, though not exclusively *interpreted*, with relation to antecedent events, kindred in principle, if not parallel in fact, to that which is mainly the subject of prediction.

Now, this may be exemplified by a comparison of "the tribulation," as given by Matthew and Luke. St. Matthew's description of it, chap. xxiv. 21–27, may be compared to an object glass closed. St. Luke draws it out, joint by joint. He first enlarges our view of it by stating, "These be the days of vengeance, that all things which are written may be fulfilled." (Verse 22.) He then explains one step further: "There shall be great distress in the land, and wrath upon this people." (Verse 23.) Then, with still additional particularity, he declares that there shall be a massacre: "They shall fall by the edge of the sword;" and a leading into captivity: "they shall be led captive into all nations." At last, he draws out the glass to its full focus: "And Jerusalem shall be trodden down of the Gentiles, until the times of the Gentiles be fulfilled." (Verse 24.)

Thus is the entire prophecy defined in its details, while it is marked with a particularity in reference to the prophetic history of the "great tribulation," which, having attained its culminating point, forms the *immediate* "sign" of the glorious coming of "the Son of Man."

But, that we may leave no room for a doubt in the mind of the reader, in regard to the distinction on which we insist, between those "signs" which were to inaugurate the events *before*, and those which were to *follow*, the destruction of Jerusalem by the Romans, it is indispensable that we settle the question, as to the alleged unprecedented character of the former. The point to be decided is, Were the calamities endured by the Jewish nation, during the interval between the announcement of the prophecy and the close of the Roman war, of an *unparalleled* nature, compared with all others that had preceded them?

We take the *negative* of this question. As we have said, so do we now proceed by *historic fact* to prove, that the unparalleled tribulation spoken of by Matthew and Mark, and amplified by Luke, was not only *not* confined to, but that it formed *no part of*, the

Roman siege, etc. A comparison of the besiegement of Jerusalem by the Chaldeans, as predicted by Moses, Deut. xxviii. 47-68, with that of Titus, will make this clear. It is affirmed by some writers, in reference to this latter siege, that the circumstance of women being led by hunger to devour their own children, taken in connection with all the other sufferings and horrors of the Jews at that time, show it to have been *without a parallel* in human history. If this be so, it nullifies entirely our exposition of the whole prophecy. But, let us see. Jeremiah, in his notable prophecy of the *second* Babylonish siege of the holy city, says: "I will make this city desolate and a hissing; every one that passeth by shall be astonished and hiss, because of all the plagues thereof. And I will cause them to eat the flesh of their sons and the flesh of their daughters, and they shall every one eat the flesh of his friend in the siege and straitness, wherewith their enemies (the Chaldeans) and they that seek their lives shall straiten them."[1] And, having lived himself to witness the *fulfilment* of this prophecy, in his lamentations over the destruction of the city by Nebuchadnezzar, he records the historic fact in the terms following: "Behold, O Lord, and consider to whom thou hast done this. Shall the women eat their fruit, and the children of a span long?"[2] "The hands of the pitiful women have sodden their own children; they were their meat, in the destruction of the daughter of thy people."[3] And Daniel, in alluding to the verification of the curse as denounced by Moses against them above referred to, chapter ix. 4, in the 12th verse adds concerning it, "The Lord hath confirmed his words which he spake against us, and against our judges that judged us, by bringing upon us a great evil: *for under the whole heaven* hath not been done as hath been done upon Jerusalem."

Evidently, therefore, we must look *beyond* the siege of Jerusalem by Titus, for the unprecedented character of that "tribulation," spoken of by the Evangelists. On this subject, and as introductory to a proper understanding of it, we observe, that though Moses and Daniel, in the passages already quoted (Deut. xxviii. 47-68, Dan. ix. 12), refer primarily to the second Babylonish siege of Jerusalem; yet the former predicts (Deut. xxviii. 63, 64), "And ye shall be plucked from off the land whither thou goest to possess it; and the Lord shall scatter thee among all

[1] Jer. xix. 8, 9.   [2] Lam. ii. 20.   [3] Ib. iv. 10.

people, from one end of the earth even to the other," etc. And this, he declares, together with their "plagues and sore sicknesses," shall be of *"long continuance"* (verse 59), alluding doubtless to the previously predicted "seven times," chastisement with which they were threatened in Lev. xxvi.; while Daniel (chap. ix. 26, 27) says of "the people of the prince that shall come to destroy the city and the sanctuary," that they "shall make it desolate, *even until the consummation*," etc.: so that the unparalleled character of the "tribulation" of Matthew and Mark respect their being led away captive into all nations, and the treading down of Jerusalem by the Gentiles *after* the invasion of the holy city by Titus in A. D. 70, "until the times of the Gentiles be fulfilled." Hence the Holy Spirit saith of its consummation, that "Jerusalem hath received of the Lord's hand *double* for all her sins."

If, however, additional evidence be required, in proof that the above prophecies looked *beyond* the calamities connected with the siege of the holy city under Titus, for a verification of their unparalleled character, we will place in juxtaposition the two following passages from Jeremiah and Daniel, in relation to it:

Jer. xxx. 6-9.	Dan. xii. 1, 2.
"Ask ye now and see, whether a man doth travail with child? Wherefore do I see every man with his hands on his loins, as a woman in travail, and all faces turned into paleness? . . . Alas! for that day is great, so that there is none like it; it is even *the time of Jacob's trouble:* but he shall be saved out of it. For it shall come to pass in that day, saith the Lord of hosts, that I will break his yoke from off thy neck, and will burst thy bonds, and strangers shall no more serve themselves of him; *but they shall serve the Lord their God and David their king*, whom I will raise up unto them."	"And at that time shall Michael stand up, the great prince which standeth for the children of thy people: and there shall be *a time of trouble*, such as never was since there was a nation, even to that same time: and at that time thy people shall be delivered, every one that shall be found written in the book. And many of them that sleep in the dust of the earth *shall awake;* some of them to everlasting life: and some to shame and everlasting contempt."

Now here, the "more sure word of prophecy, as a light which shineth in a dark place," in speaking of *"the manner of time"* revealed to these Old Testament saints by "the spirit of Christ which was in them" (comp. 1 Pet. i. 11 with 2 Pet. i. 19), evidently refers to that which forms THE CRISIS of the "great tribulation."

In conclusion, it only remains that we *harmonize* this prophecy of our Lord in Matthew and Luke, with that of Jeremiah and Daniel. The predicted *chastisement* of Judah, as we have seen, commenced with the captivity of the nation in the reign of Manasseh, A. M. 3480, reaching down to the siege of Jerusalem by Titus, as a signal, though *not* an unprecedented act of the divine "vengeance" against the Jews. But there was a *season of* "*affliction*" allotted to the covenant seed on account of their sins during "the times of the Gentiles," which, compared with any that had preceded it, should have *no* parallel. St. Luke fixes its commencement at the captivity of the nation under *Titus*, and continues it down to the *close* of the period called "the times of the Gentiles." This "affliction," however, was to *increase* in intensity, "until the times of the Gentiles be fulfilled," when its unparalleled character as the "great tribulation" should begin more especially to develop itself. The period therefore to which it belongs, is the *interval* between the consummation of the Gentile age—"the end of the world" (της συντελειας του αιωνος)— and the *coming* of the Son of Man in clouds.

It is here, however, to be particularly noted, that, unlike the predicted events which precede and run out at A. D. 1868, we have *no* definite chronological data by which to determine the length of this interval. In other words, it is *a short unchronological period.* This furnishes the reason, why it is declared of *the time* of the second coming of Christ, which falls within this period, " Of that day and hour knoweth no man, no, not the angels in heaven, neither the Son, but the Father."[1]

Again. It is of equal importance to observe, that, while Matthew and Mark describe the character of this "great tribulation,"[2] Luke's appendix to it[3] furnishes the *prolonged period* of its continuance. To be a little more precise: while Luke omits, in part, those "signs" enumerated by Matthew (verses 23-26), the appearance of false Christs and false prophets, etc., whose great signs and wonders should, "if possible, deceive the very elect," he joins those which he mentions (verses 25, 26) immediately to the *closing up* of the prolonged period of the Gentiles spoken of in verse 24; thus showing, that the time which *he* appropriates for the appearance of the darkening of the sun, moon, and stars, *syn-*

---

[1] Matt. xxiv. 36; Mark xiii. 32. [2] Matt. xxiv. 21, 22; Mark xiii. 19, 20.
[3] Luke xxi. 24.

chronizes exactly with that mentioned for the appearance of the same signs, Matt. xxiv. 27-29, and Mark xiii. 24, 25; i. e., at the close of "the times of the Gentiles" in A. D. 1868.

It follows incontrovertibly, that the "signs" enumerated, first, by Luke, of the persecutions of the disciples of Christ, chap xxi. 12-19 (and which are parallel with Matt. xxiv. 9-14 and Mark xiii. 11-13); second, by Matthew, of wars and rumors of wars, with national conflicts, etc., chap. xxiv. 5-7 and 14 (and which are parallel with Mark xiii. 7, 8, and Luke xxi. 8-11); and third, of the destruction of the Jews by the edge of the sword, etc., in his (Luke's) appendix, xxi. 24, were, one and all, to *precede*, and are to be distinguished from, the appearance of the celestial phenomena mentioned by each. The first in order were chronologically to precede the compassing of Jerusalem with armies. (Luke xxi. 12.) The second were to accompany and accomplish the work of the siege. (Luke xxi. 20; Matt. xxiv. 15; Mark xiii. 14.) And the third were to follow, as the *result* of that siege, down to the period of the "consummation" of the Gentile age. (Compare Dan. ix. 27 with Luke xxi. 24.)

With the subject before us thus divested of the obscurity which has so long overshadowed it in the writings of the learned, we reach the inevitable conclusion, that whatever of *resemblance* may be traced between the events portrayed by these "signs," the unparalleled character of the "great tribulation" spoken of by Matt. xxiv. 21, 22, and Mark xiii. 19, 20, "such as was not from the beginning of the creation which God created unto this time, nor ever shall be," commences its development from the period of the exhibition of the celestial and terrestrial phenomena *at the close* of the Gentile age in A. D. 1868, and continues *until* the Jewish nation shall exclaim, "Blessed is he that cometh in the name of the Lord." (Matt. xxiii. 39.) For, as Matthew has it, "*Immediately after* the tribulation of those days"—ευθεως δε μετα την θλιψιν—"shall the sun be darkened,"[1] etc.; while St. Mark says, "*In* those days, *after* that tribulation,"[2] etc.; while all the three Evangelists unite in the statement, "This generation,"—meaning, of course, the generation existing *at the time* of the darkening of the sun, moon, and stars, etc.,—"This generation shall not pass away, till all these things be fulfilled."

Thus, then, is harmonized the respective declarations of Jere-

---

[1] Matt. xxiv. 29. [2] Mark xiii. 24.

miah, Daniel, and our blessed Lord, regarding *the time*, and the characteristics connected with the crisis, of the unparalleled tribulation. It is emphatically styled by Jeremiah as "the great day, even the time of Jacob's trouble;"[1] by Daniel as "a time of trouble, such as never was since there was a nation, even to that same time;"[2] and by our Lord, "The days of vengeance, that all things which are written might be fulfilled."[3]

But it may be asked, how, if this season of unparalleled tribulation is to constitute "the time of Jacob's trouble" *after* the close of "the times of the Gentiles," is this to be reconciled with the *ending* that period in A. D. 1868 ? To this we reply, that though St. Luke's statement is, that the Jewish tribulation is to close when "the times of the Gentiles are fulfilled," yet we are not to understand that they are *ended* in the absolute sense. Like "the rest of the beasts" in Dan. vii. 12, who "had their dominion taken away," while "their lives were *prolonged* for a season and a time;" so, while the prolonged captivity of the Jewish nation, which is exclusively spoken of by St. Luke, will end at the time assigned to it, yet it by no means necessarily follows that their *sufferings* will then altogether terminate. This will appear from the peculiar phraseology in St. Mark's Gospel: "But, *in* those days, *after* that tribulation," etc.; thus clearly indicating that the days of the tribulation, though drawn to a close, are not absolutely *passed away:* not that this is a distinct tribulation in contrast with or in addition to that which preceded it, but only the *climax* of it. It is, so to speak, the last act, the last scene of the drama, in which occurs the grand catastrophe of the whole.

Nor, further, are we to lose sight of the momentous fact that this "great tribulation," in its *last* form of development, is to "*come as a snare* on all them that dwell on the face of the whole earth;" that is, "the days of vengeance," having reached their crisis coincident with the period when God has his controversy with the Gentiles, all the inhabitants of the world will be exposed to its fury, in accordance with the prophecy following: "The earth also is defiled under the inhabitants thereof; because they have transgressed the laws, changed the ordinance, broken the everlasting covenant: therefore hath the curse devoured the earth,

---

[1] Jer. xxx. 7. [2] Dan. xii. 1. [3] Luke xxi. 22.

and they that dwell therein are desolate: *therefore the inhabitants of the earth are burned, and few men left.*" [1]

But, in the midst of the general consternation and dismay that shall *then* seize upon all classes of the ungodly—"men's hearts failing them for fear, and for looking after those things that are coming on the earth" [2]—the jealousies of the crowned heads of Gentile rulers against the house of Judah, now dwelling nationally, but in their unconverted state, in the holy city, shall incite them to arms; when, once more, but for the *last time,* an *unprecedented* storm of persecution, like the devastations of a resistless tornado, shall be brought down upon the heads of Daniel's people. The prophet Zechariah, alluding to this very persecution, chap. xiv. 1, 2, says: "Behold, the day of the Lord cometh, and thy (Judah's) spoil shall be in the midst of thee. *For I will bring all nations against Jerusalem to battle;* and the city shall be taken, and the houses rifled, and the women ravished; and half of the city shall go into captivity, and the residue of the people shall not be cut off from the city."

This, then, is "the time of Jacob's trouble, so that there is none like it," spoken of by Jeremiah, Daniel, and Christ. "But, *he shall be saved out of it.*" For, says Zechariah, chap. xiv. 3, "Then shall the Lord go forth and fight against those nations, as He fought in the day of battle." And, adds the prophet (verse 4), "*His feet* shall stand in that day upon the mount of Olives which is before Jerusalem," etc.

Now, this period of the deliverance of Daniel's people, Isaiah makes *exactly coincident* with the appearance of the darkening of the heavenly luminaries referred to by Matthew, Mark, and Luke. In chap. xxiv. 21–23, Isaiah, having said, "And it shall come to pass *in that day*, that the Lord shall punish the high ones that are on high, and the kings of the earth upon the earth," adds, "*Then* the moon shall be confounded, and the sun ashamed, when the Lord of hosts shall reign in mount Zion, and in Jerusalem, and before his ancients gloriously." And, mark, reader: this event exactly synchronizes with the smiting of the colossal metallic image upon the feet of iron and clay by the Messianic "stone cut out without hands," Dan. ii. 34, 35; and also with "one like the Son of Man coming in the clouds of heaven to the ancient of days," and to whom is given dominion, and glory, and a king-

---

[1] Isa. xxiv. 6, 7. [2] Luke xxi. 26.

dom," etc., Dan. vii. 13, 14. See also Dan. ii. 44, and vii. 26, 27. Does not this therefore clearly demonstrate that the second personal coming of our Lord is *pre-* and not *post-*millennial? What will our opponents answer?

This, therefore, is the period when "all the kindreds of the earth shall wail," at *beholding* "the Son of Man come in the clouds of heaven with power and great glory."

And now, in conclusion on the subject of the *last* closing scene of the above unparalleled tribulation, and its *results* to the Jews and their Gentile oppressors; the prophet Jeremiah presents us with the following succinct and beautifully graphic picture:

"Israel is a scattered sheep; the lions have driven him away: first, the king of Assyria hath devoured him; and last, this Nebuchadnezzar king of Babylon hath broken his bones. Therefore, thus saith the Lord of hosts, the God of Israel: Behold, *I will punish* the king of Babylon and his land, as I have punished the king of Assyria. And I will *bring Israel again* to his habitation, and he shall feed on Carmel and Bashan, and his soul shall be satisfied on mount Ephraim and Gilead. *In those days, and in that time*, saith the Lord, the iniquity of *Israel* shall be sought for, and there shall be none; and the sins of *Judah*, and they shall not be found: *for I will pardon them whom I reserve.*"[1]

In taking our leave of the theory that has called forth these somewhat extended remarks, we feel that, however imperfectly the task has been executed, we have fully exposed the fallacy of the alleged fulfilment of Christ's prophecy, Matt. xxiv. 27-30, in reference to His second coming and the establishment of His kingdom in the world, by the judgments inflicted upon the Jewish nation and polity, at the destruction of Jerusalem by the Roman army in A. D. 70. We repeat: this theory, devised and advocated by the most eminent commentators and writers of the last and present century; and, until within the last half century almost universally adopted by all the Protestant churches; when subjected to the ordeal of impartial criticism, logical analysis, and historic fact, is shown to be in every way *unworthy* of the great minds who embraced it. And yet, such is the tendency of the human mind to be swayed by the imposing authority of great names, that unless the Lord by his grace, as in

---

[1] Jer. l. 20.

the case of Lydia, *opens the heart* to attend unto the things here spoken of,[1] *men will not receive them.*

We now pass to a consideration of those theories which affirm that the second coming of Christ is still future.

CHAPTER IV.

FOURTH THEORY.

THIS THEORY ALLEGES, THAT THE PROPHECIES RELATING TO THE KINGDOM OF HEAVEN AND THE REIGN OF CHRIST ON EARTH, REFER TO THE FIRST INTRODUCTION AND ESTABLISHMENT OF THE CHRISTIAN CHURCH; THE DISPENSATION OF WHICH MERGES INTO, FORMS A PART OF, AND ENDS WITH, THE CLOSE OF THE MILLENNIAL STATE; WHEN, IT IS AFFIRMED, CHRIST WILL PERSONALLY APPEAR AT THE JUDGMENT-DAY, AND SIMULTANEOUSLY RAISE FROM THE DEAD BOTH THE RIGHTEOUS AND THE WICKED, WHEN THE ONE SHALL BE REWARDED AND THE OTHER PUNISHED, ETC.[2]

We have at length reached the last but one of the theories connected with our examination of those prophecies which relate to the important subject of *the second coming and kingdom of Christ.*

The theory now under review, unlike the *first,* which alleges the fulfilment of all the above prophecies by the restoration of the Jews from the Babylonish captivity, affirms, with perhaps here and there an exception, the *literal* return of Judah and Israel to their own land as *still future.*

Unlike that of the *second,* while its advocates generally admit that the prophecy of Christ in Matt. xxiv. 27–30, denotes the providential or judicial coming of our Lord to destroy the nation and polity of the Jews by means of the Roman army under Titus; yet contend for the *spiritual* presence or reign of Christ as the King of saints, *during* the Christian dispensation; and that this spiritual presence, which they call His *second* coming, is to be more signally manifested, in the *conversion* of all nations, Jewish and Gentile, as preparatory to the introduction and establishment of the Church in all the privileges and blessings of her millennial state under the continuous spiritual reign of Christ. And hence,

[1] See Acts xvi. 14.   [2] See the four theories, etc., p. 55.

Unlike the *third*, they insist that the millennial state of the Church is *still future*.

These may be regarded as the *popular views* on this subject, by the Church of the present day.

For thirty years last past, however, we have been led to regard this theory, in several particulars, as essentially erroneous.

But in saying this, we at the same time distinctly avow it as our conviction, that the gulf which spans the points at issue, is of much *narrower* dimensions than what is generally apprehended. There is, for instance, an exact agreement of views in reference to two important points, viz., *the future literal return of* Judah and Israel to Palestine, and the *millennial state* of the Church as yet to come. The main point of difference relates to the *time* and *mode* of the second coming of Christ in connection with these events. Is it to be *pre*-millennial and *personal?* or is it to be *spiritually pre*-millennial and *personally post*-millennial?

Difficulties.—The Question Stated.

With these remarks premised, we now proceed to point out what, at least in our view, has *occasioned* the questions at issue in the Church on this subject. It is simply this:

First. The advocates of the theory under review, maintain that both the second personal coming of Christ, and the universal conflagration of the earth, are *post*-millennial.

Second. On the other hand, some of the most distinguished *millenarian* writers maintain, that the second personal coming of Christ, and the universal conflagration of the earth, *are both pre-millennial*.

Third. *We*, on the contrary, affirm, against the first class of writers, that the second personal coming of Christ is *pre*-millennial; and against the second class, that the universal conflagration of the earth is *post*-millennial. Our next remark is this:

That the *post*-millennialists, being unable to reconcile the scriptural moral and physical representations of the thousand years of blessedness of the Church, with the universal conflagration of the earth as *pre*-millennial, have thereby been led to *reject* the second personal coming of Christ as *pre*-millennial. In other words, as they allege that the universal conflagration is *simultaneous* with the second personal coming of Christ; they cannot reconcile that event with what the Scriptures teach of the state and character of the *millennial* dispensation; and hence deny that the second personal coming of Christ is *pre*-millennial. Accordingly, in order to square their theory with the above, they allege,

First, that the scriptural "times of the Gentiles" is *identical* with the Christian dispensation.

Second, that the Christian Church, during this dispensation, is *identical* with "the kingdom of heaven," "of God," "of the Son of Man," etc.; and that, forming a part, it is to run onward to the *end* of, the millennial state of the Church. And yet,

Third, as the idea of a kingdom involves the presence and reign of a king; so, throughout this prolonged period of "the times of the Gentiles" or Christian dispensation, they insist that Christ *has* reigned, and will *continue* to reign over this kingdom, the Church, by his *spiritual* presence.

But, in the next place: It is to be specially noted, that as both the pre- and the post-millennialists admit that the second personal coming of Christ is to take place *at the close of* "the times of the Gentiles;" therefore, if it can be shown, first, that the Christian dispensation *is not* identical with "the times of the Gentiles," however it may in part run parallel with it; and second, that the Christian Church, as "the kingdom of heaven *in mystery*," is entirely separate and distinct from "the kingdom of heaven" *in manifestation;* it will follow, 1st, that "the times of the Gentiles" end *before* the commencement of the millennial period of the Church; 2d, that the Christian dispensation forms *an entirely different era*, in all its peculiar characteristics and purposes, from the millennial; and 3d, that as, at the *end* of "the times of the Gentiles," by the admission of both classes of writers, the second personal coming of Christ is to take place, that event must be *pre-* and *not post*-millennial.

And, finally. If it can be shown, first, that in the scriptural representations of the moral and physical *changes* that are to distinguish the millennial from the Christian state of the Church, as the *sequences* of the pre-millennial personal coming of Christ, there is nothing incompatible with the universal conflagration of the earth as *post*-millennial; it will follow, second, that the reign of Christ during the millennial period of the Church, must be **a** *personal* and not a spiritual reign.

With these statements of the positions respectively of the parties concerned, we shall now proceed to an examination of the *theses* of our post-millenarian brethren, as above indicated, seriatim.

FIRST THESIS.

OF THE ALLEGED IDENTITY OF "THE TIMES OF THE GENTILES" WITH THE CHRISTIAN DISPENSATION AND THE MILLENNIAL ERA.

Relying upon the candor of the reader to extend to this subject that respectful consideration which its importance demands, we submit the following, in proof of the distinction between "the times of the Gentiles," the Christian dispensation, and the millennial era. Having, in a previous part of this work, treated at length of the scriptural evidence relating to the chronology of this period, as denoted by the mystical "seven times" of Lev. xxvi. and Dan. iv., showing the 2520 years of that prophetical number to have commenced with the captivity of the Jewish nation under Manasseh, their king, in A. M. 3480, and that it will close at the termination of the 6,000th year from the creation and fall, in A. D. 1868;[1] we now adduce the following, demonstrative of the commencement and end of the Christian dispensation as distinguished from it, and from the millennial era.

This period dates from the nativity, 652 years after the commencement of "the times of the Gentiles," and, according to the corrected Hebrew chronology, in the year A. M. 4132.[2] It is "determined" by the "seventy weeks," or 490 years of Daniel's prophecy of the time of "Messiah's" first advent, chap. ix. 24–27. This notable prophecy commenced with the edict issued in the seventh year of Artaxerxes Longimanus to Ezra, to "restore and to build Jerusalem," A. M. 3679, and ended with the "confirmation of the covenant with many" by the conversion of Cornelius,[3] at the close of the *last* of the "seventy weeks," A. M. 4169, the interval being exactly 490 years. We have only, therefore, to deduct the 33 years and 6 months of our blessed Lord's life and ministry from the *middle* of the last week, i. e., between A. M. 4165 and 4166, in order to reach the true date for the commencement of the dispensation under which we live.[4]

Nor is this less uncertain as to the time of its close. The pro-

---

[1] See pages 163-174. [2] See Note C. [3] Acts x. [4] *Our Bible Chronology*, p. 142.

phetical number of "*time, times, and the dividing of time*," or 1260 years of Daniel (chap. vii. 25), with the additions thereto of 30 and of 45 years, making a total of 1335 years—for the 1260, 1290, and 1335 years, all have a common commencement (see Dan. xii. 7, 11, 12)—refer, as all our most judicious expositors of prophecy admit, to the rise, career, and end of the "little" persecuting "horn" of the Papacy, which was to "make war with" and to "prevail against the saints" of God. . . . How long? The answer is, "*until* the ancient of days came, and judgment was given to the saints of the Most High, and the time came that the saints possess the kingdom." (Dan. vii. 21, 22.) For, it is at the *end* of the 1335 days (or years) of Dan. xii. 11, 12, that he is to "*stand in his lot*," i. e., be raised from the dead.[1]

Again. These three dates, as we have said, having a common commencement, by the almost unanimous consent of the learned, began in A. D. 533, with the edict of Justinian, constituting the bishop of Rome, in the person of John II., the vicegerent of Jesus Christ on earth; and they end at A. D. 1868, thus extending over the *whole period* of the 1335 years' career of the antichristian Papal "horn," down to the period of his being "*smitten*" by the Messianic "stone;" and hence, from A. M. 4132, runs parallel and ends coetaneously with the prophetic "seven times," or 2520 years assigned to "the times of the Gentiles."

Again. When the time comes that "the saints possess the kingdom," the prophet tells us that "one like the Son of Man comes with the clouds of heaven to the ancient of days," and that *then* "there is given Him dominion, and glory, and a kingdom, that all people, and nations, and languages should serve him."[2]

Here, then, we have a *literal* kingdom on earth, under the sway of *a real personal king*—"the Son of David," seated on "David's throne."[3] It follows that, when this event takes place, *then* will be verified the saying, "The kingdoms of this world are become the kingdom of our Lord and of his Christ." Yea, then "HE SHALL REIGN ON THE EARTH."

And, mark: as we here see, all this takes place at the simultaneous close both of "the times of the Gentiles" and of the present Christian economy; and that, in order to the introduction to, and establishment of, the Church of Christ in the enjoyment of her *millennial* glory.

[1] Compare 1 Thess. iv. 13-17, 1 Cor. xv. 23 with Rev. xx. 4-6.
[2] Dan. vii. 20, 22, and verses 13, 14.   [3] Luke i. 32; and Rev. v. 10.

Hence the inference that these two periods, thus terminating together, expire *before* the commencement of the millennial era. That there is no escape from this conclusion, take the following in proof:

1. The whole Church admits the scriptural doctrine of *the second personal coming* of Christ. Also,

2. That this event takes place at the close of the *Christian* dispensation, which, as we have seen, is coetaneous with the close of "the times of the Gentiles."

Now, take the argument following, as decisive of the point whether the Christian dispensation merges into, forms a part, and closes with the termination, of the *millennial* age.

(1.) The whole Christian Church of this day (or if there be exceptions they are of no account) professedly believes in, and is earnestly praying for, the ushering in of the latter-day glory, or millennial era; which, she affirms, will consist of a thousand years' enjoyment of that universal righteousness, peace, prosperity, and blessedness, that is to result from *the conversion of all nations*, Jewish and Gentile, to Christ. With this admission before us, let us now turn,

(2.) To that notable prophecy of our Lord, Luke xxi. 24, where, having referred to that portion of the Jewish race who should *escape* "the edge of the sword" of the Roman legions at the destruction of Jerusalem, He said: "And ye shall be led captive into all nations; and Jerusalem shall be trodden down of the Gentiles, until the times of the Gentiles be fulfilled;" or, as in the words of St. Paul (Rom. xi. 25), "until the fulness of the Gentiles be come in." Now here, the terms "fulfilled" and "fulness," by common consent, are used to denote *the close* of this period, coincident with which is also *the close* of the present Christian age. We ask, therefore,

(3.) As this prophecy can only be verified by the *continued* subjection of the Jews and of Jerusalem to the dominancy of the Gentiles over them, down to the *end* of this period, how is this to be reconciled with the declared state of *universal* righteousness, peace, prosperity, and glory, of the millennial age of the Church, as forming an integral part of "the times of the Gentiles?" In other words, where are we to find these *oppressors* of the Jews, during the millennial age, when *all nations*, Jewish and Gentile, are converted to Christ?

From this dilemma, according to the popular theory on this subject, we can see no possibility of escape.

Two inferences follow, viz.:

First. That the Christian dispensation, which ends coincident with "the times of the Gentiles," is brought to a close *before* the commencement of the millennial age; and,

Second. That, taking the admission of the whole Church, that the second personal coming of Christ is to transpire *at the close* of the Christian dispensation, *alias* "the times of the Gentiles," that event must be *pre-* and not *post-*millennial. But we pass to the

SECOND THESIS.

THIS THESIS ALLEGES THAT THE CHRISTIAN CHURCH, DURING "THE TIMES OF THE GENTILES," IS IDENTICAL WITH "THE KINGDOM OF HEAVEN"—"OF GOD"—OF "THE SON OF MAN," ETC.; ALSO THAT, FORMING A PART, IT IS TO RUN ONWARD TO THE CLOSE, OF THE MILLENNIAL ERA.

We respectfully demur to this statement. Our argument is founded upon the scriptural distinction between "the kingdom of heaven" in *mystery*, and "the kingdom of the Son of Man" in *manifestation*. It is to be observed, that, in accordance with the stipulation of the covenant of God with Abraham, "In thee, and in thy seed, shall all nations, families, and kindreds of the earth be blessed,"[1] it became necessary, as we have shown in another part of this work,[2] temporarily *to set aside* the unbelieving Jews, in order to the ingathering of the Gentiles. It was to this end that Jesus Christ was "the minister of the circumcision for the truth of God, to confirm the promises made unto the fathers," even "that the *Gentiles* might glorify God for his mercy; as it is written: for this cause I will confess thee among the Gentiles, and sing unto thy name. And again he saith, Rejoice, ye Gentiles, with his people. And again, Praise the Lord, all ye Gentiles, and laud him, all ye people. Esaias also saith, There shall be a root of Jesse, and he that shall rise to reign over the Gentiles: in him shall the Gentiles trust."[3] Yea, and this, "according to the eternal purpose of God which he purposed in Christ Jesus our Lord,"[4] involved the necessity of *the "fall"* of

---

[1] Gen. xii. 3; Acts iii. 25. [2] See pages 84, 85 of this work.
[3] Rom. xv. 8-12. [4] Eph. iii. 11.

the Jews, that they might be "the riches of the world;" and the "*diminishing* of them," that they might be "the riches of the Gentiles."[1]

Hence the reasoning of St. Paul in the eleventh of the Romans, in reference to the *exscinding* of the Jewish "national branches" from the "good olive tree" on account of their "unbelief." It was in order that the believing Gentiles of "all nations," though "wild by nature," might be graffed into their place.

And hence, also, the divinely ordained process for the "*taking out of* (or from among) the Gentiles, a people for Christ's name," through those ordinary instrumentalities of the Church, which were to follow the extraordinary ministry of the twelve apostles. This process, we shall now proceed to show, was to continue coeval, and to close, with the *Christian* dispensation.

The first argument to this end, is derived from the promise appended to the great commission of Christ to "the twelve," "Lo, I am with you alway, even unto *the end of the world*"—αἰῶνος— i. e., age, or dispensation. The meaning here is, not that Christ was personally to continue with, or that the twelve apostles were to live to, "the end of the world," or age; but that He was to be present by *divine energy and power* with those, who, as their successors, should constitute the divinely appointed "ambassadors for Christ," *during* that period.

Now, this great truth, we remark in the next place, is enunciated by our Lord for this express purpose. The first to which I would direct the thoughts of the reader is,

The parable of *the marriage of the King's Son*, Matt. xxii. 2–10. Indeed, there are two other parables, which, when considered in their connections with this, illustrate the progressive developments of the kingdom of God's "MYSTERY" OF GRACE, during the whole of man's period of trial, onward to the close of the present age. The first, the parable of the "*great supper*," given in the early part of Christ's ministry, is explanatory of the first call of the gospel to Jew and Gentile; and exhibits the exclusion from its blessings of the former class, whose unbelief and hardness of heart led them to reject it. The second, that of "*the wicked husbandmen*," as occupants of the "vineyard" committed to their care, runs parallel with the first, and delineates their growing enmity to Christ, until it results in their crucifixion of "the Lord

[1] Rom. xi.

of life and glory." And the third, the *parable in hand*, given at the close of Christ's ministry, while it covers the ground of both the others, points out the judgments of God which were to overtake the murderers of those of his servants sent to extend to them the second gospel call, at the destruction of their nation, polity, and city, in A. D. 70; and thence, through the period assigned to the ingathering of the GENTILE BRIDE for the King's Son, down to the utterance of "the midnight cry" of preparation to meet him.

We learn, therefore, from these three parables, the long-continued exercise of God's forbearance toward the Jewish nation, on the one hand; and the "taking out of (or from among) the Gentiles a people for his name" during the gospel economy of grace, on the other. This, however, is more especially to be drawn from the imagery introduced into the parabolic *marriage of the King's Son*, which is both retrospective and prospective.

First. In its *retrospective* aspect, it includes the first class of the King-Father's "servants," viz., "John the Baptist" and "the seventy," who were sent to call the Jewish nation "to the wedding." But "they would not come." "Again he sent other servants," viz., the twelve apostles, to whom Jesus said, "Go not into the way of the Gentiles, neither into any city of the Samaritans enter ye not: but go rather to the lost sheep of the house of Israel," and "tell them, behold, I have prepared my dinner . . . . come unto the marriage." But, "they made light of it," etc. Yes. *If they would*, they might have been the accepted "bride" of the King's Son, who was then personally with them. *If they would*, the Theocratic "first dominion," or "kingdom of Israel," which, in the time of Samuel, they rejected for an earth-born dynasty, might then have been "restored to them." But the King's Son "came to his own, but his own *received him not*." And so, repeating these acts of "rejecting the counsel of God against themselves," they were "cast out of the vineyard," which is thenceforth "let out to *other* husbandmen;" while the King-Father, in his "wrath, sent his armies, and destroyed those murderers, and burned up their city."

Nor this only. For, mark: the judgments of God against that guilty nation, so far from being arrested at the destruction of Jerusalem by the Roman legions in A. D. 70, still pursued those of them who *escaped* "the edge of the sword," by leading them into a long-protracted "captivity among all nations," and dooming

"Jerusalem to be trodden down of the Gentiles, *until* the times of the Gentiles be fulfilled."[1]

This, therefore, *spans the whole period* of proffered mercy and of merited judgment toward the Jewish nation, from the time of John the Baptist to the close of the above period, and with which, as we have shown, synchronizes the close of the *Christian age,* and "the times of the Gentiles."

Meanwhile, in accordance with "the eternal purpose of God which he purposed in Christ Jesus our Lord," seeing that those— the Jews—for whom the wedding was *first* made ready, by their twice-repeated rejection of it "were not worthy," the command is given to his "servants," " *Go ye therefore into the highways, and as many as ye shall find, bid to the marriage.* So these servants went out into the highways, and gathered together all, both bad and good, and the wedding was furnished with guests."

The obvious meaning here is, that the first class of invited guests to the wedding, viz., the Jews, unconscious that their perseveringly malicious machinations against the King's Son were working out the accomplishment of that very "eternal purpose which God purposed concerning Him," continued in their love of worldly barter and gain, and in hatred of Christ and his servants, until it ended in their merited doom—*they* "*were not worthy*" to be constituted "the bride, the Lamb's wife." No. She must be sought for *elsewhere.*

And, oh the stupendous "MYSTERY" of redeeming love! She is to be found, not "in the streets and lanes" of the gorgeous Jewish "city;" she is to be selected, not from the self-styled "wise, and mighty, and noble of this world;" but from among "the poor, and the maimed, and the halt, and the blind," that are found *in the highways of the earth's population;* not of one country, but of every country under the whole heaven; and not of one grade of character, but of every grade, "the bad and the good;" that is, those who are reputedly so, at the time when they are welcomed to the marriage: the "*good,*" as Nathanael, Nicodemus, Cornelius, and others; the "*bad,*" as "the woman that was a sinner," the "malefactor" on the cross, "Saul of Tarsus," the "jailer," etc.

Thus, as our Lord declared to the unbelieving house of Israel, 'Seeing that " ye will not come unto me that ye might have life,"

[1] Luke xxi. 24.

therefore, "the kingdom of God," i. e., the heavenly, which is in reserve for the *resurrected* dead in Christ and the *raptured living* saints, and which, *if ye would*, ye might have retained as its legitimate subjects and "heirs," "is *taken from you*, and given to a nation" (THE GENTILES) "bringing forth the fruits thereof." And so, although the earthly "first dominion" shall finally be restored to you, my Gentile bride alone shall be accounted "worthy" to "*sit* with me on my throne," and to "*reign* with me on the earth," "judging the twelve tribes of Israel."'

We have only to add to this, that *the period* assigned to the ingathering of the Gentile bride to Christ, runs parallel with that allotted for the prolonged judgment upon the Jews, and *ends* with it.

If, however, additional evidence be required to confirm this fact, it may, we submit, be found in the further instructions imparted by our Lord in the parable of "*the talents*, five, two, and one;"[1] and in that of the "*ten pounds.*"[2] In both cases, a distribution is made in goods or in money, as *tests* of the fidelity or slothfulness of the respective "servants" of the "householder" and the "nobleman," during their absence "in a far country:" the things denoted by the imagery employed, being that of the *improvement* or *abuse* of the means of grace to man, during the probationary period of trial allotted to him under this dispensation; the extreme points of which, as signified by the withdrawal and return of the two personages in the parables, indicating that they extend from the *ascension* to the *second coming* of Christ at which latter event, like them, He calls his servants to a reckoning, rewards the faithful, and punishes the guilty.

But what is decisive of this fact, is the lesson taught us in the parable of "*the wheat and the tares.*"[3] This parable is interpreted by many to denote that the visible Church is analogous to the "field" therein spoken of; her members, good and bad, to the "wheat and tares;" her ministers, to the "servants;" the anxiety of the ministry, on their discovery of the tares among the wheat, at once to separate the one from the other by the discipline of the Church; and the course of conduct on the part of the "servants" to "gather up the tares," etc., to the act of excommunication.

The *incongruity* of these views, however, to the things sig-

---

[1] Matt. xxv. 14-29. [2] Luke xix. 11-27. [3] Matt. xiii. 24-30.

nified by the imagery of the parable, we think will appear obvious on the following grounds. Keeping in view the fact, that our blessed Lord himself *interpreted* all those parts of the parable which required it, we remark, first, that though both the wheat and the tares grow together in the same soil, yet He does not say, "The field" is the visible Church; but, "The field is *the world*." Second. The "wheat" is interpreted to denote "*the children of the kingdom*," and the "tares," "*the children of the wicked one*." Third. Although all the other parts of the parable are interpreted by Christ, the "servants" are passed over in *silence*, a circumstance only to be accounted for on the ground that they are identical with the *angelic* "*reapers*," etc. And fourth, the express command of the "householder" to the "servants" respecting the "wheat" and the "tares," to "let both grow together *until the harvest*," can never be made to mean the exercise of discipline in the Church.

The import of the parable, then, is simply this: in exact harmony with all the others which precede it as above, though much more explicitly, it exhibits the diversified effects of "the gospel of the grace of God," as it is dispensed to mankind *during the Christian dispensation*, between the first and second comings of Christ, *as a test* of its acceptance or rejection by them. Hence, first, the two classes of sowers presented to view, He of the "good seed," who is interpreted to signify "*the Son of Man*," who commenced sowing it, first, personally, and then by His apostles and their successors; and he of the "tares," who is interpreted to denote that "enemy" of Christ, "*the devil*," and his emissaries, who commenced scattering the "tares" simultaneously with that of the "good seed."

Second. The two classes of seeds, the "wheat" and the "tares," signify the *mixed state* or character of the Church, during this dispensation, whose entire history is identified with the existence of mingled good and evil, yet of so marked a *resemblance*, as scarcely to be distinguished.

Third. "The field is the world," *in* which is to be found *the Church*, gathering, as it were, the human race into one lifetime, as they will be gathered in one "harvest," which is interpreted to mean "*the end of the world*" (αἰῶνος, age), at the close of this dispensation. And hence,

Fourth. The repression of the zeal of the angelic "servants" as the "reapers" of the "harvest," *until* the aggregate of the plants in the "field of the world," good and bad, shall have attained to full maturity. Then, and not *until* then, will the "tares" be separated from the "wheat." The angelic reapers or "servants" have been taught patiently to await the *return* of the "household" sower of the "good seed"—"*the Son of Man*"—to "the field," lest, by a premature attempt to "gather up the tares," they "root up also the wheat with them."

Nor is it out of place, in this connection, to refer to the *vast disproportion* of the "wheat" to the "tares" in this "field of the world," from apostolic times down to this present. Our design here is to show that (in opposition to the theory, that by and through the *ordinary* agencies of the Church, all nations are to be subjected to the obedience of Christ, in the order of a *geometrical succession* of conversions, under the Christian dispensation) the moral characteristics both of the Church and the world at the close of the present economy, were to furnish an exact copy to those which marked the close of the antediluvian age. This will appear from the prophecy of our Lord, in reference to *the two periods.* In Matt. xxiv. 37-39, he says: "*But as the days of Noah were*, . . . they were eating and drinking, marrying and giving in marriage, until the day that Noah entered into the ark, and knew not, until the flood came, and took them all away: *so shall also the coming of the Son of Man be.*"

Now, true. The setting aside for a time of the unbelieving Jewish nation by their excision from the good olive-tree, was "*to the intent*, that now unto the principalities and powers might be known by the Church," i. e., by the instrumentalities of the Church, "the manifold wisdom of God, according to the eternal purpose which he purposed in Christ Jesus our Lord . . . that the *Gentiles* should be fellow-heirs, and of the same body," i. e., with the believing Jews; and thus, "be made partakers of his promise by the gospel," under the *Christian* economy. Hence the commission of Christ to his apostles and their successors to evangelize the world: "Go ye, therefore, into all the world, and preach the gospel to every creature." "Go, teach all nations," etc. Not, observe, that they were expected, during this economy, to effect the *individual* conversion of all in every nation; but, that they and their successors after them should be "*a witness* unto all nations,"[1] "to take out of (or from among) them *a people for his name.*"[2]

Accordingly, during the apostolic age, the Church acted *fully up to* her sense of responsibility in these premises. "Beginning at Jerusalem," she faithfully "preached repentance and remission of sins in Christ's name among all nations."[3] True to their mission, their trumpet "voice went out into all the earth, and their words unto the end of the world."[4] The result was, that "there were added to the Church daily, of such as should be saved," so that a "goodly number" "continued steadfastly in the apostles' doctrine and fellowship," and "in breaking of bread and prayers."[5]

But, in pursuance of this great work, the apostle Paul laid down the following *test* of the Church's fidelity to Christ her Head, during this dispensation. Speaking of the excision of the natural Jewish branches from the good olive-tree on account of their unbelief; and of the grafting into their place of the believing Gentile scions, he says: "On them which fell," i. e., the Jews, "*severity;* but towards thee," i. e., the Gentile Church of all nations—Christendom—"*goodness, if thou continue* in God's goodness: otherwise," he adds, "*thou also* shalt be cut off."[6]

The question therefore is, Has the Church from apostolic times *continued* in God's goodness, in the sense here intended? Our fidelity as a writer compels us to say that, like the Sethite "sons of God" in unholy alliance with the Cainite "children of men" in Noah's day; *so is the Church throughout Christendom,* by her criminal dalliance with the world, according to the prophecy of Christ. All history attests, that by her gradual degeneracy from the doctrinal purity and catholic unity of apostolic times, the *analogy* to that which befell the Church of the antediluvian age, is complete in all its parts. While, on the one hand, the early and numerous conversions under the apostles correspond with those of the days of Enos, when "men began to call themselves by the name of the Lord;" on the other it must be conceded, that, like its remote type in the days of Noah, there commenced a *defection* in the Church, which, though at first scarcely discernible, yet at length assumed the most gigantic proportions.

---

[1] Matt. xxiv. 14.   [2] Acts xv. 14.   [3] Luke xxiv. 47.
[4] Rom. x. 12.   [5] See Acts ii. verses 41-47 inclusive.   [6] Rom. xi. 22.

We see indications of this apostasy, not only in the divisions and contentions of the Corinthian, the Roman, and the Galatian Churches, but also in the condition of the seven Asiatic Churches in the days of St. John. And who does not know, that no sooner was the Church translated, in the early part of the *third* century, from her former condition of obscurity, ignominy, and suffering during the ten pagan persecutions, to the *worldly* prominence, honors, and wealth to which she was raised under Constantine, than she entered upon her downward course? Yes. Beguiled by the smiles of courtly favor, she continued ignominiously to succumb to the policy of the state, until, in A. D. 533, by the infamous edict of Justinian, ecclesiastical ambition for the "*pre-eminence*" having attained its culminating point, John II., bishop of Rome, was permanently seated in the chair of St. Peter, as Christ's accredited vicegerent upon earth!

Thenceforward, during the succeeding ten centuries, down to the period of the Reformation in A. D. 1517, what, we ask, are the heart-sickening annals of this prolonged period, but details of the rapid progression of *primitive Christianity perverted*, in doctrine, ceremonials, church order, and moral degeneracy, to the extent that, at its close, it may be truly said, that "*the earth* was corrupt before God, and that it was filled with violence?"

Nor this only. For although, at length, the thundering voice of a *Luther*, at the portals of the Vatican of old Rome, disturbed the long-protracted quiet of the antichristian "little horn" in his lair; and much as we have cause for thankfulness to God, in view of the *fruits* of the great Reformation which followed; still, I submit, we are not to overlook the fact of the *failure* of that Reformation, both on the Continent and in England, in effecting more than *a very partial* emancipation of Christendom from the tyranny, spiritual and temporal, of the Papal See. (Notes A & E.)

And now, to bring this matter still nearer home. What evidence have we, I ask, that the Church, *since that time*, has "continued in God's goodness" as "*a witness*" to the nations? Her commission, if it did not impose upon her the obligation to effect the conversion of each individual of the "all nations" to whom she was sent; *yet it did* enjoin upon her the duty to leave not one individual of them without the *offer* of salvation through faith in Christ. Hence, a reformation in this period or that, cannot make amends for *unfaithfulness* in any previous period. Besides, that which continues has no need to be, and indeed cannot be, restored.

We appeal, then. Has God *no* controversy with the Church of this day on the subject of the unevangelized, compared with the evangelized portions of the earth, as they now present themselves in a moral aspect in bold relief before us? The following statistics will evidence the *vast proportion* of the "tares" over the "wheat," as they now prevail in the "field of the world." Take a view,

Of *the population of the earth*, scattered over a surface of at least 96,000,000 of square miles. The aggregate number is near 1,225,000 000 of souls! These may be divided into the following religious systems, viz.:

1. Of Brahminical Pagans, in Asia, ... 650,000,000
2. Of Mohammedans, in Asia and Africa, ... 150,000,000
3. Of Pagans, in a purely savage state, ... 100,000,000
4. Of Jews (the kingdom of Judah), dispersed, . . 14,000,000
5. In Christendom, there are,
   (1.) Of the Western, or Romish Church, . . 170,000,000
   (2.) Of the Eastern, or Greek Church, ... 60,000,000
   (3.) Of Protestants, throughout the world, . . 80,000,000

This gives a total population of 1,224,000,000

It results from these statistics,

First. That less than *one fifth* of the earth's population are included within the pale of Christendom.

Second. That of these latter, only about *one third* bear the Protestant name. Nor is this all.

Third. Computing, as we must, the real numerical strength of Protestant Christianity by the *communion statistics* of all the various branches of the Church scattered over "the field of the world," and they do not yield us a total of over 15,000,000 of souls!

Here then, so far as figures, based upon the most recent and best-authenticated statistical facts, are concerned, we are presented with a true picture of the *moral* condition of the populations of earth *as they now are*. And, what a picture! What a vast disproportion between the respective devotees of the various systems of religion—Pagan, Mohammedan, and Jewish

—compared with those who bear the *Christian* name! Considerably more than *two thirds* of the whole, or 914,000,000 of souls now on earth, either lie buried in the grave of a stupid and beastly idolatry, or are the dupes of a superstitious Islamism or Judaic blindness! And, of the remaining 310,000,000 of *Christendom*, as Protestants maintain that the systems both of the Roman and Greek Churches, amounting to 230,000,000, are forms of a corrupt Christianity, and that they are equally in an unconverted state with those outside of the pale of their respective communions, it reduces the actual *evangelical* element, compared with the others, to the appallingly small proportion of about 15,000,000 of souls!

Thus much, then, of the *proportion* of the "wheat" with the "tares," in the great moral "field of the world."

Now, if we take into view,

First, *the fact* that, in the parabolic teachings of our Lord, as above exhibited, they all point to *the period* of man's probation under the gospel economy of grace, from its first dispensation by Christ and His apostles, with their successors, down to the time of "the harvest at the end of the world," or "times of the Gentiles;" and if,

Second, we can show, *chronologically,* that our Lord's predicted analogy between the moral characteristics of the days of Noah, and those which are immediately to precede His second coming, are applicable to *the age in which we live;* it will follow,

Third, that those prophecies which relate to "the kingdom of heaven," and the coming and reign of Christ on earth, do not, and cannot by any possibility (as alleged by the theory under review), be made to refer to *the first establishment* of the Christian Church, and of Christ's spiritual presence with her onward to the close of the millennial age. Instead, it will result that the time of the great "harvest" of the world which is to transpire at the close of the present Christian economy, *is just at hand!*

But before we proceed to demonstrate this last-named proposition, we must once more remind the reader of the *magnitude* of the work to be achieved by Protestants, on the alleged hypothesis of the evangelization of the world by *ordinary* Church instrumentalities, to which we have already adverted. To say nothing of the numerous *obstacles* to be encountered in the conversion of

Pagans, Mohammedans, and Jews; and in being brought into collision with the vast machinery of Papal propagandism, which, with more men, and more money, and more zeal, as *twenty* to *one*, compared with Protestants; we repeat, to say nothing of these, here are more than 1,200,000,000 of souls, spread over at least 96,000,000 of square miles of the earth's surface, to be subdued to the obedience of Christ, through the process of a "*geometrical progression* of conversions," by 15,000,000 of Protestant Christians!

The difficulty, therefore, which here presses upon us from the outset is, that from a comparison of the present *Christianized* and *unchristianized* portions of the globe with the past, the progress of the Church in effecting the evangelization of the world, if not decidedly retrograde, does not certainly encourage the hope of *a very speedy* consummation of her work. The discussion of this subject on its merits must be reserved for a subsequent page, when we shall come to treat of the present fondly cherished expectations by the Church of the speedy conversion of the nations to Christ, as alleged of the moral and political revolutions of the day at home and abroad. For, aside from every other consideration, our abiding conviction is, that on the principle of the theory under review, of a "geometrical progression of conversions" by *ordinary* Church agencies—e. g., preaching; missionary operations, domestic and foreign; Bible distribution; tract, Sabbath school, and other societies, etc., etc.—even under the most favorable auspices, we cannot expect the ushering in of the millennial era of the Church this side of 500 years! And further: inasmuch as, *on this theory,* we must add 1000 years for the period of the Church during the millennium, it will follow that—as the whole Church contends—the second coming of Christ being deferred to the *end* of "the times of the Gentiles," the Church is doomed to at least 1500 years of *deferred hope,* before that event can take place!

The question to be settled, therefore, is—and we appeal that it is one of momentous interest—whether this is in accordance with "the mind of the Spirit," *as the revealed faith and hope* of the Church in regard to either the one event or the other? That it is not, we have only to refer the reader to what we have already offered in proof,

1. Of the *distinction* to be drawn between "the times of the

Gentiles" and the Christian dispensation; and also between this latter and the millennial period of the Church.[1] And, to these results, we have now only to add in further confirmation of them,

2. The *exact coincidence* therewith of the chronology of Holy Scripture, historic and prophetic. This will verify that the predicted moral characteristics which were to *immediately precede* the second coming of our Lord in analogy to "the days that were before the flood," belong to the days *in which we now live*. In this comparison of the remote original with the predicted copy, it is scarcely necessary to say, that the *special design* of our blessed Lord was, to direct our thoughts to the culminating point of wickedness, *in both ages*, as the sure and certain "*signs*" of their respective close. As the moral characteristics "in the days of Noah," taken as *signs*, marked the approach, and finally instigated the catastrophe of the flood; *so*, the corresponding moral characteristics predicted by our Lord, taken as *signs*, must relate to, and can only transpire at, *the close* of this age, as the *harbingers* of His second personal coming from heaven.

Nor this only. As the *time*, according to the Divine purpose, for the closing up of the antediluvian age, was definitely and unalterably fixed by the chronological limit of 120 years, as a respite from, and a warning of, the impending judgment of the flood; *so*, with the termination of the corresponding Gentile Christian age, *immediately preceding* "the coming of the Son of Man."

And now, that we of this day occupy a PROXIMITY to the second personal coming of the Lord Jesus Christ corresponding with that of the 120 years to the flood, in Noah's time, will appear from the following *chronological summary* of Holy Scripture, historic and prophetic, which will be found to encircle the entire period of the world's history, from the creation and fall of man to the close of time, under four distinct dispensations, Patriarchal (antediluvian and postdiluvian), Levitical, Christian, and Millennial.

We have now, however, only to do with the *first three* of the above-named dispensations. Requesting the reader to turn to pages 180–182 of "Our Bible Chronology," where we have furnished the scriptural evidence that God has revealed to the Church the unalterable period of 6000 years as the interval within

---

[1] See pages 185-188, with which compare pages 188-200.

which, under the *three dispensations*, Patriarchal, Jewish, and Christian, all His *ordinary* purposes of providence and grace were to be accomplished, we herewith append the following tabular view of the chronology of Scripture, *historic* and *prophetic*, from the creation and fall of man to the close of the 6000 years.

We would here premise, that the *prophetic* chronology, though not exclusively, yet is more especially concerned with "*the times of the Gentiles*," which, interlocking with a definitely determined period in the *historic*, viz., A. M. 3480, B. C. 652,[1] reaches down to, and closes with, those "times" in A. D. 1868.

We cannot here enter into this matter in detail. The reader will find that in my recently published work on "Our Bible Chronology, Historic and Prophetic, Critically Examined and Demonstrated," etc. We will, however, insert the *six* following tabular summaries of the different periods, including a view both of the historic and prophetic numbers, all of which, though formed of *different* combinations, amount to precisely 6000 years. Take,

1. *The several periods of the* HISTORIC *chronology.*

    (1.) From the Creation to the Deluge, - - - 1656 years.
    (2.) From the Deluge to Abraham, - - - - 427 "
    (3.) From Abraham to the Exodus, - - - 430 "
    (4.) From the Exodus to the close of the time of the Judges, - - - - - - - - 587 "
    (5.) The Regal Age, from Saul to the Babylonish Captivity, 430 "
    (6.) The Babylonish Captivity, - - 70 years, ⎫
    (7.) Thence to commencement of Daniel's ⎬ 149 "
    "Seventy Weeks," - - - 79 " ⎭
    (8.) The "Seventy Weeks" of Daniel, - - - 490 "
    (9.) Add A. D., from the close of "Seventy Weeks," 1831 "

    Total, - - - - - - - - 6000 years.

2. *The* HISTORIC *and* LONGER PROPHETIC *periods combined.*

    (1.) From the Creation to commencement of the mystical "Seven times" of Lev. xxvi., - - 3480 years.
    (2.) The "Seven times," - - - - - - 2520 "

    Total, - - - - - - - - 6000 years.

---

[1] See pages 169-170 inclusive, of this work, where the *longest* of the prophetical periods, revealed under the mystical form of "*seven times*" (Lev. xxvi. and Dan. iv.), amounting to 2520 years, is shown to have commenced at the above date, with the captivity of the Jewish nation in the time of Manasseh.

3. *Another, of the same* TWOFOLD *combinations.*

(1.) From the Creation to commencement of Daniel's
 "Seventy weeks" (chap. ix. 24–27), - - 3679 years.
(2.) The "Seventy weeks," - - - - - 490 "
(3.) Add from the close of the "Seventy weeks" in A. M.
 4169, the years A. D. - - - - - 1831 "

Total, - - - - - - - 6000 years.

4. *The* HISTORIC *and* SHORTER PROPHETIC *periods combined.*

(1.) From the Creation, set down for commencement of
 the 2300 years of Dan. viii. 14, - - - 3652 years.
(2.) Add from thence to Nativity, - 480 years.
(3.) Add years A. D. to the close of the
 2300 years, - - - 1820 "
(4.) Add years for gradual exhaustion of   } 2348 "
 the mystical Euphrates, Rev. xvi.
 12, - - - - - - 40 "
(5.) Add to A. D. 1868, - - - 8 "

Total, - - - - - - - 6000 years.

5. *Another, of the same* TWOFOLD *combinations.*

(1.) Set down for commencement of the 2300 years, 3652 years.
(2.) Add years of the 2300, down to
 commencement of its first integral
 period of "five months," Rev. ix.
 5, or 150 years, - - - 1572 years.
(3.) Add the "five months" as above, 150 "
(4.) Add for Turkish repose, from A. D.
 937 to A. D. 1057, - - - 120 "
(5.) Add interval between the departure
 of the Turks from Bagdad, A. D.   } 2348 "
 1057, to the capture of Constan-
 tinople, A. D. 1453, — 396 years,
 as the second integral of the 2300
 years above, of "a day, an hour,
 a month, and a year," Rev. ix. 14,
 15, - - - - - 396 "
(6.) Add for continued drying up of the
 mystical Euphrates, Rev. xvi. 12, 110 "

Total, - - - - - - - 6000 years.

Finally,

6. *Table, showing the* SUM TOTAL *of the Historic Chronology down to the present year of our Lord.*

(1.) From Creation to Nativity (Heb. Chron. corrected),	4132 years.
(2.) From Nativity to A. D.,	1864 "
Total,	5996 years.
(3.) Add to close of the 6000 years from A. D. 1864,	4 "
Total,	6000 years.

True, in the tabular summaries, we are compelled to assume as reliable, what we claim to have proved in our recently published work, "Our Bible Chronology, Historic and Prophetic, Critically Examined," etc. Referring the reader, therefore, to our *verification* of them as therein set forth, we most earnestly point his eye to the *result* here reached. We see, from these tables, that while *five* of them all concur in filling up *to a year* the divinely predetermined period of 6000 years as allotted to the history of man down to the close of "the times of the Gentiles;" the last one, the *sixth,* shows that we have reached that limit to within *four years* from the present time!

Well, you will ask, *and what then?* The reply is, that unless the scriptural arguments and historical facts which have been brought to bear upon our review of the theory in hand can be set aside, *that theory is proved to be founded in error on all the points at issue;* and we are found to be standing ON THE VERY VERGE of that tremendous crisis, in which *all* the prophecies converge,[1] in regard to the interests and the destinies both of the Church of God and the nations of earth, at the time of the great "harvest" at "*the end* of the world" or "times of the Gentiles."

But these *first two* theses, along with the denial, by those who advocate them, that the second personal coming of Christ is *pre*-millennial, being, as we have said, hypothecated of their inability to *reconcile* the alleged universal conflagration of the earth as *pre*-millennial, with what the Scriptures teach of the *physical condition* of the earth during that period; we have at

---

[1] The reader is requested to turn to pages 189-199 where this subject is explained at length, showing that the eye of the faith and hope of the believer has been directed toward that crisis *from the beginning.*

length reached the proper place in these discussions for an **examination** of that mooted question:

Is the Universal Conflagration of the Earth Pre- or Post-Millennial?

This is a great subject. It involves an inquiry into the *state* or *condition* of the heavens and the earth *during the millennial era*, when "the kingdoms of this world," it is declared, "shall have become the kingdoms of our Lord and of his Christ." It is undeniable, that the Scriptures teach us to look for *a most signal change* as awaiting "the world" or earth, together with its surrounding atmosphere or heavens as compared with what they "now are," which shall adapt them to that blessed era. The question is, as to the *nature* and *extent* of that change, and the *agencies* to be employed in effecting it.

Now, in direct opposition to what some distinguished Millenarian writers allege respecting it, we affirm that this change, though it will extend to the removal of the original curse from the ground, and also from the circumambient air which envelops the earth; yet that it is not to be confounded, as it is often confounded, with that final παλιγγενεσία, i. e., "regeneration" or renovation of the globe and the heavens, which is to transpire *after* the thousand years' career of the saved nations in the flesh as its occupants shall be "finished."[1]

As we have said, not a few of our expositors of prophecy, by insisting that the universal conflagration of the globe is *pre*-millennial, have greatly damaged that system of revealed truth, of which they are otherwise the able advocates. The *truth* of the matter is simply this: it by no means follows, as we shall show, that because the second coming of Christ *is pre*-millennial, *therefore* the universal conflagration of the earth *is also pre*-millennial. To maintain that it is so, forms the great stumbling-block in the way of inquirers after truth in these premises. For example: the great body of evangelical Christians of this day (the Baptists excepted), profess to believe in and to pray for the ingathering and conversion of both Jews and Gentiles to Christ, and of their introduction to a state of happiness on earth during the period of *a thousand years.* But, being unable to reconcile an

---

[1] Rev. xx. 5, compared with chap. xxi. 1–5.

alleged *pre*-millennial conflagration *of* the earth, with a continuance of men *on* the earth, they *reject* the doctrine of the second coming of Christ as *pre*-millennial. The *error* on the part of both is, that of supposing the two events to be *necessarily coetaneous*. The result is, that while the *pre*-millennial conflagrationist inevitably deprives the earth of inhabitants during that era; the *post*-millennialist, who, on that ground, *denies* the *pre*-millennial personal coming of Christ, leaves the *subjects* of the millennial kingdom on earth WITHOUT A VISIBLE KING! To escape from these two horns of a dilemma, we shall lay down the following proposition, namely:

That the universal conflagration of the earth *is not pre-* but *post-*millennial.

In the support of this proposition, we shall now proceed to the proof, that the *nature* and *extent* of that change to which the physical heavens and earth will be subjected at the *pre*-millennial coming of Christ to judgment, *precludes the possibility* of a universal conflagration as the agent to effect it. We must here premise, that in the covenant entered into with Noah, the Lord said, "I will not curse the ground any more for man's sake...... While the earth remaineth, seedtime and harvest, and cold and heat, and summer and winter, and day and night, *shall not cease.*"[1]

Now, under this covenant with creation, of which the bow in the clouds is the sign or token, the earth has continued *till the present time*. If then it can be shown that the above stipulations regarding the earth will characterize the state or condition of things during the millennial epoch down to the *delivering up* of the kingdom to the Father; it will follow that the millennial era is *the last* of those dispensations under which the earth and its inhabitants were to be placed, *during the continuance* of God's covenant with creation after the flood; and therefore that the universal conflagration to which the earth and its elements are destined, *cannot* take place till the end of the thousand years. Take the following in proof:

1. St. Peter, in his 2d Epistle, chap. iii. 6, 7, having stated that "the world that was before the flood," being overflowed with water, perished, adds, "but the heavens and earth which are now, by the same word are kept in store, *reserved unto fire against*

[1] Gen. viii. 22.

the day of judgment and perdition of ungodly men," etc. That "the day of judgment" here is to be understood, *not* of a natural day of twenty-four hours, but as running *coeval with* the thousand years of the millennial era, is evident from the apostle's statements regarding it. As he stands "looking for and hasting unto the coming of the day of God," he speaks of it as that day "in the which," or WHEREIN "the heavens, *being on fire*, shall be dissolved, and the elements shall melt with fervent heat," etc. (verse 12). Then, by way of explaining what he meant by this "day of God," he says, verse 8, "But, beloved, be not ignorant of this one thing, that *one day* is with the Lord as a thousand years, and *a thousand years* as one day." As though he had said— "You are not to understand this 'day of the Lord,' as though it were limited to the short space of a natural day of twenty-four hours; for, 'the heavens and the earth which are now, *are reserved* unto fire, against (or for) the day of judgment and perdition of ungodly men.'" And then, to guard their minds against the insalutary effects which this statement of so long an interval between the time then present, and the "day of judgment and perdition of ungodly men" might produce, he adds, "The Lord *is not slack* concerning his promise, as some men" (e. g., those "scoffers who should come in the last days, saying, *Where is the promise of his coming?*" etc.) "count slackness." (Verses 3, 4, compared with verse 9.) In other words, notwithstanding this long delay in "*reserving* the heavens and the earth" to this ordeal by "fire," what the Lord hath spoken concerning that "new heavens and earth wherein shall dwell righteousness" eternal, *He most surely will fulfil*, "according to His promise." (Verse 13.)

With this exposition, therefore, of the import of the terms "*day of God*," and "*day of judgment*," as given by the apostle, kept in view, it will be found exactly to harmonize with the expression in reference to that period in which he says, verse 12, "in the which," that is, *during which*, "the heavens and elements being on fire, shall be dissolved," etc. That is to say, inasmuch as this "day of God" of "*a thousand years*," being synchronous with that of Rev. xx. 1–5, viz., the MILLENNIAL ERA, has its morning and evening; so the *final* παλιγγενεσία or regeneration of "the heavens and the earth which are now" by "fire," does not take place at the commencement, but *at the close*, of this "day of God:" for, it is not *until then*, that He who is seated on His "great white throne". of judgment says, "Behold, I make all things new." (Rev. xxi. 1, 5.)

But, that the final conflagration of the earth *is not* pre- but *post*-millennial, we remark,

2. That the *uses* to which the term "fire" is employed in Holy Scripture, when applied to "the heavens and the earth which are now," furnish additional evidence of it. Now, both Moses and St. Paul, in speaking of the infinite God in his character as Judge, declare that "He is *a consuming fire*."[1] In Scripture, however, the term "fire" is used both in a *figurative* and *literal* sense, the purposes to which it is applied being determinable only by being taken in connection with the subject spoken of. The figurative and literal sense may readily be distinguished thus: the declaration of our Lord in Luke's gospel is, "I am come to send *fire* on the earth;"[2] in Matthew, the term "*sword*" is used.[3] These parallel passages are employed to denote, as in a *figure*, that great moral warfare, "not against flesh and blood, but against principalities and powers," or those "spiritual wickednesses in high places,"[4] which was to ensue upon the propagation of the gospel, in defence of which, when carnal instead of spiritual weapons were used, Christ said, "they that fight with the sword," i. e., literally, "shall *perish* with the sword."[5] So the "baptism by fire"[6] signifies, both figuratively and literally, first, the *sufferings* of Christ in soul and body;[7] and of His followers *after* Him who "shall drink of *His* cup and be baptized with *His* baptism."[8] In this double sense also, it is declared that "the Lord shall purge the blood of Jerusalem from the midst thereof by the spirit of judgment, and by the spirit of burning."[9] And this is preëminently true of that "*fire*" of which St. Paul speaks, which, "in the day that shall declare (or reveal) it, shall *try* every man's work of what sort it is;"[10] for, the Judge himself having come, "burning coals proceed before His feet,"[11] and "a whirlwind is His chariot," accompanied with "fire,"[12] with "the spirit of burning,"[13] with "pestilence," and with "thunder,"[14] etc.

Now, it is in these forms that "with *fire* and with the *sword* shall the Lord," *at the commencement* of His judgments upon the wicked,

[1] Deut. iv. 24; Heb. xii. 29. [2] Luke xii. 49. [3] Matt. x. 34. [4] Eph. vi. 12. [5] Matt. xxvi. 52. [6] Matt. iii. 11. [7] Compare Matt. xxvi. 38 with Luke xxii. 44; xxvii. 50. [8] Matt. xx. 22. [9] Isa. iv. 4. [10] 1 Cor. iii. 12–15. [11] Habak. iii. 5–13. [12] Isa. lxvi. 15, 16. [13] Ib. iv. 4. [14] Habak. iii. 5–13.

plead with all flesh, and the *slain* of the Lord shall be *many*."[1] This is when He comes "*in flaming fire* with His mighty angels," —not, mark, to encircle *the earth* in the flames of the last conflagration; but, to "*take vengeance* on them that know not God, and that obey not the gospel of our Lord Jesus Christ;"[2] and who, being numbered with the "*many slain*" in that day, "shall be punished with everlasting destruction from the presence of the Lord and from the glory of His power,"[3] and who shall be "*reserved for chains* under darkness, against (or unto) the day of judgment and perdition of ungodly men."[4] The obvious meaning here is, that these "many slain of the Lord by fire and by the sword" (referring, as they do, to the destruction of the last antichrist and his confederates who fall on the battle field of Armageddon[5]), being placed among those wicked "dead" who St. John tells us "shall not live again until the thousand years are finished;"[6] I say, in view of these inspired statements, the obvious meaning is, that the "*perdition*" to which they are "reserved," does not and cannot take effect upon them until *at the close* of "the great day of the Lord's"[7] judgment. For, then it is, and not *until* then, that the Lord Jesus, having judged "*the quick*" or living saints "in righteousness" for a thousand years; *as the same* Judge, will appear "seated on His great white throne;" and, raising the wicked "dead," who have *no part* in "the first resurrection," from the "sea," and from death or the grave, and from hell (rather $ᾅδης$, the state and place of departed spirits), and arraigning them before His bar of judgment, and trying them by "the things written in the books according to their works;" He will "cast them into the lake of ($γεεννα$) fire and brimstone, where the devil and the false prophet are, to be tormented day and night for ever and ever."[8]

Taking into view, therefore, these two classes of passages, the one referring to the destruction of the wicked "by fire and by the sword" *at the commencement* of "the day of the Lord's" judgment; and the other to the destruction (not annihilation) of the raised wicked dead *at the close* of it; and it is clear, that the two acts of judgment are entirely separate and distinct *in the order of time*.

The *objection* of the *post*-millenarian against those who main-

---

[1] Isa. lxvi. 15, 16.   [2] 2 Thess. i. 8, 9.   [3] Ib. i. 8.   [4] 2 Pet. ii. 7.
[5] Compare 2 Thess. ii. 8 with Rev. xvi. 13–16.   [6] Rev. xx. 5.   [7] Mal. iv. 5.
[8] Rev. xx. 7–15.

tain that the universal conflagration is *pre*-millennial, is this: "*What*," demand they, on this hypothesis, "*become of those* who are to constitute the saved nations in the flesh, *during* this general subjection of the earth to the action of this last fiery ordeal?" And recourse has been had to the most pitiful subterfuges to meet it. And this, on the simple ground of the failure of its advocates to distinguish between the *two acts* of judgment upon the wicked at the commencement and the close of that day. As we have seen, "the slain of the Lord by fire and by the sword" in the first instance, are not *all* of the wicked, but "*many*."[1] There are "*a few men left*."[2] These are, those who "*escaped* of the nations which came against Jerusalem," both Jewish and Gentile, at the time of its invasion as described Zech. xiv. 1–3; and who, like the Noahic family saved from the flood, by their conversion to Christ, form the *nucleus* of the saved nations in the flesh during the millennial era.

Here, therefore, we have, first, an answer to the above objection as founded on the *mistaken* hypothesis, that the universal conflagration of the earth is *pre*-millennial; and second, a refutation of the *post*-millenarian, who denies, on that ground, that the second personal coming of Christ is *pre*-millennial. For, the destruction of the wicked at the commencement of the day of judgment does not take effect otherwise than by *the personal* "coming of the Lord Jesus in flaming fire with His mighty angels."[3]

Still, we have not yet reached the point which more immediately relates to the subject in hand, namely—*the change* to be effected, in adapting the physical state or condition of the earth to *the era* of millennial blessedness; as contrasted with that which adapts it to the *eternal* "new heavens and earth" state.

This can only be done by taking into the account the *agencies* to be employed in regard to each. These agencies, it will be found, are entirely separate and distinct.

Now true, in the descriptions given by the prophet Habakkuk, chap. iii. 5–13, and the apostle Peter, 2 Epist. iii. 3–9, 10–12, 13, 14, there is an *apparent simultaneousness* of the destruction of the ungodly, and the change to be effected on this globe by the action of "fire," *at the coming* of the Lord to judgment.

[1] Isa. lxvi. 15, 16.   [2] Ib. xxiv. 6.
[3] Compare 2 Thess. i. 8 with 2 Thess. ii. 8.

And this would seem to derive additional strength from the statements of the prophet Isaiah, chapters lxv. 17 and lxvi. 22, and of St. John, Rev. xxi. 1–5, concerning "the new heavens and the new earth which the Lord will create." It will amply repay us to devote a few moments to a critical exegesis of these passages *seriatim*. We observe then,

First. That, in regard to Habakkuk's description of the Lord's coming to judgment, while He "marches through the land in indignation to break to pieces his adversaries, or the people of His curse;" yet, having accomplished their overthrow, there is a *pause* or *suspension* in the work of judgment: for the prophet tells us that "He stood, and measured the earth," etc.; and the purpose of this pause of God's judgment he informs us was this: "Thou wentest forth *for the salvation* of thy people, even for salvation with thine anointed," etc. Now, reference can here be made to none other event than *the miraculous national conversion* of the Jews, by their "looking upon" their Messiah as the "anointed" of God "whom they pierced," as described by Zechariah, chap. xii. 9, 10; and the *equally* miraculous conversion of those Gentile nations, who will be gathered to and united with the restored houses of Judah and Israel, as spoken of by Isaiah, chap. lx. 1–5, and lxvi. 15–19. Hence, while "the Lord will come with fire, and with His chariots like a whirlwind to render His anger with fury, and His rebukes with flames of fire," yea, although "by fire and by the sword the Lord will plead with all flesh, and the slain will be many;" yet, saith He, "it shall come, that I will gather all nations and tongues, and they shall come and *see my glory :*" which "glory" is none other than that which shall characterize "THE PEACEABLE KINGDOM OF THE BRANCH," the Messiah, during His millennial reign over the saved nations in the flesh on the renewed earth. And now,

1. In regard to the nature and extent of the change which awaits "the heavens and the earth, which are now," in adapting them to the inhabitants of earth *during the millennial era*. This will involve along with it a consideration of those *physical agencies* that will be employed in restoring them to their paradisiacal salubrity and fertility; for, the time will then have come for *the lifting from off the earth* of that dread malediction of God, "Cursed is the ground for thy sake . . . thorns also and thistles

shall it bring forth to thee."[1] *How* He will do this, may be gathered from the following:

Bearing in mind that both stages of the earth's renovation, pre- and post-millennial, is the work of the Lord Jesus Christ, when He comes to effect its *normal* renascence, Zechariah, having stated that "*His feet* in that day shall stand upon the mount of Olives which is before Jerusalem on the east;"[2] and, being clothed in "brightness as the light," while "burning coals go forth at His feet," He will "*stand and measure the earth.*"[3] And, as "His glory will then cover the heavens,"[4] He whose way is in the whirlwind and the storm;" who "rebuketh the sea, and maketh it dry, and drieth up all the rivers;" and "at whose presence the mountains quake, and the hills melt, and the earth is burned, yea, the world, and all that dwell therein:"[5] "before Him the everlasting hills shall be *scattered*, and the perpetual hills shall *bow:*"[6] for, "in that day the mount of Olives shall cleave in the midst thereof towards the east and towards the west, and there shall be a very great valley; and half of the mountain shall remove toward the north, and half of it toward the south," even as it was in the time of "the earthquake in the days of Uzziah king of Judah."[7]

We must here keep specially in view the fact, that these terrible mundane convulsions take place *at the opening* of the Sixth Apocalyptic Seal, which being *chronologically* synchronic with the "seven vials" and "seven last plagues" under the blast of the "seventh" or last trumpet,[8] there is "a great earthquake,"[9] accompanied "with voices, and thunders, and lightnings . . . such as was not since men were upon earth, so mighty an earthquake and so great."[10] Hence, such will be *the change* produced by these physical phenomena upon the surface of the earth compared with what it now is, that "*every island shall flee away, and the mountains shall not be found.*"[11]

And now, as to the *ulterior result* of all this. It may be gathered from the following prophetic utterances, having a direct bearing upon the state or condition of "the new heavens and new earth of" Isaiah, chapters lxv. 17 and lxvi. 22, during the millennial era. The prophet Joel opens the subject thus: "Fear

---

[1] Gen. iii. 17, 18.   [2] Zech. xiv. 4.   [3] Habak. iii. 3–6.   [4] Ib. verse 3.
[5] Nahum i. 3–5.   [6] Habak. iii. 6.   [7] Zech. xiv. 4, 5.   [8] Compare Rev. x. 7, with xv. 1, 6–8; xvi.
[9] Rev. vi. 12.   [10] Ib. verse 18.   [11] Ib. verse 20.

not, *O land:* be glad and rejoice: *for the Lord will do great things.* . . . I will restore to you the years that the locust hath eaten, the canker-worm, and the catterpillar, and the palmer-worm, my great army which I sent among you." And, these destroying hosts of insects being removed, "the Lord will answer and say unto his people, Behold, I will send you corn, and wine, and oil, and ye shall be satisfied therewith. Be not afraid, ye beasts of the field; for the pastures of the wilderness do spring:" also, "the tree beareth her fruit, the fig-tree and the vine do yield their strength. And the floors are full of wheat, and the fats shall overflow with wine and oil."[1] And again: "It shall come to pass in that day, that the mountains shall drop down with new wine, and the hills shall flow with milk, and all the rivers shall flow with waters, and a fountain shall go forth of the house of the Lord, and shall water the valley of Chittim."[2] So also EZEKIEL: "And I will make them and the place about my hill a blessing; and I will cause the shower to come down in his season; there shall be showers of blessings."[3] And ISAIAH: "Instead of the thorn shall come up the fir-tree, and instead of the briar shall come up the myrtle-tree; and it shall be to the Lord for a name, for an everlasting sign that shall not be cut off."[4] And again, "I will plant in the wilderness the cedar, the shittah-tree, and the pine and the box together; that they may see, and know, and consider, and understand together, that the hand of the Lord hath done this, and the Holy One of Israel hath *created* it."[5] Yea, "the wilderness and the solitary place shall be glad for them; the desert shall rejoice and blossom as the rose. It shall blossom abundantly, and rejoice even with joy and singing: the glory of Lebanon shall be given unto it; the excellency of Carmel and Sharon: they shall see the glory of the Lord, and the excellency of our God."[6] "The glory of Lebanon shall come unto thee, the fir-tree, the pine-tree, and the box together, to beautify the place of my sanctuary; *and I will make the place of my feet glorious.*"[7] Yes, *then* shall be realized to the saved nations in the flesh, that glorious vision of prophecy, "*The earth shall yield her increase*, and God, even our own God, *shall bless us.*"[8] For, "Behold, the days come, saith the Lord, that the ploughman shall overtake the reaper, and the treader of grapes him that

---

[1] Joel ii. 21-24. [2] Ib. iii. 18. [3] Ezek. xxxiv. 26. [4] Isa. lv. 13.
[5] Ib. xli. 19, 20. [6] Isa. [7] Ib. lx. 13.

soweth the seed; and the mountains shall drop wine, and the hills shall melt; and I will bring again the captivity of my people Israel, and they shall *build* the waste cities, and *inhabit* them; and they shall *plant* vineyards, and *drink* the wine thereof; they shall also make *gardens*, and *eat* the fruit of them."[1] For "the seed shall be prosperous; the vine shall give her fruit, and the ground shall give her increase, *and the heavens* shall give her dew: and I will cause the remnant of the people," both *Jewish* and *Gentile*, "to possess all these things."[2]

And, finally. The earth and its surrounding atmosphere or heaven being thus restored to their original salubrity and fruitfulness, the prophet EZEKIEL declares that "the people shall say, This land that was desolate, *is become the garden of Eden*, and the desert *like the garden of the Lord:* joy and gladness shall be found therein, thanksgiving, and the voice of melody."[3]

Thus much then in reference to the state or condition of the earth and heavens as adapted to the *millennial era*, produced, as we have seen, by a class of physical agencies, neither of which involves the *impossibility* of man's occupancy of the earth during their respective processes. Let us now proceed, therefore, to compare,

Second, "the *new heavens* and *new earth*" in the prophecy of ISAIAH lxv. 17 and lxvi. 22, with that of ST. JOHN, Rev. xxi. 1-5. Now, it is by confounding these passages, as though they referred to *one* and the *same* state or condition of the earth during the millennial era, that has betrayed those writers already alluded to, into the adoption of the false theory, that the universal conflagration of the earth is *pre*-millennial. Doubtless, St. Peter's words, 2 Pet. iii. 13, "We, according to his promise, look for new heavens and a new earth wherein dwelleth righteousness," refer to the prophecies of ISAIAH as above, they being the *only* passages in the Old Testament where such a "promise" is recorded. But, a due examination of the passages in Isaiah will show, that his statements of "the new heavens and new earth which God will create," are accompanied with circumstances furnishing unquestionable evidence that he refers, *not* to the everlasting state, but to the *millennial era*. In other words, that "the new heavens and earth" of which he speaks, as a matter of "promise," are *typical* of, or bear a *resemblance* to, those of ST. PETER and

[1] Amos ix. 13, 14.   [2] Zech. viii. 12.   [3] Ezek. xxxvi. 35 and Isa. li. 3.

St. John. Hence his expository addition of their meaning in chap. lxv. 18: "But be glad and rejoice forever in that which I create; for, behold, *I create Jerusalem* a rejoicing, and *her people* a joy." The evident meaning here is, that the *physical* constitution of the earth and the *moral* condition of its inhabitants will both have undergone such a "*renovation,*" that, compared with the "former" state of things under the curse of sin, "they will not be remembered nor come into mind." This is further evident from chap. lxvi. 22–24: "For as the new heavens and the new earth which I will make, shall *remain* before me, saith the Lord, so shall your *seed* and your *name remain.* And it shall come to pass, that from one new moon to another, and from one sabbath to another"—agreeably to the covenant made with Noah—"*shall all flesh come and worship before me,* saith the Lord. And they shall go forth, and *look upon the carcasses* of the men that have transgressed against me: for their *worm shall not die,* neither shall their *fire be quenched;* and they shall be an *abhorring* unto all flesh." Circumstances these, I repeat, *totally incompatible* with the "new heavens and new earth" state of St. Peter and St. John. For, *then,* the Noahic covenant with creation will have *expired.* Then, "the city shall have no need of the sun, neither of the moon, to shine in it: for the *glory* of God shall lighten it, and the Lamb shall be the *light* thereof. *And the nations of the saved shall walk in the light of it; and the kings do bring their glory and honor into it,*" etc.[1] Nor this only. For, as the millennial heavens and earth, glorious as they will be, shall have "fled away," so that "*no place* shall be found for them"[2]—in others words, like a "changed vesture" shall disappear to be no more seen—so, "God shall then wipe away all tears from all eyes; and there shall be no more death, neither sorrow, nor crying, neither shall there be any more pain: *for the former things,*" that is, as they were either before or during the millennial era, "*shall have passed away.*"[3]

To conclude. The *agency* to be employed in effecting this *last* act of almighty power in the regenerating of the heavens and the earth, viz., "fire," will be found to differ both in *nature* and *extent,* compared with the other. St. Peter, speaking of the *process* by which this work shall be consummated, says: "The heavens shall pass away with a great noise, and the elements shall

[1] Rev. xxi. 23, 24.   [2] Ib. xx. 11.   [3] See Note B.

melt with fervent heat; the earth also, and the works that are therein, *shall be burned up.*" (2 Pet. iii. 10.)

Now, if it be asked, "*How* this mighty work is to be effected?" we answer, by the *post*-millennial universal conflagration. If it be again demanded, "But *how* is the conflagration to take place?" we answer: that it will be under those same general laws of nature, by which they were *first* created and destroyed by *water*. By this we do not mean a natural, in the sense of an atheistic, stoical fatality. No. The *causes* will be natural; but the *application* of them is from a Higher Hand. "Fire" is the standing agent in God's hand, as we have seen, for the accomplishment of his purposes of vengeance on that world which, under every dispensation, has by sinful creaturehood been subjected to his just displeasure. A *new occasion* for the display of that vengeance will have been furnished by the *post*-millennial "Gog and Magog" apostasy.[1] And, the time—that is, *at the close* of the thousand-years "day of the Lord"—having at length come, it will be found that there is *no want of fuel* to dissolve this mighty fabric!

1. Penetrate the bowels of the earth, and there behold the exhaustless stores of *fossil coal.* See from this fact the evidence of the predisposition of the earth *internally*, through the medium of her long pent-up fires, to a conflagration, by the effects produced from its central candescent heat on matter which is combustible, and which seeks to disgorge its mass of burning lava by the creation of *volcanic eruptions.* In addition to this, behold, *externally*, scattered over all parts of the earth, and particulaly in the regions of the Mediterranean Sea, *burning volcanic mountains*—Ætna, Vesuvius, etc.; yea, and some, of which Hecla is the principal, even lying within the polar circle, in Iceland! And to these agencies you may add those numerous *lakes of pitch and brimstone*, together with *oily liquors* dispersed in several parts of the earth (whence our modern wells of oil?); and all its *vegetable* productions, as trees, and grass, and shrubs, and such like; which last, brought under the influence of drought, immediately preceding this final catastrophe, will be rendered the more combustible. Then, also, we must not overlook the predicted *earthquakes*, which are immediately to precede and prepare the way for the conflagration, by cracking, and rending, and tearing open

[1] Rev. xx. 7-9.

its *outer* crust, that its flames may feed upon its *inner* vitals. Nor should we forget, in this connection, to add the agency of the *angel hosts*, of which those sent for the destruction of Sodom and Gomorrha may be viewed as a *type*.

To all this, however, it is urged by some, that the immense body of water within, and the vast oceans on the *surface* of, the earth, form insuparable barriers to its destruction by "fire." To this it might be sufficient to reply: that we have GOD'S WORD for it, that the present earth and heavens are "reserved unto fire, to be burned up." But to this we add, by way of refutation of the above cavil, that water, being composed of two elements, *oxygen* and *hydrogen*, united by the laws of chemical affinity, it is only necessary to *suspend* these laws by the fiat of the Almighty, to render it the *most powerful agent* of either or all the others combined, to accomplish that end. It is the very nature of oxygen to *promote* combustion; in other words, to produce and support the element of "FIRE:" while the other constituent of water, viz., hydrogen, is the *most combustible* substance in nature. We repeat, therefore, *divorce* those chemical laws which unite them in an aqueous state, and the vast bodies of water both *inside* and *outside* the earth, would at once become a source of combustion commensurate with their extent.

Nor must I here omit, in conclusion, to add, that Mr. Boyle, one of the most profound and judicious naturalists in the scientific world, declares, on the authority of an experiment made by himself, that *water* is ultimately convertible into *oil* and into . . . "FIRE."

Thus, then, we submit—The objection of the *post*-millennialist to the second personal coming of Christ as *pre*-millennial, as founded upon the erroneous hypothesis that the final conflagration of the earth is *pre*-millennial, is fully met and answered by the evidence above adduced, in proof that that event is *post*-millennial. One of two alternatives, therefore, is left to him. Either, first, to refute our arguments showing the *marked distinction* between the "new heavens and earth" state of Isaiah during the Millennial Era, as contrasted with the eternal "New heavens and earth" state of St. Peter and St. John; or, second, to admit the compatibility of the second personal coming of Christ as *pre*-millennial, with those physical and moral changes that are to transpire "at his coming."

PART III.

An Examination of the Question— Will the Second Coming of Christ, as an event still future, consist of an Allegorical or Spiritual Coming, or will it be literally a Corporeal or Personal Coming; and will it be Pre- or Post-Millennial?—Scripturally and Philosophically Considered.

HAVING thus disposed of the question, Is the universal conflagration of the earth pre- or post-millennial? we now resume the discussion of this fourth theory in connection with the

THIRD THESIS.

THIS THESIS ALLEGES THAT, AS THE IDEA OF A KINGDOM INVOLVES THE PRESENCE AND REIGN OF A KING; SO, THROUGHOUT THE PROLONGED PERIOD OF "THE TIMES OF THE GENTILES," ONWARD TO THE END OF THE MILLENNIUM, IT INSISTS THAT CHRIST HAS REIGNED, AND WILL CONTINUE TO REIGN OVER THIS KINGDOM OR CHURCH AFTER AN INVISIBLE OR SPIRITUAL MANNER.

Before going on, it may be well briefly to recapitulate the ground over which we have already passed. We have presented to the reader in Part I. an abstract scriptural view of the second coming of Christ, in its *doctrinal* and *practical* aspects. In Part II. we have considered the question: Is the second personal coming of Christ an event *past* or *future?* We have examined at length the four popular theories respecting it, namely:

I. That which alleges that all the prophecies which point to that event, in its relation to and connection with the two houses of Judah and Israel, were fulfilled by the *return* of the Jews from the Babylonish captivity.

II. That which alleges that all the prophecies in reference to the second coming of Christ and the establishment of His kingdom in the world, were verified by the judgments inflicted upon the Jewish nation and polity, at the destruction of Jerusalem *by the Romans* under Titus, in A. D. 70.

III. That which alleges that the same prophecies were verified in the overthrow of Paganism and the establishment of Christianity in the Roman empire, *under Constantine the Great*, in A. D. 323. And,

IV. That which alleges that the prophecies relating to the kingdom of heaven and the reign of Christ on earth, refer to the first introduction and establishment of the Christian Church; the dispensation of which is to merge into, form a part, and end at the close of, the millennial state. It also makes the Christian Church identical with "the kingdom of heaven," "of God," of "the Son of Man," etc.; and affirms Christ's *spiritual reign* in and over it from the beginning to the end of time at the close of the millennial era: when, they say, Christ will *personally appear* at the judgment-day, and simultaneously raise from the dead both the righteous and the wicked, when the former shall be rewarded and the latter punished, etc.

Now, we claim to have candidly weighed both the scriptural arguments and facts adduced in the support of these several theories (with the exception of that part of the Fourth Theory which alleges the *spiritual reign* of Christ in and over the Christian Church and the millennial era *as a king*, down to the end of time), and to have proved their fallacy.

But, the arguments and facts adduced by us thus far, we have designed to be taken simply in the way of deduction or inference, reserving the more direct proofs to that end, for the important subjects which remain to be discussed in Part III. of this treatise.

We now, therefore, enter upon a discussion of the topics connected with this important branch of the subject in hand.

This embraces an examination of the question: Will the second coming of Christ consist of an allegorical or spiritual coming, or will it consist of a literally corporeal or personal coming? and involving along with it the question: Is that event to be pre- or post-millennial?

We here *join issue* with the advocates of the Fourth Theory, as above, who, in their *third* thesis, allege,

That, as the idea of a kingdom involves the presence and reign of a king; so, throughout the prolonged period of "the times of the Gentiles" onward to the end of the millennium, they insist that Christ *has reigned*, and that He will *continue* to reign over His Church, Christian and millennial, after an *invisible* or *spiritual* manner; and hence affirm that His second *personal* coming will be *post*-millennial.

The subjects of remark relating to this thesis will be ranged under the following sections:

SECTION I.

AN EXAMINATION OF THE ALLEGED IDENTITY OF THE CHRISTIAN CHURCH WITH "THE KINGDOM OF HEAVEN," ETC.; AND OF CHRIST'S SPIRITUAL REIGN OVER IT AS KING.

This is a subject of momentous import. It involves a *correct* interpretation and application of all those prophecies of the Old and New Testaments in connection with the phraseology, "the kingdom of God;" "the kingdom of heaven;" "the kingdom of the Son of Man," etc. The question regarding them is this:

Are the *phrases*, "the kingdom of God," etc., and the Christian Church, or "Church of God," used interchangeably in the Scriptures to denote the *same thing?*

We answer emphatically, *They are not*. True, they may exist in *alliance* with each other, but are nevertheless entirely *separate and distinct*. Where such a union exists in its purest and most perfect form, as under and during the original theocracy of Israel, the kingdom, with its sovereign, administers laws to, governs, and protects the Church, as its *loyal subjects*. But, if they *revolt* against their sovereign, and drive him into exile, and set up a *usurper* in his place, while the CHURCH continues to exist, the original theocracy, for the time, *ceases to be*, until it is again *restored*. Thus it was with the Israelitish Church State in the time of Samuel, when she *abjured* the theocracy and set up an *earth-born rival* in the place of God. Hence, saith He to Samuel, "they have not rejected thee, but they have rejected me, that *I should not be king over them*."[1] Hence, too, though "God

[1] 1 Sam. viii.

gave them a king in his anger," viz., Saul, "and took him away in his wrath,"[1] and caused David to be anointed in his place, and appointed a succession of *kings* in the line of descent from him, that arrangement was not a *restoration* of the original theocracy; but, David being of the tribe of Judah, the design of it was, to lay *a foundation* to that end, to be accomplished in due time in the person of David's royal son, THE MESSIAH.

And so, when John the Baptist entered upon his mission as the harbinger of Messiah, he found the Jewish nation, *politically*, tributary to the Roman power. Yet the Jewish Church State existed, and to them he preached, "Repent ye, for the kingdom of heaven," or the *restoration* of the original theocracy, "*is at hand.*" Also, our blessed Lord, on entering upon His public ministry, presented Himself to the same Church, and took up the same theme with that of John, "Repent ye, for the kingdom of heaven *is at hand.*" Yea, more. He actually declared Himself to be their KING, the long-expected Messiah. And the nation being thrown upon their own responsibility in accepting or rejecting Him as such, we are not saying more than the truth to affirm, that, *if they would*, Messiah had *then* restored the original theocracy to them. Yea, it was their bounden duty to have done so; just on the same principle that it is the bounden duty of every man to render perfect obedience to the law of God. But, as in this latter case, so with them. As "the carnal mind is enmity against God, is not subject to his law, neither indeed can be:"[2] so we read, though Messiah "came to his own" world, "yet his own" people, the Jews, "*received Him not*,"[3] but rejected and crucified Him!

We see, then, from this, that during the personal ministry of Christ at His *first advent* to the Jewish nation, the original theocracy, or "kingdom of God," was not *then* restored. Still, *the Church* did not cease to exist.

But, it may be asked, Was not "the kingdom of God" restored or "set up" *immediately after* the ascension of our Lord? and if so, does not this make it certain that "the kingdom of God," or of "heaven," and the Christian Church, *are one and the same?*

This is the popularly received view of the Christian Church of this day. The prevailing theory on this subject is, that "the

---

[1] Hosea xiii. 11.   [2] Rom. viii. 7.   [3] John i. 11.

kingdom of God," or the Church, is a *spiritual* establishment. And this on the ground, that our blessed Lord declared to the unbelieving Jewish nation that "the kingdom of God should be *taken from them*, and be given to a people" (the Gentiles) who should "bring forth the fruits thereof."[1] Also that St. Paul said to them, "Seeing ye put these things from you, and judge yourselves unworthy of everlasting life, *lo, we turn to the Gentiles*."[2] The objection amounts, in other words, to the assertion, "that Christ *is now* reigning as king in His own proper kingdom; and that this kingdom formally commenced on His ascension to the right hand of God, and that it will continue *unchanged*, both in character and form, till the end of the millennial age." In support of this theory, we are reminded that Christ and his apostles spoke of the "kingdom of God" or of "heaven" as *at hand;* as *about to be* established, etc.; and that the apostles, immediately after Christ's ascension, represent it as *actually* set up, etc.

A formidable array of objections these, to the views we have advocated of "the kingdom of heaven" *as still future!* The importance of the subject will require an examination into the import of the principal passages resorted to by our opponents in the support of their theory.

And here permit me to explain, in the outset, that we by no means object to the sentiment so generally expressed, so to speak, in the sermons and psalmody throughout Christendom, that "Christ *reigns in the hearts* of his believing people." Undoubtedly He does; but the *figurative* use of the word "reign," in such an application of it as this, is no authority for displacing the true, scriptural doctrine of Christ's kingdom, as *contradistinguished* from that church state under this dispensation, into which the predestined subjects of it are "*gathered out of* (or from among) the Gentiles," and prepared *spiritually* for their final admission into it-*as future.*

Hence, the present church state is called in the New Testament "the kingdom of heaven *in mystery;*" that is, it is that period during which God *by his Spirit* effectually calls, and enlightens, and regenerates, and justifies, and sanctifies his chosen people, in order to render them meet for their *ultimate* introduction into the everlasting kingdom of our Lord and Saviour Jesus

---

[1] Matt. xxi. 43.   [2] Acts xiii. 46.

Christ, at its *manifestation*. Thus St. Paul: "For the earnest expectation of the creature *waiteth* for the manifestation of the sons of God. . . . And not only *they*, but *ourselves* also, which have the first-fruits of the spirit, even we ourselves groan within ourselves, *waiting* for the adoption, to wit, the redemption of our body." [1] This, of itself, might be taken as decisive of the point at issue; for it teaches us, that it is only in *resurrection*, that the Church is to be admitted to the possession of the kingdom. No, it is not Christ *personally*, but it is the Divine Paraclete, the "Comforter," the *Holy Spirit*, dispensed by Him to the Church on the day of Pentecost, *who now "reigns"* in the hearts of believers. Christ is now *personally absent from* the Church; nor, until He "comes again" according to His promise to receive her to himself, can He "*reign*" over her in His kingdom. A due examination into the import of the passages already alluded to, will be found to confirm this view.

1. The first passage alleged in proof that the Church in its present state constitutes the *spiritual* kingdom over which Christ is said to "reign," is the following, John xviii. 36: "My kingdom *is not of this world:* if my kingdom were of this world, then would my servants fight, that I should not be delivered to the Jews: but *now* is my kingdom *not from hence.*"

The difficulty in understanding this passage lies in the Greek words κοσμος (world) and νυν (now). The κοσμος (world) here, evidently means the *aggregate population* of the earth. But, there is another Greek word mistranslated "world," viz., αἰων, in the passage, "Lo, I am with you alway, even unto the end of the (αἰωνος) *world.*" It should have been *age* or *dispensation*. Thus, κοσμος refers to the *people;* αἰωνος, to the *age*, or period of time, when the people lived. The passage in question was Christ's reply to Pilate, "Art thou the king of the Jews?" And when our Lord said, "My kingdom is not of this world," and also added, "but (νυν) *now* is my kingdom not from hence;" and Pilate asked him the second time, "Art thou a king, then?" Jesus answered him, Thou sayest that I am a king;" that is, it is so; *I am a king:* "to this end was I born, and for this cause came I into the (κοσμος) world," etc., i. e., to the Jewish and Gentile world, "that I should *bear witness* unto the truth." And, for this reason, as Peter and John declared, "both Herod and Pontius

[1] Rom. viii. 23.

Pilate, with the Gentiles, and the people of Israel,"[1] conspired to put him to death. Proof this, that "His kingdom *was not of* this world,"—not only, that is, it is not composed of men (the collective body of mankind) *now* dwelling on the earth; for *if* this were so, "then would my servants *fight*, that I should not be delivered to the Jews;" but, as "My kingdom is not (νυν) *now* from hence,"—that is, does not *now* take its commencement (ἐντεῦθεν) from hence, or from this point of time, *it is still future.* In a word, it is as though Christ had said to Pilate, "My kingdom is not" *of* the "generation of vipers," Jewish and Gentile, of *this age:* nevertheless, though not of this κοσμος, it will be *on this earth*, agreeably to the declaration of Daniel, chap. vii. 27, that the kingdom of Messiah, when "set up,"[2] will be "*under the whole heaven;*" and also of St. John, Rev. xi. 15, that the kingdoms of this (κοσμος) world *are* (or will) *become* the kingdom of our Lord and of his Christ." We pass to another passage:

2. "The kingdom of God is *within you.*"[3] Positive evidence this, it is alleged, that Christ's *spiritual* kingdom, the Church, *then existed;* or how could it be said to have been "*within*" those whom he addressed? But who, pray, were these? Not his disciples, but the *Pharisees.*[4] And was it "within" them, suppose you, that this *spiritual* kingdom was set up? Nor this only. For, if this be so, then it follows, that Joseph of Arimathea, who was at this very time "*waiting* for the kingdom of God,"[5] was *without* this inward grace! To escape this dilemma, several eminent writers[6] render εντος υμων, not within, but *among* you. But, that our Lord was not speaking of his kingdom as then present, but *future*, is evident from the fact that he here speaks of two events which must take place *before* his kingdom could be established. The first was, that he must "*suffer* many things, and be *rejected* of that generation;"[7] and the second, that His future personal advent would be preceded, "*not with observation*," or that fixed, attentive, and prolonged expectation of a coming event of which we know nothing as to either how or where,[8] whether at Bethlehem, Jerusalem, or Galilee; but, "as the lightning that lighteneth out of one part under heaven shineth unto another part under heaven, *so* should the coming of

---

[1] Acts iv. 27.   [2] Dan. ii.   [3] Luke xvii. 21.   [4] Ib. verses 20, 21.
[5] Mark xv. 43.   [6] Beza, Grotius, Doddridge, Whitby, Macknight, and a host of others.
[7] Compare Luke xvii. 25 with chap. xv. 43.   [8] See Luke xvii. 21-23.

the Son of Man be." [1] That is, it shall be both instantaneous and irresistible. Then, in the next place,

3. We are referred to that class of passages which speak of Christ's kingdom as "*nigh at hand*"—"*even at the doors*,"[2] etc. Granted. But this is equally true of other events, e. g., "*The Lord* is at hand"[3]—"*The coming* of the Lord draweth nigh"[4]— "The *end* of all things is at hand,"[5] etc., which all Christians admit and know are *still future*. And, as there can be no kingdom without a king, it follows, that as Christ has not yet *returned*, "the kingdom" has not yet been "*set up*."

4. But, we are also reminded of other passages which speak of Christ's kingdom, as *about to be* established, that is, *during* the apostolic age. Such as,

The declaration of the angel to Mary: "And the Lord God *shall give unto Him* (Christ) *the throne* of His father David,"[6] etc. To this we reply, first, that the above angelic prophecy illy applies to the popular notion of Christ's kingdom as being *spiritual;* for, during the time of Christ and his apostles, the Davidic throne was *a delegated earthly monarchy*. Besides, it had been, and was *then*, utterly supplanted by the Roman Cæsars. But second, Jehovah had made oath to David, that He would *raise up his seed* after him, that is, MESSIAH, *to sit upon his throne*, which should be established *forevermore*.[7] Hence David, being a prophet, in view of the oath made to him, "that of the fruit of his loins according to the *flesh*, God would raise up Christ to sit on his throne, he spake of the *resurrection* of Christ,"[8] etc. But third, the Davidic throne as above was not restored *immediately after* the resurrection. For Christ, after forty days, ascended to heaven, and sat down on His *Father's throne*,[9] whither "David *is not yet* ascended."[10] No, brethren, David's throne is still "fallen down;"[11] nor will it be reërected, until Christ *returns* from heaven, wearing His "many crowns."[12]

5. Another alleged passage to the same end, is that wherein Christ says to his disciples, "There be some standing here which shall not taste of death, *till they have seen* the kingdom of God come with power." This, our opponents affirm, was verified by the descent of the Holy Ghost upon the assembled disciples on

---

[1] Luke xvii. 24.   [2] Matt. iii. 2, iv. 17, x. 7; and Mark i. 15; Matt. xxiv. 33.
[3] Phil. iv. 5.   [4] James v. 8.   [5] 1 Pet. iv. 7.   [6] Luke i. 32, 33.
[7] 1 Chron. xvii. 11-15.   [8] Acts ii. 30, 31.   [9] Rev. iii. 21.
[10] Acts ii. 34.   [11] Amos ix. 11; Acts xv. 16.   [12] Rev. xix. 12.

the day of Pentecost,[1] when, they say, the *spiritual* "kingdom of Christ," or the Church, was established. Again we repeat: No, brethren, the Church existed *before*. That event was a fulfilment of the promise of Christ to his disconsolate disciples when He was about to *leave them:* "I will send you another comforter.... *even the Spirit of truth,*"[2] etc. And this, in accordance with the prophecy of Joel: "And it shall come to pass in *the last days*, saith God, I will pour out my Spirit upon *all flesh* . . . and I will show wonders in heaven above, and signs in the earth beneath; blood, and fire, and vapor of smoke: the sun shall be turned into darkness, and the moon into blood, *before that great and terrible day* of the Lord come,"[3] etc. But, surely, these latter "wonders" and "signs" did not transpire at the time of the effusion of the Spirit on the day of Pentecost. For, that effusion of the Spirit did not descend upon "*all flesh*" at that time. It was confined to the apostles and disciples, and on those believers upon whom they conferred it. That, therefore, was but an inchoate or *first* fulfilment of the prophecy of Joel. Hence the true and only consistent meaning of this passage. It refers to a *visible* earnest and specimen of the kingdom of heaven *as yet future*. Accordingly, three of the Evangelists who record it, speak of it in immediate connection with the account given, that *eight* days after this saying, "Jesus took Peter, James, and John into a mountain apart, and was *transfigured* before them," etc., together with the appearance to them of Moses and Elias talking with him.[4] Here we have a *complete pattern* of the coming kingdom. Christ, transfigured in His glorified humanity, together with Moses as the representative of the raised dead in Christ, and Elias of the living saints who shall be changed and glorified at His second appearing.[5] And, what is decisive of this matter is, that St. Peter, who was one of the three, calls this very transaction "the *power* and *coming* of our Lord Jesus Christ;" that is, it was an earnest or pattern of His final coming, the "majesty" of which, he says, he was an "eye-witness of, when he was *with Him in the mount*."[6] We pass to another passage.

6. It occurs in connection with the institution of the last supper, when our Lord said, "I will no more eat thereof, until it is

---

[1] Acts ii. 1-4. [2] John xiv. 1-4, and verses 16, 17. [3] Acts ii. 16-20.
[4] Compare Matt. xvi. 27, 28, with xvii. 1-3; Luke ix. 27 with v. 28; Mark ix. 1 with v. 2.
[5] 1 Thess. iv. 13-18. [6] 2 Pet. i. 16-18.

fulfilled *in the kingdom of God;*" and also, "I will not drink of the fruit of the vine, until the kingdom of God *shall come.*"[1] These passages, it is alleged, prove that the spiritual kingdom of God was about to be established *in the time* of Christ. But, surely, such expositors must have overlooked several important facts in this connection, the first of which is, the *design* of the institution of the Christian "passover," or last supper, as set forth by St. Paul, which was, that it was to be a standing memorial of Christ's passion, while *personally absent* from the Church. Hence the command: "Do this in remembrance of me. . . . For as often as ye eat this bread, and drink this cup, ye do show the Lord's death *till He come.*"[2] A second fact overlooked by them is this, viz., that at the institution of the last supper, Jesus said to His disciples, "I will not drink henceforth of the fruit of the vine, until that day when I drink it *new* with you in my Father's kingdom."[3] And when, pray, is that to be? The answer is, not until the twelve apostles shall be admitted to "eat and drink at Christ's table *in His kingdom,* and sit on thrones judging the twelve tribes of Israel."[4] Yea, more. Not until the "*many*" besides them shall come from the east and west, and shall sit down with Abraham, and Isaac, and Jacob, *in the kingdom of heaven.*"[5] I repeat: then, and not *until* then, will Christ celebrate His "passover" *anew* with His chosen followers. For, then "the tabernacle of God *shall be with men,* and He shall *dwell with them,* and they shall be His people."[6] We now pass to a number of passages which are alleged to speak of the kingdom of heaven *as already set up.* For example, those words of Christ:

7. "If I cast out devils" (demons) "by the Spirit of God, *then* the kingdom of God *is come unto you.*"[7] All that is necessary to say by way of reply, is this: these words were spoken in the *very same year* in which the kingdom of God was declared to be "nigh," as "at hand," and "even at the doors," etc.; and also about the time when the disciples were taught to pray, "*Thy kingdom come;*"[8] which shows it to have been *still future.* Nor was this prayer answered by the setting up of the kingdom at any time *before* the crucifixion; nay, nor *after* the resurrection. For, to the question of the disciples to the risen Saviour, "Lord, wilt

---

[1] Luke xxii. 15-18. [2] 1 Cor. xi. 23-26. See also Luke xxii. 19, 20; Matt. xxvi. 26-28; Mark xiv. 22-24. [3] Matt. xxvi. 29. [4] Luke xxii. 28-30. [5] Rev. xxi. 3.
[6] Rev. xxi. 3. [7] Matt. xii. 28. [8] Matt. vi. 10.

thou *at this time* restore the kingdom to Israel? He said unto them,"—not, mark, the kingdom never will be restored thus, but —" it is not for *you* to know the times or the seasons which the Father hath put in his own power."[1] Clearly, therefore, this passage must be understood of that dispensation—" the kingdom of God *in mystery* "—which is to *prepare the way for* its final establishment. Another passage:

8. "The Son of Man shall send forth his angels, and they shall gather *out of his kingdom* all things which offend, and which do iniquity."[2] *Ergo*, it is affirmed, this must refer to the *veritable* "kingdom of God," or the Christian Church. We reply: this passage occurs in the parable of the sower and the seed. It is here to be specially borne in mind, (see the 36th to the 40th verses of this chapter), that our Lord interprets all the parts of this parable. " The field " in which the seed, good and bad, is " sown," He tells us, " *is the* (κοσμος) *world.*" That is, as we have already explained, the inhabitants dwelling on the earth during the dispensation of " the kingdom of God " *in* " *mystery.*" Accordingly, *in this kingdom*, while it lasts, " the good seed," which denotes " the children of the kingdom," and which was sown by " the Son of Man ; " and " the tares," which were sown by the " enemy," i. e., the " Devil," and which denote " the children of the wicked one," " both grow together until "—when ? " *until the harvest,*" which Christ interprets to mean " the end of "—what ? Now mark here. Not the end of the κοσνος or world of mankind, as in verse 38, but *the end of the* αἰῶνος, i. e., *the age or dispensation* under and during which mankind have enjoyed the advantages of a preached gospel, as in verse 40.

And now observe. The " harvest " in this parable points us to that " great day of the Lord," called " *the day of judgment.*" But I pray you to mark here, that neither in this parable, nor in that of the ten talents, or ten pounds, or of the drag-net—all of which were given to illustrate the conduct of mankind during this dispensation in accepting or rejecting the gospel offers of mercy, together with the *final separation* between the two classes at the time of the " harvest,"—I repeat: I pray you to mark here, that not one word is said about the resurrection and judgment of the dead. True, *a resurrection* will have taken place. But it will be confined to those who " have a part in the *first resurrection ;*"[3]

---

[1] Acts I. 6–7. [2] Matt. xiii. 41. [3] Rev. xx. 1–5.

those who "sleep in Christ,"[1] and with whom will be united the changed and raptured saints, who were "alive and remained unto the coming of the Lord."[2] But this event transpires *prior* to the visible appearance of Christ as Judge, with His angels, "at the time of the harvest." The risen and glorified living saints, St. Paul tells us, "will God *bring with him*"[3] *to* this very "harvest." "For, know ye not," saith he, "that the saints," that is, as "joint-heirs with Christ,"[4] "*shall judge the world?*"[5]

The inevitable conclusion, therefore, is, that "the harvest" in this parable will consist of the judgment, not of the risen dead, but of the "quick," that is, of the *living nations* at the end of this αἰῶνος, age or dispensation. These will consist, first, of the *converted nations*, both Jewish and Gentile, who, as the saved nations in the flesh, will be admitted to that *restored "dominion"*[6] in the earth which was lost by the sin of the first Adam,[7] now wrested forever from the hand of his "serpent" seducer by, and which thenceforward becomes "*the kingdom of the Son of Man*"[8] *under the whole heaven.*"[9] The other will embrace the *antichristian confederacy* of the nations whom Christ will "consume by the Spirit of his mouth, and destroy with the brightness of his coming."[10] Yea, these are they who *then* "know not God, and that obey not the gospel of our Lord Jesus Christ;" and "who shall be punished with everlasting destruction from the presence of the Lord, and from the glory of his power."[11] Thus, and in no other way, will be verified the "*gathering out of his kingdom* of all things that offend, and that do iniquity."

There are several other passages to which we are referred, as alleged proofs of the same view with that affirmed of the one in this parable. These are: "He that receiveth not *the kingdom of God* as a little child shall not enter therein."[12] Another: "Except a man be born again, he cannot enter into *the kingdom of God.*"[13] And yet another, which speaks of our being "delivered from the power of darkness, and *translated* into the kingdom of God's dear Son."[14] There are also a few more passages similar to these, e. g.: Matt. vi. 33; xi. 11; xiii. 11, and verses 24 to 41; 52; xix. 12; Luke xviii. 29; 1 Cor. vi. 9, 10; xv. 24; Col. iv. 11; and James ii. 5. In view, however, of the expositions given

---

[1] 1 Thess. iv. 13-16. [2] Ib. verse 17. [3] Ib. verse 14. [4] Ib. verse 14. [5] Rom. vi. 2.
[6] Mic. iv. 8. [7] Gen. iii. 22-24. [8] Col. i. 13. [9] Dan. vii. 27. [10] 2 Thess. ii. 8.
[11] 2 Thess. i. 7-9. [12] Mark x. 15. [13] John iii. 3, 5. [14] Col. i. 12, 13.

of the preceding passages, demonstrative of the *fallacy* of the popular view, that "the Church" under this dispensation and "the kingdom of God" or "of heaven" are *one* and the *same;* no further evidence is necessary to prove that the above passages are all susceptible of a similar interpretation than the following, than which it is not possible for language more clearly to set forth the *distinction* between the present Church state as "the kingdom of God" in "*mystery*," as contrasted with the future "kingdom of Christ" in *manifestation*. Take these two passages from St. Paul and St. Peter, both of whom, it is presumed it will be allowed, were in a state of grace. St. Paul says: "And the Lord shall deliver me from every evil work, and *preserve me unto* his heavenly kingdom."[1] And St. Peter exhorts his brethren, thus: "Wherefore the rather give diligence to make your calling and election sure; for if ye do these things, ye shall never fail: for *so*," he adds, "an entrance *shall be* administered unto you abundantly, into the everlasting kingdom of our Lord and Saviour Jesus Christ."[2]

The sum of the matter, then, is this, to wit: that Christ is *the divinely constituted* "*Head*" over all things to the Church, which is his body,"[3] even that Church which had existed from the period of the first promise down to His day, and which still exists. But Christ was also born a king—"*the King of the Jews*." He also declared Himself to be such before the bar of Pilate. He, however, was *rejected* as a king, and was finally crucified by the Jews and Gentiles. Ay, envy and malice laid Him in the sepulchre of Joseph of Arimathea. But the third day He rises again. For what purpose? Was it to set up His kingdom *then?* Nay, verily. But, like the *exiled nobleman* in the parable, who, having committed his ten pounds to his servants, accompanied with the command, "*Occupy till I come*," "took his journey into a far country, *to receive* a kingdom, and to *return*," at which time he called them to a reckoning: *so* the risen Christ. Having commissioned His apostles to go to all nations, and preach the gospel to every creature, as His "witnesses," and "to take out of (or from among) the Gentiles a people for His name," He ascended, as an *exiled king*, to the far-off heavens, there to await, at the hand of His Father, the *investiture* of His royal prerogatives, when He will return with, and set up, His own rightful kingdom, and call

[1] 2 Tim. iv. 18. [2] 2 Pet. i. 10, 11. [3] Eph. i. 22.

all His servants to a reckoning for the *use* or *abuse* of the talents committed to their keeping during His prolonged absence from them.

We affirm, then, readers—and on this point we challenge refutation—that though Christ is styled "the Head of the Church," yet in the New Testament He is nowhere called the *King* of the Church. It is this circumstance, more than any other, that stamps the Church of Rome with the brand of an infinitely infamous apostasy, in that her long line of pretended popes claim to be the vicegerents of Christ in His Church as *temporal sovereigns!* If I am here reminded, however, that in Rev. xv. 3, Christ is styled "*the King of saints*," it is no exception. In the margin it reads, King of *nations.* But waiving this: "King of *saints*" is not "king of *the Church.*" The Jews, *before* New Testament times, were called "saints."[1] No. *He is their King*, and as such is ordained by the oath of God "to sit on David's throne." And on this account it is, that He is styled "the minister of the *circumcision* for the truth of God, to *confirm* the promises made unto the fathers."

But here arises a question, a proper answer to which is fundamental to a correct interpretation and application of that portion of the prophecies now before us. It is this: *What is the position or relation* of Israel and Judah to the Church of God under the Christian dispensation? An answer to this question renders it necessary to remind you,

First. That while the Messiah, Jesus, as "the minister of the circumcision for the truth of God," was the foundation, not only but the *surety* and *pledge* given to the lineal multitudinous seed of Abraham, to "confirm the promises made to their fathers;" *God the Father*, as the Author and Rectoral Head of that covenant, united Himself to Israel as her *husband.* This is evident from the following: "The word of the Lord came to Jeremiah, saying, Go, and cry in the ears of Jerusalem, saying, Thus saith the Lord; I remember thee, the kindness of thy youth, *the love of thine espousals,* when thou wentest after me in the wilderness, in a land that was not sown."[2] For, saith He, "*I am married unto you.*"[3] But, as we have seen, when Israel forsook the Lord, and provoked the Divine jealousy by her idolatrous practices, the two names, Lo-ruhamma and Lo-Ammi,[4] were applied to her. That is, the

---

[1] Dan. vii. 21. [2] Jer. ii. 2. [3] Ib. iii. 14. [4] Hosea i. 6-9.

Jehovah of Hosts as her husband, *put her away*, by removing her out of His sight. In other words, she was *divorced* from Him. The same holds true of Judah, who, on account of their "unbelief," as "the natural branches," were *broken off* "from the good olive-tree."¹

We have showed you, however, that this act of divorcement against Israel and Judah was not to be perpetual. For God, by the prophet Hosea, says: "And it shall come to pass *in that day*," that is, the day of their restoration, etc., "saith the Lord, that thou shalt call me *Ishi*" (my husband); "and thou shalt no more call me *Baali*" (my lord). Yea, saith He, then "will I betroth thee unto me *forever:* yea, I will betroth thee unto me in righteousness, and in judgment, and in loving kindness, and in mercies."²

But, brethren, this is not all. "The King's Son," the Lord Jesus Christ, must have *His bride* also. Hence it has transpired that as the *literal* Israel, to whom the invitation to the marriage feast of the King's Son was first given, "all with one consent began to make excuse," and, upon being further urged, finally "*refused to come;*" the King-Father, in His "wrath," "said to His servants, The wedding is ready, but they which were bidden *were not worthy.*" And then was straightway issued the command: "Go ye therefore into the *highways*, and as many as ye shall find, bid to the marriage." And the *result* was, that "the wedding was furnished with guests."³ Now, collateral with this, is St. Paul's address to the unbelieving Jewish commonwealth: "Seeing ye put these things from you, and judge yourselves unworthy of everlasting life, *lo, we turn to the Gentiles.*"

Yes. Thus the Jewish nation, *for the time*, was set aside. That is, she was *divorced* from her former relation to "the King" as her husband. Not that the Jews were to be *totally* excluded from the privileges of the gospel under this dispensation. For, from the time of St. Paul down to the present day, they have lived in the midst of it, and, in common with the Gentile nations, it has been offered to them. So that, in their *position* or *relation* to the Church state under this economy, "Whether Jew or Greek, barbarian or Scythian, bond or free, they are *all one* in Christ."⁴

But, what is to be specially noted in this connection, is, the *design* of this arrangement, according to that "eternal purpose

---

¹ Rom. xi. 20.   ² Hosea ii. 19, 20.   ³ Matt. xxii. 1-10.   ⁴ Col. iii. 11.

which God purposed in Christ Jesus."[1] "Simeon" stated this when he "declared how that God did at the first visit the Gentiles, to take out of" (or from among) "them, *a people for His name.*"[2] Now these, collectively, constitute that "holy nation, and royal priesthood, and peculiar people,"[3] who shall finally be presented unto the King-Father's "Son," as His elect or redeemed "bride," "THE LAMB'S WIFE."[4] And the marriage nuptials shall be celebrated when the "five wise virgins," who denote her, shall hear the "midnight cry, BEHOLD THE BRIDEGROOM COMETH, GO YE OUT TO MEET HIM."

Having, therefore, in the preceding section, demonstrated, as we deferentially claim, first, the fallacy of the theory that the phrases, "the kingdom of God," "the kingdom of heaven," "the kingdom of the Son of Man," etc., are identical with the Christian Church and the millennial era; and, second, having proved that the second coming of Christ, when it does take place, will be a literally personal and *not* a spiritual coming; we now proceed to a like direct argument, under

SECTION II.,

DEMONSTRATIVE, THAT THERE IS TO BE NO INTERVENING MILLENNIUM BETWEEN THE SECOND PERSONAL COMING OF CHRIST AND THE DAY OF JUDGMENT. IN OTHER WORDS, THAT THAT EVENT, WHEN IT DOES TAKE PLACE, WILL BE PRE- AND NOT POST-MILLENNIAL.

We shall divide this section into two parts.

PART I.

Direct Scriptural and Historical Proof, that there is to be no Intervening Millennium between the Second Personal Coming of Christ and the Day of Judgment.

This point, however conclusive as a matter of inference—as derived from the facts and arguments adduced in refutation of the several theories already examined in opposition to it—we now proceed, by *a direct* scriptural argument, to demonstrate;—that the second personal coming of Christ, when it does take place, will be *pre*-millennial.

We flatter ourself that, with those who receive the teachings of Holy Scripture as authoritative on the subject, first, of the

---

[1] Eph. iii. 11.   [2] Acts. xv. 14.   [3] 1 Pet. ii. 9.   [4] Rev. xxi. 9.

abstract doctrine of the second personal coming of Christ; second, of the fact that that event is yet *future;* and, third, of the *mode* or *form* in which it is to take place, etc.; will conclude with us, that it is "not following cunningly devised fables" to tax their further indulgence, while we proceed, on the same authority, to place this matter beyond the reach of further controversy. Indeed, when we take into account the infinitely momentous interests at stake in this issue, in reference alike to the Church of God, to the nations of the earth, and to every living soul, all must unite, as with one voice, in condemnation of the thought that it is a matter of *indifference,* whether this august event transpires within ten, or twenty, or fifteen hundred years! We proceed, therefore, to a demonstration of this point on its abstract merits, our first argument being predicated of that notable prophecy of Daniel, chapter ii. 44, 45:

"*In the days of these kings,* shall the God of Heaven *set up a kingdom, which shall never be destroyed:* and the kingdom shall not be left to other people, but it shall *break in pieces and consume* all these kingdoms, and it shall stand forever. Forasmuch as thou (i. e., Nebuchadnezzar) sawest that the stone was cut out of the mountain without hands, and that it brake in pieces the iron, the brass, the clay, the silver, and the gold; the Great God hath made known to the king what shall come to pass *hereafter:* and the dream is certain, and the interpretation thereof sure."

In order to a proper understanding of this prophecy, we must here premise,

I. That this vision of the colossal metallic image, taken in connection with Daniel's interpretation of it, *spans the entire period* called in the New Testament, "the times of the Gentiles."[1] This period, as was shown in a previous part of this work,[2] *commenced* with the loss to the Jewish nation of her independence under Manasseh, king of Judah, in A. M. 3480, B. C. 652, and that it *ends* in A. D. 1868, embracing the whole interval denoted by the mystical "seven times" of Lev. xxvi. and Dan. iv. With these also synchronizes the vision of Daniel's four rampant beasts, chapter vii. 1-8. We observe in the next place,

II. That Daniel's interpretation of this vision teaches us to look for *the final and total extermination* of all earth-born monarchies, and the *restoration* of that theocracy under which the

---

[1] Luke xxi. 24; Rom. xi. 25.   [2] See pages 165, 186.

Jewish nation was placed prior to the period of Saul. Yes; notwithstanding the enormity of their sin in casting off that government; and though they were destined, as the just punishment of their iniquity, to be subjected to a long period of the most cruel oppressions at the hands of those earth-born monarchies whose *rival* national polity to the government of God they had adopted under Saul, yet their covenant God gives them the assurance, "For the Lord will not forsake his people for his great name's sake; because it hath pleased the Lord to make them his people."¹ Hence, in vindicating them against the "rod" of their oppressors, He declares, that, when "the Desire of nations," i. e., the Messianic "stone," "*shall come*," He will "*destroy*" all those nations by whom, from generation to generation, they have been "scattered and peeled," reproached and oppressed. For, "Thus saith the Lord, To Jacob whom I have chosen, and Israel my servant, I will surely make a *full end of all nations* whither I have driven thee; . . . I will make Jerusalem a *cup of trembling* to all nations that are round about; and on that day I will make Jerusalem *a burdensome stone* to all nations, and they shall be cut in pieces and broken, though all the people of the earth be gathered together."²

But you will ask, *Wherefore this?* The answer is, because, *subsequently* to their abjuration of their original theocracy under Saul, who was anointed with oil out of a *vial*, to indicate the instability and short-lived tenure of the kingdom of Israel during his administration, God was graciously pleased to establish the *perpetuity* of the Israelic throne in the person of their second king, DAVID, who was anointed with oil out of a "*horn*,"³ the tenor of the covenant with whom was, that out "of the fruit of his loins, according to the flesh, God would raise up CHRIST *to sit on his throne.*"⁴

1. To return now to the prophecy under consideration. The four metallic compartments of the *colossal image*—the gold, the silver, the brass, and the iron mingled with clay; together with the four corresponding *wild beasts* of Daniel—the lion, the bear, the leopard, and the nondescript monster; taken in connection with the two little horns, and the ram and he-goat of chapters vii. and viii., symbolize THE FOUR GREAT GENTILE MONARCHIES that were to bear rule in the earth during "the times of the Gen-

---

¹ 1 Sam. xii. 22.   ² Zech. xii. 3.   ³ 1 Sam. xvi. 1.   ⁴ Acts ii. 30. See also Psalm ii.

tiles," viz., the *Babylonian, Medo-Persian, Grecian,* and *Roman:* setting forth also, in reference to this last-named power (the Roman), the division of that empire into east and west, as denoted by the two iron legs of the image; and its subdivision into ten principalities, as symbolized by the ten toes of the image and the ten horns of the nondescript beast; while, on the other hand, " the little horn " of chap. vii. 8 represents the PAPAL POWER, and that of chap. viii. 8-12 the MOHAMMEDAN IMPOSTURE. In the next place,

2. The prophecy points out *the destruction* of these four Gentile monarchies, together with all those anti-Christian powers emanating from them, by a certain irresistible agent, called " A STONE cut out of the mountain without hands," etc. And, in the last place,

3. *The period,* when these four monarchies with their dependencies shall be destroyed, is explicitly signified. It is to take place " *in the last days of these kings,*" during the *last stage* of their existence. The " stone " smites the image, not on the head of gold, but on the feet of iron and clay.

Hence we find, that in the Bible, as comprehending the Old and New Testaments, we are furnished with a prophetic account of the *origin,* the *career,* and *final destiny* of all the nations of earth, heathen, Jewish, anti-Christian, and Mohammedan, not only, but of their *political* and *ecclesiastical* constitutions, whether autocratic, despotic, monarchical, or democratic ; or whether idolatrous, Papal, Mohammedan, Judaic, or Protestant.

It has been well said by the learned Bossuet and Bishop Porteus, that these above-named four monarchies "form, as it were, *one vast map of Providential administration,* delineated on so large a scale, and marked with such legible characters, that it cannot possibly escape our observation;" and that "this map has been held up before the eyes of all nations for the space of nearly 3000 years, to confront the feeble cavils of atheism, and to confirm the scriptural doctrine of *a national Providence.*" Ay, however we may have overlooked this fact, IN THE BIBLE is to be found the most extensive and complete system of *political economy* of which the world can boast!

It is not our purpose, however, to enter into an application of the above prophetico-symbolic imagery denotive of the rise, etc., of these four monarchies, in detail. It must suffice to observe, that the *first three* of them, viz., the Assyrio-Babylonian, Medo-Persian, and Grecian, are specifically designated *in Scripture*, as having followed in the order of succession symbolized by the gold, silver, and brass, and by the lion, bear, and leopard, of the two visions of Nebuchadnezzar and Daniel. With the simple remark, therefore, that the term "*king* and *kingdom*" are used interchangeably to denote the *same* thing,[1] I observe,

That it is evident from Dan. i. 1, that the *first* empire, of which Nebuchadnezzar was "king," was the *Babylonian;* that is, he as its sovereign, with unlimited autocratical power, was considered as representing in his person the kingdom of Babylon. The same holds true of the *second*, the MEDO-PERSIAN. By comparing Dan. v. 1, 2, and verses 28, 30, 31, with chap. vi. 1, it will be seen that Belshazzar, the son and successor of Nebuchadnezzar, was king. Now, to this king it was, that the prophet, in interpreting the mysterious handwriting on the wall of his palace, said, "God hath numbered *thy* kingdom, and finished it;" and, "*thy* kingdom is divided, and given to the Medes and Persians," etc. (See also Dan. viii. 20.) So also of the *third*, the GRECIAN. "The he-goat" of Dan. viii. 5, 8, 21, the prophet tells us, "is the king of Grecia, and the great horn that is between his eyes is the first king," etc., i. e., Alexander. And, in regard to the *fourth*, or ROMAN empire, though it is not specially designated *by name* in either of the above visions, yet that it was that which immediately succeeded to the Grecian, is evident from the *chronology* of the rise and fall of the first three empires. The Babylonian existed from B. C. 612 to 538, a period of 74 years; the Medo-Persian, from B. C. 538 to 331, a period of 207 years; and the Grecian, from B. C. 331 to 168, a period of 163 years.

Now, at this last-named date, viz., B. C. 168, the Roman empire (as every schoolboy knows), which was founded by Romulus B. C. 753, came to maturity, and that the last stroke in its course of conquests consisted of its subversion of Egypt, as the last of the four divisions of the empire of Alexander, as symbolized by the four-headed leopard[2] of Dan. vii. 6, and the "breaking of the

[1] For example, compare chap. i. 1 and ii. 37, 38, with verse 39: "After THEE (*King* Nebuchadnezzar) shall arise another KINGDOM inferior to THEE," etc.

[2] At the division of the empire of Alexander, as denoted by the four heads of the leopard, it was parcelled out among his four generals thus: *Cassander* reigned over Macedon, Greece, and Epyrus; *Lysimachus* over Thrace and Bythinia; *Seleucus* over Syria; and *Ptolemy* over Egypt, Libya, Arabia, Cœlo-Syria, and Palestine.

great horn," in the place of which there "came up four notable horns," chap. viii. 8. But further evidence of this fact will appear from the following: First, that both Cæsar and Augustus were titles of the *Roman* emperors; second, that Judea, being tributary to the prefecture of Syria when Christ was upon earth, the chief priests declared, "We have no king but *Cæsar;*"[1] third, that our blessed Lord himself enforced upon all the injunction, "Render therefore unto Cæsar the things that are *Cæsar's,*"[2] etc.; and finally, fourth, that the chief priests and Pharisees, apprehending the powerful influence which might accrue to Christ from the miracles wrought by Him before the people, said, "If we let Him alone, all men will believe on Him: and the *Romans* shall come, and take away both our place and nation." I would only add on this subject,

(1.) That the ten toes of the metallic image, and the ten horns of the fourth or nondescript monster, denoted the subdivision of the Roman empire into TEN KINGDOMS, which was verified by the eruption of the Gothic and other barbarous tribes from the north into the western branch of the empire, and its final division into the various principalities of *modern* Europe. Nor is the matter of determining which are the ten kingdoms represented by these symbols, one of mere conjecture. The principle of *territorial* division—a principle adopted by Sir Isaac Newton, and sanctioned by all the most distinguished interpreters of prophecy of the present day—will be found to mark them out with almost infallible certainty.

The boundaries of the western empire at the time of which we now speak, namely, in A. D. 532, were as follows: It extended toward the west as far as Britain, which was included in it; toward the south to the Mediterranean; northward as far as the Danube and the Rhine; and eastward to the limits of the German empire. To these limits, therefore, we are to look for the ten kingdoms or subdivisions of this once mighty empire. And there, accordingly, we find them. They are as follows: 1st, *Lombardy*, the seat of a powerful kingdom; 2d, *Ravenna*, the seat of the exarch, who reigned over a great part of Italy; 3d, *the State of Rome*, the seat of the empire. To these are added, 4th, *Naples*, and 5th, *Tuscany*, forming a division of Italy into five

[1] John xix. 15. [2] Matt. xxii. 21.

parts. The other five kingdoms are, 6th, *France;* 7th, *Austria;* 8th, *Spain;* 9th, *Portugal;* and 10th, *Great Britain.*

(2.) Now, as there are *no other* ten kingdoms that can be named on this principle of a territorial division within the limits of the Roman empire, we may conclude with certainty that the above are the *identical kingdoms,* whose destinies are involved in the prophetic dream of Nebuchadnezzar, and the corresponding vision of Daniel. But,

(2.) The " little horn " of Dan. vii. 8, 20, 21, 25, etc., all Protestant expositors admit, symbolizes the *ecclesiastical* and *ecclesiastico-political* power of the Papacy. And,

(3.) The " little horn " of Dan. viii. 9-25, which sprang out of one of the four notable horns of Daniel's he-goat, from the description given of him, evidently denotes a power *entirely separate and distinct* from the " little horn " of chap. vii. 8. This will appear from the fact (without entering further into details) that the time of the appearance of the power represented by this " horn," was to be " in the *latter*" *period* of the " kingdom " of *one* of the " four notable horns" of Alexander's divided empire. Whereas, the other " little horn came up among the ten horns" of Daniel's fourth or nondescript beast. Suffice it to say, that this last " little horn " arose out of the *Arabian* branch of Ptolemy's kingdom, that province having fallen to him by the previous conquests and union of the Arab tribes under Alexander; and, that it refers to none other than the great MOHAMMEDAN power, Yemen being the birthplace of the notorious Islam Impostor. For, though at that time it was a province of the Persian empire, yet it subsequently formed his own more distant *Arab* territory, from which, according to the prophet Daniel, was seen to issue those hordes of northern and northwestern Saracens—the " little horn" of *Islamism*—which finally " waxed exceeding great, toward the south, and toward the east, and toward the pleasant land," i. e., *Palestine.* Again:

(4.) The career of the Papal " little horn " of Dan. vii. 8, 20, 21, 25, was to prepare the way for the introduction upon the prophetical platform of another power, viz., Daniel's " WILFUL KING," chap. xi. 3, 4, 35-39. The papal " little horn," though he was to have " a *mouth* speaking great things," chap. vii. 8, and was to " speak *great words* against the Most High," etc., verse 25; yet this " wilful king" is to " exalt himself, and magnify himself *above every god*," i. e., the true God as well as the false, and is to "speak marvellous things against *the* GOD *of gods*," and is to "prosper *till* the indignation be *accomplished*," etc. Now, though the Papacy be *an* antichrist, yet he has never reached this excess of abomination. This "wilful king," therefore, can be none other than St. Paul's "wicked," or "*the* man of sin and son of perdition," or in other words, *the last antichrist*, whose coming (παρουσια) is after the working of Satan, with all power and signs, and lying wonders, and with all deceivableness of unrighteousness in them that perish;" and "who opposeth and exalteth himself *above all* that is called God or that is worshipped, so that he as God sitteth in the temple of God, showing himself that he *is God*."

Now, if we except the "little horn" of the Papacy, Dan. vii. 8, 20, 21, 25; and the "little horn" of Dan. viii. 9–25, the symbol of the Turco-Ottoman power of Islamism, and which, at the *last end* of the indignation, "is to be broken without hand by THE PRINCE *of princes*," (see Dan. viii. 19, 25), and whose destruction is to *immediately precede* that of the others; we have in the prophecy before us, the *four monarchies* denoted by the four metallic components of the image which is to be *smitten by* "the stone cut out of the mountain without hands," "*in the days* of these kings."

Now, then, comes to be considered *the point* of principal interest in this discussion. Our text declares THE TOTAL DESTRUCTION of these four gigantic monarchies and their ten subdivisions, by the power of the Messianic stone, "IN THE DAYS OF THESE KINGS," etc.

If, therefore, the *mission* of the Messianic stone, or the second coming of Christ, as we have already proved, is still *future*, it follows that *at the time* of that mission, all these four monarchies and their ten kingdoms *must occupy their places on the platform of the prophetic earth*. Otherwise, there is swept away the entire fabric of the prophetic word, and Christianity is left without a shield of defence against the bold and blasphemous taunt of the infidel: "*Where is the promise of His coming?*"

The question then is, *Do these four monarchies still exist?* Some affirm that they do not: that they have, one and all, long since passed away, leaving nought behind them but the historic records of their former power, magnificence, and territorial extent. *Is this so?* So far from it, "the sacred calendar and great almanac of prophecy" represent them as extending *from the beginning* of the captivity of Israel under Tiglath-Pilezer,[1] A. M. 3263, "until the mystery of God shall be *finished*," when "the kingdoms of this world," by the *direct agency* of the Messianic stone in their complete overthrow, "shall have become the kingdom of our Lord and of His Christ."[2]

As I would not, however, even seem to palm upon the reader my *ipse dixit* as authority in so important a matter, I respectfully submit the following as a *solution* of the difficulty in these premises.

Originally, the *first* of the above-named monarchies in its geographical territory, population, and government, was *Babylonish*. Under the *second* dynasty, the territory and population of Medo-Persia were *annexed*, and the government of the two made *Medo-Persian*. Under the *third*, in like manner, the territory and population of Greece were *annexed*, and the government of the three made *Grecian*. And, under the *fourth*, the territory and population were completed by the *annexation* of Rome, and the whole made *Roman*. These therefore form what, for the sake of distinction, we term THE PLATFORM OF THE PROPHETICAL EARTH. Nationally and politically, this platform attained its ultimate (which is its present) dimensions, by the process of annexation of the one to the other successively, retaining, *throughout*, their national, political, and ecclesiastical characteristics—as signified by the several symbols which denote them—as so many *rods* in God's hand, for the chastisement of the Apostate Church, Judaic and Christian.

I repeat, therefore, that the prophetic colossal image of Nebuchadnezzar *now exists in all its parts*—gold, silver, brass, iron and clay; or the same, as denoted by the four corresponding beasts of Daniel—the lion, the bear, the leopard, and the nondescript beast; together with the powers denoted by the ten toes of the image and the ten horns of the fourth beast, and the two little horns of the great beast and of the rough goat. They *began* on the great river Euphrates, whereon stood *Nineveh*, the capital of Assyria, with *Babylon* on the Tigris. From these two cities proceeded the power which destroyed the national existence of the *Ten Tribes*, and brought the *Two Tribes* into captivity. And it is notorious, that both these ancient capitals, Nineveh and

---

[1] 2 Kings xv. 29, 30; xvi. 9. [2] Rev. xi. 15.

Babylon, together with the countries which they ruled, have now for eight centuries, down to the present day, been under the dominion of the *Turkish* or Mohammedan little horn of the rough goat.

On the other hand, the Grecian leopard, Alexander, added to the territory of the great image that very portion of *Greece* which, *in our times,* has arisen out of oppression and political death, into the state of an independent kingdom, such as it was when it *first* came on the prophetic stage.

And we have the *Roman,* still subsisting in the *ten kingdoms* of the west, namely, Lombardy, Ravenna, Italy, Naples, Tuscany, France, Austria, Spain, Portugal, and Great Britain.

The colossal image of Nebuchadnezzar, therefore, *at this very moment,* stands erect in all its parts, subjected, it is true, during the lapse of ages, to several transmutations, and undergoing various modifications, but preserving nevertheless, through all, its *original* metallic and beastly identity of character and of work.

Now, it is "*in the days* of these kings" (or kingdoms), i. e., while they *still* occupy their respective places and play their respective parts on the platform of the prophetic earth, that the prophet declares "THE GOD OF HEAVEN SHALL SET UP A KINGDOM, THAT SHALL STAND FOREVER." This kingdom, it would be superfluous to argue, is identical with the *millennial* state.

But, the setting up of this kingdom "in the days" of these "kings," is to be brought about by the mission of THE MESSIANIC "STONE cut out of the mountain without hands." This symbol, the "stone," I now observe, denotes Christ, in His official character as a JUDGE and a "KING."

With a view, however, to escape the admission which this interpretation involves, viz., that the second coming of Jesus Christ is *pre-*millennial and *personal,* it is urged that the "stone" in the text is *identical* with the "mountain," and that the mountain, being symbolical of *the Church,* which, by her numerous agencies, is finally to evangelize the whole world; therefore, the symbolical "stone" *cannot* refer to Christ, but to the universally established millennial kingdom of Christ, over which He is to reign *by His Spirit,* till the end of a thousand years, when He is to come to raise the dead and judge the world, etc.

This view, so generally prevalent, and sanctioned by the

authority of names both of the living and of the departed which we all revere, is to be respected. I respect it. Nevertheless, I would deferentially submit, first, if the *head of gold* of the colossal image, and the corresponding first beast, the *lion* of Daniel, symbolized, *personally*, the Babylonian king Nebuchadnezzar,[1] on what principle of interpretation are we to withhold the *personal* application of the symbolical "stone" to the King Messiah, THE LORD JESUS CHRIST? Again, second: as Daniel, after interpreting the head of gold to signify the Babylonian king, says, "after *thee* shall arise another *kingdom* inferior to *thee*," thereby using the terms "king" and "kingdom" interchangeably, i. e., as denoting *the same thing*, how can we consistently avoid a similar use of the terms "stone" and "mountain," as symbolic of CHRIST and his KINGDOM?

Until, therefore, our rule of interpretation of the symbolic "stone," and its application, *personally*, to Christ the Messiah, is proved to be unsound; we must insist, that, *when* the destruction of the *still existing* colossal image takes place, it will be effected by no less, no other, agent, than THE GLORIOUS PERSONAL DESCENT OF THE SON OF GOD FROM HEAVEN. Yes, by Him,

1. This colossal image, *in all its parts*, is to be demolished. "The stone that was cut out of the mountain without hands," is to "break to pieces the *iron*, the *brass*, the *clay*, the *silver*, and the *gold*." And, mark. The *period* in the history of these four monarchies when this destruction is to take place, is designated. It is to be in the *divided state* of the last or Roman dominion. The "stone," the prophet tells us, "smites the image on the feet" —*the ten toes*—"which were of iron and of clay."[2] EUROPE, as embracing the ten horns of the nondescript beast, *the present prophetical earth*—Lombardy, Ravenna, the Roman State, Naples, Tuscany, France, Austria, Spain, Portugal, and Great Britain—is here intended. When, therefore, the "stone" *comes*, "the iron, the clay, the brass, the silver, and the gold, shall be broken in pieces *together*, and become like the chaff of the summer threshing-floors; and the wind shall carry them away, that no place shall be found for them: and the "stone" that smites the image

---

[1] And so of all the others—the breast and arms of silver of the image, and the second beast of Daniel, the bear, etc., personally to Cyrus, the first Medo-Persian king; the belly and thighs of brass of the image, and the leopard of Daniel, to Alexander of Greece; and its four heads to his four generals, Cassander, Lysimachus, Ptolemy, and Seleucus, etc.

[2] Dan. ii. 34.

shall become a great mountain, and shall fill the whole earth." [1] Yes, then it is, that "the judgment shall sit, and they"—that is, Christ, and His co-judges [2] and rulers,[3] the risen saints [4]—"*shall take away* the dominion of the Beast, to consume and to destroy it unto the end. And the kingdom and dominion, and the greatness of the kingdom *under the whole heaven*, shall be given to the people of the saints of the Most High; whose kingdom is an everlasting kingdom, and all dominions shall serve and obey Him." [5]

In conclusion. Our next direct, and *exclusively scriptural* argument, in proof that the second personal coming of Christ is *pre-* and not *post-*millennial, will be shown in

PART II.

A demonstration, That the ideas and language of the New Testament writers in reference to the second personal coming of Christ and the judgment of the great day, were derived from and founded upon the prophetic statements of the inspired pre-Christian Jewish writers regarding them.

In illustration of this subject, we shall adopt the following passages as a stand-point:

Jude, verses 14, 15. "And Enoch of old, the seventh from Adam, prophesied of these, saying, *Behold, the Lord cometh with ten thousand of His saints*, to execute judgment upon all, and to convince all that are ungodly among them of all their ungodly deeds which they have ungodly committed, and of all their hard speeches which ungodly men have spoken against Him."

And St. Jude prophesied, saying—verses 20, 21: "But ye, beloved, building up yourselves on your most holy faith, praying in the Holy Ghost, keep yourselves in the love of God, *looking for the mercy of our Lord Jesus Christ* (i. e., at His second coming) unto eternal life."

Here it is to be observed in the outset as not a little singular, that only six out of the forty-one prophets of the Old and New Testaments, viz., Jacob, Moses, Isaiah, David, Daniel, and Malachi, predicted of *the first* coming of our Lord; while most of these, together with the others, prophesied of His *second personal* coming. (See Note D.)

[1] Dan. ii. 35. [2] Rev. iii. 21; 1 Cor. vi. 2, 3. [3] Rev. ii. 26-28.
[4] Rev. xx. 3-6. [5] Dan. vii. 26, 27.

So also, while the first class of prophets point out Christ to us in the aspect of His *suffering* humanity as a sin-atoning sacrifice under the law; the second class treat exclusively of His *resurrected* humanity, as connected with "the glory that is to follow" His sufferings, as our TRIUMPHANT KING.

And now, in regard to the *purposes* of the second coming of Christ as presented to view in the two passages already cited, they embrace two separate and distinct parts, or *acts*—those of judgment and of mercy. Of *judgment* for the ungodly: of *mercy* for those who, in faith and hope, "keep themselves in the love of God, looking" for the final conferment upon them of "eternal life" *at His second coming.*

These two prophecies of Enoch and St. Jude, therefore, both relate to *one and the same event,* called in Scripture "the day of judgment"—"the day of the Lord"—"that great day of God Almighty," etc., which is to take place *at the time of* the Second coming of Christ.

But on this, as on other momentous questions in connection with it, as we have seen, the Church of this day is unhappily at issue with herself, as to what the Scriptures teach of *the nature* and the *order of events*, etc., of "THE DAY OF JUDGMENT." Inasmuch, therefore, as that event hinges, so to speak, on all those numerous prophecies which foretell of the second coming of Christ in the clouds of heaven,

"In pomp and majesty ineffable,"

it is absolutely impossible rightly to interpret and apply them, until we shall have ascertained in what that day of judgment *consists,* as inclusive of both the particulars named above.

To explain. The prevailing doctrine of the Church on this subject is, that as, *at the instant* of the death of the righteous and the wicked, the one is immediately admitted to the *perfect fruition* of heavenly blessedness, and the other immediately consigned to endless *consummate* misery; so, there will be a *universal simultaneous* resurrection of both classes, that is, of the just and the unjust, by the second personal coming of Christ *at the end* of the millennium, as the Judge of the quick and the dead: when, having assembled all, both small and great, before His great white throne, He will open the books, try them, etc.; and, having passed sentence upon each order according to the deeds done in the body while in this life, He will say to the *righteous*, "Come, ye blessed of my Father, enter ye into the joys of your Lord;" and to the *wicked*, "Depart, ye cursed, into everlasting fire, prepared for the devil and his angels."

This theory also connects with it the additional idea, that the trial, sentences, etc., etc., of the myriads of myriads of the raised dead, will be disposed of *within the limits* of a natural day of twenty-four hours, or of a very short period.

It is here also in place to remark, respecting this theory, that the *millennium, at the end* of which the second coming of Christ, or the day of judgment, is alleged to take place, is that state of universal peace, prosperity, and triumph of the Church on earth of a thousand years, which the great body of Protestant Christians profess to look for *as still future*. Consequently, this theory, by placing the second coming of Christ *at the close* of that period, teaches that it is *post*-millennial, and that we are not to look for that event until some 1500 years to come; or according to the Rev. Samuel H. Cox, D. D. (who interprets the thousand years of the Apocalypse as a *mystical* number [1]), not until 365,000 years!

On the other hand, there are many in the Church—not confined to any one of, but who may be found among *all*, the different branches of evangelical Christians in both hemispheres, and those too most eminent for their learning, piety, position, etc.—who affirm that the second personal coming of Christ is *pre*-millennial; also, that "the day of judgment" commences and runs *parallel with* the thousand years of millennial rest to the Church.

They also deny that there is to be a *simultaneous* resurrection both of the righteous and the wicked at the end of the millennium; but maintain that the Scriptures speak of *two acts* of raising the dead, the first of which takes place at the instant of Christ's second coming, at the commencement or "*morning*"[2] of the millennium, agreeably to that passage, Rev. xx. 6, "Blessed and holy is he that hath part *in the first resurrection*," for "on such the second death shall have no power; but they shall be priests of God and of Christ, and shall reign with him *a thousand years*," etc.: the second, at the end or *evening* of that period, according to Rev. xx. 5, "But the *rest of the dead*," i. e., of the wicked dead, "lived not again until the thousand years were *finished*."

Hence they teach, that the "day of judgment" which takes place

[1] See *Christian Intelligencer*, New York, 1864. [2] Ps. xxx. 5; xlix. 14.

at the time of the second coming of Christ, instead of being limited to a natural day of twenty-four hours, opens with an act of *mercy* to the righteous, both dead and living, agreeably to the statement of St. Paul, 1 Thess. iv. 13-17: "But I would not have you ignorant, brethren, concerning them which are asleep, that ye sorrow not, even as them which have *no hope*," i. e., the wicked dead; "for, if we believe that Jesus died and rose again, even so them also which *sleep in Jesus* will God bring with Him. For this we say unto you by the word of the Lord, that we which are alive and *remain unto* the coming of the Lord, shall not prevent them which are asleep," i. e., from being raised: "for the Lord himself shall descend from heaven with a shout, with the voice of the archangel, and with the trump of God: *and the dead in Christ* SHALL RISE FIRST." Nor this only.: for the apostle adds: "*Then,*" i. e., at the time of the second coming of Christ, "we which are alive and remain, shall *be caught up together with them*," i. e., the raised dead in Christ, "*in the clouds, to meet the Lord in the air;* and so shall we ever be with the Lord."[1]

But, this "great day of God Almighty" also opens with an act of *judgment* upon the wicked, who shall *then* be alive upon the earth. We again quote from St. Paul, 2 Thess. i. 7-10: "And to you who are troubled rest with us, when the Lord Jesus shall be revealed from heaven with His mighty angels in flaming fire, *taking vengeance* on them that know not God, and that obey not the gospel of our Lord Jesus Christ; *who shall be punished with everlasting destruction* from the presence of the Lord, and from the glory of his power: WHEN HE SHALL COME to be glorified in His saints, and to be admired in all them that believe . . *in that day,*" i. e., the day of their *first* resurrection, etc., as above described.

This act of judgment, therefore, takes effect, not upon the wicked dead, but upon *the living nations* who, "*in that day,*" "know not God and obey not the gospel of Christ." It will fall upon all those who are then found within the pale of the *apostate Christian Church,* and of *the last great Democratico-Atheistic Confederacy* against Christ and His saints, who, being "consumed"—as St. Paul (2 Thess. ii. 8) says it will be— "with the spirit of the mouth, and destroyed by the brightness of the coming" of the Lord Jesus; and, thus numbered with the

[1] 1 Thess. iv. 13-17.

dead, they "*shall not live again*," i. e., be raised from the dead, "*until*" *at the close* of the same second coming of Christ, when He shall appear "seated upon His great white throne," to execute upon them *the final act* of judgment, by causing all of them, "both small and great," gathered from the "sea," and "death" or the grave, and from hell (ᾅδης), "to stand before God" when "the thousand years are *finished*." (See Rev. xx. 5.)

Consequently, this latter class of prophetical interpreters affirm of this "day of judgment," inasmuch as it comprehends the twofold acts of rewards and of punishments, that it *spans the whole period* of the thousand years of millennial blessedness. This is founded on what they claim that the Scriptures teach in regard to the *official* character and functions of the risen and glorified saints, to wit, that, being "a chosen generation, a royal priesthood, an holy nation and a peculiar people;"[1] as the "heirs of God and joint-heirs with Christ,"[2] they are constituted "*kings* and *priests* unto God and his Father;"[3] and that, as such, they shall wear "crowns,"[4] "sit on thrones with Christ,"[5] and that "*judgment* shall be given unto them,"[6] to "*judge* the twelve tribes of Israel,"[7] and also to "*rule the nations* with a rod of iron,"[8] etc.

Thus they "shall live and reign with Christ a thousand years *on* the earth and *over* the saved nations, Jewish and Gentile, in their millennial state. The prophet Isaiah, speaking of Messias in direct reference to this period as "the Branch that was to grow out of the root of Jesse," says, "With righteousness shall He *judge* the poor, and *reprove* with equity for the meek of the earth." And to this he adds, "and He shall *smite the earth*"—the four Gentile monarchies—"with the rod of His mouth, and with the breath of His lips *shall he slay* the wicked."[9]

Here then, we submit, we have a clearly defined *double act* of mercy and judgment, such as is to characterize the entire millennial period of the Church as that "great day of the Lord" called "*the day of judgment*," of which the Scriptures speak. And, *at the close* of this day, when the wicked dead are raised, tried, and condemned, "Death," i. e., he that "had the power of death, which is the Devil;" and hell (Hades, ᾅδης), where the *spirits* of the wicked dead, *prior* to the resurrection of their bodies, had

---

[1] 1 Pet. ii. 5-9. [2] Rom. viii. 17. [3] Rev. i. 6. [4] Ib. iv. 4-10. [5] Ib. xx. 4.
[6] Ib. ib. [7] Matt. xix. 28. [8] Rev. ii. 27. [9] Isa. xi. 4.

been "*reserved for chains* under darkness against the day of judgment and perdition of ungodly men;"[1] together with *all* who are not then "found written in the book of life," shall be "cast into the lake of fire," which is "the *second* death."[2]

This latter exposition of the nature and order of events, etc., of "the day of judgment," we shall now proceed to demonstrate, furnishes *the only method* by which to harmonize that large portion of the prophecies of the Old and New Testaments, which relate to THE SECOND PERSONAL COMING OF CHRIST. In doing this, we shall show, in support of the thesis which forms the subject of this section, that the ideas and language of the New Testament writers regarding it, were all derived from and founded upon the prophetic statements of it, as made by *the inspired pre-Christian* Jewish writers. In other words, it will be seen that the *doctrine* of a future judgment, with its antecedents, accompaniments, and consequents, as taught by our blessed Lord, and by the apostles St. Peter, St. Paul, and St. John, in the Epistles and the Apocalypse, all *synchronize throughout* with that of the Book of Daniel. We will begin with the following comparison:

1. When the prophetical times of Daniel are fully expired, *the Son of Man comes in the clouds of heaven to the Ancient of Days*, and having smitten the metallic colossal image on the feet of iron and clay, and destroyed the Papal and last antichristian powers, there is "*given unto Him dominion, and glory, and a kingdom*, that all people, and nations, and languages should serve him," etc. (Dan. ii. 34, 35, 44; vii. 11–14.)	When St. Luke's "times of the Gentiles" are fulfilled, the "signs in the sun, moon, and stars, together with distress of nations, men's hearts failing them for fear and for looking after those things that are coming on the earth," etc.; *then* shall the budding of the fig-tree presage "*the coming of the Son of Man in a cloud with power and great glory*," to indicate that "*the kingdom of heaven is nigh at hand*," and that the time is come for the redemption of Israel. Compare Luke xxi. 24, 25, 27, 28, with Rom. xi. 25, 26.
2. The whole period of "the times of the Gentiles" runs coeval with the prophetical "seven times," or 2520 years of Israel's chastisement, Lev. xxvi. 18, 21, 24, 28, *at the close* of which, Daniel's 1335 days or years *run out* (Dan. xii. 12), when the angel declares to him, that "God will *accomplish* to scatter the power of his holy people," i. e., the Jews, etc. (Dan. xii. 7.)	This latter period of Daniel, is *the same* with St. Paul's "fulness of the Gentiles," Rom. xi. 25; see also Luke xxi. 24; which being "come in," i. e., *ended*, he tells us that "the Deliverer shall come to Zion, *and shall turn away* ungodliness from Jacob," etc., and so, "**all Israel** shall be saved," etc. (Rom. xi. 26.)

[1] 2 Pet. iii. 7. [2] Rev. xx. 14, 15.

We shall now proceed to show, that as the *first* coming of Christ was to be while the fourth or *Roman kingdom*—symbolized by the two iron legs of the image, Dan. ii. 33, and the nondescript monster of chap. vii.—*was yet in being;* so the *second* is to take place *when it shall end.*[1]

'On this subject, the profoundly learned Mr. Mede says:

'The mother text of Scripture, whence the Church of the Jews grounded the name and expectation of *the great day of judgment,* with the circumstances thereto belonging, and whereunto almost all the descriptions and expositions thereof in the New Testament have reference, is, that vision of the viith of Daniel of *a session of judgment* when the fourth beast came to be destroyed: where this great assizes is represented after the manner of the *great sanhedrin,* or consistory of Israel; wherein the Pater Judicii had his assessories, sitting upon seats placed semi-circular before him from his right hand to his left. "I beheld," saith Daniel, (chap. vii. 9, 10), "till the thrones were pitched down," (namely, for the senators to sit upon), "and the Ancient of Days did sit. . . . I beheld, *till the judgment was set*" (that is, the whole sanhedrin), "*and the books were opened,*" etc.

'Here we see both the *form* of judgment delineated, and the *name* of judgment expressed; which is afterward yet twice more repeated; first, in the amplification of the tyranny of the wicked horn (verses 20, 21), the symbol of *the Papacy,* which (it is said) continued "*till the Ancient of Days came, and judgment was given to the saints of the Most High,*" i. e., *potestas judicandi ipsa facta:* and the second time, in the angel's interpretation, (verse 26), "But the judgment shall sit, and they shall *take away his dominion,* to consume and to destroy it *unto the end.*" Where, observe also, that cases of dominion, of blasphemy, and apostasy, and the like, belonged to the jurisdiction of *the great sanhedrin.*

'From this description it came that the Jews gave it the name of the day of judgment and *the day of the great judgment:* whence, in the Epistle of St. Jude (verse 6), it is called "*The judgment of the great day.*"

'From the same description they learned that the destruction then to be should be *by fire;* because it is said (verse 9), "His throne was like a fiery flame, and his wheels as burning fire;"

---

[1] See Mede's Works, Book IV. Ep. 8, p. 744, 745; also Book III. p. 709.

(and verse 11), "The beast was slain, and his body destroyed, and given to *the burning flame.*"

'From the same foundation are derived those expressions *in the gospel,* where this day is intimated or described: "The Son of Man shall come in the clouds of heaven"—"the Son of Man shall come in the glory of the Father, with his holy angels:" forasmuch as it is said here, "Thousand thousands ministered unto him;" and that Daniel saw "*One like unto the Son of Man coming with the clouds of heaven,* and He came unto the Ancient of Days, and they brought Him near before Him."

'Hence *St. Paul* learned that "the saints should judge the world" (1 Cor. vi. 2); because it is said that "*many thrones were set;*" and (verse 22), by way of explanation, that "judgment was given *to the saints* of the Most High."

'Hence the same apostle learned to confute the false fears of the Thessalonians, that the day of Christ's second coming was nigh at hand; because that day could not be, till the man of sin were *first come,* and should have reigned an appointed time, etc., (2 Thess. ii. 3); forasmuch as *Daniel* had foretold that it should be so, and that his destruction should be *at the appearing* of the Son of Man in the clouds; whose appearing, therefore, should not be *till then.* This επιφανεια της παρουσιας αυτου in St. Paul, "whom the Lord" (saith he) "shall destroy at the επιφανεια *of his coming.*" Daniel's wicked horn is St. Paul's man of sin [rather, we should say, the *forerunner*], as the Church from her infancy interpreted it.

'But, to go on. While this judgment sits, and when it had destroyed the fourth beast by the coming of the Son of Man in the clouds of heaven, He receives "*dominion, and glory, and a kingdom,* that all people, nations, and languages should serve and obey him" (verse 14); which kingdom is thrice explained afterwards to be *the millennial kingdom* of "the saints of the Most High." (Verses 18, 22, 27.)'

These grounds being laid, Mr. Mede proceeds.

'I argue as follows:

'The kingdom of the Son of Man and of the saints of the Most High in Daniel's vision, *begins* when the great judgment sits.

'The kingdom in the *Apocalypse,* wherein the saints reign with Christ a thousand years (Rev. xx. 4, 6), *is the same* with the kingdom of the Son of Man and of the saints of the Most High in the vision of Daniel.

'*Ergo.* It also *begins* at the great judgment.

'That the kingdom in Daniel and that of a thousand years in the Apocalypse are one and the same kingdom, appears thus:

'First, because they begin, *ab eodem termino,* viz., *at the destruction* of the fourth beast: that in *Daniel,* when the beast (then ruling in the eleventh little wicked horn) is slain, and his body destroyed, and given to the burning flame" (Dan. viii. 11, 22, 27): that in the *Apocalypse,* when "the beast" [i. e., the two-horned beast from the earth, having a mouth like the Dragon],[1] "and the false prophet" (i. e., the Papal wicked horn in Daniel), "were taken, and both cast alive into a lake burning with fire and brimstone." (Rev. xix. 20, 21.)

'Secondly. Because *St. John* begins the *regnum* or kingdom of a thousand years *from the same session* of judgment described in *Daniel,* as appears by his parallel expression borrowed from thence:

Daniel says, chap. vii. 9: "I beheld, till *the thrones* were pitched down . . . and *the judgment* (i. e., the judges) *sat.*" 22. "*And judgment* was given to the saints of the Most High." "And the saints *possessed the kingdom:*" viz., with the Son of Man who came in the clouds.	St. John says, chap. xx. 4: "*I saw thrones, and they* (i. e., the risen and raptured saints), *sat upon them.*" "*And judgment* was given unto them." "And the saints *lived and reigned with Christ a thousand years.*" "To him that overcometh, will I grant *to sit with me in my throne,*" etc. (Rev. iii. 21.) "And I will give them power *over the nations,*" etc. (Rev. ii. 26.)

'Now, if this be sufficiently proved, viz., that the thousand years *begin* with the day of judgment, it will appear further out of the Apocalypse, that the judgment is not consummated till they are *ended:* for Gog and Magog's destruction, and the universal resurrection of the *wicked dead,* together with the *final* conflagration which is to change and purify the globe, etc., *will not be till then:* therefore, the whole thousand years is *included* in the day of judgment.

'Hence it will follow, that, whatever Scripture speaks of a kingdom of Christ to be at His *second* appearing, or at the *destruction* of [the last] antichrist, it must needs be *the same* which Daniel saw should be *at that time;* and so, consequently, the kingdom

---

[1] Rev. xiii. 11.

of a thousand years, which the Apocalypse includes *between* the beginning and consummation of *the great judgment*.'

Finally. To sum up the whole in a few words. The day of Christ's second coming, and the great day of judgment which opens it, commence *at the close* of the 1335 days or years of Dan. xii. 12, when the vengeance of God *begins* to be poured out upon the little Papal horn ; is *continued* upon the last antichristian or atheistic confederacy, headed by the two-horned Apocalyptic beast from the earth (Rev. xiii. 11–17), or St. Paul's " man of sin and son of perdition " (2 Thess. ii. 3) ; extends through the period of the MILLENNIUM, and *terminates* with the final destination of all mankind, by the *reward* of the redeemed in their admission to that " inheritance which is incorruptible," [1] in the " new earth and heavens" which " God will create; " [2] and by the *punishment* of the wicked in the γεεννα (Gehenna) fire of everlasting torments.

It hence follows, that this second coming of Christ comprehends not *two separate and distinct* comings, but *two manifestations* of one and the same event: the one at the *commencement* of the millennial period, to raise the sleeping dead in Christ, and change and glorify the living saints, and to destroy the last antichrist and his God-denying confederacy ; and the other, *at the close* of it, to punish the Gog and Magog hosts that compass the camp of the saints and the beloved city, by fire from heaven ; to raise the wicked dead, both small and great, from their graves, and the sea and Hades (ᾅδης) ; and, arraigning them before the Judge, who now appears, *for the first*, seated on His great white throne, to try them according to the deeds done in the body, and to consign them, together with death and Hades, to the perdition of ungodly angels and men.

At this point, therefore, *time closes*, and *eternity begins*. Of this St. Paul spake when he said : " Then cometh *the end*, when He (i. e., Christ) shall have *delivered up* the kingdom (millennial) to God, even the Father, when He shall have put down all rule, and all authority and power ; " for, " He must reign, *until* He hath put all enemies under His feet ; " [3] and, as " *the last* of these enemies is " Death," [4] so, " when all things shall be subdued unto Him, *then* shall the Son also himself be subject unto Him that put all things under Him, THAT GOD MAY BE ALL IN ALL." [5]

[1] 1 Peter i. 4. [2] Rev. xxi. 1–5. [3] 1 Cor. xv. 25.
[4] Ib. verse 26. [5] 1 Cor. xv. 24, 28.

Thus much, then, in regard to the *opposite views* prevalent in the Church of this day, as to what constitutes the scriptural doctrine of the *second coming* of Christ and of the *future judgment*.

But we now deferentially submit, that we have pointed out the *fallacy* of the various theories:

I. That all that the prophetic Scriptures teach on this subject, were verified by the return of the Jews from the Babylonish captivity.

II. That they were *verified* by the events which preceded, accomplished, and followed the invasion and destruction of Jerusalem, etc., by the Roman army, in A. D. 70.

III. That they received their *accomplishment* by the overthrow of paganism and the establishment of Christianity in the Roman empire under Constantine the Great at and after A. D. 323; and also,

IV. Of those who allege, that the kingdom and reign of Christ on earth at His second coming will be *spiritual;* and that "the times of the Gentiles" are *identical* with the establishment of the Christian Church, the dispensation of which is to continue until the close of the millennial age, etc. And finally,

V. In addition to the *inferences* derivable from our scriptural arguments and historical and philosophical facts against the second personal coming of Christ as being *post*-millennial; what we have advanced by way of a *direct argument*, as demonstrative that, when that event does take place, it will be *pre*-millennial; we have adduced the scriptural proof, that the *ideas* and *language* of the New Testament writers in reference to the second personal coming of Christ and the judgment of the great day as future, *were all derived from and founded upon* the prophetical statement of the inspired pre-Christian Jewish writers regarding them. This last-named circumstance of itself, unless it can be shown to be fallacious, settles forever the question as to the foundation of the *synchronisms* of the Gospels, Epistles, and the Apocalypse, with the Book of Daniel, in regard to this great fundamental doctrine of the judgment-coming of the Lord; and it cannot fail to appeal, with a corresponding force and power, to the heart and conscience of every lover of the truth as it is in Christ.

It may, however, be of service here to present the *divergence* between the prevailing theory and its opposite, in juxtaposition, thus: it is maintained

By the Church at large,	By us,
1. That the second personal coming of Christ is *post*-millennial, and that the day of judgment does not commence *until the close* of that period.	That the second personal coming of Christ is *pre*-millennial, and that the day of judgment commences *at the opening* of that period.
2. That *all the dead*, both righteous and wicked, are then to be *simultaneously raised*, and being tried, are justified or condemned, the righteous being taken to heaven, and the wicked consigned to hell. And,	That then " *the dead in Christ are raised first*, and *the living saints changed and glorified;* while " the rest of the dead " (i. e., the wicked dead) are not raised " *until the thousand years are ended.*" (Rev. xx. 5.)
3. That the day of judgment is limited to the short period of *a natural day of twenty-four hours*.	That the day of judgment runs coeval with *the whole period* of the millennium of a thousand years.

In conclusion, then, we observe,

First. It is clear that these conflicting views, so absolutely antipodal, *cannot* both be according to "the mind of the Spirit," as revealed in Holy Scripture. Nor can it be pretended on any legitimate principles of scriptural interpretation, that the voice of the many *against* the comparatively few, is any evidence of *the truth* of the popular theory on this subject. To admit this, would be to *reverse* the order of evidence in proof of any doctrine of Holy Scripture. "Vox populi, vox Dei"—*the voice of the people is the voice of God*—is not the *criterion* by which to decide the question, "What is truth?" It was the voice of the people, both Jews and Gentiles, that *crucified* God's dear Son![1] while, except the weeping Mary, and Joanna, and Susanna, etc., who clung around the cross to the last, even *the few* timid disciples who had followed Jesus during his ministry, "*stood afar off!*"[2] Indeed, all history shows, that *the true faith* of the Church, doctrinally, has always been found, not with the *many*, but with the *few*. It was so at the time of the flood.[3] It was so in the time of Abraham.[4] It was so in the time of the prophet Elijah.[5] It was so at the time of the first coming of our blessed Lord,[6] and also during His ministry and that of His apostles. And Christ himself declared *prophetically*, that so it shall be *immediately before* and *at the time of* His second appearing: "As

---

[1] Acts ii. 23; iv. 10-55.   [2] Matt. xxvi. 58; xxvii. 55.   [3] 1 Pet. iii. 20.
[4] Josh. xxiv. 2, 3, and verses 14, 15.   [5] 2 Kings xix. 18.   [6] Luke xii. 32.

it was in the days of Noah," etc., "even so shall it be in the days of the Son of Man."[1] And to this St. Paul *prophetically* adds that "that day shall not come, except there come *a falling away* (αποστασια) *first.*"[2] While St. Peter, speaking *prophetically* of the same event, declares, that "in the last day shall *scoffers arise*, walking after their own lusts, and saying, *Where is the promise of His coming?* For since the fathers have fallen asleep, all things continue as they were from the beginning of the creation."[3]

Does it not then behoove us to beware, lest *we at this day* should be found among the "scoffers" of *these* "*last times?*" And,

Second. We may see from this subject the error, yea more, the palpable injustice of confounding, as many do, the *millenarian* system of interpreting the prophetic Scriptures—which is that substantially advocated by us—with that of *Millerism*. The truth of the matter is, that Millerism differs *in nothing* from the popular theory respecting the day of judgment *as future*, except in the single article of *anticipating the time* of Christ's second coming. Both affirm that Christ is to come *at the close of* "the times of the Gentiles," with this difference: according to the popularly received views, that event is not to transpire for some 1500 years or more; whereas the Father of *Millerism*, alleging that "the times of the Gentiles" *closed* in A. D. 1843, as terminating the 6000 years from the creation and fall, affirmed that Christ would come *then*, simultaneously raise the dead, both just and unjust, save the righteous, destroy the wicked, and wrap the globe in the flames of the last universal conflagration, etc.; having done which, mankind were to enter upon their *eternal state* of bliss or of woe.

On the other hand, *millenarianism* maintains that "the times of the Gentiles," and the millennial period of the Church, *are two separate and distinct dispensations;* and also, that while Christ's second coming is *pre*-millennial, the universal conflagration is *post*-millennial. And hence, that *time does not close*, and *eternity begin*, at the termination of the "times of the Gentiles;" but that it continues to run on *to the end of* the peace, prosperity, universal

---

[1] Matt. xxiv. 37-39. [2] 2 Thess. ii. 1-3. See Note A. [3] 2 Pet. iii. 2-4.

righteousness and glory to man, of the mild and benignant reign of "THE PRINCE OF PEACE."

The way is now prepared, for the discussion of the only remaining topic directly connected with "the great theological question" in reference to the Second Coming of Christ, as indicated by the following chapter.

CHAPTER V.

SACRED PHILOSOPHY, CONSIDERED IN ITS APPLICATION TO THE SCRIPTURAL DOCTRINE OF THE RESURRECTION OF CHRIST, AND OF THE RIGHTEOUS AND THE WICKED DEAD, AS DEPENDENT UPON, AND CONNECTED WITH, HIS SECOND COMING.

HAVING, in the preceding pages, agreeably to my original design, discussed at considerable length the various theories which relate to THE SECOND COMING OF CHRIST, whether it is to be *pre-* or *post-*millennial; the subject of the *mode* or *manner* of that coming calls for additional remark.

The question regarding it involves a more extended inquiry into THE NATURE OF THE RESURRECTED STATE, in its application to our blessed Lord and Saviour Jesus Christ, and to the dead, both just and unjust.

The question is, Does it consist of a *purely spiritual*, or of a *literal* or *corporeal* resurrection? On this subject we premise,

1. That, whatever was the mode or form of the *resurrection* of our Lord, that mode or form will characterize the resurrection of "*all* that are in their graves" generally; and, in respect to *the saints* in particular, there will be an exact correspondence between *it* and the resurrected state of CHRIST, in accordance with the explicit declaration of the Apostle John, 1st Epis., chap. iii. 2: "Beloved, now are we the sons of God, and it doth not yet appear what we shall be, but we know that when He shall appear, *we shall be like Him*, for we shall see Him as He is." But,

2. The popularly received theory of the Church of this day is, that the righteous, *at the instant of death*, enter upon a state of

perfect and consummate blessedness of God in heaven, and of the wicked in hell, and that their *resurrection* will consist of their being changed into a *purely spiritual* state. It follows, therefore, on the principle of homogeneity,

3. That the resurrection of CHRIST, in its mode or form, was of a *purely spiritual* nature. For, to argue that the resurrection of Christ was a *literal* or *corporeal* resurrection, while that of the saints is *purely spiritual*, is totally irreconcilable with, and ignores the above statement of St. John.

But, this popular theory of a *purely spiritual* resurrection, we maintain, tends to cut up, root and branch, what we affirm to be the scriptural doctrine of a *literal* or *corporeal* resurrection of the dead, whether in respect either of Christ, or of the just and unjust.

It is necessarily founded upon the hypothesis, that "*the soul only is the man,*" that is, the PERSON.

But in direct opposition to this theory—which we hold to be of the species of ancient Sadduceeism [1]—we maintain, that *the soul*, plus *the body*, is the man, that is, the PERSON. In other words, we mean, that man, at his creation, was constituted a *complex* being, consisting of *body* and *soul;* and hence that, in order to preserve the *personality* of man in its integrity *after* death, the body must be *literally* raised from the dead, and *reunited* to the soul ; and also, that *such* a resurrection is *common* to both Christ and the saints, together with "the rest of the dead" spoken of in Rev. xx. 5. We shall treat the subject under the following sections :

SECTION I.

AN INQUIRY INTO THE IMPORT OF THE TERMS, SPIRITUAL, CORPOREAL, AND PERSONAL.

I. By the term SPIRITUAL, I mean that which is not cognizable to the senses, *immaterial, incorporeal, invisible.* To illustrate its nature, operations, etc., our blessed Lord employs the following striking metaphor: "The *wind* bloweth where it listeth, and thou hearest the sound thereof, but canst not tell whence it cometh,

---

[1] See Matt. xxii. 23-33; 2 Tim. ii. 16-18 ; 1 Tim. i. 18-20.

and whither it goeth; so is every one that is born of the SPIRIT."[1] Here, that material element, the "wind" or air in motion, from its most powerful but subtle and invisible properties, is used to denote the *nature* of THE INFINITE AND ETERNAL GODHEAD, whose existence, however attested by the magnitude and grandeur of *creation's* work, or by the *fruits* of man's regenerated being, is nevertheless, in His DIVINE ESSENCE, *hidden* from mortal eye, "The blessed and only Potentate, the King of kings, and Lord of lords, who only hath immortality, dwelling in light, which no man can approach unto; *whom no man hath seen, nor can see.*"[2] Hence the word *spirit*—in Hebrew רוּחַ, *ruach*, in Greek πνευμα,[3] *pneuma*, and in Latin *spiritus*[4]—as significant of the divine essence, is applied, first, to THE FATHER,—" God is a *spirit* "[5]—and of whom Jesus declared, "*No man hath seen God at any time:*" and second, to THE THIRD PERSON of the adorable Trinity, who, proceeding from the Father and the Son, energized the chaotic elements of the *material* world, bringing order out of confusion;[6] and in the *moral* world, inspires, illumines, regenerates, and sanctifies the redeemed. I only add on this subject, that our Lord, by way of contrasting His *complex* nature with that of a Being *purely spiritual*, says to the eleven disciples among whom He appeared in His resurrected body, "Why are ye troubled? and why do thoughts arise in your hearts? Behold my hands and my feet; it is I myself. Handle me, and see: *for a spirit hath not flesh and bones, as ye see me have.*"[7] This brings me to a definition of the word,

II.—CORPOREAL.

This word means, that which is opposed to spiritual or immaterial, as, *a material* or *corporeal body*. Such a corporeity, however, is not to be understood as excluding from it all connection

---

[1] John iii. 8.   [2] 1 Tim. vi. 15, 16.
[3] Applied by the Greek writers to the *wind* (*Theophanes*, Hom. xlvii., p. 325), " Αυτος ὁ χινουμενος αηρ λεγεται πνευμα; The *air* itself in motion, is called πνευμα."
[4] From spiro, *to blow, breathe*, etc. : (*Virgil*, Æn. xii., line 365) :

——————Boreæ cum *spiritus* alto
Intonat Ægæo——

——————When the northern *Blast*
Roars in the Ægean——

See *Parkhurst's* Gr. Lex., word Πνευμα.

[5] John iv. 24.   [6] Gen. i. 2.   [7] John.

with what is *spiritual*. They may *coexist* with each other. In MAN, they *do* so coexist. Hence the term πνευμα is applied to the *human* SOUL or SPIRIT, *breathed into* the newly-created corporeal form of man by God himself,[1] expressly to distinguish it on the one hand from his BODY, σωμα, *soma;* and on the other from his SOUL, ψυχη, *psuche.* Man, indeed, is constituted of three parts, *body, soul,* and *spirit;* the latter, the *spirit,* consisting of the *animal life,* as forming *the connecting link* between the body and the soul, and which, though composed of matter, yet being refined and attenuated to its utmost capacity, like caloric or heat—which is material—is invisible and intangible, a refined, active substance, subject to the laws of matter, and, though differing from every other modification of it, yet is equally liable to decomposition. This is in exact harmony with the *philosophy* of the inspired Paul on this subject, 1 Thess. v. 23, where he says, "I pray God your whole *spirit* and *soul* and *body* be preserved blameless *unto the coming of our Lord Jesus Christ.*"

From the very intimate but yet inscrutable affinities subsisting between the *soul* and *spirit,* however, man for the most part has come to be regarded simply as constituted of *body* and *soul,* or the *corporeal* and the *spiritual:* the body, the vehicle of the soul's manifestations; the body, originally created immortal, yet, on account of sin, subject to DEATH; the soul, immaterial, indestructible.

Such, then, is MAN. And such a man—I would utter the sentiment with the deepest solemnity—such a man, sin excepted, was our BLESSED LORD AND SAVIOUR, JESUS CHRIST. Yes. "According to the eternal purpose" of *self-manifestation,* which the spiritual "invisible God" the Father "purposed in Christ Jesus our Lord,"[2] "*a body,*" corporeal, visible, was "prepared" FOR HIM; and, "in the fulness of the time," was assumed by Him of the Virgin Mary, by "the power of the Holy Ghost." Of that "body," that of the newly-created Adam was "THE FIGURE."[3] Nor of the body only. For, as "God breathed" into the "nostrils" of "the first man" who "was of the earth, earthy,"[4] and he thereby "*became* a living soul;"[5] so we read of the Lord Jesus, that "His *soul* was exceeding sorrowful."[6] Nor does the corresponding relation between "the first man" as the figure or

---

[1] Gen. ii. 7; see also Rev. xi. 11. [2] Eph. iii. 11. [3] Rom. v. 14.
[4] 1 Cor. xv. 47. [5] Gen. ii. 7. [6] Matt. xxvi. 38.

type of "the second Adam, the Lord from heaven"[1] as the antitype, end here. Did the first Adam *die?* So did the second. The following Pauline statements illustrate and confirm these points: "HE (Christ) took not on Him the nature of angels, but He took on Him *the seed of Abraham.* Wherefore it behoved Him, *in all things,* to be made *like unto* His brethren." "Forasmuch, then, as the children are partakers of flesh and blood, He also himself likewise took part of the same; that, *through death,* He might destroy him that had the power of death, that is, the Devil; and deliver them who, through fear of death, were all their lifetime subject to bondage."[2]

With this distinction, therefore, between the nature of the *purely spiritual,* and that which is *corporeal,* kept in view, I now remark, that, whenever the Scriptures speak of the *first* and the *third* persons of the adorable Trinity, namely, the FATHER and the HOLY GHOST, whatever be their acts and operations, either in the world of nature or of grace, they are always presented to the mind in their incorporeal, indivisible, and infinitely *spiritual* essence. That is, that they are not cognizable to the senses.

It remains to be seen whether the same holds true of what the Scriptures affirm of the *second* person of the Trinity, the Lord Jesus Christ, as the MANIFESTED GOD-MAN MEDIATOR.

The whole question, therefore, *philosophically* considered, turns upon the single point as to what constitutes,

III.—PERSONALITY, AND PERSONAL IDENTITY.

1. *Personality.* On the principle that the soul *plus* the body is the man, then, the *soul* cannot say to the body, "I have no need of thee;" nor can the *body* say to the soul, "I have no need of thee." This reciprocity of dependence each upon the other, as arising from the joint connection of the two, constitutes *essential personality.* And, as the person consists of soul *and* body conjointly, so,

2. *Personal Identity,* taken in connection with the scriptural doctrine of the resurrection, is dependent on two circumstances: the first, the *perpetuity* of the material body in its connection with

---

[1] 1 Cor. xv. 47. [2] Heb. ii. 16, 17; and verses 14, 15.

the soul *during life;* and the second, the *resurrection* of the *same body,* and its REUNION with the soul *after death.*

Now, in reference to the first of these conditions, viz., *the perpetuity of the material body during life,* it is provided for by a law of nature adapted by the Creator to that end. "Life is maintained by continued combustion. The oxygen of the air we breathe combines with the food we eat. Carbonic acid is given out by the breath and the pores of the skin. Fresh carbon is required to maintain the supply, and to compensate for the waste thus produced. The sensation of hunger urges us to eat, and thus fresh fuel is added to the fire. Every time we breathe we inhale oxygen. Every time we eat we swallow carbon. By this simple process, *life is maintained.*" And, whatever changes may occur in the physical constitution of man, as produced by these chemical combinations from infancy to old age, the *supply,* as seen in the *gradual growth* of the body, *exceeding the waste,* his material nature is *sustained* in its entire integrity. At DEATH, "the oxygen is inspired for the last time, and the combustion which maintains life, of course, ceases. The fire is put out, to be *rekindled* once for all [and, so far as *the dead in Christ* are concerned, after a *heavenly* manner] *at the resurrection.*" As to the allegation that, under the above-named law for the maintenance of animal life, the body undergoes *an entire change* every seven, or as some say, every three years, so that we have not the same body *now* that we had three, or seven, or ten years ago; a *scar,* contracted in childhood, and retained to old age, is a sufficient refutation.

And, what is true of the "*children*" as "partakers of flesh and blood,"[1] is equally true of that ADORABLE REDEEMER, who took upon Him their nature. Of the child Jesus, we read, that He "*grew, and increased in stature,*"[2] etc.

The *second* condition of personal identity, I said, consisted in *the resurrection of* THE SAME *body, and its* REUNION *with the soul, after death.*

Now, observe here. By the phrase, the resurrection of the same body, I mean, not that it (i. e., the body of the believer) will be the same as to its *corporeal condition,* both before and after the resurrection; for we read that "we shall all be *changed,* at the last trump."[3] This "vile body shall be *made like unto* CHRIST'S GLORIOUS BODY."[4] By the phrase, the same body, then,

[1] Heb. ii. 14.   [2] Luke i. 80; ii. 52.   [3] 1 Cor. xv. 51, 52.   [4] Phil. iii. 21.

I mean the *identity* of the PRE-*resurrection* body with the POST-*resurrection* body, when it shall be REUNITED to the soul.

PERSONALITY, then, as we have seen—understanding the soul as including that of the spirit—consists of two parts, *body* AND *soul*. At death, these two parts are *dissociated* from each other. The body is laid in the *grave*. The soul is in *hades* (ἅδης), the place of the departed, whether of happiness or misery. The body, taken separately, though not ourselves, is *a part* of ourself, and it is that part which *dies*. But, THE SOUL NEVER DIES. Nothing is more irrational and absurd, therefore, than to talk of the *resurrection* of the *soul*. True, the soul, if saved, must also be changed in its moral character, and this change in Scripture is called both a *new creation*[1] and a *resurrection*.[2] But, *this* new creation and resurrection of the soul must take place *in this life*.[3]

It follows, that, in order to *complete* our personality, the *same body* that is laid in the grave, subject to such *a change* as is necessary to fit it to that end, must be *raised*, and *reunited* to the soul. This introduces us to,

SECTION II.

A DEMONSTRATION OF THE SCRIPTURAL DOCTRINE OF A LITERAL RESURRECTION OF THE DEAD.

Our first argument in proof of it is derived,

1. From *analogy*. The apostle Paul, in answer to the question, "*How are the dead raised up? and with what body do they come?*" answered: "Thou fool, that which thou sowest is not quickened, *except it die:* and that which thou sowest, thou sowest not that body that shall be, *but bare grain*,"[4] etc. Here we are plainly taught, that the seed which *dies*, is the seed that is *quickened*. This representation accords with fact, and is sanctioned by common consent. The *difference* of the raised body, viz., "*that body that shall be*," from the body *as dead*, is illustrated by the difference between the *seed sown*, and the *plant* which springs from it. The plant, the raised body, has a *pericarp*, whereas the seed sown has none, but is a "*naked seed*." It

---

[1] Eph. ii. 10; iv. 24.   [2] Eph. ii. 1; Rom. vi. 4.
[3] 2 Cor. vi. 2; Heb. ii. 3.   [4] 1 Cor. xv. 35-37.

has been objected to the *personal identity* of the dead with the raised body, as drawn from St. Paul's analogy between the seed sown and quickened, that *insect transformation*, e. g., that of the *butterfly*, is against it. But, let us see. The following comparison, if I mistake not, will show that there is *a perfect analogy* between them. On close examination, each will be found to pass through the four following stages. Thus—

The Insect. (BUTTERFLY.)		MAN.
1. The *egg*.		1. Man, in *embryo*.
2. The *larva*, or caterpillar.	corresponding to	2. ——, at *birth*—a crawling worm.
3. The *pupa*, or chrysalis.		3. ——, at *death*, his *pupa*, or *chrysalis* state.
4. The *imago*, or perfect insect.		4. ——, at the *resurrection*, his *imago*, or perfect state, when he comes forth *clothed with* an immortal body.

The fallacy of the above objection consists in its making the soul to pass *at once* from the second, the *larva*, or caterpillar state, to that of the fourth, or the *imago* or perfect state; thus overlooking the important fact that the third, the *pupa* or chrysalis state, is *intermediate* between the two. Nothing therefore is more evident than the *perfect analogy* which exists between the *insect* and the *human* transformations; for, "The butterfly, the representative of the *soul*, is prepared in the *larva* for its future state of glory; and if not destroyed by the ichneumons and other enemies to which it is exposed, symbolical of the vices that seek to destroy the *spiritual life* of the soul, it will come to its state of repose in the *pupa*, which is its *hades* ; and at length, when it assumes the *imago*, break forth with new powers and beauty to final glory, and the reign of love. So that, in this view of the subject, well might the Italian poet exclaim,

"'Non v' accorgete voi, che noi siam vermi,
  Nati a forma l' angelica farfalla ?'
Do you not perceive that we are caterpillars,
Born to form the angelic butterfly ?"

I pass to another argument.

2. The resurrection of "dead persons" *is an elemental doctrine.* Thus St. Paul, Heb. vi. 1, 2, makes "*the resurrection of*

the dead" one of the first "principles of the doctrine of Christ." And no marvel. For Jesus himself had declared, "The hour is coming, in the which *all that are in their graves shall come forth,"* [1] &c.

Now, whether we understand the expression, a dead person, to denote *a dead body ;* or the *soul* of a dead person ; or the soul and body *conjointly ;* the Scriptures will be found to treat the subject *under all these aspects,* to show that the resurrection from the dead consists of a REVIVISCENCE to life, *by a* REUNION *of soul and body.*

(1.) Take the first sense—where a dead *person* is understood in the sense of a dead body. "One who had DIED was carried out, the *only son* of his mother." [2] "DEAD PERSONS are raised." [3] "Women received THEIR DEAD raised to life again." [4] In these and numerous other passages, a dead *person* means a dead *body* raised to life.

(2.) Take the second sense—where the *soul* is used to denote *a dead person.* "I saw under the altar *the* SOULS of them that were SLAIN for the word of God, and for the testimony which they held," [5] etc., viz., the martyrs of Jesus.

(3.) Take the third sense—where *a dead person* is understood of the soul and body *conjointly.* Such are all those passages which speak of *a resurrection of* (or from among) dead persons." Thus, "THE DEAD *in Christ shall rise first."* [6] Here, as predicated of the *resurrection,* the meaning is, that those who shall share in the blessedness of *" the first resurrection,"* [7] are raised by a RE-UNION *of soul and body,* the former being redeemed from *hades,* the latter, from the *grave.* This *reunion,* therefore, both of body and soul, is *essential* to the integrity of the ENTIRE PERSON. Further comment on this article is superfluous.

3. But, I pass to a third argument. It is this: This *identity* of the dead body with the raised body, is proved from those passages in which " the *person* " is expressed, and *" the body "* is intended. Man, after death, does not *cease to exist.* True, a change has taken place in *the mode* of that existence. The soul and body are *separated.* But to say, on this account, that the soul and spirit *alone* constitute man in the *whole integrity* of his

---

[1] John v. 28, 29.   [2] Luke vii. 12.   [3] Ib., v. 22.   [4] Heb. xi. 35.
[5] Rev. vi. 9.   [6] Thess. iv. 16.   [7] Rev. xx. 5, 6.

complex nature, is as contrary to sound philosophy as it is repugnant to Scripture.

The Mosaic account of man's creation is decisive of this. "The Lord God formed man of the dust of the ground; *and breathed into his nostrils the breath of life,* and man BECAME A LIVING SOUL." Here is man in the integrity of his nature as constituted of *body* and *soul* WHILE LIVING. There must, therefore, in order to *retain* that integrity in man's RESURRECTED state, be a complete parallelism thereto. Otherwise, man *loses* his personal identity. Paul's argument of analogy in the fifteenth of 1 Cor., between the dead seed sown and quickened, and the dead body buried and raised, proves this parallelism. I have said that the *soul,* when separated from the body at death, *still lives* in a state of perfect consciousness in hades. On the other hand, the popular idea regarding *the state* of the dead body when laid in the grave is, that *life is totally extinct.* And yet, death, in Scripture, is represented figuratively as a state of *sleep.* Speaking of the dead in general, Daniel styles them "*the sleepers in the dust of the earth.*"[1] So the martyr Stephen is said to "*have fallen asleep.*"[2] And Christ said of Lazarus, "Our friend Lazarus *sleepeth.*"[3] All that I would suggest as intended by these and similar passages, is, that they illustrate the *minuteness* of the analogy between the *seed sown* and the *buried body.* The seed contains within itself *a vital principle,* which, when sown, lies in a *dormant* or *torpid* state, and this state the apostle calls DEATH.[4] Can the apostle, then, mean anything less, anything else, than that the dead bodies of those who "*sleep in the dust of the earth*" are also possessed of *a principle of vitality?* Is the latter case *less possible* with God than the former?[5] So thought not St.

---

[1] Dan. xii. 2.   [2] Acts vii. 60.   [3] John xi. 11.   [4] 1 Cor. xv. 36.

[5] But to this it is objected: "Does not the plant [seed?] whose germ has been destroyed, lose its productive power? Throw a seed into the fire, and what prospect of its germination?" . . . . "Submit a human body to the action of the flames, and then say whether the effect upon the vital principle or the vital portion, whatever it may be, is not the same as in the case of the plant" [seed?].

Our reply is, that, even admitting this to be true in regard to the plant [seed?] under the circumstances here represented—and no one will deny it—yet the argument *fails,* in its application to "a *human* body submitted to the action of the flames." The reasoning of the apostle in the above analogy, evidently comprehended *the death of the body under all possible circumstances,* whether dying in a bed, or burnt at a stake, or engulfed in an ocean, or blown to atoms by gunpowder. The "earth to earth, ashes to ashes, dust to dust" of the dead, whether reposing in a tomb, or scattered to the four winds of heaven, or borne away by the current of the Ganges, or consumed by the inhabitants of the mighty deep; in either case, it is written, "*The sea shall give up the dead that is in it; and death*

Paul: But, recognizing the *identity* of the *dead* with the *living* body, he says, "*and I pray God your whole* SPIRIT *and* SOUL *and* BODY *be preserved blameless, unto the coming of our Lord Jesus Christ.*"[1]

The above facts I have adduced simply to show *why it is* that the Scriptures, when speaking of the dead, make mention of "*the person,*" when "*the body*" only is intended. I give the following illustration: In the twenty-third chapter of Genesis, the phrase, *burying the dead,* occurs seven times; and at the close of it we read, "Abraham *buried* SARAH his wife." Again. "ISAAC *died*. . . . and his sons Esau and Jacob BURIED *him.*"[2] "MIRIAM *died,* and was BURIED."[3] "AARON *died,* and was BURIED."[4] "God BURIED MOSES in a valley in the land of Moab."[5] "DAVID *was* BURIED in the city of David."[6] And, coming to the New Testament, we read of TABITHA or DORCAS who had *died,* that when Peter entered the chamber where the *corpse* was laid, "turning him to THE BODY, he said, TABITHA, *arise!*"[7] In the account of the death of LAZARUS (John, chap. xi.), the expressions, "HE *had lain in the grave four days already*" (v. 17); "*Where have ye laid* HIM?" (v. 34); "They took away the stone, *where* THE DEAD MAN *was laid,*" etc. (v. 41), all go to show that the evangelist, in speaking of the *dead body* of Lazarus, spake of him PERSONALLY.

And this mode of speech, I now remark, is in perfect harmony with that in common use on this subject. Thus we say: "WASHINGTON lies buried in the family vault at Mount Vernon." "PITT and Fox lie side by side in Westminster Abbey," etc.

But, in addition to the above fact, there is yet one other which I must not pass over. It is the following:

4. PERSONALITY is applied to *the bodies* of those who were *raised from the dead.* Says our Lord, "*Our* FRIEND LAZARUS *sleepeth: but I go that I may awake him out of sleep.*"[8] And when He had prayed, "He cried with a loud voice, LAZARUS,

---

and hell (ᾅδης) *shall deliver up the dead which are in them,*" etc. (Rev. xx. 13.) "THE LORD GOD" is as able to *re-form* man after death "*from the dust of the ground as at the first,*" however that dust may have been scattered. No conceivable circumstances, therefore, resulting in the *death* of the body, can destroy *the principle of vitality* which God has implanted in it. Hence the appropriateness of the inspired analogy *minus* the fact, that there is nothing in nature which affords *a perfect parallel* to the resurrection of the body—between the *conditions* of the seed sown and quickened, and the dead body when raised to life.

[1] 1 Thess. v. 23. [2] Gen. xxxv. 29. [3] Numb. xx. 1. [4] Deut. x. 6.
[5] Deut. xxxvi. 6. [6] 1 Kings ii. 10. [7] Acts ix. 36-41. [8] John xi. 11.

come forth! and HE *that was dead, came forth,*" etc.[1] So also, at the time of the crucifixion, we read that "*the graves were opened; and many* BODIES OF THE SAINTS *which slept* AROSE, etc., *and went into the holy city, and* APPEARED *unto many.*"[2]

In the light, therefore, of the above facts, namely, the distinction between that which is *spiritual* and that which is *corporeal*, the latter only being cognizable to the senses; the nature of man, as constituted of *body* and *soul* conjointly; the evidences of man's *personal identity* as such while *living*, and of the same in his *resurrected state;* and the proof of it furnished by what is recorded of some *who were actually raised from the dead;*—these facts, I submit, demonstrate *the real, visible, corporeal*, and therefore THE LITERAL, *resurrection of man.*

SECTION III.

A SPECIAL INQUIRY INTO THE MODE OR FORM OF CHRIST'S RESURRECTED STATE.

Reverting once more to the great question before us—Will the second coming of Christ, when it does take place, be a *purely spiritual*, or a *visible, corporeal,* or *personal* coming?—I remark that, in order to an intelligent understanding of it, we must necessarily go back to the *stones* which compose the foundation on which we build.

One—and that the Lord Jesus Christ, "the chief corner-stone" thereof, has been already examined, as to what constitutes His *complex* Being, as "EMMANUEL—God with us"[3]—"God," as "MANIFEST IN THE FLESH."[4] The result is, that He is presented to our view as possessed of the two component parts of *proper humanity,* namely, a *material* or *corporeal body,* and a *reasonable soul.*

A *second stone* in this foundation. Of Christ's complex incarnate nature as our sin-atoning sacrifice, the "exceeding sorrow of His soul,"[5] and the crucifixion of His body on the cross, subjected him to an actual *organic death,*[6] and He was *buried* in Joseph's tomb.[7] But,

In this foundation is a *third stone,* to which I now for the first would call your special attention. It is this, viz.:

[1] John xi. 41–44. [2] Matt. xxvii. 51–53. [3] Matt. i. 23. [4] 1 Tim. iii. 16.
[5] Matt. xxvi. 38. [6] Ib., xxvii. 50. [7] Ib., vs. 57–60.

That, whatever the Scriptures reveal, as to the MODE or FORM of the *second coming* of Christ—whether it be spiritual or personal—THE RESURRECTION OF CHRIST ON THE THIRD DAY, according to His own word affords *the only key* to its solution. For it is clear that the resurrection of our Lord, *if a purely spiritual one*, could have had no connection whatever with that *corporeal body* in which He was born of the Virgin Mary, in which He labored, suffered, and died, and which, after His crucifixion, was laid in the sepulchre. On this hypothesis of *the purely spiritual* nature of Christ's resurrection, it may reasonably be demanded, *What became* of the entombed body of Christ after His resurrection? Was it *cast aside* as a thing of nought? Was it *annihilated?*

I cannot, reader, spend my time, and tax your patience, with a wire-drawn exhibit of the *philosophy "falsely so called,"*[1] of the above theory. Suffice it to say, that it is but *the fruit* of that system of scriptural hermeneutics introduced into the Church in the early part of the third century by ORIGEN, who, though a man of distinguished eminence in his day and generation, and of great apparent holiness and zeal, as he was also of profound scholarship; yet, having committed himself to the guidance of a *fanciful imagination* in his interpretations of Scripture, "was permitted of the Lord to be drawn away from *the true sense* of God's word, even while avowedly engaged in the study and exposition of it." The result to the Christian world for the most part from that day to the present has been, the substitution of the ALLEGORICAL or SPIRITUAL, in the place of the LITERAL, sense of Scripture,[2] as THE RULE *of interpretation.* In its application to the subject in hand, it inevitably involves a *denial* of the resurrection of the material body of CHRIST, and hence affords a plausible pretext for the support of that theory which alleges that *man*, immediately after death, rises again in a *purely spiritual* state, in which he lives *as a man*, throughout eternity, either in heaven or hell.

The *fallacy* of this theory has been already exposed, in our definitions of the terms *spiritual, corporeal*, and *personal*, in proof of the complex nature of man, as constituted of a material body and a rational soul. And, having also demonstrated the scriptural doctrine of the *perpetuity*, intact, of man's personal identity after death, by and through the process of a *literal* resurrection of the body from the grave, and its reunion with the soul, I hence argue

---

[1] 1 Tim. vi. 20.

that, if this be true of OUR *personal identity of body and soul after death*—on the principle that our blessed Lord and Saviour Jesus Christ, though VERY GOD, was also TRULY AND VERILY MAN; as He suffered death upon the cross, and was also buried, and rose again—so, *His resurrection, in the* MODE *or* FORM *of it, must also have been a* REAL, VISIBLE, CORPOREAL, and therefore A LITERAL *resurrection.*

Let us, however, enter here a little into detail. As preliminary to what is to follow, I observe, that as "*in all things* it behoved Christ to be made like unto His brethren,"[1] during His life, ministry, sufferings, betrayal, trial, death, burial, resurrection, etc.; as "THE MAN CHRIST JESUS,"[2] He must have possessed their entire complex nature, corporeal and spiritual, in all its integrity, sin excepted; or, if "*the soul*" only "IS THE MAN"—if "*the soul*" only *was raised from the dead*, it follows that Christ is only *half a Saviour!* that while He atoned for the sin of man's *soul*, He left *the body* to be consigned to *an eternal sleep!* that the inspired Paul committed an unpardonable blunder, and imposed upon the credulity of his Thessalonian brethren, when he prayed that their "*whole body* and *soul* and *spirit* might be preserved blameless unto the coming of our Lord Jesus Christ."[3] But, as evidence of the fallacy of these hypotheses, in His *proper personality*, as constituted of *body* and soul (equally as when he conversed, and walked, and ate, and slept, and sorrowed, and rejoiced, and wrought His many miraculous "deeds and wonders among men"[4]), He predicted,

1. *His own death by crucifixion.* "And they shall scourge Him, *and put Him to death*."[5] "And the Son of Man shall be betrayed unto the chief priests and unto the scribes, . . . and to the Gentiles to mock, and to scourge, *and to crucify Him*."[6]

2. *That prediction was literally fulfilled.* "The chief priests, and the rulers, and the people, cried out all at once, saying, *Away with this man* . . . and they cried, saying, *Crucify Him! crucify Him!*"[7] "Then Pilate delivered Him to be *crucified*."[8] "And they led Him away to *crucify* Him."[9] "And He (Jesus), bearing His cross, went forth into a place called the place of a skull . . . Golgotha, where they *crucified* him."[10]

---

[1] Heb. ii.   [2] 1 Tim. ii. 5.   [3] 1 Thess. v. 23.   [4] Acts ii. 22.
[5] Luke xviii. 33.   [6] Matt. xx.   [7] Luke xxiii. 13–21.   [8] Matt. xxvii. 26.
[9] Ib., verse 31.   [10] John xix. 17, 18; see Rev. xi. 8.

3. *He was buried.* "And after this, Joseph of Arimathea (being a disciple of Jesus) . . . besought Pilate that he might take *the body* of Jesus: and Pilate gave him leave. . . . Now, in the place where He was crucified, there was a garden: and in the garden *a new sepulchre,* wherein was never man yet laid. *There laid they Jesus;*"[1] i. e., the *corpse,* or *body,* of JESUS. For we read that "Joseph took it down, and wrapped it in linen, and laid it in a sepulchre hewn in stone,"[2] etc.

Now then, having proved that the *personality* of Christ, whom "it behoved to be made like unto His brethren," consisted of His endowment of a *material body* and a *rational soul;* and that His *soul* did not and could not either *die* or be *raised;* it follows, that, in order to preserve that personality in its *integrity,* the SAME BODY of Christ that was buried in the sepulchre must have risen, and must have been REUNITED to His soul. I remark,

4. *That it was predicted of Christ, that it should so be.* David, personating Christ prophetically, says, "*My flesh* shall rest in hope. For thou wilt not leave my *soul* in (ᾅδης) hell" (i. e., the place of the departed), "neither wilt thou suffer thine Holy One to *see corruption.*"[3,4] Both Peter and Paul quote these words of David as prophetic of Christ's *resurrection,* declaring that "God *raised Him up,* having loosed the pains of death, because it was not possible that He should be holden of it."[5] "*David,*" says Paul, "*saw corruption:* but He whom God raised up *saw no* corruption."[6] And so also, Jesus Himself declared, "I have power to lay down my life, and I have power to take it again."[7] And he predicted, "I will *destroy* this temple" (meaning His *body*), and in three days I will *raise it again.*"[8]

This, therefore, brings us to the question direct:

5. *Were these several predictions verified, by* THE ACTUAL RESURRECTION OF THE SAME BODY OF CHRIST FROM THE DEAD, *that was crucified on the cross? And if so, what evidence have we of it?*

Now, we take the *affirmative* of this question, in the advocacy of the LITERAL, in opposition to the so-called *spiritual* or *metaphorical,* resurrection of CHRIST. The evidence in support of such

---

[1] John xix. 38-42.   [2] Luke xxiii. 33.   [3] Ps. xvi. 9, 10.

[4] In this respect the dead body of Christ (if we except those who shall be "alive," and immediately "changed" at His coming, 1 Thess. iv. 13-18) *differed* from that allotted to our common humanity, which *does* see corruption.

[5] Acts ii. 23-27.   [6] Acts xiii. 34-37.   [7] John x. 18.   [8] Mark xiv. 58.

a claim, I admit, must be express, positive, leaving *no* room for further doubt or cavil, or it is of *no* account. In adducing this evidence, therefore, I refer you,

(1.) *To the action taken by the enemies of Christ, regarding His dead body.* Calling to mind the "deceiver's" predicted resurrection of Himself on "the third day;" and to protect the sepulchre against His thieving disciples; having obtained leave of Pilate, the scribes and pharisees "made sure the sepulchre, sealing a stone, and setting a watch."[1] My purpose in referring to this fact is, simply to prove that the Jews understood a "*resurrection from the dead*" to mean a "*resurrection of the body.*" The *design* of the above procedure, however, was to prove that Christ was an *impostor*. But, behold! at the end of the third day, an earthquake ministers to a celestial visitant from heaven, in rolling away the sealed stone from the mouth of the tomb, while the sentinels, overpowered with fear, become as dead men. Some of this same "watch," on their recovery, "went into the city, and showed unto the chief priests all the things that were done." And *they* not only believed that Christ had actually risen; but the *bribery* of the soldiers by the chief priests, to say that Christ's disciples came by night and stole Him away *while they slept*,"[2] is proof that *they also* believed it. For, if these soldiers were *awake* at the time of the alleged act, why did they thus suffer the corpse to be removed? And if they were *asleep*, how could they tell that it was *stolen?* Alas! Their "last error was worse than the first."[3]

(2.) The next evidence of this fact is the testimony of *some who had themselves been raised from the dead*. "They came out of their graves after the resurrection, and went into the holy city, and *appeared* unto many."[4]

(3.) But, I am now about to refer you to the most astounding moral phenomenon known in the history of man. I refer to *the incredulity of Christ's own disciples*, as to the fact of His actual, literal resurrection from the dead. Now, when we reflect that these men had been *associated with* Christ for more than three years; that they had *listened* to, and believed in, His doctrines; that they had witnessed his miracles (especially those connected with His raising several from the dead; e. g., the young maid of

---

[1] Matt. xxvii. 62–66.   [2] Matt. xxviii. 2-4; 12-15.
[3] Matt. xxviii. 64.   [4] Ib., xxvii. 52, 53.

Cyrophenicia, and Lazarus who had lain in the grave *four days*); that they had *heard Him* predict His resurrection from the dead on the third day; and that they had all professed the most *firm adhesion* to Him and His cause in life and in death: I say, when we reflect on all this, how reasonable is it to infer that they would have awaited, in the exercise of a strong faith and unflinching hope, the approach of the resurrection morn, to hail with joy their risen Master!

But, so far from this, their conduct throughout evinced an apparent determination, at all hazards, to prove that Christ *was an impostor!* But, under God, this very circumstance is made to furnish *the only evidence* demonstrative of the fact of Christ's *literal* resurrection. This will appear most conspicuous in every event which furnished them with the proof that "THE LORD IS RISEN INDEED."[1] The *nature* of the evidence demanded by them was of the highest order. In the case before us, that evidence may be gathered from the following facts, namely,

FIRST. The eleven disciples first doubted the *credibility* of those who reported that Christ was actually risen.

SECOND. When they could no longer resist this evidence, they then doubted the *reality* of the appearance of Christ, which was declared to have been *seen*. And, to this,

THIRD, *tangible evidence* must be added, before *all* the eleven would admit the fact.

If therefore it can be shown, that all these species of evidence *were afforded them* in proof of Christ's LITERAL resurrection from the dead, it will place that fact beyond the reach of further controversy. You will here again bear in mind, however, that in speaking of the resurrection of the *same body* of Christ from the grave that was crucified on the cross, I speak of that body as *changed*. In what that change *consisted*, must be a subject of after consideration. I now conduct you back to the sepulchre. It is at "the end of the Sabbath" (Jewish), as it merged into the opening dawn of "the first day of the week,"[2] the morning of the resurrection, and hence, the Christian Sabbath. At the mouth of the open sepulchre—for the great stone had been rolled away—stood a solitary female mourner. It was Mary Magdalene. She had come "while it was yet dark," seeking the body of Jesus.

---

[1] Luke xxiv. 34. [2] Matt. xxviii. 1; John xx. 1.

But, behold, *it was gone!* And, still incredulous as to the fact of Christ's resurrection, even she, supposing the body to have been *stolen*, ran to bear the sad tidings to Peter and John, " They have taken away THE LORD (meaning His *body*) out of the sepulchre, and we know not where they have laid Him." To satisfy themselves on this point, both these disciples ran to the sepulchre, and looking in, saw nothing but the shroud and napkin of the dead body. Peter, however, still remained *incredulous*. John *only*, believed that He was *risen*. [1]

But, what, meanwhile, became of Mary Magdalene? Why, being now joined by "Joanna, and Mary the mother of James, and other women with them," [2] she returned to the sepulchre to weep there. Yes, women were *last* at the cross, and *first* at the sepulchre. And now, superadded to the previous witnesses of Christ's resurrection, namely, His enemies the sepulchral sentinels, and the risen dead, we add,

(3.) *The testimony of the angels*, who to these weeping and " perplexed " female disciples of Christ, said, " Fear not ye: for I know that ye *seek* JESUS, *who was crucified*. HE is not here: *for* HE *is risen*, as HE said. Come, see the place where THE LORD (that is, the *body*) lay." And now,

(4.) As last at the cross and the first at the tomb of Christ, *so these women are the first of His disciples to proclaim His resurrection to others*. Yes. Of them it may be said,

> " The morn the Saviour rose,
> Ah what, true saints, was then thy meet reward?
> The eyes that watched His woes,
> Were *first* to hail the *rising of the Lord!*
> Oh, when were tears so pure, so blest as those
> Which gushed, when at His feet they knelt—
> Gazed—wept—and adored! ".

Obedient to the angelic command, these women at once wend their way quickly to His disciples as heralds of His resurrection.[3] But, "their words seemed to them as *idle tales*, and they *believed them not*."[4] No. With them the above evidence was not sufficient. Though they personally *knew* these witnesses, and had every reason to *confide* in their veracity, yet they doubted the

---

[1] John xx. 1-11. [2] Luke xxiv. 10.
[3] Matt. xxviii. 7, 8. [4] Luke xxiv. 11.

credibility of these reports. They had been furnished with the FIRST species of evidence in this matter. But it had proved entirely unsatisfactory. They demanded,

SECOND, *ocular demonstration* of the fact. This, we must admit, was reasonable. For they well might, and indeed must have argued, "*If risen, where is He?* Has He, like Enoch or Elijah of old, been escorted to heaven, without having afforded His anxious, trembling, desponding disciples that evidence so essential to a proof of the fact, *that of His having been seen?*" etc. If so, this had been a direct violation of a promise made by Christ to them *before* His crucifixion. "After I am risen again, I will go before you into Galilee."[1] But no. This could not be. And I now proceed to the evidence, that our blessed Lord, after His resurrection, *appeared visibly*, not only to *one*, but to *many persons:* not only in *one*, but in *several places*.

1. The first person by whom he was seen, was *Mary Magdalene*. As she stood weeping at the sepulchre, still in doubt as to His actually having risen, JESUS *spake to her*. But she, supposing it was the gardener, said, "If ye have borne Him away, tell me where ye have laid Him, and I will take Him away... Jesus saith unto her, *Mary!*" It was enough. She exclaimed, "RABBONI!"[2]

2. After this, as Mary and the other women were on their way to Galilee to bear the joyful tidings to their brethren, "Jesus met them, saying, All hail! And they came and held Him by the *feet*, and worshipped Him. Then said Jesus unto them, Be not afraid: go tell my brethren that they go into Galilee, and there shall they *see me*."[3] Accordingly, "Mary Magdalene cometh to tell the disciples that *she had seen* the Lord." Still, they were *incredulous*. "And they, when they *heard* that He was alive, and *had been seen* by her, *believed not*."[4]

3. The risen Christ was next *seen by the two disciples*, who were on their way to Emmaus. To these, though "their eyes" at first "were holden, that they *should not* know Him," that they might stand self-convicted of their "slowness of heart to believe all that the prophets had spoken" concerning Christ; yet "their eyes were" finally "*opened*, and they *knew* Him; and He vanished out of their sight."[5]

[1] Matt. xxvi. 32. [2] John xx. 14–16. [3] Matt. xxviii. 9, 10.
[4] Mark xvi. 11. [5] Luke xxiv. 13–31.

Nor is the circumstance to be overlooked, that Christ made Himself known to these two disciples in the "*breaking of bread*," thereby showing, that though risen from the dead, He was still possessed of *real corporeity*. Yes, to a conviction of their judgment by *reason*, was added a conviction of their *senses*. They saw Christ *eat* before them. No doubt as to His *literal* resurrection found any further place in their minds. And hence, returning to Jerusalem, they at once made known these things to "the eleven disciples, and those that were with them, saying, *The Lord is risen indeed*."[1] "And, as they thus spake,"

4. "Jesus stood in the midst of them" (i. e., *the eleven*, etc)., "and said unto them, Peace be unto you." The circumstances connected with *this* personal appearance of Christ to the eleven, introduces us to

The THIRD kind of evidence demanded by them, before they would believe. When these disciples could no longer resist the *credibility* of the REPORTS of Christ's resurrection by those who had *seen* Him, they then doubted the *reality* of the appearance of Christ to them. Hence, upon our Lord's presenting Himself in their midst, we read that "they were terrified and affrighted, and supposed that they had seen *a spirit*."[2] This is a proof of their determination to reject all previous evidence, unless fortified by what was TANGIBLE. Our Lord knew this. And therefore "He said unto them, Why are ye troubled? And why do thoughts arise in your hearts? Behold my hands and my feet: it is I myself. *Handle me*, and see: *for a spirit hath not flesh and bones, as ye see me have*." .... Besides, He "partook of their broiled fish, and did *eat* before them."[3]

5. But, on this occasion, "Thomas, one of the twelve, *was not with them*, when Jesus came." Eight days after, however, Thomas being present, "came Jesus, the doors being shut, and stood in the midst of them, and said, Peace be unto you."[4] This occasion of Christ's appearance furnished the opportunity for the dissipation of *the last* lingering doubt, as to the LITERALITY of His resurrection. "The other disciples had said to Thomas, *We have seen the Lord*."[5] Now, mark. They did not declare to him whether or not they *had handled the body* of Christ. My own impression is, that they *had not*. This I think is borne out by the recorded

[1] Luke xxiv. 33, 34.   [2] Luke xxiv. 37.   [3] Ib., verses 38-43.
[4] John xx. 24-26.   [5] John xx. 25.

effect of Christ's challenge to them, "*Handle me*," etc., which is, that "they believed not for joy, and wondered,"[1] etc. Surely, the above demonstrations of the fact were sufficient to produce convictions in their minds without it. But, *if* their declaration as above to Thomas, "We have *seen* the Lord," was still accompanied with a lingering doubt in any of their minds, the *result* of the declared incredulity of that disciple set it at rest forever. Hear him. Saith he, "*Except I shall see in His hands the prints of the nails, and put my finger into the print of the nails, and thrust my hand into His side*, I WILL NOT BELIEVE." Yes, the evidence of the sense of *touch*, with him, must be added to that of *sight*, before he will be convinced. The condescending Saviour therefore says to him, "*Thomas, reach hither thy finger, and behold my hands: and reach hither thy hand, and thrust it into my side: and be not faithless, but believing!*"

And now, what could the doubting Thomas do, *but yield?* and he *did* yield. In holy faith and worshipful adoration he exclaimed, "MY LORD, AND MY GOD!"[2]

I only add to the above that, as we have no account that any one of the disciples informed Jesus of the declaration made by the unbelieving Thomas, either *before* or *after* He entered the chamber where they were assembled; and as He entered that chamber while the doors were closed, *without divesting Himself* of that glorified body which had been recently raised from the tomb; taken in connection with the above evidence of His ACTUAL LITERAL resurrection; we are furnished with a demonstration beyond which nothing can be demanded or given, of THE PERSONAL IDENTITY, DIVINE AND HUMAN, OF OUR BLESSED LORD AND SAVIOUR JESUS CHRIST, BY A REUNION OF HIS BODY AND SOUL, IN HIS RESURRECTED ESTATE.

And now, in conclusion, the risen Christ, having subsequently appeared to the eleven disciples while engaged in fishing on the sea of Tiberias;[3] then to the five hundred brethren on a mountain in Galilee;[4] and once more to the eleven, when He gave them their commission and sent them forth to preach the Gospel;[5] and having "been seen of them forty days, and speaking to them of the things pertaining to the kingdom of God;"[6] in that *same body* in which He was born of the Virgin Mary, and which was

---

[1] Luke xxiv. 41.   [2] John xx. 28.   [3] John xxi. 1-6.
[4] 1 Cor. xv. 6.   [5] John xx. 19-21.   [6] Acts i. 3.

crucified, and was buried, and was raised again on the third day:—in that same body, but *changed*, "while the disciples beheld, He was taken up" into heaven, "and a cloud received Him out of their sight."

This then, that is, the CORPOREAL, VISIBLE, PERSONAL, but *changed* and *glorified* mode or form in which Christ was raised from the dead, and in which he ascended to Heaven, will be the mode or form in which he will return.

SECTION IV.

A SCRIPTURAL EXHIBIT OF THE NATURE, ATTRIBUTES, AND OFFICIAL DIGNITY OF THE LITERAL OR PERSONAL RESURRECTED AND GLORIFIED HUMANITY OF CHRIST.

We shall select, as the basis of an illustration of this subject, the following passage, 2 Pet. i. 16, 17:

"For we have not followed cunningly devised fables, when we made known unto you the power and coming of our Lord and Saviour Jesus Christ, but were eye-witnesses of His Majesty. For He received of God the Father honor and glory, when there came to Him such a voice from the excellent glory, This is my beloved Son, in whom I am well pleased."

This section we shall divide into two parts:

PART I.

OF THE NATURE OF CHRIST'S RESURRECTED HUMANITY.

This is a subject that may well be placed in the category of "the deep things" of God's revealed mysteries—the "some things hard to be understood" of St. Paul, and which, as we have seen, on the principle of the allegorizing or spiritualizing theory of interpretation, "they that are unlearned and unstable *wrest*, as they do also the other scriptures."[1] Our prayer is, that it may not be "to their own destruction;"[2] but, that "the eyes of their understanding being enlightened, they *may know* what is the hope of

---
[1] 2 Pet. iii. 16.   [2] Ibid.

their calling, and what the riches of the glory of their inheritance in the saints."[1]

Nor is the subject of our present inquiry to be classed with those "foolish and unlearned questions" which, "engendering strifes," we are called upon to "avoid."[2] Still, while meditating on what "the wisdom of God" has been graciously pleased to reveal to us in these premises, we would not forget that it is " *a mystery*," which, like the river disclosed to Ezekiel in prophetic vision, issuing from under the threshold of the temple, gradually expands into a width that "cannot be passed over."[3] While, however, we are not presumptuously to intrude into those "secret things which belong alone to the Lord our God," we are not to be deterred from a diligent and prayerful investigation of "the things that are revealed to us and our children"[4]—"*the things which the angels desire to look into.*"[5]

The subject then in hand, relates to the NATURE OF THE RESURRECTED HUMANITY OF CHRIST. In reference to it, I remark,

1. NEGATIVELY, That it was not a *spiritual* resurrection. This could not be. The body of our Lord that was interred in the sepulchre, was *material*. And matter even when attenuated to its utmost capacity, cannot be transformed into that which is *purely* spiritual, or incorporeal. And, could it have been so transformed, as Christ was also possessed of a reasonable or spiritual *soul*, this spiritual resurrected body would have become so absorbed into, and so identified with, his material body, as to have destroyed all personality. Besides, it would involve the dilemma, that Christ had *two spiritual* human natures! which is an absurdity. But, take a view of the subject,

2. POSITIVELY. And here I must premise, as necessary to an intelligent view of the matter, that we must distinguish between a *purely spiritual* body, and a body *spiritualized*. The former consists of a being immaterial, incorporeal, and hence, not tangible to the senses. That is, it can be neither *seen* nor *handled*. On the other hand, a body SPIRITUALIZED, is a material substance *changed*, or transformed from a *lower* to a *higher* state, thereby adapting it to a *new*, and a more exalted and glorious sphere of action. And if this be so, a body may be spiritualized or changed, without ceasing to be *material*. Such a body, however refined or

[1] Eph. i. 18.   [2] 2 Tim. ii. 23.   [3] Ezek. xlii. 1-5.
[4] Deut. xxix. 29.   [5] 1 Pet. i. 12.

transparent it may become, does not necessarily lose its *inherent elements* of corporeity. On any other hypothesis, *personal identity*, so essential to *the whole man*, as I have just said, would be destroyed.

Now,[1] apply this principle to our blessed Lord and Saviour Jesus Christ, and I argue that, as neither His *body* alone, nor His *soul* alone, but both *conjointly*, made up *His whole manhood*, unless *the same* material body that was crucified and buried was also *raised*, and REUNITED to His soul, His manhood or personal identity was *not* sustained in its integrity. But, as has been already abundantly demonstrated, that *same body* of Christ that was crucified and buried in, also *emerged from*, the tomb, on the third day. Ay, and by the act of the resurrection power of God, it was *changed* also. Christ's *mortal body*, as "the first-fruits of them that slept,"[1] at that instant "*put on immortality.*"[2] And, as I shall now proceed to prove, when Christ's body was *raised* from the dead, it consisted, not in being a *purely spiritual*, but, in being,

3. A SPIRITUALIZED BODY. That is, it was *changed*. In treating of this deep mystery of God, however, let me not awaken expectations beyond what was designed. I do not mean to venture into this shoreless and fathomless ocean beyond my depth. I would also scrupulously avoid all metaphysical subtleties and amusing speculations regarding it. I say, then: of *the mode of the hidden process* by which the dead body of Christ was both raised and changed; in other words, HOW the *material corporeity* was *spiritualized*, we know nothing. And, of the *actual nature, qualities*, etc., of that spiritualized body, we know but "in part." A thick film spreads over the "glass" through which we are now compelled to look at it.[3] And hence, under the most favorable circumstances, it is a much easier task to tell in what it *does not*, than in what it *does*, consist. To this method, then (at least in part), I shall resort, in my endeavors to illustrate this subject. I therefore remark,

That Christ's body, when raised, and changed, *did not become angelic.*" HE TOOK NOT ON HIM THE NATURE OF ANGELS"[4]— and, unless He *lost* His entire personal identity in passing through the grave to His resurrected state—which we have proved an im-

---

[1] 1 Cor. xv. 20, 23.   [2] 1 Cor. xv. 53.
[3] 1 Cor. xiii.   [4] Heb. ii. 16.

possibility—He must have *retained*, AFTER *His resurrection*, that same nature, in which He died and was buried. Now if, *before* His resurrection, His nature *was not* angelic, how, I ask, could it become so *after* that event?

The advocates of the theory of Christ's *spiritual* resurrection, have labored to support it on the ground of an alleged *exact correspondence* between the nature of CHRIST's raised body, and that of the *angels*. But this theory, while it is in direct contradiction to the inspired Pauline statement as above, that Christ "*took not on Him* the nature of angels," rests on the assumption that "angels," in their nature, are *incorporeal* or *purely spiritual* beings. This, however, is contrary to fact. This can *only* be said to be true of the *two Persons* in the infinite and eternal Godhead—the FATHER and the HOLY GHOST. We are to bear in mind, that "*angels*," whatever be their nature, are *created* beings. And creation is *the great boundary-line* which separates between that which is *purely spiritual*, as the Invisible Godhead, and that which is *corporeal*, as angels and men. If it be urged, but angels are called "spirits,"—"*who maketh his angels spirits;*" I reply, in the same passage we read, "*and his ministers a flame of fire.*"[1] Here, the terms "*angels*" and "*ministers*" denote the same thing. While, therefore, the term "spirits" may be understood to refer to the *rational*, the term, "a flaming fire," which we know to be a *material* element, is used to signify the *corporeal* vehicle, through which to *manifest* themselves. That *their* corporeity differs from the *human*, is admitted. It is of a vastly higher, more refined, and ethereal nature. But, it were as consistent to deny the *materiality* of the air we breathe, as, on this account, to deny angelic *corporeity*. Besides, the Scriptures abound with instances of *visible* and *corporeal* angelic visitations to men on earth,[2] thereby illustrating the adaptedness of their compound nature, rational and corporeal, to answer the heaven-devised purposes of "ministering angels, sent forth to minister to them who shall be heirs of salvation."[3]

Still, the nature of angels as thus defined, though corporeal, and that of the resurrected body of Christ, *are not identical.*

[1] Ps. civ. 4; Heb. i. 7.
[2] Gen. xvi. 7, 9; xix. 1, 15; xxii. 11; Exod. xxiii. 20; Numb. xx. 16; xxii. 23; Judg. ii. 1, 4; 2 Sam. xxiv. 16; 1 Kings xix. 15; Dan. iii. 28; Zech. i. 9; Luke i. 13, 19; xxii. 43 Acts x. 7, 22; xii. 8; and numerous other instances.
[3] Heb. i. 14.

The difference is this: their nature, as they are not subject to *death*, is not susceptible of any *change*. This is true, not only of "the elect," but of the "fallen angels."[1] True, by their *sin*, they lost the *holiness* of their character. But we nowhere read of their *dying*. In the same nature in which they rebelled, "are they *reserved* in chains under darkness, against the day of judgment."[2] It is this circumstance which renders their salvation an impossibility. CHRIST did not assume their nature. "*But he took upon Him the seed of Abraham.*" That is, He assumed *the grosser corporeity of human nature*, which, having *sinned*, became subject also to *death*. But, in order to *accomplish* the great object of His mission into our world as "GOD MANIFEST IN THE FLESH" (which was, "to destroy him that had the power of death, that is, the Devil, and deliver them who through fear of death were all their lifetime subject to bondage"[3]), "the Son of God" must *die*, not only, but RISE AGAIN.

Now, as "an *angel* cannot be actually transformed into a human being without *ceasing* to be an ANGEL;" so, by parity of reason, a *material* body cannot be actually transformed into the angelic, without *ceasing* to be HUMAN. It follows, that as our Divine Redeemer ("who in all things, sin excepted, it behooved to be made like unto us") suffered, died, and was buried in His proper *human* nature; so, when He *rose* from the dead, He must have risen in *the same proper human* nature. That He *did so arise*, is evident from the angel's declaration to the weeping Mary, at the sepulchre. "*He* (CHRIST) *is not here.* HE IS RISEN? *Behold the place where* THE LORD (i. e., the corpse) *lay.*"[4]

Nor, again, did *the difference in the condition*, between the body of Christ as crucified and buried, and of the same body as raised and changed, *destroy His real corporeity*. The question before us now, is not "as to the link that united God and man in one person, namely, Christ;" but it is as to the *spiritualized* nature of His *risen body*. And, however we may reason analogically from *our* resurrection, as illustrated by the dead seed sown and quickened, in proof of *the fact* of the resurrection of Christ, at this point *all coincidence* between *us* and HIM *ceases*. "In all things, He must have the PRE-EMINENCE." As, even in His

[1] Tim. v. 21; Jude, ver. 6. [2] 2 Pet. ii. 4, 17; Jude 6.
[3] Heb. ii. 15. [4] Mark xvi. 6.

death, " He saw *no* corruption," and which differs from that of the saints, who *do* see corruption; so, as "the first-fruits of them that sleep in Christ," *our* resurrection state is to be inferred from His, not His from ours. "Who shall change our vile body, and fashion it like unto His own glorious body."

But, notwithstanding the proofs adduced in pages 271–278, of the *actual corporeity* of the raised and spiritualized body of our blessed Lord on the third day, the *spiritualists* would have us to believe that all the above instances were mere *ocular illusions.* We are told, that "an *appearance* generally denotes the opposite of *reality.*" And hence, when we read that "Christ *appeared*, to put away sin by the sacrifice of Himself," it was *a mere phantom!* That when He said to Mary, "Touch me not," there was *nothing to touch!* And, that, when the women "worshipped" the risen Saviour, "holding Him by the feet," they were actually clasping less *than a shadow!* Reader, are you prepared to receive such teaching as this?

4. But, finally, on this topic of the *spiritualized body* of the risen Christ. With a view to obviate an *alleged difficulty* arising from our exposition, namely, that *the same* body of Christ that was raised from the dead ascended to heaven; it is contended by some, that while they *admit a literal* resurrection to have taken place on the third day, yet that our blessed Lord, when He *left* his disciples and ascended to heaven, *laid aside that raised body,* or in some way *changed it into a purely spiritual body,* totally distinct from that seen by His disciples after his resurrection. And this is argued from the facts following:

That there are *a number of extraordinary circumstances and actions,* connected with these ocular manifestations of Christ, in His resurrected spiritualized body. For example: His appearing to Mary *under the aspect* of a gardener. His talking and eating, etc., with His disciples, *without being recognized* in His true character. And His entering the room where the eleven were assembled, *while the doors were closed,* etc. The question therefore is, *How are these extraordinary circumstances and actions to be explained?* Not, I submit, (as some allege,) by his resurrected body *undergoing a change;* or by His *assumption,* alternately, *of a material and ethereal form at will;* or by *a transformation* of His risen spiritualized corporeity into different shapes to suit the occasion, from that with which He left the sepulchre. Doubtless, during the interval of the forty days that elapsed between the resurrection and the ascension, while the Saviour was employed "in speaking" among His disciples "of the things pertaining to the kingdom of God,"[1] there was to them an *eclipsing* of the full glory of His beatified risen body, which, however, no more argued *any change* in the glorified body *itself*, than an eclipse of the natural sun in the heavens argues a change in its *physical organism* as the bright ruler of the day. The *ostensible* reason of this, on the part of the risen Saviour was, that the time had not yet come for the *full* "restoration of the kingdom to Israel."[2] A *subordinate* reason was, to produce in their minds a conviction of the *reality* of His resurrection, *by appeals to their understanding*, rather than by *a brilliant display of His full glory to their senses*. They had criminally forgotten "all that the prophets had spoken concerning Christ, how He should suffer, and die, and rise again on the third day,"[3] etc. And, as we have seen, such was their "slowness of heart to *believe*" that He was *actually risen*, that they pertinaciously refused to admit it, except on the highest evidence that could be given—that of *tangible* demonstration. It may well be doubted, therefore, whether *the brightest instantaneous exhibit* by Christ to them of His risen glorified humanity, would have led them to believe in and receive Him as such. Hence, while "He showed himself alive" to them "after His passion" as above recited, it was "*by many infallible proofs*,"[4] i. e., MIRACLES, wrought, not on *Himself*, but on *them*. Take a single example in illustration. As our Lord was walking with the two disciples on their way to Emmaus, it is recorded of them, that "*their eyes were holden, that they should not know Him*."[5] And so, He whose *look* was sufficient to remove the bolts and bars of closed doors, could also *lock up* the senses of the eleven against a perception of His presence, *till* He was seen standing in their midst. And, finally, if the Saviour, *before* His crucifixion, to escape the stoning of the Jews, could "*hide Himself*," and yet pass by "*through the midst of them* out of the Temple;"[6] surely we can have no difficulty as to His "*vanishing*" out of the sight of the two disciples, *after* that event.[7]

In this article, therefore, of the changed or spiritualized body of our risen Redeemer by the power of God, (limited as is our

[1] Acts i. 3.   [2] Ib., 6, 7.   [3] Matt. xvi. 21.   [4] Acts i. 3.
[5] Luke xxiv. 16.   [6] John viii. 59.   [7] Luke xxiv. 31.

knowledge of its nature, yet,) enough is revealed to us of its peculiar properties or qualities, to enable us to adopt the language of our text, and say, "we have not followed cunningly devised fables" in our endeavors thus to analyze it. Nor is the *same veil* that eclipsed its brightness during the brief sojourn of the risen Christ with the early Church, drawn over the present eye of faith. In evidence of this, I pass to consider,

PART II.

WHAT IS REVEALED OF THE ATTRIBUTES AND OFFICIAL DIGNITY OF THE RESURRECTED HUMAN NATURE OF CHRIST.

I. An exemplification of this "glory" was made on the mount of TRANSFIGURATION. The *humiliation* of Christ was His transfiguration as "*the word made flesh,*" with its accompaniments of poverty, obscurity, and suffering. On the other hand, the transfiguration on the mount, was an exhibit and an earnest of His *glorified risen humanity*, and the power and splendor of His future reign. The *design* of it was, to furnish to the three disciples who witnessed it, a proof of His MESSIAHSHIP, and to fortify their minds against the influence of the ignominies of His life and death. But, alas, *how soon* was this resplendent display of the glory of Christ obliterated from their minds! Their conduct, subsequently to the trial, crucifixion, and resurrection of their Divine Master, was evidence of this. And, as has been shown, even amid the "many infallible signs" afforded them of His resurrection glory, their perceptions of it were greatly obscured. Nor was this obscurity removed, till the descent of the Holy Ghost upon them on the day of Pentecost. Then, "*all things,*" which Christ either did or said respecting Himself, or which had been said of Him by the prophets, "*were brought to their remembrance.*"[1] Hence, thirty-five years after the transfiguration on the mount, the apostle Peter writes, "We have not followed cunningly devised fables, when we made known unto you the power and coming of our Lord Jesus Christ, but were eye-witnesses of His MAJESTY. For He received from God the Father, HONOR AND GLORY, when there came to Him such a voice from the excellent glory, This is my beloved Son, in whom I am well pleased."

[1] John xiv. 26.

Now, observe here. The apostle, in speaking of the incarnate Christ *before* His passion, declares that He "received of God the Father *honor* and *glory*," and immediately connects it with His *transfiguration*. The question then is, *what was transfigured?* And the answer is, the INCARNATE BODY of Christ. Otherwise, I ask, what *became* of the material body of Christ meanwhile? And, this transfiguration the apostle calls "the *power* and *coming* of our Lord' and Saviour Jesus Christ." Matthew, Mark, and Luke, in *describing His appearance*, tell us that "His countenance was altered;" that "His face did shine as the sun;" and that "His raiment was white as the light," "shining," "glistening," "exceeding white as the snow."[1] Daniel, to whom He was revealed in prophetic vision in His resurrected "glory" as the Christ of God, thus speaks: "I beheld, till the ANCIENT OF DAYS did sit, *whose*[2] garment was white as snow, and the hair of His head like the pure wool,"[3] etc. And so also the prophet Ezekiel, speaking of the Lord (*Jehovah*) in human form, says that, "upon the likeness of the throne was the likeness as the appearance of A MAN above upon it," . . . "from the appearance of His *loins* even downward, fire: and from His *loins* even upward, as the appearance of brightness, as the color of amber." And, speaking of His *voice*, the same prophet says, that it was "like the noise of great waters, as the voice of the Almighty, the voice of speech, as the noise of an host." And "*this*," he adds, "*was the appearance of the likeness of the glory of the Lord.*"[4] Again we turn to the prophet Daniel, who says of Him, "Then I lifted up mine eyes and looked, and behold, a certain MAN"—referring to Christ's resurrected glorified humanity—"a certain MAN clothed in linen, whose loins were *girded with fine gold* of Uphaz; His body also was like the *beryl*, and His face as the appearance of *lightning*, and His eyes as *lamps of fire*, and His arms and His feet like in

---

[1] Matt. xvii. 1, 2; Mark ix. 2, 3; Luke ix. 28, 29.

[2] This vision contains a *double allusion*. It reveals to us a view of "*God IN Christ*,"—the FATHER, as "the ancient of days," and who, in His essential spiritual essence is *invisible*, "whom no man hath seen nor can see," being exhibited under the visible form and character of God the Son, who therefore testifies, "He that hath seen me, hath seen the Father also." This distinction between the Father and the Son is more emphatically shown in the 13th verse of this viith chapter: "I saw in the night visions, and behold, *one like unto the Son of man* came with the clouds of heaven, and came to *the ancient of days*, and they brought Him (Christ the Son) near before Him (God the FATHER); and there was given Him (Christ the Son) dominion, and glory, and a kingdom," etc.

[3] Dan. vii. 9. [4] Ezek. i. 26-28.

color *to polished brass,* and the voice of His words *like the voice of a multitude.*"[1] Finally, we turn to the Revelator John, who says of Him, "And I turned to see the voice that spake with me. And being turned, I saw seven golden candlesticks: and in the midst of the seven candlesticks ONE LIKE UNTO THE SON OF MAN, *clothed with a garment down to the foot,* and girt to the breasts *with a golden girdle.* His head and hairs *white like wool, white as snow;* and His eyes as *a flame of fire;* and His feet *like unto fine brass,* as if they had been burned in a furnace; and His voice as *the sound of many waters:* and holding in His right hand *seven stars:* and out of His mouth *a sharp two-edged sword* proceeding: and His countenance as *the sun shineth in his strength.*"[2]

But, from this brief exhibit of THE GLORY of the resurrected humanity of Christ, let us pass to a view of that same glory, as connected with,

II. HIS DIVINE ATTRIBUTES. The *effect* of the above vision of Christ to John in His resurrected "glory" was, that he "*fell at His feet as dead.*"[3] It is not our purpose to enter here into a proof and defence of the proper Deity of Christ in detail. That necessity is avoided by the very attributes claimed by our Lord, in His address to His servant John on the above occasion. He laid His right hand upon him and said, "*Fear not,* I AM THE FIRST, AND THE LAST: *I am He that liveth, and was dead; and, behold, I am alive for evermore, Amen: and have the keys of hell and of death.*"[4]

Of the *identity* of Christ as above, with "*the Son of Man*" who was revealed in the visions of Daniel and Ezekiel, there can be no doubt. The 8th verse of this chapter may be taken as *expository* of the attributes claimed by Christ in the passage just quoted. Saith He, "I AM ALPHA AND OMEGA, *the beginning and the ending,* saith the Lord, *which is, and which was, and which is to come,* THE ALMIGHTY." These titles, therefore, namely, "the *first* and the *last,*" or their equivalent, "the *Alpha* and *Omega,*" being the first and last letters of the Greek alphabet (and which are also used as numerals), are designed to signify the *eternity* of the Being who claims them.

Now, of "*the Almighty God,*" saith Isaiah, "Who hath

---

[1] Dan. x. 5, 6. [2] Rev. i. 12-16.
[3] Ib. ver. 17. [4] Ib., verses 17, 18.

wrought and done it, calling the generations from the beginning? I, JEHOVAH, the *first*, and with *the last*, I am He."[1]

But St. Paul declares concerning Christ, that "*He is before all things*," and that "by Him *all things consist*."[2] That is, that Jesus Christ, as the Son of God, is "THE Being through whom creation received its origin, and who conducts it through the ages of ages to its final destination."

Hence, in this book (chap. iv. 8), St. John applies the ineffable name of JEHOVAH to Christ, and which, in that passage, is a paraphrase of that name as used in the corresponding song of the Seraphim in the sixth chapter of Isaiah. We will compare them.

St. John.	Isaiah.
"And the four living creatures rest not day and night, saying, HOLY, HOLY, HOLY, LORD GOD ALMIGHTY, who is, and who was, and who is to come:" or who is THE COMING ONE.	The six-winged Seraphim cried one unto another, saying, "HOLY, HOLY, HOLY, IS THE JEHOVAH of hosts; the whole earth is full of His glory."

I remark in conclusion in reference to this ineffable name, that it is not a word, but the *monogram* of an appellation consisting of several words, of which it contains *all the letters*, as well as the *initials*, in their order:

וְהֹוֶה - הָיָה - יִהְיֶה

(YIHYEH–HAIYEH–VEHOVEH); that is, ἔσται καὶ ἦν, καὶ ὤν; or, more properly as an appellation of the Greek tongue, ὁ ὤν, καὶ ὁ ὤν, καὶ ὁ ἐρχόμενος, "THE IS, THE WAS, AND THE COMING ONE."

What a Name! It is expressive of the summing up of all existence, in all time and mood, in His own infinite Being, which is of all existence the source and centre, and of life, past, present, and to come, the all-comprehensive, all-sustaining ocean!

Such, then, are the *attributes* of the resurrected and ascended Personal Christ! It only remains that we notice,

III. His resurrected OFFICIAL DIGNITY. This is threefold. It relates,

1. To Christ's INTERCESSION in our behalf at the right hand of God. In His humiliation Christ appeared as a *Prophet*. Now

---

[1] Isa. xli 4. [2] Col. i. 17.

that He is risen and glorified, He appears in heaven as a *Priest*, to intercede for us. "But this man, after He had offered one sacrifice for sins, for ever sat down on the right hand of God."[1] "Wherefore He is able also to save them to the uttermost that come unto God by Him, seeing He ever liveth to make *intercession* for them. For, such an *High Priest* became us, who is holy, harmless, undefiled, separate from sinners, and made higher than the heavens,"[2] etc. This intercession of Christ in our behalf extends from the time of the *ascension*, to the period when He shall descend from heaven,

2. As our JUDGE. This is the second official work of the risen Christ in his resurrected human nature. Thus, the apostle says, "and He commanded us to preach unto the people, and to testify, that it is He which was ordained of God to be *the judge* of quick and dead;"[3] "because He hath appointed a day, in the which He will *judge the world in righteousness*, by THAT MAN whom He hath ordained."[4] And, as such, He will judge *the fallen angels*, who are "reserved in chains, under darkness, against the day of judgment."[5] Also *Antichrist*, "the man of sin" and "son of perdition," whom He will "consume with the spirit of his mouth, and destroy with the brightness of His coming."[6] And He will also judge *the poor*, and all their *wicked oppressors.* "He will judge the poor of the people, He will save the children of the needy, and He will break in pieces the oppressor."[7] "He will not judge after the sight of His eyes, neither reprove after the hearing of His ears; but with righteousness shall He judge the poor, and reprove with equity for the meek of the earth; and He will smite the earth with the rod of His mouth, and with the breath of His lips shall He slay the wicked."[8] And, finally, connected with Christ's dignity as risen, is,

3. His office as KING. Isaiah, in predicting of Him, says, "He shall be called, ... THE PRINCE OF PEACE."[9] He is elsewhere styled "the Prince of the *kings of the earth*."[10] Hence, as David's son, who is to sit upon His throne, He was "*born a king*," "THE KING OF THE JEWS."[11] And, at His first coming, had they received Him as such, He had *then* established Himself

---

[1] Heb. x. 12.   [2] Ib., vii. 25, 26.   [3] Acts x. 42.
[4] Acts xvii. 31.   [5] 2 Pet. ii. 4, 17; Jude, 6, 13.   [6] 2 Thess. ii. 8.
[7] Ps. lxxii. 4.   [8] Isa. xi. 4.   [9] Ib., ix. 6.
[10] Rev. i. 5.   [11] John xviii. 37; xix. 19.

on David's throne. But, "by the determinate counsel and foreknowledge of God, they, with *wicked hands*, crucified and slew Him."[1] And now, see the wisdom of God in all this. Christ's rejection by the Jews, opens the door for His expiating human guilt by the sacrifice of Himself on the cross; and for His burial, resurrection, and ascension to heaven, whither He has gone to receive a kingdom, and to return."[2]

I close, by a reference to that event, as described by the revelator John. "And I saw heaven opened," says he, "and behold, a white horse; and He that sat upon him was called FAITHFUL and TRUE, and in righteousness He doth judge and make war. His eyes were as a flame of fire, and on His head were many crowns. And He had a name written, that no man knew but Himself. . . . And out of His mouth goeth a sharp sword, that with it He should smite the nations: and He shall rule them with a rod of iron: and He treadeth the wine-press of the fierceness of the wrath of God. And, He hath on His vesture, and on His thigh, a name written—KING OF KINGS, AND LORD OF LORDS."[3]

Blessed be God! "Behold! A KING"—Jesus, in His risen and glorified humanity—"shall reign and prosper, and shall execute judgment and justice in the earth."[4]

SECTION V.

CONCLUDING SCRIPTURAL PROOF THAT THE SECOND COMING OF CHRIST WILL BE BOTH PRE-MILLENNIAL AND PERSONAL.

I. Proof that it will be PRE-MILLENNIAL.

To relieve this important doctrine from all misapprehension, I propose to present it in the following syllogistic aspects, namely:

That only can be *restored to* the Church, which has been *withdrawn from* the Church.

But the SPIRITUAL presence of Christ *never has been* withdrawn from the Church.

---

[1] Acts ii. 23. [2] Luke xix. 11, 12. [3] Rev. xix. 11-16. [4] Jer. xxiii. 5.

Therefore, the spiritual presence of Christ *is not the thing* to be restored to the Church at the second advent.

Take another form:

That only can be *restored to* the Church, which has been *withdrawn from* the Church.

But the PERSONAL PRESENCE of Christ, at His ascension, *was withdrawn from* the Church.

Therefore, the personal presence of Christ IS THE THING TO BE RESTORED TO THE CHURCH at the second advent.

Here, then, I might well rest the whole merits of this question. What follows, is added simply by way of *illustration* of the latter conclusion.

I have, on a previous occasion,[1] considered those passages which *distinguish* between the immaterial or spiritual, and hence invisible essence of the *first* and *third* persons of the Infinite Godhead—the FATHER and the HOLY SPIRIT—" whom no man hath seen nor can see;"[2] and the visible manifestations of the same eternal Godhead to man, in the person of the IMMACULATE JESUS, "*the* WORD *made flesh*,"[3] "*Emmanuel*, GOD WITH US,"[4] and of whom St. John, who *saw Him*, bare witness, "THIS IS THE TRUE GOD, *and eternal life.*"[5]

I have also explained the sense in which the Scriptures represent Christ's *spiritual coming* to His people. I now refer you to several passages which distinguish between the *fellowship* which His people hold with Christ in virtue of this SPIRITUAL presence, during His intercession in their behalf " at the right hand of the majesty in the heavens;"[6] and His VISIBLE APPEARING " the second time, without sin, unto salvation."[7] Thus, the apostle exhorts the Corinthians to " see that they come behind in no gift;" for, inasmuch as "God is faithful, by whom they were called " (i. e., by the Spirit) " unto the *fellowship* of His Son Jesus Christ our Lord, He would also confirm them *unto the end*, that they might be blameless IN THE DAY of our Lord Jesus Christ;" and this he urges as *a motive* for their constant " WAITING FOR THE COMING of our Lord Jesus Christ."[8] Here, clearly, while the "*coming*" spoken of was to them, *future;* the *spiritual* "*fellowship*" was to them, *present*.

This brings us to *another stand-point*, absolutely indispensable

---

[1] See pp. 258, 259. [2] 1 Tim. iv. 16. [3] John i. 14. [4] Matt. i. 23.
[5] 1 John v. 20. [6] Heb. i. 3. [7] Heb. ix. 28. [8] 1 Cor. i. 7–9.

to a proper understanding of the subject in hand. It is this: *That all the prophecies of Scripture which speak of Christ, relate exclusively to His* HUMANITY, *either in His* SUFFERING, *or His* GLORIFIED *estate*. They point us,

I. To HIS SUFFERING ESTATE. And here we are directed,

1. To *His parentage*. As the "SEED" of the woman,[1] He was to be "born of a virgin," "of the house and lineage of David."[2]

2. To *His birth-place*—Bethlehem.[3]

3. To *the scene of His personal ministry*—"The land of Zebulun, and the land of Nephthalim."[4]

4. To *His prophetic and priestly functions*. The first, as the great "Teacher sent from God:"[5] and the second, as a sin-atoning sacrifice;[6] and hence, they point us also,

5. To *His death*. To this end, "a *body* was prepared Him,"[7] in which He "bare our sins on a tree,"[8] thereby procuring for us "peace," "reconciliation," "sanctification," and free access into the holiest of all, "in the body of His flesh through death."[9]

But, in connection with the prophetic and priestly offices of Christ, the Scriptures also treat of His *kingly* or *regal* prerogatives, all of which relate,

II. To HIS GLORIFIED HUMANITY. And here, permit me again to remark, that the Deity, abstractedly considered—the Deity, considered in reference to His ineffable, spiritual essence, *cannot be* the subject of prophecy. He is only such as "Deity *manifest in the flesh*." And the class of prophecies now under consideration—those relating to Christ's KINGLY or REGAL prerogatives—all stand directly connected with His SECOND COMING, in His estate of GLORIFIED HUMANITY.

Accordingly, it will be found that the prophetic Scriptures specify with the greatest minuteness the *details* of that event. They point out the *place* of His descent;[10] the *seat* of His Government;[11] the *extent* of His Dominion;[12] the *happiness* of His subjects;[13] the *duration* of His reign;[14] and the *time*, both when He

---

[1] Gen. iii. 15. [2] Matt. i. 23; ii. 1. [3] Micah v. 2; Matt. ii. 5.
[4] Matt. iv. 12, 13; see Isa. ix. 1, 2. [5] John iii. 2. [6] John i. 29, 36.
[7] Heb. x. 5. [8] Isa. liii. 12; 1 Pet. ii. 24. [9] Col. i. 22, 23.
[10] Zech. xiv. 4; Acts i. 2.
[11] Jer. iii. 17; Isa. xxiv. 23; Ezek. xliii. 5-7; Mic. iv. 7.
[12] Gen. xv. 18; Exod. xxiii. 31; Ps. lxxii. 8.
[13] Ps. lxxii. 7; Isa. xl. 1-9; lx. 15-22; lxvi. 12-14; Rev. xxi. 1-5.
[14] Ps. lxxxix. 20-37; comp. x. 1-7.

will *commence* His millennial reign,[1] and when it will *terminate*, by the *delivering up* of that kingdom to the Father.[2]

The only point which at present concerns us, however, is the office of Christ as KING. In this capacity it was predicted of Him, that "He shall be great, and shall be called the Son of the Highest, and that the Lord God shall give unto Him *the throne of His father David.*"[3] For, "God had sworn by an oath unto David, that, of the fruit of his loins *according to the flesh*" (not according to the spirit), "He would *raise up Christ to sit on his throne.*"[4] It is however urged by many, that as the sitting of Christ on David's throne was *to follow* His *resurrection*, He commenced His kingly reign as David's son *immediately on His ascension to heaven*. Hence the foundation of the popular idea, that Christ NOW REIGNS AS KING over His saints; in support of which, the two following passages are quoted: "Sit Thou on my right hand, until I make thy foes thy footstool."[5] And, "He must reign, till He hath put all enemies under His feet."[6] But, I submit, as the first passage has reference to the exercise of Christ's office in heaven as the *intercessor* of His people "*till*" His and their enemies are subdued unto Him; so the last regards His *providential government* over the kings and nations of the earth,[7] *till* "the kingdoms of this world are become the kingdom of our Lord and of His Christ."[8]

To the above I add that, if Christ, *at the time of His ascension*, sat on DAVID's throne, it follows, that there are *two thrones* in heaven. For St. Paul tells us that our Lord, upon His *return* to heaven, "sat down on the right hand of *the throne of God.*"[9] At least, this result follows, unless it can be shown that the phrases, "throne of David" and "throne of God" are convertible terms. But, that they are not, and that our blessed Lord *has not yet taken possession* of "the throne of His father DAVID," the apostle Peter most explicitly declares respecting "the patriarch David, that he is both *dead* and *buried*, and that his *sepulchre* (not his throne) is with us unto this day."[10]* And, as though this were not sufficient, the same apostle adds, that "David *is not*

---

[1] Dan. ii. 31–35; 36–45; vii. 15–28; 2 Thess. ii. 1–12. [2] 1 Cor. xv. 24–28
[3] Luke i. 32, 33.   [4] Acts ii. 30.   [5] Acts ii. 34, 35.
[6] 1 Cor. xv. 25.   [7] Dan. ii. 20, 21; iv. 26.   [8] Rev. xi. 15.
[9] Heb. i. 1–3; viii. 1; Acts ii. 34.   [10] Acts ii. 29.

* Yea, and even in *our day*. For "the tomb of David" retains its original locality, just outside of the southern wall of "the Hill of Zion" or "City of David," in Jerusalem.

ascended into the heavens."[1] How, then, I ask, can his *throne* be there?

In conclusion, therefore, on this subject, I remark, that when Christ ascended to heaven, and sat down on the throne of God, it was not to commence His reign as KING, but to exercise His office as our INTERCESSOR. Hence says St. Paul, "Now, of the things which we have spoken, this is the sum: We have such an HIGH PRIEST, who is set on the right hand of the throne of the majesty in the heavens,"[2] whose office-work *now* is, *not to reign* over His people as KING, for He has not yet "*received* his kingdom;"[3] but, to make *perpetual* INTERCESSION for us."[4]

The sum of the whole matter, then, is simply this: David has *no throne* in heaven. And Christ, though born a king, and crucified as a king—"THE KING of the Jews"—yet, "the kingdom, and dominion, and greatness of the kingdom under the whole heaven,"[5] *has never yet been given to Him or to His saints.*[6] But, there stands the immutable oath of God to David, that CHRIST, as his Son "ACCORDING TO THE FLESH"—mark, not according to *the spirit*—"SHALL SIT ON HIS THRONE"![7]

It follows inevitably, that *when* this oath is *verified* to David, it must be by Christ's sitting on David's throne *at the commencement* of the millennium.

II. Proof that Christ's second coming will be PERSONAL.

I now observe, that the New Testament scriptures harmonize with the old, on this subject. Seeing that it is only in His HUMAN NATURE, that the Saviour can be said to "*come*," to "*appear*," to be "*sent*," etc.; the phrase, the "COMING OF THE SON OF MAN,"[8] inasmuch as He is *always spiritually present* with His people, must involve a VISIBLE, PERSONAL coming. For example: That the following and similar passages—"Waiting for *the coming* of the Lord Jesus Christ,"[9]—"and to wait for His Son *from heaven*,"[10]—"Blessed is that servant whom His Lord, *when He cometh*, shall find watching,"[11] etc., all denote a VISIBLE and PERSONAL coming, is evident from the following:—

In the New Testament there are three nouns substantive used to signify that event, the first of which is, Αποκάλυψις, *Revela*-

---

[1] Acts ver. 34. [2] Heb. viii. 1. [3] Luke xix. 11–27.
[4] Heb. vii. 25. [5] Dan. vii. 26, 27. [6] Ib., ver. 21.
[7] Acts ii. 30. [8] Matt. xxiv. 27. [9] 1 Cor. i. 7.
[10] 1 Thess. i. 10. [11] Luke xii. 43.

tion ; the second, Επιφανεία, *appearance ;* and the third, Παρουσία, *coming,* or *presence.*

1. Now, though the word Αποκαλυψις may be employed to signify the discovery of *spiritual truth* to the mind,[1] yet it is never so applied in reference either to the *first* or *second comings* of Christ. As it regards the last-named event, in the sense of *uncovering, revelation, disclosure, display,* etc., it occurs in the following passages: "Waiting for the *revelation* of Jesus Christ."[2] "At the *revelation* of Jesus Christ, with His mighty angels."[3] "Might be found unto praise, and honor, and glory, at the *revelation* of Jesus Christ."[4] "Hope for the grace that is brought unto you, at the *revelation* of Jesus Christ."[5]

The second term, Επιφανεια, which signifies *appearance, display, splendor,* etc.—" apparitio rei corporeæ et lucidæ,"*—"the appearance of a thing corporeal and resplendent,"—occurs in relation to Christ's *second coming,* in the following passages: "Until the *appearing* of our Lord Jesus Christ."[6] "Who shall judge the quick and the dead, at His *appearing* and kingdom."[7] "Unto them that love His *appearing.*"[8] "Looking for that blessed hope, the glorious *appearing* of the great God, even our Saviour, Jesus Christ."[9]

3. The third term, Παρουσία, which signifies *presence, coming,* etc., occurs, in all, *twenty-five* times. Now if, when this word is applied to *others* than the Saviour, it can mean, and is admitted to mean nothing short of a *personal* coming, with what consistency, I ask, can it be interpreted to mean quite a different thing when applied to Him?

1. In the following passages, it is applied to *different individuals*: "I am glad (ἐπὶ τῇ παρουσίᾳ) of *the coming of Stephanus.*"[10] "God ... who comforted me (ἐν τῇ παρουσίᾳ) by *the coming of Titus.*"[11] "And not by (ἐν τῇ παρουσίᾳ) *his coming only.*"[12] "But his—i. e., Paul's—(ἡ δὲ παρουσία τοῦ σώματος) *bodily presence is weak.*"[13] "That your rejoicing may be more abundant in Christ Jesus for me, (διὰ τῆς ἐμῆς παρουσίας) *by my coming to you.*"[1] "Wherefore, my beloved, as ye have always

[1] Matt. xl. 27.   [2] 1 Cor. i. 7.   [3] 2 Thess. i. 7.
[4] 1 Pet. i. 7.   [5] Ib., ver. 13.   [6] 2 Tim. vi. 4.
[7] 2 Tim. iv. 1.   [8] Ib., ver. 8.   [9] Titus ii. 13.
[10] 2 Cor. xvi. 17.   [11] 2 Cor. vii. 6.   [12] Ib., ver. 7.
[13] 2 Cor. x. 10.   [14] Philipp. i. 20.   * Schleusner.

obeyed, not (ἐν τῇ παρουσίᾳ μου) *as in my presence only*, but now much more *in my* (ἀπουσία) *absence*,"[1] etc. And, in the following passage, the same word is applied to THE LAST ANTICHRIST, who, both before and since the time of the Reformation, has been regarded as the Papistico-Infidel Leader of iniquity, who was to appear in the last "perilous times" to come. "And that *man of sin* be revealed, (Οὗ ἐστιν ἡ παρουσία) *whose coming* is after the manner of Satan,"[2] etc. Yes. As JESUS CHRIST, as "GOD *manifest in the flesh*," was *the embodied visible personification of* ALL GOOD ; so SATAN, through this *incarnate* " *son of perdition*,"[3] at the close of "the times of the Gentiles," will be *the embodied visible personification of* ALL EVIL.

2. I pass now to those passages—in all, *seventeen*—where the word παρουσία is applied to THE SECOND COMING OF CHRIST. "What is the sign (τῆς σῆς παρουσίας) *of thy coming*."[4] "As the lightning . . . so shall (ἡ παρουσία) the coming of the Son of Man be."[5] "As the days of Noah, so shall also (ἡ παρουσία) *the coming* of the son of man be."[6] "Till the flood came . . . so shall (ἡ παρουσία) *the coming* of the son of man be."[7] "They that are Christ's (ἐν τῇ παρουσίᾳ) *at His coming*."[8] "What is our hope . . are not even ye, in the presence of our Lord Jesus Christ (ἐν τῇ αὐτοῦ παρουσίᾳ) at His coming?"[9] "To the end that He may establish your hearts unblamable . . . (ἐν τῇ παρουσίᾳ) *at the coming* of our Lord."[10] "We which remain (εἰς τὴν παρουσίαν) *unto the coming* of our Lord."[11] "And I pray God your whole body and soul be preserved blameless (ἐν τῇ παρουσίᾳ) *unto the coming* of our Lord Jesus Christ."[12] "Now we beseech you, brethren, (ὑπὲρ τῆς παρουσίας) *by the coming* of our Lord."[13] "That wicked" —the last personal Antichrist—"whom the Lord shall destroy with (τῇ ἐπιφανείᾳ) *the brightness* (τῆς παρουσίας αὐτοῦ) *of His coming*."[14] "Be patient, therefore, brethren, (τῆς παρουσίας) *unto the coming* of the Lord."[15] "For (ἡ παρουσία) *the coming* of the Lord draweth nigh."[16] "We made known unto you the power (τὴν παρουσίαν) *and coming*, of our Lord Jesus Christ."[17] St. Peter here alludes to the TRANSFIGURATION ON THE MOUNT, which

---

[1] Philipp. ii. 12. [2] 2 Thess. ii. 3, 9. [3] Ib., ver. 3.
[4] Matt. xxiv. 3. [5] Ib., ver. 27. [6] Ib., ver. 37.
[7] Ib., ver. 39. [8] 1 Cor. xv. 23. [9] 1 Thess. ii. 19.
[10] Ib., iii. 13. [11] Ib., iv. 15. [12] Ib., v. 23.
[13] 2 Thess. ii. 1. [14] 2 Thess. ii. 8. [15] James v. 7.
[16] James, v. 8. [17] 2 Pet. i. 16.

was *personal* and *visible*. "Where is the promise (τῆς παρουσίας αὐτοῦ) *of His coming?*"¹ "Looking for, and hasting unto (τὴν παρουσίαν) *the coming* of the day of God."² "And now, little children, abide in Him . . . and not be ashamed before Him (ἐν τῇ παρουσίᾳ αὐτοῦ) at His coming."³

In the view, therefore, of all that has been offered on the subject of *the mode or form* in which the second coming of Christ will transpire, I think we may affirm, without either breach of modesty or fear of refutation, that, when that long-predicted event does take place—a prediction reaching back to the time of "Enoch, the seventh generation from Adam,"⁴ A. M. 687, or 5309 years ago—it can be understood of none other than a REAL, VISIBLE, PERSONAL coming. That "SAME JESUS," which was "TAKEN UP" from earth to heaven forty days after His resurrection, in His *glorified human body*, "shall," WITH THE SAME BODY, "SO COME AGAIN IN LIKE MANNER."⁵

"Spirit of Grace"! through Thine enlightening, regenerating, and sanctifying power, may we all "LOVE HIS APPEARING," ⁶ and "BE ACCOUNTED WORTHY TO STAND BEFORE THE SON OF MAN." ⁷

¹ 2 Pet. iii. 4.   ² Ib., ver. 12.   ³ 1 John ii. 28.   ⁴ Jude, ver. 14.
⁵ Acts i. 9-11.   ⁶ 2 Tim. iv. 8.   ⁷ Luke xxi. 36.

CHAPTER VI.

A HAND-BOOK TO MILLENARIANS,

BEING

A COMPLETE SYNOPSIS OF THE MILLENARIAN SCHEME OF THE SECOND PERSONAL COMING OF CHRIST AND OF THE MILLENNIAL ERA, AS TAUGHT IN HOLY SCRIPTURE.

REMARK. *The contents of this chapter embraces also such parts of the subject-matter in the "* REPLY *" which follows, as was deemed necessary to complete the synopsis.*

THE various theories of *anti* and *post*-millenarians on the subject of the second personal coming of Christ and the millennium, as the discussions in this treatise show, are based upon a series of *negatives*. We claim to have *historically* demonstrated upon the authority of "Holy Scripture and ancient authors," that the millenarian scheme is founded upon and derived from the prophetic announcements of the Old Testament prophets, and of Christ and His apostles, and that it was believed in and became universally prevalent among the orthodox as the Catholic faith of the Church during the early post-apostolic age. Also, that it met with no opposition, until the substitution of the *allegorical* in the place of the *literal* interpretations of "the teachings of Isaiah and St. John concerning the second coming of Christ," as introduced into the Church by Origen in the early part of the third century.

Now, it was this unauthorized change in the *original law* prescribed for the interpretation of "the Messianic prophecies," which necessitated those who adopted it to frame their respective *exegeses* in such wise as to stand out in *antagonism* to the LITERAL INTERPRETATIONS of the prophecies regarding the coming and kingdom of Christ, as taught. by the primitive chiliasts. In analogy to the future assault upon the *pre-existing* "camp of the saints and the beloved city" by the *post*-millennial "Gog and Magog" hosts, the citadel of the *pre*-Christian Jewish, apostolic, and early primitive millenarians, has been the object of attack, on widely different grounds, by its *anti* and *post*-millenarian opponents. Hence, in accordance with the rule of Tertullian—"that which is *first* is true, that which is *later* is adulterate"—the advocates of millenarianism have occupied the position of the *defensive* against the objections of its assailants of every name. Again: Whatever may be said of the *variations* that have obtained among LITERALISTS, in their interpretations of "the teachings of Isaiah and St. John concerning the second coming of Christ," yet, compared with the *numerous contradictory theories* of the ALLEGORISTS, we submit, we are furnished with a strong presumptive argument in behalf of the former. For, differ as they may in some of the minor details of the millenarian scheme, *literalists*, ancient, mediæval, and modern, have always substantially maintained the same great fundamental tenets required by the law of their adoption. On the other hand, the *allegorists*, surrendering themselves to the caprice of fancy, have originated theories between no two of which can be traced the remotest resemblance.

Take, for example, the ancient theories of Origen, Eusebius, and Augustine. Or take the more modern theories of Grotius, Prideaux, Vint, and Bush, and of the Millerites, together with that based upon the popular interpretations of Matt. xxiv. 27–30, and of the Whitbyan "New Hypothesis" as founded upon Rev. xx. 1–6: and who, we deferentially ask, will venture to affirm that a law of interpretation of "the Messianic prophecies" such as that adopted by the *allegorists*, could by a possibility have been given by inspiration from God? This would be to argue that THE LAW of sacred hermeneutics given by the Holy Spirit, instead of "guiding us into all truth," was designed to allure us into a wilderness of uncertainty and conjecture in the interpretations of that "more sure word of prophecy" to which we are admonished to "take heed, as unto a light which shineth in a dark place." The fair inference is, that ORIGEN, as the originator of the *allegorical* theory of interpretation, as Mosheim declares, "by an unhappy method, opened a secure retreat for all sorts of errors which a wild and irregular imagination could bring forth;" and that, as Milner says, "no man, not altogether unsound and hypocritical, ever injured the Church more than Origen did;" and that hence, in the words of Luther, "the allegorical sense is commonly *uncertain*, and by no means safe to build upon; forasmuch as it usually depends on *human opinion and conjecture only*, on which, if a man lean, he will find it no better than an Egyptian reed."

And hence, having exposed the fallacy of the various theories which, as built upon Origen's "unhappy method" of interpreting "the teachings of Isaiah and St. John concerning the second coming of Christ," allege that they were all fulfilled, either first, by the return of the Jews from the Babylonish captivity; or second, by the overthrow of paganism and the establishment of Christianity in the Roman Empire under Constantine the Great in A. D. 325, as founded upon Rev. xx. 1–7; or third, that the second coming of Christ was verified by the judgments inflicted upon the Jewish nation and polity by the Roman army in A. D. 70, as founded upon our Lord's prophecy, Matt. xxiv. 27–30; or finally fourth, as predicated of the Whitbyan "New Hypothesis" of a spiritual coming of Christ, as founded upon Rev. xx. 1–6; I repeat, having exposed the fallacy of these absolutely conflicting theories of "the Messianic prophecies," I proceed to lay before the reader a brief synopsis of the millenarian scheme of the second coming of Christ and of the millennial era, as taught in Holy Scripture, that he may have a more complete view of it *as a whole*, than was compatible with our original plan and design in the "Sequel." Millenarianism teaches,

I. That the *faith* and *hope* of the Church, in every age, have been directed to and centred in THE SECOND PERSONAL COMING OF CHRIST, as that event which is to consummate her redemption from all physical and moral evil. Heb. xi. 13–16; 35, 39, 40; xii. 1, 2; 1 Cor. i. 7; Phil. iii. 20, 21; 2 Tim. iv. 8; 2 Pet. iii. 12–14; Titus i. 1, 2; ii. 11–13; iii. 7; Rom. v. 5; viii. 24, 25; xv. 13; Col. i. 27; 2 Thess. ii. 16; Heb. vi. 18, 19; 1 Pet. i. 3; 1 John iii. 3; Job xix. 25–27; Isa. xxv. 9; Matt. xvi. 27; xxv. 31–34; Mark xiv. 62; 1 Tim. vi. 13, 14; Heb. ix. 27, 28.—1 Thess. i. 10; Rom. viii. 23; 1 Cor. i. 7; 2 Thess. iii. 5.[1]

II. That the present Christian dispensation is that part of "the times of the Gentiles" called "*the gospel* of the kingdom," or the kingdom of God IN "MYSTERY," during which the gospel is to be preached to all nations as "*a witness*" of the truth, "to take out of (or from among) the Gentiles a people for Christ's

---

[1] It will, of course, depend upon the reader to turn to the numerous references to the Scriptures under each head, in order to *verify* the correctness of their application to the subjects treated of.

name," as preparatory to their admission to "the kingdom of God" IN MANIFESTATION. Luke xxi. 24; Rom. xi. 25.—Matt. xiii. 11; xxiv. 14; Mark iv. 11; Luke viii. 10; Rom. xvi. 25, 26; Eph. iii. 3, 4, 9; 1 Tim. iii. 16; Rev. x. 7.—Acts xv. 14; (Matt. xxviii. 18-20; Mark xvi. 15, 16, 17-20.)—1 Pet. i. 1-9; 2 Tim. iv. 6-8; Matt. xxv. 31-34.

III. That we are now living toward that *close* of "the times of the Gentiles" called "*the time of the end*," Dan. xii. 9. That is, not THE END OF TIME, but of the αἰῶνος (*world*), the present *age* or *dispensation*. See on this, the chronology of the world, "Sequel," pages 201-203, and of "the times of the Gentiles," *ib*., pages 167-172, and 185-188. And also as more fully set forth in " Our Bible Chronology, Historic and Prophetic, Demonstrated," etc. And hence,

IV. That as, by the acknowledgment of the whole Church, the second coming of Christ is to take place *at the end* of "the times of the Gentiles," we are now occupying a position *proximate* to that event. Dan. ii. 35, and verse 44; vii. 11, 12, and verses 13, 14; 2 Thess. ii. 3, 4, and verse 8, etc. (See also references above.) Accordingly,

V. That there is *no ground for the popular expectation* of a millennium of universal righteousness, prosperity, and peace, as alleged to be effected by the conversion of all nations to Christ through ordinary church instrumentalities BEFORE *His second coming*. So far from it, that event is to be *immediately preceded* by the following portentous SIGNS:

1. A prevalent *ignorance of divine things* among all classes. Isa. lx. 2; Dan. xii. 10; Isa. xxxii. 6, 7; Hosea xiv. 9; Rom. xi. 8-10; 2 Thess. ii. 10-12; Rev. ix. 20, 21.

2. A *general apostasy* from that "faith once delivered to the saints," and especially in the article of the Lord's second coming. Luke xviii. 8; 2 Thess. ii. 1-3; 2 Pet. iii. 1-4.

3. A state of *religious formalism, abounding iniquity, national and political revolutions, tyranny, anarchy, war, infidelity, and blasphemy*. Matt. xxiv. 12; James v. 1-6; 1 Tim. iv. 1-3; 2 Tim. iii. 1-7.—Isa. ii. 10-22; v. 26-30; xxiv. 1-20; Jer. xxv. 15-29; Ezek. xxi. 24-27; Haggai ii. 7; Luke xxi. 7-11, and verses 25, 26.—Daniel vii. 8, 11, 20, 25; 2 Pet. ii. 12-15; Jude 10, 17-19; Rev. xiii. 1, 5, 6. Nevertheless,

4. That, in the midst of these general commotions in church

and state, the gospel will accomplish *its second circuit through the earth*, when its office-work as "A WITNESS" to the nations will end. See first, Matt. xxviii. 19; Mark xvi. 15. Then compare Rom. x. 18, and Col. i. 6, with Matt. xxiv. 14, and Christ's promise, Matt. xxviii. 20, which extends down to "the *end* of the world" (*i. e.*, αἰῶνος), *age* or *dispensation*.

5. That there will also be *an extensive spirit of inquiry among the true followers of Christ* on the subject of His second coming. Dan. iv. 4, 9; Habak. ii. 1-3; Matt. xxv. 6, 7.

6. That these "signs" will be attended with *numerous corresponding physical phenomena* in the earth and the heavens. Micah vii. 15, 16; Luke xxi. 25, 26. See also verse 11; and Rev. xvi. 18.

7. That there will be *an unprecedented manifestation of the power and malice of the Devil*, in exciting the worst passions of national rulers and their subjects to acts of mutual violence, and of blasphemy against God. Rev. xii. 12; xiii. 4-8; followed by the *effects*, as symbolized in Rev. xvi. 13, 14. See also Ps. ii. 2, 3; and Rev. xvi. 9-11; 21.

8. That while there will be *a waning of the temporal power* of the Popedom, the *spiritual superstition* of the Papacy will *revive and become dominant* throughout Christendom, down to the *close* of "the times of the Gentiles," when it will be *totally exterminated* by the very power which has so long promoted and upheld it. Compare Dan. vii. 12, particularly the last clause, with Rev. xvii. 12, 15; and verses 16-18; taken in connection with chap. xviii. 1-21; 22-24.

9. That the same will apply to *the wasting and decay* of the Turco-Mohammedan Imposture, the *total extinction* of which, as the only impediment to the restoration of the Jews to Palestine, will be coetaneous with the destruction of the Papal power. Compare Dan. viii. 8-12, and verses 21, 22; 23-25; with Rev. ix. 14, and xvi. 12. See also "Sequel," pages 92, 93, and *note*.

10. That as the Turkish power approaches the destiny that awaits it as above, the ruling powers of Europe and America will be more and more inclined to *remove existing disabilities, and withdraw the hand of oppression from off the Jewish nation*, which will indicate the *preparatory steps to their return* to their own land. Isa. xiv. 2; xlix. 22; lx. 9; lxvi. 18-20.

11. But, notwithstanding the marked character and signifi-

cancy of these "signs" as the immediate harbingers of the Lord's second coming, that the nominal church and the world, heedless of their premonitory warnings, *will be involved in a state of stolid indifference, carnal self-security, and sensual indulgences.* Matt. xxiv. 37-39; 1 Thess. v. 1-3; 2 Thess. i. 4-9; Rev. xviii. 7, 8.

Now, these last Scriptural references undeniably connect Christ's second coming *with the moral and physical phenomena as above indicated*, and hence demonstrate the *impossibility* that a millennium of universal righteousness and peace is to *precede* that event. Nor this only. The 8th and 9th of the above "signs," taken in connection with the others, *when viewed in their relation to* the second coming of Christ, prove irrefragably,

VI. That that event is PRE and not post-millennial. In other words, inasmuch as the *final destruction* of the Papal and Turco-Mohammedan powers is to take place *at the close* of "the times of the Gentiles;" and this being, by the admission of the whole Christian Church, *the time* of the second coming of Christ; it follows, that *no* millennial kingdom or other power *can come in between* their destruction and that event. First. Of the *Papal* power. Compare Dan. vii. 11, 12, with verses 13, 14: also 20, 21, with verse 22: also verses 24, 25, with verses 26, 27. Second. Of the *Turco-Mohammedan* power. Compare Dan. viii. 9, 14, 23, with verse 25, last clause.

NOTE.—It is quite superfluous to add, that this second PRE-millennial coming of Christ, not in the sense of a *providential*, or an *ecclesiastical*, or a *spiritual*, but a PERSONAL coming, form the corner-stone in the base and the key-stone in the arch of the millenarian scheme. It is founded upon the fact, that the following and similar passages, viz., 1 Cor. i. 7, 1 Thess. i. 10, and Luke xii. 43, all denote a VISIBLE and PERSONAL coming. Proof, as derived from the three following nouns substantive, used to denote that event. First. Ἀποκάλυψις (apokalypsis, or *Revelation, Disclosure, Display*, etc.), 1 Cor. i. 7; 2 Thess. i. 7; 1 Pet. i. 7; and verse 13. Second. Ἐπιφανεία (epiphaneia, *Appearance, Display, Splendor*, etc.), 2 Tim. vi. 4; 2 Tim. iv. 8; and verse 8; Titus ii. 13. Third. Παρουσία (parousia, *personal presence, coming*, etc.), Matt. xxiv. 3; and verse 27; and 37; and 39; 1 Cor. xv. 23; 1 Thess. ii. 19; iii. 13; iv. 15; and verse 23; 2 Thess. ii. 1; and verse 8; James v. 7; and verse 8; 2 Pet. i. 16. The millenarian scheme also teaches concerning that event,

VII. That while "of that day and hour knoweth no man—no, not the angels in heaven, neither the Son, but the Father only" (Matt. xxiv. 36), yet that prophecy reveals the PROXIMATE period when it will take place. All the *eleven* "*signs*" above enumerated, and especially the 8th and 9th, are designed to indicate *its near approach*. (See references under No. VI.) Further, it teaches,

VIII. That the great event that is to *immediately accompany* the second personal coming of Christ, is, the *resurrection* of those who sleep in Him, and the *change and translation* of those living saints who shall remain unto His coming, according to 1 Thess. i. 13-18; 1 Cor. xv. 23; and which is called " THE FIRST RESURRECTION," Rev. xx. 5, 6. Also, that *this* coming of Christ in the first instance will be, *not openly or visibly* to all the world, but as it were SECRETLY, like "a thief in the night," to steal away His waiting and watching saints, when "two shall be in one bed, the one shall be *taken* and the other *left*," etc. Matt. xxiv. 43; Luke xii. 39; 1 Thess. v. 2; 2 Peter iii. 10; Rev. xvi. 15; Luke xvii. 34-36.

NOTE.—Let us now look at those events that will be *contemporaneous with* this INVISIBLE coming of the Lord.

The dead in Christ and the living saints, as above, having been taken up from the earth "*to meet the Lord in the air*" (1 Thess. iv. 17), those of the apostate church and the nations of Christendom that are "*left*" *behind*, will not be idle. But, being surrendered up to the power of Satanic influence (See No. 7), and being characterized by the *moral* "signs" of the last times described in Nos 1, 2, 3, and 11, and influenced by the *political* commotions and revolutions set forth in Nos. 8, 9, and 10, the way will have been prepared for the introduction upon the prophetical platforms *at the close* of "the times of the Gentiles," or the termination of the 6,000 years of the world, in A. D. 1868,

1. Of the *last great democratico-atheistic confederacy*, under the leadership of THE LAST ANTICHRIST, or St. Paul's "man of sin and son of perdition," etc., and which will constitute that unprecedented "*falling away first*," or APOSTASY from the faith of the Gospel, that is to immediately precede that OPEN and VISIBLE manifestation of the Lord Jesus, when "every eye shall see Him, and they also that pierced Him, and all kindreds of the earth shall wail because of Him." Compare 2 Thess. ii. 1-3; Rev. i. 7. Observe,

First. In reference to this *last Antichrist*,

(1.) His *titles*. Isa. xiv. 4, 25; Ezek. xxviii. 2, 12; Dan. xi. 21; Matt. xxiv. 15; Rev. ix. 11; xiii. 11, 18; 2 Thess. ii. 3, 8.

(2.) His *characteristics*. Isa. xiv. 29, 30; Ezek. xxviii. 3-5,

11–19; Dan. xi. 21–23, 32, 36–39; Matt. xxiv. 15, 24; 2 Thess. ii. 9, 10. Notice,

Second. The *confederacy* under him—how formed. See Rev. xvi. 13, 14.

The way having been prepared therefor, as indicated under "sign" No. 10, the next event *contemporaneous* with the above will be,

2. *The restoration of the Jews to their own land*, in verification of the following prophecies: Lev. xxvi. 40–45; Isa. xi. 11, 12; xxvii. 12, 13; xliii. 5–7; xlix. 11–13; lx. 4; Jer. iii. 18; xvi. 14, 15; xxiii. 3; xxxi. 7–10; Ezek. xxxiv. 22–31; Zech. viii. 7, 8; x. 8–10, and numerous other places. Their restoration will be brought about under the circumstances following:

(1.) The last Antichrist having made his appearance upon the prophetic stage, the JEWS, captivated by his display of miraculous powers (Rev. xiii. 11–17), will make *a league* with him to restore their nation to Palestine, by which they will virtually acknowledge him as their MESSIAH. Compare Hosea v. 13, with Dan. xi. 23.

NOTE.—The prophet Hosea speaks of the last Antichrist under the title of the *Assyrio*-Babylonian king, by whom "*the house of Judah*" was carried into captivity, while Daniel styles him that "*vile person*" with whom the Jews make the compact above spoken of. History attests that the *Assyrian* monarchs dictated the terms for the adjustment of all disputes and other matters appertaining to inferior powers, with the authority of despots. We shall presently see that this personage is *identical* with St. John's "*beast from the earth*, having two horns like a lamb, with the mouth of a dragon" (Rev. xiii. 11), or the "*eighth*," which is "OF the seventh" head of the Roman beast from the sea (Rev. xvii. 11), and also with St. Paul's "*wicked*," or "man of sin and son of perdition" (2 Thess. ii. 3, 8).

(2.) The Jewish nation will be restored to Palestine *in their unconverted state* by this mystical Assyrian or Antichrist, in alliance with *a great maritime power*. Isa. xviii. 1–3. This passage, instead of "Woe to," etc., should read, "Ho! the land of overshadowing wings," etc. This prophecy refers to that nation which shall hold *a maritime preëminence* over all others, and which can refer to none other so emphatically as to *the United States of America*.

(3.) The Jewish nation, when thus restored, *will rebuild their temple in Jerusalem after the model prescribed by Ezekiel, and will rapidly rise to national and political distinction*, etc. First.

See Ezek. xli.–xliii., inclusive. Second. Isa. xliii. 5; Zech. viii. 7, 8; Isa. lxv. 21; Jer. xxix. 5, 28; Isa. lx. 10; Amos ix. 11, 14; etc. But,

(4.) The Jews will remain *tributary* to the false Messiah, he having obtained possession of their kingdom by flatteries (Dan. xi. 21, 22); and after the league he will work deceitfully; and will forecast his devices against the strongholds (verses 23, 24), and divide the land for gain (verse 39), and select Jerusalem as his capital, etc. (verse 45, Ezek. xxviii. 2, 14); and, true to his characteristics as already portrayed, he will not only utter the most horrid blasphemies against the FATHER and the SON (verse 36, and 1 John ii. 22, 23; iv. 3; 2 John 7; Jude 4), and appropriate to himself divine honors in the temple of God (Ezek. xxviii. 2; Dan. xi. 36; Isa. xvi. 13, 14; 2 Thess. ii. 4), and establish idolatry (Dan. xi. 38, 39); but he will also deprive the Jews of their restored daily sacrifices (verse 31; ix. 27), and sorely oppress and persecute them (Dan. xi. 32–35). And, under these circumstances of his treachery, they will *revolt* against his authority (Isa. xxiv. 16), which will result,

(5.) *In his invasion of the Holy Land and the city of Jerusalem* by his confederate hosts. Isa. xiii. 4, 5; xvii. 12–14; Ezek. xxxviii. 1–17; Joel iii. 2; Zech. xiv. 1, 2; Rev. xvi. 13, 14, 16.

NOTE.—Thus, as "the house of Judah had dealt *treacherously* against their covenant God (Isa. xlviii. 8; Jer. iii. 20; v. 11), and especially in that they will have hailed the mystical Assyrian Antichrist as their MESSIAH, so will *the same measure* be meted out to them at his hand. (Matt. vii. 2.) This will constitute, preëminently, "*the time of Jacob's trouble*" (Jer. xxxi. 7; Dan. xii. 1), or that UNPARALLELED TRIBULATION predicted by our Lord, Matt. xxiv. 21; Mark xiii. 19. (See also "Sequel," pages 166–179.) But, both Jeremiah and Daniel declare that "*he shall be saved out of it.*" (See references above.) Accordingly, at this point, THE ENTIRE PROPHETIC SCENERY CHANGES. The above invasion of Jerusalem by the Antichrist and his Magogean army, *is identical with that war* waged by the beast and the kings of the earth and their armies against the rider on the white horse whose name is Faithful and True, and the armies who followed Him *from heaven* upon white horses, etc., described Rev. xix. verses 19 and 11. Hence, millenarianism teaches,

IX. That it is *in connection with this war*, that the mighty conflict takes place between the TRUE MESSIAH and his army, and the ANTICHRISTIAN USURPER of His kingly rights and his confederates, which is attended with Christ's PERSONAL AND VISIBLE MANI-

FESTATION OF HIMSELF, when "*every eye shall see Him, and they also which pierced Him, and when all the kindreds of the earth shall wail because of Him*" (Rev. i. 7). Let us now look at the events which follow this PERSONALLY VISIBLE coming of the Lord in their regular consecutive order.

1. *The destruction of the Antichrist and his Magogean army*, by Christ and His heavenly attendants. (For these latter, see 1 Thess. iv. 13–17). Then turn to, first, Isa. xiv. 10–25; Ezek. xxviii. 7, 8, and verses 21, 22; Dan. xi. 45. Second, the *manner* of their destruction, Zech. xiv. 3–5; 2 Thess. ii. 8; Rev. xix. 11–16; 17, 18, 20, 21. Third, the *extent* of their destruction, under the name of the mystical king of *Babylon*, Isa. xiv. 4–25; also of *Pharaoh*, Ezek. xxxi. 2–18. But, fourth, this destruction of the enemies of Christ and His people, though *complete* in kind, is not *total* in number. 1st, some of the *Jews* shall escape, Zech. xiv. 2, last clause, Rom. xi. 5, 28; 2d, also some of the *Gentiles*, Zech. xiv. 16.

NOTE.—The reader will here bear in mind the fact, that "the times of the Gentiles" and the Christian dispensation at the time here spoken of have *ended*, and with them the *ordinary* means of grace and salvation to man, and that the events just described transpire *at the opening* of the seventh millenary of the world.

The *erection* of the millennial kingdom had commenced with the resurrection of the dead in Christ, and the change and translation of the living saints, when He came *invisibly* as a thief in the night, and separated them as a shepherd divideth his sheep from the goats. It was *the dividing and complete ingathering of the elect Bride of Christ*, from the *wicked dead*, and the *unbelieving but still living* nations. The Bridegroom, whose near approach had been announced by the midnight cry, *had come*, and they that were ready *went in with Him* to the marriage, when, the door being shut, the others were left *without*. (Matt. xxv. 1–12.) The things set forth in this parable of the ten virgins, and further elaborated in verses 31–46, together with the intervening parable given in verses 14–30, taken as a whole, were intended to illustrate the nature and design of the Christian dispensation as "*the gospel*" of "*the kingdom of heaven*" *in mystery*, down to its termination by THE JUDGMENT-COMING OF THE LORD.

For the *details* connected with the PARTICULAR PROCESS of this "day of judgment," however, we must take into account other prophetic announcements which hold a direct relation to it. These furnish the evidence that there will be,

First, the *universal ingathering of all the redeemed, both dead and living, of all ages of the world*, at the second personal but INVISIBLE coming of the Lord, who will "be caught up together in the clouds, to meet Him in the air, and so to be ever with Him," and which is called "THE FIRST RESURRECTION." (1 Thess. iv. 13–17; Rev. xx. 4–7.)

Second, This accomplished, will be followed by the VISIBLE appearing of Christ (Rev. i. 7), accompanied by His risen and glorified saints (Zech. xiv. 5, last clause), to consume and destroy the last Antichrist and his confederates, when "the slain of the Lord shall be *many*." (Zech. xiv. 1–3 ; 2 Thess. i. 6–9; Isa. lxvi. 6.)

Third, These, being numbered among the wicked dead, "shall be *reserved* for chains under darkness against the day of judgment and perdition of ungodly men," which *final* act of judgment will not take place "until the thousand years are *finished*." (Compare 2 Pet. ii. 4–9, and iii. 7, with Jude 6, 14, 15, and Rev. xx. 5, 11–15.) Then,

Fourth, as there will be a *remnant* of the Jews, and *some that will be "left"* of the nations that invaded Jerusalem, they, together with the yet *unrestored* ten tribes of Israel, and the vast nations of *heathendom* that formed no part of the antichristian confederacy, will constitute the NUCLEUS for the peopling of the millennial earth, in analogy to the family of Noah, etc., who were preserved during the flood. And hence the next tenet in the millenarian scheme—

X. That these nations, Jewish and Gentile—the latter both nominally Christian and heathen—*will be converted to Christ, and become the mortal subjects of the earthly millennial kingdom during a thousand years*, UNDER THE PERSONAL REIGN OF CHRIST AND HIS RISEN AND GLORIFIED SAINTS. The following predictions relating to these stupendous events, will indicate the order in which they are to occur.

1. *Preliminary prophecies* of the world's conversion, etc., Isa. xxvi. 9 ; xxvii. 7–9 ; Hosea v. 15 ; the *Jews:* Jer. xxxi. 9 ; the *Gentiles:* Isa. lx. 3 ; lxvi. 18 ; see also Gen. xii. 3 ; xviii. 18 ; Ps. lxxii. 17 ; Acts iii. 25, 26 ; Gal. iv. 8.

2. *Special prophecies* of, specifying *the order* of these national conversions, and the *agencies* to be employed in effecting them. These will consist of a series of MIRACULOUS displays of the Divine power to that end.

(1.) Of the *Jewish nation*. Their conversion to take place *after* Christ's return, compare Zech. xii. 8, 9 ; Micah ii. 12, 13 ; and Ps. cii. 16 : with the *agencies* by which it will be accomplished, viz. : first, *an unprecedented outpouring* of the Holy Spirit, Joel ii. 28–32 ; second, the *personal presence* of Christ, Zech. xii. 9–14 ; Rom. xi. 26.

NOTE.—As St. Paul's conversion as a Jew was by Christ's *personal* manifestation to him (Acts ix. 3–5 ; 1 Cor. ix. 1), and he tells us that he was "as of one *born out of due time*" (1 Cor. xv. 8), it was doubtless designed as a *type* and *earnest* of the spiritual birth of the Jewish nation as it were in a day. (Isa. lxvi. 7, 8.)

(2.) Of the *Gentile nations of Christendom.* Compare Zech. xiv. 17, and Isa. xxvi. 9, with Isa. lvi. 8; lxvi. 18; lx. 3-12. *Miraculous agencies* employed in—Isa. xlix. 12, 22; lxvi. 19. These converted Gentiles shall be sent,

(3.) To the *idolatrous nations.* Compare Isa. lxvi. 18, 19, with chap. ii. 18-22, and Ps. i. 8. See also Rev. xiv. 6.

(4.) Of the conversion of the *ten tribes of Israel;* who are still captives in ASSYRIA. Compare 2 Kings xv. 29, and xvi. 9, with chap. xvii. 20. Their conversion to *precede* their return. Jer. xlvi. 27, 28; xxxi. 1-14; Ezek. xxviii. 24-26; xxxvi. 1-6; 7-15; Isa. xliv. 1, 2. Their *continental restoration follows.* See Jer. xvi. 16-21; Isa. xi. 11, 12; 14-16; lxvi. 19, 20.

(5.) The conversion of *Egypt* and *Assyria,* etc. See Isa. xix. 18-25. Consult also Isa. xi. 10; xlii. 1-17; Jer. xvi. 16-21; Micah iv. 1-5; Zech. viii. 20-23; Isa. lx. 1-10. Finally,

(6.) This work of converting the nations, Jewish and Gentile, will be accomplished in *a short period of time.* Rom. ix. 28; Matt. xxiv. 34.

Thus will be verified the prophecy, "THE KINGDOMS OF THIS WORLD ARE BECOME THE KINGDOMS OF OUR LORD AND OF HIS CHRIST; AND HE SHALL REIGN FOR EVER AND EVER" (Rev. xi. 15; see also Dan. ii. 44; vii. 13, 14, and verses 22, 27). And this leads, first, to an exhibit of,

XI. The *physical changes of the earth and heavens,* in adapting them to the millennial era of the world.

1. The earth, with its surrounding atmosphere, *will be restored to their Paradisiacal salubrity and fertility.* Compare Gen. ii. 8-14, with Ezek. xxviii. 13; xxvi. 35; Isa. li. 3; lx. 13; Ezek. xlvii. 12.

NOTE.—This is that "new heavens and earth" of the MILLENNIAL ERA predicted by Isaiah, chaps. lxv. 17-20, and lxvi. 22-24, and are the type and earnest or "*promise*" of the *post*-millennial "new heavens and earth" predicted by St. Peter and St. John. Compare 2 Pet. iii. 8-13; Rev. xxi. 1-5. (See Sequel, pages 204-216.)

2. The original curse will be removed from the *animal creation.* Rom. viii. 19-23; Isa. xi. 6-9; Isa. lxv. 25; Hosea ii. 18; Zech. xiv. 11, 20, 21.

3. *Antediluvian longevity* of human life will be restored. Compare Gen. v. 5, 27; with Isa. lxv. 20, 22, and Ps. xcii. 12.

4. The earth shall be blessed with *uninterrupted prosperity*

and national peace. Ps. lxvii. 6, 7 ; xcvi. 11-13, first clause; Isa. xxxii. 15, 16 ; xxxv. 1-7 ; lii. 9, 10 ; and ii. 4. And,

5. There will be *a new division of* Palestine among the twelve tribes, see Ezek. xlviii. Jerusalem and the Temple will be *rebuilt,* Jer. xxx. 18-24 ; xxxiii. 10-16 ; Zech. xii. 6, xiv. 11 ; Ezekiel, chapters xxxvii. 26-28, and xl. and xliii. inclusive; and building and agriculture will *flourish,* Isa. lxv. 21-24 ; lxii. 8, 9 ; lx. 6, 7. The second change relates to,

XII. The *moral* aspect of the world.

1. The knowledge of the Lord will be *diffused through the whole earth.* Ps. xxii. 27 ; Isa. xi. 9 ; Habak. ii. 14 ; Heb. viii. 10, 11.

2. The restored covenant seed of Abraham, JUDAH and ISRAEL, will be *the medium of great blessing* to all the families of the earth. Gen. xii. 2, 3 : compare Jer. xxxi. 33, 34, and Ezek. xxxvi. 24-33, and Heb. viii. 10-12, with Rom. xi. 12-15 ; Zech. viii. 20-23 ; and Micah iv. 1, 2. The third change—

XIII. *Politically*—Take the following prophecies :

1. The *national schism* between the two houses of JUDAH and ISRAEL, or the ten tribes shall be *healed.* Ezek. xxxvii. 1-14 ; 15-28 ; Isa. xi. 10-13 ; Jer. iii. 18, 19 ; xxiii. 3-8 ; Hosea i. 10, 11 ; Zech. viii. 9-15 ; Rom. xi. 25-29. And, thus again *united into one nationality,*

2. The *earthly "first dominion,"* lost by the first Adam, shall be *restored* to them. Micah iv. 8. See Gen. ii. 26 ; iii. 1-6 ; 20-24.

3. God will establish *a new covenant* with them, adapted to their regenerated state. Jer. xxxi. 31-34 ; xxxii. 39-44 ; Deut. xxx. 6 ; Ps. xxxvii. 31 ; Ezek. xi. 19, 20 ; xxxvi. 25-27 ; 2 Cor. iii. 3, 7, 8 ; Gal. v. 22, 23 ; Heb. viii. 10 ; x. 16, 17. Compare also Rom. viii. 2-8, with vii. 22.

4. There will be *a restoration of ceremonial observances, the offering of sacrifice,* etc. Jer. xxxiii. 18. Compare Ezek. xliii. 13-27, with Isa. lxvi. 21, 23 ; lvi. 3-7 ; lxi. 6. See also Ezek. xl. 38-42; and xlii. 13. Of the *priests* who are to officiate. Ezek. xliv. 10-30. See also specially verse 9. Their *observance* positively enforced. Ezek. xliii. 10, 11, and xliv. 5, 6. (See on this subject, "Sequel," pages 73-75.) And,

5. Under these circumstances of the physical, moral, and political changes of the earth and heavens and of the Jewish race, *all other nations will be subordinated to them.* Isa. lx. 3-7 ; 8-12 ;

13, 14; 15, 16; Jer. iii. 16, 17; Zech. xiv. 16-19. And, superadded to the above,

6. During the millennial era, *mankind will be exempted from the power of Satanic influence.* Rev. xx. 1-3. See also Isa. xxvii. 1. Hence,

7. *Israel's song of praises to God,* for the fulfilment of these long-deferred prophecies of their national restoration, conversion, and political preëminence in the earth. Isa. xii. 1-6.

RECAPITULATION.—We have now presented an exhibit, Ist, of those prophecies of the events that are *immediately to precede* the second personal coming of the Lord—the second universal promulgation of the Gospel as a witness among all nations; the unprecedented prevalence of formalism and apostasy in the Church, and of iniquity in the world; and the overthrow of the Papal and Mohammedan powers. IId, of that stupendous event which will *accompany* Christ's INVISIBLE return from heaven —the resurrection of the dead in Christ, and the change and translation of His living saints to meet Him in the air. And IIId, of those *subsequent* events, which transpire down to the time of His VISIBLE manifestation to all nations—the introduction upon the prophetical platform of the last Antichrist and his confederate Magogean army. The "league" entered into between him and the Jews as their acknowledged Messiah to restore them to their own land. Their restoration, rebuilding of the temple, and exalted position among the nations. Antichrist's after treachery toward them, their revolt, and his invasion of Palestine and Jerusalem, followed by the VISIBLE APPEARANCE OF CHRIST ON MOUNT OLIVET, accompanied by His risen and glorified saints. The destruction of the antichristian legions by Christ personally on the battle field of Armageddon. The escape of a remnant of the Jews and a portion of the Gentile antichristian hosts. The subsequent universal miraculous conversion of all nations to Christ; together with those signal changes in the physical, moral, and political conditions of the world, by which it is introduced into and fitted for, the millennial era. The restoration of the earth and atmosphere to a state of Paradisiacal salubrity and fertility. The removal of the curse from the animal tribes. Antediluvian longevity of human life restored. Judah and Israel reunited into one nationality, and blessed with their recovery of the "first dominion" given to man. A new covenant made with them, together with a renewal of ceremonial observances, and the subordinating to them of all other nations.

It only now remains, therefore, in the light of prophecy, to present a view of the millennial scheme in reference to—

THE ORGANIC STRUCTURE OF THE MILLENNIAL HIERARCHY.

REMARKS.—First. In analogy to other earthly kingdoms, the Millennial Kingdom must have its *King*, its *officers of state*, its *subjects*, and a *territorial domain*.

Second. Thus it was in *innocence*. "The earth and the fulness thereof," created by the self-manifested "GOD IN CHRIST"[1] as the *territorial domain* of his kingdom, and of which "they that dwell therein," viewed representatively in their federal head, were the *subjects*, were "the Lord's"[2] by rightful possession and sovereign rule.[3] Hence,

Third. The "*dominion*" given to man in Eden, was not a dominion over *his own kind*.[4] And, as his sin was an act of treason and rebellion against his only rightful sovereign, THE CHRIST OF GOD, and he was delivered over as a vassal to the Satanic usurper of his Lordly rule down to the time of the predicted "restitution of all things;"[5] when *restored* from the ruins of the fall, it will consist of his recovery to and acknowledgment of his allegiance to THE ONLY RIGHTFUL KING, the "woman's Seed," CHRIST. Or, as in the instance of Israel's abjuration of the THEOCRACY in the time of Samuel, when GOD HIMSELF WAS THEIR KING;[6] having "abode *many days*" (the mystical "seven times" of Lev. xxvi., or 2520 years—see "Sequel," pages 167–171) "without a king, or a prince, or a sacrifice, or an image, or teraphim," when they shall "*afterward* seek the Lord their God in the latter days," that THEOCRACY shall be restored to them under the reign of David's royal son, "THE PRINCE OF PEACE."[7] True, in accordance with God's convenant promise to Israel when restored to their own land—"I will restore thy *judges* as at the first, and thy *counsellors* as at the beginning,"[8] etc.; and again: "I will make thy *officers* peace, and thy *exactors* righteousness;"[9] and also that, in matters of "controversy, the *priests*, the *Levites*, the sons

---

[1] John i. 1–3; Col. i. 15–17.   [2] Ps. xxi. 1.   [3] Gen. ii. 16, 17.
[4] Gen. ii. 24, 26–28.   [5] Acts iii. 21.   [6] 1 Sam. viii.
[7] Hos. iii. 4, 5; Isa. ix. 6.   [8] Isa. i. 26.   [9] Ib., lx. 17.

of Zadok, shall stand in judgment," [1] etc., it is evident that they shall be invested with *governmental* powers. As with Israel of old, they will be constituted of a church and state union, with a ritual form of worship, and a corresponding system of government for the regulation of their civil, social, judicial, and religious affairs. But I now add,

Fourth. That when "the *first dominion* shall come to the daughter of Zion, and the *kingdom* to the daughter of Jerusalem," [2] as above, it will constitute the *lowest*, inasmuch as it will be the SUBORDINATE form of Government, under the restored THEOCRACY of Israel. I now observe, therefore, that in the organic arrangement of the Millennial Hierarchy,

I. The son of David, THE LORD JESUS CHRIST, who is to sit upon his throne, is the Divinely appointed KING, or HEAD, around which, as the source of all authority, and the Centre of Unity, all the lesser orders, like the planets around the sun, will revolve. First, compare Ps. lxxxix. 4, 5, with Acts ii. 29–35. See also Ps. xc.; Matt. xxii. 42–45; 1 Cor. xv. 25; Eph. i. 22; Heb. i. 13. Second, 2 Sam. vii. 12–16; Ps. ii. 6–12; Isa. ix. 6, 7; Jer. iii. 17; xxxiii. 17, 20, 21; Ezek. xxxiv. 23, 24; xxxvii. 24, 25; Zech. xiv. 9; Luke i. 31–33; 1 Cor. xv. 25; Heb. ii. 6–8.

All the nations of the earth, Jewish and Gentile, *shall be subjected to His Divine Authority.* Dan. ii. 44, 45; vii. 13, 14; 22, 26, 27; Isa. xxxii. 1, 17, 18; Ps. lxxii. 8–19; Micah iv. 1–7; Zech. ix. 10; Rev. xi. 15–18.

II. The raised and translated living saints *share with Christ in the government of the nations of earth.* Ps. xlvii. 3; xlix. 14; Isa. xxxii. 1; Dan. vii. 21, 22; Matt. xix. 28; Luke xix. 17, 19; xxii. 29, 30; 1 Cor. iv. 4, 5; vi. 2, 3; ix. 25; 2 Tim. iv. 8; 1 Pet. v. 4; Rev. i. 6; ii. 10, 26, 27; iii. 21; v. 10; xx. 4, 5, last clause, and verses 6, 7.

NOTE.—It is important here to observe, that as not a few writers on this subject, by confounding things which differ, have indiscriminately amalgamated those of the *mortal* with the *immortal* or resurrected state, *as equally and in the same sense the occupants of* the millennial new earth—which circumstance, by the way, more than any other, has subjected millenarians to the imputation of *Judaizing and carnalizing the future state of Christ and His glorified saints*—it becomes necessary to point out,

---

[1] Ezek. xliv. 15, 24.   [2] Micah iv. 8.

III. *The* DISTINCT PROPHETIC RELATION *that will exist between the saved nations in the flesh, and Christ and His co-reigning saints, during the millennial era.* This will involve an exhibit,

1. Of the *territorial domain* assigned to the newly erected millennial kingdom of Christ. As this "kingdom" is said to be "*under the whole heaven,*" Dan. vii. 27, of course it must be *on this earth.* Compare Isa. ix. 6, 7, with Ps. xxii. 28; and lxvii. 4; ii. 8; lxxxii. 8; Rev. iii. 21; v. 10; xx. 4, 6.

This refers to the earth, etc., as *renewed or regenerated by "fire" at the last day,* i. e., the seventh millenary of the world, in the *morning* of which it will be *partial* only, preparing it for the MILLENNIAL "new heavens and earth" state predicted by Isaiah, chap. lxv., compare verse 17, with 18, 19; and chap. lxvi., compare verse 22 with 23, 24. See also Ezek. xxxviii. 18-23; xxxix. 6. But in the *evening* of that day, it will be *total,* corresponding with the state of the "new heavens and new earth" of St. Peter and St. John. Compare 2 Peter iii. 8, with verses 9-12, and 13; and Rev. xxi. 1-5, and chap. xx. 9. This will prepare it for the ETERNAL ABODE of the redeemed.

The *distinction between these two states* of the renewed earth will appear from the following comparison. The former *will not be totally exempt* from existing evil, sin, and death, see Isa. lxv. 20, and lxvi. 23, 24: circumstances, these, *absolutely incompatible* with the latter. See Rev. xx. 1, 4; xxii. 3-5; 11, 15.

2. The *metropolis of the millennial earth.* Isa. ii. 2-4; xxiv. 23; lx. 8-14; Joel iii. 16, 17, 20; Zech. xiv. 17-21; Ezek. xliii. 7. Reference is here made to *the ancient city of Jerusalem* when rebuilt. It is to be located in the "*holy oblation or portion,*" upon the division of the land, on the *north* next to JUDAH, Ezek. xlv. 1-3; xlviii. 7, 8; 30, 31. In this city is to be erected the *new* '*sanctuary*" or *temple,* Ezek. xlv. 3; xlviii. 21. And also a "*tabernacle,*" Ezek. xxxvii. 25-27.

But there is to be *a second city,* Ezek. xlviii. 15. This "city" is located in the "holy portion" on the *south,* next to BENJAMIN, whose "border," like that of Judah, extends from east to west, verse 23.

Then there is to be *a third city,* called "THE HOLY CITY, NEW JERUSALEM," etc., Rev. xxi. 2, 10. In this "city" there is also to be a "*tabernacle,*" Rev. xxi. 3.

And finally, both Ezekiel and St. John speak of *a new river,* whose borders on either side will be lined with fruit-bearing trees, etc. Compare Ezek. xlvii. 12, with Rev. xxii. 2.

Now, an attentive perusal of the above references will show, that these three cities, together with the sanctuary, or temple, and tabernacle, and the river of Ezekiel and of the Apocalypse, *are totally separate and distinct* each from the other as it regards their respective *localities*, their *uses*, and the *order of time* in which they are to appear. As it is perfectly apparent that the " new heavens and earth " state of Isaiah, chap. lxv. and lxvi., is *pre*-millennial, and that of St. Peter and St. John, 2 Pet. iii., and Rev. xxi. 1, 5, is *post*-millennial, with the period of a thousand years intervening; so, the *first two cities*, together with the *sanctuary* or *temple*, the *tabernacle*, and the *new river* of Ezekiel, belong to the MILLENNIAL NEW EARTH STATE: while the *third city*, and the *tabernacle* and *new river* of St. John, belong to the ETERNAL NEW EARTH STATE.

But, *from the time* that Messiah VISIBLY appears to Israel, when they shall exclaim, " Lo, THIS IS OUR GOD, we have waited for Him, and He will save us: THIS IS THE LORD, we have waited for Him, we will be glad and rejoice in His salvation " (Isa. xxv. 9), the prophets declare that " JERUSALEM shall be called THE THRONE OF THE LORD " (Jer. iii. 17), and that he will " DWELL IN THE MIDST of them," etc., Zeph. iii. 14, 15; Zech. ii. 10–12; and viii. 3; Ps. cxxxv. 21; and Isa. xxiv. 23. Also, that " THE NAME OF THE CITY from that day shall be, THE LORD IS THERE " (Ezek. xlviii. 35). And again, that both Ezekiel and St. John declare that His " SANCTUARY shall be IN THE MIDST of them," and His " TABERNACLE shall be WITH MEN," etc., Ezek. xxxvii. 25–27; Rev. xxi. 3. And finally, as of the saints it is declared that they shall be " *kings* and *priests* unto God and the Lamb," so they are to " sit with Him IN HIS THRONE," and " REIGN ON THE EARTH," etc., Rev. iii. 12; and verse 21; also chap. v. 10; xx. 4.

Now, expositors, not a few, having confounded the " new heavens and earth " states of Isaiah, St. Peter, and St. John, insisting that they are *identical;* have also, first, confounded the two cities of Ezekiel with the Holy City or New Jerusalem of St. John. Second, the same with the tabernacles of Ezekiel and St. John, insisting that they are *identical* with the New Jerusalem of the latter prophet. And then, third, alleging that " the holy city, or new Jerusalem " of the Apocalypse, will be *the abode* of Christ and his co-reigning saints DURING THE MILLENNIAL ERA, from the above descriptions of their PRESENCE in the Jerusalem and second city of Ezekiel, they insist, fourth, *that all the above-named phrases refer to one and the same thing*, as denotive that THE FUTURE INHERITANCE of the raised and changed saints during the millennial era, is *identical* with that of the occupants of the earth in the flesh.

If this be so, it renders the millenarian scheme justly obnoxious to the charge, that it is a Judaizing and carnalizing the future state and condition of Christ and His glorified saints.

But, a careful discrimination between things which differ, as connected with the several cities spoken of, their occupants, the relations of rulers and the ruled as predicated of the organic structure of the millennial hierarchy, and the distinction to be drawn between the millennial and the eternal state portrayed in the above prophecies, will sufficiently evidence the *fallacy* of the above theories, and with it the *injustice* of the imputation against the millenarian scheme thence arising. To this end, it is only necessary to take into account,

1. The distinction drawn between the millennial new heavens and earth state of Isaiah, and that of St. Peter and St. John, after an intervening period of a thousand years.

2. That the two cities, together with the sanctuary and the tabernacle of Ezekiel, appertain to the *millennial* state of the renewed earth.

3. That the two cities, together with the sanctuary and tabernacle, located in the holy oblation or portion of Ezekiel, form the *metropolis of the millennial earth state*, occupied by the saved nations in the flesh. I next observe, that,

4. Between these, as the SUBJECTS of the millennial kingdom, and the Lord Jesus Christ as their KING, together with his co-ordinate immortal and glorified saints, there will be kept up *a continued intercourse* from His seat or throne "IN THE AIR" (see 1 Thess. iv. 17), AS THE CAPITAL of His universal earthly empire, onward to the period of "*the end*, when He will *deliver up*" the millennial "kingdom to God, even the Father . . . THAT GOD MAY BE ALL IN ALL." (1 Cor. xv. 24–28.)

It hence follows, that there is a wide distinction in the prophetic writings, *between the respective relations and spheres of action* of the living races of men, and of the risen and glorified redeemed Church of Christ. The former are of the *lineal multitudinous seed of Abraham*, and of the *Gentile nations* gathered unto them, during the millennial era. The latter, in virtue of their *prior* faith in Christ, who is emphatically THE "SEED" of Abraham, and who are of the "Jerusalem that is above," have a union with Zion's King that is not of an earthly, but of a *heavenly* origin, and are hence of the "*election*" according to grace, whether they be Jews or Gentiles by nature, all being ONE in Christ Jesus; so that, when they are gathered into one "at the appearing of Christ," on the morning of "the first resurrection," they will constitute the MYSTICAL BODY of the glorious Head—His SPOUSE—His BRIDE, whose high destiny is, not to be ruled over, but to *rule*, as kings and priests unto God. The scriptural meaning of the word "INHERITANCE," in its application to the two classes of the *literal* and *spiritual* seed of Abraham, will afford additional light on this important subject. Apply it,

First, To the *literal Israel* as the LORD'S inheritance. Deut. xxxii. 8, 9; Ps. cxxxv. 4.

Second, *To the land of Canaan* as THEIR inheritance, in connection with the *Gentile strangers* among them, etc. Ezek. xlvii. 13, 14; 22, 23. So on the other hand,

First. Christ has a glorious inheritance IN HIS SAINTS. Compare Eph. v. 27, with chap. i. 18, and verses 15–23 inclusive. This will be *revealed* when He appears the second time, etc. Compare Heb. ix. 28, with 2 Thess. i. 10. But,

Second. The saints also have an inheritance IN CHRIST. See Eph. i. 11–14.

Now, this "inheritance," for which the saints of the "first resurrection" have an "earnest" or title deed IN CHRIST, is entirely separate and distinct from that of the Jewish and Gentile saved nations in the flesh. It is typified by that which the *priests* and *Levites* had IN GOD under the law, as occupying the place and enjoying the privileges of the *first-born*, as the Lord spake unto Moses, Numb. iii. 12, 13; and Deut. xviii. 1, 2; and also by Ezekiel, chap. xliv. 28. With these passages, compare James i. 18; Rev. xiv. 4; Heb. xii. 23. In the enrolling of names in this last passage, allusion is made to the numbering and recording the names of the *first-born* among the Israelites, etc., Numb. iii., and chap. viii.; and, as such, they are said to be "*redeemed from the earth*," Rev. xiv. 3, i.e., in resurrection glory, Rom. viii. 23, and hence belong to Christ as his "*jewels*," Mal. iii. 17, and shall be admitted to that "INHERITANCE incorruptible, undefiled, and that fadeth not away," 1 Pet. i. 3, 4, which, now "*reserved* in heaven for them," shall be "*revealed* in the last time . . . AT THE APPEARING OF CHRIST," verses 4, 5, 7.

It is hence evident, that the elect saints—THE CHURCH OF THE FIRST-BORN—as the espoused Bride of the Lamb, *never will have an abiding inheritance upon the restored Paradisiacal* "*new earth*" *of Isaiah during the millennial era.* The reason is obvious. Those in mortal flesh, whose "inheritance" *is on the earth*, as we have seen, being of the *natural seed* of Abraham, are to some extent subject to both *sin* and *death*. Whereas the saints of the resurrection, being "heirs of God, and joint-heirs with Christ," who is the divinely constituted "HEIR OF ALL THINGS," will be exalted to resurrection life "*in the air to be ever with Him.*"

And now, as to *the mode of the intercourse* to be kept up between Christ as ZION'S KING in conjunction with the "*firstborn*" *of the resurrection* as His "kings and priests," and the *saved nations in the flesh.* Though our knowledge of it is limited, still, with the ladder in Jacob's vision present to our minds, with its foot resting on earth and its top reaching to heaven, and THE LORD standing above it, while the *angels* of God were seen *ascending and descending upon it* (Gen. xxviii. 10–13), we may consider ourselves as furnished with some useful suggestions in elucidation of this subject; and especially when we take into account the numerous statements already given of CHRIST'S PERSONAL PRESENCE with His people on earth during the millennial era, and of the statement regarding the resurrected saints, that they will be "*equal unto the angels,*" i. e., in *wisdom*, and in the powers of *locomotion*, etc., by which they will be qualified to *descend from* and *ascend to* their aerial thrones (See Rev. xx. 4), in the execution of the commands of Zion's King, among the millennial inhabitants of earth. Why, did not Jesus, in His resurrected and glorified humanity, appear among, and eat and drink with, His disciples? And when He arose, did not many of the saints which slept arise with Him and enter into the Holy City and appear unto many? Yea more, has not the earth often been trodden by angels' feet? And do we not find that everywhere in the universe of God there are ranks and degrees? Among the *angels* there is an HIERARCHY. And so also, "in the resurrection" state, "one star will differ from another star in glory." In the world to come, therefore, there will be those who *rule*, and those who are *ruled;* JESUS CHRIST, seated upon His father David's throne, swaying His righteous sceptre OVER ALL; "*the apostles*, sitting on twelve thrones, judging the twelve tribes of Israel;" and the *resurrected saints*, also enthroned; and which, taken together, will constitute that GLORIOUS MILLENNIAL HIERARCHY OR THEOCRACY OF THE WORLD TO COME, whereof we speak.

And finally, on this subject of the *intercourse* between Christ and His saints with the occupants of the millennial earth. It is not necessary, in order to meet the requirements of the prophecies in reference to it, that it should be *uninterrupted*. It may be illustrated by the condition of our blessed Lord, *during the forty days' interval between His resurrection and ascension*. He had then *no fixed habitation*, nor did He *associate with men* as He was wont to do before His crucifixion. It was *seldom* that He showed Himself even to His own disciples, and all His appearances were *miraculous*. They knew not whence He came, nor whither He went. It might be in a room, where the doors were closed, that He *suddenly stood in the midst of them*, they not perceiving *how* He obtained admittance. Or it might be on the public highway, or in the open fields, or by the seaside, that He joined their circle and their converse. But in every case they were taught that their risen Lord's resurrected human body had acquired superhuman or supernatural power of *concealment* or of *manifestation*.

As so, we are warranted to expect that THE SAINTS, when raised in their spiritualized bodies, and made *like unto Him*, shall also possess this extraordinary power as above intimated, of *appearing* and *disappearing* at will. To conclude:

5. The two cities of Ezekiel, though possessing several marks of *resemblance* (compare Ezek. xlviii. 31-34, with Rev. xxi. 12, 13), yet, besides other points of dissimilarity, while the former are to be located within the bounds of the "*Holy Oblation*," St. John saw the latter "*descending from God out of heaven*," etc., Rev. xxi. 2, 10. Besides, this follows, *in the order of time*, the creation of the POST-millennial "new heavens and earth" by the "fire" of the last conflagration. (Compare 2 Pet. iii. 7-13, with Rev. xxi. 1, 5.) This stands connected with,

6. *The closing scene of time*—the last Gog and Magog apostasy—their attempted assault upon "the camp of the saints and

the beloved city "—their destruction by "fire from God out of heaven"—the resurrection of the wicked dead when the millennial thousand years are "finished"—the assemblage of "the dead small and great" before "the great white throne"—their trial and condemnation, which have so long awaited them, even unto this "*the day of judgment and perdition of ungodly men*," when "death and hell shall be cast into the lake of fire, which is the second death;" and when "whosoever shall not be found written in the book of life, shall be cast into the lake of fire." Then will follow,

7. The great voice from heaven, saying

Behold, the tabernacle of God is with men, and he will dwell with them, and they shall be His people, and God himself shall be with them, and be their God. And God shall wipe away all tears from their eyes; and there shall be no more death, neither sorrow nor crying, neither shall there be any more pain: FOR THE FORMER THINGS ARE PASSED AWAY.

This is that ETERNAL STATE in the "new heavens and a new earth wherein dwelleth righteousness."

Trusting to the indulgence of the reader for the space occupied in the "Sequel" on this momentous subject of our blessed Lord's pre-millennial coming, in the language of St. Paul, "I commend him to God, and to the word of his grace, which is able to build him up, and to give him AN INHERITANCE among all them that are sanctified."

REPLY TO AN ARTICLE

ON

"ESCHATOLOGY,

OR THE

SECOND COMING OF CHRIST,"

IN CONNECTION WITH

THE "MILLENARIANISM OR CHILIASM OF THE ANCIENT, MEDIÆVAL, AND MODERN CHURCH," ETC.,

AS CONTAINED IN THE

REV. PROF. SHEDD'S "HISTORY OF CHRISTIAN DOCTRINE."

BY

THE REV. RICHARD CUNNINGHAM SHIMEALL,

MEMBER OF THE PRESBYTERY OF NEW YORK,

AUTHOR OF, OUR BIBLE CHRONOLOGY, HISTORIC AND PROPHETIC, DEMONSTRATED; AN ILLUMINATED SCRIPTURAL CHART OF HIST., CHRON., GEOG., AND GENEALOGY; A CHART OF UNIVERSAL ECCLESIASTICAL HISTORY; WATT'S SCRIPTURE HISTORY ENLARGED; END OF PRELACY; A TREATISE ON PRAYER, ETC., ETC.

NEW YORK:
PUBLISHED FOR THE AUTHOR,
By JOHN F. TROW, 50 GREENE STREET,
AND RICHARD BRINKERHOFF, 48 FULTON ST.
1866.

Entered according to Act of Congress, in the year 1864, by

REV. R. C. SHIMEALL,

In the Clerk's Office of the District Court of the United States for the Southern District of New York.

JOHN F. TROW,
PRINTER AND STEREOTYPER,
50 Greene Street.

CONTENTS.

	PAGES
SUMMARY OF SUBJECTS	iii–vi
PREFACE	vii, viii

CHAPTER I.

SEVERAL COLLATERAL POINTS, WHICH HAVE AN IMPORTANT BEARING ON THE MAIN SUBJECTS AT ISSUE.

SECTION I. The Dogmatical—Necessity of Defining the Two Laws of Prophetic Interpretation, the Literal and the Allegorical . . 9–21

SECTION II. The Introduction of Side Issues into these Discussions—Illustrations of 21–36

CHAPTER II.

THE DIRECT HISTORICAL VIEW, AS PRESENTED BY PROF. SHEDD, EXAMINED, ETC.

SECTION I. The Ancient Era 37–48
SECTION II. The Mediæval Era 48, 49
SECTION III. The Modern Era 49–52

CHAPTER III.

BRIEF SKETCH OF THE ORIGIN AND DEVELOPMENT OF MILLENARIANISM, ANCIENT, MEDIÆVAL, AND MODERN, IN ACCORDANCE WITH AUTHENTIC HISTORY.

Introductory Remarks 53, 54

Section I. Ancient Millenarianism.

	PAGES
I. Of the JEWISH NATION at the Time of Christ's First Advent—On What Founded	54–56
II. Of the PAGAN WRITERS—Persians, Etruscans, etc., as Founded on Tradition, Derived from the Hebrew Prophets	56, 57
III. Of the CHRISTIAN CHURCH.	
1. The *Apostolic Age*	57–59
2. The *Ancient Jewish Uninspired* Writers	59, 60
3. The *Early Post-Apostolic Era*—Barnabas—Clement of Rome—Ignatius—Polycarp—Hermas—Papias—Justin Martyr—Irenæus—The Churches of Vienna and Lyons—Melito—Tertullian—Clement as Bishop of Alexandria—Methodius—Nepos and Coracion.	60–71

Section II. Era of the Commencement of Apostasy from Ancient Chiliasm.

The Circumstances which led to it	72–75
Epiphanius—Hilary—The Augustinian Theory—Dr. Lardner—Quotation from, on the Millenarianism of the Early Ages—Chillingworth, do.—Mosheim, do.—Bp. Russell, do.—Dr. Burton, do.—Dr. Neander, do.	76–78

Section III. Millenarianism of the Mediæval Age.

Paul's predicted Apostasy—In What it was to Consist—How Promoted—Origen—Augustin—Bp. Russell on—Eunapius the Pagan—Dr. Burnet—The Augustinian Theory—Baronius—The Ancient Vaudois or Waldenses—Concessions of Romish Writers respecting Them—The Vaudois were Millenarians—Rev. Mr. Gilly and M. Peyrani, a Vaudois, in A. D. 1823, etc.	78–83

Section IV. History of the Revival of Modern Millenarianism.

The Reformation—Prof. Shedd on, etc.—Divided into Three Parts	83, 84
I. *From the Reformation*, A. D. 1517, to A. D. 1720—Examination of Prof. Shedd's Statements of—Luther—Melancthon, Piscator, Osiander, Flacius, Chytræus, Bullinger, and Pareus, adopt Luther's Views—John Calvin, etc.—All *Anti*-millenarian	84–86
Millenarianism Revived by the Anglican Reformers—Cranmer—Latimer—Ridley—An Extraordinary Coincidence—Nicene	

	PAGES
Creed—Catechism of Edward VI.—Westminster Assembly of Divines—Fox and Brightman—John Knox . . .	86–90

II. *From the Middle of the Sixteenth to the Eighteenth Century, embracing an Interval of 150 Years*—Prof. Shedd on—His Statements Examined—Joseph Mede—Dr. Wm. Twiss—Archbp. Usher—Rev. Robert Maton—Milton—James Janeway—Jeremy Taylor—Rev. Thomas Watson—Richard Baxter—and many others 90–94

III. *History of Millenarianism during the Eighteenth Century*—Peter Jurieu—Robert Fleming—Sir Isaac Newton—Increase Mather—A NEW ERA—Daniel Whitby—His "New Hypothesis"—Bp. Russell on—Whitby's Concessions to Ancient Chiliasm—State of the Churches at this Time—Rev. Alexander Pirie, A. D. 1700, Opposes the Whitbyan Theory—Cotton Mather—Edmund Wells—Charles Daubuz—John Albert Bengel—Dr. Isaac Watts—Joseph Perry—William Lowth—Sayer Rudd, M. D.—Joseph Hussey—Robert Hort—Dr. John Gill—John Wesley—Charles Wesley—John Fletcher—and others—Augustus M. Toplady—Bp. Newton—Archbp. Newcome—Dr. B. Gale—William Cowper—William Romaine—Joshua Spaulding—Robert Hall—Reginald Heber . . 94–110

CONCLUSION.

State of the Churches and of Millenarianism at the Opening of the Nineteenth Century.

Prevalence of the Whitbyan Theory—Revival of Millenarianism in England—Depressed State of, in the American Churches—Commenced Revival of—Present Prospects 111–117

NOTE A.

PAGE

Observations on the Distinction between the ECCLESIA and the APOSTASIA of the Christian Dispensation. (See Reply.) . 119–122

NOTE B.

The Millennial Era not to consist of a Moral and Physical *absolutely indefectable* State 122–125

NOTE C.

Adjustment of the *Chronological Discrepancy* between 1 Kings vi. 1, and Acts xiii. 17–22 125–132

NOTE D.

Animadversions on "*The Messiah's Second Coming*," by the Rev. Edwin E. Hatfield, D. D., New York City . . . 132–143

NOTE E.

On the *Extent* and *Results* of the Continental and Anglican Reformation from A. D. 1517 . . . . 143, 144

PREFACE.

In the "Sequel to Our Bible Chronology," Part III. was devoted to an examination of the question, Will the second coming of Christ, as an event still future, be *pre-* or *post*-millennial; and will it consist of an *allegorical* or *spiritual*, or of a *literally* corporeal or personal coming?

This subject involved an inquiry into the correctness of the popular theory of the day, which alleges the *identity* of the Christian Church with "the kingdom of the Son of Man," etc.; and of Christ's *spiritual* reign over it as King onward to the end of the millennium, when He is to personally appear at the judgment day, etc.

Against this theory, we urged two arguments: the first was founded upon the *direct* scriptural and historical proof, that there is to be *no* millennium intervening between the SECOND PERSONAL coming of Christ, and the day of judgment. And the second, upon the scriptural proof that the ideas and language of the New Testament writers in reference to the second personal coming of Christ and the judgment of the great day, were derived from, and were founded upon, the prophetic statements of the *inspired pre-Christian Jewish* writers regarding them.

But, on all these points, as we shall see, the Rev. Dr. SHEDD, in his recently published work on the "History of Christian Doctrine," joins issue with us. To this end, in his "Sixth Book" (vol. ii., pages 389–399), in which he claims to have furnished us with a "History of ESCHATOLOGY," "chapter i." treats of the "Second Coming of Christ," which he divides into two sections —"§ 1. Millenarianism," or "Chiliasm;" and "§ 2. Catholic Theory of the Second Advent," etc.[1] And in summing up the *result* of his "History" in these premises, he tells the reader—"The facts,

---

[1] See pages 389 and 398.

then, established by this account of *Millenarianism*[1] in the ancient, mediæval, and modern Churches, are the following: 1. That millenarianism *was never the ecumenical* faith of the Church, and *never entered as an article* into any of the creeds. 2. That millenarianism has been the opinion of *individuals and parties only* —some of whom have stood in agreement with the *Catholic* faith, and some in opposition to it." (See page 398.)

Now, this elaborate work, emanating from the pen of a divine so distinguished for scholarship as a minister of the Presbyterian Church (O. S.), and a Professor in the Union Theological Seminary in this city, cannot but claim the respect, and exert a most potent influence in *shaping the opinions*, of both the clergy and the laity of the churches, in accordance with the theory advocated in the above alleged historic facts.

It is this circumstance that has called forth the following Reply. We are forced to demur to both the *character* of the tenets of "Millenarianism or Chiliasm in the ancient, mediæval, and modern Churches," and to the *historic facts* by which they are attempted to be supported, as set forth in said "History of Christian Doctrine."

The method of our Reply will necessitate, first, a notice of several *collateral points*, which have an important bearing upon the main subjects at issue. These disposed of, we shall proceed, second, to an examination of the *more direct historical* view of millenarianism as presented by this writer. And third, add thereto a *brief sketch* of the origin and development of millenarianism, ancient, mediæval, and modern, in accordance with authentic history.

This combined view, *pro* and *con*, of the subject in hand, will be found to furnish the reader with all that is essential to a proper understanding of the rise, progress, and present state and prospects of millenarianism, in both its doctrinal and historical aspects.

As we write for the benefit of none but candid and unbiassed minds, we leave it for the reader to decide as to where *the truth* lay in these premises.

R. C. S.

NEW YORK, *July*, 1864.

[1] We have taken the liberty to use small capitals and italics, not found in the original text of the author.

REPLY.

CHAPTER I.

SEVERAL COLLATERAL POINTS WHICH HAVE AN IMPORTANT BEARING ON THE MAIN SUBJECTS AT ISSUE.

SECTION I.

The Dogmatical—Necessity of defining the Two Laws of Prophetic Interpretation, the Literal and the Allegorical, etc.

BEFORE entering upon the *historical facts* in these premises as alleged by this writer, it will be in place to advert to several *collateral points*, which have an important bearing upon the main subjects at issue.

The first deserving notice is, the assiduous endeavors of anti-millenarian writers to *prejudice* the mind of the reader against the system of their opponents, by a species of dogmatizing, and the introduction of side issues, in their discussions on this subject. This, we regret to say, is preëminently characteristic of the writer in hand. Take the following in illustration of the first point here indicated, viz.:

1. The *Dogmatical*. Speaking of "millenarians," Dr. Shedd says, "the testimony of history goes to show that the *literal* and *materializing* interpretations" which they "put upon the teachings of Isaiah and St. John concerning the second coming of

Christ, was not the most authoritative one" (p. 391). For that, we must look to "the Alexandrian school, under the lead of Clement and Origen," etc. (p. 395).

We introduce these quotations in this place, because of their important bearings on the question regarding the TWO THEORIES of scriptural hermeneutics, applied by millenarians and anti-millenarians, in their "interpretations" of "the teachings of Isaiah and St. John." Millenarians adopt and apply the *literal* law of interpretation; anti-millenarians, the *allegorical* or so-called spiritual law. The learned writer need not to be reminded, that these two theories of "interpretation" of the prophetic Scriptures are *absolutely antipodal*. It is, therefore, we submit, an unwarrantable assumption for either the one or the other, to attempt a settlement of the question as to which of these two laws of interpretation is "the most *authoritative* one," by a mere *ex cathedra* announcement. This may answer the purpose of reliance upon a blind and servile credulity to the mere *ipse dixit* of priestly arrogance; never as a motive of "obedience to the faith" by a reasonable appeal to a "thus saith the Lord."

Our limits will not allow of a discussion of the laws of scriptural interpretation *in extenso*. They relate to the Natural, the Typical, the Figurative, and the Symbolical portions of Scripture. It is in place here to observe, that the Scriptures everywhere abound in the *figurative* modes of speech and of writing, of which there are nine orders: 1. The Comparison or Simile; 2. The Metaphor; 3. The Metonymy; 4. The Synecdoche; 5. The Hyperbole; 6. The Hypocatastasis; 7. The Apostrophe; 8. The Prosopopœia or Personification; and 9. The Allegory or Parable. Not so with the *symbols*. They are fewer in number, and are only to be found in connection with the *prophecies* of Scripture. The difference between figures and symbols may be distinguished thus:

Figures of speech are used only for purposes of *illustration* and *ornament*. Hence, the agents or objects to which they are applied, are always the agents or subjects of the acts or qualities which they ascribe to them. And the *law* for their interpretation is, that the nominatives of the propositions which affirm the resemblances between the figure and the agents, objects, qualities, acts, or conditions of the facts set forth by them as they appear to our senses or reason, require the *language* to be taken in its natural or grammatical sense, and applied *literally*. For example:

Assyria is used by metonymy to denote, not the country, but the *inhabitants;* and the hand, by synecdoche, refers to the *person* to which the proposition respecting the hand belongs.

To *confound* the nominatives or subjects of these figures of speech with the affirmations themselves, therefore, as though, by a trope, they contained another figure, is a violation of this law. To speak of the figure *of* a figure would be absurd.

Accordingly, the advocates of the allegorical or so-called *spiritualizing* theory of interpretation, having discovered the absurdity of employing one figure to illustrate another of the same class, have resorted to the conversion of *figures* into *symbols*, as though they were the *representatives* of those of another class; the figure *or* symbol being but the *shell*, under which a mystical or *spiritual* sense, which they allege is the true sense, is to be found.

This theory of interpretation is founded on the principle, that, as the symbolical imagery of the Old and New Testaments is connected with the prophecies of events that are *still future;* and, as they allege that both figures and symbols are identical; therefore, both are to be interpreted *mystically* or *spiritually*.

Of course, then, consistency requires that *all* these prophecies should be interpreted uniformly by the same principle, or law. Take, for example, the following prophecy of Isaiah, chap. ii. 1–5: "And it shall come to pass in the last days, that the mountain of the Lord's house shall be established in the tops of the mountains, and shall be exalted above the hills, and all nations shall flow unto it. And many people shall go and say, Come ye, and let us go up to the mountain of the Lord, to the house of the God of Jacob, and he will teach us of his ways," etc. Now, here, by identifying the figurative *with* the symbolical, in the application of the above theory to this prophecy, the *subjects* of which the affirmations are made, namely, "the *mountain* of the Lord's house"—"*all nations* shall flow into it"—"*many peoples*"—"Jehovah's *house*," etc., are all interpreted and applied in a mystical or spiritual sense, to denote the *conversion* of the Gentiles to the Christian faith, and their *ingathering* into the Christian Church, etc. Then let the reader place beside this, all that numerous class of prophecies in both Testaments which foretell the *various judgments* which were to overtake the Jewish nation on account of their sins. Take, for example, that of our Lord, Luke xxi. 24: "And ye shall be *led captive into all nations,* and Jerusalem shall *be trodden down of the Gentiles until the times of the Gentiles be fulfilled.*" What now? Is *this* prophecy interpreted by our allegorists in a mystical or spiritual sense? So far from it, there is not one of them who does not interpret it *literally!*

And, reader, it is this *inconsistency* in the application of their own rule of interpreting the prophecies, which forms the great stumbling-block in the way of the Jew. He says to them, "You Protestants take all those prophecies which point out that long train of *calamities* that were to overtake our race on account of their rebellions against God, and interpret them *literally.* And you are right. But when you come to those numerous *precious promises of our future* national restoration, reconciliation, and preëminency and peace in our own dear Palestine under the reign of MESSIAH, straightway you take and apply them *spiritually,* as belonging to you Gentiles!" Consistency, thou art a jewel! But perhaps Dr. Shedd will explain.

Having thus briefly defined the nature and office of figures, together with the law for their interpretation, we next observe that, on the other hand,

SYMBOLS, instead of being mere names or predicates of agents or objects, etc., are *themselves* agents, objects, qualities, acts, conditions, or effects, that are used as representatives of agents, etc., etc., generally of a different but resembling class. Thus: in Daniel's vision, the four wild beasts are employed as *prophetic representatives* of cruel, bloody, and destroying men; powerful and ferocious creatures in the animal world, that preyed on inferior beasts, being put in the place of men in the *political* world, of a *corresponding* character toward mankind; and the destructive acts of the one employed to *represent* the resembling acts of the other. The reverse of this is seen in the passage, Isa. ii. 1–5 · "The mountain of the Lord's house"—"all nations flowing into it"—"many peoples"—"Jehovah's house," etc., are an assemblage of beautifully appropriate *figures,* setting forth what shall *literally* transpire in relation to God's covenant people, the Jews, when, again *restored* to their own land, "the Lord shall arise upon them, and His glory shall be seen upon them," etc. For, then shall the "*all nations,*" i. e., "the Gentiles, come to *their* light, and *kings* to the brightness of *their* rising." Yea, then "the abundance of the sea shall be *converted unto them ;*

the forces (or wealth, marg.) of the Gentiles shall come unto *them,*" the figures *illustrating* the things signified.[1]

And this brings us to the special design of these remarks on the two above-named theories of interpretation. It is this: we affirm, and herewith challenge refutation, that *prior* to the time of " Clement and Origen, of the Alexandrian school," the former of whom flourished between A. D. 188 and 218, and the latter between A. D. 204 and 254, the allegorical or spiritual law of interpreting the prophecies *was totally unknown to the Church.* Clement first laid the foundation, upon which Origen reared the superstructure, of that allegorical or spiritual theory of scriptural interpretation, which soon swept away almost the last vestiges of that *original law of literal* interpretation which, till their time, had been followed by the Church, both Jewish and Christian. Every ecclesiastical scholar knows that the mind of Origen became early and deeply imbued and corrupted from the simplicity of the gospel, through his passionate fondness for the Platonic philosophy. So completely did he *Platonize* Christianity, that there was left of it scarcely the semblance of its original features. History ascribes to him the following, among his other errors: he asserted the inequality of the Father and the Son, in which respect he may be considered as a forerunner of *Arius.* He indulged in the most ambiguous and inadequate expressions concerning the work of redemption, making but faint and *indefinite* mention of the incarnation, life, and sufferings of Christ, His sacrifice and satisfaction, and the forgiveness of sins. He also maintained the mutual relation of human power and divine grace, on which point he paved the way for the doctrine of *Pelagius.* He also resolutely denied the eternity of future torments, and taught, in accordance with the views of *Plato,* that the souls of good men will hereafter (i. e., at the day of judgment) pass through a *purgatorial* fire. That he was distinguished as much for his profound scholarship as for his zeal in defending and propagating his various tenets, no one will deny. But, it was not until A. D. 232, that, having matured his NEW THEORY OF INTERPRETATION, he urged its adoption by the Church with all the energy of his exalted genius.

His theory was founded on the *principle* that, as he alleges, "the source of many evils lies in adhering to the literal and external part of Scripture;" therefore, "the true meaning of the

[1] See D. N. Lord's Essay on the Characteristics and Law of Proph. Interp. Theol. and Lit. Journal.

sacred writers was to be sought in a mysterious or *hidden* sense. Hence, as a disciple of *Plato* (whose philosophical system was a sort of compound of Paganism, Judaism, and Christianity), having committed himself to the guidance of a fanciful imagination in his expositions of Scripture, he substituted the allegorical or mystical in the place of the literal, as the standard rule of interpretation. This latter law of interpretation, the *literal*, we repeat, was the *only* principle that had been applied in the exposition of the Old Testament prophecies, together with those of Christ and His apostles, by the whole Church, pre-*Jewish*-Christian, *Apostolic*, and *early post*-Christian, down to his time! And we now affirm, that the circumstance which mainly led Origen to adopt his new theory of interpretation, was *his* stern and unbending opposition to "Chiliasm," or the doctrine of *the pre-millennial personal reign of Christ on earth over the saved nations in the flesh for a thousand years*, as founded upon the *literal* interpretation of prophecy.

The consequence has been, *the loss*, to the Christian Church, at least for the most part, until the time of the Reformation, of this the only true law of scriptural hermeneutics, and with it, the "Chiliasm" or millenarianism of the "ancient, mediæval, and modern Church," from the close of the fourteenth century to this day, together with her subjection to all the evils of an unbridled fancy in the interpretations of God's word.

But I would not call upon the reader to receive so momentous and emphatic an averment as the above, on the authority of *my ipse dixit*. I will therefore take the liberty to place beside the Rev. Dr. Shedd, the testimony on this point of the three following writers, all of whom are held in the *highest repute* by the whole Protestant Church, namely, Luther, the great reformer, and the two standard ecclesiastical historians, Mosheim and Milner.

1. LUTHER. He says: "That which I have so often insisted on elsewhere, I here once more repeat, viz., that the Christian should direct his first efforts toward understanding the *literal* sense (as they call it), which *only* is the substance of faith and of Christian theology: and which *alone* will sustain him in the hour of trouble and temptation; and which will triumph over sin, death, and the gates of hell, to the praise and glory of God. The *allegorical* sense," he adds, "is commonly uncertain, and by no means safe to build upon; forasmuch as it usually depends on *human opinion and conjecture only*, on which, if a man lean, he will find it no

better than an Egyptian reed. Therefore ORIGEN," he continues, together with "Jerome, and similar of the fathers, *are to be avoided*, with the whole of the Alexandrine school, which, according to Eusebius, formerly abounded in that [the allegorical] interpretation. For," says Luther, "later writers having unhappily followed their too much praised and prevailing example, it has come to pass that men *make just what they please* of the Scriptures, until some accommodate the word of God to the most *extravagant* absurdities; and (as Jerome complains, even in his own times), they extract from Scripture *a sense repugnant* to its meaning: of which offence, however, Jerome himself was also guilty."[1]

2. DR. MOSHEIM. This ecclesiastical historian says: "After the encomiums we have given to ORIGEN.... it is not without a deep concern we are obliged to add that he also, by an unhappy method, opened a secure retreat for all sorts of errors which a *wild* and *irregular imagination* could bring forth." After noticing that he had abandoned the literal sense, and divided the hidden (i. e., the allegorical) into moral and mystical, he adds, "a prodigious number of interpreters, both in this and succeeding ages, *followed the method of* ORIGEN, though with some variations; nor could *the few*, who explained the sacred writings with judgment and a true spirit of criticism, oppose with any success the *torrent of allegory* that was overflowing the Church."[2]

3. DR. MILNER. This writer, in his Ecclesiastical History, says: "No man, not altogether unsound and hypocritical, *ever injured the Church more than* ORIGEN *did*. From the *fanciful mode of allegory* introduced by him, and uncontrolled by scriptural rule and order, arose a *vitiated* method of commenting on the sacred pages (which has been succeeded by a contrary extreme, viz., a contempt of types and figures altogether); and in a similar way," he adds, "Origen's fanciful ideas of letter and spirit, tended to remove from men's minds *all just conceptions* of genuine spirituality. A thick mist *for ages* pervaded the Christian world, supported and strengthened by his *allegorical* manner of interpretation. The learned alone were considered for ages implicitly to be followed; and the vulgar, *when the literal was hissed off the stage*, had nothing to do, but to follow their authority wherever it led them."[3]

---

[1] Annot. in Deut. cap. l. folio 55.
[2] Mosheim's Eccles. Hist., Cent. III., Part II., sec. v–vi.
[3] Milner's Eccles. Hist. vol. i. p. 409.

With these facts in view, we appeal, first, How are "the teachings of Isaiah and St. John"—and to which we would add, those of Daniel and all the other prophets—to be understood, separate from a determination of the question regarding THE RULE by which they are to be interpreted? And we appeal, second, whether we have not made good our statement, that, *prior* to the time of "Clement and Origen of the Alexandrian schools," between A. D. 188 and 254, the literal law of interpretation was *the only law* of prophetical exegesis known to the Church? We have seen when, and with whom, and the circumstances under which, the allegorical, mystical, or spiritual theory of interpreting "the teachings of Isaiah and St. John" *originated;* that it sprang from an amalgamation of the Christian with the *Platonic* system of "science falsely so called,"[1] at the hand of the renowned Origen, in the early part of the third century; who, we have shown, *in consequence*, laid the foundation for the introduction into the Church of the worst forms of error and heresy—Arianism, Pelagianism, Romish purgatory, and Restorationism. And finally, these statements have been confirmed by the united testimony of three acknowledgedly standard writers. Luther affirms that "the literal sense *only* is the substance of faith and of Christian theology;" that "the allegorical sense is commonly *uncertain*, as it usually depends on human opinion and conjecture only;" and that, therefore, Origen as the father of it, with others, "is to be *avoided*, with the whole Alexandrian school," etc.; and that for the reason, that it leads "to the most *extravagant* absurdities," and "extracts from Scripture a sense *repugnant* to its meaning;" while Dr. Mosheim declares that Origen, "by an *unhappy method*, opened a secure retreat for all sorts of errors which a wild and irregular imagination could bring forth;" and Dr. Milner, that "no man *ever injured* the Church more than Origen did," from whose "fanciful mode of allegory, arose a *vitiated* method of commenting on the sacred pages," and by which ultimately "the literal was hissed off the stage."

And hence, another appeal. Third. Should not a writer, claiming to give a true and faithful "History of Christian Doctrine," *Ancient, Mediæval,* and *Modern* (and especially on the momentous subject of "Eschatology," or "*the second advent of Christ*," in connection with an account, particularly, of early post-

[1] Tim. vi. 20.

apostolic "Millenarianism" or "Chiliasm"), have clearly and distinctly pointed out *which of the two laws*, the literal or the allegorical, had *precedence* in the Church? From what we have said on this subject, it cannot but be obvious to the plainest mind, that the *entire merits* of the points at issue between millenarians and anti-millenarians, hinges on the important question as to the *legitimate* law by which "the teachings of Isaiah and St. John" are to be interpreted. And this depends solely upon the historic fact, as to which of the two theories of interpretation, the literal or the allegorical, *had prevailed* in the pre-Christian-Jewish, the Apostolic, and the early post-Apostolic Church. On this point we have most emphatically affirmed and proved, that it was exclusively the *literal* law of prophetic interpretation, and that it remained so until it was supplanted by the Platonico-Christianized sophistry of Origen.

But, the only allusion made to this subject by the learned Professor, is the following: speaking of "the later-Jewish doctrine of the Messianic kingdom upon earth," he says, p. 389, "The Jews *at the time* of the incarnation were expecting a personal prince, and a corporeal reign, in the Messiah who was to come." Well, of course, then, *they* were *literalists.* The Professor adds: "And one of the principal grounds of their rejection of Christ was the fact that he represented the Messiah's rule as a *spiritual* one in the hearts of men, and gave *no* countenance to their literal and materializing interpretation of the Messianic prophecies." He continues: "The *disciples* of Christ, being themselves Jews, were at first naturally infected with these views, and it was not until *after* the Pentecostal effusion of the Holy Spirit which so enlarged their conceptions of the kingdom of God, and with which their inspiration properly begins, that they *rose above* their early Jewish education. In *none* of their inspired writings do we find such an expectation of Christ's speedy coming as prompted the question: 'Lord, wilt thou at *this* time restore the kingdom to Israel?'" etc. (p. 390).

Our reply to the above is this: the phrase "Messianic prophecies," takes in its scope "*all* that was written in the law of Moses, and in the Psalms, and in the Prophets, concerning Christ."[1] Now, "the later-Jewish doctrine of the Messianic kingdom upon earth" which prevailed among "the Jews at the time of the incar-

---

[1] Luke xxiv. 44.

nation," was *founded upon* those prophecies. The question is, were they in *error*, in looking for a literal verification of them when Christ appeared to the nation at his first coming? The writer under review maintains that they were. "Christ represented the Messiah's rule as a *spiritual* one in the hearts of men, and gave *no* countenance to their literal and materializing interpretation of the Messianic prophecies," etc.

Beg pardon, Doctor. In the first place, it is undeniable that Christ, who declares that He was "born a King,"[1] was *literally* present as such among these "later Jews." In the next place, it is very reasonable to expect from this circumstance that they should be "*naturally infected*" with the idea that He came to set up that *literal* kingdom foretold in Daniel, chap. ii. 44, and vii. 13, 14, and in numerous other places, over which He, as "the son of David," who was to "sit upon his" (David's) "throne,"[2] should "rule." Now, we deferentially *deny* that either our Lord or the "inspired writers" *ever* discountenanced, by word or deed, "the later-Jewish doctrine," in its *most literal sense*, "of the Messianic kingdom upon earth." Otherwise, how are we to account for His triumphant entry into Jerusalem, unresisted and unreproved by our Lord, amid the acclamations of the people, "*Hosanna:* blessed is He that cometh in the name of the Lord;" "blessed be the *kingdom* of our father David;" and "blessed be the *King* of Israel that cometh in the name of the Lord."[3] Was this giving "*no* countenance to their *literal* interpretation of the Messianic prophecies?"

Again: *After* the resurrection of Christ, when the disciples said to Him, "Lord, wilt thou at *this* time restore the kingdom to Israel?" (Acts i. 6), so far from treating their expectation of a literal king and kingdom under their Messiah as an *error*, He simply intimated to them that *the time* of its manifestation was not yet come. "It is not for *you* to know the times or the seasons, which the Father hath put in His own power" (verse 7). They, as His "*witnesses*," were to await their endowment with "power," by the descent upon them of "the Holy Ghost" on the day of Pentecost, and to preach the gospel "both in Jerusalem, and in Judea, and in Samaria, and unto the uttermost parts of the earth" (verse 8); for, "this *gospel of* the kingdom must be preached in all the world for a witness unto all nations; and *then* shall the end come." (Matt. xxiv. 14.) The end of what? Surely, not the

---

[1] John xviii. 37.   [2] Acts ii. 30.   [3] See Matt. xxi. 9, 15; Mark xi. 9, 10; John xii. 13.

end of the *millennial era.* For, as a prolonged punishment of the *nation* for having rejected and crucified the Lord, following the destruction of their city and polity by the Romans in A. D. 70, those of them that escaped the edge of the sword were to be "led captive into all nations, and Jerusalem to be trodden down of the Gentiles."—How long? " *Until the times of the Gentiles be fulfilled.*" (Luke xxi. 24.) Well, and what then? Why, St. Paul, when speaking of the *literal* Israel, having said that "there is a remnant according to the election of grace," and that, "as touching the election, they are beloved for the fathers' sakes" (Rom. xi. 5, 29); and also, that " blindness *in part* is happened to Israel, until the fulness of the Gentiles be come in," (verse 25), he adds, "and so, all Israel shall be saved: as it is written" (Isa. lix. 20), " *There shall come out of Zion* THE DELIVERER, *and shall turn away ungodliness from Jacob,*" etc. (verse 26). And Prof. Shedd himself says, page 398, that "the Jews" shall be "converted to Christianity," *after* " the fulness of the Gentiles be brought in " (Rom. xi.). But he also says (same page), " The *personal* coming of Christ . . . is not to take place *until the final day of doom;* until the gospel has been preached ' unto the uttermost parts of the earth,' " etc. And, as "the final day of doom" is not to take place until the *close* of the millennial era, so " the gospel is to be preached to the close of the *same era!* "

With the preceding facts as a whole, therefore, kept in view, taking it for granted that the Rev. Professor admits that the terms "Israel," " Jacob," "Jew," etc., are to be understood *literally,* we respectfully ask, first, by what law of interpretation does he deny that " the Deliverer," who "turns away ungodliness from Jacob," is not also to be understood *literally ?* Again: as the Professor says that the *Jews* are to be converted to Christianity *after* " the fulness of the Gentiles be brought in ; " and as, in addition to this, the *Gentiles* also are "to come to their light, and kings to the brightness of their rising," by their being "converted unto them" (see Isa. lx. 3, 5); our next question is, How is this to be reconciled with our Lord's prophecy, that the Jews are to be " *led captive* into all nations, and Jerusalem to be *trodden down* of the Gentiles until the times of the Gentiles be *fulfilled,*" *if* that period is not to end " until the final day of doom ? " In other words, *by what Gentile nations* are the Jews to be oppressed and Jerusalem trodden under foot *down to* " the final day of doom," when they, together with the Jews, are *all* to be "converted" *after* "the fulness of the Gentiles be brought in?"

The reader will readily perceive, that the only escape from this dilemma is to be found in the following inferences: 1. That as the conversion of the Jews and Gentiles is to take place "*after* the fulness of the Gentiles be brought in,*"* the millennium, during which "there shall be *nothing to hurt or destroy* in all God's holy mountain,"[1] must come in *between* the close of that period and "the final day of doom." And 2. That, as the whole Church admits that the second *personal* coming of Christ is to take place *at the close* of "the times of the Gentiles," that second personal coming *must be* PRE-millennial. Will the Professor please answer?

Then further. The above will help to clear away the mist which surrounds the learned Doctor's statement, page 389, that "Christ represented the Messiah's rule as a *spiritual* one in the hearts of men," etc. The meaning here is, that the term "*rule*" is to be taken in the sense of Christ's spiritual reign *as King* in and over the CHRISTIAN CHURCH as His *kingdom*, DURING the times of the Gentiles down "to the final day of doom."

Beg pardon, Doctor. And to explain, we submit to his candid consideration the following: First. In the adorable Trinity, the FATHER, in the plan of human redemption, sustains to it the relation of Rectoral Head. The SON, that of Mediator. The HOLY SPIRIT, that of Regenerator and Sanctifier. Second. The SON, in His work as Mediator, sustains the threefold office of Prophet, Priest, and King. 1. As a *Prophet*, He taught the people during His public ministry. As a *Priest*, combining in His God-man-hood both the antitypal altar and the victim, He made an atonement for sin. But His *office* of priesthood did not *end* there. In analogy to the entrance of the Levitical high priest into the most holy place in the tabernacle and temple, to *intercede* for the people; so, as "the High Priest of our profession," at His ascension, "He entered into the holiest of all," "into heaven itself,"[3] "there to make *intercession* for us at the right hand of God;"[4] thence "expecting, *until* His enemies be made His footstool."[5] In other words, though "born a King," "THE KING OF THE JEWS," yet, in analogy to the "nobleman" in the parable, whose citizens, hating him, and sending a messenger after him, saying, "We will not have this man to reign over us," "took his journey into a far

---

[1] Isa. xi. 9. [2] Heb. iii. 1. [3] Heb. ix. 24. [4] Heb. vii. 25. [5] Heb. xvi. 3.

country to receive a kingdom and to return;"[1] so our blessed Lord. He is now *a King in exile*. And, until He *receives* His kingdom at the hand of "the Ancient of Days," as described by Daniel, chap. vii. 13, 14, and *returns* to "set it up" (Dan. ii. 44), He *cannot* exercise His kingly prerogatives over the nations. Meanwhile, during His *personal absence from* the Church, the door is opened for the exercise, third, of the *special* office-work of the Holy Spirit, which He "shed down" upon the Church "on the day of Pentecost,"[2] and whose office-work is "to receive" of the things that are Christ's, and to "show them unto us,"[3] by the application of the benefits of His atonement to our souls. Hence, *during* the Christian dispensation, or "the times of the Gentiles," whilst the Jewish nation, as such, for the time *is set aside*, "Simeon hath declared how God at the first did visit the Gentiles, *to take out of* (or from among) *them* a people for His name,"[4] as "the spouse," or "BRIDE of the Lamb."[5] It results, therefore, that the present dispensation is "the kingdom of God in *mystery ;*" the time during which "the gospel of the kingdom is to be preached to all nations," for the purpose above indicated. Doctor, is this orthodox? Please answer.

We now pass to the next characteristic of this writer, in his attempts to prejudice the mind of the reader against millenarianism. This will appear under

SECTION II

THE INTRODUCTION OF SIDE ISSUES INTO THESE DISCUSSIONS.

We adduce the following in evidence:

1. This learned writer brands the system of millenarianism as a "*materializing*" of the "teachings of Isaiah and St. John concerning the second coming of Christ," page 391. He says, that they "subject them to *a very sensuous* exegesis," etc., page 392. He also represents "Nepos and Coracian" as "advocating *a very gross form* of millenarianism in the diocese of Dionysius, bishop of Alexandria," etc., page 395. He further affirms, that "during the middle ages, it can hardly be said to have had *any existence*

---

[1] Luke xix. 12. [2] Acts ii. 1-4. [3] John xvi. 14. [4] Acts xv. 14. [5] Rev. xxi. 9.

as a doctrine, though at the close of the tenth century there was an undefined fear and expectation among the masses that the year 1000 would witness the advent of the Lord." Also, that "in the period of the Reformation, millenarianism made its appearance in connection with the *fanatical and heretical* tendencies that sprang up along with the great religious awakening," etc., page 396. And finally, he makes millenarianism identical with "the system of the *Judaistic-Gnostic Cerinthus,* the contemporary and opponent of the apostle John," page 390; and also with the "tenets held by the *Anabaptists,*" etc., page 396. And yet, speaking "of the apostolical fathers," he says, "only Barnabas, Hermes, and Papias exhibit in their writings *distinct traces* of this doctrine, the latter teaching it in its *grossest* form, and the first two holding it in a *less* sensuous manner," etc., page 390. And again, referring to "Cyprian," he says, that he "maintains the millenarian theory with his usual candor and moderation." That is, as we take it, "Cyprian," "Barnabas and Hermes were *less* materializing," *less* "gross in form," and *less* "fanatical and heretical" in the system of millenarianism which *they* "maintained," than Papias and the others!

In what, then, we ask, does the *difference* between the *two classes* of millenarians, as implied in the last quotations, consist? Surely, the reader should have had the benefit of a well-defined distinction, if there be one, on the subject of the "*Eschatology*" of "Millenarianism" or "Chiliasm," at the hand of a writer claiming to give a fair and impartial "history of Christian doctrine." The only light, however, that the writer has been pleased to reflect on this subject, is the following: "Some Millenarians have stood in *agreement with the Catholic faith*, and some in *opposition* to it," page 398. Is this, then, intended by the writer as a concession that millenarianism forms *a part* of "the Catholic faith?" To determine this point, let us turn,

First, to his *definition* of millenarianism. "Millenarianism, or Chiliasm," he says, "is the doctrine of two resurrections (Rev. xx.); the first, that of the righteous dead at the time of the second advent of Christ, and the second, that of the righteous and the wicked dead at the end of the world; and a personal and corporeal reign of Christ between them of a thousand years, upon the renovated earth." (Page 389.) Again: "Irenæus and Tertullian give glowing descriptions of the millennial reign. Antichrist, with all the nations that side with him, will be destroyed. All earthly empires, and the Roman in particular, will be overthrown. Christ will again appear, and will reign a thousand years in corporeal presence on earth, in Jerusalem, which will be rebuilt and made the capital of His kingdom. The patriarchs, prophets, and all the pious, will be raised from the dead, and share the felicities of His kingdom. The New Jerusalem is depicted in the most splendid colors. The metaphors of Isaiah (liv. 11, 12) are treated as proper names. Irenæus describes the foundations of the rebuilt Jerusalem as *literally* carbuncle and sapphire, and its bulwarks crystal; and regards it as *actually* let down from heaven, according to Rev. xxi. 2. (Pages 292, 393.)

Now, we presume the Rev. Doctor will admit that Barnabas and Hermes, and even Papias, together with Irenæus and Tertullian, were among the "*some* who stood in agreement with the Catholic faith?" and yet, so far as their *millenarianism* is concerned, he places them in the *same* category with the heretic Cerinthus of the first century, the deluded "masses" of the tenth century, and the " fanatical and heretical Anabaptists " in the early part of the sixteenth century! For, having told us there is an "*affinity* between millenarianism and the *later*-Jewish idea of the Messiah and His kingdom," i. e., "*at the time* of the incarnation;" and that "it appears *first* in the system of the Judaistic-Gnostic Cerinthus," at the close of the first century" (pp. 389, 390), etc.; this very learned divine and theological Professor tells us that *this* is the "materializing," "very gross," and "fanatical and heretical" system of "exegesis" to which "Christ gave *no* countenance!" Ay, and more than this: inasmuch as the millenarianism of the "*modern* Churches" is, in all its essential features, precisely the same with that of the "*ancient*," as alleged to have been the "*invention* of Cerinthus " (p. 394); to those who have adopted it "in union with an intelligent and pious orthodoxy," as given by this writer; e. g., "Delitzsch and Auberlin, in Germany; and by Cumming, Elliott, and Bonar, in Great Britain," (p. 397), we can add to the list of this learned author of the " History of Christian Doctrine," the following:

Baillie says of the *Westminster divines* (1643), that " the *most* of the chief divines here, not only the Independents, but others, such as Twisse, Marshall, Palmer, and many more, are *avowed chiliasts* (i. e., millenarians)." And so *after* them, Dr. John Gill,

Bishops Clayton, Horsley, Newton, and Newcome, Dr. Greswell, Dr. Hopkins, Dr. Thomas Chalmers, J. Knight, A. Toplady, Sir Isaac Newton, Frere, Cuninghame, Edward Bickersteth, Burgh, Fry, Gurdlestone, Hooper, Melville, McNeil, Pym, and the eloquent Robert Hall, who, on his deathbed, regretted that he had not preached the millenarian views that he had entertained. And to these may be added the following *American* divines: the late Bishops Henshaw and Meade, the living Bishops Hopkins of Vermont, McIlvaine of Ohio, and Southgate of this city, together with Drs. S. H. Tyng, Francis Vinton, etc., of the Protestant Episcopal Church, and Drs. C. K. Imbrie, R. McCartee, W. R. Gordon, J. T. Demarest, and many others of the different Protestant Evangelical Churches.

Surely the reader, and especially those *living* divines named above, must be specially indebted to the very charitable estimate made by the learned Professor Shedd of their "intelligent and pious orthodoxy." For, be it observed, their "materializing," "gross," and "fanatical and heterodox exegeses" of "the teachings of Isaiah and St. John concerning the second coming of Christ," are all alleged to be traced to their "*literal* interpretation of the Messianic prophecies!" Ay, gentlemen, and if you want ample proof of it, the Professor informs you, page 393, that "Irenæus cites with approbation from Papias the statement, that there would be vines having 10,000 branches, and each branch 10,000 boughs, and each bough 10,000 shoots, and each shoot 10,000 clusters, and each cluster 10,000 berries, and each berry would yield 25 measures of wine." Verily, Professor, a tolerably large vine, this! But we suppose that the literalizing fanatic Papias had in his eye the *Mosaic* account of those "grapes of Eshcol, *one cluster*" of which, gathered from Canaan by the spies, was "borne between *two men upon a staff*," who reported, "*This is the fruit of it.*"[1] Then, too, we may suppose that Papias also took into his reckoning the difference between the fruit-bearing productiveness of the vine of Canaan *in the time* of Moses, compared with what it will be when the millennial heavens and earth will be *restored* to their paradisiacal salubrity and fruitfulness. This, however, by the way. The Professor goes on: "Irenæus," he tells you, "describes the rebuilt Jerusalem as *actually* let down from heaven, according to Rev. xxi. 2;" and

[1] Num. xiii. 23, 27.

adds: "Tertullian puts the same interpretation with Irenæus upon this text, and for confirmation refers to the report, that in the Parthian war, in Judea a city was observed to be lowered down from the sky every morning, and to disappear as the day advanced," etc. (page 393). Wonderful! But we suppose this to be about on a footing with the alleged "vision of the cross in the heavens" to the Emperor Constantine the Great in A. D. 311, and which it is presumed the Professor, in common with the Christian Church generally, regards as having *literally* taken place.

But let us suppose, reader, that the *facts* above narrated of Papias and Irenæus are true. Does that prove that the doctrine of *millenarianism*, taken as a whole, is false? The Professor himself concedes that they were *orthodox* in all other respects. Why then should millenarianism as advocated by them be condemned in the score, because, forsooth, a fervid imagination may have betrayed them on some points into a substitution of the *ideal* for the *real?* It is, after all, simply a question of *interpretation*, and no one will pretend that the ancient fathers of the Church were infallible. We think that Papias's estimate of the millennial vine and grapes, even with the "one cluster" brought by the spies from "Eshcol" in Canaan present to his mind, savors rather of the fanciful than the actual. And as to "the rebuilt Jerusalem" being "actually let down from heaven," as alleged of the interpretation of Irenæus, it obviously arises from his having *confounded* the holy city, Jerusalem, as "*rebuilt*" upon the restoration of the Jews to their own land, with that "holy city, *new Jerusalem*," which St. John, Rev. xxi. 2, 10, declares he "saw coming down or descending out of heaven from God," and which he describes "descending *as*," or *like unto*, "a bride adorned for her husband." This latter is a figure of speech; and it is *literal*. It follows therefore that the thing illustrated by it must be literal also. Else what is the meaning of the additional words, "Behold, the tabernacle of God *is with men*, and he will *dwell with them*, and they shall be his people, and GOD HIMSELF shall be *with them*, and be their God?" While, therefore, "the rebuilt Jerusalem" will constitute the metropolis or "*capital* of his [Christ's] kingdom on earth" (p. 393), the seat or *throne* of His empire, in conjunction with His risen and translated living saints, will be "*in the air.*" (See 1 Thess. iv. 13–17.) And, to those who would still persist in adhering to the *allegorical* Origenic rule of "exegesis" of the above passage against the literal, we will leave them to settle the matter in dispute as best they may, with the statements made respecting them by Luther, Mosheim, and Milner, in a preceding page.

We now proceed to another point, in connection with the learned Professor's side issues.

2. This consists of his endeavor to *lower the claims* of the ancient fathers to the respect and confidence of the reader, by representing them as "by no means of such a weight of character and influence, as would entitle them to be regarded as the principal or sole *representatives* of orthodoxy. On the contrary," he says, "these minds were comparatively uninfluential, and their writings of little importance. The ecclesiastical authority of Clement of Rome, Ignatius, and Polycarp, is certainly *much greater* than that of Barnabas, Hermes, and Papias" (p. 391). And yet, he says of these latter fathers, that their "*general catholicity* [or orthodoxy] was acknowledged" (ib.). And again: quoting from "Eusebius," who "describes the opinion of *Papias*," although the writer says that "he was very limited in his comprehension, as is evident from his discourses;" he nevertheless adds, "yet he was *the cause why most writers*, urging the antiquity of the man, were carried away by a similar opinion, as, for instance, Irenæus, or any other that adopted similar sentiments" (pp. 395, 396).

The above, reader, is a fair specimen of the summary manner in which the millenarianism of these ancient fathers, and especially that of *Papias*, is attempted to be got rid of by those who do not admit the doctrine. They represent that this doctrine originated in the literal and materializing notions of men warped by *Jewish* prejudices, of whom Papias, a person of shallow mind and weak judgment, is selected as a *specimen;* and then produce an extract from a writer who lived 200 years *after* him (and he a zealous opponent of the doctrine), together with others in the third, fourth, fifth, and sixth centuries—as Origen, Ambrose, Hilary, Chrysostom, Jerome, and Augustine—to denounce it as *heretical!*

Keeping in view, then, the fact that we have not yet reached the *historic* question regarding the origin of millenarianism, we observe, that if it were some difficult, abstruse, metaphysical matter—the mysteries of the Divine existence, or the dark and intricate plan of God's providential government of the world—that were involved in these premises, there might perhaps be some ground for calling in question *Papias's* capacity to cope with them.

At the same time, considering that his critics, both ancient and modern, measure his mental capacities through optics *jaundiced* by a deeply seated prejudice against his system, their testimony, we submit, should be received with some degree of caution.

What then is that system? Why, simply this: St. John tells us, Rev. xx. 4, that, in view of St. Paul's statement in 1 Thess. iv. 13-17, respecting the risen dead in Christ and the changed and glorified living saints at his coming, "he saw *thrones*, and they who *sat* upon them, to whom judgment was given," viz., "the souls of them that were beheaded for the witness of Jesus"— and which he had before seen "*under the altar*" at the opening of the fifth seal (Rev. vi. 9-11)—together with them "which had not worshipped the beast, neither his image, neither had received his mark upon their foreheads or in their hands," and whom he declares "lived and reigned with Christ a thousand years." Also further, that, as to the resurrection of "the rest of the dead"—that is, the *wicked* dead—"they *lived not again till* the thousand years were *finished*." To which the apostle adds, "THIS IS THE FIRST RESURRECTION" (v. 5). And all that Papias does is, to *avow* this doctrine, and to tell us that there is nothing mysterious or unintelligible in it, but that it is to be understood in its plain, straight-forward, *literal* sense.

Now, Eusebius, in speaking of this doctrine of Papias, says: "These views however I think he has taken up from a misconception of the statements of the apostles, not seeing the meaning of what they spoke *mystically in figures*, (or examples). For he seems to be *very weak* in intellect,"[1] etc. But surely, we have here but the "*individual*" *opinion* of Eusebius, that the apostles are to be understood in an allegorical or spiritual, rather than in a literal sense. He "*thinks*," and Papias "*seems* to be," etc. We are willing, however, on this point, to compare *Eusebius's* claim to soundness of judgment, etc., with that of Papias. We will quote but a single clause from this same section of his history. He has been saying that Papias mentioned John the elder, a person *posterior* in date to John the apostle; and that hence the circumstance of there being *two* tombs at Ephesus inscribed with the name of John, may be accounted for. And he then goes on: "To these circumstances it is necessary to pay attention: for it is likely that the *second* John, unless any one *chooses* to say it is the first,

---
[1] Euseb. Eccles. Hist., lib. iii., sec. 39.

saw the revelation which goes forth under the name of John." Now, *we* had much rather trust the judgment of simple old Papias, than that of a man who can, to say the least, thus lightly and groundlessly *throw a mantle of doubt* over the inspiration and authenticity of the APOCALYPSE. Then, too, history affirms that this same Eusebius, bishop of Cæsarea, favored the Origenist *semi-arian* views respecting the Trinity, A. D. 321; and, on the adoption of the Nicene creed, in A. D. 325, though he subscribed this confession, yet he interpreted it in accordance with his *own* views, and persuaded other Origenist or semi-arian Oriental bishops to do the same! But, enough of this. We pass to another side issue of the learned Professor.

3. He says: "A further incidental proof of the position, that millenarianism was not the received and authoritative faith of the Church from the death of the apostles to the year 150, is found in the fact, *that it does not appear in the so-called Apostles' Creed*" . . . in which "symbol," he affirms, "there is not the slightest allusion to *two* resurrections and a *corporeal* reign of Christ between them. The only specifications are, that Christ shall come from heaven 'to judge the quick and the dead;' and that there is 'a resurrection of the body,' and a 'life everlasting' [*immediately succeeding*, is the implication]" (pp. 391, 392). And again: "Cyprian maintains the millenarian theory with his usual candor and moderation. Yet, millenarianism does not appear in the Catholic creed as an article of faith. Both Irenæus and Tertullian, in their writings against heretics, present brief synoptical statements of the authorized faith of the Church; but *in none of them* do we find the millenarian tenet. In their synopses, there is *nothing more* said upon eschatological points than is contained in the Apostles' Creed" (p. 394).

We reply. The creed says nothing about "everlasting punishment," or "the second death." Nor is there "the slightest allusion to" faith and repentance, as necessary to "the forgiveness of sins;" nor to a holy life as necessary to salvation; nor to the ministry, ordinances, and polity of "the holy Catholic Church," etc., etc. And yet no one will doubt that they are not one and all *implied in it as parts of* that "faith once delivered to the saints." And so, in regard to the "*eschatology*" of that creed. *Isolate* it from the general scope of what the Scriptures teach on the subject of the second coming of Christ and the resurrection of the dead, etc., and, like some isolated passages, e. g., Dan. xii. 2 and John v. 28, 29, and there is apparent countenance given to the current theology of the day, that there is to be a *simultaneous* resurrection of the righteous and the wicked when Christ comes to "judge the quick and the dead." But, when taken in connection with the *whole scheme* of God's revelation on these points, we maintain that "the so-called Apostles' Creed," when or by whomsoever compiled, so far from *denying* "two resurrections" and a corporeal reign of Christ between them, "*by implication*" must have included both.

For example: St. Paul believed in the resurrection of *all* the dead from their graves by the power of Christ. But in his Epistle to the Philippians, chap. iii. 11, he says that he sought to know the fellowship of Christ's sufferings, etc., "*if by any means* he might attain unto THE resurrection of the dead;" which earnest desire and striving on his part is without meaning, unless he believed that there were "*two* resurrections," the one of the *just* and the other of the *unjust*. True, he does not anywhere state the precise period that is to intervene between the two acts of resurrection; but he does most emphatically declare that "every man" shall be raised "*in his own order:* Christ the first fruits; *afterward* they that are Christ's *at his coming*" (1 Cor. xv. 23), and also in 1 Thess. iv. 16, that "the dead *in Christ* shall rise *first*." It was reserved for St. John to inform us of the *exact period* that is to come in between the "two resurrections" of the righteous and the wicked, in Rev. xx. 4, 5. St. Paul therefore sought to "attain unto *the* resurrection of (or *from among*) the dead," on the ground that it is written, "*Blessed* and holy is he that shall have a part in the *first* resurrection:" and that for the reason, that "on such the second death shall have no power, but they shall be *priests* of God and of Christ, and shall *reign with him* a thousand years:" which is that very "*corporeal* [or personal] reign of Christ" that comes in "*between* them," so positively denied by Professor Shedd.

Our time and space will not allow of a further argument on this point. Suffice it to say, that we cannot accept the Professor's confident *ex cathedra* statement, that by "*implication*," a "resurrection of the body," i. e., simultaneously of the just and the unjust, "and a life everlasting" "*immediately succeeding*," can be drawn from "the so-called Apostles' Creed."

And as to the alleged *omissions* in "the brief synoptical statements" of the early fathers mentioned, to refer to "the millenarian tenet," which, as we shall prove in the proper place, is not historically true of those fathers named by him, it is sufficient to say, that there was *no necessity* for "more to be said upon eschatological points, than is contained in the Apostles' Creed." These "points," as we shall presently show, were generally received and well understood by the Church *at the time* referred to. We pass to another, and the last side issue of the Professor, to wit:

4. His reference to those who were *opposed* to millenarianism. We shall notice these in their chronological order. The first in the list is one " GAIUS [Caius?], a presbyter of Rome about the year 200," who, the Doctor informs us, "attacks the millenarian views of the Montanist Proclus, and declares millenarianism to be the *invention* of Cerinthus" (p. 394). Indeed! Well, this must be decisive against it, and especially so, as our author tells us of this same Gaius, that he "declares the *Apocalypse* a writing of this heretic." Did Eusebius obtain his cue regarding this last book of the New Testament from Gaius? The learned Professor introduces this statement of Gaius in reference to that book without comment. Does he *indorse* that statement? Gaius was certainly consistent with himself on that score. He clearly perceived that the *logical* workings of his anti-millenarian theory involved a *repudiation* of the canonicity of the Apocalypse!

The next in order is "the Alexandrian school," which, "under the lead of CLEMENT and ORIGEN, made a vigorous attack" upon millenarianism in the early part of the third century (p. 395). For an explanation of the nature and design of this "attack," the circumstances under which it originated, and its results, we hand the Professor and the reader over to the care of the reformer Luther, and the two ecclesiastical historians, Mosheim and Milner.[1] The Professor goes on:

"In the last part of the third century, DIONYSIUS, bishop of Alexandria, succeeded by dint of argument in suppressing a very gross form of millenarianism that was spreading in his diocese, under the advocacy of *Nepos* and *Coracion*" (p. 395). As we have seen,[2] Origen having, in the early part of this century, introduced his new theory of *allegorical* interpretation of the Scriptures,

---

[1] See pages 14, 15.   [2] See pages 13, 14.

directed all the weight of his influence and authority in opposing the *literal* rule of exegesis as adopted by the chiliasts. Hence the *origin* of the controversy respecting it. And, having fallen into comparative discredit, Nepos, an Egyptian bishop, attempted to *restore* it, in a work written against the allegorists, (for so he called, by way of contempt) the adversaries of the chiliastic or millenarian system. This work, and the system it defended, was extremely well received by great numbers in the canton of Arsinoë; and, among others, by Coracion, who, if Mosheim is of any authority, was a presbyter of no mean influence and reputation.[1] But, in A. D. 262, Dionysius, bishop of Alexandria, and a *disciple* of Origen, "succeeded," as Professor Shedd tells us, "by dint of argument"—that is, as based upon "a vitiated method of commenting on the sacred pages" (Milner); "which opened a secure retreat for all sorts of errors which a wild and irregular imagination could bring forth" (Mosheim); and which "accommodated the word of God to the most extravagant absurdities," by "extracting from Scripture a sense repugnant to its meaning" (Luther); in a word, by "following *the method* of Origen," than whom, "no man ever injured the Church more than he did" (Mosheim and Milner):—we repeat, this is the man who "succeeded by dint of argument in suppressing" that "*very gross form* of millenarianism that was spreading in his diocese, under the advocacy of Nepos and Coracion."

Nor is this all. For, as Luther says, "*later* writers having followed the too much praised and prevailing example of the Alexandrian school, it has come to pass that men *make just what they please* of the Scriptures;" to which Milner adds, that in consequence, "*a thick mist for ages* has pervaded the Christian world, supported and strengthened by Origen's allegorical manner of interpretation;" until, as now, for the most part, "the *learned alone* are considered as implicitly to be followed;" so that the vulgar, seeing that "*the literal is hissed off the stage*," consider that they "have nothing to do but to follow their authority, wherever it leads them." Luther in his day, speaking of the ancient allegorists, told the people that "Origen and Jerome, and similar of the fathers"—Dionysius, bishop of Alexandria, for example—"*are to be avoided*, with the whole of the Alexandrian school." No, exclaim our *modern allegorists*. Close your eyes and shut your ears

---

[1] Mosheim's Eccles. Hist., Cent. III., i. 284.

against the so-called "materializing," "gross," and "fanatical exegeses" of the millenarians of this day, who, by their *literal* interpretations of "the teachings of Isaiah and St. John," affirm that the second personal "coming of the Lord *draweth nigh*," and that "the kingdoms of this world" are *soon* to become "the kingdom of our Lord and of his Christ."

But the learned Professor Shedd goes on: "The AUGSBURG CONFESSION condemns *chiliasm*, in conjunction with the doctrine of limited future punishment; both tenets being held by the *Anabaptists* of that day"[1] (p. 396.) He also adds, page 397, that "the ENGLISH CONFESSION OF EDWARD VI., from which the Thirty-nine Articles were afterward condensed, condemns it in nearly the same terms as the Augsburg."[2] Before remarking on these passages, we must recall the notice of the reader to two others of a similar character and design, in the preceding pages of this "History of Christian Doctrine." The first is that in which the author, treating of "millenarianism at the close of the *first century*, says, p. 390, that "it appears first in the system of the *Judaistic-Gnostic* Cerinthus, the contemporary and opponent of the apostle John." And, in confirmation of this, p. 394, he refers the reader to "Gaius, a presbyter of Rome about the year 200," who "declares millenarianism to be the *invention* of Cerinthus," etc.

Now, what are the *facts* of history in this case? Why, that this said Cerinthus, the Ebionite, of apostolic times, distinguished himself, in the first place, by a heretical denial of the *proper deity* of the Lord Jesus Christ, and of the Holy Spirit, and against whom St. John directed his Epistles. But he was also the *first* who attempted to "turn away the ears" of the primitive Christians from the teachings of Paul, Peter, and John, and to "turn them unto fables," by claiming that Christ descended *upon him* in the form of a dove, and to *turn them from the scriptural* doctrine of the millennium, by investing that economy with all the carnal and sensual attributes of a Mohammedan Paradise. The consequence is, that the circumstance of his antiquity, and of his advocacy of the voluptuous elysium of which he was the advocate, have been made available by *anti*-millenarians, both ancient and modern, to invent and prefer against the *chiliasts* of

---

[1] See quotation from Hase, Libri Symbolic., page 14 (Shedd, vol. ii., p. 396).
[2] Niemour, Collectio, page 600.

the first four centuries, and those of later times who have revived and brought to light the long-neglected and almost forgotten system taught by them, the charge of advocating *the same* gross, carnal, and sensual absurdities and abominations respecting the millennium, with that arch-heretic! Reader, turn to the list of modern "chiliasts," as given in pages 23, 24 of this reply, and we appeal, *is this fair?*

But we pass to the next passage, page 396, where the Rev. Doctor, speaking of millenarianism "during the *middle ages*," having stated that "it can hardly be said to have had any existence as a doctrine," adds, "though at the close of the tenth century, there was an undefined fear and expectation among the masses that the year 1000 would witness the advent of the Lord," etc. Again, we ask: What are the *facts* of history in this case? Why, according to Mosheim, the priests and monks of the Latin Church openly taught the people the *immediate* approach of the day of judgment, on the false assumption, that the 1000 years millennial rest of the Church spoken of in the Apocalypse (as hypothecated of the theory advocated by Origen, Ambrose, Hilary, Chrysostom, Jerome, Augustine, and others of a similar class who preceded them), had *then* expired; and, spreading itself with amazing rapidity throughout the European provinces, it produced among them the deepest anguish, consternation, and despair. Prodigious numbers, under this delusion, flew with the utmost precipitation to Palestine, as the place designated for the appearance of Christ as the Judge of men. And ... what? Ah, reader, here you discern the *design* of all this on the part of these crafty priests and monks. It was to gratify their avarice. For, while the frenzied multitudes deserted their homes, these their spiritual guides remained quietly behind, on the one hand to seize upon the luxurious lands and abundant treasures of their former occupants and owners; and on the other, as the professed vicegerents of Christ upon earth, to reduce vast numbers of the remainder to the condition of the most abject spiritual bondage. We must presume that the learned Professor of the "History of Christian Doctrine" was not entirely ignorant of this historic fact. We therefore again appeal, is it fair, even upon his own showing, to place millenarianism on the *same platform* with the delusion of these Latin priests and monks of the tenth century?

We now return to the two above-quoted *condemnations* of millenarianism by the "Augsburg" and "English Confessions." Well, admit that they did so. The question is, are *their acts* to be received as authoritative and decisive in this matter? This would argue that they were *infallible* in their judgment. Will the Professor claim this in their behalf? Have not confessions, and creeds, and Church courts, yea, and the Church herself, *erred* in their decisions as to matters of doctrine? It remains therefore to be decided, whether the *grounds* on which this condemnation of millenarianism by the two above-named "Confessions" were just and equitable. The learned Professor has decided that they were so. Before discussing the merits of their acts in the premises, therefore, inasmuch as millenarianism is again gaining ground extensively in *all* our Evangelical Protestant Churches; we would respectfully suggest to the Professor, as an instructor in one of our principal schools of the prophets, and especially holding, as he does, that millenarianism is a "materializing," "gross," and "fanatical and heretical" system of interpreting "the teachings of Isaiah and St. John concerning the second coming of Christ," yea, and press it upon him as a bounden duty, to set himself about convoking an ŒCUMENICAL COUNCIL of all the Churches in Protestant Christendom, to *test* this momentous question on the principles of a *legitimate* law of scriptural hermeneutics.

And now, as to the *merits* of the acts of condemnation of millenarianism, as above. They are alleged to have been hypothecated of the "*conjunction* of chiliasm with the doctrine of limited future punishment; both tenets being held by the Anabaptists of that day," etc. That is, the "Anabaptists" were "*chiliasts*," and both taught "the doctrine of future limited punishment. Thus, chiliasts or millenarians are alleged to be *identical* with the Anabaptists!

We most positively affirm, that, so far as "chiliasm," ancient or modern, is concerned, the above statement *is a most unjust and malicious libel* against that system. First. As to the article of "*limited* future punishment," individuals, under that name, tinctured by the *Origenist heresy*—for as we have said, he zealously *denied* the eternity of future torments of the wicked—may have advocated it. But, so far from its forming *a part* of that system as held by the orthodox early post-apostolic or modern advocates of it, we confidently assert that it furnishes *the only* effectual antidote to the heresies both of the Universalist and the Restorationist. On this point, we challenge refutation.

Then, second, as to the alleged *identity* of "chiliasts" with the "Anabaptists." Now *who* and *what* were these Anabaptists? Take the following historic facts: Their name is derived from the Greek word ανα, "*new*," and βαπτιστες, "*a baptist*," from their practice of baptizing infants *anew*, by *immersion*. But in addition to this, particularly, the Anabaptists of Germany advocated the possibility of attaining to a *perfect* Church state, both in its internal purity and external organization. Under the guidance of this delusion, and excited by the success—not the example—of Luther, whose principles of the Reformation they viewed as defective, they determined upon the erection of a new Church state, "*entirely spiritual and divine.*" Their leaders, Munzer, Stubner, Storick, and others, claiming to be moved by a divine impulse, and also the power to work miracles, by their discourses, visions, and predictions, excited commotions in various parts of Europe; and, having at length become quite numerous, the weapon of *persuasion* was exchanged for that of the *sword;* and their leaders, at the head of a large army, declared war against *all* existing laws, civil and ecclesiastical, under the pretext that Christ was *then* to take the reins of government in his own hands. But, under the auspices of the Elector of Saxony and other princes, the army was dispersed, and Munzer, their principal leader, was put to death, in A. D. 1525. Subsequently, however, in A. D. 1533, first under one Matthias, who was cut off by the bishop of Munzer's army; and then under Bockholdt, who gave the city of Munzer the name of *Mount Zion*, and claimed by special designation from heaven to be its *king*, and that he was invested with legislative powers like *Moses;* the Anabaptists again attempted to establish themselves. But the city being finally taken, and Bockholdt put to death, this absurd and wretched delusion expired with the causes which originated it.

Thus ends our animadversions on the insidious and assiduous endeavors, as we have said, of *post*-millenarian writers to prejudice the mind of the reader against the system of their opponents, by a species of dogmatizing, on the one hand, and the introduction of side issues in their discussions of this subject, on the other. In regard to the first, the *dogmatical*, involving, as it does, the determination as to the *priority* of the two rules of interpretation of "the teachings of Isaiah and St. John concerning the second coming of Christ," viz., the literal or the allegorical: we submit that we have historically verified that claim in behalf of the former, no other rule of scriptural "exegesis" having obtained in the Church *till the time* of Clement and Origen. And as it respects the second, the *side issues* resorted to, to the same end: these prefer against millenarianism the allegations: 1. That it is a "materializing," "gross," and "fanatical and heretical" system of *interpreting* "the Messianic prophecies." 2. Of the attempt *to lower the claims* of the early chiliastic fathers to the respect and confidence of the reader, by representing them as "by no means of such a weight of character and influence as would entitle them to be regarded as the principal or sole representatives of orthodoxy." 3. That "millenarianism *does not appear* in the so-called Apostles' Creed," nor in "the brief synoptical statements" of the early fathers. 4. That it has been opposed by various writers, e. g., Gaius, Origen, Dionysius, etc. And finally, 5. That it was *condemned* by "the Augsburg Confession," and also by the Confession of Edward VI., on the ground of its alleged *identity* with "the Judaistic-Gnostic heresy of Cerinthus, of the first century;" also of the *fanatical* Latin priests and monks of the tenth, and of the deluded "Anabaptists" of the sixteenth century.

Hence the somewhat extended space devoted to a *vindication* of millenarianism in these premises. Whether it be true or false, does not rest upon the mere *ipse dixit* of any man. Nor will all the efforts of its impugners to bring it into disrepute and arrest its onward march in these "last days," by scandal and reproach, avail. The pious and candid inquirer after truth, estimating the muck and mire with which its adversaries are wont to bespatter it at their true value, will ask, What saith *authentic* history in its behalf? We, therefore, leave the impartial reader to decide on the *merits* of the points at issue, so far as already noticed in connection with Professor Shedd's exhibit of millenarianism, and proceed to his more direct *historical* statements regarding it, ancient, mediæval, and modern.

CHAPTER II.

SECTION I.

THE ANCIENT ERA.

Professor Shedd gives the following as his historic account of the *origin* of millenarianism. On this point he informs us, that "it is substantially the same with the *later*-Jewish doctrine of the Messianic kingdom on earth. The Jews, *at the time* of the incarnation, were expecting a personal prince, and a corporeal reign, in the Messiah who was to come." To this he adds, "the *disciples* of Christ, being themselves Jews, were at first naturally infected with these views." Again: "There being this *affinity* between millenarianism and the later-Jewish idea of the Messiah and His kingdom, it is not surprising to find that millenarianism was a peculiarity of the *Jewish* Christian, as distinguished from the *Gentile* Christian Church, at the close of the *first century*. It appears *first* in the system of the Judaistic-Gnostic Cerinthus, the contemporary and opponent of the apostle John." (See pages 290, 291.) "Gaius . . . declares millenarianism was the invention of *Cerinthus*." (P. 394.)

Our first remark in reference to these statements, relates to the *distinction* drawn between "the Jewish-Christian and the Gentile-Christian branch of the Church, at the close of the first century." *None* of "the *Gentile*-Christian branch," it would seem, were "infected" by millenarianism. In the next place, "the *disciples* of Christ," it appears, who *were* "infected" by it, derived said infection from the later-Jewish doctrine "*at the time* of the incarnation." And yet the learned Professor gravely tells us that millenarianism "appears *first* in the system of Cerinthus, the Judaistic-Gnostic" Ebionite in the time of St. John, by whom it was "*invented!*" Here, then, we have the "later-Jewish doctrine" of millenarianism *existing* in the Jewish nation between A. D. 1 and 34, which was not "*invented*" till the time of "Cerinthus," in A. D. 96. So much for the *first* century.

We pass on to the next step in the Professor's historic development of millenarianism. The reader is doubtless curious to know when and how "the *Gentile*-Christian branch of the Church" first became "infected" with this system. Our author introduces this matter by the statement, that "although prevalent among the Jews, as distinguished from the Gentile Christians," yet millenarianism "gradually became prevalent in the Church *generally*, from a cause"[1] which he explains in a subsequent page. The *period* he is now treating of is that between "the death of the apostles and the year 150," during which, he says, "millenarianism *was not* the received and authoritative faith of the Church."[2] It is not until he reaches "the period between the year 150 and 250," that he throws light upon the "*cause*" of this mighty change. It was on this wise: "Some minds," he says, "*now* adopt the *literal* interpretation of the Old Testament prophecies, and subject them to a *very sensuous* exegesis." Well, were these "some minds" *the first* to adopt the literal interpretation of the prophecies? By turning back to page 390, the Professor says: "Of the *apostolical fathers*, Barnabas, Hermes, and Papias exhibit in their writings *distinct traces* of this doctrine," all of whom flourished between A. D. 40 and 163. Of course, then, the *literal* interpretation must have prevailed in the Church *prior* to A. D. 150.

But there is another passage to which we must refer, having a bearing upon the subject of the *originating cause* of millenarianism. "The millenarian tendency," says our author, "became stronger, as the Church began, in the last half of the second century, to feel the *persecuting hand* of the government laid upon it. The distressed condition of the people of God led them to desire and pray for *an advent* of the Head of the Church that would extinguish all His enemies. It was natural," he adds, "that the doctrine of the *personal* reign of Christ should be *most prevalent*

---

[1] See page 391. [2] Ib. 391.

when the earthly condition of the Church was *most intolerable*," etc.

But we deferentially ask here, if there is in "*persecution*" a "natural tendency" to originate and promote "the doctrine of the personal reign of Christ" among "the people of God" in their "distressed condition," how happens it that this "natural tendency" to millenarianism was not *long before* developed? For, surely, the persecution of the Church was not limited to "the *last half* of the second century." The first general Pagan persecution commenced under the bloody *Nero*, in A. D. 64. The second, under *Domitian*, in A. D. 95. The third, under *Nerva*, in A. D. 100. And the fourth, under *Antoninus Philosophus*, in A. D. 162. And each, with scarcely any relaxing interval, was equally severe with the last. On this hypothesis, therefore, we submit, *the whole Church* could not have failed, by this "*natural*" process, to have adopted the millenarian faith; aye, and that, maugre their "subjection to a very sensuous exegesis," by the "adoption of the *literal* interpretation of the Old Testament prophecies" which it involved.

But no. *Directly the reverse* of this is the truth. Like the old patriarchs, all of whom "*died in the faith*" of those "promises which they beheld afar off,"[1] so with those "people of God" who suffered under their Pagan persecutors. Their *belief in* "an advent of the Head of the Church that would extinguish all His enemies," *supported them under* those trials of cruel mockings, and scourgings, and bonds, and imprisonments, and martyrdoms, *that they might obtain* a better resurrection."[2] On the other hand, the *exemption* of the Church from persecution, when, basking in the sunshine of earthly pomp, and ease, and luxury, she adopts the language of the Church of the Laodiceans, and says: "I am rich, and increased with goods, and have need of nothing;"[3] *then it is*, that we find the "natural tendency" of the doctrine of the personal reign of Christ to be the "*least* prevalent." In other words, we mean to say, that the "*natural* tendency" of outward worldly prosperity *to* the Church is, to *crush out* what remains of millenarianism *in* the Church. In proof that we are not mistaken on this point, we quote the following from page 398, where Dr. Shedd, on the "Catholic theory of the second advent," says: "The pressure of persecution being *lifted off*, the

[1] Heb. xi. 13.   [2] Ib., verses 36–40.   [3] Rev. iii. 17.

Church *returned* to its earlier and first exegesis of the Scripture data concerning the end of the world, and the second coming of Christ," etc. We presume that our author here alludes to the *cessation* of the ten Pagan persecutions, and the wafting of the Church from the sea of bloody suffering to the court of princely favor under Constantine the Great. Yes, *then it was*, that that alleged period of the "materializing," "gross," and "fanatical and heretical" literal system of interpreting the Old Testament prophets "was *hissed* off the stage"—aye, and that the very *era* of the "martyrs of Jesus," which the Church has been wont to regard as "*the golden age*" of her history—to give place, not, as we shall presently show, "to its *earlier* and *first* exegesis of the Scripture data concerning the end of the world and the second coming of Christ," which is the very point to be proved; but—to give place to the Origenic "fanciful mode of *allegory*," from which, as Milner says, "arose a vitiated method of commenting on the sacred pages," and, as a consequence of which, "a thick mist for ages has pervaded the Christian world."

Thus much then as to the "*cause*," or rather *causes*,—viz., the adoption by "some men" of the *literal* interpretation of prophecy, and "the hand of *persecution*"—which originated the millenarian system. We now turn to the Professor's account of the different stages of its prevalence.

1. *The first period.* "This tenet" (i. e., millenarianism) "was not the received faith of the Church certainly down to the year 150. It was held only by individuals."[1] "Of the apostolical fathers, only Barnabas, Hermes, and Papias exhibit traces of this doctrine. . . There are *no traces* of chiliasm in the writings of Clement of Rome, Ignatius, Polycarp, Tatian, Athenagoras, and Theophilus of Antioch."[2]

Barnabas was a Levite, and was born in the Island of Cyprus, and flourished between A. D. 40–75. He first introduced Paul to the other apostles,[3] and subsequently became his companion in labor.[4] "He was a good man, and full of faith and of the Holy Ghost."[5] He wrote an Epistle which is still extant, and which was read in the Churches, and was cited by Clement of Alexandria, Origen, and others, the latter styling it "the Catholic epistle of

---
[1] Page 391.
[2] Hegenbach, History of Christian Doctrine, § 75, note 6 (see Shedd, vol. ii., page 391).
[3] Acts ix. 27. [4] Ib., xiii. 1-7. [5] Ib., xi. 24.

Barnabas." *Hermas,* says Dr. A. Clarke," is generally allowed to be the same that Paul salutes," Rom. xvi. 14. Hagenbach remarks that his work, "The Shepherd or Pastor," "enjoyed a high reputation in the second half of the second century, and was even quoted as a part of Scripture;"[1] and Eusebius says that it was regarded as a part of the sacred canon in the time of Irenæus,[2] in A. D. 176—202, which last writer, with Jerome, says it was read in the Churches. Dr. Burton and Prof. Stuart, however, date its production about A. D. 150. *Papias* was bishop of Hierapolis, where he was probably born. Irenæus, Eusebius, and Jerome all testify that he was the disciple and pupil of the revelator St. John, and the companion of Polycarp. He wrote five books, entitled "A Narrative of the Sayings of our Lord."[3] These books are not now extant, except as they come to us through Eusebius, who, though, in speaking of him as a millenarian, represents him as "very weak in intellect," and that his writings contain "matters rather too fabulous;" yet says that on other points he was "eloquent and learned in the Scriptures." He flourished between A. D. 119 and 163.

Let us now pass on to those other "fathers," in whose "writings" Professor Shedd tells us that "*no traces* of chiliasm" are to be found. It is proper to premise in this place, that the learned Professor represents that Gaius, a presbyter of Rome about the year 200, was the *first* to "attack millenarianism," etc. (p. 394). Now, all the above-named "fathers" flourished between A. D. 98 and 178. Suppose, then, that "*no traces of chiliasm* are to be found in any of their writings. The fair inference is, that "chiliasm" in their day, was so "far the *received* faith of the Church," as to form *no part* of those controversies in which they were engaged. And, as it respects the "writings" of Clement of Rome, Ignatius, and Polycarp, we refer the reader to our quotations from their writings in subsequent pages, in refutation of the above statement of Dr. Shedd.

Clement of Rome was the "fellow laborer of St. Paul," whose name is "in the book of life." (Philip. iv. 3.) Eusebius says of him, "Of this Clement there is one Epistle extant, acknowledged as genuine, of considerable length, and of great merit. This we know to have been read for common benefit in most of the

---

[1] Hist. of Doctrines, vol. I., p. 56.   [2] Eccles. Hist. B., V., ch. viii.
[3] See on this, Library of the Apostolical Fathers, Oxford translation.

Churches, both in former times and in our own."[1] As to his Second Epistle, he speaks less confidently of its genuineness. He flourished between A. D. 68 and 100. *Ignatius* was bishop of Antioch. Of his parentage and birth, nothing is known. Chrysostom, Echard, Mosheim, Chalmers, Fox, and others affirm that he was the disciple and familiar friend of the apostles, and was educated and nursed up by them. He wrote seven Epistles, viz., to the Churches of Ephesus, the Magnesians, Trallians, Romans, Philippians, Smyrnians, and to Polycarp,[2] which are almost universally acknowledged to be genuine. He flourished between A. D. 70 and 107. *Polycarp.* Spanheim, on the authority of Baronius, affirms that he was ordained the bishop of Smyrna by St. John in A. D. 82; and Usher and others, that John in the Apocalypse addresses him as "the Angel of the Church of Smyrna."[3] He wrote an Epistle to the Thessalonians, which is admitted to be authentic and genuine. Eusebius bears the highest testimony concerning him, and makes him a pattern of orthodoxy. He lived to a great age, being 100 years old. He professed to the proconsul of Asia, Statius Quadratus, that he had served Christ eighty-six years.[4] He was hence contemporary with Ignatius, Papias, and Irenæus.

As it respects the other "fathers" referred to by Professor Shedd: "*Tatian*, a Syrian, well versed in the Greek philosophy, was converted at Rome by Justin, and," as Spanheim says, "wrote a useful work; but after the martyrdom of Justin [i. e., in A. D. 168], he returned into the East, and having imbibed much of the *pernicious heresy* of Marcion and Valentine, he endeavored to spread his new opinions very widely."[5] His followers were called Tatianists; or, from their fastings, celibacy, and abstinence, encratites, "temperate," hydroparastates, "water-drinkers," and apotactics, "renouncers." *Athenagoras*, in A. D. 175, is said to have been at the head of the catechetical school of Alexandria. In A. D. 177, on account of the revival of the persecution under the Emperor Antoninus, he addressed to him an apology in behalf of the Christians, in which, besides other matters, "he also treated of several of the *doctrines* of Christianity, in *all* which," says the *anti*-millenarian Echard, "he is supposed not to have been *nicely*

---

[1] Euseb. Eccles. Hist., B. III., chap. xvi.   [2] Echard's Eccles. Hist., vol. ii., p. 440.
[3] Rev. ii. 8.   [4] Spanheim's Eccles. Hist., p. 192.   [5] Echard, vol. iii., p. 497, 498.
[6] Spanheim, p. 187, and note.

orthodox." Query : Do Echard's exceptions to his orthodoxy relate to "*chiliasm?*" It would so seem from the fact that he states, he also " wrote a *particular treatise on the resurrection of the dead*, in which he endeavored to prove that the thing [i. e., as we suppose, the *first* resurrection in contradistinction from the *second*, see Rev. xx. 4, 5] was so far from being impossible, that it was *extremely credible*," etc.[1] For surely, it cannot be pretended that the "nicely orthodox," in these early times, denied the doctrine of "the resurrection of the dead." *Theophilus of Antioch.* Echard's account of this writer is, that in A. D. 181, he, as bishop of Antioch, and " one of the most vigorous opposers of the *heretics* Marcion and Hermogenes, now wrote an excellent treatise against a learned pagan called Autolycus, which is all we have remaining of his works. It is divided into three books; consisting of a great variety of learning and reasoning, with which he clearly vindicated the Christian religion against all the exceptions of Autolycus and the heathens; and demonstrated the history of Moses was more ancient, and more true, than any among them; and that their poets had borrowed their principal stories from the Holy Scriptures."[2] We ask, therefore, in view of the obvious character and design of this work, is it fair to assume, that because "no trace of chiliasm" is to be found in it, *ergo*, Theophilus *was not* a chiliast ?

But, to go on. Our author says: " The period between the year 150 and 250 is *the blooming age of millenarianism;* and yet," he adds, "even in this period it does not become the *Catholic* faith, as embodied in the Catholic creed " (page 392). This, according to the learned Doctor, was produced by "some minds" who "now adopt the *literal* interpretation of the Old Testament prophets," and also by " the *natural* tendencies of persecution." Aye. And of this "blooming period of millenarianism," he says : " *So general had the tenet become in the last half of the second century*, that Justin Martyr declares that it was the belief of *all* but the Gnostics " (page 394). "But," he adds, "Irenæus, on the contrary, speaks of *opposers* of millenarianism, who held the Catholic faith, and who agreed with the Gnostics only in being anti-millenarians; although he is himself desirous to make it appear that anti-millenarianism is of the nature of *heresy*" (page 394).

[1] Echard's Eccles. Hist., vol. ii., pp. 508, 509.   [2] Ib., 519.

Well. According to the Professor, although he alleges "that millenarianism *was not* the received and authoritative faith of the Church from the death of St. John to the year 150;" yet, the next hundred years, down to A. D. 250, this "materializing," "gross," "sensual," and "fanatical" system, which he affirms is identical with the *heresy* of the "Anabaptists," *had become general "in the Church*," etc.

But, this "blooming era of millenarianism" was not of long continuance. "Irenæus speaks of *opposers* to millenarianism," and says that "their system was of the nature of *heresy*."

Thus, then, eschatologists, *millenarian* and *anti-millenarian*, mutually prefer against each other's system the charge of HERESY. And, indeed, there is no other alternative. *If* millenarianism is what Professor Shedd represents it to be—a "materializing," "gross," "sensual," and "fanatical" system of interpreting "the Messianic prophecies" "concerning the second coming of Christ" —the "*orthodoxy*" of its advocates cannot shield it from the charge that it is *heretical*. So, on the other hand, the "*orthodoxy*" of anti-millenarianism cannot avert from it a similar charge. There is no *via media* principle of compromise between them. They are absolutely *antipodal*.[2] So thought and taught and felt the great "Irenæus." And so, the *normal* elements of opposition to millenarianism, having prepared the way therefor toward the close of its "blooming era;" "that spirit of hostility to it, *commenced* by the "attack of Gaius about the year 200," was gradually fanned into a flame by those two leading catechists of the Alexandrian school, Clement and Origen. Then followed in their track that redoubtable disciple of Origen, Dionysius of Alexandria, who, as the author of the "History of Christian Doctrine" tells us, "succeeded by dint of argument, in repressing that very gross form of millenarianism that was spreading in his diocese, under the advocacy of Nepos and Coracion." So that, adds he, "*after* the third century the tenet *disappears very generally*" (page 395).

Now, on the subject of this *early* millenarian collapse, it is opportune to repeat what we claim to have demonstrated in a previous part of this reply,[1] viz., that the *literal* interpretation of "the teachings of Isaiah and St. John concerning the second coming of Christ," was the *only law* of prophetical "exegesis" known to the Church, Jewish and Christian, until it was supplanted by

[1] See page 13.   [2] See Note A.

the *new* theory of allegorical exposition of the Scriptures, matured and propagated by the *Platonico*-philosophical speculations of Origen. And, so far as *we* are concerned, we are willing to risk the entire merits of the question as to which of the two systems as predicated of these divergent laws of interpretation, the *literal* or the *allegorical,* is subject to the charge of *heresy.* Let the reader take Professor Shedd's own definition of millenarianism, as advocated by those writers who he admits have exhibited it "in *unison* with an intelligent and earnest orthodoxy" (page 397), and place them beside what we have shown to have been the heresies of Origen,[1] on the one hand; with what Luther, Mosheim and Milner declare of the truth-perverting and disastrous results to the Church of his *allegorizing* system of interpreting the word of God, on the other.

We come now to the fourth century. "The third century" having "witnessed a very decided opposition to millenarianism— a fact which evinces," says our author, "that its blooming period was a brief one of about a hundred years;" he adds—"*Lactantius* († 330) is the *only* man of any note in the fourth century, who defends the system. *Augustine* adopted the theory in his earlier days, but rejected it afterwards. That chiliasm could not have been *generally* current in the beginning of the fourth century, is proved by the manner in which Eusebius speaks of it," in "describing the writings of Papias," etc., which has been already noticed. Had it been otherwise, "a writer like Eusebius, whose respect for every thing Catholic and ecclesiastical was very high, would not have spoken of it as '*fabulous.*'" (Pages 395, 396.)

Lactantius. He flourished between A. D. 310 and 330. He was tutor to Constantine's heir, and the purity of his Latin gained for him the title of "the Christian Cicero." Mosheim styles him "the most eloquent of the Latin fathers." Professor Stuart allows him to have been "a zealous *chiliast.*" Jerome ridiculed his millenarianism, as he did that of Irenæus, Tertullian, and other Christians who held the same sentiments. He charged Lactantius with the error of the Manichees, but Dr. Lardner satisfactorily vindicated him against that charge.[2]

In reference to Professor Shedd's statement, "that chiliasm *could not* have been generally current in the beginning of the fourth century," it is in place here to remark, that he must have

---

[1] See page 13.   [2] Lardner's Cred. of the Gospel Hist., vol. iii., pp. 316, 319, 520.

overlooked the well-known historic fact (inadvertently, of course) that the NICENE COUNCIL, which was convened in A. D. 325, and which consisted of some 318 bishops collected from all parts of Christendom; in their ecclesiastical forms and constitutions (and from which the form now used in the communion service of the Anglican and American Episcopal Church, called the *Nicene Creed*, was derived), the "Creed" drawn up by them concludes as follows: "*I look for the resurrection of the dead and the life of the world to come;*" which the council thus expounds (the *Greek* text of Gelasius Cyzicenus, de Actis Consilii Nicæni, from which it is extracted, being placed side by side with the *English* translation, thus):

"Μικροτερος ὁ κοσμος εγενετο δια την προγνωσιν· προεγνω γαρ ὁ Θεος ὁτι ἁμαρτησει ὁ ανθρωπος. Δια τουτο καινους ουρανους και καινην γην προσδοκωμεν κατα τα ἱερα γραμματα, φαινομενης ἡμιν επιφανειας και βασιλειας του μεγαλου Θεου και σωτηρος ἡμων Ιεσου Χριστου. Και παραληψονται τοτε, κατα φησι Δανιηλ, την βασιλειαν ἁγιοι Ὑψιστου. Και εται ἡ γη καθαρα, ἁγια, γη ζωντων, και ου νεκρων. Ην προεωρακως Δαβιδ τω της πιστεως οφθαλμω βοα. Πιτευω του ιδειν τα αγαθα του Κυριου εν γη ζωντων· γη πραεων και ταπεινων. Μακαριοι γαρ φησιν [ὁ Χριστος] οἱ πραεις, ὁτι αυτοι κληρονομησουσι την γην. Και ὁ προφητης φησι, και πατηρουσι αυτην ποδες πραεων και ταπεινων."	The world was made *inferior* because of foreknowledge: for God foreknew that man would sin. Therefore we expect *new heavens and a new earth* according to the Holy Scriptures: the *Epiphany and kingdom* of the great God and our Saviour Jesus Christ *then appearing*. And as Daniel says (chap. vii. 18) *the saints of the Most High shall take the kingdom*. And there shall be a pure and holy land, *the land of the living* and not of the dead: which David foreseeing with the eye of faith, exclaims, I *believe* to see the goodness of the Lord in the land of the living—*the land of the meek and humble*. Blessed, saith Christ (Matt. v. 5), are the *meek*, for they shall *inherit the earth*. And the prophet saith (Isa. xxvi. 6), *The feet of the meek and humble shall tread upon it.*"[1]

Indeed, even at a *later* period, between A. D. 375 and 420, Jerome (who, as we have seen, was no friend to millenarianism, but the contrary) admits that "*many* Christians and martyrs had affirmed the things which he denied; and that *a great multitude* of Christians agreed in them *in his own day:* so that though he could not *follow* them, he could not *condemn* them." It is here to be borne in mind, that ROME had been considered by Christians as *the seat of antichrist* and destined to destruction. Hence, Lactantius, who lived in the time of Constantine, in his

---

[1] See Investigator and Expositor of Prophecy, vol. 1., pp. 14, 51. London, 1831-'2.

Book on the Divine Institutes, says: "The Roman authority, by which now the world is governed (my soul dreads to speak it—but it will speak it, because it shall come to pass), shall be taken from the earth, and the empire shall return into Asia, and again the *East shall rule* and the *West obey.*"

Mosheim in his "History of the Church" admits, "that *long before* this controversy, an opinion had prevailed, that Christ was to come and reign a thousand years among men, *before the entire and final* dissolution of the world;"—"that this opinion had hitherto (i. e., up to the middle of the third century) met with *no* opposition;"—and that "now its credit began to decline, principally through the influence and authority of Origen, who opposed it with the greatest warmth, *because it was incompatible with some of his favorite sentiments.*" But, notwithstanding this opposition, the facts above adduced prove that millenarianism still formed "*the Catholic faith* of the Church" till the *latter end* of the fourth century.

We say, therefore, fearless of successful confutation, that Professor Shedd's statement "that chiliasm *could not* have been generally current in the beginning of" (and we add, throughout) "the fourth century," cannot be sustained by the *facts* of history.

Again. Because, forsooth, "*Augustine* adopted millenarianism in his earlier days, but rejected it afterward;" therefore, millenarianism is a "materializing," "gross," "sensual," and "fanatical heresy!" And so, the *truth* or *falsity* of a system turns upon its *repudiation* by this or that distinguished ancient "father" of the Church. On this hypothesis, the theory substituted in its place, *whatever it may be,* must be received by us as the *true* one. Does Professor Shedd then adopt the *anti*-millenarian theory of Augustine, of "a *spiritual resurrection,* commencing from the epoch of the nativity; and which affirms, that as at the *first* coming of Christ, Satan having been bound, and the strong man disarmed and ejected from the hearts of men, it is to continue from the middle to the end of the *sixth* chiliad?"

Finally. On the subject of this "ancient" period of millenarianism. "A writer like Eusebius, whose respect for everything Catholic and ecclesiastical was very high, could not have spoken of it as *fabulous,*" if it were not so. Of course then, "*everything*" put forth by this writer as "Catholic and ecclesiastical," must be *unconditionally* received by us as authoritative. If this be so, then Eusebius, who followed in the track of Gaius, the presbyter of Rome, and Dionysius, bishop of Alexandria, at least in casting a shade of doubt over the canonical authority of the *Apocalypse*, is to regulate *our* faith in that particular. But, we must pass on to

SECTION II.

THE MEDIÆVAL AGE.

The Professor says: "The history of millenarianism after the year 400, is reducible to a very short compass. During the middle ages, it can hardly be said to have had *any existence* as a doctrine." Indeed, none whatever, except that, "at the close of the tenth century, there was an undefined fear and expectation among the masses, that the year 1000 would witness the advent of the Lord"[1]—such, reader, for example, as that which we have shown to have characterized that master-device of the Latin priests and monks, to delude and ensnare the "masses" of that day?[2] Let it then be conceded that, although we have historically demonstrated the *general prevalence* of millenarianism in the fourth century, and that "a great multitude" of them were still existent in the time of Jerome, between A. D. 375 and 420, yet that subsequently it began to decline. This involves an inquiry into the *causes* which operated to produce that result. We observe then,

That Constantine the Great, soon after his accession to the imperial sceptre of Rome, having professed his conversion to Christianity, became the *patron* of the Church: and, having assumed a headship over its affairs, and formed A CHURCH AND STATE UNION, he proceeded to mould it after the model of the previously existing constitution of things in *pagan* Rome. Hence the laying of the foundation upon which was erected the superstructure of that stupendous ecclesiastical hierarchy which, in A. D. 533, culminated in the elevation of John II., the Patriarch of Rome, in the chair of St. Peter, as the universal Bishop or Head of all the Churches, by the edict of the emperor Justinian. The reader therefore will readily perceive how antagonistic to all this

[1] Page 396. [2] See page 33 of this Reply.

was the *millenarian* doctrine enunciated by Lactantius as already stated.[1] The policy of Constantine, while it tended to eradicate the last remaining vestiges of the *primitive* landmarks of Christianity and the Church, contributed also to pander to the ambition of an aspiring clergy after "THE PRE-EMINENCE."[2] Hence the gradual suppression of that doctrine, which the open hostility of some, and the timid and temporizing policy of others, succeeded to effect. This was brought about by their adoption of the *Origenic* rule of interpreting "the teachings of Isaiah and St. John concerning the second coming of Christ," on the one hand; and the explaining of them in accordance with the theory of *Eusebius*, which made Rome the *New Jerusalem* of the Apocalypse, on the ground that Constantine turned the heathen temples into Christian churches, etc., on the other. Then too, the Popes, in after ages, *discountenanced* millenarianism, inasmuch as it militated against their antichristian usurpation and dogma, that the millennium *commenced* with Romish domination in the Church.[3] Thus we are brought down to

SECTION III.

THE MODERN ERA.

We again quote from the "History of Christian Doctrine." The Professor says: "In the period of the REFORMATION, millenarianism made its appearance *in connection with the fanatical and heterodox* tendencies that sprang up along with the great religious awakening," etc. (page 396). We have already shown that reference is here made to the *Anabaptists* in the time of Luther, in A. D. 1525 and 1533, thus making millenarianism *identical* with that sect. Query: Why did not the Professor think to bring in also the *fifth-monarchy men* of this century? It would doubtless have contributed much, on the same hypothesis, to strengthen his cause. We are willing, however, to leave our vindication of the millenarianism of this period in a previous page,[4] against the above unscholarly aspersion of it by the Professor, to

---

[1] See pages 45–47.
[2] 3 John v. 9.
[3] See Sequel, Chap. II. Second Theory, p. 99.
[4] See Sec. II, pp. 34, 35.

the decision of the unbiased inquirer after truth; only reiterating, by the way, that millenarianism was as *foreign* from the fanaticism and heresy of the "Anabaptists," as was "the great religious awakening along with which" it is declared to have "sprung up." In other words we affirm, that millenarianism was no more *connected* with, nor *occasioned* by, nor was *accountable* for, that delusion, than was "the great religious awakening *itself*."

We admit, then, that, in view of the *causes* adverted to at the close of the preceding era, millenarianism, down to the time of the Reformation, was thrown into the background. But we also affirm, that as that work progressed, millenarianism was again *revived*. Not that it became "general," or that even "great multitudes" adopted it, as in the time of Jerome in the fourth century. For, owing to the fanatical turbulence of the "*Anabaptists*" on the continent; the equally fanatical *fifth-monarchy men* in the time of Cromwell in England in A. D. 1645; and the so-called *French Prophets*, who made their appearance in Dauphiny and Vivarias in France in A. D. 1688; this tenet again fell into comparative disrepute. Just as it is now again on the American continent, owing to the delusions of the Irvingites in England, and of the Millerites, etc., etc., in our own country, attempted to be brought into disrepute, by a disingenuous *identifying* of it with those delusions. Nevertheless, to go back to the era of the Reformation, we observe, that though many through timidity concealed their "light under a bushel," yet the doctrine in its purity was by no means *denied*. Many men—as we shall show in its proper place—were raised up from time to time who advocated these truths in the Established Church; and the Dissenters still continued to hold it so *generally*, that at last to broach these opinions exposed a man to the imputation of being a Dissenter.

We have reserved for this place Professor Shedd's mention of "the *Belgic Confession*," first published in A. D. 1561, and which he affirms "guards the statement respecting the second coming of Christ, by teaching that *the time* of its occurrence is unknown to all created beings, and that it will not take place until the number of the elect is *complete*," etc. (page 391). But this surely is a 'begging the question.' For, millenarians affirm their belief in *both* these facts. The real question at issue is, whether the second coming of Christ is *pre-* or *post*-millennial? And that the Belgic Confession leaves undecided.

Before passing on, we must again advert to the Professor's statement respecting the *condemnation* of millenarianism by "the English Confession of Edward VI." Now, Edward VI. ascended the throne in A. D. 1547, and was vacated by his death in A. D. 1553. We introduce this matter here, simply to refresh the memory of the learned Professor regarding an historic fact which he seems to have overlooked, viz., that in *addition* to said "Confession," which was ratified in the early part of his reign, there was a work drawn up by his prelates, and authorized by himself, May 20th, 1553, in the *last year* of his life, called "THE CATECHISM OF EDWARD VI.," from which we make the following extracts:

"*Question.* How is that petition, *Thy kingdom come*, to be understood?

"*Answer.* We ask that His kingdom may come, for as yet we *see not all things* subject to Christ: we *see not yet* how the stone is cut out of the mountain without human help, which breaks into pieces and reduces to nothing the image described by Daniel;[1] or how the only rock, which is Christ, doth obtain and possess *the whole world* given Him of His Father.[2] As yet, antichrist is not slain: whence it is that we desire and pray that at length it may come to pass and be *fulfilled;* and that *Christ alone may reign with His saints according to the divine promises;*[3] and that He may live and have *dominion in the world*, according to the decrees of the holy gospel, *and not* according to the traditions and laws of men and the wills of the tyrants of the world.

"Q. God grant that His kingdom may come most speedily, etc.

*　　*　　*　　*　　*　　*　　*

"Q. The sacred Scripture calls the end of the world the *consummation* and *perfection* of the mystery of Christ, and the *renovation* of all things: for thus the apostle Peter speaks in his 2d Epistle, chap. iii.: 'We expect *new heavens and a new earth*, according to God's promise, *wherein dwelleth righteousness*.' And it seems agreeable to reason, that the corruption, mutability, and sin, to which the whole world is subject, should at last *cease*. Now, by what means, or ways of circumstances, those things shall be brought to pass, I desire to know of thee?

"*A.* I will declare, as well as I can, the same apostle attesting. The heavens, in the manner of a stormy tempest, shall pass away, and the elements estuating shall be dissolved, and the earth and the works that are therein shall be burnt. As if the apostle should say, *the world*, like as we see in the refining of gold, *shall be wholly purged with fire, and shall be brought to its utmost perfection;* which the little world, man, imitating it, shall likewise be freed from corruption and change. And so, *for man's sake*, for whose use the great world was created, being at length *renovated or made new*, it shall put on a face that shall be far more pleasant and beautiful."[4]

---

[1] See Dan. ii. 34, 35.　　[2] Dan. vii. 12–14; 21, 22.　　[3] See Rev. xx. 4, 5, 6.
[4] See Investigator and Expositor of Prophecy, vol. i., p. 15, 1831–'2.

Now, this is *pure millenarianism*, as entertained and taught generally by chief persons in the Church in the time of the Reformation. Were the English prelates, who compiled it, and King Edward VI., who indorsed it, fanatical and heretical "Anabaptists" and fifth-monarchy men? Will the Professor please answer?

Having at some length concluded our *animadversions* on the subject of "Eschatology" by Professor Shedd, we now propose to follow it up by a sketch of the origin and development of millenarianism.

CHAPTER III.

BRIEF SKETCH OF THE ORIGIN AND DEVELOPMENT OF MILLENARIANISM, ANCIENT, MEDIÆVAL, AND MODERN, IN ACCORDANCE WITH AUTHENTIC HISTORY.

It is maintained, in the sequel to "Our Bible Chronology," etc., and also in this reply to Dr. Shedd's chapter on "Eschatology," that, independently of the details of Scripture chronology, historic and prophetic, God has revealed in His word the precise period of 6000 years,[1] (which that chronology will be found exactly to fill up *to a year*), between the creation and fall, and the Christian dispensation, as that within which all His *ordinary* purposes of providence and grace toward mankind were to be accomplished, and which is to be immediately followed by the *seventh* millenary of rest, in exact analogy to the *six days* of formation of the earth and heavens, and the *seventh day* of the Divine Sabbatic repose.

But in determining the *terminus a quo*, or *commencing* period, and the *terminus ad quam*, or *closing* period of the seventh millenary of the world, we must repair to the *historic* and *prophetic* chronology of Scripture.

There is, however, a *variation* between the Hebrew and the Greek Septuagint chronologies. There are also variations in the computations of both by different chronographers. The first point to be settled, therefore, is, which of the two, the original Hebrew or the Greek Septuagint is *authoritative* in determining the true chronology of the world's history from the creation and fall of man. We adopt the HEBREW as our standard, the reasons for

[1] See Our Bible Chron., chap. vi., sec. i., pp. 79-82.

which are exhibited at length in "Our Bible Chronology," etc., Chap. VI., sections ii. and v. inclusive, pages 82–89. And, as to the Hebrew chronology for the *nativity*, we have demonstrated the *true* date to be 4132 years, instead of 4004, as that adopted in our common version from Archbishop Usher. (See as above, sections vi. and vii., pp. 89–96.)

The difference between the Hebrew chronology and that of the Septuagint, stands thus:

To the Nativity, according to the *corrected Hebrew*, ... 4132 years.
" " " *Septuagint*, ... 5871 "

This gives an *excess* of the Septuagint over the Hebrew of 1739 years, leaving only 129 years to the close of the 6000.

The *important connection* which the chronology of Scripture holds in settling the question of the commencement and close of the seventh "chiliad," is our apology for introducing it in this place. Some of the ancient writers, as Augustine and others, and some of modern times, as Grotius, Prideaux, etc., adhere to the chronology of the *Septuagint*, which circumstance (as no two of them agree in their computations) accounts for their commencing what they call *the millennium*, from so many different standpoints. But more of this anon.

With these remarks premised, we would respectfully commend to the special notice of the author of the "History of Christian Doctrine" what we deferentially claim as a demonstration, that the *ideas* and *language* of the New Testament writers in reference to the second personal coming of Christ and the judgment of the great day, were all derived from and founded upon the prophetic statements of the inspired *pre-Christian-Jewish* writers regarding them; e. g., Isaiah, Jeremiah, Ezekiel, and especially the prophet Daniel. (See Sequel, etc., Part II., pp. 243–252)· To proceed.

SECTION I.

I. ANCIENT MILLENARIANISM.

Now, Professor Shedd admits that "the Jews, *at the time* of the incarnation, were expecting a personal prince, and a corporeal reign, in the Messiah who was to come, etc. (page 389). We, of course, here take it for granted that the Professor speaks,

I. Of the JEWISH NATION, *as it was*, when Christ appeared among them. The question, therefore, is, on what was their expectation *founded?* what but the following and similar prophecies, too numerous to quote in this place? First, in reference to their *restoration:* "Thus saith the Lord God, I will even gather you from the people, and assemble you out of the captivities where ye have been scattered, and I will give you the land of Israel."[1] Second. The *dominion* and *kingdom* that was to be restored to them: "And thou, O tower of the flock, the stronghold of the daughter of Zion, unto thee shall it come, even the *first dominion;* the *kingdom* shall come to the daughter of Zion."[2] Third. The *King* who should reign over them: "Behold, the days come, saith the Lord, that I will raise unto David a righteous BRANCH (Messiah), and a *King* shall reign and prosper; and shall execute judgment and justice in the earth."[3] And again: "THE LORD shall reign in mount Zion, and in Jerusalem, and before His ancients gloriously."[4] Then too, fourth. *All the Gentile nations* were to be gathered to restored Judah: "And the *Gentiles* shall come to thy light, and *kings* to the brightness of thy rising."[5]

These examples must suffice. The "later Jews," in Christ's time, interpreted these prophecies *literally*. Hence our account of the origin of millenarianism. We repeat: it *antedated, by thousands of years*, the time of these "later Jews." It reaches back to the *first promise* of redemption by Christ,[6] which promise was renewed in the covenant of God with Abraham and his seed,[7] through whom all the families and kindreds of the Gentiles were to be blessed,[8] and of whom "Christ is the minister of the circumcision for the truth of God, to *confirm* the promises made unto the fathers."[9]

Thus much, then, as to the *source* whence these "later Jews" derived their expectation of "a personal prince, and a corporeal reign, in the Messiah which was to come." What does the Professor think of it?

But this is not all. The belief that the *earth*, and the moral and religious state of its *inhabitants*, were to undergo a great change at the end of 6000 years, has been detected in the *tradi-*

---

[1] Ezek. xi. 17.   [2] Micah iv. 8.   [3] Jer. xxiii. 5.   [4] Isa. xxiv. 23.
[5] Isa. lx. 3.   [6] Gen. iii. 15.   [7] Gen. xii-xv.   [8] Gen. xii. 3; Acts iii. 25.
[9] Rom. xv. 8.

tionary writings of the Pagan nations. On this subject, Bishop Russell, of Scotland, though an anti-millenarian, says: "With respect to the millennium, it must be acknowledged that the doctrine concerning it stretches back into antiquity so remote and obscure, that it is impossible to fix its origin."[1] Not quite, Doctor. Let us see what may be gathered,

II. From PAGAN writers. The *Chaldeans*, according to Plutarch, believed in a struggle between good and evil for a space of 6000 years, "and then Hades is to cease, and men are to be happy, neither wanting food nor making shade." True, Plutarch assigns no reasons for their belief; but it was, without doubt, like all their other notions regarding the origin of all things, derived by *tradition* from the inspired patriarchal writings. The learned Mr. George Stanley Faber affirms it to have been the doctrine also of the *Persians* and *Etruscans*, particularly the latter, who taught that the world was formed in the course of *six periods*, each period forming a millenary; while 6000 years is allotted to a *seventh period*, viz., that of its duration. "Zoroaster, an ancient *Persian* philosopher, the author of the Zendavesta, or Persian Bible, and the founder of the Magians, also taught the same thing. Dr. Prideaux supposes him to have been a contemporary of the prophet Daniel,[2] from whom, as also from the other Hebrew prophets, Dr. Hengstenberg thinks he stole and adulterated the truths of revelation. He taught that in "the last times," after much evil of every kind had afflicted the earth, two beings of supernatural powers would appear and extensively restore mankind. In the end another superior personage, viz., Sociach—a name resembling in sound the Hebrew word Messiah—would make his appearance, under whose reign the dead would be raised, the judgment take place, and the earth be renovated and glorified. And finally, a still superior righteous judge, Ormuzd, from an elevated place, commands Sociach to render to all men their deserts, and take the pure to his own presence. He also taught the *sex-millennial* duration of the earth. Bishop Russell also states, that Theopompus, who flourished 340 years B. C., relates that the Persian magi taught that the present state of things would continue 6000 years, after which Hades, the place and state of departed spirits, would be destroyed, and that mankind would then live

---

[1] Discourse on the Millennium, p. 39.
[2] Prideaux's Connections, vol. i. p. 205.

happy. But, from these pre-Christian-Jewish and Pagan writers, let us now turn to,

III. Those of the CHRISTIAN CHURCH, and

1. Of the *apostolic age.* On this subject, as we have already seen, Professor Shedd makes the following statement: "The disciples of Christ, being themselves Jews, were at first naturally affected with these [millenarian] views." But that *after* the day of Pentecost they *rose above* their early Jewish education: and that "in *none* of their inspired writings do we find such an expectation," etc. (pages 389, 390).

We must here premise, in the first place, that our blessed Lord himself, when predicting of the *restoration of Israel at the close* of the "times of the Gentiles" (Luke xxi. 24), directs them to "look up and lift up their heads at their approaching redemption," when they shall see the "SIGNS" immediately preceding His "coming in a cloud," "*begin* to come to pass." (Luke xxi. 27, 28.) Or, if He alludes to the millennial kingdom which the God of heaven shall set up at the destruction of the anti-Christian nations (Dan. ii. 34, 35; compare verses 44, 45), when "the *kingdom,* and dominion, and greatness of the kingdom under the whole heaven shall be given to the saints of the Most High (Dan. vii. 13, 14, 27), still this "kingdom of God is nigh at hand," *only* when the indications of *His return* are observable. (Luke xxi. 27–31.) Or, if to correct a misapprehension on the part of his "disciples," as though "the kingdom of God was *then* nigh at hand," He rehearses to them the parable of the "nobleman, who went into a far country, *to receive a kingdom and to return,*" etc. (Luke xix. 11–27); the obvious purport of it was, to teach them that in the case of a nobleman going into a far country, intrusting his servants with money, that they may testify their love to him by a right occupation of his property in the interval, and returning *after* he has received a kingdom, to reward the obedient and punish those wicked "citizens" who had driven him into exile; I repeat: the obvious purport of it was, to suggest to them the idea of *subsequent continued residence,* which ill comports with the popularly received view of Christ's returning merely for the purpose of pronouncing sentence upon all *at the close* of the millennium.

Now then we appeal,—in view of these teachings of Christ himself—all of which are in perfect harmony with what "Moses in the law, and David in the Psalms, and all the prophets wrote concerning Him"[1]—can it be believed that "the disciples of Christ," *because* they were "Jews," were "naturally infected with these views," *only* on the ground that it was the "doctrine" taught by the "*later-Jewish*" *nation in Christ's time?* More than all: is it to be credited that those glorious things which all the older prophets have announced concerning the *future* redemption of Israel and Judah, and of which prophetic bards have sung in strains of highest rapture—which sustained them in the hour of their fiery trial—to picture forth which, imagery the most splendid has been employed—and the prospect of which cheered them during their long and weary pilgrimage, and enabled them to "*die in faith*" of those promises which they "beheld afar off," together with the above prophetic utterances of our blessed Lord:—is it to be credited that "*none* of the inspired writings" of the apostles treat of the doctrine of the second personal coming of our Lord *in accordance with* those teachings? If such predictions *really* contain allusions to the millennium, so also are they intimately connected with the Saviour's return, and resurrection of his saints. But if *these do not* contain allusions to the millennium, then are there *no* references to it in either the Gospels or Epistles. But, so far from this, the only difficulty arises from not knowing where to begin the citations. We must confine ourselves mostly to the *epistolary* writings.

First, then. In the exercise of their faith in the return of that Master for whom they took joyfully the spoiling of their goods, and in testimony to whose Messiahship they cheerfully laid down their lives, that they *fully believed* in the realization of the Church's hopes, to be accomplished *only* by the establishment of the predicted "*kingdom,*" Peter declared concerning Christ, "whom the heavens must receive, *until* the times of restitution of all things, which God hath spoken by the mouth of all his holy prophets since the world began." (Acts iii. 21.) And in harmony with this, Paul declares that unto them was "made known the *mystery* of God's will according to his good pleasure, which he hath purposed in himself, that *in the dispensation of the fulness of times,* he might gather together in one all things in Christ, both which are in heaven and which are on earth." (Eph. i. 9, 10.) And further, as to the *process* of this: 1st. A large portion of the eleventh chapter of the Romans is devoted by the

---

[1] Luke xxiv. 44.

apostle to demonstrating the final restoration, conversion, etc., of the "*remnant* of Israel according to the election of grace," when "the DELIVERER shall come to Zion, and shall turn away ungodliness from Jacob:" for *then*, "all Israel shall be saved." And Peter, speaking of the *Gentile* believers, says: "And when the Chief Shepherd *shall appear*, they shall receive a crown of glory that fadeth not away." (1 Pet. v. 4.) And this shall be, says Paul, "when the Lord himself shall descend from heaven with a shout, with the voice of the archangel, and with the trump of God: *and the dead in Christ shall rise first*," while they "which are alive and *remain* unto the coming of the Lord, *shall be caught up to meet the Lord in the air*, and so shall ever be with the Lord." (1 Thess. iv. 13–17.) Then also, in reference to the millennial "new heavens and new earth" predicted by Isaiah, when the Lord will "create Jerusalem a rejoicing and her people a joy" (Isa. lv. 17, 18, and lxvi. 20–22), Paul speaks of the *removal from the inferior creation* of the burden that they have been made to endure, in immediate connection with "the adoption," or "redemption of our body," at "the *manifestation of the sons of God*." (Rom. viii. 19–23.) And again: when Paul speaks of the destruction of the Man of Sin, which shall immediately precede the millennium, he asserts that "him shall the Lord destroy with the brightness of *His coming*." (2 Thess. ii. 8.) So also, in treating of that "*rest* (σαββατισμὸς) which remaineth for the people of God" (Heb. iv. 9), he refers to that *seventh* millenary in "the world to come" (οικουμενην την μελλουσαν—*habitable earth to come*) (Heb. ii. 5), during which, as John declares, Satan shall be bound and the saints shall reign with Christ *a thousand years*." (Rev. xx. 1–3, 4–6.) And yet, according to Professor Shedd, "in *none of their inspired writings* do we find such an expectation" of Christ's second coming and kingdom on earth, as that spoken of by the old prophetic seers and by Christ himself! But we now pass on, to introduce in this place what may be gleaned from,

2. THE ANCIENT JEWISH UNINSPIRED WRITERS, on this subject. Speaking of these, Bishop Russell says there is "no room for doubt that the notion of a millennium preceded by several centuries the introduction of the Christian faith."[1] RABBI ELIAS, a Jewish doctor of high celebrity, whose opinion is called

[1] Discourse on the Millennium, p. 32.

by the Jews "a tradition of the house of Elias," and who flourished about 200 years before Christ, taught that the world would be "2000 years void of the law; 2000 years under the law; and 2000 years under the Messiah. He limited the duration of the world to 6000 years, and held that in the *seventh* millenary, "the earth would be renewed and the righteous dead raised; that these should not again be turned to dust, and that the just *then alive* should mount up with wings as the angels," etc.; "so that in that day they would not fear, though the mountains be cast into the midst of the sea." (Ps. xlvi. 3.) On this passage Bishop Russell observes, "that by this resurrection he meant a resurrection *prior* to the millennium is evident," etc. Dr. Gregory also, a learned mathematician and astronomer in Oxford, England, who died in A. D. 1710, says: "In the first verse of the first chapter of Genesis, the Hebrew *Aleph*, which in the Jewish arithmetic stands for 1000, is *six times* found. From hence the ancient cabalists concluded that the world would last 6000 years. Because also, God was *six days* about the creation, and a thousand years with Him are but as one day. (Ps. xc. See also 2 Pet. iii. 8.) Therefore after six days, that is, 6000 years' duration of the world, there shall be a *seventh* day, or millenary sabbath of rest,"[1] etc. Baal Katturim observes: "That at the end of 6000 years the world shall return to its old state, without form and void, and *after* that, it shall wholly become a sabbath." The author also of Cespar Mishna, in his notes on Maimonides, writes: "At the end of 6000 years will be *the day of judgment*, and it will also be a *sabbath*, the *beginning* of the world to come. The sabbath year, and year of jubilee, intend the same thing." And finally (though these quotations might be greatly extended): in the Gemarah, or comment on the Mishna, we read: "Rabbi Katina has said, that in the last of the thousands of years of the world's continuance, the world shall be destroyed; of which period it is said, 'the Lord alone shall be exalted in that day.' (Isa. ii. 11.) And tradition agrees with Rabbi Katina; for even as every *seventh year* is a year of *release*, so of the *seventh thousand year* of the world, it shall be a thousand years of *release*." We now resume the regular chain of history from the close of the New Testament age, by passing on to,

3. The early Post-Apostolic Era. We here observe that,

---

[1] Hale's Anal. of Chron., vol. I., p. 79.

in addition to the tradition of the *pre*-Christian Jewish writers, that the *six days* of creation were designed to typically adumbrate 6000 years, to be followed by a *seventh* millenary of rest and triumph over their enemies, the *New Testament* Scriptures also recognize the same principle of analogy of the one with the other. We ask: Was not the first Adam created as "the *figure* of Christ the coming One?"[1] If then, we can go back to the fountain-head of time, and find a *type* of "the second man, the Lord from heaven," as He who by a second creation is to restore all things from the ruins of the fall; why should it be thought a thing incredible, that the *six days* of formation of the material heavens and earth, and a *seventh* of rest, should bear a like character? Wherefore did God create the world in six days, and rest on the seventh? Why did He not employ five, or ten, or twenty instead? And so, accordingly, St. Paul, Col. ii. 16, 17, alluding to the *typical* character of the preceding dispensation, speaks especially "in respect of the sabbath days"—of which, the *seventh day* of the Creator's repose from His six days' work was the *first*—and denominates them a "*shadow of good things to come.*" Or, if this be thought an unwarrantable stretching of a type in regard to this first sabbath, we would direct the reader to St. Paul's use of the word σαββατισμὸς—SABBATISM—in Hebrews iv. 9, where, especially considering that it was Hebrew Christians whom he was addressing, and that, from long-continued usage, they could not do otherwise than associate it with a *chronological septenary*, he employed it to designate the saints' anticipated and ardently prayed-for season of glorious rest with Christ.

If, therefore, as is undeniable, the inspired apostle applied this seventh day or *first sabbath* of creative rest as a type of the heavenly rest to come, how can we consistently withhold from the previous *six days* of creative labor a similar typical character, as denotive of the 6000 years that were to precede the seventh of rest? As "a *shadow* of good things to come," the apostle refers primarily to that MILLENNIAL "REST which remaineth for the people of God" under the reign of Messiah and his saints, which is most explicitly declared to consist of "a thousand years;"[2] while both David and St. Peter declare that "one day is with the Lord as a thousand years, and a thousand years as one day."[3]

[1] Compare 1 Cor. xv. 47 with Rom. v. 14. [2] Compare Heb. iv. 1-11 with Rev. xx. 1-6.
[3] Ps. xc. 4; 2 Pet. iii. 8.

But, to the above may be added the fact, that the *primitive fathers* of that purest age of the Church immediately following the apostles, continued to put forth the same sentiment; and that, observe, not as mere opinions based upon the uninspired pre-Jewish-Christian traditions regarding it; but, with the additional light reflected upon it by the teachings of the New Testament writers *as an article of Christian faith.* In the quotations which follow, will be found a number of those early millenarian fathers, who spoke directly to the point under consideration. The first to be introduced to the reader's notice is

BARNABAS.[1] Of the Epistle still extant which bears his name, though Eusebius and Jerome pronounce it apocryphal, it is nevertheless esteemed genuine by such writers as Archbishops Wake and Usher, by Bishop Fell, and Drs. Mill, Cave, Burnet, S. Clarke, and Mr. Whiston and others. In this Epistle (which doubtless Eusebius and Jerome wished to bring into disrepute on account of the millenarianism of its author), sec. xiv. and xv., Barnabas, having argued that the Abrahamic covenant was *perpetual*, and that it had been *fulfilled* so far as it related to Christ's *first coming* in the flesh; from Isa. xlii. 6 and lxi. 21, he exhibits Christ as the covenant pledge for the accomplishment of the *remaining part* of its stipulations at "the times of restitution of all things." He then goes on to say: "Furthermore it is written concerning the *Sabbath*, 'sanctify the sabbath of the Lord with pure hands and a clean heart.' And elsewhere he saith, 'if thy children shall keep my sabbaths, then will I put my mercy on them' (alluding to the mercy promised to Abraham). And even in the beginning of the creation he makes mention of the Sabbath: 'And God made in *six days* the works of his hands, and finished them on the *seventh day*, and he *rested* on the seventh day and sanctified it.'" And he then adds: "Consider, my children, what this signifies: 'He finished them in six days.' The meaning is this: that in 6000 years the Lord will bring all things to an end. 'For with him one day is as a thousand years,' etc. Therefore, children, in *six days* (i. e., 6000 years) shall all things be *accomplished*. And what is that he saith, and *rested on the seventh day?* He meaneth, that WHEN HIS SON SHALL COME, and abolish the wicked one, and judge the ungodly, and change the sun and moon and stars, that He shall gloriously rest on the

---

[1] See pages 40, 41.

seventh day. Behold, therefore, when we have received the righteous promise, when iniquity shall be no more, all things being *renewed* by the Lord, we shall be able to sanctify it, ourselves being holy." Barnabas wrote in A. D. 71. He is supposed to have been martyred about A. D. 75, being stoned to death by the Jews.

Professor Shedd tells us that "there are *no traces* of chiliasm in the writings of Clement of Rome, Ignatius, Polycarp," etc. But, let us see.

CLEMENT OF ROME.[1] In his first Epistle he says: "Let us be followers of those who went about in goatskins and sheepskins, *preaching the coming of Christ.* Such were the prophets." Again, alluding to some who scoff at the apparent delay of Christ's second coming, he says: "Ye see how in a little while the fruit of the trees come to maturity. Of a truth, yet a little while, and His will shall be accomplished *suddenly,* the Holy Scripture itself bearing witness that *He shall come quickly* and not tarry; and the Lord shall suddenly come to his temple, even the Holy One whom ye look for." In his second Epistle he says: "If therefore we shall do what is just in the sight of God, we shall *enter into his kingdom.* . . . Wherefore let us *every hour expect* the kingdom of God in love and righteousness, because we know not the day of *God's appearing.*" Clement was martyred under the emperor Trajan about A. D. 100, by being thrown into the sea.

IGNATIUS.[2] To the Ephesians he expresses his faith thus: "*The last times* are come upon us; let us therefore be very reverent and fear the long suffering of God, that it be not to us condemnation." To Polycarp he wrote: "Be every day better than another; consider the times, *and expect Him* who is above all time," etc. Writing to the Smyrnians on the resurrection of Christ, He tells them that Peter and the other apostles did actually prove the same by the sense of touch, "being convinced both by the flesh and spirit." This belief, in connection with his hope of having a part in *the first resurrection,* was what led him to despise death and aspire after martyrdom, which was a general characteristic of the Christians of that age. Hence he thus expresses himself: "If I suffer, I shall then become the free

---

[1] See pages 41, 42.   [2] See page 42.

man of Jesus Christ, *and shall rise free.*" He was devoured by lions in the amphitheatre of Rome in A. D. 107.[1]

POLYCARP.[2] Dr. Burnet pronounces him a decided millenarian, and Eusebius hints the same. In his Epistle he taught that God had raised up our Lord Jesus Christ from the dead, and that he will come to judge the world and *raise the saints,* and that if we walk worthy of him we shall *reign together with him.* "Every one," says he, "that confesses not that Jesus Christ is come in the flesh, is *antichrist.* . . . And whosoever shall say that there is *neither resurrection nor judgment to come,* that man is the first-born of Satan."[3] Being a disciple of St. John, he must have received the doctrine directly from him. He was burned at the stake about A. D. 167. The next in order comes

HERMAS.[4] This early father, having predicted great tribulation as awaiting the Church, says: "Happy ye, as many as shall endure the great trial at hand." He also says: "This world is also as the winter to the righteous men, because they are not known, but dwell among sinners; but *the world to come* is a summer to them." Again he says: "The great God will remove the heavens, and the mountains, the hills and the seas: and the end will be accomplished that all things may be filled with His elect, *who will possess* the world to come." . . . "This age must be destroyed by fire, but *in the age to come* the elect of God shall dwell."

PAPIAS.[5] In the preface to his "Narratives of the Sayings of our Lord" already alluded to, Papias says that "he did not follow various opinions, but had *the apostles* for his authors; and that he considered what Andrew, what Peter said, what Philip, what Thomas, and other disciples of the Lord; as also what Aristian and John the senior, disciples of the Lord, what they spoke; and that He did not profit so much by reading books, as by the *living voice* of those persons which resounded from them." This is Jerome's account of Papias. Eusebius thus records his words: "Nor will you be sorry, that, together with our interpretations, I commit to writing those things which I have formerly learned from the elders and committed to memory. For I never (as many do) have followed those who abound in words, but rather those who taught the truth; not those who taught certain *new* and unaccustomed precepts, but those who remem-

---

[1] Apost. Fathers, pp. 60-137.   [2] See page 42.   [3] Apost. Fathers, p. 56.
[4] See page 41.   [5] See page 41.

bered the *commands of our Lord,* handed down in parables, and proceeding from truth itself, i. e., the Lord. If I met with any one who had been conversant with the elders, from *him* I diligently inquired what were *the sayings* of the elders . . . The elders who had *seen* John, the disciple of our Lord, taught concerning those times (the millennium), and said, the 'days come, when the vine shall bring forth abundantly,'[1] . . and all other fruits, . . and all animals shall become peaceful and harmonious, one to the other, being perfectly obedient to man. But these things are credible only to those who have faith.' Then Judas, the betrayer, not believing, and asking *how* such fertility should be brought about, our Lord said, 'They shall see who come to those times.' And, of these very times Isaiah prophesying said, 'The wolf and the lamb shall dwell together.'" This is recorded by Papias as a discourse of our Lord, handed down by John the Evangelist. Eusebius himself thus speaks of Papias: "Other things also, the same writer has set forth, as having come down to him by unwritten tradition, some new parables and discourses of our Saviour. Among these, he says, that there will be a certain thousand years *after* the resurrection of the dead, *when the kingdom of Christ will be established visibly in the earth.*" Papias here alludes to the seventh millenary *after* the 6000 years of the world's history. Eusebius affirms that "*most of the ecclesiastical writers*" *believed* with Papias;[2] and Dr. Whitby admits that he taught concerning the millennium, that "it shall be a reign of Christ bodily on earth." While Dr. Burton allows that Papias's "proximity to the apostolic times, if not his personal acquaintance with some of the apostles, would put him in possession of many facts;" the learned Greswell observes that "Papias's honesty has *never* been impeached, and his antiquity makes his testimony to the millennium so much the more valuable."

JUSTIN MARTYR. He was a Greek, born at Annapolis or Sichem, in the province of Samaria, in Palestine, about A. D. 89. As a writer, he flourished between A. D. 148–165. He was therefore contemporary in part with Polycarp, Papias, and Irenæus. Eusebius says his works stood in high credit among the early Christians. In his "Dialogue with Trypho," the Jew, which is

---

[1] This is that marvellous vine of Papias, referred to by Prof. Shedd. See page 24.
[2] Eusebius, Eccles. Hist., B. III., chap. 39.

held to be authentic and genuine, having become a convert to "chiliasm" of a pure character, he looked for *no* millennium during this dispensation. He speaks of those as "destitute of just reason who did not understand that which is clear from all the Scriptures, that *two* comings of Christ were announced;" and he maintained that the millennium would be *beyond* the resurrection [i. e., of the saints], and *in* the restitution of all things, quoting Isa. lxv., and others of the prophets, as proof, especially verses 17-19, "Behold, I create new heavens and a new earth," etc. And in reference to those in his time who denied this doctrine, in answer to the question of Trypho in regard to his faith, he says that, among other things, "I have demonstrated to thee that these are indeed called Christians, but are atheists and infamous heretics, because that in all things they teach what is blasphemous, ungodly, and unsound." We presume he here refers to the *Gnostics* of that age, whose system was a combination of Oriental and Platonic philosophy, and also, in some cases, as that of Cerinthus, of Judaism, with certain elements of Christian doctrine. He also adds: "But I, and whatsoever Christians are ORTHODOX IN ALL THINGS, *do know that there will be a resurrection of the flesh, and a thousand years in the city of Jerusalem, built and adorned, and enlarged according to the prophets.*" He further continues thus: —"For thus hath Isaiah spoken of the thousand years: '*for there will be a new heavens and earth,*' etc. He then quotes Isa. lxv., making the "tree" of verse 22 the tree of life [or, as we suppose he meant, the restoration of *patriarchal longevity* to the human race]; and adds, "We believe a thousand years to be figuratively expressed. For it was said to Adam, 'In the day that thou eatest thereof, thou shalt surely die,' Gen. ii. 17; so that we know that he did not live a thousand years. We believe, also, that this expression, 'The day of the Lord is as a thousand years,' Ps. xc. 4, and 2 Pet. iii. 8, relates to this." And then, quoting from Rev. xx. 1-5, in proof, he says: "We may conclude from many places in Scripture, that those are right who say that 6000 years is the time fixed for the duration of the present frame of the world."

Eusebius admits that Justin Martyr's writings stood in high esteem among the early Christians. Also Milner, Semisch, a German writer, and Drs. Cave, Burton, Elliott, and Adam Clark, all confess that this writer held the "*chiliasm*" *of the second century,* which constituted so decidedly an article of the Christian faith, to be *a criterion of orthodoxy.* Also, that "he abounds in solid, sound sense, the product of an acute and well-cultivated mind;" that he was "a witness beyond all exception," and that his learning and piety as such has been testified to by nearly all the succeeding fathers." He was crowned with martyrdom at Rome by being beheaded, A. D. 165.

IRENÆUS, bishop of Lyons. He was born, it is supposed, near Smyrna, and flourished as a writer between A. D. 176-202. Basil styles him "one near the apostles." He was pupil to and trained up under the tutelage of Papias and Polycarp, both of whom were disciples of the revelator John. For learning, steadfastness, and zeal, he was among the most renowned of the early fathers. Milner highly commends him, and calls him a man of excellent judgment. It may hence seem to the reader not a little singular, that Professor Shedd, when speaking of *Papias,* should represent his "mind as comparatively uninfluential, and his writings as of little importance," and quote Eusebius as saying that they "contain matters rather too fabulous,"[1] while at the same time he admits that "he was *the cause why most* of the ecclesiastical writers, urging the antiquity of the man, *were carried away* by a similar opinion, as, for instance, Irenæus, or any other that adopted his sentiments."[2] Such statements carry with them their own refutation. It is not in the nature of things, that a man like Irenæus should have been led to adopt the millenarian system at the hand of a shallow-minded fanatic.

The works of Irenæus, still extant, consist of five books on the heresies of the times. These Mosheim calls "a splendid monument of antiquity." We must here again quote from Professor Shedd. "Irenæus and Tertullian, in their writings against *heretics,*" says he, "present brief synoptical statements of the authorized faith of the Church; *but in none of them* do we find the millenarian tenet."[3] Now, let us first put this to the test in reference to Irenæus. He affirms, that certain heretical opinions had arisen, proceeding from ignorance of the arrangements of God, *and the mystery of the first resurrection and the kingdom of the just;* and it therefore became needful to speak of them. And, having given a lucid and scriptural exposition of the Abrahamic covenant as embracing in its stipulations, first, Abraham's *lineal*

---

[1] See pages of his History, 391, 395. [2] Ib., page 396. [3] Ib., page 391.

multitudinous seed, and second, the *Gentile* nations as blessed through them; and for the security of which, Christ as Abraham's seed was the surety and pledge, he says: "For true and unchangeable is God; wherefore also he said, '*Blessed are the meek, for they shall inherit the earth.*'" And to show how fully he supported his prophetical exegeses by quotations from the Old and New Testaments, we give the following in his own order of the subjects treated: Isa. xxvi. 19; Ezek. xxxvii. 12-14; xxxviii. 25, 26; Jer. xxiii. 7, 8; Isa. xxx. 25, 26; lviii. 14; Luke xii. 37-40; Rev. xx. 1-6; Isa. vi. 11; Dan. vii. 27; Jer. xxxi. 10-15; Isa. xxxi. 9; xxxii. 1; liv. 11-14; and lxv. 17-28.

Dr. Burton, in speaking of these doctrines of Irenæus, says, that he "goes to *the fountain head.*" He relates it as from St. John, and John from our Lord. And he adds: "Irenæus, like Justin (Martyr), calls those '*heretics*' who expected the saints' glorification *immediately after death* and *before* their resurrection. He also made the *Roman kingdom* to be the fourth beast described by Daniel, seventh chapter. And on the *duration* of the world, he says: "In as many days as the world was made, in so many thousand years it is perfected; for if the day of the Lord be as it were a thousand years, and in *six days* those things that are made were finished; it is manifest that the perfecting of these things is *in the six thousandth year*, when ANTICHRIST, having reigned 1260 years, . . . then the Lord shall come from heaven in the clouds with the glory of His Father, casting him and them that obey him into a lake of fire; but bringing to the just the time of the kingdom, that is, the *rest*, or *Sabbath*, or *seventh day* sanctified, and fulfilling to Abraham the promise of the inheritance."[1]

The Churches of Vienna and Lyons. These Churches addressed an epistle to the Churches in Asia and Phrygia in A. D. 177, which Eusebius inserts at length in his Ecclesiastical History. Professor Moses Stuart thinks it probable that it was written by Irenæus, though Dr. Elliott ascribes it to one of the Lyonese Christians. After narrating the martyrdoms of Ponticus, a youth of fifteen years, and Blandina, a Christian lady, it says: "The bodies of the martyrs having been contumeliously treated and exposed for six days, were burned and reduced to ashes, and scattered by the wicked into the Rhone, that not the least particle

---

[1] Irenæus Adversus Hereses, Lib. V., chap. xxxv., pp. 452-464.

of them might appear on the earth any more. And they did these things as if they could prevail against God, *and prevent their resurrection*, and that they might deter others, as they said, 'from *the hope of a future life*, relying on which, they introduce *a strange and new* religion, and despise the most extraordinary tortures, and die with joy. Now let us see if they will rise again, and if their God can help them and deliver them out of our hands."[1] Mr. Faber, on this testimony from their enemies of the *practical* bearing of the doctrine of the resurrection of the body, as held by the primitive martyrs, says: "The doctrine of the *literal* resurrection of the martyrs prior to that epoch certainly prevailed to a considerable extent throughout the early Church, and often animated the primitive believers to seal the truth with their blood." And on the same subject, the learned Dodwell writes: "The primitive Christians believed that '*the first resurrection*' of their bodies would take place *in the kingdom of the millennium;* and as they considered that resurrection to be peculiar to the *just*, so they conceived the martyrs would enjoy the *principal share* of its glory,"[2] etc.

Irenæus sealed his testimony with his blood, by being beheaded, under the reign of Severus, in A. D. 202.

Melito, bishop of Sardis. He was born in Asia, and was contemporary with Justin Martyr. Tertullian and Polycrates both testify to his preëminent piety and eloquence.[3] Besides an Apology and Canon of the Old Testament, he wrote a treatise on the *Apocalypse*. Jerome and Gennadius both affirm that he was a *decided millenarian*. The time and manner of his death are unknown.[4]

Tertullian. He was born at Carthage, in Africa, and flourished as a writer between A. D. 196–218. Cyprian thought much of him, and never passed a day without reading some portions of his works. Spanheim calls him "one of the first of the fathers." Others, as Professor Stuart, Mosheim, Neander, and Milner, differ in their estimates of his excellencies and defects. In reference to his views of the Apocalypse, he writes thus: " We confess that *a kingdom is promised us on earth before* that in heaven, but in another state, namely, *after* the resurrection; for it will be *one*

---

[1] Eusebius's Eccles. Hist., Book V., chap. l.   [2] Dodwell's Dissertations, sec. 20.
[3] Eusebius's Eccles. Hist., Book V., chap. xxiv.
[4] Cave's Lives of the Fathers, p. 337; Burnet's Theory of the Earth, vol. II., p. 166.

thousand years in a city of divine workmanship, viz., Jerusalem brought down from heaven; and this city Ezekiel knew, and the apostle John saw, etc. This is the city provided of God to receive the saints *in the first resurrection,* wherein to refresh them" [not in the "materializing," "gross," and "sensual" pleasures of the elysium of a Cerinthus, but] "with an abundance of *all spiritual* good things, in recompense for those which in the world we have either despised or lost. For it is both just and worthy of God, that his servants should there triumph and rejoice, where they have been afflicted for His name's sake. This is the manner of the heavenly kingdom."[1] Where or how he died is uncertain.

Clement, bishop of Alexandria. Professor Shedd had come a little nearer the mark, had he claimed Clement of Alexandria as having taken no notice of "the millenarian tenet." Dr. Burnet says: "He has not said anything that I know of, either for or against the millennium: but," he adds, "he takes notice 'that the *seventh day* has been accounted sacred both by the Hebrews and Greeks, because of the revolution of the world, and *the renovation of all things.*'" And from this Burnet argues, that "it can be in no other sense than that the seventh day represents the *seventh millennium,* in which the kingdom and renovation are to be."[2] And in his address to the heathen, Clement says: "Therefore Jesus cries aloud, personally urging us, *because the kingdom of heaven is at hand:* He converts men by fear,"[3] etc. "This," says Dr. Duffield, "is Peter's argument (1 Peter iv. 7), and it proves that he regarded the kingdom of heaven, as the prophets testify, to be *introduced by judgment:* his ideas of that kingdom must have been radically different from those of the *spiritualists.*"[4] And some others regard him as a millenarian. But, be that as it may, although Eusebius calls him an "incomparable master of the Christian philosophy," and Neander attributes to him "great knowledge about divine matters," we regard the preceding as of too *equivocal* a character to justify the inferences drawn from them. As we have already intimated, Clement, first at the head of the catechetical school (A. D. 188), and then bishop of Alexandria, laid the foundation for that NEW THEORY of Scriptural her-

---

[1] Tertullian against Marcion, Lib. III., p. 680.
[2] Burnet's Theory of the Earth, vol. ii., p. 188.   [3] Cave's Lives, etc., p. 355.
[4] Duffield on Prophecy, p. 29.

meneutics by which the *literal* interpretation of the prophets was finally "hissed off the stage." We have the explicit declaration of Dr. Murdock, that "he construed the Bible *allegorically and fancifully.*" This with us is decisive.

Clement flourished as a writer between A. D. 193–218. Of the place and manner of his death we know nothing.

Methodius, bishop of Olympus. He flourished between A. D. 260–312. Dr. Whitby, who was at antipodes with his sentiments, allows that "Methodius held to a *pure millennium,* free from everything sensual." He was also admitted by Neander to have been a chiliast.[1] He was a firm opponent of Origen, and charged that fanciful interpreter with heresy. The following passage is quoted from his work by Produs in Epiphaneus: "It is to be expected that at the conflagration, the creation shall suffer a vehement commotion, as if it were about to die: *whereby it shall be renovated, and not perish;* to the end that we, then also renovated, *may dwell in the renewed world free from sorrow.* Thus it is said in Psalm civ.: 'Thou wilt send forth Thy Spirit, and they shall be created, and Thou wilt *renew* the face of the earth.' For seeing that after this world there shall be an earth, of necessity there must be inhabitants; and these shall die no more, but be as angels, irreversibly in an incorruptible state, doing all most excellent things."[2] He was crowned with martyrdom, under the emperor Decius, in A. D. 312.

Nepos and Coracion.[3] Nepos was a learned Egyptian bishop, and all writers, ancient and modern, admit that he was a millenarian, in which Coracion coincided with him. Dr. Cave says, that "he was a man skilled in the Holy Scriptures, and also a poet; and that he had fallen into the *error of the millenarians,* and had published books to show that the promises made in the Scriptures to good men, were, according to the sense and opinions of the Jews, to be *literally* understood,"[4] etc. Even Whitby allows that he taught that, "*after* this (first) resurrection, the kingdom of Christ was to be upon earth for a thousand years, and the saints were to reign with Him. According to Mr. Brooks, "he wrote a book entitled 'The Reprehensions of *Allegorizers,*' which was specially directed against those who *now* began (A. D. 262) to explain the millennium *figuratively.*"

---

[1] Neander's Church History, vol. i., pp. 451, 452. [2] Epiphaneus Her., 74.
[3] See pages 30, 31. [4] Cave's Lives, etc., p. 510

SECTION II.

ERA OF THE COMMENCEMENT OF APOSTASY FROM ANCIENT CHILIASM.

Having traced the *origin* of millenarianism through the inspired pre-Christian-Hebrew Church, as founded upon the Abrahamic covenant—which was itself but a revised and enlarged form of the *first promise* of redemption made to fallen man—also that it was recognized by the uninspired Jewish writers, and in the traditional theology of Pagan nations *prior* to the first coming of Christ; and that it abounds in the epistolary writings of the New Testament age, and constituted the received faith of the Church during the early post-apostolic age: we now approach that period of the COMMENCED APOSTASY from the said "faith delivered to the saints," as set forth in the following noted prophecy of St. Paul, 2 Tim. iv. 3, 4:

"*For the time will come when they will not endure sound doctrine; but after their own lusts shall they heap to themselves teachers, having itching ears; and they shall turn their ears from the truth, and shall be turned unto fables.*"[1]

We have already shown that the millenarian controversy that sprung up in the early part of the third century, was instigated by the introduction into the Church of the *new allegorical* theory of Origen, in opposition to the *literal*, as the standard rule of scriptural exegesis.[2]

We have also proved the *error* of the historical statements alleged by Professor Shedd, to wit: that millenarianism "was not the received faith of the Church certainly down to the year 150;" that "it was held only by individuals;" "that its blooming period was a *brief one* of about a hundred years;" and "that the third century witnessed a *very decided* opposition to it." Indeed, the *main reliance* of anti-millenarians in their assaults upon this system, consists in holding it up to view as a "materializing," "gross," "sensual," and "fanatical heresy," and decrying its followers as a small and insignificant sect. Thus the learned Dr. Hamilton, in his work against the millenarians, says (page

---
[1] See Note A.   [2] See pages 13, 14.

308), "that its principles were opposed and rejected by almost every father of the Church, with the *exception* of Barnabas, Clement, Papias, Justin Martyr, Irenæus, Nepos, Apollinarus, Lactantantius, and Tertullian!" That is, with the exception of *all* the fathers whom he knows before, and some who were contemporary with and subsequent to, *the time of Origen!* And this, reader, on the ground that he prefers the fathers of *later* date, because "their learning and talents *far surpassed* any in the first centuries of the Church." But we have only to ask, first, what must have been the *extent* to which millenarianism must have prevailed between the time of St. John in A. D. 96 and that of Origen in A. D. 232 (the date at which his *new* allegorical theory first began to obtain in the Church), when ALL the fathers were its avowed advocates? And second, when, in A. D. 325, at the Council of Nice, 318 bishops, collected from all parts of the Church, *incorporated in the Nicene Creed* adopted by them, the distinguishing tenets of millenarianism?[1] And finally, third, when Jerome admits that "*many* Christians and martyrs had affirmed the things which he denied;" and that, toward the close of the fourth century, "*a great multitude* of Christians agreed with them in his own day?"

But we have also admitted that, *after* this date, millenarianism began to decline. We have already explained the *causes* which led to this result.[2] It now comes in place to observe, that this system was not opposed by all *on the same grounds*. Some writers, as Dionysius, of Alexandria, and Eusebius, of Cæsarea, acting on the principle that, *if* the Apocalypse of St. John is to be received as canonical, millenarianism is a scriptural doctrine, *repudiated* that book as spurious. Others, however, of whom Origen was one, while they admitted that it *was* canonical, and actually declared their belief that the second personal coming of the Lord was *imminent in their day*, and also admitted that the earth, in its renovated state after the conflagration, would be the *seat* of the redeemed, yet *opposed* millenarianism.

Now, how is this to be explained? Simply, we reply, on the ground of their adoption of the *Septuagint chronology* of the world, in the place of the original Hebrew text. The Septuagint, as we have seen,[3] places the nativity in *excess* of the Hebrew date at A. M. 5871, which leaves only a fraction over 1100 years to the close of the 7000th year from the creation and fall of man. And,

---
[1] See pages 45, 46.   [2] See pages 48, 49..   [3] See pages 53, 54.

as all writers admit that at the close of the *seventh* chiliad time ends, and the redeemed Church enters upon her *eternal state*, so the class of interpreters here referred to regulate the commencement of the millennium in accommodation to their *variant* computations of the Septuagint chronology. Of the chronological calculus of the writers of the early Church, as founded on the *Septuagint* version, Clement of Alexandria terminated the 6,000 about A. D. 374; Cyprian earlier, in A. D. 243; Eustathius, Lactantius, Hilarion, Jerome, etc., in A. D. 500; Sulpitius Severus, in A. D. 581; and Augustine, in A. D. 650. Indeed, while some of these writers deny *any* millennium at all, the above system of chronology of those who were *anti*-millenarian has originated all those theories of a *spiritual* millennium which have infested the Church from the time of Origen. These theories, one and all, as a matter of course, ignore that fundamental principle of millenarianism, viz., the *literal* restoration, conversion, and national preëminence of the Jews, and the blessing of the Gentile nations through them, together with the personal reign of Christ and His saints over the saved nations in the flesh for a thousand years. And yet, singular as it may appear, while all the spiritualizing theorists *rightly* place the universal conflagration of the earth at the *end* of the seventh chiliad, some otherwise able expositors of millenarianism, by confounding the judgments of God upon the wicked at the *commencement* of the millennial era with that event, erroneously represent it as *pre*-millennial. Several of the ancient fathers,[1] together with those of modern date, have fallen into this mistake. On the other hand, *anti*-millenarians, both ancient and modern, in one form or another, have incorporated in their theories one or other of the *distinguishing tenets* of millenarianism. Thus *Jerome*. "God will make *new heavens and a new earth:* not other heavens and another earth; but the former ones changed into better." And even as late as Gregory the Great, we find him saying: "Others are not to be created, *but the same renewed.*" And again, on Eccles. iii. 14, he says: "They will pass as to their present figure or appearance, but as to their substance, they will *remain forever.*"[2] And so *Origen.* In the thirteenth book of his work against Celsus, he says: "We do not deny the purging fire of the destruction of wickedness, *and the renovation of all things,*" etc. And

---

[1] Eusebius's Eccles. Hist., B. VI., ch. xxxv.; Ward's Hist. Millen., p. 19.; Stuart, vol. i., p. 344.
[2] Lib. XVII., ch. ii. and v.

again: "The earth, *after* its conflagration, *shall become habitable again and be the mansion of men*,"[1] etc. And finally, he affirms in his thirteenth Homily on Jeremiah, "If any man shall preserve the washing of the Holy Spirit, he shall have his part *in the first resurrection:* . . . Let us lay the Scriptures to heart, that we may be raised up *with the saints*, and have our lot with Jesus Christ."

But the question is, Did the above facts make these writers millenarians? Our reply is, By no means. Though they are *cardinal points* in that system, yet, this amalgamating of the *allegorical* with the *literal* in the interpretation of "the teachings of Isaiah and St. John respecting the second coming of Christ," strikes at the very vitals of that system. For, the *order* of events, as well as the *nature* of the things predicted, being hypothecated of the chronology of the *Septuagint*, aims to "*sweep from off the stage*" the last vestiges of the "chiliasm" of the Church.

We are not ambitious, therefore, to augment the number of millenarians by accessions from the ranks of such. The preceding remarks are predicated of the conviction that the time has fully come, when there is a need-be *to distinguish between things which differ* in these premises. Our object and aim is to present millenarianism before the Churches of this day *on its merits as a whole* according to "the law and the testimony" of Holy Writ. On this subject, we are willing to abide the issue in accordance with what Origen himself admits: that "they who *deny* millenarianism, are they who interpret the sayings of the prophets *by a trope;* but they who *assert* it are styled disciples of the *letter* of Scripture only." With these explanations, which the reader will do well to keep in view, we now resume the thread of our history.

Notwithstanding Professor Shedd's confident statement, that "Dionysius, bishop of Alexandria, succeeded by dint of argument in *repressing* a very gross form of millenarianism that was spreading in his diocese" (page 395); yet, that the chiliastic party was still strong after this, is evident from the declaration of Burnet, that "we do not find that Dionysius's opposition *had any great effect.*" He also states that "the millennial kingdom of Christ was the *general doctrine* of the primitive Church from the *times of the apostles to the Council of Nice,* inclusively."[2]

[1] Encyc. of Rel. Knowledge.   [2] Burnet, vol. ii., p. 184.; Mosheim, ch. v.

Epiphanius, bishop of Constantia or Salamis in Cyprus, and who flourished between A. D. 367–403, was a millenarian, and testifies that the doctrine was held by *many in his time*. Quoting the words of Paulinus, bishop of Antioch, concerning one Vitalius, whom he highly commends for his piety, orthodoxy, and learning, he says, "Moreover, others have affirmed that the venerable man would say, that in the first resurrection we shall accomplish a certain millenary of years;" on which Epiphanius observes, "And that indeed this millenary term is written in the Apocalypse of John, and is received of *very many* of them that are godly, is manifest. Besides, in A. D. 402, he vehemently contended against the Origenists." But from his time, millenarianism began to grow unpopular, and to fall into general desuetude.

Hilary, bishop of Poictiers, A. D. 368, Ambrose, bishop of Milan, A. D. 374–397, Chrysostom, bishop of Constantinople, A. D. 370–407, and Jerome of Rome, A. D. 363–420, all of the Origenist school, form the connecting links between Epiphanius and AUGUSTINE, bishop of Hippo, A. D. 390–430. While the Church was now becoming more and more corrupted by the growing superstitions of the age, and the doctrines of grace continued to degenerate, Augustine remained comparatively free from the one and a zealous advocate of the other, and, as Milner says, "the light from his writings glimmered through many ages, down even to the Reformation." He was once a chiliast, but owing to its perversion by many and the misrepresentations of his enemies, he abandoned it, and adopting the *Septuagint* chronology, developed what is usually called the AUGUSTINIAN THEORY of the millennium, which afterwards became very prevalent, and which formed *a new era* in its history. The world's duration he accordingly made *sex*-millennial, and affirmed that the resurrection was *spiritual*, which he dated from the *first coming* of Christ, and with the other *anti*-millenarian fathers of the fourth and fifth centuries, explained the seventh sabbatical day, not of a seventh sabbatical millennium of rest, but an *eternal sabbath*—a view generally adopted afterwards.[1]

But in regard to the millenarian faith of the *early Church*, DR. LARDNER, though an anti-millenarian, testifies, "The mil-

---

[1] Augustine De Civit., Lib. XX., c. v., xiv., xvi. Homily, vol. i., pp. 43, 358, 252, 83, 70. Oxford ed.

lennium has been a favorite doctrine of *some ages*, and has had the patronage of the learned as well as the vulgar among Christians."[1] CHILLINGWORTH says: "Whatever doctrine is taught by the fathers of any age, not as doctors, but as witnesses, etc., of the doctrine of the Church of their time, neither did any contradict them in it; *ergo*, it is doubtless to be esteemed." Again he says: "It appears manifest out of this book of Irenæus, that the doctrine of the *chiliasts* was in his judgment apostolic tradition, as also it was esteemed (for aught appears to the contrary) by all the doctors, and saints, and martyrs of, or about his time; for all that speak of it, or whose judgments in the point are any way recorded, are for it; and Justin Martyr professeth, that all good and orthodox Christians of his time believed it, and those that did not, he reckons among *heretics*."[2] MOSHEIM gives substantially the same testimony.[3] BISHOP RUSSELL says: "The Jews and their followers, in primitive times, understood the millennium *literally;* the word had *no double sense* in their creed; it was not in their estimation the emblem or shadow of better things to come; on the contrary, it denoted the actual visible appearance of the Messiah, and the establishment of his kingdom upon earth as the Sovereign of the elect people of God,"[4] etc. DR. BURTON says: "It cannot be denied that Papias, Irenæus, Justin Martyr, and all the other ecclesiastical writers, believed, *literally*, that the saints would rise in the first resurrection, and reign with Christ upon earth *previous* to the general resurrection,"[5] etc. DR. NEANDER, speaking of the early Church, says: "They were accustomed to consider that ... as the world was created in six days, and according to Ps. xc. 4, a thousand years in God's sight is but as one day, so the world was supposed to endure 6,000 years in its present condition; and as the Sabbath day was the day of rest, so this millennial reign was to form the seven thousandth year period of the world's existence, at the close of the whole temporal dispensation connected with the world,"[6] etc.

Quotations to the same effect might be made from other *anti*-millenarian writers, but with all those "whose respect for everything Catholic and ecclesiastical," like that of Eusebius, is "very high," and who are wont to repair to the fountain head of early

---

[1] Cred. of the Gosp. Hist., fol. ed., vol. iv., p. 513; see also pp. 640, 641.
[2] Chillingworth's Works, fol. ed., p. 174, and p. 347.
[3] Eccles. Hist., vol. i., p. 89, ch. iii., sec. 2.   [4] See Disc. on the Millen. pp. 47, 84, 89, 236.
[5] Burton's Bampton Lecture for 1829.   [6] Neander's Ch. Hist., vol. i., pp. 403, 404.

post-apostolic antiquity in support of their favorite theories, the above testimony of their *anti*-millenarian compeers in regard to the faith of the primitive "chiliasts," is specially commended to their respectful consideration.

SECTION III.

MILLENARIANISM DURING THE MEDIÆVAL AGE.

We now enter upon the long and dreary interval of the dark ages. Yes, "the blooming age of millenarianism" was destined to pass away. That "falling away first" (ἡ ἀποστασία—THE APOSTASY) which was to be headed up in the revelation of "the man of sin" as the precursor of the second coming of our Lord,[1] and which is called "the mystery of iniquity,"[2] began to work in St. Paul's time. The very phraseology indicates that it was to take place *within the Church*,[3] which of course implies that, during this dispensation, she was to be a of a *mixed character*, analogous to the wheat and tares in the parable, both of which were to "grow together *until the harvest*."[4]

And we affirm that this apostasy from "the faith at first delivered to the saints" was to consist, SPECIALLY, *of a perversion and denial of the doctrine of our blessed Lord's second personal coming, as embraced in the tenets of millenarianism.*[5] When speaking of His second coming to avenge His elect of their adversaries, as illustrated in the parable of the judge and the importunate widow seeking redress at his hand, Christ said, "Nevertheless, when the Son of Man cometh, shall He find (this) faith on the earth?"[6] So far from it, maugre her boasted "orthodoxy" in other respects, the apostate portion of the nominal Church, "walking after their own lusts," will be found uttering the demand of St. Peter's predicted "scoffers of the last days, saying, *Where is the promise of his coming?*"[7]

We hold that the *tenets* of millenarianism as a matter of divine revelation, are infallible and immutable. Not so with its *uninspired* advocates, whether ancient or modern. They were

---

[1] 2 Thess. ii. 1-3.   [2] Ib., v. 7.   [3] Acts xx. 28-30.   [4] Matt. xiii. 30.
[5] See Note A.   [6] Luke xviii. 1-8.   [7] 2 Pet. iii. 2-4.

both fallible and mutable. In regard therefore to the ancient fathers, while we hold them to be credible witnesses of what *was* believed in their time, we discard them as authority as to what *should be* believed. Still we maintain that, in all the *fundamental* principles of that system, however they may have erred in its details, they interpreted "the teachings of Isaiah and St. John concerning the second coming of Christ" according to "the mind of the Spirit."[1]

We concede, then, that the "gold, silver, and precious stones" of millenarian truth in these early times, were more or less tarnished by the "wood, hay, and stubble" of man's device. Hence these latter, in the way and manner already indicated,[2] were seized upon and used by all classes and grades of *anti*-millenarians, as the weapons to "*turn away men's ears from the truth, and to turn them unto fables.*"[3] And when we consider that, along with the gradual decay of millenarianism, the insidious working of a horde of rapacious, ambitious, and aspiring ecclesiastics was inundating the Church with every species of error in doctrine and corruption of the primitive usages of the Church, and especially *after* the time of Constantine down to that of Augustine, nothing remained in order to *mature* that apostasy, but the engrafting into the theology of the Church the theory of *that father* respecting the millennium. The old system of Paganism had indeed fallen, but at the opening of the fifth century the *Papacy* was hastening to its birth, and, by the edict of Justinian I., was ushered into being in the person of John II., the then Patriarch of Rome, in A. D. 533, as the so-called vicegerent of Jesus Christ upon earth. Henceforth the *ecclesiastical* "little horn" of the Papacy[4] (and which soon after became an *ecclesiastico-political* power) commenced to "*make war* with the saints, and to *prevail* against them;"[5] and that, on the ground of their CHILIASTIC protestations against the corrupt Church of Rome as *antichristian*, and the Pope as *Antichrist*.

For this consummation, Origen, who made the Church on earth "the *mystic* kingdom of heaven," and Eusebius, who spoke of it as "the *very image* of the kingdom of Christ," and Augustine, who invested it with the appropriate form and proportions of a regular system, had prepared the way. "It is

---

[1] Rom. viii. 27.   [2] See pages 72–74.   [3] 2 Tim. iv. 3, 4.
[4] Dan. viii. 8, 20.   [5] Ib., v. 21.

worthy of remark," says Bishop Russell, "that so long as the prophecies regarding the millennium were interpreted *literally*, the APOCALYPSE was received as an inspired production, and as the work of the apostle John; but no sooner did theologians find themselves compelled to view its annunciations through the medium of *allegory* and *metaphorical* description, than they ventured to *call in question* its heavenly origin, its genuineness, and its authority. Dionysius, the great supporter of the allegorical school, gives a decided opinion *against* the authenticity of the Revelation." On the other hand, Eunapius the Pagan, even in A. D. 396, speaking of the martyr-worship in the Church of Rome, exclaimed, "These are the gods that the earth now a days brings forth; these the intercessors with the gods—men called martyrs: before whose bones and skulls, pickled and salted, the monks kneel and lie prostrate, covered with filth and dust." But the augmented corruptions and abominations of the Papal see of Rome during the fifth and sixth centuries, while they made the Pagan to blush, cast into the shade all that had preceded them. Can we then be surprised, that under such circumstances, the *true millennium* was cast aside, and with it the *Apocalypse* that taught it? "Rome," says Dr. Burnet, "always had an evil eye on the millennium," i. e., as taught by the *chiliasts*. Baronius, a Roman Catholic historian of the sixteenth century, in alluding to the chiliasm of the fifth century writes: "The figments of the *millenaries* being rejected everywhere, and derided by the learned with hisses and laughter, and being also put under the ban, were entirely extirpated!"

But wherefore this opposition of the Church of Rome to chiliasm? Let Dr. Burnet reply. "I never yet met with a Popish doctor that held the millennium. . . . It did not *suit the scheme* which they had drawn. The Apocalypse of John supposed the true Church under hardships and persecutions; but the Church of Rome supposing Christ reigns already by his Vicar, the POPE, hath been in prosperity and greatness, and the commanding Church in Christendom for a long time. And the millennium being properly a reward and a triumph for those that come out of *persecution* (i. e., the martyrs); such as have lived always in pomp and prosperity, can pretend to *no share* in it, or be *benefited* by it. This has made the Church of Rome always have an *evil eye* upon this doctrine, because it seemed to have an evil eye *upon her;* and as she grew in splendor and greatness, she eclipsed and obscured it more and more; so that it would have been lost out of the world, as an obsolete error, if it had not been *revived* by some at the REFORMATION."[1] Ay, and so, we add, just in proportion as the *Protestant* Churches of Christendom have been exempted from persecution, and have increased in worldly prosperity, have they, under one form or another, looked with " an *evil eye* upon this doctrine." Protestants, think of this!

But what *theory* did the Church of Rome substitute in the place of chiliasm? It was that of AUGUSTINE, as already explained,[2] and which was adopted and expounded in the apocalyptic writings of Tichonius of the fourth century; Primasius of the sixth; Andreas of the sixth or seventh; Ambrose, Anabert, and probably Bede of the eighth; and Berengard of the ninth. Elliott, in his "Horæ Apocalypticæ," gives the following scheme of it: "That the millennium of Satan's binding, and the saints reigning, dated from Christ's *ministry*, when he beheld Satan fall like lightning from heaven; it being meant to signify his triumph over Satan in the hearts of true believers; and that the subsequent figuration of Gog and Magog indicated the coming of Antichrist at the end of the world—the 1,000 years being a figurative numeral, expressive of the whole period intervening. It supposed the resurrection taught to be that of dead souls from the death of sin to the life of righteousness; the beast conquered by the saints, meant the wicked world; its image, a hypocritical profession; the resurrection being continuous, till the end of time, when the universal resurrection and final judgment would take place."

But if, as Baronius affirms, "the figments of the millenaries were *entirely exterminated*" in the fifth century, how comes it that it was *revived at the Reformation?* The fact is, the learned Romanist, like some others, committed a slight error in this matter. He happened to overlook the historic fact, in reference to the ancient VAUDOIS, or Waldenses, that heroic band of faithful " witnesses " for the truth, who descended from those ancient sufferers under the *Pagan* emperors, that sought for refuge from the hand of their bloody persecutors in the remote regions of the Cottian Alps, and who are known to exist down to the present day, in the secluded and extensive valleys at the foot of the Alps in the northwest corner of Piedmont.

[1] Burnet's Theory of the Earth, vol. ii., p. 193.   [2] See page 76.

Now, these ancient Vaudois form the *connecting link* between the New Testament and early post-Christian Church; and 'the primitive doctrines to which they adhered were preserved *uncorrupt*, through the Albigenses, the Lollards or Wicklifites, the Bohemian Protestants, etc., who derived those doctrines from them, down to the time of the Reformation. If any doubt this, we would refer them to the following testimony from Romish writers themselves. Thus:—Pope Alexander III., when presiding over the Synod of Tours in A. D. 1167, pronounced the doctrine of the Vaudois to be "a damnable heresy of *long standing.*" Another synod held at La Vaux, urged the Pope to exterminate "an heretical pest" (meaning the Vaudois), "*generated in olden times*, of enormous growth and *great antiquity.*" The Romish inquisitor, Reinerus Sacco, having expressed alarm at the danger which threatened his church from the heresy of the Vaudois, declared that it was "because it was *more ancient* than any other, as well as more general," etc. And Cassini, a Franciscan, writing in the sixteenth century against the Vaudois, says, "The errors of the Vaudois consist in their *denial* that the Romish is the Holy Mother Church, and in their *refusal* to obey her traditions." And he then adds, "In other points, they recognize the Church of Christ; and for my part," says he, "I cannot deny *that they have always been* members of the Church."

Now, one of the principal articles of faith of these Vaudois is, that "they have always regarded the Papal Church as Antichrist: the Babylon of the Apocalypse;" and "they also condemned the *mystical* or *allegorical* interpretations of Scripture." [1] Of course, then, they must have interpreted *literally* "the teachings of Isaiah and St. John concerning the second coming of Christ," the millennium, etc., etc. Their writings consist of a "Treatise on Antichrist," and the "Noble Lesson," the last written in the twelfth century, and both pronounced by the best judges to be genuine and authentic.[2] We have not space for further extracts. Suffice it to say, that they are purely millenarian.

We would add on this subject, that the Rev. Mr. GILLY, a distinguished Episcopal clergyman, in his valuable and instructive account of the Vaudois or Waldenses, whom he visited in A. D. 1823, gives a report of a conversation that he then had with M. Peyrani, the Moderator of their Church. This minister of

---

[1] Vide Encyc. of Rel. Knowledge. [2] See Elliott, vol. ii., p. 228.

Christ having felt great satisfaction in explaining how closely the *doctrines* of the Vaudois Church assimilate to those of the Church of England (i. e., the Thirty-nine Articles), . . . with conscious and becoming pride he said, "But remember, that you are indebted to us for your emancipation from Papal thraldom. *We led the way.* We stood in the first rank, and against us the first thunderbolts of Rome were fulminated. The bayings of the bloodhounds of the inquisition were heard in our valleys *before you knew its name.* They hunted down some of our ancestors, and pursued others from glen to glen, and over rock and mountain, till they obliged us to take shelter in foreign countries. A few of these wanderers penetrated as far as Provence and Languedoc, and from them were derived the Albigenses, or (so-called) heretics of Albi. The province of Guienne afforded shelter to the Albigenses. Guienne was then in your possession. From an English province, our doctrines found their way into *England* itself, and your WICKLIF preached nothing more than what had been advanced by the ministers of our valleys 400 years before his time."

With this account of the *preparation of the way* for the commencement of the great Continental and Anglican Reformation, we proceed to

SECTION IV.

HISTORY OF THE REVIVAL OF MODERN MILLENARIANISM.

In this portion of his "History of Christian Doctrine," Professor Shedd affects to dispose of "millenarianism or chiliasm" in a very summary manner. He says (page 378), "The history of chiliasm since the Reformation, *presents few points of importance.* During the present century, *individual* minds in England and America, and upon the continent of Europe, *have attempted to revive* the theory—in some instances, in union with an intelligent and earnest orthodoxy; in others, in connection with an uneducated and somewhat fanatical pietism. The first class is represented by Delitzsch and Auberlin in Germany, and by Cumming, Elliott, and Bonar in Great Britain; the second class by the so-called Adventists and Millerites in the United States." For the sake of convenience, we shall divide the period above indicated into three parts:

I. The first, *from the Reformation, which commenced in* A. D. 1517, *down to* A. D. 1550, *embracing an interval of* 33 *years.* One remark on the above passage, however, before passing on. Professor Shedd makes a *distinction* between those chiliasts who have flourished *since* the Reformation, some possessing "an intelligent and earnest orthodoxy," while others were "uneducated and somewhat fanatical." But to what, we ask, does this distinction amount, if the "chiliasm" *itself* of a "Delitzsch," an "Auberlin," a "Cumming," an "Elliott" and a "Bonar," is *identical* with "the so-called Adventists and Millerites"? In other words, if chiliasm or millenarianism was "*the invention* of Cerinthus" of the first century—in proof of which Professor Shedd quotes the declaration of Gaius (Caius?) of the second century (see page 394)—then what matters it whether its advocates were of the "first" or of "the second class"? In either case, the *system* is equally "materializing," "gross," "sensual," "fanatical," and "heretical"! What will the millenarians of the day at home and abroad think of this estimate of their "intelligence and earnest orthodoxy" by Professor Shedd? But no. While we have demonstrated, from the origin of millenarianism, and its distinctive tenets in all ages, the *fallacy* of its alleged identity with the unscriptural, sensual, and delusive theory of the arch-heretic *Cerinthus,* and of the fanaticism of the *Anabaptists, fifth-monarchy men,* and others since his time, on the one hand; we have shown that the "intelligence and earnest orthodoxy" of those who *wilfully and pertinaciously reject it,* cannot save them from the imputation of *heresy,* on the other.

But, "the history of chiliasm since the Reformation, presents *few points of importance.*" Indeed! *We,* however, Doctor, are not quite so sure of that. In regard, then, to the Reformation. We concede that it was a great and glorious achievement, under God, in arousing Christendom to a sight and sense of the enormities of that master-piece of satanic device for the destruction of the bodies and souls of men, the ecclesiastico-political despotism of Papal Rome. But, on *two points,* the following facts will prove that the Church of the present day is in capital error in reference to that work. The first relates to its *extent,* and the *results* growing out of it. It is to be recollected, that the Reformation, Continental and Anglican combined, contrary to the general opinion regarding it, extended to only about *one third* part of Christendom. And as to its final results, reaching down to this day, the historian Macaulay, a prince among Protestants, affirms that, "during the past 250 years, Protestantism has made no conquests worth speaking of.[1] Nay, we believe," he adds, "that as far as there has been a change, that change has been in favor of *the Church of Rome.*" This fact stands connected with and furnishes proof of the other error, to wit, that the Church of this day—which maintains that the world is to be converted during this age, to be followed by a millennium of pious rulers in the flesh, under the *spiritual* reign of Christ—occupies the *same platform* with that of the reformers. So far from it, the great LUTHER himself, in his comment on the passage, "Other sheep I have," etc., says: "Some, in explaining this passage, say, that *before* the latter days, the whole world shall become Christian. This is a falsehood, forged by Satan, that he might darken sound doctrine, that we might not *rightly* understand it. Beware, therefore, of this delusion."[2]

It is true, nevertheless, that, during the sixteenth century, considerable attention was devoted to the exposition of the prophecies. First and foremost in the ranks was the renowned LUTHER. His views of the Apocalypse, however, were somewhat meagre and obscure. On the millennium, Dr. Elliott observes, he indorsed the *Augustinian* system, somewhat modified, and made it the 1000 years between St. John and the issuing forth of the Turks; and in the language of Bengel, "he believed also, with many others, that the duration of the world, from its commencement, would be *only* 6000 years; and hence considered its end so near, that he could see no space for any *future* millennium." Other writers adopted substantially the views of Luther, e. g., MELANCTHON, who flourished A. D. 1514-1560; PISCATOR, Professor of Theology at Strasbourg, 1530-1546; OSIANDER, one of Luther's first disciples, 1530-1552; FLACIUS, Professor of the Greek and Latin Languages at Wittenberg, and a pupil of Luther and Melancthon, 1561-1575; CHYTRÆUS, of Bostock, who wrote a commentary on the Apocalypse, 1590-1600; BULLINGER, of Zurich, 1531-1575; and PAREUS, of Silesia, who also

[1] See Note E. [2] Com. on John x. 11-16.

wrote an Apocalyptic commentary, 1590–1622. Then, too, there was the celebrated reformer, JOHN CALVIN, of Geneva, in Switzerland, who flourished between A. D. 1532–1564. He repudiates the millennium, rebuking those (the chiliasts) who would limit the kingdom to a thousand years; but with Luther—in opposition to the post-millennialists of the present day—he looked for a *renewed earth*, saying, "I expect, with St. Paul, a reparation of all the evils caused by sin, for which he represents the creatures as groaning and travailing," etc.; and also allows that "the Scriptures most commonly exhibit the resurrection of the children of God *alone*, in connection with the glory of heaven, because, strictly speaking, Christ will come, not for the destruction of the world, but for purposes of salvation."[1]

According to this theory, therefore, these writers maintain that at the *commencement* of the seventh chiliad, Christ was to *personally appear* as Judge, raise the dead, reward His saints, punish the wicked, and introduce His Church into her *eternal state*. They have overlooked the circumstance, so emphatically stated by St. John, of "the *first resurrection*" of the righteous dead, as separated from "the rest of the dead which lived not again *till the thousand years* (or seventh chiliad) *were finished*" (Rev. xx. 1–6); and also the *coetaneous delivering up* of the kingdom (millennial) to God the Father, as stated by St. Paul, 1 Cor. xv. 14–28.

They were, consequently, one and all, *anti*-millenarians. Their minds, being trammelled with the *Augustinian* theory, it was reserved in the providence of God as the work more especially of the ANGLICAN REFORMERS, *to revive and recover to the Church that long-lost truth*. Passing on, therefore, we come to take a bird's-eye glance at the prophetical expositions of the English Reformers. First and foremost among them was CRANMER, archbishop of Canterbury, who flourished between A. D. 1533–1556. With him were associated Latimer and Ridley.

HUGH LATIMER was raised to the bishopric of Worcester by Henry VIII. in A. D. 1535, but soon after resigned. In his third sermon on the Lord's Prayer, he speaks of "a parliament in which Christ shall bear rule, and not man; and which the righteous pray for when they say, '*Thy kingdom come*,' because they know that therein reformation of all things shall be had;" and he adds, "Let us therefore have a desire that this day may come quickly,"

---

[1] Calvin's Inst., Book III., ch. xxv.

etc. It is also here to be specially noted, that Latimer, with the other English reformers, was among *the first* to abandon the Septuagint for that of the SHORTER HEBREW CHRONOLOGY. Hence, in the same sermon, he continues thus: "The world was ordained to endure (as all learned men affirm, and prove from Scripture) 6000 years. Now of that number there be past 5552 years; so that there is no more left but 448 years. And furthermore," he adds, "those days shall be shortened: it shall not be full 6000 years; 'the days shall be shortened for the elect's sake.'" . . . Then, he continues, "There will be *great alterations* in that day; there will be hurly-burly, like as we see when a man dieth, etc. There will be such alterations of *the earth and elements*, they will lose their former nature, and be endued with another nature. And then shall they see *the Son of Man come in a cloud*, with power and great glory. Certain it is that He shall come to judge; but we cannot tell the [exact] time when He shall come." And again: In his sermon for the second Sunday in Advent, after saying that the saints in that day "shall be taken up to meet Christ in the air,'[1] and so shall come down with Him again,"[2] he adds, "That man or that woman that saith these words, 'Thy kingdom come,' with a faithful heart, no doubt desireth in very deed that God will come to judgment, and *amend* all things in this world, and *put down* Satan, that old serpent, under our feet."

Now, what is this, we ask, but *pure millenarianism?* First: Speaking of the change that will take place in "the earth and elements," he says that "great alterations" will be made "in that day;" meaning, doubtless, not such as will be effected by the *last* conflagration, but the *restoration* of "the earth and elements" to that paradisiacal state indicated in the prophecy of Isaiah, chapter lxv. 17, 18, and lxvi. 20–24. Second: As to his *chronology*. By adding 5552 + 448 = 6000 years, which, according to his computation, would end in A. D. 1983. But, the "*shortening* of the days," of which he speaks, is, we submit, misplaced. He overlooked, as have all chronologists until within the last half century or so, the *discrepancy* in the historic chronology of the Old Testament for the period between the exode and the fourth year of Solomon, as given in 1 Kings vi. 1, and Acts xiii. 17–22, and which, when properly adjusted, adds 128 years to the 480 years

---

[1] See 1 Thess. iv. 13–17.   [2] See Zech. xiv. 4–6.

of 1 Kings vi. 1. This, when supplemented to the A. M. 4004, which is the date of Archbishop Usher for the nativity, carries forward the *true* date of that event to A. M. 4132, and places the terminus of the 6000 years at A. D. 1868.[1] And finally, third: Latimer rightly makes the *rapture* of the risen and changed living saints at the second coming of the Lord, to take place coetaneously with the binding of Satan at the *commencement of* "the thousand years."[2]

Nicholas Ridley, bishop of London, was a companion of Latimer. In his "Lamentation for the Change of Religion," written in A. D. 1554, he says: "The world, without doubt—this I do believe, and therefore I say it—*draws toward an end.* Let us, with John, the servant of God, cry in our hearts unto our Saviour Christ, 'Come, Lord Jesus, come!'" He here comprehends in a few words all that is set forth in the above extracts from Latimer. He, with his companion Latimer, suffered martyrdom at the stake, under the bloody reign of Queen Mary, in A. D. 1555.

We come now to note *a very extraordinary coincidence* in the history of "chiliasm," between the early part of the fourth century, and that which marked the state of things connected with it in the middle of the sixteenth century. In regard to the first, Professor Shedd tells us (page 395) that "Lactantius († 330) is the *only man of any note* in the fourth century who defends the system," etc. Whereas we have shown, that at the *Council of Nice*, held in A. D. 325, and which was composed of some 318 bishops, collected from all parts of Christendom, the "Nicene Creed" then drawn up by them, concludes with that extract from it which we have inserted in Greek, with an English translation, in page 46 of this work, and which contains a declaration of the purest chiliastic tenets. So *now again* in the middle of the sixteenth century, although the learned Professor positively affirms that "the history of chiliasm since the Reformation presents *few points of importance,*" etc., yet we find that, in exact harmony with the millenarianism of Latimer and Ridley, the same doctrine is most lucidly and fully set forth in the *Catechism of Edward* VI., in the last year of his reign (May 20, 1553), of which catechism, indorsed by the king himself, Bishop Burnet declares that Cranmer owned that he was the author.[3] We refer the reader to pages 51, 52 for extracts from it.

---

[1] See "Our Bible Chronology," etc., ch. vi., sec. vi., vii., pp. 89-96, and Note C.
[2] See Rev. xx. 1-6.   [3] Burnet's Hist. of the Ref., vol. iii., p. 4.

EDMUND SANDYS, archbishop of York in Queen Elizabeth's time, who flourished between A. D. 1550-1588, in his sermon on "The end of all things is at hand," says: "As His (Christ's) coming is most certain, so the hour, day, month, and year is most uncertain. Now, as we know not the day and the time, so let us be assured *this coming of the Lord is near*. . . . That it is at hand, may be probably gathered out of the Scriptures. The signs mentioned by Christ in the gospel" [see Luke xxi. 24-31], "which should be the *foreshadows* of this terrible day, are almost already *all fulfilled.*"

The next in order is the WESTMINSTER ASSEMBLY OF DIVINES, convened by Parliament during the reign of Charles I., in A. D. 1543. They were appointed to frame "The Directory for Public Worship," "The Confession of Faith," "The Larger and Shorter Catechisms," and to sign "The Solemn League and Covenant." Besides 10 lords and 20 commoners, there were 121 divines, Episcopalians, Presbyterians, Independents, etc. Now, while it is not pretended that this learned "assembly" did incorporate into the Confession of Faith or the Catechisms compiled by them the tenets of millenarianism, yet Brooks, Anderson, Duffield, and others affirm that a *majority* of the "chief divines" of that body were millenarians. Indeed, Robert Bailee, one of the members, and a strong *anti*-millenarian, writing to his friend William Spang at that time, admits that "*the most* of the chief divines here, not only Independents, but others, such as Twiss [who was moderator of the assembly], MARSHALL, PALMER, and many more, *are express chiliasts.*"[1] Among these "many more," were such men as the celebrated JOHN SELDEN, the erudite HENRY AINSWORTH, D. D., the learned THOMAS GATAKER, the admired DANIEL FEATLY, D. D., THOMAS GOODWIN, JEREMIAH BURROUGHS, JOSEPH CARYLL, SIMEON ASH, WILLIAM BRIDGE, A. M., WILLIAM GOUGE, D. D., J. LANGLEY, and PETER STERRY. To these we may add Rev. WILLIAM PERKINS, rector of St. Andrew's parish, England, who flourished between A. D. 1580 and 1602.

On the other hand, Fox, the martyrologist, and who also wrote a commentary on the Revelation, was the *first modern writer* who made the binding of Satan for a thousand years to commence from the time of Constantine. He was born in A. D. 1517, and died in A. D. 1587. And Thomas Brightman, rector of Hawns,

---

[1] Letter 117, vol. ii., p. 156.

England, between A. D. 1585–1600, who also wrote an exposition of the Apocalypse, followed in the track of Fox.

And finally, in reference to this period, we shall claim that dauntless reformer and founder of the Presbyterian Church in Scotland, JOHN KNOX, whose prayers, Queen Mary said, she feared more than an army of 20,000 men, as a chiliast. On the doctrine of the earth's renovation, Knox writes: " *To reform the face of the whole earth,* which never was, nor yet shall be *till* the righteous King and Judge appear for the restoration of all things." Acts iii. 21. In his letter to the faithful in London, dated 1554, he, on the Redeemer's advent, asks: "Has not the Lord Jesus, in despite of Satan's malice, *carried up our flesh into heaven? and shall He not return?* We know He shall return, and that with expedition."

What now says the reader of the above interval from the time of Luther in A. D. 1517? Is he prepared to indorse Professor Shedd's statement, that " the history of chiliasm since the Reformation presents *few points* of importance?" But we proceed to consider, briefly, the next period:

II. *That from the middle of the sixteenth to the eighteenth century, embracing an interval of* 150 *years.* In his history, the Professor says: " During the *present century,* individual minds in England and America, and upon the continent of Europe, *have attempted to revive* the theory," etc. Besides, then, that the Professor totally ignores the historic facts connected with the *preceding revival* of chiliasm from Luther's time, he also would limit said revival to attempts made by *a few "individual minds,"* e. g., "Delitzsch and Auberlin in Germany, and Cumming, Elliott, and Bonar, in Great Britain," etc., " *during the present century!*" If, however, the learned Professor had penetrated the pages of history about fifty years farther back, he might have hit upon such a millenarian as the profoundly learned JOSEPH MEDE, B. D., styled "the illustrious Mede," who flourished as a writer between A. D. 1612 and 1638. His principal work is the "Clavis Apocalypticæ," of which, in connection with his other works, Dr. Elliott says, that they " have generally been thought to constitute AN ERA in the solution of the Apocalyptic mysteries," and " for which," particularly his " Clavis Apocalypticæ," " he has been looked upon and written of as a man almost inspired." [1]

[1] Horæ Apoc., vol. iv., p. 450.

The biographer of Mede assures us, "that he tried all ways imaginable to place the millennium elsewhere than *after* the first resurrection, and, if it were possible, to begin it at the reign of Constantine. But after all his striving, he was forced to yield," etc. And he says of himself: "When I first perceived that millennium to be a state of the Church *consequent* of the times of the beast, I was averse from a proper acceptation of that resurrection [i. e., of Rev. xx. 4, 5], taking it for *a rising of the Church from a dead estate*" (which has formed the basis of interpretation of all orders of *anti*-millennarian allegorists from the time of Origen to the present day) ; "yet *afterward*," says he, "more seriously considering and weighing all things, I found no ground or footing for any sense but the *literal*."[1] Our space will not allow of even a synopsis of his scheme. It must suffice to remark, that while his system of interpretation was founded upon the "all scripture given by inspiration of God,"[2] or that "testimony of Jesus which is the spirit of prophecy;"[3] his writings furnish the most ample evidence of his extensive, if not indeed unexampled familiarity with the fathers of antiquity, both Christian and Jewish. And, although we do not set up the claim of *inspiration* in his behalf as an interpreter of "the teachings of Isaiah and St. John concerning the second coming of Christ;" yet, from his acquaintance with all the extant theories, both *true* and *false*, from the earliest times down to his day, he may be said to approach nearer to "the mind of the Spirit" than that of any other. It has hence been truly said of him, that his works have done more to *revive* the study of the prophecies, and to furnish *guides* to others in promoting millenarianism, than any other one man before or since his day.

We leave the reader therefore to decide as to the consistency or justness of Dr. Shedd in this attempt to cast such a chiliastic writer *into the shade*. Why, Delitzsch and Auberlin, in Germany, and Cumming, Elliott, and Bonar, in England, were and are but the *copyists*, so to speak, of Joseph Mede. Nor they only. Other millenarians sat at his feet as did Paul at the feet of Gamaliel. Dr. WILLIAM TWISS, A. D. 1625, in a letter to him, writes: "O Mr. Mede, I would willingly spend my days in hanging upon your lips," etc., "to hear you discourse upon the glorious kingdom of Christ here on earth, to begin with the ruin of anti-

---

[1] Works, Book III., p. 604.   [2] Tim. iii. 16.   [3] Rev. xix. 10.

christ."[1] So too the erudite Archbishop Usher, though somewhat shy of committing himself on the subject, yet observes of Mede's work on the Apocalypse, "I cannot sufficiently commend it." The fact is, that Usher, though for a time trammelled with the *Augustinian* theory, yet Mr. Mede, in writing to Dr. Twiss, says of him, that "he did not discover any aversion or opposition to the notion I represented to him thereabout." And Mr. Wood told Mr. Mede, after the archbishop had read his (Mede's) papers, that he said, "I hope we shall meet together *in resurrectio prima.*"

So also the Rev. ROBERT MATON, minister and commoner at Oxford, A. D. 1642; the Rev. THOMAS ADAMS, a learned tutor in Cromwell's time, A. D. 1650; the seraphic poet, MILTON, A. D. 1660; the Rev. James Janeway, a dissenting divine of Oxford, A. D. 1660; and Bishop JEREMY TAYLOR, though he condemned the early chiliastic belief, yet most inconsistently; for, while he admits the *catholicity* of the doctrine, he maintains in his writings a cardinal point in *pre*-millenarianism, as may be seen from the following: "The resurrection," he says, "shall be universal; good and bad shall rise; *yet not all together:* but *first* Christ—*then* we that are Christ's—and then there is *another* resurrection . . . they that are *not* his: 'Blessed and holy is he that hath a part in the *first resurrection.*' There is a *first* and a *second* resurrection, even after this life,"[2] etc. So also the Rev. THOMAS WATSON, in A. D. 1670, and the famous RICHARD BAXTER, minister of Kidderminster, in A. D. 1670–1691. Besides other passages in his writings, which indicate the leaning of his mind favorably to the chiliastic tenets, but yet undecided "about the thousand years' reign of Christ on earth before the final judgment;" "yet I must say," adds he, "that I cannot confute what such learned men as Mr. Mede, Dr. Twiss, and others (after the old fathers) *have hereof asserted.* . . . But I *believe* there will be *new heavens and earth,* on which will dwell righteousness."[3]

If our space would allow, to the above *scores* of other witnesses might be added, who bore the most emphatic testimony to the *pre*-millennial doctrine during the seventeenth century. True, in A. D. 1657, DR. HOLMES's chiliastic work, published in 1654,

---

[1] Letters in Mede's Works, Book IV., p. 845. [2] Sermon on 1 Cor. xv. 23.
[3] Baxter's Works, vol. xvii., pp. 500, 555; vol. ii., p. 513; vol. iv., p. 164; and Saints' Rest., ch. ii.

under the title of "The Resurrection Revealed," etc., was virulently attacked by Thomas Hall, B. D., pastor of Kingsnorton, England. But we have the testimony of Dr. Adam Clarke, in reference to a work on the Revelation by that Scottish nobleman LORD JOHN NAPIER, issued about A. D. 1575 or 1580, and in which he advocated *the near coming* of the Lord, that, "so very plausible were the reasonings and calculations of Lord Napier, that there was scarcely a Protestant in Europe who read his works [i. e., at the opening of this century], who was not of the *same opinion*."[1]

Accordingly, the writings of the most eminent divines of this century not avowedly chiliastic, were so *tinged* with its tenets, as to render them *utterly irreconcilable* either with the *anti*-millenarian or *post*-millennial theories. Such was the case with Isaac Ambrose, a divine of some notoriety in England in A. D. 1650. And, though SAMUEL RUTHERFORD, professor of divinity at St. Andrew's in Scotland, who flourished between A. D. 1643 and 1661, is claimed by both parties, yet the following never can be reconciled with the present popular views of the conversion of the world *before* the second coming of Christ. He says: "The Lord's Bride will be up and down, above the water swimming, and under the water sinking, *until* her lovely and mighty Redeemer and Husband set His head through those skies, and come with His fair court to settle all their disputes and give them *the hoped-for inheritance*." Again he says, on the doctrine of Christ's *personal reign*, that the Church ought to "*avouch* the royal crown and absolute supremacy of our Lord Jesus Christ, 'the Prince of the kings of the earth,' as becometh; for certain it is *Christ will reign the Father's King in Mount Zion*, and his sworn covenant will not be buried." And, on the *bringing in of Israel*, he says: "Oh for a sight *in this flesh of mine* of the prophesied marriage between Christ and them." And of the *ingathering of the Gentiles*, he adds, "The kings of Tarshish, and of the isles, *must bring presents* to our Lord Jesus," etc. . . "It is our part to pray, *that the kingdoms of the earth may become Christ's*,"[2] etc. Now, these sentiments are purely millenarian.

The same holds true of the general character of other writers, e. g., THOMAS VINCENT, a dissenting minister of London between

---

[1] Clarke's Com., vol. I., p. 22, preface.
[2] See Rutherford's Letters, pp. 111, 460, 549; also pp. 37, 62, 77, 84, 89, 94, 276, 349, 367 460, 549, etc., etc.

1656–1661. Of Dr. Stephen Charnock, who flourished between A. D. 1650–1680. In his work on "The Attributes of God," he stoutly maintains, *not* the destruction, but the *restitution* of the world, inanimate, irrational, and rational, which is a cardinal point in the millenarian scheme.[1] Also of Dr. Matthew Henry, who flourished between A. D. 1685 and 1714. On Rom. viii. 19–23, he says: "At the second coming of Christ, there will be a *manifestation* of the children of God. Now, the saints are God's hidden ones, the wheat seems lost in a heap of chaff; *but then they shall be manifested*. . . . All the curse and filth that now adheres to the creature shall be done away then, when those that have *suffered* with Christ upon earth, *shall reign with Christ upon earth*. This the *whole creation* looks and longs for." And, on Luke xii. 45, 46, he writes: "Our looking at Christ's second coming *as at a distance*,"—the *very attitude and sin* of the Church generally of this day—"is the cause of all those irregularities which render the thought of it *terrible* to us."

Of those whose chiliastic tenets were of a more decided cast, we may reckon John Davenant, bishop of Salisbury, A. D. 1630. John H. Alstead, an erudite professor of divinity and philosophy in Transylvania, A. D. 1627, in his "Prophetical work," affirmed that *a majority* of the divines of his day held that "the last judgment was even at the doors." Dr. Prideaux, about A. D. 1670, admits that the Dissenters of his day took the word "*souls*," Rev. xx. 4, as meaning "*souls and bodies united*," etc., which is purely chiliastic. Tillinghast, in A. D. 1665, taught that the second coming of Christ was but "*a little way* from the door." Thomas Beverly, in A. D. 1687, maintained the doctrine of a *literal* first resurrection, and expected a millennium to follow. The Baptists, in their confession of faith presented to Charles II. in A. D. 1660 signed by 41 elders (among which names was enrolled the world-renowned John Bunyan), deacons, etc., and approved by more than 20,000 others, was thoroughly millenarian. Dr. William Ames, of Norfolk, England, A. D. 1641; John Cocceius, professor of theology at Bremen, A. D. 1650; John Howe, A. D. 1660; and Dr. Cressener, who wrote a work in A. D. 1690 on the "Protestant Applications of the Apocalypse," were *pre*-millennialists.

III. We come now to consider, briefly, the history of millen-

[1] See Charnock on the Divine Attributes.

arianism *during the eighteenth century.* At the *opening* of this century, PETER JURIEU, who flourished between A. D. 1660 and 1713, and who was styled "the Goliath of Protestantism," and who for the most part followed Mr. Mede as his master, writes that "many divines in this country (England) have greatly murmured at it [i. e., millenarianism], even so far as to threaten to complain of me. I am sorry for it, for I should be glad not to displease my brethren." This shows that the *spirit of hostility* to these tenets must have been of an exceedingly virulent character, thus to have intimidated even this "Goliath of Protestantism." But, as we shall see, the present age is not unfruitful of a similar class of millenarian "Goliaths" among ourselves.

The following expounders and advocates of chiliasm, however, appeared upon the stage about this time, in both hemispheres. ROBERT FLEMING, the son of a Scotch minister, was the great-grandson of the celebrated John Knox, on his mother's side. A pious and learned divine, he was the pastor first of the Leyden and Rotterdam churches, and afterward of the Presbyterian church in Lothbury, Scotland. Besides other works, he is the author of the remarkable treatise of "The Rise and Fall of the Papacy," published first in A. D. 1701. He fixed the date of the former event at A. D. 552, *Julian* time, from which, however, he deducted 18 years, to accommodate said date to *prophetical* time, thus making the "*rise*" of the Papacy to correspond with A. D. 533, when, by the edict of Justinian I., John II., the then bishop of Rome, was constituted the universal head of all the Churches in Christendom.[1] From this date, by the addition of the 1260 years of Dan. vii. 25, he placed the period of its "*fall*" at A. D. 1794 (or rather 1793). The astonishing accuracy of this date was verified in those signal judgments which took effect upon the Papal power during the troubles of the *first French Revolution*, when Louis XVI., king of France, was beheaded, and the Robespierrean "Reign of Terror" commenced, a circumstance which, when remembered, produced a most thrilling sensation throughout Great Britain. Not that that event was to *complete* the destruction of the Papacy under the fifth vial, "though it would exceedingly weaken it." Its final overthrow *awaited* the effusion of the seventh vial. But Mr. Fleming was less happy in his adjustment of the *chronology* of events connected with the seals, trumpets, and

---

[1] Rise and Fall, etc., pp. 27, 61.

vials of the Apocalypse. This arose from his having overlooked that important *discrepancy* in the chronology of the Old Testament between 1 Kings vi. 1 and Acts xiii. 17–22, relating to the period from the Exode to the fourth year of Solomon,' in consequence of which, by the addition of 2000 years to A. M. 4004, in order to complete the 6000 years, he carried that period beyond the A. D. 1793 to the extent of 207 years. At the same time, he observes, "Seeing the 1260 days (or years) are the *whole time* of the Papal authority, it is not to be totally destroyed until *the great and remarkable appearance of Christ*, upon the pouring out of the seventh vial; and that, therefore, Christ will have the honor of destroying him finally HIMSELF (though this iniquity began to work in the apostolic times); wherefore, we may certainly conclude . . . that though the Lord will gradually consume or waste this great adversary by the *spirit of his mouth*, yet he will not sooner abolish him than by THE APPEARANCE OF HIS OWN PRESENCE."[2] (2 Thess. ii. 8.) And again: speaking of the seventh vial being poured out on the air, he says: "As Christ concluded his sufferings on the cross with this voice, '*It is finished;*' so the Church's sufferings are concluded with the voice out of the temple of heaven, '*It is done.*' And therefore, *with this doth the blessed millennium of Christ's spiritual reign on earth begin.*"[3] These extracts from Mr. Fleming's work are decidedly millenarian.

Contemporaneous with this writer was the renowned SIR ISAAC NEWTON, who flourished between A. D. 1665–1727. Of his millenarianism it is unnecessary to enlarge. "His praise," as such, is, or should be, "in all the Churches."

INCREASE MATHER, D. D., was born in Dorchester, Massachusetts, in A. D. 1639. He was minister of the North Church in Boston for 62 years, which included 15 years presidency of Harvard College. From his biographer, we learn that he became a student of prophecy, and when made aware that the early Church, till the fourth century, taught the *pre*-millennial advent and kingdom of Christ on earth, "he found himself under the necessity of becoming a sober chiliast." He furnishes a synopsis of his millenarian views in a work entitled the "Remarkables of Mather's Life," page 68, which Mather himself fully verifies in his "Mystery of Salvation," page 138, published in A. D. 1668, and

---

[1] Rise and Fall, p. 81, and Note C.   [2] Ib. pp. 21–25.   [3] Ib. p. 69.

also in his sermon on Titus ii. 13. His biographer adds: that "he mightily looked up to heaven for direction and assistance in all his inquiries into the character and approaches of the *holy kingdom*," and that, "by studying the prophecies, and meditating upon the paradisiacal state which will *then* be at the restitution of all things, he sailed so near to the land of promise, that he felt the balsamic breezes of the heavenly country upon his mind."[1]

This, however, we suppose, is rather too "materializing," "gross," and "sensual," to suit the refined tastes of the modern school of *allegorists*. Thus it was at the opening of this eighteenth century. The teachings of a Fleming and a Sir Isaac Newton in England and Scotland, and of a Mather in America, did not avail to prevent the introduction of A NEW ERA in the department of prophetical exposition. For this, the Church is indebted to DR. DANIEL WHITBY, who flourished between A. D. 1660–1680. He himself styles his millennial theory "A NEW HYPOTHESIS." Yes, an *hypothesis*, i. e., a system that is founded on conjecture, or an opinion, or something supposed but not *proved:* directly the opposite of a *thesis*, which is defined to be a proposition, a position, a statement, etc. Well, let us see what this "New Hypothesis" is. Bishop Russell, who is an impartial witness (being himself an *anti-*millenarian), says: "For example, the phrase, 'coming of Christ,' which in former times conveyed the most exalted ideas in respect to the destinies of the world, is conventionally employed in our day to mean *the hour of every individual's death*. The first resurrection, according to Whitby and his followers, implies nothing more than *the conversion of the Jews;* the reign of the saints with the Redeemer a thousand years on earth, denotes simply *the revival of evangelical doctrine;* and by the rest of the dead we are to understand *a generation of bad men,* who are to be born about the end of the millennium, and to appear to annoy the congregation of the faithful. Those very persons who were not to have fathers or mothers for 900 years afterward, are, agreeably to this "hypothesis," described as *the rest of the dead,* at the moment the martyrs were raised to live and reign with Christ . . . Every person who reads the Book of Revelation without any *bias* on his mind, and then turns to the *farfetched* commentaries of Dr. Whitby and his pupils, will perceive either that *undue liberties* have been used by them in expounding

[1] Remarkables, etc., p. 64.

the original, or that John the Divine *did not know* the meaning of his own words."[1]

Nor this only. Take the following, from Dr. Whitby himself, which, says the London Quarterly Journal for A. D. 1850, " comes to us with the weight of an irresistible testimony" in *condemnation* of his own "New Hypothesis." In his "Treatise on Tradition," he says: "The doctrine of the millennium, or the reign of saints for 1000 years, is now rejected by all Roman Catholics, and by the greatest part of Protestants; and yet it passed among the best Christians for 250 years for a tradition *apostolical;* and as such is delivered by many fathers of the second and third centuries, who spake of it as the tradition of our Lord and His apostles, and of *all the ancients* that lived before them; who tell us the *very words* in which it was delivered, the Scriptures, which were then so interpreted, and say that it was held by *all Christians who were exactly orthodox.*" Then, quoting the fathers in proof, he sums up with the following statements: "It was received not only in the eastern parts of the Church by *Papias* (in Phrygia), *Justin* (in Palestine), *Irenæus* (in Gaul), *Nepos* (in Egypt), *Apollinarius, Methodius* (in the west and south), *Cyprian, Victorinus* (in Germany), by *Tertullian* (in Africa), *Lactantius* (in Italy), and Severus, *and by the Council of Nice,*" i. e., in A. D. 323. And he continues: "These men taught this doctrine, not as doctors only, but as *witnesses* of the tradition which they had received from Christ and His apostles, and which was taught by the elders, the disciples of Christ. . . . . They pretend to ground it upon numerous and manifest testimonies both of the *Old* and *New* Testaments, and speak of them *as texts* which admit of no other meaning."

Now, in view of the universally admitted rule of Tertullian in these premises, that "whatever is *first,* is *true,* whatever is *later,* is *adulterate;*" what are we to think of those modern writers " whose respect for everything Catholic and apostolic," like that of " Eusebius," is declared to be " very high," yet *ignore* the testimony of such a cloud of " witnesses " in behalf of *primitive chiliasm,* and substitute in its place " the *far-fetched* " " New Hypothesis " of Dr. Whitby? Ay, and that in the face of the following statement of Archdeacon Woodhouse, a decided *post*-millennialist, who justly observes: " It is remarkable that Dr. Whitby, who

[1] Bishop Russell's Dis. on the Millennium, pp. 113, 115.

had *declined* to comment on the Apocalypse, assigning as his motive, *that he felt himself unqualified for such a work*, has ventured to explain *this particular* prediction of the millennium [i. e., Rev. xx. 4-6, on which his entire theory is founded], which being, as all agree, a prophecy *yet unfulfilled*, is, of all others, the most difficult!"[1]

It is, however, nevertheless a fact, that during this eighteenth century, "*the greatest part of Protestants of this day*, as Dr. Whitby affirms of his own times, have *indorsed* this "far-fetched" and novel "hypothesis" of that writer! But we affirm that, maugre the professed "*orthodoxy*" of these "Protestants," by whatsoever name they may be called, at this very point THE GREAT BOUNDARY LINE is drawn, which demonstrates the *apostasy* of the modern Church from that cardinal "faith" regarding the *second personal* coming of the Lord "at first delivered to the saints" by the ancient patriarchs and prophets, and by Christ and the New Testament writers!"[2] Its principal advocates since the time of Whitby have been Hopkins, Scott, Dwight, Bougue and others. But we herewith confidently challenge the production of any one writer in its defence *before* the commencement of this eighteenth century. Will the Churches heed it?

It may here be in place to state, that the REV. ALEXANDER PIRIE, of Newburgh, Scotland, a stanch millenarian, about A. D. 1700, controverted the statement of "Dr. Whitby and his numerous followers, that a proper and literal resurrection is *never* in the whole New Testament expressed or represented by the living of the *soul*, but by the living, raising, and resurrection of the dead —the rising of the *bodies* of the saints," etc. Pirie, quoting the prophecy of David by Peter, concerning Christ, that "His *soul* was not left in hell (ᾄδης), neither did His flesh see corruption" (Acts ii. 27-31); having argued that "here is a proper and *literal* resurrection expressed in the New Testament, by the living again of the *soul*;" and that, "as the resurrection of the first-born from the dead is so expressed," that it was "proper to express the resurrection of his younger brethren in the same way," etc., he adds: "When we hear John saying, 'I saw the *souls* of them that were beheaded, etc., and *they* lived and reigned with Christ a thousand years,' we must necessarily understand this as spoken of their *reanimated and risen bodies*, because Peter has taught us

---

[1] Woodhouse on the Apoc., p. 470. [2] See Note A.

so to explain the resurrection of the *soul of Christ*, the Lord and Head of the resurrection. Besides," he continues, "how could John *see a soul* separated from the body?"[1] He hence concluded that "the above remark of Dr. Whitby is *unfounded* in truth." What say the Whitbyites?

It is not, however, to be supposed that the light of millenarianism expired with Pirie. *Throughout this entire century*, England, Scotland, and America have produced numerous advocates of it, who have shone among the brightest luminaries in the ecclesiastical firmament. Arranging these in their chronological order, we begin with

COTTON MATHER, D. D., a son of Increase Mather, already noticed. He succeeded his father as minister of the North Church, Boston, and was the most distinguished and learned clergyman of his day in New England. His writings are numerous, the most celebrated of which is his "*Magnalia*." Like his father, he was an eminent chiliast. All its cardinal tenets are fully exhibited in his work entitled "The Student and Preacher, or Directions for a Candidate of the Ministry." EDMUND WELLS, professor of Greek in Oxford, in A. D. 1720, was a decided millenarian. CHARLES DAUBUZ, of France, a scholar of the first rank, published an Apocalyptic commentary in A. D. 1720, which is pronounced to be "the ablest of all the commentaries on the visions of St. John." He mainly followed Mede and Jurieu, and maintains throughout the purest chiliastic tenets. JOHN ALBERT BENGEL, of Wurtemberg, Germany, A. D. 1720. He is celebrated as a prophetical writer, and united in himself, as Dr. Adam Clarke affirms, "the deepest piety and the most extensive learning." His "memoirs and writings show him to be thoroughly millenarian." Dr. ISAAC WATTS's Psalms and Hymns abound in the doctrines of the *personal* advent, the *literal* resurrection of the saints, the *terrestrial reign*, the *recreation* of the earth, and the *descent* of the New Jerusalem, etc. It may truly be said that "Watts has sung in noblest strains of the bright hope of a fallen, ruined world." JOSEPH PERRY, of Northampton, England. In his work called "The Glory of Christ's Visible Kingdom in this World," published in A. D. 1721, he lucidly sets forth the *pre*-millennial reign of Christ and His saints.

WILLIAM LOWTH, distinguished as a theologian and commen-

[1] Posthumous Works, pub. 1805.

tator, A. D. 1730, was a chiliast. See his commentary on Ezek. xi. 23; xliii. 2; Dan. vii. 9, and verse 27. SAYER RUDD, M. D., London, wrote an "Essay on the Resurrection, Millennium, and Judgment," which was published in A. D. 1734, and in which he confuted, in a masterly manner, as a *pre*-millennialist, the theory of Whitby."[1] JOSEPH HUSSEY, an author of some distinction, in Cambridge, A. D. 1730, wrote a work entitled "The Glories of Christ." He was a most decided millenarian. ROBERT HORT, A. M., chaplain to his grace Josiah, Lord Archbishop of Tuam, in A. D. 1747, was an able advocate of chiliasm.[2]

DR. JOHN GILL, also, who flourished between A. D. 1750–1771, was a Baptist, and rose to high eminence as a divine, theologian, and orientalist. All who are conversant with his extensive Prophetical Sermons, Body of Divinity, and Commentary, are aware that he was a thorough millenarian. Would not our Baptist brethren of this day do well to call to mind the millenarianism of good old Bunyan and the 20,000 brethren of his time, and also that of their great Dr. Gill, of whom they may be so justly proud?

We now come to the time of the Wesleys and of Fletcher, who flourished between A. D. 1723 and 1788. JOHN WESLEY was a decided millenarian. His views on this subject may be found in his published works (N. Y. ed.), vol. v., pp. 726, 727, and vol vi., p. 743, and also in his "Notes on the New Testament," published in A. D. 1754. See his comments on Matt. xxiv. 36, and 2 Peter iii. 12. As it respects the Apocalypse, while he does not "pretend to understand or explain *all* that is contained in this mysterious book," yet he remarks that it "reaches from the *Old* Jerusalem to the *New*," and also that the seven trumpets extend " nearly from the time of St. John to the end of the world;" by which he meant, *not* the end of time, but (αἰῶνος),[3] this *age* or *dispensation;* for, says he, the dominion of Christ "appears *in an entirely new manner,* as soon as the seventh angel sounds." Again: while he says that "some have miserably handled this book," he severely rebukes those who "are afraid to touch it. . . . They inquire after anything rather than this, as if it were written, 'Happy is he that *doth not* read this prophecy;'" to which he says, "Nay, but happy is he *that readeth,*" etc. Rev. i. 3. . . . And then adds:

[1] Rudd's Essay, etc., p. 406.   [2] Rudd's Tracts on Prophecy.
[3] Consult Greek text of Matt. xxviii. 20; and xiii. 30.

"It behooves every Christian at all opportunities to read what is written in the oracles of God, and to read this precious book *in particular*, frequently, reverently, and attentively; for the time *is near*—even when St. John wrote. *How much nearer to us* is even the full accomplishment of this weighty prophecy!" See also comments on Rev. v. 4; and chapters xiv.–xxii. 17 *et seq.* This eminent divine, and the founder of Methodism, evidently adopts the *main* tenets of the early chiliastic fathers, but in interpreting the Revelation, like Bengel, whose views he adopted for the most part, he singularly gathers two millenniums from Rev. xx. 1-6: the *first*, "a flourishing state of the Church *on earth;*" the *second*, "a reign of the saints with Christ *in heaven*," allowing verse 6 to teach a *literal* resurrection of the martyrs and saints. This, however, arose from a confounding of things which differ, a peculiarity of many of the writers both before and after his time. We would only add, that Mr. Wesley fully indorsed Mr. Hartley's book, called "Paradise Restored: a Testimony to the Doctrine of the blessed Millennium;" a book wholly and positively millenarian, being written expressly in defence of it.

We here introduce to the notice of the reader the name of JOHN FLETCHER, vicar of Madely, an associate of Mr. Wesley, a most pious and learned man, a close student of the prophecies, and a stanch millenarian. He addressed a "Letter on the Prophecies" to Mr. Wesley, dated A. D. 1775, in which he refers to a certain "great and learned man," who, with Sir Isaac Newton, held that "we are come to the last times," and that Christ was coming to destroy the wicked, and raise the righteous dead a thousand years *before* the final judgment, etc. These views Mr. Fletcher fully indorses, and proceeds in said letter and in his other writings to elucidate them at considerable length; and, on the subject of the chronology of "the time of the end" (Dan. xii. 9), he reaches a conclusion nearly coincident with the most reliable writers of the present day. "If," says he, "Jesus told his disciples that it was not *theirs* to know the times when these things should be accomplished, it does not follow that it must be hid from *us* who are far nearer concerned in them than they were." And he adds: "I know many have been grossly mistaken as to the years; but because they were *rash*, shall we be *stupid?* Because they said '*to-day*,' shall we say '*never*,' and cry 'peace, peace,' when we should look about us with eyes full of expectation?" And then, exhorting us "to hasten by our prayers that glorious kingdom," and adding the exclamation, "What a glorious prospect is this!" he says: "Let us then often think of our Lord. '*Behold I come quickly.*' 'Blessed is he that mindeth the sayings of this prophecy.' Let us join 'the Spirit and the Bride,' who say, 'come.' Oh, 'let him that heareth say, come; and let him that is athirst, come; for he that testifieth these things saith, Surely I come quickly. Amen: even so, come, Lord Jesus!"[1]

That CHARLES WESLEY'S views coincided with those of John on these subjects, is evident from his numerous hymns, in which he shows great familiarity with millenarian doctrines, and refers frequently to them as topics of warm personal expectation. Thus, on the text, "I know that my Redeemer liveth," he says:

> "Jesus shall reappear below,
> Stand in that dreadful day unknown,
> *And fix on earth His heavenly throne.*"

On Isaiah xlix: 23, he represents the Saviour as proclaiming His glorious advent and the setting up of His future kingdom, thus:

> "Then, Sion, thou shalt fully know
> The King of kings revealed below.
> In glorious majesty Divine,
> * * * * *
> *Expecting Me on earth to reign,*
> *My people shall not wait in vain.*"

On Isaiah lx: 13, he sings in the same strain:

> "That place where once I walked below,
>   On Olivet, I will appear:
> My bleeding feet to Israel show,
>   While those who pierced, behold me near
> *Again* I will forsake My throne,
>   And to My footstool earth descend:
> And fill the world with peace unknown,
>   With glorious joy, that ne'er shall end."

So, on Isaiah lxv. 17, he prays:

> "Come, Divine, effectual power,
>   Fallen nature to restore:

[1] See Fletcher's Works, vol. x.

> Wait we for Thy presence here,
> Lord, to see Thy throne appear;
> Bid the new creation rise,
> Bring us back our Paradise.
>
> "Now our universe create,
> Fair beyond its first estate,
> When Thine eyes with pleasure viewed,
> When Thy lips pronounced it good:
> Ruined now by sin, and curst,
> Speak it fairer than at first."

Thus, again, he celebrates the restoration of the literal Israel in the latter day:

> "We know it must be done,
>   For God hath spoke the word;
> All Israel shall their Saviour own,
>   To their first state restored.
> Rebuilt by His command,
>   Jerusalem shall rise;
> Her temple on Moriah stand
>   Again, and touch the skies."

And his continuation of the same theme is equally clear and decisive:

> "When the house of Jacob's sons
>   Their Canaan repossess,
> Shall not all thy chosen ones
>   Abide in perfect peace?
> *Trusting in the literal word,*
>   *We look for Christ on earth again;*
> Come, our everlasting Lord,
>   With all Thy saints to reign!"

Again:

> "When wilt Thou on Thy throne appear,
> Triumphant with Thine ancients here!"

Again:

> "Lord, as taught by Thee, we pray
>   That sin and death may end;
> In the great millennial day,
>   With all thy saints descend."

Again:

> "Dismissed, I calmly go my way,
>   Which leads me to the tomb;
> And rest in hope of that great day,
>   When my DESIRE shall come.

> Happy *with those that first arise*,
>   Might I my lot obtain,
> When Christ, descending from the skies,
>   Begins His glorious reign."

It is plainly not a spiritual reign alone, but a personal one, preceded by the resurrection of the just only, which he here anticipates, as the following also shows:

> " Come, my God, Jehovah, come,
>   With all Thy saints appear;
> Antichrist expects his doom,
>   *And we, Thy kingdom here.*
>   *   *   *   *   *
> Thee, Jesus, Lord of lords we know,
>   The kingdoms of the earth are Thine;
> Hasten t' erect *Thy throne* below,
>   *That last great monarchy divine.*"

The same is embraced in his hymns on Malachi, where he also asserts his belief that Elijah is yet to reappear on the earth, to testify again for the living God:

> " *Once he in the Baptist came,*
>   And virtue's path restored;
> Pointed sinners to the Lamb—
>   Forerunner of his Lord.
> Sent *again* from Paradise,
>   *Elijah shall the tidings bring:*
> ' Jesus comes ! ye saints arise,
>   And meet your Heavenly King."

Again:

> " Previous to the dreadful day,
>   Which shall Thy foes consume;
> Jesus, to prepare Thy way,
>   *Let the last prophet come.*
> When the seventh trumpet's sound
>   Proclaims the grand sabbatic year:
> *Come Thyself*, with glory crowned,
>   *And reign triumphant here.*"

> " Come, then, our Heavenly Friend,
>   Sorrow and death to end;
> Pure millennial joy to give,
>   *Now appear on earth again:*
> Now thy people, saved, receive,
>   Now begin thy glorious reign."

> "Before the final general doom,
> We know Thou wilt to judgment come;
> *Thy foes destroy,* Thy friends maintain,
> *And glorious with Thine ancients reign.*"

And yet once more sings this prolific and often enrapturing songster:

> "Mightier joys ordained to know,
> *When Thou com'st to reign below:*
> We shall at Thy side sit down,
> Partners of Thy great white throne;
> Kings a thousand years with Thee,
> Kings through all eternity."

Do the admirers and followers of these Wesleys and Fletchers think that these devout and able men were *altogether in error* on these topics? Are they prepared to take *issue* with their own greatest authorities and leaders? Have they learned the Scriptures *better* than these through whom they have been taught the way to heaven, and by whom their songs before the face of God in His sanctuary are led? We find many of our Methodist and Wesleyan contemporaries very strongly *adverse* to millenarian doctrines, and unwilling even to entertain the subject for examination. Will they please tell us what they think of their fathers in these matters? Will they bear with us in quoting for them the admonition of the prophet: "Stand ye in the ways, and see, and *ask for the old paths, and walk therein;* and ye shall find rest for your souls?" (See Prophetical Times, Vol. ii, No. 9).

Dr. George Benson, an eminent Dissenting divine in England, from A. D. 1750 to 1763, in his notes on Ps. xcvi. 10–13, and xcviii. 4–9, is clearly millenarian. Here also looms up a *Roman Catholic* ecclesiastic in France, Francis Lambert, who flourished between A. D. 1750 and 1763, the author of a work on the prophecies, first published in Paris, 1806, in which, contrary to the doctrines of his Church, he gives a striking testimony in favor of millennial views. In this work, having dilated upon the punishments which were to fall on apostate Gentiles—among whom he includes Roman Catholic nations as well as Protestant—and dividing them into three periods, which the Scriptures call worlds, the *first*, the antediluvian, which perished by the flood; the *second*, from Noah to the close of this corrupted world (or age), respecting which our Lord said to Pilate, "My kingdom is not of this world;" he adds, "in fine, the *third*, which is yet future, is that which the apostle calls 'the world to come;' or (Greek) '*the habitable earth to come.*'" Heb. ii. 5,¹ etc., etc. Allowing for some errors in his details, the above is a tolerably fair exposition of chiliasm. THOMAS PRINCE, pastor of the Old South Church, Boston, Massachusetts, from A. D. 1728 to 1758, of whom Chauncey said, "he was second in learning to none but Cotton Mather," was an eminent pre-millennialist.² JOHN GLAS, of Scotland, whose works consist of four volumes, published in Edinburg, A. D. 1761, show him to have been a strong advocate of chiliasm.³ N. LANCASTER, D. D., A. D. 1770, was a pre-millenarian.⁴

The next distinguished writer of this century is AUGUSTUS M. TOPLADY, A. D. 1765 and 1778. The following declaration, besides what appears in his voluminous writings, sufficiently attests his millenarianism. He says: "I am one of those old-fashioned people who believe the doctrine of the millennium, and that there will be two distinct resurrections of the dead: *first*, of the just, and *second*, of the unjust; which last resurrection of the reprobate will not commence till a thousand years *after* the resurrection of the elect. In this glorious interval of a thousand years, Christ, I apprehend, *will reign in person* over the kingdom of the just; and that during this dispensation (i. e., the millennial), different degrees of glory will obtain, and every man shall receive his own reward according to his own labor."⁵

THOMAS NEWTON, D. D., bishop of Bristol, England, from A. D. 1725 to 1784, the well-known author of "Newton's Dissertations on the Prophecies." That he was a millenarian, is evident from the following: "Nothing is more evident," he observes, "than that this prophecy of the millennium, and of the first resurrection, [meaning that of Rev. xx. 1–6] *hath not yet been fulfilled*, even though the resurrection be taken in a *figurative* sense." And he argues: "If the *martyrs* rise only in a spiritual sense, then *the rest of the dead* rise only in a spiritual sense; but if the rest of the dead *really* rise, the martyrs rise in the *same* manner. There is no difference between them, and we should be cautious and tender of making the *first* resurrection an *allegory*, lest others should reduce the *second* into *allegory too*, like Hymeneus and

---

¹ See Lambert's Expositions, vol. 1., pp. 97, 98.
² See Life of Mather ; also Spaulding's Lectures.
³ Glas's Works, vol. ii., pp. 425, 429, 430.   ⁴ Lancaster's Perpetual Com., p. 568.
⁵ See Toplady's Works, vol. iii., p. 470 et seq.

Philetus," etc. From these premises he draws the conclusion —"*that the kingdom of heaven shall be established upon earth*, is the plain and express doctrine of Daniel, and all the prophets, as well as of St. John; and we daily pray for the accomplishment of it in praying, '*Thy kingdom come.*'"[1]

WILLIAM NEWCOME, the eminently learned archbishop of Armagh, Ireland, A. D. 1780 to 1799. On Rev. xx. 4, he thus speaks: "I understand this *not figuratively* of a peaceable and flourishing state of the Church on earth, but *literally* of a real resurrection, and of a *real* reign with Christ, who will display His royal glory in the New Jerusalem. This is the *great sabbatism* or rest of the Church."[2]

DR. B. GALE, of Killingworth, Connecticut, from A. D. 1725 to 1795. He was a laborious student of the prophecies. John W. Barber, in his "Historical Collections of Connecticut," p. 531, in a comment on his epitaph, says: "It appears by this inscription, that Dr. Gale was a believer in the ancient doctrine of millenarians, a name given to those who believe that the second coming of Christ will *precede* the millennium, and that there will be a *literal* resurrection of the saints, who will reign with Christ on earth a thousand years. This appears to have been the belief of pious persons *at the time* of the first settlement of New England. Even as late as the great earthquake, 1775, *many Christians* were looking for and expecting the second coming of Christ."

WILLIAM COWPER, England's "Christian poet," of imperishable fame, flourished from about A. D. 1756 to 1800. A thorough millenarian, in his "Task" he has sung in glorious numbers of the signs of the times, the world's age, the second coming of the Lord, the restitution of all things, the reign of Christ and his saints on earth, the New Jerusalem, and of all those "scenes surpassing fable" but just before us:[3]

> "The world appears
> To toll the death-bell of its own decease—
> . . . . The old
> And crazy earth has had her shaking fits
> More frequent, and foregone her usual rest ;
> And nature seems with dim and sickly eye
> To wait the close of all.
>   *   *   *   *   *   *   *

[1] See Dissertations, vol. iii., 331, etc. [2] Quoted by Bickersteth on Prophecy, p. 106.
[3] Cowper's Task, Books II. and VI.

> Six thousand years of sorrow have well nigh
> Fulfilled their tardy and disastrous course
> Over a sinful world: and what remains
> Of this tempestuous state of human things,
> Is merely as the rocking of a sea
> Before a calm that rocks itself to rest.
>
> * * * * * * * *
>
> Behold the measure of the promise filled;
> See Salem built, the labor of a God!
> Bright as a sun the Sacred City shines:
> All kingdoms and all princes of the earth
> Flock to that light: the glory of all lands
> Flows into her; unbounded is her joy,
> And endless her increase.
>
> * * * * * * * *
>
> Come then, and added to Thy many crowns,
> Receive yet one, the crown of all the earth,
> For Thou alone art worthy.
>
> * * * * * * * *
>
> Thy saints proclaim Thee King; and Thy delay
> Gives courage to their foes, who, could they see
> The dawn of Thy last advent, long desired,
> Would flee for safety to the falling rocks."

That the eminently learned theologian and divine, WILLIAM ROMAINE, who flourished between about A. D. 1736 and 1795, could not have embraced the Whitbyan theory, is evident from the following: he writes thus—"The marks and signs of Christ's second advent are fulfilling *daily*. His coming cannot be far off. If you compare the uncommon events which the Lord said were to be the forerunners of his coming to judgment, with what hath lately happened in the world, you must conclude the time is *at hand*."

JOSHUA SPAULDING was minister of the Gospel at the Tabernacle in Salem, Massachusetts, A. D. 1796. The "Lectures" of this pious and able divine, which are well known, abundantly attest his advocacy of the millenarian tenets. We have already spoken of the Rev. ROBERT HALL, a Baptist minister and writer of great talent, and one of the most eloquent and extraordinary men of his time. That he was a millenarian, is testified to by MR. THORP, of Bristol, England (himself an able advocate of that doctrine), certifying that he fully avowed himself to be such in a conversation with him on the subject a few days before his death, but, like some others, hid his light under a bushel, which he greatly regretted on his dying bed. DR. THOMAS COKE, LL. D., an associate of the Wesleys, was a thorough chiliast. In his Commentary he follows and quotes Mede, Daubuz, Newton, and others, firmly advocating the *pre*-millennial view of the second coming of our Lord. We close the above partial galaxy of witnesses "for the word of God and the testimony which they held" in behalf of the truth, with the name of

REGINALD HEBER, the eminently pious bishop of Calcutta, distinguished alike as a divine and poet. He died suddenly at Trichinopoly in India, A. D. 1826. His millenarianism stands out in bold relief in many of his poetical effusions and other writings. We limit ourself, however, to the following extract from his spirited poem, "Palestine," which gained for him the prize at Oxford:

> "And who is He? the vast, the awful form (Rev. x. 1, 2),
> Girt with the whirlwind, sandall'd with the storm!
> A western cloud around his limbs is spread,
> His crown a rainbow, and the sun his head.
> To highest heaven he lifts his kingly hand,
> And treads at once the ocean and the land:
> And hark! His voice amidst the thunders roar,
> His dreadful voice, that time shall be no more.
> Lo! thrones are set, and every saint is there. (Rev. xx. 4–6.)
> Earth's utmost bounds confess their awful sway,
> The mountains worship, and the isles obey:
> Nor sun, nor moon they need—nor day, nor night;—
> God is their temple, and the Lamb their light (Rev. xxi. 22);
> And shall not Israel's sons exulting come,
> Hail the glad beam and claim their ancient home?
> On David's throne shall David's offspring reign,
> And the dry bones be warm with life again. (Ezek. xxvii.)
> Hark! white-robed crowds their deep hosannas raise,
> And the hoarse flood resounds the sound of praise;
> Ten thousand harps attune the mystic song,
> Ten thousand thousand saints the strain prolong!
> Worthy the Lamb, omnipotent to save,
> Who died, who lives triumphant o'er the grave."

CONCLUSION.

Hall (a Baptist), and Thorp (an Independent), and Coke (a Methodist), and Heber (an Episcopalian), formed a sort of *quadruple millenarian link*, between the close of the eighteenth and the opening of the nineteenth centuries. That talented French divine and master of eloquence, John B. Massillon, who died in A. D. 1742, while he admits that in the first ages it would have been deemed a kind of apostasy not to have sighed after "the day of the Lord," yet says it was very difficult *in his day*, on account of the worldly minded and lukewarm state of the Church, "to call up the minds of the people to attend to the subject of the Lord's advent."[1] Dr. Gill, too, testifies that the Churches in this (the eighteenth) century, had a name to live, and were dead: "a sleepy frame of spirit," he says, "having seized upon us, both ministers and Churches are asleep." Bengel also called it "a poor, friged, slumbering age, that needed an awakener."

Such was the complaint, both in England and on the Continent. And there was *a cause* for this coldness. WHITBY had lived and wrote, and his "*New Hypothesis*," by which *the personal coming* of the Lord is necessarily postponed for 1000 years, had stifled the warning note of, "*Behold, I come quickly.*" That "belief in the speedy advent of the Saviour and habitual contemplation of the last things, which adds weight and impressiveness to the ordinary preaching of the Gospel, giving it earnestness, fervor, and solemnity not often attained,"[2] was now getting *unpopular*, and, as in the fourth century, truth measurably dimmed before wide-spread error, and, with the *decay* of pre-millennialism, spiritual life, too, died away.

Such, then, was the disastrous effect resulting from the prevalence of the *Whitbyan* "New Hypothesis" in England and on the Continent at the opening of the nineteenth century. But, thank God, in that extensive field, and especially in Great Britain—and of which *England* is the principal seat—within the last half century, and particularly within the last 25 years, many of the leading pulpit orators, or who are so regarded by the mass of the people, are the decided advocates of the *millenarian* doc-

---

[1] See Massillon's Sermons, p. 1.   [2] See New York Independent, for 1850.

trine of the speedy personal coming of Christ, and his reign upon the earth. Hundreds of voices and of pens, in the pulpit and through the press, have been and are still engaged in their endeavors to *rescue the Church* from the delusion of the Whitbyan theory, and to recover her to the acceptance and belief of those truths of the New Testament and early post-apostolic times, for which so many millions of martyrs bled and died. Many of the pulpits in Great Britain are employed in raising "the midnight cry, BEHOLD THE BRIDEGROOM COMETH, GO YE OUT TO MEET HIM." Nor are these pulpits confined to one class only. They are occupied by scores of the clergy of the established Churches of nearly equal celebrity, but of whom Dr. Elliott, Dean Alvord, Dr. Margoliouth, Dr. Tregelles, Dr. Hugh McNeile, and Dr. Ryle, take the lead. In the Scotch Church, besides many others, are Dr. Bonar and Dr. Cumming, the latter one of the most voluminous and eloquent writers of the age. Then there are the Rev. Mr. Spurgeon and the Rev. Mr. Cox, of the Baptist Church; and the Rev. Denham Smith, of the Independents. Nearly all of these have also employed their pens in the same cause, thus placing themselves in the ranks of the most eminently learned and extensive writers of the day. In addition to these may be added, among the most recent authors in defence of millenarianism, the following: Rev. Dr. French, Rev. W. Wood, Rev. E. Nangle, Rev. Wm. Harker, Rev. E. Auriol, Rev. C. I. Goodhart, Rev. Dr. Leask, Rev. Mr. Chester, Rev. A. Dallas, Rev. E. Gillson, Rev. T. R. Berks, Rev. James Kelly, Rev. J. G. Gregory, Rev. C. Molineux, Rev. David Pitcairn, Rev. Frederic Fysh, M. A., George Ogilvie, Esq, etc., etc. There are also large numbers of books and tracts issued by several of the leading publishing houses in London. Among these may be noted Wm. McIntosh, Paternoster Row; S. W. Partridge, do.; James Nesbitt & Co., Bernners street; and Wm. Yapp, Walbeck street. And to these may be added several periodicals devoted to the same cause, among which are, "The Quarterly Journal of Prophecy," edited by Dr. Bonar; and "The Rainbow," an interesting and sprightly monthly, edited by Dr. Leask.[1]

This augurs well for the cause on the other side of the Atlantic. The Churches there have been aroused from that "poor, frigid,

---

[1] See Prophetical Times, article "Words from Europe," vol. ii., Sept., 1864, pp. 140, 141, Philadelphia.

slumbering" state, as Bengel expresses it, into which "a worldly-minded and lukewarm" spirit had involved them, and the minds of the people have been awakened to attend to the subject of the Lord's second coming as nigh at hand.

With the *American Churches*, however, it is otherwise. The state of the Churches as described of the times of Bengel, Massillon, and Dr. Gill, on this momentous subject, is, to a lamentable extent, applicable to our own times. We have only to refer, I submit, to what Professor Shedd says of the alleged *circumstance* under which the Church has been recovered to his so-called "Catholic theory of the second advent," to obtain a clue to *the cause* of this state of things. Speaking of the Church in the time of Constantine, he says: "*The pressure of persecution being lifted off*, the Church returned to its earlier and first exegesis of the Scripture data concerning the end of the world, and the second coming of Christ. . . . The personal coming of Christ, it was now held, is not to take place *until the final day of doom*," etc. (page 398). But we have demonstrated that nothing is further removed from the truth than this. Why, what said the covenant God of Israel to his chosen people? "Behold, I have refined thee, but not with (or *for*, marg.) silver: *I have chosen thee in the furnace of affliction*. For mine own sake, even for mine own sake, I will do it," etc. (Isa. xlviii. 10, 11.) And what saith Jesus concerning his followers? "*In the world ye shall have tribulation*," etc. (John xvi. 33. See also Acts xiv. 22.) And of the redeemed in "the world to come" it is said, "*These are they which came out of great tribulation*," etc. (Rev. vii. 14.) As, therefore, it *was not* "persecution" which made the early post-apostolic martyrs chiliasts; so, just in proportion as persecution was "*lifted off*" from the Church, and the tide of worldly prosperity and its concomitants set in, did she adopt, not, as Professor Shedd affirms, the "*earlier* and *first* exegesis of the Scripture data concerning the end of the world and the second coming of Christ," but the *unscriptural* theory of Augustine.

And so, we now affirm that, just in proportion as a similar tide of *worldly prosperity and exemption from suffering for Christ's sake* has marked the progress of the American Churches, —Episcopal, Presbyterian, Dutch Reformed, Methodist, and Baptist—while they have *ignored* the ancient Augustinian theory, they have adopted the *equally unscriptural* and, as Bishop Russell of Scotland styles it, the "*far-fetched*" "*New Hypothesis*" of Dr. Whitby; which, removing that great event, the second personal coming of Christ, at least 1000 years hence, or, as the learned Professor states it, "*until the final day of doom,*" they have settled down into "*a poor, frigid, slumbering*" *state*—that very state indicated by the "five foolish virgins" in the parable—regarding that crisis! We repeat: that "belief in the *speedy advent* of the Saviour and *habitual contemplation* of the last things, which adds weight and impressiveness to the ordinary preaching of the gospel, giving it earnestness, fervor, and solemnity not often attained" (we quote from the New York Independent for A. D. 1850), by having been rendered *unpopular*, has nearly died out. The Whitbyan "New Hypothesis" holds the decided *predominance* among us over both the clergy and the laity. Alas! over the laity, *because* of the tenacity with which the *clergy* still cling to it.

Nor this only. Our duty to God compels us to advert to the fact of the consequent *lamentable neglect*, on the part of most of the clergy of this day, to "*study* to show themselves approved unto God, workmen that need not to be ashamed,"[1] in the article of that "diligent inquiring and searching into *what*, or *what manner of time* the spirit of Christ which was in the old prophets did signify, when it testified beforehand the sufferings of Christ, and the glory that should follow."[2] The writer could give the names of not a few of the most distinguished of these, who urge the pressure of *other duties* in justification of their neglect in familiarizing themselves with "the teachings of Isaiah and St. John concerning the second coming of Christ." And this is attempted to be fortified by the plea, that the prophecies are so dark, obscure, and enigmatical, that they lay beyond the reach of *ordinary* scriptural "exegesis;" that the most learned and pious divines *differ* in their interpretations of them; that they can only be understood by us as they are *fulfilled;* and finally, that, as their ultimate accomplishment is removed at *too great a distance* to interest our inquiries, therefore, all attempts to lay open these alleged secret councils of Jehovah's will, only tend to produce disquietude among sober-minded Christians, and to lead to fanaticism and delusion. It is in vain we plead, in the plain and emphatic language of Peter, that "we have a more sure word of

---

[1] 2 Tim. ii. 15. [2] 1 Pet. i. 10, 11.

prophecy, *to which we all do well that we take heed*, as unto a light which shineth in a dark place, *until* the day dawn, and the day-star arise in our hearts."[1] In vain that we quote that benediction, "BLESSED is he that *readeth*, and they that *hear* the words of this prophecy, and *keep* those things which are written therein, *for the time is at hand*,"[2] that is, for the *commenced* accomplishment of "all those things which God hath spoken by the mouth of all His holy prophets since the world began."[3]

Pardon us, therefore, reader, if we once more repeat, that it is to the wide-spread prevalence and influence of the "far-fetched" "New Hypothesis" of Dr. Whitby throughout the Churches of this land, that we are indebted for that spirit of indifference, not only, but of open and covert hostility to the cause we advocate, so generally characteristic of these "last times." And so—the assertions of some to the contrary notwithstanding—the consequence is, that "the spirit of God seems to be withdrawn from the Churches," and that "they are dead, dead, dead:" words uttered in the hearing of the writer, by two of the most distinguished pastors of Churches in this city.

At the same time, we have cause for thankfulness that some efforts have been and still are being put forth—and they are gradually assuming larger proportions—both through the pulpit and the press, *to arouse the Churches in this country* to a view of the coming crisis before them. As in the record already given of those bright and shining lights in the Church, ancient, mediæval, and modern, who have avowed their belief in and have advocated the millenarian tenets, so with those of the *present* generation. Their deep piety, " in union with an intelligent and earnest orthodoxy," and the eminence of their positions in the Church of Christ, form an *invulnerable shield* against those shafts of invective and satire hurled against them by their opponents. Associated as they were or are with one or other of the leading evangelical Churches of Christ, furnishes the evidence that, amid the *general defection* of said Churches in these premises, from that " faith at first delivered to the saints," " the God of mercy has preserved a remnant according to the election of grace," as so many *beacon lights* to those who, with sincere hearts, " stand in the ways," that they may " see, and ask for the old paths, where is the good way," with a desire to " walk therein."[4] Such,

[1] 2 Pet. i. 19.   [2] Rev. i. 3.   [3] Acts iii. 18.   [4] Jer. vi. 16.

surely, need be neither ashamed nor afraid to pay a respectful deference to the "interpretations put upon the teachings of Isaiah and St. John concerning the second coming of Christ," by such servants of Christ as the late millenarian Bishop Henshaw, of Rhode Island, and Bishop Meade, of Virginia; nor of such living divines and theologians as Bishop Hopkins, of Vermont, Bishop McIlvaine, of Ohio, and Bishop Southgate, of this city. To these may be added, of the Episcopal Church, the Rev. S. H. Tyng, D. D., rector of St. George's, Rev. Francis Vinton, D. D., assistant minister of Trinity Church, New York city, and Rev. Edward Winthrop, Norwalk, Ohio; also Rev. Richard Newton, D. D., and Rev. William Newton, West Chester, Pennsylvania, of the same Church. Of the Old School Presbyterian Church, Rev. Robert J. Breckinridge, D. D., of Danville, Kentucky, Rev. Robert McCartee, D. D., Yonkers, N. Y., Rev. Charles K. Imbrie, D. D., and Rev. J. Harkness, Jersey City, N. J., Rev. William Lee, Rev. Nathaniel West, and Rev. Hugh S. Carpenter, Brooklyn, L. I., and others. Of the New School Presbyterian Church, Rev. George Duffield, D. D., of Detroit, Michigan, and Rev. Robert Adair, D. D., Philadelphia. Of the Dutch Reformed Church, Rev. John Forsyth, D. D., Rev. William R. Gordon, D. D., and Rev. J. T. Demarest, D. D., New Jersey, and others. Of the Lutheran Church, Rev. Joseph A. Seiss, D. D., Philadelphia. Of the Moravian Church, Rev. Edwin E. Reinke, Philadelphia. Of the Congregational Church, Rev. Thomas Wickes, Marietta, Ohio, Rev. Henry F. Hill, Geneseo, N. Y., Rev. Alfred Bryant, Presbyterian, Niles, Michigan, Rev. J. S. Oswald, York, Pennsylvania. In all these Churches, there may be found among the laity also not a few who are avowedly millenarians. Of the most distinguished of these, may be named Mr. David N. Lord and Eleazar Lord.

Others might be added to this list, but the above are sufficient to commend this subject to the serious consideration of every candid and unbiassed inquirer after truth. Most of them have employed their pens in the form of prophetical expositions and defence of primitive and modern millenarianism, and, for learning, chasteness, and eloquence of style, will compare with those of any other. The only extant journals devoted to the exposition and defence of millenarianism proper in this country—at least the only ones that we could commend as reliable—are, "*The Israelite*

Indeed," edited by G. R. Lederer, New York city, and "*The Prophetical Times,*" under the editorial supervision of the Rev. Drs. Seiss, Newton, Duffield, and others, published in Philadelphia.

We here close our somewhat extended reply to Professor Shedd's article on "Eschatology," or "the second coming of Christ," in connection with his historical exposition of "millenarianism, or chiliasm," ancient, mediæval, and modern. We intreat one and all, and especially the clergy, to pause, and "read before they strike." The whole subject is now before them. The points at issue, scriptural and historical, are thoroughly defined. The writer holds that, viewing this matter in connection with and as applicable to these "last perilous times" in which we live, the destiny of each one for weal or woe, for time and for eternity, depends upon a right understanding and acceptance or rejection of THE TRUTH in these premises. And, in whatsoever that truth consists, of this we are assured, that it is only those who *rightly* "LOOK FOR HIM" (Christ) according to a "Thus saith the Lord," to whom "*He will appear the second time without sin unto salvation.*" (See Heb. ix. verses 27, 28.)

Finally. Seeking to imitate the faith and hope of the New Testament saints, as centred in Christ as "THE COMING ONE," may God, of His infinite mercy, stir up our hearts to "*love His appearing*" (2 Tim. iv. 8; Titus ii. 13); and to "*hasten unto the coming of the day of the Lord*" (2 Pet. iii. 12); so that " we may be *accounted worthy* to escape all these things that shall come to pass, *and to stand before the Son of Man,*" (Luke xxi. 36,) "*and not be ashamed before Him at His coming*" (1 John ii. 28).

NOTE A.

Observations on the Distinction between the Ecclesia *and the* Apostasia *of the Christian Dispensation.*

In our "APPEAL" to the Clerical Representatives of the leading Evangelical Protestant Denominations on the momentous subject of the Second Personal Coming of Christ, having alluded to the question involving *the time* of that Event (page xxx.), whether it be *pre* or *post*-millennial, we remarked that the difference implied HERESY on the part either of the one or the other. That we are not mistaken on this point, will appear from the fact, that while Prof. Shedd, in his "History of Christian Doctrine," page 394, says that "Irenæus," in speaking of those "*opposers* of millenarianism" in his day, "who held the *Catholic* faith, and who agreed with the Gnostics only in being *anti*-millenarian," is "desirous to make it appear that *anti-millenarianism* is of the nature of *heresy*;" and Dr. Burton says that "Irenæus, like Justin Martyr, calls those *heretics* who expected the saints' glorification *immediately after* death and *before* the resurrection," etc.; he himself represents the system of the *pre-millennialists* as "materializing," "gross," "sensual," "fanatical," and "*heretical*," yea, and that, even though it is found "in union with an intelligent and earnest *orthodoxy*," (page 397).

Hence, as we have said (see Reply, etc., p. 44), Eschatologists, *millenarian*, and *anti* and *post-millenarian*, mutually prefer against each other's system the charge of HERESY. And, indeed, from this charge there is no escape. *If* millenarianism is what its opponents represent it to be—a "materializing," "gross," "sensual," and "fanatical" system of interpreting "the Messianic prophecies concerning the Second Coming of Christ"—the professed "*orthodoxy*" of its advocates in other respects cannot shield it from the charge that it is *heretical*. So, on the other hand, *if* millenarianism constitutes the only true system of expounding said Messianic prophecies in reference to that event, it will follow that the professed "*orthodoxy*" of those who impugn it, cannot save them from a similar charge.

In this view, it is a matter of the highest importance to ascertain on what principle, if there be one, we are to determine the *criterion* which is to test the charge of heresy in these promises.

So far as we know, there is none other save that which is to be found in the distinction between the *Ecclesia* and the *Apostasia* of the Christian Dispensation.

I. The ECCLESIA. By the Ecclesia, or Church, is to be understood those who were called of God from among men, both Jews and Gentiles, and which, separated from the rest of the world, formed the first Christian Society, and was governed by the Laws of God—the Scriptures of the Old and New Testaments.

But this Ecclesia or Church, as a visible society, was of a *mixed character*, that is, it was composed of those who were *effectually called* or chosen of God, as the *wheat;* and the *nominal* professors of Christ's religion, called the *tares*.

II. The APOSTASIA. That portion of the Ecclesia, the effectually called or "the *Election*" of the Church of God, "are *kept in the faith* by the power of God *through faith*, UNTO" that "salvation ready to be revealed in the last time" (1 Peter i. 5), that is, *at the appearing* of Jesus Christ" (verse 7). But St. Paul, speaking of "the *coming* of our Lord Jesus Christ" (2 Thess. ii. 1), predicted that it should be preceded by "*a falling away*"—ἡ ἀποστασία, THE APOSTASY—"*first*," which, as "the mystery of iniquity," he tells us began to "*work*" even in his time (verses 3, 7). Now, this apostasy appertains to the *mere visible professing* part of the Church, which, though having "a name to live," yet are spiritually "dead;" though having "a form of godliness," yet "deny the power thereof" (Rev. iii. 1; 2 Tim. iii. 5). Hence, this portion of the visible Church, with all its zeal and pretensions, cannot but degenerate into the APOSTASIA, or those who "*fall away*" from "the faith once delivered to the saints," of which St. Paul and St. John so vehemently warn us (2 Thess. iii. 1–4, 6–12; see also verse 5; and Rev. xii.–xvii., and xviii. 1–7.)

But the question is—In what was to consist the *retaining* or *renunciation* of "the faith" as originally "delivered to the saints"? The answer is, that it could not respect that "faith" in reference to the "*first principles*" of doctrinal truth; for to these *both classes* have professed adherence; but to the great, cardinal, fundamental truth relatively to *the period* fixed in the Divine purpose for THE SECOND PERSONAL COMING OF THE LORD JESUS CHRIST TO JUDGMENT, taught by the Old Testament prophets, by the pre-Christian Jewish writers, by Christ and his apostles, and by the early post-Christian fathers for the first four centuries, as being PRE-MILLENNIAL.

Undeniably, St. Paul connects the *Apostasia*, which is to result in the revealing of "the man of sin and son of perdition," with *the coming of the Lord* to consume and destroy him (comp. 2 Thess. ii. 3, 4, with verse 8); while the *chief characteristic* of this Apostasia will consist of *a denial* of Christ's coming, agreeably to His own words—"*When the Son of Man cometh, shall he find* (this) *faith on the earth?* " (Luke xviii. 8). Nay, says St. Peter : for "there shall come *in the last days* scoffers, walking after their own lusts, and saying, *Where is the promise of his coming?* " etc. (2 Pet. iii. 3, 4).

At least, we submit, that, until our scriptural arguments and historical facts in defence of this great truth can be shown to be fallacious, it will follow that its *opposite*, or that theory which alleges that the Second Coming of Christ is POST-MILLENNIAL, constitutes that portion of the visible Ecclesia or Church called the APOSTASIA.

Now, that *defection* from "the faith at first delivered to the saints" as connected with this cardinal truth, as we have shown, developed itself in the first instance towards the close of the second, and more fully in the early part of the third centuries, upon the establishment of Christianity in the Roman Empire by Constantine the Great. Certain it is, that that portion of the *Ecclesia* which denied and condemned what we claim to have been the original creed of the whole Christian Church before that time, being greatly in the majority, and clothed with plenitude of power, anathematized all bearing the name of chiliasts or millenarians as *heretics*.

Nor this only. From the fourth century onward to this day, the same *mark* of the Apostasia in the visible Ecclesia or Church, though on different grounds, holds true of both the Romish and Protestant branches throughout Christendom. For example: The Romish Ecclesia, affirming that the Christian Church under this dispensation constitutes the very "kingdom of heaven," "of God," " of Christ," etc., spoken of by all the Old Testament prophets, and by Christ and his apostles; and adhering to the *literal* interpretation and application of the symbolic imagery employed by them to denote it, insist that they refer to the triumphs of the said Ecclesia under Constantine over Paganism, whence commenced her MILLENNIAL STATE, over which Christ *personally* reigns, by a delegation of all his prophetic, sacerdotal, and kingly powers to an unbroken line of Popes as his vicegerents on earth.

On the other hand, the Protestant Churches throughout Christendom since the Reformation, at least for the most part, affirm, as do the Romanists, that the Ecclesia is, *de facto*, " the kingdom of heaven," " of God," " of Christ," etc. ; but differ with her in this respect, viz.: that Christ as King reigns *spiritually* in the hearts of his people; while both agree in denying and denouncing what we claim as the original doctrine of His PRE-MILLENNIAL PERSONAL COMING.

We offer these remarks on the distinction between the import of the *Ecclesia* and the *Apostasia* of the Christian dispensation, with no other than the kindest feelings toward all of every name, who are interested in the subject, our only motive being to awaken such inquiry regarding them as will elicit the truth. If founded in error, no one, on evidence, will be more ready to recant than the writer.

NOTE B.

The Millennial Era not to consist of a Moral and Physical absolutely Indefectible State.

As we have more than once intimated in the preceding "Sequel," not a few prophetical expositors, though from the best of motives and a commendable zeal in their occupancy of this field, *by confounding things which differ*, have occasioned the greatest confusion and perplexity to inquiring minds in regard to many important subjects. Now, this may be said to hold true especially in reference to the following particulars, namely:—

That of an indiscriminate amalgamation of those in the mortal and the immortal or resurrected state, as being equally, and in the same sense, the OCCUPANTS *of the Millennial " New Earth."*

In addition, therefore, to what has been adduced as demonstrative (if we mistake not) of the difference between the physical and moral condition of the renewed earth, etc., of Isaiah (chaps. lxv. and lxvi.), in adapting it to the *Millennial Era*, as contrasted with that of St. Peter (2 Epis. chap. iii. 7-13, and of St. John, Rev. xxi. 1-5), which appertains to the same earth in its *eternal* state subsequently to the universal conflagration, etc. (see "Sequel," pages 203-216); we now observe, that it is to the circumstance above alluded to, more than to any other, that we are indebted to the impugners of our faith, both *anti* and *post*-millenarian, for the charge preferred against *millenarianism*, that it is a "materializing," "gross," "sensual," "fanatical," and "heretical" interpretation of "the Messianic prophecies concerning the second personal coming of Christ." We readily concede that, *if* what is above alleged by these writers respecting the *mortal* and *immortal* or resurrected saints as the *joint* occupants of the renewed millennial earth *be true*, there is no escape from the above imputation. For,

1. Of the latter it is said—"IN THE RESURRECTION, they *neither marry nor are given in marriage*, but are as the angels of God in heaven;" the *reverse* of which holds true of mankind in their still *mortal* state during the millennial age (Matt. xxii. 30). And although, from Ps. lxxvii. 25, it is evident that "*angels eat food;*" yet, those "children of God" who are

"the children of the *resurrection*," not only "neither marry nor give in marriage," "neither can they *die* any more," but being made "*equal* unto the angels," that is, in their intellectual, moral, and physical powers, whatever be the "*food*" adapted to angelic natures—and of which they doubtless will partake—in all these respects there is *no* correspondence between *their* condition, compared with those of the saved nations in the flesh, or *mortal* state, during the millennium. As we have said, it arises from a neglect to properly discriminate between *things which differ* on this subject, that has led to the confused and contradictory statements of not a few otherwise reputable writers in regard to it.

Thus the Rev. Mr. Begg, having in one part of his work labored to make the new heavens and earth of Isaiah *identical* with that of St. Peter and St. John,[1] says, that "the 'promise' of new heavens and a new earth recorded by Isaiah, is, as we have seen, *to have its fulfilment* AT *the millennium*" (p. 215). Now, this "new heavens and new earth," as he alleges, being the *same* as that "to which the apostle [Peter] refers in the words, 'Nevertheless, we, *according to his promise*, look for new heavens and a new earth wherein dwelleth righteousness' (2 Pet. iii. 13); it follows, of course, that *the earth* that "shall be inhabited by the saints" of the resurrection, will be that predicted alike by Isaiah and by *Peter*. And yet, we have only to pass on to pages 220, 221, of this work, and the same Rev. Mr. Begg writes as follows: "Much confusion has resulted from applying to *the inhabitants of the new earth*, the character of the *citizens of the New Jerusalem* which descends out of heaven *unto it*. The distinction, he adds, "is obvious. While, in the *new earth*, Isaiah predicts there shall be both *sin* and *death*, the apostle John declares the *exclusion* of both from the HOLY CITY," the Apocalyptic account of the descent of which from God out of heaven, he rightly makes to be "*after* that of the *final* resurrection and general judgment," etc., described Rev. xx. 5, and verses 12–15.

This, we now observe, is the only true ground upon which to *harmonize* those numerous prophecies of the Old and New Testaments, which foretell of the *physical* changes that await the present earth and heavens, in adapting them to the *moral* state of its *mortal inhabitants* during the Millennial Era, as predicted by Isaiah, and the relation to and connection with them, of the *immortal* or resurrected and translated saints, spoken of by St. Paul, 1 Thess. iv. 13–17. The former are constituted of those *living nations in the flesh*, both Jewish and Gentile, who, having *escaped* those judgments which shall result in the destruction of the last Antichrist and his confederates by the power of Christ on the battle field of Armageddon, at the *commencement* of the seventh millenary of the world (compare 2 Thess. ii. 3, 4, 8; Rev. xvii. 13–16; xix. 11–21, with Zech. xiv. 1–5), shall be *converted* to Christ (compare Zech. xii. 9, 10, with Isaiah lx. 1–7, etc.), and

---

[1] Begg's Connected View, etc., pp. 110–117.

who make up the *subjects* of that millennial kingdom *on earth*, over whom Christ will thenceforth exercise His kingly reign. On the other hand, the latter are the *risen dead* in Christ of the first resurrection, together with those *living saints* who, having remained unto his coming, are changed and translated to "meet Him *in the air*" (compare 1 Thess. iv. 13-18, with Rev. xx. 5), and who, as "priests of God and of Christ, shall reign" *conjointly* "*with him*" over the saved nations in the flesh for "a thousand years (Rev. xx. 4, 6).

In view of these facts, therefore, to wit, *first*, the difference as to the nature and extent of the physical changes of the new heavens and earth of Isaiah, compared with those of St. Peter and St. John, as to the order of time; and *second*, the distinction between the local habitation and moral condition and relations of the saved nations in the flesh during the millennium, when contrasted with those of the risen and glorified saints; I repeat, in view of these facts, it is perfectly clear, that, as stated at the head of this Note, *the Millennial Era will not consist of a moral and physical absolutely indefectible state*. So far from it, although it will be a period of unprecedented holiness and happiness, still, from the express declaration of the prophet Isaiah, neither *sin* nor *death* will be wholly excluded from it. For although, when speaking of "Jerusalem" in millennial times, he declares that "the voice of weeping shall be no more heard in her, nor the voice of crying," and that "there shall be no more thence an infant of days, nor an old man that hath not filled his days," etc.; yet in immediate connection he adds—"the child shall *die* an hundred years old; but the *sinner*, being an hundred years old, shall be *accursed*" (Isa. lxv. 19, 20).

Allusion is here made to the restoration of the antediluvian patriarchal *longevity* to the occupants of the millennial earth, as in verse 22—"for as the days of a tree, *are the days of my people*, and mine elect shall *long enjoy* the work of their hands." The age of a "child" at one hundred years, will hence be in proportion with that of an "old man" at one thousand. The following reading will perhaps more clearly express the sense of the last clause of verse 20. "The child of an hundred years old, who is a *sinner*, being accursed, shall *die*." And thus, by a wise arrangement of providential retribution, *sin*, during the Millennial Era, will not be permitted to propagate.

On the other hand, the moral and physical condition of the new heavens and earth of St. Peter and St. John that are to follow the final conflagration *at the close* of the millennium, or the *eternal* state of the redeemed, will be characterized by *a total removal of the last and the least vestiges of the curse*. For, the *post*-millennial Gog and Magog apostasy having run its course and met its fate (Rev. xx. 7-9); and the general resurrection of "*the rest of the dead*" (chap. xx. 5) from the sea and death, or the grave, and hell (ᾅδης), together with their trial and condemnation and consignment, with the devil and the false prophet, into the *gehenna* (γεέννα) "perdition" of final torments, called "the lake of fire," being ended (compare Rev. xx. 5, with 2 Pet. iii. 7; Rev. xx. 10, 12-15); and the last renascency or purification of the heavens and the earth by fire being consummated (compare 2 Pet. iii. 10-13, with Rev. xxi. 1, 5); *then* it is, that St. John *sees* in vision "the holy city, new Jerusalem, coming down from God out of heaven, prepared as a bride adorned for her husband: and *hears* a great voice out of heaven, saying, Behold, *the tabernacle of God is with men*, and he will *dwell with them*, and they shall be his *people*, and GOD HIMSELF shall be *with them*, and be *their God*. And God shall wipe *all tears* from their eyes; and there shall be *no more* death, neither sorrow, nor crying, neither shall there be any more pain: FOR THE FORMER THINGS," *i.e.*, sin and death, etc., which prevailed, though to a limited extent, even during the Millennial Era, "ARE PASSED AWAY." . . "And the nations of them that are saved shall walk in the light of it; and the kings of the earth do bring their glory and honor into it. And the gates of it shall not be shut at all by day; *for there shall be no night there*. And they shall bring the glory and honor of the nations into it. *And there shall in no wise enter into it anything that defileth, neither whatsoever worketh abomination, or maketh a lie:* BUT THEY WHICH ARE WRITTEN IN THE LAMB'S BOOK OF LIFE."

NOTE C.

Adjustment of the Chronological Discrepancy between 1 *Kings* vi. 1, *and Acts* xiii. 17-22.

HAVING had occasion, in the progress of the preceding "Sequel to Our Bible Chronology," etc., and now again in this "Reply," to advert to the important *discrepancy* of the Old Testament date in reference to the period intervening between the Exode and the fourth year of Solomon, as given in 1 Kings vi. 1, and Acts xiii. 17-22, the following *adjustment* of it is herewith inserted, as explanatory of the grounds of our adoption of A. M. 4132 (instead of the Usherian Chronology of A. M. 4004 in the margin of our English version), as the *true* date of the NATIVITY of Christ. We must here premise,

I. That the correction of what we deem to be an *error* in the chronology of Archbishop Usher in reference to this period, is based upon *the authority of the Hebrew text*, as the foundation of the chronology of human history.

II. As to the *origin* of the above discrepancy, the date in 1 Kings vi. 1 being set down at four hundred and eighty years, when, as we maintain, it is more than one hundred years *too short*, must have been occasioned either by the carelessness of an early transcriber, in substituting the Hebrew numeral ד *dauleth*, 4, instead of ה *hay*, 5 (and which, from the *similarity* in the formation of the two letters might readily have been done), or by design.

III. We observe, in the next place, that the above discrepancy in this part of the Old Testament chronology, compared with St. Paul's account of the same period, has constituted THE GREAT CHRONOLOGICAL GORDIAN KNOT, which, until within a few years last past, has baffled the skill of many a master in Israel, who, failing to untie it—like the knot in the harness of the Phrygian King Gordius at the hand of Alexander—have attempted to *cut* it asunder. This summary process, however, in view of the important *issue* involved—that of a difference of more than one hundred years in the current chronology of our English version in settling the *true* date of the NATIVITY—will not do. This *discrepancy*, we repeat, taken in connection with the *conjectural* dates appertaining to the times of the anarchy after Joshua, and of Eli, Samson, and Samuel, must be satisfactorily adjusted, and the *true* period determined from reliable data. In order to this, we shall first place the two above-named passages in opposite columns:

1 Kings vi. 1.	Acts xiii. 17-22.
"And it came to pass, in the *four hundred and eightieth year* after the children of Israel *were come out of the land of Egypt*, in the *fourth year of Solomon's reign over Israel*, in the month of Zif, which is the second month, that he began to build the house of the Lord."	"The God of this people of Israel chose our fathers, and exalted the people when they dwelt as strangers *in the land of Egypt, and with a high arm brought he them out of it*. And about the time of *forty* years suffered he their manners in the wilderness. *And when he had destroyed seven nations in the land of Canaan, he divided their land to them by lot*. And after that, he gave to them judges *about the space of four hundred and fifty years, until Samuel the prophet*. And *afterward* they desired a king; and God gave to them Saul, the son of Cis, a man of the tribe of Benjamin, *by the space of forty years*. And *when he had removed him*, he raised up David unto them to be their king," etc.

We shall now proceed to *verify* what we claim to be the *true* chronology of this period. by a direct appeal to the events detailed in the sacred narrative *as a whole*. It will be well, however, to furnish, in the first place, the following *analysis* of 1 Kings vi. 1, and Acts xiii. 17-22 :

1. Both passages begin with the *Exode*, in A. M. 2513.
2. But, the passage in 1 Kings vi. 1, carries the events narrated *beyond* those of Acts xiii. 17-22; while, on the other hand, the dates of this last passage *exceed* the whole number of years of 1 Kings vi. 1, by more than one hundred years. It hence follows,
3. That if the chronological links in connection with the detailed events of this period are found to *agree with St. Paul's dates*, as given in Acts xiii. 17-22, the chronology of 1 Kings vi. 1 must be an *error*.

We must preface our *tabular* exhibit of this period by a reference to the phraseology of Acts xiii. 20, where St. Paul says—" And after that, *he gave them* JUDGES, *about the space of four hundred and fifty years*, until Samuel the prophet," etc. In view of this passage, it is objected against what we affirm of this discrepancy, that the apostle's phraseology—" *he gave them* JUDGES," etc., requires that we commence the four hundred and fifty years with *Moses*, at the time of his slaying the Egyptian, and of his attempted mediation in settling the quarrel between the "two men of the Hebrews who strove together," when " he that did the wrong said to him, *Who made thee a prince and a* JUDGE *over us*," etc. It is hence argued, that, as Moses was at this time *called a judge* by the offending Hebrew,[1] the *line of* "*judges*" spoken of by St. Paul down to the time of " Samuel the prophet," which he says was " *about* the space of four hundred and fifty years "—and whether *longer* or *shorter*, is immaterial—we must begin the reckoning so as to include *Moses* as one of the number. And thus, it is maintained, the two passages in 1 Kings vi. 1, and that of Acts xiii. 17-22, may be harmonized. And, in proof of this, we are referred to St. Stephen's speech before the Jewish council as recorded in Acts, chapter vii., etc. But to this we reply,

1. That it is scarcely to be supposed, certainly it is contrary to the Divine procedure, that so important an office as a "JUDGE" over the commonwealth of Israel, should have originated simply in the *calling* Moses a *judge*, by an exasperated and pugilistic Hebrew. The act of Moses in killing the Egyptian whom he saw smiting one of his Hebrew brethren,[2] and also that of his proffered mediation between the two Hebrews, were doubtless *preintimations* of God's purpose to *deliver* the enslaved Israelites at his hand. *But the time had not yet come* for his designation to that high office. Instead, Moses, now being forty years of age,[3] on finding that he was discovered as the *murderer* of the Egyptian, instead of acting as *judge* over Israel, fled to Midian,[4] where, as a *shepherd* of the flock of his father-in-law, Jethro, the priest of Midian,[5] he

---

[1] Exod. ii. 13, 14.   [2] Exod. ii. 11, 12.   [3] Acts vii. 23.
[4] Exod. ii. 14-25.   [5] Exod. iii. 1.

passed another forty years, when, at the age of eighty years,[1] in a manner worthy of God and his momentous mission, he was inaugurated into his office—mark, not then as a *judge*, but as the MIGHTY DELIVERER of God's chosen covenanted people from the bondage of Egypt, *by the voice of God to him from the midst of the burning but unconsumed bush in Horeb*.[2]

That part of the defence of St. Stephen which relates to this matter, fully accords with this statement. Referring to God's appearance to Moses in the burning bush, verses 30, 32, he says—" *Then* said the Lord to him . . . Now come, *I will send thee into Egypt*" . . . for what? as a *judge?* No. But to be "A RULER AND A DELIVERER by the hand of the angel which appeared to him in the bush," verses 33-35.

I repeat. Moses was appointed as a *judge*, not in his fortieth year, when so *called* by a belligerent Hebrew, but in his eightieth year, as recorded in Exodus, chap. xvii. 13-27. True, Moses, while yet connected with the Court of Pharaoh,[3] had *visited* his suffering Hebrew brethren, and had "*looked on their burdens*."[4] And when he smote the Egyptian oppressor of one of them, "he supposed his brethren would have understood how that God by his hand would deliver them: *but they understood not*." Neither is there any evidence that Moses himself thought that the time had *then* come for its accomplishment. He knew also that his brethren would demand the fullest *credentials* of his appointment as their deliverer. The *slaying* of a single Egyptian was not sufficient to that end. The demand, therefore, of his querulous brother—"Who made *thee* a prince and a judge over us?" is proof decisive that he looked upon his proffered interposition as *unauthorized*, and hence rejected it with disdain, or, to use the words of Stephen, "*thrust him away*."[5] But,

2. Let us look at this matter in its *chronological* aspect. And in the first place, it is impossible to *evade* the fact, that St. Paul starts his period of the four hundred and fifty years—not from the killing of the Egyptian by Moses, nor from his inauguration at Horeb into his office as the commander of the hosts of Israel, nor from his subsequent appointment by Jethro to the judgeship—but, "*from the division of the land of Canaan by lot*" *among the twelve tribes*, forty-five years *after* their departure from Egypt (see verses 18-20). The Israelites wandered in the wilderness forty years, and five years were occupied in its division among the tribes.[6]

Then, in the next place. It is equally impossible to harmonize the *commencement* of the period from the fortieth year of Moses at the slaying of the Egyptian in A. M. 2473, and the *end* of it at the close of Samuel's judgeship in A. M. 3036, with that part of St. Paul's period given in Acts xiii. 18-20.

---

[1] Exod. vii. 7. [2] Exod. iii. 1-6 *et seq*. [3] Acts vii. 22. [4] Exod. ii. 11.
[5] Acts vii. 27. [6] Compare Numb. xiv. 30, 33, 34, with Josh. xi. 18, xiv. 10.

The *former period* embraces the following:

1. Moses, Acts vii. 30, ...	40 years.	
2. Wanderings, Josh. v. 10, ...	40 "	
3. Division of Land, Josh. xiv. 10, ...	5 "	=559 years.
4. After that, Acts xiii. 20, ...	450 "	
5. Time of Samuel (conjectural), ...	24 "	

The *latter period* embraces the following:

1. Exode—Wanderings, Acts xiii. 18, ...	40 years.	
2. Division of Land, Acts xiii. 19, ...	5 "	=519 "
3. After that, Acts xiii. 20, ...	450 "	
4. Time of Samuel, Acts xiii. 20, ...	24 "	

Excess of the former over the latter, ... 40 "

Again. Take St. Paul's dates from the *Exode* to the *end* of Samuel's judgeship, ... 523 years.

1. Add for reign of Saul, Acts xiii. 21, ...	40 "	
2. " " David, 2 Sam. v. 4, 5, ...	40 "	=607 "
3. " " Solomon, 1 Kings vi. 1, ...	4 "	

Take whole period from the fortieth year of Moses to end of Samuel's judgeship, ... =563 "

Excess of the former over the latter, ... 44 "

Here we have, first, an excess from Moses' fortieth year *over* that of St. Paul to end of Samuel's judgeship of.................... 40 "
Thence, an excess of St. Paul *over* Samuel of .... 44 "

Which gives a *difference* between the two aggregate periods, of ... 84 "

It is hence clear, that, to *commence* the four hundred and fifty years of St. Paul, Acts xiii. 20, from the slaying of the Egyptian by Moses in his fortieth year, utterly fails to *harmonize* 1 Kings vi. 1 with Acts xiii. 17-22. It also settles the question of the *discrepancy* between the two passages as affirmed by us.

It now remains, therefore, to *adjust* the chronology of this period, by a direct appeal to the *detailed events*, etc., connected with it, as furnished in the sacred narrative. In order to this, we submit the following. Requesting the reader to keep in view the fact, that both passages—1 Kings vi. 1, and Acts xiii. 17—*commence* this period from the *Exodus of the Israelites out of Egypt*, we append the following tabular facts:

1. Deduct A. M. 2513, the year of the *Exodus*, from the commencement of Samuel's judgeship in A. M. 2993,.................. } thus, 2993 yrs. 2513 "

And you have the precise years of 1 Kings vi. 1, of .... 480 "

2. In the following table, you will find *all the chronological links* appertaining to this period from the Exodus to the fourth year of Solomon, with the Scriptural references in proof.

	DATA.	REFERENCES.	YEARS.	
1	Exodus—Wanderings	Comp. Numb. xiv. 30, 33, 34..	40	
2	Division of Land	With Josh. xi. 18, xiv. 10	5	
3	Joshua—After this	Comp. Josh. xiv., xxiv. 29	25	
4	Time of Anarchy—(Interreg.)	(Conjectural)	20	
5	First Servitude	Judges iii. 8	8	
6	Othniel—(Rest)	" — 10, 11	40	
7	Second Servitude	" — 12–14	18	
8	Ehud—Shamgar	" — 15–30	80	
9	Third Servitude	" iv. 1–3	20	
10	Deborah and Barak	" — 6; v. 31	40	
11	Fourth Servitude	" vi. 1	7	These links make up the 450 years of St. Paul, Acts xiii. 20.
12	Gideon—(Rest)	" viii. 28	40	
13	Abimelech	" ix. 22	3	
14	Tola	" x. 2	23	
15	Jair	" — 3	22	
16	Fifth Servitude	" — 6–8	18	
17	Jephtha	" xii. 1–7	6	
18	Ibzan	" — 8–10	7	
19	Elon	" — 11, 12	10	
20	Abdon	" — 13, 14	8	
21	Sixth Servitude. (This includes the time of *Eli* and *Samson*)	" xiii. 1, and 1 Sam. iv.—etc. (conject.)	40	
22	Seventh Servitude	" vii. 2	20	
23	Samuel	(Conjectural)	24	
24	Saul	1 Sam. x. 1,; Acts xiii. 21	40	
25	David	2 Sam. v. 4, 5	40	
26	Solomon	1 Kings vi. 1	4	

Total, ... 608 years.

Now, of this table, we remark,

1. That it begins with the Exodus, and ends with the fourth year of Solomon, thus including *the whole period* given in 1 Kings vi. 1.

2. By deducting from 608, the aggregate of the links, the 480 years of 1 Kings vi. 1, it gives an excess over that date of 128 years!

3. As to the *phraseology* of St. Paul in Acts xiii. 20, "And after that he gave unto them judges *about the space* of four hundred and fifty years, until Samuel the prophet," the table, between the *division* of the land by lot among the twelve tribes (this being the starting point with St. Paul, see verse 20), and the *commencement* of Samuel's judgeship at Mizpeh after the seventh servitude (see 1 Sam. chap. vii.), corresponds exactly with the four hundred and fifty years of St. Paul, Acts xiii. 20, thereby demonstrating that he meant to speak of it as a fixed and definite period. Then,

4. In reference to the *conjectural* links in the table.

(1.) The first relates to the five years inserted for the division of the land, and the twenty-five years for Joshua *after* that. They are adjusted as follows:

Joshua's age at his death (Josh. xxiv. 29) was .... 110 yrs.
At the close of the division of the Land (Josh. xiv. 10) he was 85:
When sent as a spy (Josh. xiv. 7), he was .... 40 yrs. ⎫
In the Wilderness after that .... 40 " ⎬ =80 "
⎭

Division of the Land, ... 5—85 "

Hence Joshua lived *after* the division of the Land, ... 25 "

(2.) The next *conjectural* link relates to the *anarchy*, between the death of Joshua and the first servitude. On this date, the Scriptures are entirely silent. But, the number of years from the Exode to the death of Joshua, of seventy years, and that between the commencement of the first servitude and the fourth year of Solomon. of five hundred and nineteen years, which give a total of five hundred and eighty-seven years; when deducted from the aggregate period of six hundred and seven years, leaves twenty years space for the *anarchy*. All that we know of this interval is, that that generation of "Israel" who is said to have "served the Lord all the days of Joshua, and all the days of the elders that overlived Joshua" (Josh. xxiv. 31; Judg. ii. 7), were *very soon* after his death "gathered to their fathers," and were succeeded by another "who knew not the Lord" (Josh. ii. 10), and whose idolatrous defection, as described verses 11–13, soon followed. Even the priesthood of the pious Phinehas, who succeeded his father, Eleazar, soon after the death of Joshua, and who lived in these troublous times (Judg. xx. 28), utterly failed to effect a reformation; which opened the way for their subjection to the *first servitude*, under Cushan-Rishathaim, king of Mesopotamia (Judg. iii. 8).

(3.) The next *conjectural* date relates to the chronological times of *Eli* and of *Samson*. That it is included in the forty years of the sixth servitude of Israel under the Philistines, will appear from the following:

In 1 Sam. iv. 18, *Eli*, at his death, is said to have judged Israel forty years. The number of years between the death of *Abdon*, Judg. xii. 14, and that of *Eli*, 1 Sam. iv. 18, is just forty years. Eli, therefore, was his *immediate successor*, as one of the *judges* of Israel. The sacred narrative furnishes no other mode than this of determining the *commencement* of Eli's administration as judge. Now, it is evident that the narrative which immediately follows the death of ABDON, gives an account of the *birth* of Samson, Judges xiii.; not of the *commencement* of his *judicial* administration. At the time of Samson's *marriage*, "the Philistines had *dominion* over Israel," Judges xiv. 4. Samson was then a *young man*, verse 10; say about twenty years of age. But it was at this *very time*, when his career as defender and deliverer of Israel *commenced*. "The spirit of the Lord began to move him at times in the camp of Dan, between Zora and Astaol;" and when he came to his father and mother, asking them to procure as his wife the woman of Timnath, they "knew not that it was *of the*

Lord," and "that he sought an occasion *against* the Philistines," Judg. xiii. 25; xiv. 1–4. To this it may be added, that it is expressly declared (Judg. xv. 20), that "Samson judged Israel *in the days of the Philistines* twenty years." Nor will this be thought singular, when, in addition to the *official inefficiency* of Eli, we add the consequent *misrule* of his two sons, Hophni and Phinehas.

The conclusion, we submit, is, that the *interval* between the death of Abdon and that of Eli, includes *all* that is narrated of the career of Samson, and of Hophni and Phinehas. In other words, that the forty years of *Eli*, and the twenty years of *Samson*, are to be included in the forty years of the SIXTH SERVITUDE. Then,

(4.) The *conjectural* date in reference to the time of Samuel. We are to bear in mind in this connection, that Samuel's official character was threefold: he acted as *prophet*,[1] as *priest*,[2] and as *judge*.[3] In the next place we are to note that he is said to have "judged Israel *all the days of his life*,"[4] meaning, that reference is made to his *whole complex administration*, the exercise of which was commenced *before* the death of Eli, as occasioned by the declared *inefficiency* of the early as well as of the latter part of his administration.[5] Now, it was during *this part* of Samuel's joint judgeship with Eli, and which probably embraced some eight or ten years—transpired those events which ended in the capture of the ark, etc. (1 Sam. iv.–vi.); its final removal to Kirjath-jearim; and the assemblage of the people by Samuel at Mizpeh (1 Sam. vii. 1–5), where we have express mention of the fact, that "Samuel *judged* the children of Israel at Mizpeh," indicating that *then* and *there* he commenced his SEPARATE administration. And, from the circumstance that we are told (1 Sam. vii. 2), that the ark remained at Kirjath-jearim for a *long time*, i. e., some twenty years, at least, and also—that Samuel having "*grown old*, he made his sons judges over Israel;" but who, "not walking in his ways, but turning aside after lucre, taking bribes, and perverting judgment," etc.; the elders of Israel assembled at Ramah, and demanded of Samuel to "*make them a king*, to judge them like other nations" (1 Sam. viii. 1–5). Hence the anointing of *Saul* by Samuel, as the first king of Israel, in the twenty-fourth year after the arrival of the ark at Kirjath-jearim.

Finally. Inasmuch as the *aggregate* chronology of the period between the Exodus and the fourth year of Solomon as given by St. Paul (Acts xiii. 17–22), *exceeds* that of the same period as recorded in 1 Kings vi. 1, by one hundred and twenty-eight years, it follows, that these years must be *added to* the current chronology for the NATIVITY of Christ as given on the authority of Archbishop Usher, viz., A. M. 4004, thus: 4004 + 128=4132, as the *true* date of that event.

Then again. We claim to have demonstrated, not only by the *tradition*

---

[1] 2 Sam. ii. 11, 18, 19; iii. 1.   [2] Josh. xxiv. 29.   [3] 1 Sam. iii. 14–18, 15–20.
[4] 1 Sam. vii. 15.   [5] See 1 Sam. iii. 11–18.

of the pre-Christian Jewish writers,[1] and the early post-Christian fathers, but also by *Scripture*,[2] that God has revealed to the Church the unalterable period of six thousand years, as the interval *within* which, under the three dispensations, Patriarchal, Jewish, and Christian, ALL his *ordinary* purposes of providence and grace were to be accomplished. The six chronological tables, historic and prophetic (see Sequel, pages 201-203), which, though formed of different combinations, yet all give the *same aggregate* of six thousand years—and which may be *verified* by reference to "Our Bible Chronology," etc.—are referred to in proof. It only remains, therefore, that we set down,

1. From Creation and Fall to close of " the times of the Gentiles,"[3] 6000 yrs.
2. Insert from Creation to Nativity, ...A. M. 4132 yrs................. ⎫
3. Add thereto the present year, ... A. D. 1864 " .... ⎬ =
4. Deduct from the 6000 years, ... 5996 "
                      Leaves...................................... 0004 "
5. Add four years to A. D. 1868................... ⎫
6. Add A. M.................... 4132................... ⎬ =6000 yrs.

The inevitable conclusion therefore is, that, unless these chronological deductions, and especially our adjustment of the above discrepancy between 1 Kings vi. 1 and Acts xiii. 17-22 can be shown to be fallacious, the generation of those now living are they upon whom " the ends of the world " (αἰώνων, i. e., *age* or *dispensation*) " are come " (1 Cor. x. 11) ; and that —mark, NOT THE END OF TIME, but—" THE TIMES OF THE GENTILES " will close in A. D. 1868.

NOTE D.

Animadversions on " The Messiah's Second Coming," by Edwin F. Hatfield, D. D., New York City.

JUST as the stereotyper had completed the plates of our " Reply to Prof. Shedd's Article on 'Eschatology,'" etc., we were informed by a brother clergyman of an essay on " *The Messiah's Second Advent*," from the pen of the Rev. Edwin F. Hatfield, D. D., of New York city, published in " The

---

[1] See Reply, etc., pp. 59, 60.
[2] See Sequel, etc., pp. 167, 168 ; and Reply, pp. 60, 61.
[3] See Sequel, etc., on the phrase " *Times of the Gentiles*," pp. 167-170, also pp. 182-188.

American Presbyterian and Theological Review," in the April and July Nos. of 1864. This article purports to be founded on the following works: "An Inquiry into the Nature, etc., of Prophecy, by Samuel Lee, D. D.," Cambridge, 1849. "The Second Advent, etc., by Alpheus Crosby," Boston, 1850. "Christ's Second Coming: Will it be Pre-Millennial? by the Rev. David Brown, A. M.," Edinburgh, 1849. "Dissertations on the Prophecies, etc., by George Duffield, Detroit," New York, 1842. "Outlines of Unfulfilled Prophecies, etc., by the Rev. T. R. Birks," Kelshall, London, 1854, and "The Coming and Reign of Christ, etc., by David N. Lord," New York, 1854.

We were hence led to expect a thorough and candid canvassing of the whole subject, *pro* and *con*, as put forth by these writers, for the edification of the readers of said "Review." But, on the perusal of the learned writer's lucubrations, with the exception of one or two brief quotations from the *first work* in the above list, the others are passed over in silence. This circumstance, together with the fact, that—with the exception of *two important points* to which we propose to direct the reader's thoughts—the Rev. Dr. Hatfield occupies the same ground in his assault upon Millenarianism, with that covered by Prof. Shedd, will save the necessity of anything beyond a few animadversions on the article above referred to.

This learned divine devotes considerable space to an exhibit of what the *Scriptures* teach concerning the Second Advent of Christ.[1] He opens the subject by the statement, that "The Church of Christ has, *from the first*, been taught to expect a Second Personal Advent of the Messiah." Now this statement, at first view, would seem to intimate that this had been *the faith of the Church through all time,* in accordance with the *Pædo*-baptist creeds of all evangelical Churches in Christendom, which simulate with the doctrine of the *perpetuity* of the ONE Church of God under the *three* dispensations, Patriarchal, Jewish, and Christian. This doctrine is set forth in the Presbyterian "Confession of Faith," chap. vii., pages 38–43, as the *foundation* on which the Church rests, under the head of "God's covenant with man," and is founded upon what is styled the "*second*" covenant, "commonly called THE COVENANT OF GRACE," as contradistinguished from the *first*, or "Covenant of works," and which is the *same* covenant in a revised and enlarged form as that made with Abraham.[2] But, so far from his indorsing this scriptural view, the writer, by the phrase, "*from the first,*" makes the Church's expectation of a Second Personal Advent of Messiah to be limited to what is taught concerning it in "the Apostles' Creed," "the Nicene Creed," and "the Athanasian Creed," etc., as derived from "the teachings of Scripture *subsequently* to the First Advent."[3] And, that he confines these teachings of Scripture on this sub-

[1] See Review for April, pp. 197–204.
[2] Gen. xii.–xv.–xvii. See also Rom. xi.; Gal. iii. 7–9, 14, 15–29; Col. ii. 17.
[3] Review, pp. 197, 198.

ject to *a very small portion only* of the New Testament prophecies, will appear from his positive and reiterated *denial*, that the Old Testament prophets ever uttered a single prophecy in relation to *a second personal coming*, or that they ever thought of or knew anything about it. Nor this only. He also affirms that all the predictions of Christ himself in reference to his second coming, received their fulfilment *prior* to the close of the Apostolic age.

Now, these are startling averments. If we except the Rev. Samuel Lee, D. D., upon whom he relies for support, we know of no writer who has ventured to avow them in the same positive form. And, while we admire Dr. Hatfield for his boldness, we join issue with him on this,

I. As the *first point* of our animadversions. That the reader may have a clear view of this matter, we will place our position in the premises side by side with Dr. Hatfield's averments, thus:

Our Position.

There are in the Old and New Testaments, embracing the old prophets, and Christ and his apostles, from *Enoch* to *St. John*, in all FORTY-ONE. Of these, in our "Sequel," etc., pp. 243, 244, we have said:

"It is not a little singular, that only *six* out of the forty-one prophets of the Old and New Testaments, viz., Jacob, Moses, Isaiah, David, Daniel, and Malachi, predicted of the *first* coming of our Lord; while most of these six, together with the others, prophesied of his *second* coming.

"So also, while the *first class* of prophets point out Christ to us in the aspect of his SUFFERING HUMANITY as a sin-atoning sacrifice under the law;[1] the *second class* [with the exception of the disclosures made by Christ in reference to His approaching sufferings at Jerusalem, Matt. xv. 21; xvii. 12; Luke xxii. 15] treat exclusively of His RESURRECTED HUMANITY, as connected with 'the glory that is to *follow*' His sufferings as our TRIUMPHANT KING."

Dr. Hatfield's Averments.

In answer to his own question, "Whence does she," i. e., the Church, "derive this doctrine?" viz., the doctrine of the second coming of Christ, as incorporated in the Apostles', the Nicene, and the Athanasian Creeds, the doctor says:

"The glowing descriptions of peace, plenty, and prosperity, and of the glorious and universal triumph of the principles of truth and righteousness which so abound in the HEBREW ORACLES, *had distinct reference, beyond all question,* TO THE FIRST ADVENT." . . . "What the old prophetic seers beheld, in these visions, was simply the Messiah coming *to inaugurate the new dispensation of the kingdom of grace.*" . . . "That these messengers of the Divine will and purposes *had any distinct perception of* A SECOND ADVENT, *or any thought of such an event,* is by no means certain," etc. . . . "Nothing can be more obvious, than that ALL the Old Testament predictions relative to Christ and his Church, *were originally understood of his* FIRST ADVENT," etc., etc. (Review, pp. 198, 199.)

---

[1] See Luke xxiv. 46; Acts iii. 8; xxvi. 23.

To facilitate the reader's reference to the two classes of prophecies alluded to in the first column, bearing in mind that they all form *integral parts of*, and consequently are *founded upon*, that great promise, " the seed of the woman shall bruise the serpent's head, while the serpent was to bruise his heel " (Gen. iii. 14, 15), we herewith insert a collection of all the passages in both Testaments relating to this subject. Of those which foretell—

First, THE FIRST COMING OF CHRIST: are 1st. *Jacob:* Gen. xlix. 10. 2d. *Moses:* Deut. xviii. 15; Acts iii. 22. 3d. *Isaiah:* Isa. vii. 10-16; ix. 6; and chap. xl.-liii. 1-9. 4th. *David:* 2 Sam. vii. 11-17; Ps. lxxxix. 3, 4; 19-37. 5th. *Daniel:* Dan. ix. 24-27. 6th. *Malachi:* Mal. iii. 1.

Second. THE SECOND COMING OF CHRIST: 1st. "*Enoch,* the seventh from Adam": Jude, verses 14, 15. 2d. *Noah:* Gen. ix. 26, first clause. 3d. *Job:* Job xix. 25-27. 4th. The covenant with *Abraham,* and his faith in it as " *the heir of the world* " (Rom. iv. 13), Gen. xii.-xv.-xviii. 5th. *Jacob:* Gen. xlix. 22-26; compared with Ps. lxxx. i; 1 Pet. ii. 4-8. 6th. *Moses:* Deut. xxx. 1-16; c. w. Rom. xi. 26-29. 7th. *Balaam:* Numb. xxiii. 7-10; 18-24; xxiv. 3-9; 14-19. 8th. The prophecy of *Hannah,* the mother of Samuel, in which, for the first time, MESSIAH is distinctly spoken of as " THE ANOINTED OF GOD," the whole passage evidently referring to His *second coming,* 1 Sam. ii. 10. 9th. *David:* Ps. l. 3, 4; see also Ps. lxxii. and xcvi. to cii. inclusive. The major and minor prophets. 10th. ISAIAH: Isa. i. 21-31; ii. 1-5; iv. 3-6; vi. 8-10; ix. 1-7; x. 20-23; xi.-xii.-xiv. 1, 2; 3-23; xix. 18-25; xxiii. 15-18; xxiv. 13-15; 22, 23; xxv. 1-6; 6-12; xxvi.-xxvii. 1-6; 7-9; 12, 13; xxviii. 5, 6; 10; xxix. 17-24; xxx. 18-26; xxxi. 4, 5; xxxii. 1-8; 15-20; xxxiii. 2, 5, 6; 17-24; xxxv.-xli. 8-20; xlii. 1-17; xliii. 1-7; xliv. 1-8; xlv. 21-25; xlvi. 3, 4; xlix. relates to the ingathering of *Jews* and *Gentiles* and the overthrow of the *last Antichrist* by Messiah; l. the same, but takes in both advents; li. 17-23; lii. the same; liii. 1-9; 10-12, takes in both advents; liv. includes *Jews* and *Gentiles;* lv. 1-5; 6-13; lvi.-lvii. 15-21; lviii. 5, 6, 7; 8-14; lix. 17-21; lx. includes *Jews* and *Gentiles,* and so to the end of the book. 11th. *Joel:* Joel iii. 14-17. 12th. *Amos:* ix. 8-10; 11-15. 13th. *Hosea:* Hos. 8, 9; 10, 11; iii.; v. 15; vi. 1-3; xi. 8-15; xiii. 9-14; xiv. 14th. *Micah:* Mic. ii. 12, 13; iv.-v.-vii. 8-17; 18-20. 15th. *Zephania:* Zeph. iii. 8-13; 14-20. 16th. *Jeremiah:* iii. 12-19; iv. 1-4; 31; xii. 14-17; xvi. 14-21, includes *Jews* and *Gentiles;* xvii. 19-27; xxiii. 5-8; *Jews* and *Gentiles;* xxx. 18-24; xxxi. xxxii. 6-15; xxxiii. 1-13; 14-26; xxxv. 18, 19; xlv. 1-4, 5; xlvi. 27, 28; xlviii., the restoration of *Moab,* ver. 47; l. 4-8; 18-20; 33, 34. 17th. *Habakkuk:* Hab. 1-3, reference to the *prophetical numbers* of " the vision," and the *certainty* of their fulfilment; iii. 5-15. 18th. DANIEL: compare Dan. ii. 31-43, with verses 44, 45; also vii. 9, 10, and 11, 12, with verses 13, 14; also 20, 21, with verse 22, and 23-25, with verses 26, 27; and chap. xii. verse 7, with verses 8-13. 19th.

Obadiah: Obad. i. 17–21. 20th. *Haggai:* Hag. ii. 1–9; 10–19; 20–23. 21st. EZEKIEL: xi. 14–21; xii. 26–28, certainty of the fulfilment of the *prophetical time* set to Israel's calamities; xiv. 22, 23; xvi. 60–63; xvii. 22–24; xx. 33–44; xxviii. 24–26; xxix. 21; xxxiv. 11–16; 17–22; 23–31; xxxvi. 8–15; 16–24; 25–38; xxxvii. 1–15, 16–24; the *reunion* of Judah and Israel in their own land. See also verses 25–28; xxxviii. 1–17; 18–23, overthrow of the *last Antichrist*, under the name of "Gog and Magog;" xxxix. 1–24, the same; see also verses 25–29. The following chapters foretell the rebuilding of the Temple and the restoration of sacrifices, etc. Chaps. xl.–xli.–xlii.–xliii. from verse 9, xliv.–xlv.–xlvi. Return of the SCHECHINAH, etc., xliii. 1–5: compare Haggai, chap. ii. 6–9. See also Ezek. xlvii. 1–12, and verses 13–23, enlargement and new division of the land. See also chap. xlviii. 22d. *Zechariah:* i. 1–6; 7–11; 12–17; 18–21; ii. 1–5; 10–13; iii. 8–10; vi. 9–15; viii. 1–8; 20–23, refers to *Jews* and *Gentiles;* ix. 9–12; 13–17, predicts both advents; x. 4–12; xii. 1–5; 6–8; 9–14. This last prophecy points to the *conversion* of the Jews by the PERSONAL appearance of Messiah to them; xiii. the same; xiv. 1–6, the last sacking of Jerusalem by Antichrist and his confederate hosts, and their destruction by Messiah's PERSONAL presence. Compare Dan. ii. 34, 35, and 2 Thess. ii. 3, 4, and verse 8. See also Zech. xiv. 7–11; 12–15; 16–19; 20, 21. 23d. *Malachi:* i. 1–5; chaps. iii. and iv. refer to both advents.

THE NEW TESTAMENT. 24th. By an *angel* to Mary, Luke i. 26–33. 25th. Predictive song of *Elizabeth*, Luke i. 41–45. 26th. Also of *Mary*, verses 46–55. 27th. Also of *Zacharias*, verses 67–80. 28th. Also of *Simeon*, Luke ii. 34, 35. 29th. Also of *Anna*, verses 36–38. 30th. Of *John the Baptist*, Luke iii. 16, 17. 31st. Of CHRIST, having foretold His sufferings and death at the hand of His enemies, Matt. xvii. 22, 23, and the sufferings of His *Church*, Mark x. 35–40, together with the *judgments* that would overtake the Jewish nation down to the time when they should say, "Blessed is he that cometh in the name of the Lord," Matt. xxiii. 13–39, which is to be *at the close* of "the times of the Gentiles," Luke xxi. 24; Rom. xi. 25; our blessed Lord predicted of his *resurrection* from the dead, Matt. xii. 38–40; xvi. 1–4, 21; xvii. 23, 24; xx. 17–19; and also on different occasions, and especially in that crowning prophecy of all others, recorded Matt. xxiv., Mark xiii., and Luke xxi., of *the mode or manner of His second coming;* Matt. xvi. 21, 28; Mark viii. 31, 38; Luke ix. 22–27; Matt. xxiv. 3–27, 30, 34; xxv. 31, 32; John xiv. 2, 3, 18, 28; Matt. xxvi. 64; Mark xiv. 62; Luke xxii. 69; John xxi. 23; Acts i. 6, and verse 11. And of the *design* of His second coming, Luke xix. 27; 2 Thess. i. 6–9; 2 Thess. ii. 3, 4, 8; the *punishment* of His enemies, Matt. xix. 27–29; 2 Thess. i. 10; the *establishment* of His kingdom and the *reward* of the just. 32d. *St. Peter:* Acts iii. 20, 21; 1 Pet. i. 1–7; iv. 7, 13; v. 1–4, and 2 Pet. iii. 1–4; 8–12. 33d. *St. Paul:* 1 Cor. iv. 5; xi. 26; xv. 22–24; Philipp. iii. 20, 21; Col. iii. 4; 1 Thess. i. 10; iv. 15, 16, 17; 2 Thess. i. 7, 8, 10;

ii. 1–4, 8; 2 Tim. iv. 1; Titus ii. 13; Heb. ix. 28. 34th. *St. James:* v. 7, 8. 35th. *St. John:* 1 John iii. 2; Rev. i. 4, 7, 8; iii. 11; iv. 8; xvi. 15; xxii. 7, 12, 17, 20.

Let the reader now turn back to Dr. Hatfield's averments in reference to the Old Testament " prophetic seers," or " messengers of the Divine will and purposes "—that " the glowing descriptions of peace, etc. which so abound in the Hebrew oracles, had distinct reference, beyond all question, to the first advent; " that " what they beheld in their visions, was simply the Messiah coming to inaugurate the new dispensation of the kingdom of grace ; " that whether they " had any distinct perception of a second advent, or any thought of such an event, is by no means certain ; " and finally, that ALL the Old Testament predictions relative to Christ and his Church, were originally understood of his first advent," etc. Then let him *apply* these averments to that of " *Enoch* the seventh from Adam," who stands as *the very first* in the list of the Old Testament " prophetic seers," and I ask, has the " thought " ever before entered the head of man or child, that that prophecy, " *beyond a question*," refers to " the FIRST ADVENT "? It will set at defiance the most tortuous exegesis, to harmonize the context of Jude with Enoch's " prophecy," being founded, as it is, upon the *future and final destiny*, not only of the fallen angels (verse 6), but of the Sodomites, etc., mentioned verses 7–13 inclusive. Nor this only. The reader is desired to turn miscellaneously to any of the numerous passages selected from the " Hebrew oracles " of the old " prophetic seers," and especially to the copious prophecies of Isaiah, Jeremiah, Ezekiel, and Daniel, to satisfy himself that they take in their scope those prophecies which relate to " THE FIRST ADVENT," not only, but that *by far the larger portion of them* foretell the restoration of Judah and Israel to their own land—the destruction of their enemies—the final universal ingathering of the Gentiles—and the ultimate preëminent national supremacy, "peace, plenty, and prosperity," of the Hebrew Commonwealth, IN CONNECTION WITH, AND AS THE RESULT OF, THE SECOND PERSONAL COMING OF THEIR MESSIAH. Again. Let Dr. Hatfield, if he can, refute our exegesis of those prophecies from the Old Testament in regard to the SECOND PERSONAL COMING OF CHRIST, as found in pages 33–39 of the " Sequel." On the prophecy of Haggai, chap. ii. 2, 9, in reference to the *second temple*, etc., see remarks in the " Sequel," pages 71–73.

We therefore maintain, that it is in *direct violation* of all the known legitimate laws of prophetical interpretation, to affirm that " what the old prophetic seers saw in their visions, was simply the Messiah coming to inaugurate the new dispensation of the kingdom of grace ; " and we *deny* " that all the Old Testament predictions relative to Christ and his Church, were originally understood of his first advent." (See on this subject, " Reply," etc., section I., Ancient Millenarianism, pages 54–71.)

And so, in reference to CHRIST'S prophecies of his Second Coming, inclusive of that connected with his reply to the questions of his disciples on the occasion of His prediction of "the calamities that were coming upon their city and nation" (Matt. xxiv. 3), as given in verses 27 and 30; the learned doctor says that our Lord, "to *limit* the application of what he *then* said, adds: 'This generation [ἡ γενεὰ αὕτη] shall not pass [παρέλϑη] till all these things be fulfilled.'" Or *if* he makes any exception, even in reference to Matt. xxv. 31, 32, it is given in the following equivocal form: "In the description of the scenes that follow, reference, *it is commonly thought*, is made to the transactions of the day of judgment." (See Review, pp. 200, 201.)

The reader will find this whole matter discussed at length in the "Sequel," by turning to chapter III., commencing at page 118, under the article, "Third Theory," which furnishes a view of the popular interpretations of Matt. xxiv. 27–30, and our reply, etc. Our "direct literal exposition of this prophecy, taken in connection with its chronological standpoints," pages 160–182, may possibly supply the Rev. Dr. Hatfield with material for another article for "The Am. Presb. and Theol. Review."

And finally, in regard to the prophecies of the APOSTLES on this subject, Dr. Hatfield says: "In these passages, the *only ones* that seem expressly to teach the doctrine of the *second advent*, that event is spoken of as a παρουσία, an ἐπιφάνεια, a φανέρωσις, an ἀποκαλυψις, or by some forms of the verb, ἔρχομαι;" to which he adds, "*all* of which terms are also used in relation to his *first advent*," etc. Exactly so. Well, the first advent, we presume it will be admitted, was a PERSONAL advent? The writer proceeds: "A portion of them," i. e., of these apostolic prophecies, "must be interpreted, evidently, of the generation *coeval* with our Lord himself; while yet another portion *seem* to demand a reference to a period *yet future*—the completion of the fulfilment of all prophecy—'the end of the world' [συντέλεια τῶν αἰώνων], the finishing of the ages—the winding up of the grand drama of redemption." Then, inasmuch as there was *no second personal* coming of Christ during "the generation coeval with our Lord himself," the learned doctor explains: "In respect to the former" [passages], "the terms are necessarily to be interpreted *figuratively;* in the case of the latter, a *literal* interpretation has uniformly, or with rare exceptions, been given; as *seems* to be required by the address of the two angels, on the occasion of the ascension."[1] But we would respectfully ask our reverend friend, if "ALL" the above Greek terms "as also used in relation to Christ's *first advent*," denoted and were verified by His *personal* coming, by what *law* of scriptural hermeneutics, are the *same* Greek terms, when applied to those passages which refer to his *second coming*, "necessarily to be interpreted *figuratively* "?

On the subject of the difference between the *literal* and *figurative* laws

---

[1] See Review, etc., for April, pp. 203, 204.

of interpretation, as applied to the *events* of prophecy in general, and of the *second coming* of Christ in particular, we can only now refer the reader to our expositions of them in the "Sequel," pages 127-130, and in the "Reply," etc., pages 9-21.

As already intimated, from the general coincidence of the *historical* developments of millenarianism or chiliasm, ancient, medieval, and modern, which mark the productions of Dr. Hatfield and Professor Shedd, we deem the "Reply" to the latter writer sufficient to meet all the points at issue in their relation to the former. We proceed, therefore, to offer a few remarks on the *next point* regarding which we are at issue with the Rev. Dr. Hatfield. This relates,

II. To what is technically called the YEAR-DAY theory of interpretation of the *prophetical numbers* in the book of Daniel and the Apocalypse. The principal prophetical numbers or dates are, 1st. The "time, times, and dividing of time," Dan. vii. 25, and xii. 7, together with the synchronico-Apocalyptic dates following: the "forty and two months," or the "thousand two hundred and threescore days," Rev. xi. 2, 3; and xii. 6; and xii. 5, and the "time, times and half a time," Rev. xii. 14; 2d. The "thousand two hundred and ninety days," Dan. xii. 10; 3d. The "thousand three hundred and five and thirty days," Dan. xii. 11; and 4th. The "two thousand three hundred days," Dan. viii. 14. The simple question is, are these prophetical dates to be understood to denote *literal* time, i. e., a *day* for a *day?* or are they to be interpreted *prophetically* to denote a *day* for a *year?*

Dr. Hatfield maintains the *former* theory. He affirms that the "chief originator" of "the *year-day* system of prophetic interpretation" was one "Joachim, a Calabrian monk, born A. D. 1111, near Cosenza, in the southern part of the kingdom of Naples;" and he speaks of this said Joachim on this wise—" that he was a wild enthusiast, unlettered, a pretender to a sort of divine inspiration, whose commentaries are beneath criticism, are wholly dogmatical, and visionary to the last degree, unsupported by any references to the wisdom of twelve centuries, and in direct opposition to the teachings of all the fathers of the Church and of every ecclesiastical writer before his day," etc. Yes: this Joachim "marks out a scheme, and introduces a principle of interpretation, which Protestant interpreters have since adopted, almost without inquiry, and on which they have builded vast and magnificent structures, succeeding each other as rapidly as the clouds that flit across the vernal sky, and as shadowy and unsubstantial," etc.[1] But the learned doctor adds : " True, here and there, *before his day*, we meet with an obscure writer, or a late author, who *suggests* that the three and a half *days* of the exposure of the dead bodies of the two witnesses (Apoc. xi. 9), may mean three and a half *years*. Such were Tychonius, Prosper, Primasius, Bede,

---

[1] See Review for July, pp. 427-429 et seq.

Haymo, Ansbert, Bruno, and Rupert. None others went so far. But even they had not the least thought, *apparently*, of stretching the 1,260 *days* of the dragon's raging over the period of 1,260 *years*. Joachim was *the first* to venture on so bold an assumption, and must be credited with the invention," [1] etc.

Well. All that the doctor says of "Joachim" may be true, in which event it is certainly not very creditable to those "Protestant interpreters" who are alleged to have derived their "*year-day* system" from so disreputable a source. Inasmuch, however, as the learned doctor has promised that this subject "will receive attention in a separate article," [2] we would deferentially suggest the importance of a little more *particularity* in his historic allusions to those "obscure writers" who flourished "before his [Joachim's] day," both as to their *official* positions in the Church, and the *periods* when they lived. For, with the exception of Tychonius and Ansbert, who cannot boast of a very prominent record, *Prosper* of Aquitaine was private secretary to Leo I., in A. D., 461, and a Christian writer of some celebrity. *Bede*, called "the venerable Bede," flourished between A. D. 716 and 735. He contributed largely to the promotion of theological learning in England, wrote a history of the Christian Church, and translated the Gospel of St. John into Saxon. There were *three Brunos*. One was the apostle of Prussia, in A. D. 1007.[3] Another was bishop of Wurtsburgh in A. D. 1045. A third was the founder of the Carthusian order, in A. D. 1101. But which of the three the doctor refers to, he does not inform us. *Primasius* was an African bishop, who flourished about A. D. 553.[4] *Haymo* was bishop of Halberstadt in the ninth century.[5] And *Rupert* of Tuitium flourished in the twelfth century, was "a learned and pious man, and on some points an enlightened witness for the truth, particularly in his comments on St. John's Gospel and the Apocalypse." [6]

Now, all these "obscure writers" lived between the middle of the fifth and the opening of the twelfth centuries, and hence form a *continuous chain* of witnesses to the truth of "THE YEAR-DAY SYSTEM" of interpreting the prophetical dates "*before Joachim's day*." And yet, we are gravely told that this system of interpretation was "in *direct opposition* to the teachings of *all* the fathers of the Church and of *every* ecclesiastical writer *before* his day"!

But, though these "obscure writers" interpreted "the 3½ *days* of the exposure of the dead bodies of the two witnesses to denote 3½ *years*," yet "they had not the least thought, apparently, of stretching the 1,260 days of the dragon's raging over the period of 1,260 YEARS." "*Apparently*." But where is the proof of this? What have we in support of it but the *dictum* of this learned doctor? Surely, nothing is more natural than the

---

[1] See Review for July, pp. 429-430. [2] See Review, p. 430.
[3] Riddle's Eccles. Chron. London, Longman & Co., 1840.
[4] Spurzheim's Eccles. Hist., p. 207. [5] Ib., p. 356. [6] Ib., p. 410.

inference, that these "obscure writers," from a regard to consistency, applied the *same law* of interpretation alike to *all* the prophetical dates.

But, be this as it may. Either system depends, not on the authority of man, but on the word of God. "To the law and to the testimony: if we speak not according to this word, it is because there is no light in us."[1] We have no space to enter upon an exposure of the fallacy of the so-called *literal theory* of interpreting the prophetical dates, as denoting a *day* for a *day*. This is what we conceive to be nothing more than *literalism* run mad. Besides several advocates of this theory on the other side of the Atlantic, at the head of whom stands the Rev. S. R. Maitland, of Gloucester, England; in our own country, the late Rev. Moses Stuart, of Andover, takes the lead. For an illustration of the mode of his application of the *day* for *day* theory to the time of Antiochus Epiphanes, and its results, we refer the reader to "Our Bible Chronology, Historic and Prophetic," etc., pp. 109–111, and proceed to submit for his consideration the following in relation to

"THE YEAR-DAY SYSTEM." According to this system of interpretation, the prophetical numbers are regarded as *symbolical* indices or measurements of time; i. e., that the terms *day, week, month, time, times*, etc., are used in prophetic language to denote YEARS.

Upon the settlement of this point, therefore, depends the correct interpretation as to "*what*" (events) and *what manner of time*" are "noted" prophetically "in the Scriptures of truth." And as it would be impossible, in the *absence* of the requisite means to determine the question of the literal or symbolic import of mystical numbers, to assign to the events predicted their appropriate place in the great calendar of "the times and seasons" of Scripture, it is reasonable to expect that a suitable KEY would be provided for their interpretation.

Happily, as I shall now proceed to prove from numerous precedents in Holy Writ, there is furnished to our hand such a key, with which to unlock the otherwise hidden meaning of these mystical numbers, clearly authorizing that interpretation designated as THE YEAR-DAY THEORY. For example: Nothing is more frequent among the Old Testament writers, than to describe years under the symbol of days. Thus Moses, in speaking of the patriarchs, says, "All the *days* that Adam lived were nine hundred and thirty *years ;*"[2] where evidently, by the interchangeable use of the terms "days" and "years" in reference to the age of Adam, as denoting the same thing, he furnishes a precedent for the adoption of the word *day* to signify a *year*. So Laban said to Jacob, "Fulfil her *week*, and we will give thee this also, for the service which thou shalt serve with me yet *seven years*."[3] The *week* here, as the symbol, is used as equivalent to *seven years*. And so, in Leviticus, we read, "And thou shalt number *seven sabbaths of*

---

[1] Isa. viii. 20.   [2] Gen. v. 5.   [3] Gen. xxix. 27.

years unto thee, seven times seven years."¹ This had reference to the Jubilee, which occurred at the *end* of every forty-nine years; 7×7=49: i. e., on every fiftieth year. Hence, according to the Jews, seven weeks of *days* in prophetical language mean, not seven literal, but seven *mystical* weeks, or forty-nine years, at the end of which the Jubilee was celebrated. But, what is decisive of this point is the following direction given to the prophet Ezekiel: "Lie upon thy left side, . . . for I have laid upon thee the iniquity of the house of Israel according to the number of the DAYS, *three hundred and ninety days;* . . . and when thou hast accomplished them, lie again on thy right side, and thou shalt bear the iniquities of the house of Judah *forty days:* I have appointed thee EACH DAY FOR A YEAR."²

And so, as it respects the other symbolic phrases—the "*seven times*" of Lev. xxvi. 18, 21, 24, 28; and of Dan. iv. 16: of the "*time, times, and dividing of time,*" Dan. vii. 25, xii. 7; Rev. xii. 4: of "the *times of restitution* of all things," Acts iii. 21: of "*the times of the Gentiles,*" Luke xxi. 24: of "*the dispensation of the fulness of times,*" Eph. i. 10: and of "the appearing of our Lord Jesus Christ, which *in his times* he shall show,"³ etc.;—in respect of all which it is conceded that *chronological periods* are meant. When viewed in the aspect of the things signified in each, they will be found to contain *internal evidence,* either expressed, as in the instance of the "seven times" of Lev. xxvi., and Dan. iv., etc., or implied, as in that of "the times of the Gentiles," Luke xxi. 24—furnishing a rule for an exact calculation as to their length. For example: Understanding the term "*times,*" wherever it occurs, to signify *years,* as each year is to be reckoned at 360 days, when it is found connected with a *specified number,* as "seven," then "*seven times,*" being equivalent to *seven years* of 360 days, "each day for a year," give us a total of 2,520 years as the length of the period denoted thereby. "*Time, times,* and HALF *a time,*" *one* year, *two* years, and *half* a year, thus:

    1 year ....360 days
    2 " ....720 "
   ½ " ....180 "
                                     Total, ...1,260 days,

"each day for a year." And the *undefined* periods, as the "*times* of the Gentiles," "the dispensation of *the fulness* of times," etc., are to be determined by those events connected with prophetical dates, which the Holy Ghost has assigned to them.

Taken as a whole, therefore, these prophetical numbers, though changed in the mode or form of computation, yet when interpreted agreeably to the law of symbols as above laid down, are nevertheless *equally precise and determinable* with those reckoned by literal or current time.

¹ Lev. xxv. 8.   ² Ezek. iv. 4–6.   ³ Tim. vi. 5.

It is in place to remark here by the way, that "for the first four centuries, the days of Antichrist's duration given in Daniel and the Apocalyptic prophecies, were interpreted literally as *days*, not as *years*, by the fathers of the Christian Church.[1] From this period to the time of Luther, with the exception of occasional glimpses into the principles of the year-day theory, they remained hidden from the Church. Mr. Elliott remarks on this subject—"The year-day principle scarcely broke on Luther's mind; and he once had a curious notion of *a prophetic time* being equal to thirty years. . . But we find it hinted at by Melanchthon. And the Magdeburg centuriators fully advocated the *year-day* principle, and applied it to the papacy, as also most Protestants afterwards."

Mr. Elliott adds, that "almost immediately after Luther's publication of his Bible, it was discussed by the chief Protestant prophetic expositors that followed ; and in most cases the *year-day* principle applied to explain them." Indeed, this principle will be found to be "sustained by the soundest exegesis, as well as fortified by the high names of Mede"—of whom Mr. Elliott says, that he "was looked on and written of as a man almost inspired for the solution of the Apocalyptic mysteries"—"Sir Isaac Newton, Bishop Newton, Faber, Scott, Keith, Cunninghame, Cumming," and a host of others, and of which, to use the language of a writer of distinguished note, we may say: "*If the old established principle of the year-day theory* is wrong, not only has the whole Christian world been led astray for ages by a mere *ignis fatuus* of false hermeneutics, but the Church is at once cut loose from every chronological mooring, and set adrift in the open sea, without the vestige of a beacon, lighthouse, or star, by which to determine her bearings or distances from the desired millennial haven to which she had hoped she was tending."

NOTE E.

On the Extent *and* Results *of the Continental and Anglican Reformation from* A. D. 1517.

The Continental and Anglican REFORMATION, which was commenced in A. D. 1517, instead of sweeping away the *entire system* of the Romish APOSTASIA, and exerting its energies and influence in the restoration to the ECCLESIA of the great original fundamental faith concerning the second

[1] This arose from the prevalence in the Christian Church of the *Septuagint*, in the place of the Hebrew Chronology, on which, see " Reply," etc., pp. 53, 54.

personal coming of Christ, was content to limit itself, at least for the most part, to the recovery of the *first* "*principles* of the doctrine of Christ"— the removal of the grosser abuses and corruptions of bygone ages, and the reëstablishment of a more Scriptural and primitive ministry, polity, ordinances, and discipline, etc., in the Church.

Now, while we concede that these were all demanded by the necessities of the times, and hence were highly commendable; yet, as we must insist, they lacked one essential element, as *a bond of union* to the reformed Churches of Christ—that of directing the *faith* and *hope* of God's people to the Lord Jesus Christ as "THE COMING ONE," who was to *restore all things.* Instead, the early reformers, at least for the most part, retained the popish Augustinian theory of interpreting and applying the Messianic prophecies of the Old and New Testaments to the state of the Church *under this dispensation*, as constituting "the kingdom of heaven," "of God," "of Christ," etc.

There was, however, this difference between the two theories: While the Romanists interpreted the prophecies *literally*, and claimed, in virtue of a delegation from Christ, to have a real and *visible* HEAD in this kingdom, the Church, in the person of the Pope as the vicegerent of Christ on earth, Protestants contend only for a *spiritual* presence of the now personally absent Christ from His kingdom, the Church.

The *result* is, that the Romish theory, being the more consistent of the two, is a far more masterly and complete *imitation* of Christ's kingdom than that of the Protestants ever can be. It is this that has constituted the so-called *centre and bond of unity* to the hierarchy of Papal Rome. On the other hand, from the *absence* of a corresponding element of union to the Protestant Churches, as the results of the Continental and Anglican Reformation reached only about *one third part* of Christendom, *it has ever since been receding more and more*, until the light which then began to break out amidst the general gloom, seems again about to be absorbed and extinguished in the overspreading aggressions of reviving Popery. For, although the *temporal* "*dominion*" of the "little horn" of the Popedom has been almost entirely wrenched from its grasp, yet the *spiritual* "*life*" of the papacy is to be "*prolonged* for a season and a time" (Dan. vii. 12). While, therefore, this stupendous "mystery of iniquity" is destined to once more become dominant throughout Protestant Christendom—though, thank Heaven, it will be short-lived—so, we may look forward, as the *issue* of the struggle between these antagonistic elements—unless we greatly err—to a *continuous recession* of the latter before the giant strides of the former, until all nominally bearing the Protestant name, except the humble "remnant according to the election of grace" who shall hear and obey the command to "come out of the mystic Babylon" (Rev. xviii. 4), shall be once more embraced within her encircling pale.

INDEX.

N.B.—*s* refers to pages in the "Sequel," *r* to pages in the "Reply." C.'s S. C., is adopted for an abbreviation of *Christ's Second Coming.*

A

ABRAHAMIC COVENANT, the Covenant of Grace, etc., s. 78, 85–90.
ACTS xiii. 17–22, and 1 Kings vi. 1, discrepancy between, r. 125–132.
ἅδης, s. 208, 247.
ADVENT   See CHRIST, THE SECOND COMING OF.
AGRIPPA, Letter to Caligula, 62, 68.
Αἰῶνως, s. 177, 189, 193, 222, 227, 228.
ALLEGORICAL theory of interpretation, totally unknown before the time of Origen, r. 13, 17. See on figurative interpretations, etc.
ANABAPTISTS, r. 22, 23; 34, 35, 36, 44, 49, 50, 84.
ANTICHRIST, s. 99, 117.
ANTICHRIST, the last, s. 304, 305; his league with the Jews, 305; his treachery, and invasion of Jerusalem, 306; his destruction, etc., 307.
ANTI-MILLENARIANS, s. iv.
AMBROSE, r. 26, 76.
APOCALYPSE, its canonicity denied by Gaius, 30; and also by Eusebius, 28.
'Ἀποκάλυψις, s. 47, 295.
APOSTASY, of Israel, 84.
APOSTASY, Papal, 112.
APOSTASY, from millenarianism; causes of, s. 72–75. See also Note A. 119–121.
APOSTASY, the last?

APOSTLES' CREED, alleged silence of, on Millenarianism, Ans. r. 28, 29, 43.
APOSTASIA, its distinction from ECCLESIA, etc., r. 119–121.
APPEAL, to several leading Prot. Divines, on C.'s S. C., s., ground of, xxi, xxii., their objections to C.'s S. C. as being *pre*-millennial, xxii, xxiii. — Answers to, xxiii–xxviii. Hence our appeal, xxviii-xxxi.
ATHENAGORUS, 40, 42.
ARIANISM, s. 114.
AUGSBURG CONFESSION, r. 32, 34.
AUGUSTINE, r. 26, 45, 47, 76, 81.

B

BABYLON, the mystic, s. 66.
BAPTISM, s. 88.
BAPTISTS, the, r. 20,000, in the time of Charles II., Millenarians, s. 94.
BARNABAS, r. 22, 38, 40, 41.
BARNES, Rev. Albert, s. 120, 121, 123, 159.
BARONIUS, s. 81.
BAXTER, Rev. Richard, r. 92.
BEAST, from the Sea, Rev. xiii. 1, not identical with the Dragon, etc., 101–105.
BELGIC CONFESSION, r. 50.
BENSON, Dr. s. 120, 130, 159.

BIBLE, THE, only rule of faith for Protestants, s. xvii.
BIBLE, Cottage, s. 120.
BUNYAN, John, r. 94.
BURKITT, Rev. Mr., s. 123, 159.
BURNET, Bp., s. 80.
BUSH, Rev. Geo., theory of the Millennium, s. 99–117.

C

CALMET, 73.
CALVIN, John, s. 86, 88.
CANAAN, the land of, given in Covenant to Israel, s. 89.
"CARCASSES," etc., s. 121.—Ans. 134–136.
CERINTHUS, r. 22, 23, 32, 36, 38.
CHARNOCK, Dr. Stephen, r. 94.
CHILIASTS. See on Millenarians.
CHILLINGWORTH, s. 77.
CHRIST, a *King*, etc., s. 229, 230; 229, 230; r. 18, r. 18, 19: as the King-father's Son, must have His *Bride*, etc., s. 92: 189, 190, 192, 231, 232.
CHRIST'S SECOND COMING,—The great Theological Question of the day, s. iii. Not verified by the return of the Jews from the Babylonish captivity, 57–98: nor at the extermination of Paganism under Constantine, 99–117: nor at the destruction of Jerusalem by the Romans, 118–132. It is not a *providential*, 56, 119, 132, nor a *spiritual* or figurative, 56, 58, nor a *judicial* coming, 132, 134, 140. Proof that it is *pre*-millennial, 187, 188: also, that it is *personal*, 57, 132–134; 218–232; 294, 295. r. 20, 21. Proof that it will consist of two manifestations, the first, *secretly*, "as a thief in the night," 304. Second, *openly or visibly*, "when every eye shall see him," etc., 306, 307. The events or "signs," 1st, that are to *immediately precede* his coming, 2d, that will *attend* his coming, 3d, that will come in *between his invisible* and *visible* appearing; 4th, that will *follow* his visible manifestation. Our *proximate nearness to* his Second Coming, s. 203, 301. *No three comings* of Christ, as some writers affirm, 58.
CHRONOLOGY, variations between Hebrew and Septuagint, r. 53, 54; aggregate chro. of the world, s. 198–203.
CHRYSOSTOM, r. 26, 76.

CHURCH, the, C.'s S. C. the object of her faith and hope in every age, s. xxiii, 300.
CIRCUMCISION, s. 88.
CLARKE, Dr. Adam, s. 122, 123, 140, 143, 144, 145, 159.
CLEMENT of Rome, r. 40, 41, 42.
CLEMENT of Alexandria, r. 16, 30, 44, 70.
COKE, Dr. Thomas, s. 120, 140, 159.
CONFESSION OF EDWARD VI. 32, 34.
CONFEDERACY, the last anti-Christian, s. 305: their invasion of Jerusalem, 306: their destruction, 307.
CONFLAGRATION, the last universal, of the earth, not *pre*-millennial, s. xix, 204–216.
CONSTANTINE, s. 99, 106, 107, 110, 112, 113, 115, 116, 218, r. 48, 49.
CONVERSION, of the Nations, not to take place *before* C.'s S. C., s. 301: but is to follow, 308, 309.
CUMMING, Rev. John, alleges the last universal conflagration to be *pre*-millennial, s. xix. Error of, s. 204–216.
COVENANT, the Old or Sinaic, distinct from the Abrahamic, s. 86 et seq.
COWPER, Wm. r. 108.
COX, Rev. Samuel H., s. 245.
CRANMER, Archbp., s. 86, 88.
CREEDS, etc., all recognize the doctrine of Christ's Second Coming, s. xiii.
CYPRIAN, r. 28.
CYRUS, 60, 61, 64, 65, 66, 113.

D

DEMAREST, Rev. J. T., D.D., s. xxiii
DEUT. xxx. 3–6: 75.
—— xxviii. 36, compared with xxx. 3, 4, s. 75.
—— xxx. 6: 76.
DIONYSIUS, Bp. of Alexandria, r. 21, 30, 31, 48, 75, 80.
DISCREPANCY between 1 Kings vi. 1, and Acts xiii. 17–22, r. 125–132.
DISPENSATION, see on MYSTERY, "Kingdom of God" in.
DIX, Rev. Dr., on Church union, s. xxii.
DOCTRINAL aspect of C.'s S. C. Old Testament, s. 33–39. New Testament, 39–48.
DOGMATICAL, the, in discussions on this subject, r. 9, 10, 16–21.
DRAGON, the, of Rev. xii. 3, alleged to be identical with the Beast from the Sea, Rev. xiii. 1, 100, 101. Fallacy of, 101–105, 112.

DRAGON, the, of Rev. xii. 3, 9, xiii. 4, xx. 1-3, identical, 101-105.

E

"EAGLES," etc., alleged figurative meaning of, s. 118,—Ans. 132, 134–136.
EARTH, the millennial, *physical* changes of, s. 309, 310: *moral* changes of, 310: *political* changes of, 310, 311.
———, the present population of, in an unconverted state, etc., s. 196–198.
ECCLESIA, its distinction from APOSTASIA, etc., r. 119-121.
EDWARD VI., CONFESSION OF, Millenarian, r. 51, 52, 88.
ἡ γενεὰ αὕτη, s. 124, 147.
ELLIOTT, Dr., s. 81, 85, 90.
Ἡ ἡμέρα τοῦ Χριστοῦ, s. 46, 115.
ἐντεῦθεν, s. 223.
ἐντὸς ὑμῶν, s. 223.
Ἐπιφανεία, s. 45, 295.
EPIPHANEUS, s. 76.
Ἐρχόμενος, s. 45.
ESCHATOLOGY, or the Second Coming of Christ. Reply to the Rev. Dr. Shedd on, Preface vii, viii; 16, 22, 44.
ETERNITY, to man, when it commences, s. 252.
EUPHRATES, the great river, Rev. ix. 14; xvi. 12; symbolizes the Turkish power, or little horn of Dan. viii. 9–12; 21–25, s. note, 92, 93. Its extinction, ib., purpose of, ib.
EUSEBIUS, r. 27, 28, 30, 41, 45, 47, 48, 49, 112.
εὐθέως δὲ μετὰ τὴν θλῦψιν, s. 178.
EVENTS, the present, most portentous, s. xxviii.
EZEKIEL, chap. xxviii. 1-9, an appeal founded on, xxix. xxx.; xxxvii. 17, 65.

F

FABER, Rev. Geo. Stanley, s. 57.
FIFTH-MONARCHY MEN, r. 49, 50.
FIGURATIVE interpretations of prophecy, in contrast with the *literal*, s. Matt. xxiv. 27, s. 119-121. Ans. 131-134.
——— 28, 121. Ans. 134-136.
——— 29, 121, 122. Ans. 136-139.
——— 30, 122, 123. Ans. 159, 160.
Other passages, Matt. xvi. 27, 28, 124.—Ans. 148, 149. John xxi. 22, 125.—Ans. 149-151. Matt. xxvi. 64, 125.—Ans. 151-154. *Poetical imagery* of O. T. in support of, 125.

—Ans. 129. Allegory, s. 85. Allegorical, s. 299, 299.
1 KINGS vi. 1, and Acts xiii. 17–22, discrepancy between, r. 125–132.
FLEMING, Robert, r. 95, 96.
FRENCH PROPHETS, r. 50.
FLETCHER, Rev. John, r. 102.

G

GAIUS, r. 30, 32, 41, 44, 48.
GALATIANS, s. iii. 15-18, 85, 86; iv. 22-31, 64; 78, 79; 85.
GIBBON, 111, 112.
GILL, Dr. John, r. 101.
GORDON, Rev. Wm. R., D. D., s. xxiii.
GREAT CRISIS, etc., s. 173.
GROTIUS, s. 99, 130.

H

HAGGAI, 2, 9: 71-73.
HALL, Rev. Robert, r. 109.
HATFIELD, Rev. Edwin F. on "Messiah's Second Coming;" animadversions on, r. 132-143.
HEBER, Bp., r. 110.
HEBREW chronology, r. 53, 54.
HENRY, Rev. Matthew, r. 94.
HERESY either *pre-* or *post-*millenarian— must be heretical, s. xxx, xxxi. Hence must be discussed and settled on their merits, xxxi. r. 44. See also Note A, 119-121.
HERMES, r. 22, 26, 38, 40, 41.
HIERARCHY, the Papal, s. 114.
HIERARCHY, the millennial, structure of, s. 312-320.
HILARY, r. 26, 76.
HOPKINS, Bishop, of Vermont, s. xxiii.

I

IGNATIUS, r. 26, 40, 42.
IMBRIE, Rev. C. K., D. D., s. xxiii.
INTERPRETATION, change of the original law of, s. 298.
INTERPRETATION—two rules of, the *literal* and the *figurative*, s. xix. 127-131. See also r. 10–16. Origen the author of the allegorical theory of, 13–15.
INTERPRETATIONS OF PROPHECY, *see* under figurative and literal.
IRENÆUS, r. 22, 23, 25, 28, 43, 45, 67, 68.
ISRAEL, God a husband to—divorced—restored, s. 230, 231.

ISRAEL, and JUDAH, their divorcement not final, s. 90–92.
IRVINGITES, r. 50.

J

JER. l. 4, 17; and 33, 34: s. 60, 61, and 64–66.
JEROME, r. 15, 26, 45, 46, 48, 76.
JEWS, THE, their complete restoration under Cyrus asserted, from Jer. l. 4, 17, and 33, 34, s. 60, 61: also their independence, 64, 62: also the union of Judah and Israel into one nation, 62: also the spiritual revivals among them, etc., 63. Other arguments urged against their future literal return to Canaan. 1. It would necessitate the restoration of their Temple, sacrifices, etc., 63. 2. The silence of the New Testament on, 63. 3. The nature of the two covenants forbid it, etc. Fallacy of, I. The *foundation* of this theory. Examination and application of Jer. l. 4, 17, and 33, 34. Introductory remarks, 64–66. Direct proof, 66, 67. II. Its *superstructure*. SECTION I. Fallacy of their alleged independence on their return from Babylon, 67, 68. SECTION II., or of their reconciliation, 68–71. SECTION III., or of their spiritual revivals, 71. Other arguments. First. The rebuilding of the Temple, proved from Haggai ii. 2, 9, 71–73. Second. Restoration of sacrifices, 73–75. Proof of their future restoration, from Deut. xxx. 3–6. 1st. It will be general, verses 3, 4, 75. 2d. Also by comparing Deut. xxviii. 36, with chap. xxx. 3, 4, respecting their king, 75. 3d. Compare also the number of the captives from Babylon, with that of their predicted future return, 75, 76. 4th. Further proof from Deut. xxx. 6, as derived from their future revivals, etc., 76. Numerous other passages referring to, 76. SECTION IV. Proof that the New Testament is not silent on this subject, 77. SECTION V. Of the *two covenants*, etc. Gal. iv. 22–31. Preliminary remarks, 78, 79. Two theories respecting them. I. That the Abrahamic is *identical* with the Sinaic covenant of works, and hence related only to temporal things, 79, 80. II. That the Abrahamic is THE COVENANT OF GRACE, as contradistinguished from the Sinaic *covenant of works*, 80, 81. Israel placed themselves under the Law of works. Hence their fall, etc. 81, 82. God's mysterious purpose in this, 82. But the excision of Israel not final, 82–84. St. Paul's argument in the xith of Romans a proof of this, 84, 85. Additional proof of the Abrahamic covenant of grace as argued, first, from Gal. iv 22–31, 85. Second, from Gal. iii. 15–18, 85, 86. Third, from the nature and design of, 1st, as distinct from the covenant from Sinai, 86. 2d. That it is a *spiritual compact*, 87–89. 3d. Embraced also *temporal things*, 89, 90. Cause of Israel's rejection, and calling of the Gentiles, 90. Purpose of this, to obtain A BRIDE FOR THE KING'S SON, 19. Israel not forever divorced—WILL BE RESTORED TO THEIR LAND, 91, 92. Their conversion follows, by the personal appearance of their Messiah to them, 92, 93.
JEWS, the, their restoration, etc., *the Key* to an interpretation of all those prophecies which speak of C.'s S. C. as *pre*-millennial, 67.
JEWS, the, their restoration, s. 305: their league with the last Antichrist, 305: rebuild their temple, etc., 305: their revolt and consequent sufferings, 306: deliverance of a remnant, and also of the Gentiles, 306, 307. Their conversion follows, 308, 309.
JOEL ii. 30, 31; iii. 15, s. 142–146.
JOHN xxi. 22, s. 149–151.
xviii. 36, 222, 223.
JOSEPHUS, 60, 61, 62, 67, 68, 139, 143, 152, 156.
JUDAH, and ISRAEL, their divorcement not final, s. 90–92.
JUDGMENT, the day of, a period of 1000 years, s. 115; 227, 228. The ideas and language of the New Testament writers on, derived principally from Dan. vii. 9, etc., s. 243–253. Double act of, 247–256.
JUSTIN MARTYR, s. 65–67.
JUSTINIAN's Edict in A. D. 533, etc., the foundation of the Papal Hierarchy, s. 114, 115, r. 48.
JURIEU, Peter, r. 95.

K

"KINGDOM OF GOD," the phrase, difference between, in *mystery*, and in *manifestation*, s. 148, 189–200. See mystery.

KINGS OF THE EAST, Rev. xvi. 12—denote the Jews, s. Note, 92, 93.
KNOX, John, r. 90.
κοσμος, s. 222, 223, 227.

L

LACTANTIUS, r. 45, 46, 88.
LARDNER, Dr., 45, 76.
LATIMER, Hugh, s. 86-88.
LEIGHTON, Dr., s. 122.
LIGHTFOOT, Dr, s. 141, 159.
LITERAL interpretation of prophecy, s. xv, xix, 63, 140, 141, 142-146; 127-131; of Matt. xxiv. 27-30, 160-182, 186, 298, 299.
LIVING NATIONS, judged at C.'s S. C., s. 246.
"LITTLE HORN," the Roman Papal, s. 171, 186.
―――― The Mohammedan, s. 171.
LOWTH, Bp., s. 130, 143, 144, 145.
――, Dr. Wm., r. 100.
LUKE xvii. 21, s. 223, 224.
―― i. 32, 33, s. 224.
―― xxii. 15, 18, s. 226, 227.
LUTHER, s. 85; r., repudiates Origen's allegorical theory of interpretation, 14-16, 31; commences the great Reformation in A.D. 1517, 196.

M

MATHER, Increase, D. D., r. 96.
――, Cotton, r. 100.
MATT. xiii. 41, s. 227, 228.
―― xv. 28, 224, 225.
―― xvi. 27, 28, s. 147-149; xxvi. 64, s. 151-154.
MCCARTEE, Rev. Robert, D. D., s. xxiii.
MCILVAINE, Bishop, of Ohio, s. xxiii.
MCKNIGHT, Dr., s. 130.
MEDE, Joseph, r. 90, 91.
MELITO, s. 69.
METHODIUS, s. 71.
MILLENARIANS, wherein they agree and differ with Millerites and Post-millenarians—cause of, s. xix, xx, xxiii, xxv.
――――, anti and post, their Theories based upon negatives, s. 298.
――――, pre, their system substantially the same, s. 299.
――――, English, r. 111-113. American, 115-117.
MILLENNIAL ERA, not absolutely indefectible, r. 122-125.

MILLENNIAL HIERARCHY, structure of, s. 312-320.
MILLENNIAL KINGDOM, its erection, when and how commenced, s. 307, 308. Note. Cannot be established before C.'s S. C., s. 232-243; 303.
MILLENARIANISM, Rev. Dr. Shedd's History of, Ancient, Mediæval, and Modern, vii, viii—Collateral points. 1. The dogmatical, 9, 10. 2. Side issues, etc.—1st, denounces millenarianism as materializing, sensual, gross, fanatical, and heretical, 21, 22. Ans. 23-26. 2d. Lowers the claims of the ancient Chiliasts to respect as writers, 26. Ans. 26-28; 40-43. 3d. Alleges the silence of the Apostles' Creed on, 28. Answer, 28-30.
――――, History of—I. ANCIENT. Dr. S—'s account of the Origin of—Cerinthus, 32: the Jews in Christ's time, 37, 38, 54: cause of, 38, 39: different stages of, 40, 43, 44, 45, 47, 48: opposition to, down to the ivth century, 30, 32. Answers. 1st. Alleged origin of, Cerinthus, 32; 33: 2d. Alleged causes of, 38-40: 3d. Alleged stages of,—Proof that millenarianism existed before Christ's time, 54, 55. Pagan traditions of, 55-57. Pre-Christian uninspired Jewish writers, 59, 60. The Apostolic Church, 57-59. Early post-Apostolic Era, to A. D. 150, 40-43; 60-65. From A. D. 150 to 250, "the blooming age of," 43, 44; 65-67. Third and fourth centuries, 45-48. 4th. Alleged opposition to, down to ivth century, 30, 32. True cause of the decline of, to time of Augustine, 30-36; 48, 49; 72-76. Ends in THE GREAT APOSTASY from, 78-81. Not totally exterminated at the period of the Reformation, 81-83. II. MEDIÆVAL ERA. Dr. S—'s account of—alleged fanatical and heretical revival of, at the Reformation, 49. Also its condemnation, etc., 32. Answer, 34, 35; 49-52. Alleges that "the history of Chiliasm presents few points of importance since the Reformation," 83, 84. Answer. Different stages of—1st, from A. D. 1517 to A. D. 1550, etc., 84-90. 2d. From middle of xvith to that of the xviiith century, 90-110. Conclusion. Opening of the xixth century. State of millenarianism in England, etc., 111-113. In the American churches, 113-115. Present prospects, 115-117

MILLENNIUM, the, s. 160,—still future, 105–117.
MILLER, Mr. Wm., s. xv, xviii.
MILLERISM, s. 98—not to be confounded with Millenarianism, s. xviii, xxiii, identical with the popular view of C.'s S. C., except as to time, xviii, xix; fallacy of, 99.
MILLERITES, r. 50.
MILNER, Dr., repudiates Origen's allegorical theory of interpretation, r. 15, 16, 31.
MOHAMMEDAN POWER, its destruction to precede C.'s S. C., s. 303.
MOSHEIM, Dr., repudiates Origen's allegorical theory of interpretation, r. 15, 16, 31.
MYSTERY, "the kingdom of God" in, s. 188, 189, 227.

N

NATIONS, the living, to be judged at C.'s S. C.
———, the, who escape the overthrow of the last Antichrist, etc., Jewish and Gentile, to be converted in the order following. I. The Jewish nation, 92, 93. II. The Gentile nations of Christendom, 94. III. The idolatrous heathen, 94, 95. IV. The Ten Tribes of Israel, 95, 96. V. Egypt and Assyria, 96, 97.
NEANDER, Dr., s. 77.
NEPOS and CORACIAN, r. 21, 30, 31, 71.
NESBITT, Rev. Mr., s. 130.
NEWCOMB, Archbishop, r. 108.
NEW HEAVENS and EARTH, difference between the millennial and the eternal states of, note, s. 309.
"NEW HYPOTHESIS," Dr. Whitby's, 97–99.
NEWTON, Bishop, s. 128, 140, 149, 159, r. 107.
NEWTON, Sir Isaac, r. 96.
NICENE CREED, millenarian, r. 46.
νυν, s. 222, 223.

O

OBJECTIONS, to C.'s S. C. as *pre*-millennial. Its alleged tendency to lead to fanaticism, etc., s. xxii. Answer, xxiii. Its alleged remoteness, xxiii. Answer, xxiii, xxiv. The alleged disagreement of interpreters, xxiv, xxv. Answer, xxiv–xxvi. The plea, that it is a matter of indifference, xxvi. Answer, xxvi, xxvii. The plea, that death is the great motive to faith, etc., xxvii. Answer, xxvii, xxviii.
ORIGEN, Platonizes Christianity; the first to introduce the allegorical rule of interpreting the Scriptures; laid the foundation of several heresies, s. 13, 14. Luther, Mosheim, and Milner's repudiations of, 14, 15, 16, 17, 26; 30, 31. Other references to, s. 298, 299, r. 13, 14, 16, 17, 30, 31, 34, 36, 47, 91.
OWEN, Dr. John, s. 57.

P

PAGANISM, personified, etc., 100, 103, 104.
παλιγγενεσία, s. 204, 206.
PAPAL APOSTASY, 112.
PAPAL POWER, its destruction to precede C.'s S. C., s. 103.
PAPIAS, r. 22, 23, 24, 25, 26, 27, 38, 40, 41, 43.
PARABLES, s. 189–194.
PAREUS, s. 57.
Παρουσία, s. 45; 295, 296; 296, 297.
Φανερῶσις, s. 47.
PATRICK, Bishop, s. 143.
PEARCE, Bishop, the father of the *figurative* interpretation of Matt. xxiv. 27–30, s. 128, 159.
PERIOD, *a short unchronological*, s. 171, 177, after the close of the 6,000 years.
PETRONIUS, 62.
PHILO, 62, 68.
POLYCARP, r. 26, 40, 41, 42.
POOLE, 73.
POST-MILLENARIANS, s. iv, xix, xxiii, 183.
PRACTICAL Aspect of C.'s S. C.: the polar star of the Church's faith and hope in all ages, s. 48. Now for the most part lost to the Church, 48. Other motives substituted for, as 1st, preparation for death, 49. Answer, 49, 50. 2d, meditation on, etc. Answer, 50, 51. C.'s S. C. and not death, etc., the great motive to faith, holiness, etc. Eleven illustrations of, 51–53.
PRE-MILLENARIANS, s. iv, not Millerites, s xviii, xix.
PRIESTS AND MONKS, of the Latin Church in the xth century, r. 33, 48.
PRIDEAUX, s. 99, 73.
PROPHECIES, arguments against the study of, s. xv, xvi, xxi, xxii. Reply to, xvi, xvii, xxiii–xxxi.

PROPHETS, the O. and N. T., only *six* out of the *forty-one*, predict the FIRST Coming of Christ—all the others, the SECOND, etc., s. 213, r. 134. See copious references, *Note* D, 135-137.

PROPHECY, makes known the PROXIMATE period of C.'s S. C., s. 303.

PROPHECIES, of C.'s S. C.; first impressions on a perusal of, that it is still *future*, s. 54, 55. Three theories which allege that it is *already past*, etc. Ist Theory alleges that they were all fulfilled at the return of the Jews from the Babylonish captivity, s. 57-98. Proofs of its fallacy, 64-89.

———, of C.'s S. C. IId Theory alleges that they were verified by the overthrow of Paganism under Constantine in A. D. 32", whence commenced the Millennium of Rev. xx. 1-6—adopted by Grotius, Prideaux, Vint, and advocated by the late Geo. Bush. The Theory defined, s. 99-101. Fallacy of, 101-105. Other arguments.—I. That Rev. xx. 1-7 alone mentions a 1,000 years, etc. Answer, 105-107. Scriptural view of the millennial state, 108, 109. II. Historical examination of Prof. Bush's theory. 1. Lateness of Constantine's baptism—was a homicide—united church and state, 110, 111. 2. His theory opposed to the scriptural character of the millennium, and the period assigned to it, 111-114. 3. Further evidence of the misapplication of this prophecy, 114-116. Conclusion. Three inferences, 116, 117.

——— of C.'s S. C. The IIId Theory alleges that all were verified in the destruction of Jerusalem by the Romans in A. D. 70, as founded on Matt. xxiv. 27-30. The theory defined, s. 118, 119. I. Figurative interpretations of, 119-123. II. Arguments in support of, 119-127. I. The *figurative* and *literal* theories compared, 127-129. Difficulties of the *figurative* interpretation, 129, 130. II. Reply to, etc., 131-160. III. Direct *literal* interpretation of the prophecy, 160-182.

——— of C.'s S. C. IVth Theory, wherein it differs from the three preceding theories, s. 182, 183. The chasm between pre- and post-millenarians a narrow one, 183. Difficulties stated, 183-185. FIRST THESIS of this theory. Alleged *identity* of "the times of the Gentiles," or Christian Dispensation, with the Millennial Era, 185. Proof that these two Eras are distinct, 185-188. SECOND THESIS, alleges that the Christian Church and "kingdom of heaven," etc., are *identical*, and end at the close of the millennium, 188. Proof that the Christian Church during this Era is the kingdom of God in *mystery*, 189-200. Further evidence from the *chronology* of, 201-204. THIRD THESIS, alleges the *spiritual* reign of Christ during the Christian Era and onward to the close of the Millennium. Recapitulation, 217-219. Section I. Alleged *identity* of the Christian Church with "the kingdom of heaven," and of Christ's *spiritual* reign over it as king, etc., 219. Answer, 219-222. Particular passages adduced in support of this thesis, 1st, John xviii. 36, 222. Answer, 222-223. 2d, Luke xvii. 21, 223. Answer, 223, 224. 3d, Luke i. 32, 33, 224. Answer, 224. 4th, Matt. xvi. 28, 224. Answer, 225. 5th, Luke xxii. 15-18, 225. Answer, 225. 6th, Matt. xii. 28, 226. Answer, 226, 227. 7th, Matt. xiii. 21, 227. Answer, 227-232. Section II. Proof that C.'s S. C. is *pre*-millennial. Part I. No millennium *before* that event, 232-243. Part II. Ideas and language of the N. T. writers respecting C.'s S. C. and the Day of Judgment derived from the O. T. prophets, etc., 243-252. Summary of the Theories at issue, 253-256.

R

REFORMATION, Prof. Shedd's account of Millenarianism in connection with, r. 49, 50. Ans. 50-52. Its extent and results, etc., r. 143, 144.

RESURRECTION, the, as applied to CHRIST, and the dead *just* and *unjust*, s. 257. Quest. Is it purely spiritual, or literal? Remarks, 251, 258. SECTION I. The term, *spiritual*, what, 258, 259. II. *Corporeal*, what, 259-261. III. *Personality* and *personal identity*, what, 261. SECTION II. Arguments drawn from analogy, 263-268. SECTION III. Applied to Christ's resurrected state, 268, 269. Fallacy of the theory, that *the soul only* is the Man, 269, 270. Proofs of Christ's *literal* resurrection, 270–278. SECTION IV. Part I. Nature of, not a purely spiritual, but a *spiritualized* body, 278–280. Several extraordinary circumstances and actions of, *after* His resurrection, 283, 284. Explained, 284, 285. Part II. I. Glory of, 285–287. II. Attributes of, 287, 288. III. Official dignity of, 1, as our Intercessor, 288, 289; 2, as our Judge, 289; 3, as our King, 289, 290. SECTION V. Concluding proof that C.'s S. C. will be *pre*-millennial and personal, 290–297.

RESURRECTION, THE FIRST, s. 227, 245; r. 27, 108.

REV. xxi. 1–7, 99.

RIDLEY, Nicholas, s. 88.

ROBINSON, Dr., s. 122, 140, 159.

ROMAN EMPERORS, s. 113.

ROM. xi.—, 63.

RUSSELL, Bp., s. 77, 80, 97.

RUTHERFORD, Samuel, r. 93.

S

Σαββατισμος, s. 168.

SACRIFICES, restoration of, not a *reductio in absurdum*, s. 63, and 71, 73–75. The Millennial, commemorative, s. 74–76.

SATAN, binding of, 99.

SCOTT, Dr. Thomas, s. 57, 120, 140, 159.

"SIGNS" of C.'s S. C., darkening of sun, etc., s. 110, 124, 137. Ans. 137. Lightnings flash, 118, 119–121. Ans. 134–136.

"SIGNS" to *immediately precede* C.'s S. C., s. 301–303—to *accompany*, s. 304: that are *contemporaneous with* the interval between the invisible and visible appearing of Christ, s. 304–306: that are to *follow*, 307–311.

SIMEON, s. 57.

SINAI COVENANT of works, not identical with the Abrahamic, s. 78–90.

SEPTUAGINT, chronology, r. 53, 54.

"SEVEN TIMES," of Lev. xxvi. and Dan. iv. a mystical number, s. 160, 161. Explained, 167. Commencement of, 167–172.

SHORT UNCHRONOLOGICAL PERIOD, s. 171.

SHEDD, Rev. Dr. See on Millenarianism.

SIDE ISSUES, used in these discussions, r. 21–37.

6,000 YEARS, etc., r. 53. Pagan writers on, 56, 57. Ancient uninspired Jews, 59, 60. Early post-apostolic Christians, 60–63, 65, 68, 70, 77, 85.

SOCRATES, 112.

SOUTHGATE, Bishop, s. xxiii.

SYKES, Rev. Dr., s. 130.

SYMBOLIC IMAGERY of, Rev. xx. 1–7, a 99–101; 101–108; 108, 109.

T

TAYLORS, the, s. 130.

TATIAN, r. 40, 42.

TEMPLE, THE, rebuilding of, not *a reductio in absurdum*, s. 63, and 71–73.

TEN TRIBES, their restoration, conversion, etc., s. 95, 96.

TERTULLIAN, r. 22, 23, 28, 45, 69.

THEODOSIUS, 112.

THEOPHILUS of Antioch, r. 40, 43.

TIME, when it closes, s. 252.

"TIMES OF THE GENTILES," runs coeval with the "seven times" of Lev. xxvi., etc., s. 167–172. Embraces the whole period of Jewish desolation, 172–182. Not the same with the Christian era, though they include it, 185–188, r. 19–21.

———, the present, the period of the close of, s. xxviii, 301.

Τὸ τέλος, s. 46.

TRANSFIGURATION, s. 72, 149.

TREATISE, this, an attempt to restore the true doctrine of C.'s S. C., s. xvii, xviii.

——— Origin of, and requisites of, for such a work, s. iii, iv.

THEORIES, on C.'s S. C. various—the four principal; I. Augustine on,—Hammond and Grotius on : III. Dr. Whitby on ; IV. The popular view, s. xiii–xv, and 55, 56. The Vth system of, One only, the true, xv.

TOWER, Rev. Dr., s. 130.

"TRIBULATION, THE GREAT,"—alleged *figurative* meaning of, s. 118, 123, 124, argued from Joel ii. 30, 31, and iii. 15, 142, 143. Ans. 143–146. The *time* of, etc., 138–141. Ans. 141–149. Further proof that it is *entirely future* to the destruction of Jerusalem, 154–160. Additional evidence, from the *Chronology* of the prophecy, Matt. xxiv. 27–30, 155–160. Also pages 160–182.

TURKISH POWER, the only impediment to the return of the Jews, s. 92, 93, and note.

U

UNION of Church and State, r. 48.

UNPARALLELED TRIBULATION, s. 106.

V

VAUDOIS, or WALDENSES, Millenarians, s. 81-83.
VINT, s. 99.
VOX POPULI, VOX DEI, s. 254.

W

WARBURTON, Bishop, s. 159.
WATSON, Rev. Mr., s. 123, 130, 132, 140, 159.
WATTS, Dr. Isaac, r. 100.
WESLEY, Rev. John, r. 101.
———— Rev. Charles, r. 103-106.
WESTMINSTER DIVINES, most of the chief of them Millenarians, r. 23, 89.
WHITBY, Dr. Daniel, s. xiv, 120, 121, 122, 128, 139, 141, 159; r. 97-99.
WILLET, s. 57.

BY THE SAME AUTHOR.

OUR BIBLE CHRONOLOGY,

HISTORIC AND PROPHETIC,

CRITICALLY EXAMINED AND DEMONSTRATED,

AND HARMONIZED WITH THE CHRONOLOGY OF PROFANE WRITERS,

EMBRACING

A REFUTATION OF MODERN EGYTOLOGISTS,

AND ACCOMPANIED WITH

EXTENSIVE CHRONOLOGICAL AND GENEALOGICAL TABLES, SACRED AND PROFANE, FROM THE EARLIEST RECORDS TO THE PRESENT TIME; A MAP OF THE DISPERSION; A CHART OF THE COURSE OF EMPIRES; AND VARIOUS ILLUSTRATIONS, ETC.

In One Royal Octavo Volume.   Pages 240.   Price $2 50.

———o———

This Work forms a plain and complete Commentary on the Chronology of the Scriptures, Historic and Prophetic, and is designed especially for the use of Families.

———o———

THE PRESS, both religious and secular, has reviewed the work with favor. It has also been critically examined, and pronounced *reliable*, by many eminent Scholars and Divines, among whom are the following:

REV. THOMAS DEWITT, D. D., Collegiate Ref. Dutch Church.
REV. JOHN M. KREBS, D. D., Presbyterian Church.
REV. CHARLES K. IMBRIE, D. D., Presbyterian Church, Jersey City.
REV. FRANCIS L. HAWKS, D. D., LL. D., Calvary Church (Episcopal).
REV. SAMUEL R. JOHNSON, D. D., Dean of the General Theological Seminary of the Prot. Episcopal Church, and Professor of Divinity, etc.
REV. JOHN CUMMING, D. D., F. R. S. E., Minister of the Scottish National Church, London.

This last-named writer has furnished the author with the following testimonial:

(LONDON).   "Montague Place,   ) April 30,
"MY DEAR SIR: Russell Square, W. D. ʃ   1864.

"I have everywhere spoken of your work on Scripture Chronology *as the most able investigation I have read.*"

In evidence of this, Dr. Cumming has adopted it as his standard, with appropriate acknowledgments, in his recently published work under the title of "THE GREAT PREPARATION," reprinted from the London Edition by CARLETON & ROE, Broadway.

N. B. All orders for the above work addressed to Rev. R. C. Shimeall, No. 371 West Thirty-Fifth Street (with the price inclosed), will be promptly delivered to any part of the city, or sent by express to those abroad.

A CARD.

"OUR BIBLE CHRONOLOGY," etc., forms the *Basis* of the present work, which is designed as a "*Sequel*" to it. The two volumes will be found to impart a thorough knowledge of all that appertains to "THE GREAT THEOLOGICAL QUESTION OF THE DAY," in reference to

"THE SECOND COMING OF CHRIST."

∗ Retail price of the Bible Chronology, $2 50. Of the Second Coming of Christ, $3 00. Booksellers and agents can obtain both works of the publishers at *twenty per cent.* discount, *FOR CASH ONLY*. Either volume or both can be had of the author, No. 371 West Thirty-Fifth Street.

N. B.—The author, with a view to place these volumes within the reach of all who take an interest in the subjects of which they treat, offers them at the rate of *twenty per cent.* below the ordinary prices for works of a similar class.

The author will esteem it a favor to receive from those into whose hands these volumes may fall, any communication, (under their proper signature) on the subjects of which they treat, whether favorable or adverse to the views he advocates.

R. C. S.

New York, January.   1865.

The following works, prepared by the author within the last five years (and in good part by trimming the midnight oil), will be issued at as early a period as circumstances will permit:

I.

Arcana Prophetica, or God in Prophecy;

BEING A HARMONY OF THE DIVINE PURPOSES,

AS EXHIBITED IN THE PROPHECIES OF THE OLD AND NEW TESTAMENTS

IN THEIR CONSECUTIVE ORDER.

I. INTRODUCTION—POPULAR OBJECTIONS TO THE STUDY AND INTERPRETATION OF THE PROPHECIES CONSIDERED.
II. BIOGRAPHICAL SKETCHES OF ALL THE OLD AND NEW TESTAMENT PROPHETS, AND THE LEADING SUBJECTS OF THEIR PREDICTIONS, CHRONOLOGICALLY ARRANGED.
III. SACRED HERMENEUTICS: OR THE LAWS OF INTERPRETATION, WITH SPECIAL REFERENCE TO THE PROPHECIES—THE NATURAL, THE TYPICO-HISTORICAL, THE FIGURATIVE, AND THE SYMBOLICAL.
IV. THE NATURE, DESIGN OR END, AND GENERAL SCOPE OF PROPHECY.
V. THE DETAILS OF THE PROPHECIES: THEIR STRUCTURE AND GENERAL ARRANGEMENT, EXTENDING FROM THE COMMENCEMENT OF TIME, TO THE CONSUMMATION OF ALL THINGS.
VI. THE CHRONOLOGY ON PROPHECY.
VII. THE SEVENTH MILLENARY OF THE WORLD.

In One Volume. Large Octavo. 550 Pages.

II.

The Apocalypse Made Plain:

BEING AN EXPOSITION OF THE BOOK OF REVELATION

AS FOUNDED UPON

THE EVIDENCES OF ITS INTERNAL STRUCTURE;

WITH

A PARAPHRASE AND HARMONY OF ITS SEVERAL PARTS,

SHOWING ITS SYNCHRONISMS WITH OTHER PROPHECIES,

THE WHOLE CHRONOLOGICALLY ARRANGED,

And accompanied with a complete Diagram of the Seals, Trumpets, and Vials.

In one Super-Royal Octavo Volume.

III.

Prophetical Views of the Parables of Christ:

ANALYTICALLY ARRANGED,

CONSIDERED FROM A MILLENARIAN STAND-POINT,

SHOWING THAT THEY EMBODY A COMPLETE SYSTEM OF

THE PLAN OF HUMAN REDEMPTION,

FROM THE CREATION AND FALL OF MAN, TO THE FINAL ISSUE OF THE SAVED AND LOST.

In One Volume Octavo. 400 pages.

IV.
The Two Questions Considered:
I. WHERE AND WHAT IS HEAVEN?
II. WHERE AND WHAT IS HELL?

INCLUDING

A SCRIPTURAL AND HISTORICAL VIEW

OF THE

DOCTRINE OF THE INTERMEDIATE STATE BETWEEN DEATH AND THE RESURRECTION.

In One Volume, 12mo.

V.
The Angelic Orders, Unfallen and Fallen:

BEING A SCRIPTURAL INQUIRY INTO

THEIR ORIGIN, NATURE, FACULTIES OR POWERS,

CHARACTERISTICS, NUMBERS, AND FINAL DESTINY.

In one Volume, 12mo.

VI.
The Immortality of the Wicked after Death:

BEING A

REFUTATION OF THE MODERN THEORY OF THEIR ANNIHILATION,

AS ADVOCATED BY HUDSON, STORRS, AND OTHERS.

In One Volume, 18mo.

VII.
The Napoleonic Family:

NAPOLEON BONAPARTE I., THE FIRST EMPEROR OF FRANCE.

NAPOLEON BONAPARTE II., THE DUKE OF REICHSTADT.

LOUIS NAPOLEON BONAPARTE III., THE PRESENT REIGNING EMPEROR OF FRANCE.

THEIR RISE, CAREER, AND DESTINY,

AS VIEWED IN THE LIGHT OF PROPHECY.

In One Volume, 18mo.

N. B. The author is ready to negotiate with any publisher in New York, Boston or Philadelphia, on reasonable terms, for the publication of either of the above-named works.

Any communication addressed to Rev. R. C. SHIMEALL, 371 West 37th Street, or directed to the care of E. BRINKERHOFF, Bookseller, 48 Fulton Street, N. Y., will receive immediate attention.

New York,

R. C. S.

www.ingramcontent.com/pod-product-compliance
Lightning Source LLC
Chambersburg PA
CBHW020833020526
44114CB00040B/602